Real Possibilities

W9-BRM-395

FROMMER'S

Places for
Passion

Pepper Schwartz, PhD
Janet Lever, PhD

FrommerMedia LLC

Published by
FROMMER MEDIA LLC

ISBN 978-1-62887-150-0 (paper), 978-1-62887-151-7 (e-book)

Director, AARP Books: Jodi Lipson
Editorial Director, FrommerMedia: Pauline Frommer
Editor: Lorraine Festa
Production Editor: Kelly Dobbs Henthorne
Photo Editor: Meghan Lamb
Cover Design: Dave Reidy

AARP publishes books on a variety of topics. Visit www.AARP.org/bookstore.

For information on Frommer's other products and services, see www.frommers.com.

FrommerMedia LLC also publishes its books in a variety of electronic formats. Some content that appears
in print may not be available in electronic formats.

Manufactured in the United States of America

5 4 3 2 1

CONTENTS

1 GOING AWAY TO GET CLOSER 1

What Travel Can Do for a Relationship 2

What to Look for in a Romantic Destination 3

2 PLANNING YOUR ROMANTIC VACATION 9

Choosing Your Destination 10

Romance on a Budget 15

All About Pricing 20

Getting the Best Room 21

Getting Off to a Romantic Start 23

part 1 URBAN ROMANCE 25

3 PASSIONATE CITIES: U.S. & CANADA 26

Charleston 26

Chicago 29

Los Angeles 33

Miami 39

Montréal 43

New Orleans 47

New York City 49

San Francisco 54

Santa Fe 58

Seattle 61

Washington, D.C. & Environs 65

4 PASSIONATE CITIES: EUROPE 69

Barcelona 69

Istanbul 72

Lisbon 76

Paris 82

Venice 86

Vienna 90

5 PASSIONATE CITIES: EXOTIC LANDS 93

Bangkok & Chiang Mai 93

Buenos Aires 100

Cape Town & the South African Winelands 103

Marrakech 107

Rio de Janeiro 111

Sydney 115

part 2 NATURAL ROMANCE 119

6 EARTHY DELIGHTS: U.S. 120

Aspen, Colorado 120

Bucks County, Pennsylvania 125

The California Wineland: Sonoma & Napa Valley 128

Jackson Hole, Wyoming 135

Kentucky Horse Country 140

Montana: Glacier National Park & Whitefish 143

Sedona, Arizona 148

Walla Walla Winelands (Washington State) 155

Willamette Valley (Oregon) 159

Zion & Bryce Canyon National Parks (Southwest Utah) 164

7 EARTHY DELIGHTS: CANADA & MEXICO 169

Banff & Lake Louise (Canadian Rockies) 169

Jasper (Canadian Rockies) 175

Rancho La Puerta (Tecate, Mexico) 178

8 EARTHY DELIGHTS: EUROPE 181

Cotswolds, England 181

Ireland 186

Loire Valley (France) 193

Provence (France) 198

Tuscany & Umbria (Italy) 202

part 3 BEACH ROMANCE 211

9 SULTRY SHORES: U.S. 212

Carmel-by-the-Sea, Monterey & Big Sur 212

Florida Keys 220

Hawaii (The Big Island) 224

Martha's Vineyard & Nantucket 228

Maui, Kauai & Oahu 234

Oregon Coast 243

San Juan Islands (Washington State) 252

Santa Barbara & the Santa Ynez Valley 257

10 SULTRY SHORES: CARIBBEAN & MEXICO 261

Bermuda 261

Cabo San Lucas 266

Mayan Riviera Coast, Cancun to Tulum 270

Negril, Jamaica 275

St. Lucia 279

11 SULTRY SHORES: EUROPE 283

Amalfi Coast 283

Dalmatian Coast: Dubrovnik, Split, Hvar, & Korčula 290

Greek Isles Cruise 295

12 SULTRY SHORES: EXOTIC LANDS 303

Bali 303

Bora Bora 308

Maldives 312

Moorea & Tahiti 314

Phuket & Koh Samui 322

part 4 ADVENTURE ROMANCE 331

13 AMOROUS ADVENTURES: NORTH AMERICA 332

Alaskan Cruise 332

Colonial Mexico: Guanajuato, Santiago de Querétaro & San Miguel de Allende 340

Montana: The Luxury Ranch Experience 348

Vancouver Island 351

14 AMOROUS ADVENTURES: EXOTIC LANDS 356

Botswana 356

Great Barrier Reef & Beyond (Australia) 359

The Great Rift Valley & Zanzibar (Tanzania & Kenya) 365

Kerala & Cochin (Kochi), India 371

The Sossusvlei (Namibia) 374

Rajasthan: Jaipur & Udaipur (India) 378

The Red Centre (Australia) 382

Siem Reap, Cambodia 385

Uttar Pradesh: Agra & the Taj Mahal (India) 388

ROMANTIC INTEREST INDEX 391

INDEX 397

SPECIAL SECTIONS

Great Hotel Gestures 7

Packing Heat 18

Making Valentine's Day Special 34

The Art of Getting Away 40

Better Birthdays 63

The Healing Power of Travel 152

Planning a Destination Wedding 216

Celebrating Milestone Anniversaries 266

Romance on a Family Holiday 314

Popping the Question 326

ABOUT THE AUTHORS

Pepper Schwartz, Ph.D., and **Janet Lever, Ph.D.,** coauthored the "Sex and Health" column for *Glamour* magazine for a decade. Both appear frequently in national media as experts in intimate relationships and sexuality. Both earned their Ph.D.'s at Yale University and are Professors of Sociology at University of Washington and California State University, Los Angeles, respectively.

Dr. Pepper Schwartz has authored or coauthored 19 books, including *Prime: Adventures and Advice on Sex, Love, and the Sensual Years, The Normal Bar: the Surprising Secrets of Extremely Happy Couples,* and *Dating After 50 For Dummies.* She has been the Chief Relationship Expert for perfectmatch.com since it started helping daters meet online. Currently, she serves as AARP's Ambassador for Love and Relationships and writes a regular column for AARP.org on those topics. She has offered romantic travel advice on the nationally syndicated Peter Greenberg radio show and is the Romance Concierge at the Salish Lodge in Snoqualmie, Washington. Dr. Schwartz is a past president of the Society for the Scientific Study of Sexualities and a charter member of the International Academy of Sex Research. Pepper is one of four on-air relationship experts starring in A&E Network's FYI channel's "Married at First Sight" in 2014.

Dr. Janet Lever, after leading teams of researchers that designed the three largest magazine sex surveys ever tabulated, came to *ELLE* in 2002 to lead a series of annual surveys hosted on both the health and the business sections of NBCNews.com (formerly msnbc. com). Her "Office Sex and Romance Survey;" "Work, Sex, and Power Survey;" "Good Sex Survey;" and "Sex and Money Survey" are among the largest surveys on these understudied topics. Each of these Internet surveys has been reanalyzed for social science, management, health, and medical journals.

ACKNOWLEDGMENTS

It has been a great adventure visiting all these places and meeting the fabulous people who make them so wonderful. We are indebted to the people listed below for their guidance, creativity, and generosity. However, our work could not have been accomplished without some even more extraordinary work from two people. Cooper Schwartz from HisandHers Travel.com did much of the early research, cultivated the contacts with resort personnel and media representatives, and organized the travel itineraries, searching out exceptional properties. Kate Nolan, perhaps one of the world's best editors, helped make our early drafts into a much more polished product. Far more than an editor, Kate was a friend and lifesaver when deadline pressures loomed, and she put everything else away to pitch in. Finally, Pepper is especially indebted to Fred Kaseburg, who traveled many of these roads with her and made everything sooo romantic, but he also had to give up a lot of time together when getting the book done required solo trips and an enormous amount of writing time. Love you, Fred!

Lorraine Festa, our Frommer's editor, went far beyond anything we could have hoped for in her inventive vision of this project, diligence, and talent—even some hand-holding when needed. Our deepest thanks to Pauline Frommer who believed in this book enough to publish it, and to Jodi Lipson, director of AARP's book division, who has always been a stalwart supporter of this book. Many thanks to Beth Domingo, Kristin Palmer, and Barry Spencer, also at AARP. We are in debt to Suzy Ginsberg for her big-hearted help with publicizing our book. Several people helped sharpen our proposal, and for that we especially thank Peter Greenberg, Sarika Chawla, and our agent, Helen Zimmerman. Early help from Linda Barth helped craft the book's organization. For many other good ideas as well as technical support, we thank Brian J. Gillespie, Cynthia Cobaugh, Barbara Nellis, Monica Chavez, and Flavio Argueta. We also are grateful to our dedicated fact checkers: Angela Gee, Suzanna R. Thompson, and Jessica Weber. Jessica Y. Young assisted in fact-checking, too, and so much more. Our thanks, too, to Kelly Henthorne, our production editor.

We thank dear old friends for hosting us during some visits: Jonathan and Nancy Goodson and John and Elizabeth Haring. Other friends helped with valuable insights: Peter and Patti Adler, Tim Bagley, Deanna Fulton and Kunoor Chopra, Kristen Hunt-Greco and Rob Azevedo, Alexandria and Danny Mills, Gretchen Peterson and Mike Kozachenco, and Marcie and Kevin Spawr. For doing so much to introduce us to these special destinations, we thank the following people (and apologies to those we have inadvertently left off the list!): Sally Carson, Jolene Disalvo, Delaine and Mark Emmert, Nicki and Steve Fitzgerald, Zelda Gamson, Tarryn Gibson, Kristy Gordon, Steve and Bridget Griessel, Gil Herdt, Ed and JP Hollister, Claire Howe, Shannon Olson Johnson, Victoria Larrea, Julie Matteo, Greg Roper, Ray and Gail Sage DaMazo, Deborah Szekely, Marco Van Emden, and Michael Winfield.

We also thank all those helpful and thoughtful concierges, hoteliers, massage therapists, food servers, etc., whom we encountered during our enviable research duties—too many to be named here. A special thanks to: Lubosh Barta, Nicola Blazier, Nicola Chilton, Katie Clark, Sue Dreyer, Prhativi Dyah, Colleen Flynn, Kevin Girard, Putu Indrawatum, David Johnson, Anchalika Kijkanakorn, Howard Klein, Prachai Lertkunakornkit, Nelly Malonda, Haruethai Maneerat, Jany-Michel-Fourre, Refiloe Mokgabudi, John O' Sullivan, Nora Pary, Guido Phillips, Yanis Ratanaviosit, Selamat Makani, Anjali Nihalchand, Frank Peeters, Kantuethai Roongruang, Dao and Pat Trungprakan Patara, Kini Sanborn, Rizky Selfira, Komson Sevatasai, Sophie Sieck, Emma Silverman, Jason Stone, Wayan Susanto, Gede Widia, Wayan Winawan, Vichit Wisanjaturong, Imuthia Yanindra, and Ruth Zuckerman.

PHOTO CREDITS

GOING AWAY TO GET CLOSER

I magine the two of you just as the sun begins to set, the only ones left on the beach because the tropical breezes have picked up and it's growing dark. You cuddle together to stay warm on your oversized lounge chair, watching the moon rise as it casts a long streak of light on the sea. You wonder why it took so long to plan this getaway.

Planning a vacation with romance at its heart can be beneficial to almost any couple. These trips can help relationships that need some nourishment, and even those that don't, because even the best relationships can use a little magic.

The craving for special time together can come at all stages of a relationship. Sometimes you need that magic to show the person you have fallen in love with how amazing life can be together. You take her to Paris to propose—or you make your first vacation as a couple to the place he's wanted to go all his life. You want a setting that allows you and your new partner to see each other as special. You want the place, the food, the music—even the air you breathe and the sight of the sun rising or setting—to make your hearts stir and your attraction grow and deepen.

Long-term relationships are strongest when romantic trips are part of their history, present, and future. The happiest couples keep thinking of new things to please and delight each other. Of course, you can't avoid the routine of everyday life, nor would you want to. Some tried-and-true favorites feel great: your special table at a neighborhood restaurant, a familiar walking path, or the cozy bar where you meet old friends. Routines are comfortable and help you connect with good memories, but sometimes they become *too* familiar, and too predictable. Keeping romance—and passion—alive over the long term isn't impossible, but it isn't easy, either. It's complicated: We crave the security that comes with our committed relationship, but we also desire adventure and fresh discovery. Long-term and lifelong couples face a challenge, but it is also a solution—to maintain a mix of routines we love, along with innovations and surprises that make us feel lucky to be sharing a life with one another.

1 WHAT TRAVEL CAN DO FOR A RELATIONSHIP

Of course, any number of ways can support and enhance romance, but we firmly believe one of the best and easiest ways is to take time together as lovers and explorers of new and favorite destinations. As long-time relationship researchers and professionals, we know that a little invention and exploration go a long way to keeping love and intimacy fresh and healthy. Embracing new places—whether sharing inspiring landscapes or exciting adventures—will enrich a long-term relationship or help create a new one, whether you are 25 or 65. We've found that couples that thrive are the ones who create new experiences—who share moments of wonder and even bliss. We know it can be difficult to coordinate schedules and plan a getaway, but here are some of the reasons why you might need to put it at the top of your list.

- **You have a great history together but long for some of the sizzle your relationship had when you started.** You'll be surprised how it all comes back when you add some new scenery and shared adventures. Humans thrive on a mix of predictability and variety. An easy way to offset too much predictability is to break the routine in a new location. Enjoy the chance to surprise each other by putting yourself in some unusual, and romantic, situations. Then go native!

- **You need the right setting to put you in the mood for romance.** If you've been together a long time, you probably need a little atmosphere to get passion jump-started. If you're newly together, you need a place without distractions: no computers, smartphones, TV, chores, or unfinished projects staring you in the face. Established couples can feed off the anticipation of a forthcoming getaway to build a little more sensual electricity. Even couples in the midst of intense careers and/or child raising need to escape to remember how good sex can be when you can concentrate on each other and you are not falling into bed exhausted.

- **You need uninterrupted time together.** What is a greater luxury for you and your partner than time away together with an open agenda? For romance you need time to talk, walk, and have fun together. A trip to a better climate, or a prettier room (one that you don't have to clean) invites longer conversations and emotional connection. Indulging in a well-planned vacation or even a quick weekend getaway can energize a couple's romantic connection almost instantaneously.

Time away for couples is essential, especially for those whose home, dominated by family responsibilities, has more or less lost the capacity to be a haven for introspection and deeper communication. Getting away is especially critical for those two-career couples for whom work has become the leitmotif of their world. It can be hard, impossible even, to get work out of their heads long enough to feel what's in their hearts.

The Price of Love

When you look over all the amazing choices in this book, you might feel a thud of emotional letdown after you calculate the cost of some of these experiences. Some of these places are pricey—and pricey in any season.

But throughout this book, we include plenty of affordable options for hotels and dining. Also, see "Romance on a Budget," in chapter 2, which outlines great ways to save on your romantic getaway.

- **You need to wake up your brain.** Sharing something new as a couple can be very sexy! Getting away and seeing one another in a different context can give you energy and positions you to see each other in a new way. Taking a spa day together at a nearby luxury hotel or resort is refreshing, but staying overnight somewhere nearby can be even better. Give yourself permission to sleep in; then go to morning yoga or take a walk or run. Doing things together turns ordinary activities into something special. But embarking on a truly adventurous trip can give you a new perspective on life—and on each other. When everything is new, and nothing feels at all familiar, it awakens every one of your senses.
- **You'll feel more pride and gratitude.** How often do you talk about your dream destinations, yet never get there? When you actually do go, you feel proud that you made it happen! It's likely the gratitude you feel for that experience will carry over to how you feel about each other. It's a simple formula: Gratitude for the getaway makes you value the relationship that brought you there. Traveling carves out time to liberate—and remember—the fun part of who you are.

WHAT TO LOOK FOR IN A ROMANTIC DESTINATION

Some people love the pulse of a big city while others want the loudest sound they hear to be the measured lapping of waves against a sandy shore. Of course you need to decide as a couple what kind of location will thrill you, but we have learned that certain types of places and specific features can really create and sustain romance. We've traipsed the world looking for the perfect romantic destinations, and in the pages that follow we've identified the 75 most romantic settings. We've walked a lot of cobblestone, sifted through acres of sand, and sipped endless vintages, and we think we've discovered the top 10 traits that make a destination just right for romance. Naturally, the more of these features a place has, the better.

1. The Beauty of Nature

Beautiful, natural views set a mood. For most people, looking out at the sea, the mountains, a gorgeous canyon, or a beautiful garden resonates with their kinder, gentler, more loving side. Sometimes a magnificent view, like rugged high mountain peaks, can leave you speechless and filled with awe. We look for wondrous settings in our recommendations because these feelings can ignite all four of the so-called love hormones: dopamine, which fosters feelings of love; oxytocin, which helps create trust and bonding; serotonin, which increases feelings of pleasure and well being; and norepinephrine, which gives us energy and is part of our sexual arousal.

It may be simplistic, but it's true: Looking at something magnificent is a thrill that usually brings couples together, making them hug more and feel grateful to be able to share the moment together. So ask yourselves which natural setting will set the stage for you and your partner: the turquoise sea? a rocky coastline? craggy mountains? a luscious rain forest? ancient, mystical canyons? the bright lights of a city skyline? What will deepen your connection?

2. Indoor Beauty

Many travelers try to economize on the lodging part of a vacation, rationalizing that they will be out and about more than indoors. That's true in a lot of cases, but we believe that when you want to light a fire within (or re-ignite one) you should consider cutting other corners to allow for a reasonable splurge when it comes to your hotel room. Certain rooms invite you to linger, to stay in bed nestled in smooth satin sheets, or to take a bath or shower à deux, followed up with the sensuality of thick, soft towels. This lingering is the defining element for passion. You know the old joke that women need to have a reason to have sex but that men just need the opportunity. Sure, it's a caricature of both genders, but women will feel more sensual if a room provides a bit of luxury or charm. And, actually, an inviting room can help jump-start both partners' libidos.

When identifying some of the most romantic places to stay, we looked for hotel rooms that please the senses with details like fresh flowers and soothing or vibrant colors, and sometimes we even recommend theme rooms because they are so playful. We prize rooms with views, balconies, and patios, oversize two-person bathtubs and showers, fireplaces, and comfortable beds with sheets and pillows that are more luxurious than yours at home.

3. A Stage Set for Love

Indoors and outdoors should conspire together to make you feel lucky, well cared for, and we hope, amorous. The best destinations are designed to immediately set a mood. The scenery and hotels we love the most set the stage in the same way a well-designed set improves a play or movie. Your mood is established just by looking at the backdrop in which the action takes place.

4. A Chance to Get Your Adrenaline Pumping

The easiest way to get your hormones percolating is to get physical—whether hiking or doing something really intense (like bungee jumping). This kind of activity fuels a feeling of connectedness that, given the right stimulus, heightens your erotic feelings for one another and will keep them pumping. A classic psychology article in 1971 based on a variety of experiments demonstrated that people became more attached when they met during thrilling or scary circumstances. The researchers' conclusion: "Adrenaline makes the heart grow fonder." Now, we don't want to suggest anything too frightening—that would be counter-productive—but in the pages that follow we go out of our way to suggest a variety of activities to get your blood pumping in a way that boosts libido and makes you feel more bonded and open to love. For those less physically fit, think about what else would do this for you, such as venturing onto the glass balcony outside the 103rd floor on the sky deck of Chicago's Willis Tower (http://theskydeck.com), or taking a helicopter ride over the mouth of the famous volcano on Hawaii's Big Island (see p. 224).

5. Likelihood of Surprises

Romance flourishes best when the adventure you've planned turns out to be even more wonderful than you anticipated. If you expected a red rose, how much more wonderful the surprise when you get a dozen? If you expect nothing extra in your room and you get a bottle of wine and cheese upon arrival, you are pleased. If you go to dinner and you are seated in your own alcove in a special part of the restaurant that you didn't know existed, you are likely to be charmed. And when you come back to your room from a long day exploring wine country, and you find a fire burning in the fireplace and romantic music already playing (all done by an attentive turndown service), you are likely to feel grateful and very content.

Not every hotel or resort plans surprises or crafts a magical night you didn't expect. But we look for the ones that do—and include them in this book. Then again, you don't have to depend on the place you are staying to add magic and surprise. You can start a trip by giving your partner a gift on the first night; even the smallest token will go a long way to setting a mood of emotional generosity and love. It could be a gift massage, a sentimental card, a book of poems or one on the region reflecting a special interest, or something practical like new mini binoculars. If you didn't have time ahead of the trip, give something you saw your partner admiring earlier that day (and then circled back to buy it). Or you could just draw a bath for your partner. The fact that you thought of the gesture, and presented it as a surprise, will usually create all kinds of reciprocal kindnesses and good will. And if the gift is given in a sweet way (say, hiding a lovely nightgown under a pillow to be discovered at bedtime), it might be remembered forever.

6. Opportunities for Mutual Discovery

We love destinations that offer dramatic excursions, places to discover together, and experiences so outstanding that they inevitably turn into special memories. We also appreciate places that invite you to add new skills for the two of you to take on together. It could be learning to kayak or river raft, or taking a cooking lesson or a wine tasting tour together. We look for experiences that expand your knowledge (like seeing how experts restore paintings in Venice) or make you proud of each other (like hiking a [slightly] more rigorous trail than you are used to).

All these shared experiences are important not only in themselves but also because partners in relationships need new material to talk about to stay interesting. If you have been together for a very long time, you could easily get so predictable that you are in danger of boring each other. At their best, new experiences remind you of your early days together and how much fun it was to get to know each other. Another bonus for all couples: You work as a team creating your romantic adventure together. Trusting each other and being interdependent buoys relationships. (The only exception is when your relationship is in an unstable period, and you are going away to heal; then you need as few decisions as possible. See "The Healing Power of Travel" on p. 152.)

7. Novelty

Research shows that the very best way for couples to refresh their love for one another is to do something, *anything*, novel together. Why? Because novel experiences raise your dopamine levels, and dopamine, a neurotransmitter, tells your brain to focus on the one you love. Again, it's the basics of the chemistry of endorphins: Boost them and feel more joy and bliss. But you don't have to climb Mt. Kilimanjaro to create novelty. Sometimes just new sights will do the trick. Negotiating your way from one attraction to another in a new foreign city or watching something new (like kabuki theater—by definition, out of the ordinary) will stimulate your brain and your conversation. Novelty is easier to find than you might think.

8. Privacy—and Protection from Distraction

So imagine all these elements are in place, but you can hear your neighbors arguing through the shared wall of your hotel bedroom. Or you arrive at a resort only to find it filled with conventioneers, making the space feel crowded or chaotic. For most people, this is the end of romance and passion and the beginning of feeling cheated. We feel it is extremely important that people can enjoy where they stay without hearing other people—or being heard by them. We also think that even when you are in a city, it is much more romantic when you can find places to sit or walk where you can feel private together. In general, romantic vacations are meant to help you focus on each other, which means avoiding distractions. To us, that means finding restaurants where the noise is low and the feeling is intimate, or adult-only beaches and pools absent the screams of children and the roughhousing of teenagers.

GREAT HOTEL gestures

It's not surprising that the grander hotels provide the most over-the-top gestures, but even modest hotels and inns make gestures that facilitate feeling romantic, such as offering adult-only pools, or serving complimentary home-made cookies with wine or hot chocolate in the afternoon. The following properties go way beyond the ubiquitous chocolate on the pillow:

o A soaking pool reserved for one lucky couple for the whole night (Salish Lodge, Washington [p. 64])

o A private candlelit dinner, set around the resort's enormous pool (Amankila at Nusa Dua, Bali [p. 306]).

o A trail of rose petals lead-ing to a foaming bathtub with champagne on ice next to it (Ngorogoro Cra-ter Lodge, Africa [p. 367]).

o A wine-tasting room for a private tasting. (The Marcus Whitman, Walla Walla, Washington [p. 157]). *Note:* Check with your concierge at any wine-region hotel; many can organize a pri-vate tasting for you.

o A romantic dinner in your own lakefront gazebo with a chef and music only for you (The Four Seasons [p. 94] or The Mandarin Oriental [p. 56], Chiang Mai, Thailand).

o A small plane to a private fishing place on the river, with a picnic, readymade for a proposal along the banks (The Little Nell, Aspen, Colorado [p. 123]).

o Reserved private hours on the clothing optional sun-deck (Cambridge Beaches Resort & Spa, Bermuda [p. 263])

o Horse ride to a private pic-nic by a river or hilltop (The Resort at Paws Up, Montana [p. 349]).

o Turndown service that includes lighting the fire-place and filling the room with romantic music (Ken-wood Inn and Spa [p. 130]).

o A private dinner with white-gloved service, in a torch-lit gazebo at water's edge on Seven-Mile Beach (Azul Sensatori Jamaica, Negril [p. 277]).

We also want everything to be so wonderful and engaging that you will be able to resist the inevitable temptation to remove yourselves from the present and get trapped in endless worries about what's waiting undone at home. A getaway—whether it is for a day, a night, or weeks—needs you to be present and playful. We want to make it almost impossible not to be in the moment!

9. It's All in the Details

We like hotels that really listen to you, and we advise you to let the staff know that you are planning a romantic getaway. Don't be shy about giving them instructions about what you need. If a hotel or resort or restaurant knows that you will be celebrating an anniversary or proposing, it will usually try even harder to make your visit outstanding. Some hotels may even upgrade you if they can. Great places will, as far as possible, make sure all your preferences are met, and they let you know when they cannot. They will also suggest special things to do, for example, telling you where to enjoy a picnic (and they may provide it) or where to find a remote mountain stream or beach cove. We've found a huge difference between hotels that are proud of their hospitality and seek to always make the customer happy and places that merely check you in. When you go to a place that cares about you and seeks to make you really happy, that mood pervades your whole visit.

10. Satisfaction for All the Senses

We humans are sensual animals. Our sense of smell might not be as acute as a bear's or a wolf's, but it is still our most immediate involuntary sense. If you smell a tantalizing perfume or cologne on your partner's neck, you may always have a pleasant reaction when you smell it again. Likewise, the wrong smell can ruin a promising place. A nonsmoker walking into a room that reeks of smoke may feel nauseated or angry.

Romance is heightened if all our senses are alerted—and satisfied. We like places where the food is so yummy that the adjective "orgasmic" is only a slight exaggeration. We want each sense—smell, taste, touch, sound, and sight—to be delighted. So we pick our restaurants, walks, activities, and views with the idea that if those are all special, romance will be inevitable.

And let's not skimp on old Eros. If you are a new couple in the initial stages of scoping each other out, erotic attraction probably won't be a problem. We'll just give you some places that help you accentuate your passion for each other. But if you've been together a long time, sex may well be kind of humdrum, and let's admit it, infrequent. That may be the style you've become accustomed to, and that's comfortable for you. But if one or both of you longs for a bit more passion, the mood and feelings we will help you create could better your game significantly. At the very least, we will have you cuddling, kissing, and holding hands more often, and quite a few couples feel that is the most gratifying way they express their love.

We applied our 10-point formula to help us pick every destination in this book, but you can use them on any place you hear about and want to investigate. In the meantime, you can depend on us to bring wonderful places for romance to your attention and, we hope, this will be enough to motivate you to take advantage of them, again and again.

PLANNING YOUR ROMANTIC VACATION

Before you book a single flight or a guest room, remind yourself about the purpose of this trip: to enhance the romantic temperature of your relationship. It's not a business trip, planned with the hopes of getting a little private time on the side, or a packaged tour that has you hopping on and off buses all day, or even a ski vacation that has you on different slopes because of different skill levels, returning totally exhausted at night. Those make for great vacations—but not the shared experience we are promoting in this book.

What you want here is a getaway that gives you quality time together and that meets at least some of the criteria we wrote about in chapter 1 (a beautiful setting, privacy, special details, and so on). Your trip should also fit your budget and provide opportunities to do what you *both* like to do together. You will notice, for example, that this book isn't heavy on sport vacations where only one person in the relationship may be truly passionate about the activity. Golf, for example, can be a focal point of a great getaway vacation if you both love it, but it's a terrible idea for romance if only one of you really cares about the sport.

We trust that you and your partner have a good sense of what you like in common. We know that tenting in the Rockies would be heaven for some people, but hell for others. Or that foodies might swoon over a multi-destination tour in search of gourmet delights, but others might think of that as a supreme waste of time and money. And we recognize that different kinds of trips beguile at different times of the life cycle—and different parts of a relationship cycle. We even offer recommendations for couples with younger kids, who want to find romance on a family vacation (p. 314). In this book we've done our best to share a variety of destinations and activities to speak to the romantic in you.

CHOOSING YOUR DESTINATION

So where will it be: an alluring city? a natural wonderland? a sultry beach? a once-in-a-lifetime adventure?

We've divided our 75 destinations into four groupings: Urban Romance, Natural Romance, Beach Romance, and Adventure Romance. As you think about these very different types of destinations, keep in mind that you are looking for landscapes and places that let you concentrate on each other, the kinds of places that take you away from the distractions of work, friends, and even thoughts of the big evening news stories about what's going on in our tumultuous world. Choose a type of destination that you believe promises to let you refocus, give thanks for the most positive essence of your relationship, and make you think about the life you want to live together in the future. Our bottom line: Select your destination with care. And if you want a little more guidance, take a look at our Romantic Interest Index, beginning on p. 391.

Urban Romance

Bright lights, big city. Sometimes a getaway in a romantic room with a view, a special dinner in a celebrated restaurant, and a day window shopping on famous streets (say, Madison Avenue in New York or Michigan Avenue in Chicago) or seeing a special exhibition can be just enough time to rejuvenate romance.

What E. B. White famously said of New York City is true for all the cities we invite you to visit: Prepare to be surprised. Cities offer new restaurants, live theater and shows, romantic parks and promenades, and old historic buildings. Cities are also great for people watching. On the other hand, if *you* don't want to be seen (we won't ask why), a big city is a great place to become invisible.

Cities can be costly, though, especially if you want to be in the heart of the action. But for re-energizing with glitz and glamour, late-night dancing, comedy clubs, or a full-scale musical, no suburban or rural location can compete.

Our coverage of the most exciting cities for romance begins on p. 25.

Natural Romance

While city vacations are wonderfully rich and complex—full of museums, people, and events—we think that reviving or deepening romance often requires more solitude, space for conversation, and interdependence. The destinations in this group—natural wonderlands, countryside retreats, and winelands—promise the gifts of remote places, striking landscapes, and off-the-beaten-path gems. Being out in nature makes you appreciate what is truly important: Your relationship is the keystone to a good life, and experiencing deep intimacy is one of the best parts of it.

The destinations in this section are meant to get you out of the city, to places that can change your mood quickly from tense to relaxed and where holding hands just happens naturally. Some of the places we describe may be just a quick plane ride or a short drive from your home—it can be fun to just get in the car and go. Mutual discoveries along the way put additional pleasure and excitement in the journey. Take your time as you drive through cute or historic towns with quaint shops.

But mostly, your job is to enjoy the beautiful scenery. You may be going through blue-grass horse country, or untouched marshlands where you'll see more wildlife than humans, or valleys with gorgeous ranches or estates, or past vast panoramas of mountains and canyons. In this section we include opportunities for out-in-nature activities like superb skiing, horseback riding, or endless biking and hiking—even hot air balloon rides if you're feeling adventurous.

We recommend plenty of charming small hotels and B&Bs that are as satisfying as the 600-thread-count sheets and afternoon sherry that thoughtful innkeepers provide. We prefer newer small inns built for more private hospitality rather than dwellings that were originally built for a family—but there are exceptions to every rule. Some country inns are beyond luxe: You pay a high tariff, but besides impeccable rooms, you get world-class cuisine. But even the affordable places we suggest provide cozy rooms that ooze charm and have been set up to put you in a romantic mood.

You may find a few more mentions of winelands here than in other travel books. Just to put our authorial cards on the table, Pepper loves wine, and to her mind, few things are more delightful and romantic than a weekend spent sipping wines in a beautiful valley devoted to the culinary art and viniculture. Plus, wineries love to customize a visit; they often have private rooms and private tours, and many have romantic places you can stay.

Some of our destinations provide scenery that will stun you with its grandeur. And there is nothing like natural beauty of awesome proportion to help open hearts and minds to one another. Gorgeous wonders of nature are all over the world, and some of them are closer to home than you may have realized. In Utah, for example, the rugged country brings to mind ancient places in the Middle East or Africa. And some of these destinations are noted for their seclusion or mystical qualities that make them excellent places to heal (and we note them as such). But most of all, the places in this section offer the luxury of privacy in vast outdoor spaces where you can truly be thankful for getting away from everything, to just be together.

Our coverage of the most alluring places for natural romance begins on p. 119.

Beach Romance

Getaways that include beautiful water views seem to alleviate any pressured feelings and let you exhale and relax from the moment you arrive. We're not saying it always takes a tropical vacation, but a powdery sand beach, a rugged coast with its rocky cliffs, or a relaxing cruise can all serve as shortcuts to reconnecting and feeling romantic. Just about everything in these places cultivates romantic feelings: trading shoes for flip-flops, the smells of the ocean, the gentle breezes, and moonlight reflecting off the water during your after-dinner stroll.

Beach locations have lots of activities to keep you entertained while building your shared experiences and memories. Couples who prefer thrills and physically demanding adventures like scuba diving and water skiing will get their adrenaline happily percolating. More meditative couples can snorkel together or just hang on rafts, side-by-side in the warm, calm, crystal-clear waters—or just lie around on beach towels and feel lucky to have each other. Some places just whisper to you, "Go ahead, order that piña colada, even though it's just a little past noon."

Some of our choices in this section offer so much coastline that there are always plenty of beachfront places to stay, places like Miami and the Florida Keys, or the two coasts of Mexico (the Mayan Riviera on the east, and the 20-mile ocean corridor between Cabo San Lucas and Jose del Cabo on the west). These, and several others of our destinations, offer beach after beach, each seemingly more beautiful than the last. You'll have multiple choices for the same stretch of beach—but at vastly different price points. So even if your room doesn't equal one at the five-star resorts, you still get the views, sand, and beach walks while staying at handsome, but way cheaper, hotels.

Besides famous beaches, different kinds of aquatic beauty might never fail to move you. Driving along the cliffs of Big Sur country with the ocean on one side and rugged vistas ahead or watching the powerful waves of British Columbia's coast as they attack the craggy coastline near Tofino are two good examples. We include many mesmerizing coastlines, from the famed Amalfi Coast to the less known but equally dramatic Dalmatian Coast in Europe and closer to home, the awesome dunes between Eugene and Portland, Oregon. If thoughts of driving long distances or zig-zagging hairpin turns on narrow roads scare you, cruises offer a delightful and often cost-effective way to tour these stirring sights.

Perhaps the most classic vision of getting away for romance is being together staring at the endless sea in all directions from a tropical island. Actually any beautiful island, in any season, conjures romantic imagery that stirs the heart. We suggest faraway exotic ones like the beaches of Phuket and Koh Samui and the more familiar tropical paradises like the lush Hawaiian island of Kauai, but also remind American readers that a mere 568 miles east of the Carolinas, Bermuda offers a different kind of sun-filled, foreign-flavored island escape.

Our coverage of the most exciting beaches for romance begins on p. 211.

Adventure Romance

Travel memoirs like "Eat, Pray, Love" or "A Year in Provence" are powerful because they demonstrate how a stay in a magnificent place can change an individual in fundamental ways. We agree that travel experiences can be transformative. Most of these books, however, do not even attempt to chronicle what such experiences can do for a couple. Believe us, magical things can happen to a relationship when a major adventure or exotic destination is taken together.

Of course, you have to be careful, and you need to know your combined tolerance levels for inconvenience because of unexpected travel snafus that often happen in less developed countries. Exotic destinations often have different travel requirements (like visas and inoculations) than the United States or the EU; and you may need to be aware of the political, environmental, and health conditions of your destination. Still, if you are up for the challenge, we think the thrill of wholly new landscapes, people, and experiences is one of life's natural aphrodisiacs, and so we present some of our most treasured travel categories for you to consider.

Want to go off into the wild? Ask anyone who has done it. When you go on an African safari, all your senses are awakened, and you are as conscious and alert as you will ever be. The life you witness—a lion stalking its prey, a gazelle jumping, an elephant trumpeting (at you!) to announce his territory and show who is boss in the bush—forces you to pay attention and perhaps rethink which species is dominant in the world.

But there are also great, awe-inspiring adventures closer to home, where you'll still feel the thrill of the wild. The United States has amazing stretches of wilderness; some have been tamed a bit for those of us who want a romantic experience, not a survival challenge. Among our favorites are river-rafting and float trips, such as those on the Snake River near Jackson Hole, Wyoming, and Palouse Falls State Park near Walla Walla, Washington. The earlier in the summer season, the more whitewater you get, and the more exciting the ride. You are likely to see abundant large four-hoofed wildlife to further stir your sense of grand adventure. And each night, tenting at a beautiful site on the river, romantic feelings come easily as you ponder the millions of stars you never knew were there.

Rio de Janeiro promises another kind of wild—the wildest street party on the planet. Starting on Saturday and ending on Fat Tuesday (Mardi Gras), the city stops so everyone, at every age, can celebrate this world-famous pre-Lenten festival, Carnival. If you're willing to brave the crowds and the perfect conditions for pickpockets (leave your valuables at home!), and if you are willing to pay peak rates for your hotel, this is the place to be—at least once in your life.

And sometimes the adventure of a lifetime means entering a dream world, someplace exotic, luxurious, and whose culture is a world apart. In Asia, many countries provide the wonderful mix of spirituality and sensuality: Among them, we especially love Thailand, Indonesia (Bali, in particular), Cambodia, and India. We name locations that are so special, so ethereal, that their romance quotient is sky high.

Our coverage of the most dramatic places for adventure romance begins on p. 331.

How to Choose the Best Location

We hope you will take the time to choose the right location for *both of you* as you plan your romantic getaway. Following are a few questions to consider before you book. Have fun; make it a date night and discuss it over a quiet dinner; or just gather around a computer and fire away.

What have been your most romantic trips up to now? What features made them so romantic for you? And which of those features do you want to replicate in your next trip?

What are the top three places each of you has longed to go? If you aren't sure, this might be a good time to look through this book for inspiration. Read the descriptions of our four main types of getaway over the preceding couple of pages, or peruse our **Romantic Interest Index,** which begins on p. 391. For details such as climate and general tourist information, search online. Also online, Google Earth lets you zero in on the location of the places you are considering, showing just how close you would be to airports, restaurants, shops, adjacent buildings, and even construction sites!

Are any of your top three choices a good fit for both of you? If one of you is seeking a rigorous adventure while the other would prefer to sit on the beach, consider only the choices that would make you both happy.

How much are you willing to spend on this vacation? And is your budget in sync with your top pick? If your top choices seem too costly (or are too costly for the season you've chosen), what would be a realistic substitute?

When do you want to go? Set a date or approximate date or season for your trip. Do you want to go during high season when weather is optimal or low season when you can find bargain prices?

What research is necessary to pick the right spot for the right time of year? Divvy up the duties to follow up on everything you dreamed up at this discussion—and then schedule another planning meeting!

Is an all-inclusive resort right for you? Some travelers want to know everything is taken care of on one gorgeous site, whereas others prefer to explore an area by staying in a boutique hotel in or near town to get a better sense for local color. If you're in the former category and prefer not to get bogged down with too much planning, an all-inclusive might be right for you. Usually, they are a great bargain, but in our experience many of them are guilty of serving big quantities of low-quality food (one notable exception: Club Med, www.clubmed.com). We include few all-inclusive resorts here—only the ones that carry it off particularly well—because romance doesn't feel great when you feel like you are part of the herd.

Do you want to opt for tours or cruises? There are some wonderful packaged tours and cruises that make travel easier by doing a lot of the planning, keeping the costs down, and offering you company during the day and occasional interesting dinner companions at night, should you feel social. We include a

Throughout the book we feature sidebars and special sections that offer great advice on making your romantic getaway *unforgettable*. In these sections we offer tips on celebrating milestone events, finding romance on a family vacation, getting away close to home, saving money wherever you go, using travel for healing, and much more. Check out the Table of Contents for a complete list. Also, see our Romantic Interest Index, starting on p. 391, to help you hone in the places that speak to your personal interests.

few fantastic options among our destinations. In general, however, we think it is risky to go on a tour or a ship with assigned seating on a romantic vacation. If you do go on a ship, make sure it offers table-for-two options at the time you prefer to eat (later seatings have fewer children) and whether on a tour or cruise, be ready to guard your privacy and good mood, even if it means you have to avoid some (or all) of the people around you.

If you do choose to cruise, here's an easy way to get atmosphere, great food, and romantic ambience (without the crowds and family tables): On booking, ask how soon you can sign up for upgrades to the ship's elite specialty restaurants. Usually the upgrade is $15 to $25 per person per meal, and it yields exponential returns on your investment. Even on a deluxe all-inclusive liner, the highest quality foods, cooked haute cuisine to order by the best chefs, are found here. This is a well-known secret, so sign up as early as you can for one or two meals, which may possibly become among the most memorable meals of your lifetime.

ROMANCE ON A BUDGET

As we searched the world for its most romantic destinations, we worked hard to include affordable options in our hotel and restaurant recommendations. But beyond those specific establishments, here are a few more ways to save on your romantic getaway.

TRAVEL IN THE OFF-SEASON AND SHOULDER-SEASON. Consider visiting your dream location in the off-season, when the demand is low. You may even feel like you have the place all to yourselves, an added romantic boon that gives the place a kind of magic. That said, there are off-seasons—and there are "beware seasons." An off-season may be a little rainy, but the "beware" season has dangerous hurricanes. An off-season may be too hot, but the beware season is 120° in the shade.

We find that the so-called "shoulder season" is often ideal; these are the timeslots just before or after high season—like the Caribbean after Thanksgiving, before rates jump up for Christmas travelers; the weather is good (this is post-hurricane season), but prices are significantly lower.

One of our perennial favorites is the shoulder season for ski areas. Call it the neither season; it is neither winter nor summer, but it's got its own thing going, still offering plenty of luxury and fun things to do. For example, we talked to reservation agents at the stunning **Ritz Carlton at Bachelor Gulch** in the Vail Valley (2 hours from Denver, 2 hours from Aspen). A suite there in September after Labor Day can be yours for $179 a night; that same room mid-January goes for a whopping $799.

Additional favorite, and flagrantly underappreciated, off-season destinations are the islands and coastal regions that are crowded and expensive in summer, but are on a fire sale in winter. **Bermuda** typically has a wonderful spring, and has quite benign weather even in winter. On the East Coast, **Martha's Vineyard** and **Nantucket**—known as the summer playground to the rich—offers reduced rates in the late fall and winter. You will still enjoy the beaches, enhanced by the solitude you can find on them at that uncrowded time of year. In the West, among our favorites are the American and Canadian **San Juan Islands** near Seattle; in the summer, they are an international playground; in the late fall and winter, you can play, too—but it's all yours, even on the spur of the moment. Further south, the wonderful resorts up and down the coast of California are also available for a lot less during the off-season. And don't forget **Catalina Island,** just off the Los Angeles coast—it's warm all year, yet hotels and ferries give great deals when it's not the high summer season. Or consider the long haul to Indonesia to visit **Bali**: A January visit will definitely put you in the rainy season—but your trip will be half the price.

OPT FOR CHEAPER SLEEPS. When you find a destination that speaks to you, but the recommended hotels don't seem to perceive your budget, consider sourcing a cheaper hotel online or possibly even renting a private apartment. (Check out our sidebar, "Packing Heat," on p. 16, for ways to add romantic appeal to any guest room.) **Airbnb.com** offers privately owned apartments and rooms—even treehouses and boats—in 192 countries. Before booking, peruse the photos and guest reviews for a fairly good idea of what the place is like. The reviews often tell you about the neighborhood as well. It's estimated that Airbnb sleeps some 50,000 to 60,000 people a night. **Homeaway.com** and **VRBO.com** are known for even more luxurious private rentals. **HouseTrip.com** is another popular website. And some sites are city specific, like **Parisperfect.com.** Just check carefully to be sure you understand all the policies (including cancellation) and possible extra costs, like cleaning fees or taxes.

VISIT OUR PRICIER PLACES. We'll admit it: Some of the spots we mention in this book are extremely expensive and just a night or two lodgings here could consume most of your budget, but you should consider a visit to one of their restaurants or lounges that are open to the public. Splurge on a luxurious lunch—the most affordable meal, and when timed right it can be your main meal of the day—or Sunday brunch. Check to see whether there are happy hours in garden terraces; but even without happy hour, a single round of drinks and a shared appetizer doesn't usually break the bank. If there's a spa onsite, consider indulging in a single treatment; oftentimes, for the price of a spa treatment, you get a guest pass that lets you enjoy many of the amenities of a luxe resort.

SEARCH ONLINE RESOURCES. There's no end to the travel resources you can find online. AARP's travel website, **Travel.AARP.org**, offers destination guides, travel tips, and, of course, exclusive travel discounts for AARP members. You can visit **Frommers.com** for trip-planning information and for searching the best rates for airfare, lodging, and car rentals. We also like **PeterGreenberg.com** and **SmarterTravel.com** for their recommendations on getting good travel deals and useful travel advice and cautions. If you travel with a smartphone, Yelp.com can be helpful getting you to a nearby affordable restaurant wherever you are—it's especially useful in Europe.

CONSIDER PACKAGED DEALS. What level of planning are you willing to do? If you don't have the time or don't enjoy trip-planning work, then packaged deals are an option to consider. Joining tours, staying at all-inclusive resorts, and sailing with a cruise line all offer economical travel options. Just be aware that on cruises, day tours or area activities are usually a la carte items that can add heft to your final bill. We prefer all-inclusive packages, like the ones offered by the following companies. **Overseas Adventure Travel** (OAT; www.oattravel.com) offers small-group (up to 16 persons) trips that our friends swear by; check the website for last-minute deals to save you even more money. OAT is part of the larger **Grand Circle Travel** (www.gct.com), which features trips for larger groups (around 40); check the website for discounts. The company has won awards for their economical river cruises—a couple we know loved their Paris-to-Provence cruise so much, they did it again before trying another of Grand Circle's many destinations. **Viking** (www.vikingcruises.com) recently launched a fleet of longships (190 passengers) that offers more luxury and amenities (like real verandas); their tours are usually a little more expensive, but Viking is well known for the quality of its guides and local cuisine.

SEEK OUT AGE-SPECIFIC DISCOUNTS. If you're 50+, **AARP** (© 888/ OUR-AARP; www.aarp.org) is the go-to place for savings; members get discounts on hotels, airfares, and car rentals. Visit AARP's travel website, **Travel.AARP.org** to find current travel discounts, and read the excellent advice given by AARP travel ambassador Samantha Brown online and often in "AARP The Magazine."

Road Scholar (formerly Elderhostel; www.roadscholar.org) is the not-for-profit leader in educational travel, and it offers 5,500 educational tours in all 50 U.S. states and 150 countries. The organization has promoted lifelong learning through travel adventures since 1975.

For just $10, people age 62 and up get lifetime free admission to national parks with the **Golden Age Passport,** offered through the U.S. National Parks Service (© 888/GO-PARKS; www.nps.gov/fees_passes.htm).

Seniors Home Exchange (www.seniorshomeexchange.com) bills itself as the only home exchange company exclusively catering to people 50 and over.

Romance on a Budget

PACKING heat

You can turn any hotel room into a Place for Passion with a few simple tricks:

o **Bring candles and candle holders.** A working fireplace is a real romantic plus, but if you bring along some candles, you can get pretty much the same effect. Add a great aroma to the candles, and you can please two senses at the same time. Just be safe: Bring candles that are already in some kind of nonflammable holder. Needless to say, don't forget to blow them out before you go to sleep or leave your room.

o **Bring bath products you love.** Luxury hotels usually provide luxurious bath products. But if you're staying in a lesser hotel or renting a private apartment, you cannot expect this amenity. Pack a great selection of bath and body products, including an aromatic massage oil, just in case you want to exchange foot or full body massages.

o **Bring your own music.** Music is great for setting the right mood. If you already travel with your favorite tunes on your smartphone or tablet, check with your hotel to see whether it provides docking stations in the guestrooms. If not, bring your own, along with portable wireless

You must just become a member to use its services. There are a few other companies that offer similar services. Do some online research to discover which one might work best for you.

LOOK FOR INTERNET SPECIALS. Consolidators like Expedia.com and Orbitz.com offer package deals that combine air travel, car, and hotel; these options are worth checking out before you book. Packagers—such as Groupon Getaways, Living Social Escapes, Travelzoo, Triporati, and Vacationist—sometimes offer incredible deals online; keep a lookout for them because you'll have to grab them fast. Many airlines offer packaged trips, too. But take caution. Before you commit to any of the so-called deals, make sure it is to a place that you know is great and confirm its usual website booking price. Be sure there's still availability within the restricted dates before you commit to purchase. Finally, check the dates and make sure the weather isn't awful that time of the year. Most cruises, for example, will be discounted during the rainy season. But do you really want to experience Tahiti in the rain every day?

PICK UP THE PHONE. Plenty of places offer deep Internet discounts, but in some places personal contact will do the trick. It never hurts to call an establishment to try to get a better rate.

speakers, and consider adding some collections that will add to the mood. Who does it for you and your partner? Al Green or Marvin Gaye, or maybe Norah Jones or Sade? Do you move while you groove with Robin Thicke? Or go classic with Tony Bennett? All we're saying is be thoughtful and provide your own smooth soundtrack.

○ **Bring your own toys and other entertainments.** Sometimes you want your own sensual enhancements. If you have "aids" that enhance sensual play that you ordinarily use at home (or would like to try on this vacation), bring them along! Just remember that different countries have different values about what might be considered pornographic. So think before you pack something if you are going to have to go through Customs.

○ **Pack special clothes.** Clothes really can set a mood—for both the wearer and the admirer. Unless you are going backpacking, take at least one thing that is dressy for a special evening—and it wouldn't hurt to wear something new and special to bed (unless your version of "special" is nothing at all!).

Inexpensive Places—Even in High Season

Let's say you want to travel in the high season because you like the weather then or it's the only time you can get away for a chunk of time. You can still visit some of your coveted locations if you're willing to take the roads less traveled—that is, choose similar but less popular places. For example, instead of going to the beautiful beaches of Cabo San Lucas or San Jose del Cabo, go inland and tour the amazing cities of colonial Mexico. We recommend **Guanajuato, Santiago de Querétaro,** and **San Miguel de Allende** in Central Mexico. The climate is universally lovely, and these towns are postcard pretty with their Spanish architecture, central plazas with fountains, and charming shops and authentic restaurants.

You can even do Europe on the cheap in high season. Most seasoned travelers know that **Barcelona** is less expensive than Rome, Paris, or London, and we think it rivals any of those cities as a romantic hotspot. It's a picturesque port city, with fine restaurants, a unique culture, and a vibrant section called Las Ramblas that is full of twists, turns, local markets, cafes, flower shops, intimate small bars, and historic buildings to explore.

A less well-known and even less expensive European city to consider for summer travel is **Lisbon.** We whole-heartedly endorse this truly underrated ancient city. The Old Town, where you eat along the cobblestone streets as well as in the restaurants, is convivial and packed at night. The sounds of local *fado* singing and guitar music start wafting from clubs as the night grows late. Portugal is also extremely easy to drive. One of the most intriguing and lively towns is **Porto,** home, of course, to Port wine.

The U.S. dollar still goes farther in Eastern Europe than in Western Europe, and we love Croatia's **Dalmation Coast,** whose dramatic views rival those of the much better known Amalfi Coast in Italy—and the city Dubrovnik is not to be missed. It's touristy, yes, but going inside this perfectly preserved late-Medieval walled city is like stepping into a fairytale. No wonder Lord Byron called it "the pearl of the Adriatic." It is a jewel of a city in an irresistible setting.

ALL ABOUT PRICING

We've assigned a $ rating to all of our recommended hotels and restaurants to help you plan your romantic adventure according to your budget. Here's a key to the system used in this book.

Hotels

Price categories for hotels are based on the rack rates for a basic double room; expect those rates to rise, perhaps into the next pricing category, if you upgrade to a suite or better. Also, be aware that you can sometimes get better rates by calling the hotel directly and asking if discounts are available, or checking its website.

$ RATING	PRICE RANGE
$	up to $250
$$	$251–$425
$$$	$426 and up

Restaurants

Restaurant ratings are based on the average price of a main course (or prix fixe menu, where appropriate).

$ RATING	PRICE RANGE (MAIN COURSE)	PRICE RANGE (PRIX FIXE MENU)
$	up to $19	$35 or less
$$	$20–$36	$36–$55
$$$	$37 and up	$56 and up

Attractions

For attractions, we list exact prices in the local currency. The currency conversions quoted here were current at press time. Rates fluctuate, however, so before departing, consult a currency exchange website, such as www.oanda.com/currency/converter, to check up-to-the-minute rates.

THE VALUE OF VARIOUS CURRENCY VS. OTHER POPULAR CURRENCIES

	US$	€	A$	C$	NZ$	UK£
Argentine (Peso [ARS])	.12	.09	.12	.13	.13	.07
Australian (Dollar [A$])	.94	.69	—	1.00	1.07	.55
Brazilian (Real [R])	.45	.33	.48	.48	.52	.26
Euro	1.33	—	1.32	1.37	1.74	.85
British (£)	1.75	1.26	1.82	1.84	1.94	—
Canadian (Dollar [C$])	.93	.68	.99	—	1.06	.54
Croatian (Kuna [KN])	.18	.13	.19	.20	.21	.11
Indian (Rupee [INR])	.02	.01	.02	.02	.02	.01
Mexican (Peso [MXN])	.08	.06	.08	.08	.09	.05
Moroccan (Dirham [dh])	.12	.09	.12	.12	.13	.07
South African (Rand [R])	.09	.07	.10	.10	.10	.05
Thai(Baht [THB])	.03	.02	.03	.03	.04	.02
Turkish (Lira [TL])	.46	.33	.48	.48	.52	.26

GETTING THE BEST ROOM

Someone is going to get the best, most romantic, room in the house, and it may as well be you. Here are a few ways to stake your claim.

Tell the booking person you are there for a romantic vacation. Say you want something special, or ask for something specific. If it's available, the receptionist will try to get it for you.

Book early. We are not fans of finding romantic places once you get there; it's way too risky and can add stress to your vacation. The best rooms get booked first, so the sooner you decide where you want to go, the better chance you have of getting the most desirable rooms. All rooms are not equally large or equally charming. Call and ask the concierge's opinion and take a virtual tour of specific rooms on the website, if offered (nice B&Bs and small inns often offer this). Typically, for large hotels you can see photos from each room category (call to ask about square footage if that's important to you).

Ask about soundproofing. Not all guest rooms are acoustically desirable. Be especially wary of B&Bs. While some of their charm can be their age, they often do not have modern soundproofing. Personally, we don't think it's romantic to hear a toilet flush next door or someone's baby cry all night. When you book a room, make sure it's protected from such distractions, and if you are in a hotel, make sure you are not next to the elevator or right above the onsite nightclub. We like end units or those adjacent to a stairwell because they guarantee privacy on at least one side of the suite.

Try to get a room with an oversize tub or shower. Water is romantic. Lolling in a bathtub together is particularly romantic. If the hotel offers a room with an oversized tub, say you want it! Some of the hotels we suggest have their own plunge pools or a Jacuzzi tub. A few will have those fabulous showers that have 10 heads that blast your increasingly blissful body or rainforest shower heads that mimic the experience of being in a relaxing, soothing light rain. It's strange how a small thing like luxurious plumbing can make your vacation special, but it can!

Try to get a room refrigerator. Another small point—by no means a deal breaker—is a fridge. It's nice to be able to chill your favorite bottles of wine (without paying room service prices), or finger foods (like exotic local fruits) you picked up during your day for romantic in-bed snacks that you can feed each other. Here's another tip: If you are driving some place close to home, and you know the hotel doesn't provide fridges, bring a cooler to keep in your room—there's always plenty of free ice. *Note:* Some upscale properties are now installing motion sensors and scales in their minibars so if you so much as move an item to make room for something of yours, you are automatically charged for it. Check with front desk.

Be prepared to pay: The cheapest room is unlikely to be the most romantic. Almost every hotel or inn has a less desirable room, and you can usually tell by the price tag. In general, we would rather go to the best room or suite in a lesser hotel than the worst one in a fancy place. This is especially true with the older, grand hotels that have been reconfigured over the decades. Sometimes they end up creating some glorious suites, but amid a warren of odd-sized rooms that can feel like closets. Newer luxury chains rarely offer anything that irregular and some (like Aman, Banyan Tree, Four Seasons, Mandarin Oriental, Oberoi, Ritz Carlton, St. Regis, and other luxury properties we rave about in this book) are absolutely dependable, and you will never get a bad room. Still, there are good rooms and great rooms, and usually the great ones cost more.

Be particularly picky if your room is on a ship. All the cruise lines will show you where your room is on a ship diagram. Some people like to be in the middle of the ship, where they believe they get less motion; some want to be higher up; other people don't care much because they expect to spend little time other than sleeping in their room. It's personal taste. But by all means, if your ship has balcony rooms, spend more money or find a way to negotiate an upgrade to get one. (Early bookings will often get you the upgrade.) You will spend more time in the room if you have a balcony, and most lines offer butler service to bring you goodies or breakfast you can eat outside while gazing at the water or shoreline. We think the balconies are *essential* for romance. The bigger, the better.

GETTING OFF TO A ROMANTIC START

The concierge is your friend. The concierge is probably the most under-utilized person at most hotels and resorts. Sure, she can make dinner reservations for you, but in most properties concierges are capable of so much more. If you have any issue—such as limited mobility— tell the concierge, and he or she will find you a room that is comfortable and safe for you. Almost all the hotels in the United States have such accommodations (other parts of the world might be more problematic), but you need to know up front if the hotel suits your situation. Concierges are also a great source of information about the prices of activities or places that interest you, and they have information on money-saving tours or discounted entrance coupons.

Do not be afraid to ask the concierge ahead of time for ways to make your stay more romantic. Ask him about romance packages the hotel already has (most of the places in this book have them) or to suggest something customized to your trip. If you're planning to propose, do you want the ring placed on the top of the soufflé? (Be careful about putting rings inside food; very expensive gifts have been known to require an internal trip before they resurface.) Would you like a horse-drawn carriage or a balloon ride to drop you in a specific romantic setting? Concierges can think of some pretty amazing things for you and your honey to do. And most of them really love helping you to bring them off! (Some hotels, like the Salish Lodge & Spa in Snoqualmie, Washington, are so serious about giving you a great romantic experience that they even have a "romance concierge.")

No concierge? Make friends with the desk agent. You might be surprised at how much latitude she has to make room allocations or changes. If you are not making headway, talk to the manager or assistant manager. But don't ever discount the front desk agent if you can help it. A nice attitude (and perhaps a nice tip) may help move your stay from ordinary to amazing. A great front desk staff person would be willing to receive dozens of discreet texts or emails from a nervous man who wants to be sure every detail is in place for his proposal that evening.

Skimping and splurging both have a place. Small details matter. So don't order cheap champagne or a single rose. If you are offended by the high prices some hotels charge for any small service, then bring your own good wines and pick up a fragrant bouquet to take back to the room, rather than look like you aren't being generous. In fact, that is a general rule for a romantic interlude. There can't be any false notes. Exploring quirky places can be the best part of a vacation, but not necessarily the risk you want to take when you are on a romantic one.

Be realistic about your fitness and energy levels. We suggest a lot of places in this book that are exotic, and some require a certain level of fitness and resilience. You may be drawn to mountains, for example, but be alert and honest about how you or your partner feel at 7,000 feet—if the answer is woozy, seeing Logan Pass in Glacier National Park may not be for you. Be careful about all the suggestions that require getting physical. *Both* of you have to be in shape for skiing, hiking, climbing, river rafting, etc., or your vacation will quickly devolve into one or both of you wishing you hadn't come.

Check to see if any festivals or conventions are going on while you are there. The former might be fun, the latter, definitely not. If you are in a city that is going to be packed while you are there, you might not be able to get into events and restaurants that you want to explore, and you may end up paying top prices for your room. The ambience of even the most spectacular place can be ruined by drunk conventioneers carousing in the halls late at night. This is a good question to ask the concierge before finalizing your plan—remember to ask about the city or whole area, not just the hotel.

Let go of that long "must do" list and bring back "relax." Sure, if you are in Paris you long to see every street, cafe, museum, and market. But that's for another trip. Think about planning a trip that also offers lazy mornings in bed and a lot of cuddling and talking. Imagine sitting in a beautiful park or cute sidewalk cafe and slowly sipping a café au lait. Maybe you want just a couple hours at the Louvre, or other famous grand museum, to return another time for a different part of it rather than a marathon day that exhausts you. In other words, conserve your energy for each other.

And so, in the interest of bringing back "relax," and adding a bit of fire to the equation, we present in the following pages the 75 most romantic destinations we have discovered in the world.

Urban Romance

1 Passionate Cities:
U.S. & Canada

2 Passionate Cities:
Europe

3 Passionate Cities:
Exotic Lands

PASSIONATE CITIES: U.S. & CANADA

North America's great cities, with all their hustle, bustle, splendor, and variety, offer a wealth of pleasures—be it sophisticated museums or thrilling outdoor adventure. Who better to have it all with?

3

CHARLESTON
Ring My Southern Belle

One thing about the South: The folks here sure know how to do graceful—and gracious. That sense of easy living just flows over you in Charleston, one of the loveliest (and most historic) cities in the United States. If you like elegant 18th- and 19th-century neighborhoods, waterfront strolls, exquisitely executed Southern delicacies (crab, shrimp, fried green tomatoes, and grits), and the languor of a mostly moderate climate, you will love this city. Its romanticism is innate: Each walk inflames the senses thanks to the city's profusion of trees, flowering aromatic plants, and, in many neighborhoods, gorgeous old mansions impeccably maintained.

How should you approach the city? Tour the gentrified center with its restored historic buildings, intriguing backstreets, and intricate gardens. Walk through the Battery area via Church and Broad streets to see beautifully restored homes and hidden patios. Stop at the **RLS Gallery,** 2 Queen St. (© **843/805-8052;** www.rlsart.com), which has been selling local artists' work since the 1920s in a building restored to its 1760 origins. Then meander through Radcliffborough, Ansonborough, and other downtown neighborhoods, where old and new architectural masterpieces make for an aesthetically pleasing afternoon. Or just walk along Charleston Harbor on the banks of the Cooper River and stop at **Riverfront Park,** 1001 Everglades Ave. (© **843/740-5853;** www.northcharleston.org). It's a great place to jog or stroll; there's often a morning haze, but you'll see nearby islands and Fort Sumter in the distance, which reminds you this is where the first shots of the Civil War rang out.

When we're here, we like to imagine who walked here before us, how they lived, how plantations affected every class of person who lived on them, and how this city rose from the ashes of our Civil War to be the grand city it is today.

KEY ATTRACTIONS

Calhoun Mansion   Charleston boasts many house museums, but this is undoubtedly one of the most luxurious of them all, a lavish over-the-top Italianate mansion built in1876. Tour the house to view the opulent 35 rooms, a grand ballroom, Japanese water gardens with koi ponds, ornate chandeliers, and decorative lighting designed and installed by Louis Comfort Tiffany. And just for the fun of it, talk about what it would be like to live here together. Hey, one can always dream . . . .

16 Meeting St. ℭ **843/722-8205**. www.calhounmansion.net.

Edisto Beach   You'll encounter more wildlife than humans on this island, now connected by a bridge to the mainland. Dirt roads take you past many tall oaks, untouched marshlands, and inlets and bays where you can see incredible birds and shore creatures including huge turtles and alligators.

Gullah Tours   Alphonso Brown is the erudite and charming guide behind this 2-hour bus tour. He's a talented ranonteur who brings Charleston history to life, regaling visitors with tales of the area's first African inhabitants, the origins of the "Gullah" language (which was spoken by the slaves of South Carolina and Georgia) and more. The time just flies by when you're listening to the meliflous Mr. Brown (a former band leader and singer).

375 Meeting St. ℭ **843/763-7551**. http://gullahtours.com. Tours $18.

Plantation Tours   Head outside the city limits to see **Middleton Place,** a grand old plantation that has been partially preserved by a land trust and descendants of the original owners (the main house was destroyed during the Civil War). You can tour the glorious gardens by carriage. **Drayton Hall** is another beaut where you can see how the historic "one percent" lived.

Middleton: 4330 Ashley River Rd. ℭ **800/782-3608** or 843/556-6020. www.middleton place.org. Admission $28. Drayton: 3380 Ashley River Rd. ℭ **843/769-2600.** www. draytonhall.org. Admission $20.

HOTELS WITH HEART

Belmond Charleston Place Hotel $$ Here is *the* place to stay in Charleston. It's an eight-story landmark right in the historic district. Handsomely furnished (as you'd expect from a property formerly affiliated with Orient Express) spacious guest rooms provide a romantic retreat with southern colonial elegance. The deluxe restaurant, the **Charleston Grill** (ℭ **800/ 237-1236** or 843/577-4522; www.charlestongrill.com), is excellent.

205 Meeting St. ℭ **888/635-2350** or 843/722-4900. www.charlestonplace.com.

Fulton Lane Inn $$ Tucked away in a quiet corner of the city's renowned King Street, this boutique hotel is close to acclaimed restaurants, antique and other shops, and historic waterfront homes. Its cozy rooms have romantic touches like whirlpool tubs and fireplaces.

202 King Street. ℭ **800/720-2688** or 843/720-2600. www.fultonlaneinn.com.

Indigo Inn $$ If you are on a budget, this sweet little inn may be the right pick. It's on a picturesque street, right in the heart of the old quarter, which is exactly where you want to be. Ask for one of the rooms that looks out over the classic southern courtyard. Amenities include free Wi-Fi and late afternoon hors d'oeuvres in the lobby. You get a lot of charm, and a complimentary breakfast, for your money here.

1 Maiden Lane ✆ **843/577-5900.** www.indigoinn.com. Rates include breakfast.

King George IV Inn $ A lovely four-story wooden mansion house with heaps of character, comfortable beds, and spotlessly clean rooms, this Federal-style residence dates back to the 1790s. All rooms feature fireplaces, 11-foot ceilings, original wide-planked hardwood floors, and plenty of Victorian antiques. Note that the top-floor rooms share a bathroom. You'll be sleeping on anything from antique Gothic rope beds from the 1840s to Victorian iron or teak masterpieces.

32 George St. ✆ **843/723-9339.** www.kinggeorgeIV.com. Rates include a full breakfast.

Planters Inn $$$ You'll feel like you have been transported back to the 19th century at this elegant 1844 inn. Now a Relais & Châteaux property, the structure started life as a large cotton warehouse, just across from the City Market. The spacious, bright rooms feature comfortable four-posters, large flatscreen TVs, upholstered chairs, and beautiful furnishings. Have your afternoon tea in the lobby, home to the **Peninsula Grill,** described below.

112 North Market St. ✆ **843/722-2345.** www.plantersinn.com.

MOST ROMANTIC RESTAURANTS

Charleston Grill $$ SOUTHERN/FRENCH   This is one of the fanciest and most famous restaurants in Charleston, all marble floor and mahogany and European appointments. The service and the flavors are sublime, and it has the city's most extensive and well-curated wine list. Celebrity chef Bob Waggoner draws rave reviews for his French and Low Country cooking.

224 King St. ✆ **843/577-4522.** www.charlestongrill.com. Reservations required.

Hominy Grill $ SOUTHERN   An inexpensive, funky place in a repurposed old barbershop that serves fabulous breakfasts. We are not the only ones who find an authentic place to have breakfast romantic.

207 Rutledge Ave. ✆ **843/937-0930.** www.hominygrill.com.

Peninsula Grill $$ SOUTHERN   Some of the drooliest, drippingest, best of southern cooking is here. Get your fried green tomatoes, hush puppies, bourbon-grilled shrimp, and crab cakes in this historic restaurant that is quite frankly Old South, but not stuffy. Peninsula Grill's coconut cake has become a thing of legend.

112 N. Market St. ✆ **843/723-0700**. www.peninsulagrill.com.

CHARLESTON BY NIGHT

Jazz   Charleston is renowned as a jazz town. If you're an aficionado, head to the Voodoo Tiki Bar and Lounge, 15 Magnolia Rd. (℃ **843/769-0228;** www.voodootikibar.com), for live music. Voodoo hosts a year-round jazz series and memorable Mardi Gras and New Year's Eve celebrations.

Upper King Street   You can always find a good time in this cluster of bars just 2 miles from the city's historic center. The most talked-about spots lately are the Grocery, 4 Cannon St. (℃ **843/302-8825;** http://thegrocery charleston.com; reservations recommended), Prohibition, 547 King St. (℃ **843/ 793-2964;** www.prohibitioncharleston.com; reservations recommended), HoM, 563 King St. (℃ **843/573-7505;** www.homcharleston.com), and The Macintosh, 479 King St. (℃ **843/789-4299;** www.themacintoshcharleston.com).

Theater   See a Charleston Stage Company performance at the **Dock Street Theatre,** 135 Church St. (℃ **843/577-7183;** www.charlestonstage.com), the oldest building in America created for theatrical productions.

Vendue Inn   Did we mention we're suckers for rooftops? This inn has a great one. Charleston natives love this place too, as it is known for fine cocktails and views of Charleston's harbor, Waterfront Park, Cooper River Bridges, and Fort Sumter. Outdoor heaters keep it cozy all year. 19 Vendue Range St. ℃ **800/845-7900** or 843/577-7970. www.thevendue.com.

CHICAGO
Swept Away in the Windy City

Despite the icy winters, the miracle of the Windy City is that from May until November it's a balmy resort town, if you stick close to Lake Michigan. From Chicago's 26-mile lakefront you can observe waterfront golfers on three different courses, visit 10 boat harbors, and dig your toes into the sandy beaches. Hence the nickname, the "Third Coast."

You'll find captivating views of the city and lakefront on foot, from high-rise rooftop observation decks or from fun tourist boats that cruise the lake and Chicago River. The renovated **Navy Pier,** 600 E Grand Ave. (℃ **800/595-7437** or 312/595-7437; www.navypier.com), is a fun zone with a giant Ferris wheel rising above the shimmering lake waters. **Chicago Summer Dance** (www.cityofchicago.org) offers free dance lessons and all kinds of live music June through August. Thursday to Sunday nights in Grant Park, the city's grand lakefront commons, a Lollapalooza rock show plays every summer. Just west of the park is the famous skyline engraved by dozens of skyscrapers reminding you that Chicago is a city of world-class culture with the arts, restaurants, and romance for all seasons.

KEY ATTRACTIONS

Art Institute of Chicago   At this venerable art institution you can see "Nighthawks," Edward Hopper's famous couple-at-a-diner painting. Tour the huge Impressionist collection and bond over Degas, Renoir, or Cassatt.

111 S. Michigan Ave. ℂ **866/512-6326** or 312/443-3600. www.artic.edu. Admission $23; 65 and older $17.

Architecture River Cruise   Bob along with your sweetie on a double-decker cruiser down the Chicago River. The **Chicago Architecture Foundation,** 224 S. Michigan Ave. (ℂ **312/922-8687;** www.architecture.org; Apr–Nov; admission $38), gives a tour of famous buildings along the Chicago River and Lake Michigan. It covers old and new landmarks, plus tales of their architects. A two-hour sunset boat ride on Lake Michigan with **Wendella,** 400 N. Michigan Ave. (ℂ **312/337-1446;** www.wendellaboats.com), costs a couple around $50. For many dollars more, do it in a private sailboat (ℂ **773/710-7245;** www.gosailing chicago.com) instead.

> ## Perfect Place for a Proposal
>
> The Chicago Botanic Garden has an abundance of romantic settings for popping the question. Take your pick: Will it be beneath flowering cherries and crabapples in spring? among the roses in summer? or while strolling the Japanese and other theme gardens and beside the waterfall for romantic emphasis?

Chicago Botanic Gardens   In Glencoe, an easy drive or Metra train ride from downtown, these vast gardens have many secluded, tucked-away areas, like the breathtaking Waterfall, Sensory and English Walled gardens, in addition to peaceful lagoons and millions of plants from around the world. Small wonder so many bridal parties pose for pictures in the Rose Garden. Admission is free, but you pay to park.

1000 Lake Cook Rd. ℂ **847/835-5440.** www.chicagobotanic.org. Free admission; parking $25 per car; $10 seniors.

City Stroll #1   Day or night, from the Chicago River, a stroll north on the impressively broad **Michigan Avenue** (called the Magnificent Mile here for the 40-carat real estate and luxe shopping) to Oak Street is a heckuva lot of fun. Turn left for high-end boutiques and classy cafes or go a block north to Oak Street Beach, one of the most chic of a dozen local strands. This is the route that prom-goers ask their limo drivers to take—it's acceptable to smooch anywhere along the glitzy way.

City Stroll #2   Head north from Oak Street along the shore. At the blue boathouse, take the pedestrian overpass into Lincoln Park. Follow the path to the zoo, the Farm in the Zoo, and the Lincoln Park Conservatory, where even in winter you'll shed your wraps and surrender to the orchid-scented tropical air.

City Stroll #3   From Michigan Avenue go east on Congress Parkway to the majestic Buckingham Fountain in Grant Park; head north on Columbus Drive through the park; at Monroe Street, ogle the sailboats on Lake Michigan to the right; continue north to architect Frank Gehry's ribbon-like BP Bridge and follow it to Millennium Park and the famed Bean sculpture—it looks like a giant silver bean and distorts your reflections in wonderful ways. End your trek with a canoodling lunch at Terzo Piano, 159 E Monroe St. (**$; ℂ 312/443-8650;** www.terzopianochicago.com), an excellent moderately priced restaurant at the Art Institute of Chicago, 111 S. Michigan Ave. (**ℂ 312/443-3600;** www.artic.edu), and ask to be seated on the terrace. Or picnic at the Bean— pick up goodies at nearby Pastoral: Artisan Cheese, Bread & Wine, 53 E. Lake St. (**ℂ 312/658-1250;** www.pastoralartisan.com) and enjoy the gardens (which become an ice rink in winter).

HOTELS WITH HEART

The Drake Hotel $$ Once Chicago's most "international" hotel, the Drake may no longer be the glitziest game in town, but its lobbies and restaurants still evoke the grand European hotels of the ages. The rooms have upscale-but-comfy furniture and a relaxing sitting area with couch and chairs. As the only Chicago hotel that directly faces Lake Shore Drive, its north-facing rooms have spectacular lake views (for a price). Avoid the "city view" rooms on the lower floors that look directly onto a building. The hotel's retro restaurants include the Coq d'Or, with its atmospheric piano bar, and the cozy Cape Cod Room, an old-timey and intimate seafood spot.

140 East Walton Place. ℂ **800/553-7253** or 312/787-2200. www.thedrakehotel. com.

Millennium Knickerbocker Hotel $ This beautiful gothic building dates back to the 1920s, and legend has it that Al Capone's brother, Ralph, ran a speakeasy and casino from the penthouse during Prohibition. In 1970, Hugh Hefner and Playboy Enterprises purchased the property, and it operated as Playboy Towers until 1979. The hotel revels in that history and invites guests to do so, too, during a free Friday tour at 3pm. Rooms are small but very comfortable, and the location is ideal: close to the lake, shopping, nightlife, restaurants, and more.

163 E. Walton Place (east of Michigan Ave.). ℂ **800/621-8140** or 312/751-8100. www.millenniumhotels.com/millenniumchicago/index.html.

Ritz-Carlton Chicago $$$ This hotel's elegantly cheerful lobby is way up on the 12th floor of the Water Tower Place mall. The lovely rooms are expensive—spring for a lake view if you can, although all the views are good. It's a great place to nest when the snow is flying: Everything you need is in the hotel—a spa, several restaurants, and great room service—or in the attached luxury mall. You can even arrange for delivery of fresh-baked cookies and milk to your room.

160 E. Pearson St. ℂ **800/819-5053** or 312/266-1000. www.fourseasons.com.

Talbott Hotel $ This cozy Gold Coast boutique hotel near North Michigan Avenue straddles the line between fun and staid. Room views are relatively unobstructed and some have a lake view.

20 E. Delaware Place. ℂ **800/825-2688** or 312/944-4970. www.talbotthotel.com.

MOST ROMANTIC RESTAURANTS

Chicago is a place where flavors from around the world run rampant. Check with your concierge on where to go in Chicago's thriving ethnic neighborhoods such as Greektown, Chinatown, Mexican Pilsen, and Devon Avenue (Middle Eastern, Indian, Pakistani, and West African).

We love Chicago ribs. Frank Sinatra did, too, and would drop in for them at **Twin Anchors Tavern,** 1655 N. Sedwick St. (**$$;** ℂ **312/266-1616;** www.twinanchorsribs.com), when he played the "toddling town." This homey old neighborhood joint (once a speakeasy) in Old Town has served delectably tender baby back ribs coated in a savory sauce for more than a half-century. Order a slab and chow down together to Sinatra on the jukebox. Other good bets for ribs: **The Smoke Daddy,** 1804 W. Division St. (**$;** ℂ **773/772-6656;** www.thesmokedaddy.com), and **Honey 1 BBQ,** 2241 N. Western Ave. (**$;** ℂ **773/227-5130;** www.honey1bbq.com).

Alinea $$$ AMERICAN   Chef Grant Achatz delivers an overall sensory experience. Book well in advance and bring your adventurous spirit and plenty of time and money. Prepare for a journey through a meal that may involve 20 dishes, some served on an aromatic pastry pillow. Amazingly, the excellent service seems effortless.

1723 N Halsted St. ℂ **312/867-0110.** www.alinearestaurant.com Tickets purchased online. Priced by number of guests.

Café Spiaggia $ ITALIAN   This sleek well-priced cafe is next door to its more expensive sibling but serves some of the same tasty Tuscan cookery. While you lunch on lovely salads and pasta with wine pairings, look out the grand windows for a 5-star view of Oak Street Beach and Michigan Avenue.

980 N. Michigan Ave., 2nd fl. ℂ **312/280-2750.** www.spiaggiarestaurant.com.

Cyrano's Cafe & Wine Bar $ FRENCH   For charm, try this Paris-like cafe in the lively River North area. Its bistro cuisine and warm decor provide the perfect backdrop for the language of love. Slip downstairs to the cabaret for a nightcap.

233 E. Lower Wacker Dr. ℂ **312/616-1400.**

North Pond $$ EUROPEAN/AMERICAN   In a lovely secluded setting on a pond in Lincoln Park, this Arts and Crafts–style restaurant provides fine dining and a dramatic view of the nearby historic neighborhood. Before dinner, take a delightful stroll through the park to get there, a short taxi ride from most hotels.

2610 N. Cannon Dr. ℂ **773/477-5845.** www.northpondrestaurant.com. Reservations recommended.

CHICAGO BY NIGHT

Chicago Blues & Jazz   The city's sexy musical traditions are alive and bopping. You can easily find authentic urban blues in great clubs for under $10 at B.L.U.E.S., 2519 N. Halsted (℗ **773/528-1012;** www.chicagobluesbar.com), and Blue Chicago, 536 N. Clark St. (℗ **312/661-0100;** www.bluechicago. com). Superstar Buddy Guy has his own club, Buddy Guy's Legends, 700 S. Wabash (℗ **312/427-1190;** www.buddyguys.com), but it'll cost you. For jazz, close to most hotels and in very nice rooms, try Andy's Jazz Club, 11 E. Hubbard St. (℗ **312/642-6805;** www.andysjazzclub.com), and The Green Mill, 4802 N. Broadway Ave. (℗ **773/878-5552;** www.greenmilljazz.com).

Ravinia   This beautifully landscaped venue an hour north of the city offers outdoor summer concerts featuring top talent in all genres. It has restaurants galore with excellent wine lists, and you can order a picnic (in advance) or bring your own. Then snuggle up on a blanket (or pay a bit more for tickets in the seats) and get mellow. The Metra train from downtown stops right at Ravinia's gates. 418 Sheridan Rd., Highland Park. ℗ **847/266-5000.** www.ravinia.org.

Second City   Laughter reduces your stress hormones and laughing together is definitely bonding. The laugh laboratory that launched dozens of careers (John Belushi, Steve Carell, Tina Fey, Bill Murray, and more) is quite riotous. Come early so you can explore the interesting Old Town area and stop in for great ribs at Twin Anchors (see above), about a 5-minute walk from Second City. 1616 N. Wells St. ℗ **312/337-3992.** www.secondcity.com.

The Signature Room   Start your night high on the 95th floor of the John Hancock building, where you get the same view as on the observation deck one floor up, but in a lovely bar with drinks in your hands. No admission fee—just the tab. 875 N Michigan Ave. ℗ **312/787-9596.** www.signatureroom.com.

The Violet Hour   This chic bar's owners call it "hush and wonder." The idea: dimly lit romance in a quiet atmosphere where patrons must turn off their cell phones. High wing-backed chairs are grouped in private conversation areas partitioned by curtains. Very fancy cocktails with evocative names (a highball Dark & Stormy or a Juliet and Romeo in a martini glass) and appetizers are served in the near darkness, which is offset slightly in winter by a roaring fireplace. You enter through a mural, but first you have to identify the door within the art. The bar is in trendy Bucktown, and parking is tight, so take a cab from your hotel. 1520 N Damen Ave. ℗ **773/252-1500**. www.thevioglethour.com.

LOS ANGELES
Your Own Romantic Movie Set

Los Angeles, gritty, gaudy, or glamorous, has many personalities. Some get bad press: They don't call it Tinseltown for nothing. But there is precious gold to be found in this sprawling metropolis if you know where to look. Explore

MAKING valentine's day SPECIAL

Valentine's Day is *the* day that can re-charge a relationship.

Oh, did we hear groans? So what if it's commercial? Do you really want to just give her chocolates and roses . . . again? Frankly, Valentine's Day gets us off our collective butts and, travel-wise, focuses us on seeking out a truly a romantic experience. Nothing is better than the gift of your time and attention. Following are some of our tips to make it a perfect day, an overnight, or a weekend occasion.

Valentine Do's:

o **Pick a special restaurant.** This is a great time to try one of our recommendations for especially romantic restaurants. If you aren't near one, follow our guidelines: Think atmosphere, feeling special, great food and service, and warm lighting or candlelit tables. Or do something sentimental: Return to the restaurant where you had your first date, or the place you got engaged, or spent a special anniversary. Not possible? Then pick a place your partner has always longed to try.

o **Buy gourmet finger foods.** If you're on a budget, save money and enhance your sense of privacy by picking out the most seductive food you can find at a gourmet market. Create your own "small plates"— and tempt each other with a picnic in your hotel room. Splurge on a great wine to match the flavor profile.

in and around L.A., and only then can you properly grasp a fraction of its delightful eccentricities, beaches, mountains, and architectural gems.

While in Los Angeles, you'll come across many locations where you'll feel you've literally stepped into a movie because you know the scenery from classic films. Take, for example, the romantic cityscape at night from the iconic **Griffith Observatory,** where James Dean had his drag race in "Rebel without a Cause." The Planetarium perched above the glittering city makes a perfect place to snuggle in the dark. In one of the downtown walks we recommend, you can enter the gold and wrought-iron splendor of the 1893 landmark **Bradbury Building,** a setting for "Bladerunner," "500 Days of Summer," and "The Artist."

But it's the city's natural assets that reward the observant traveler. So many visitors spend their time inching along freeways going to Disneyland and Universal Studios that they miss out on the high mountains that ring the city and the Pacific Ocean that washes upon its shore. We will help you appreciate this vibrant place like the insiders do. Trust us: One of the authors lives here.

- **Get expert advice.** Don't be afraid to ask the hotel concierge or manager for ideas or help in creating dinners in unexpected places. We've heard of people placed at the side of waterfalls, alone in front of the fireplace, or even loaned the balcony in an unused suite. You won't know what your options might be if you don't ask.

- **Give an unexpected and thoughtful gift.** You're never wrong to give a gift. It really is the thought that counts, so it won't require great expense. Great ideas: Surprise your partner with tickets to something he or she loves, like a play, concert, or a sporting event that will be a memorable part of that trip. Or, if your partner lives to ski, golf, or play tennis or some other sport, give the gift of an equipment upgrade or a private lesson.

What's the big **Valentine's Day don't?** You can do everything right, but one big wrong can make it all implode. Don't give gifts that look like desperate last-minute choices. (Even if you forgot everything and really are desperate!) Snatch victory from the jaws of defeat and offer a certificate for a day spa together and put it in a beautiful card. If you are already on vacation, splurge on a room service dinner. If you're not, look to the future and create an "I Owe You" for a future travel getaway. Set a date, so it really happens, then enjoy a nice dinner and ponder the choices for your promised vacation.

KEY ATTRACTIONS BY FOOT

No other city in the world is as closely identified with automobile as L.A., yet there are several places to take great walks or hikes.

Catalina Island   Take the scenic ferry ride to **Catalina Island** from Long Beach, San Pedro, or Dana Point (© **800/481-3470;** www.catalinaexpress. com; $68–$77 round trip depending on port). The Catalina Express ferry company offers hotel packages and a $15 upgrade to its Commodore Lounge to start your ride over in style. You'll start your walking tour in **Avalon,** Catalina's capital, a classic California beach resort town with plenty of shopping, dining, and a few small museums strung along the harbor. Because the entire island is car-free, and buffalo roam freely in the hills, you'll have your pick of trails and walking routes leading out from Avalon. Contact **Catalina Tours,** 228 Metropole Ave., Avalon (© **310/510-0036;** www.catalinatours.com), for the low down on snorkeling and scuba diving, golf (on the oldest operating course west of the Mississippi), and hiking trails. If you want to splurge, take a helicopter taxi (© **800/228-2566** or 310/510-2525; www.islandexpress.com; $195–$390 round trip depending on location).

Downtown   In late afternoon, start at the striking **Walt Disney Concert Hall,** 111 S. Grand Ave. (© **323/850-2000;** www.laphil.com/visit), whose stainless steel waves and curves were designed by Frank Gehry. Acoustically perfect, it's worth going to an evening concert here, but even if you don't, take the self-guided tour (narrated by actor John Lithgow) of the curved wood-paneled auditorium and upper-level garden grounds. From there it's just two long blocks downhill to the **Bradbury Building,** 304 Broadway (© **213/626-1893**), with its magical lights-filled Victorian lobby and mezzanine. Now it's time for happy hour, another few blocks away in one of the most romantic bars we've ever seen. The **Edison,** 108 W. 2nd St. #101 ($; © **213/613-0000;** www.edisondowntown.com), is a re-imagined subterranean power plant that was the first to light up old Los Angeles. The mechanical artifacts are still here, interspersed with small private rooms in this dark, incredibly sexy space.

Griffith Park   Go to **Griffith Park** by day and hike up to the **Observatory,** 2800 E. Observatory Rd. (© **213/473-0800;** www.griffithobservatory. org), for sunset and a splendid 180-degree birds-eye view over Los Angeles. If you happen to be a fan of Frank Lloyd Wright architecture, the Los Feliz neighborhood sitting at the foot of Griffith Park is **Barnsdall Park,** 4800 Hollywood Blvd. (© **323/644-6275;** www.barnsdall.org), where you can tour his famous Hollyhock residence, and get a wonderful view of the famed Hollywood Hills and Observatory.

Venice Beach & Santa Monica   Plan a beach day starting with a walk on the funky **Venice Boardwalk** (© **310/399-2775;** www.laparks.org/venice) and ending at the **Third Street Promenade** in Santa Monica (btw. Colorado Ave. and Wilshire Blvd.; © **310/393-8355;** www.downtownsm.com), an upscale outdoor mall with great choices for dinner and drinks. Enjoy great people-watching with your lunch at the **Sidewalk Café,** 1401 Ocean Front Walk ($$; © **310/399-5547;** www.thesidewalkcafe.com), in Venice. The boardwalk is the place to buy trendy sunglasses and cheap L.A. T-shirts, get a henna tattoo or tarot card reading, and watch a wild variety of performers, from the freakish to the professionally freakish. The very best free entertainment has moved to evenings, year-round, on the Third Street Promenade. The biggest landmark on your walk (aside from the ocean) will be the famous **Santa Monica Pier** (© **310/458-8901;** http://santamonicapier.org). Its illuminated ferris wheel over the ocean is visible for miles at night (and you'll hear the delighted screams from the roller coaster as well). A wide, golden sand beach stretches the whole way between the two beach cities.

KEY ATTRACTIONS BY CAR

Mulholland Drive   You can do this route by day, but it's far more romantic at night to slowly drive the winding road that skims the top of the Hollywood Hills for a stunning aerial view of downtown L.A. and Hollywood on one side and the great expanse of the San Fernando Valley on the other. Several of the viewpoints (most famous is the Hollywood Bowl overlook), are historic spots for necking with the city lights extending forever into the night below. Pick up

The Getty Center

The ultra-modern **Getty Center,** 1200 Getty Center Dr. (*①* **310/ 440-7300;** www.getty.edu; free admission; parking $15), is a world-class palace for art and architecture. A monorail takes patrons up from the freeway level (it's right off 405 freeway) to this mountaintop home of the exten- sive collections of J. Paul Getty. Make a reservation in advance for the **Restaurant at the Getty Center ($$;** *①* **310/440-6810**) to dine on haute cuisine with post- card views over the Los Angeles Westside and the ocean beyond; the large cafeteria also has excel- lent food and spectacular views.

Mulholland Drive near the Hollywood Bowl. Go at least as far as Laurel Can- yon, which takes you back down to the Sunset Strip, quite possibly the world's best mile-and-a-half stretch of rock clubs and concert venues. Outdoor cafe seating along the boulevard is great for a nightcap or dessert, along with the quintessential L.A. pastime: car- and people-watching.

PCH   Rent a convertible and drive north along the **Pacific Coast Highway** (PCH–Hwy 1) from Santa Monica. This California tradition never gets old, especially if you do it with one arm around your sweetie. The drive takes you past golden beaches from Beach Boys songs, the foothills of the Santa Monica Mountains, and a few celebrity homes (albeit hidden behind massive com- pound walls). We strongly recommend a stop for the fine food and impeccable service at **Geoffrey's,** 27400 PCH (**$$$;** *①* **310/457-1519;** www.geoffreys malibu.com). Every table has an ocean view from the terraced restaurant on cliffs; fire pits warm lovers from the chill of evening ocean winds. For a brief cultural interlude, visit the **Getty Villa,** 17985 PCH (*①* **310/440-7300;** www. getty.edu/visit), a treasure trove of antiquities and art sitting right above PCH. Admission is free, however, a timed-entry ticket is required; just reserve parking ($15) online. For an overnight in Malibu, we recommend **Casa Malibu Inn,** 22878 PCH (**$$$;** *①* **800/4MALIBU** or 310/456-6444; www.malibubeachinn. com), on beautiful Carbon Beach, where the truly rich build their homes.

HOTELS WITH HEART
Channel Road Inn $ This tucked-away retreat is a half-block from a quiet stretch of Santa Monica's beach, away from the tourists and in a prime residential canyon area. Part of the Four Sisters Inn group, this historic 15-room inn seems to be a secret even to most locals. Many rooms have fire- places and spa tubs, and some have balconies. Complimentary wine, hors d'oeuvres, and fresh-baked cookies are served every afternoon. Off season (Nov–Feb) you can get half off your second night, or a "carpe diem" rate of $175 for any available room that same night.

219 W. Channel Rd., Santa Monica. *①* **310-459-1920**. www.channelroadinn.com. Rates include full breakfast.

The Culver Hotel $ This historic Art Deco hotel is not only close to the beaches, but also close to Beverly Hills and Hollywood. The national landmark building (home to the Munchkins during filming of "Wizard of Oz") is in the heart of the hippest part of Culver City and walking distance of bars, restaurants, and live theater. The rooms have luxury bedding, Art Deco furniture, and antique tubs. If you can afford it, request a suite; if not, ask for a corner room (with an unusual lay-out and terrific views). Bonus: Complimentary continental breakfast and evening happy hour in the Lobby Lounge. Live jazz plays nightly, and the lounge features swing dancing on Wednesdays.

9400 Culver Blvd., Culver City. © **888/3CULVER** or 310/558-9400. www.culver hotel.com. Rates include breakfast.

Hotel Bel-Air $$$ These lush grounds have a bit of a Florida and old Spain feel to them, yet are pure L.A. You enter over a bridge with twinkling lights and swans floating on the lake below. Our favorite rooms are the new canyon suites, which have outdoor fireplaces, spa pools, and patio views of a neighboring terraced vineyard. We especially like the multiple showerheads in the fancy marble bathrooms, which we think can be put to good romantic use. The lush grounds—the beloved oval pool has retained its signature shape and setting—and the new 4,000-sq.-ft. spa make it easy to jumpstart any getaway weekend.

701 Stone Canyon Rd. © **310/472-1211.** www.hotelbelair.com.

Shutters on the Beach $$$ The simplicity of this laidback chic hotel immediately relaxes you. The white, bright decor anchors you right on the beach to inhale the sun and sea air. It is an easy walk to the famed Santa Monica Pier and the hip Third Street Promenade.

1 Pico Blvd., Santa Monica. © **310/458-0030.** www.shuttersonthebeach.com.

Sunset Tower $$ This historic Art Deco landmark was originally a luxury apartment building that boasted of Howard Hughes, John Wayne, and Marilyn Monroe as residents. Now a fashionable place to stay on the Sunset Strip, it has floor-to-ceiling windows in rooms that open on beautiful city and hillside views. The large rooms have recessed lighting and beautiful Art Deco edging and are moderately priced for L.A. The restaurant and poolside bar feel like you are back with Lauren Bacall and Humphrey Bogart (yes, it's that glamorous) and the chance of seeing actual living celebrities is quite high.

8358 Sunset Blvd. © **323/654-7100.** www.sunsettowerhotel.com.

MOST ROMANTIC RESTAURANTS

The Little Door $$$ FRENCH MOROCCAN   It's no secret: You can't beat The Little Door for romantic atmosphere. It all starts when you find the little door itself and unfolds when you sit under the trees and dine surrounded by fragrant flowers. This is a place to order a glass of champagne and plot a getaway to Provence, or the perfect setting for a small wedding or anniversary party.

8164 W. 3rd St. © **323/951-1210.** www.thelittledoor.com.

Saddle Peak Lodge $$$ AMERICAN   In the moutains above Malibu where no city lights reach to compete with a sky full of stars (and no cell-phone service to distract you), you can eat outdoors on a gorgeous garden patio. If you prefer to be indoors, you will feel quite cozy and get the full rustic effect of this once active hunting lodge. Candlelit tables (No. 8 is recommended for a proposal) set the stage, and a celebrated wine list will help ease you into asking or responding to the question that will change your lives forever.

419 Cold Canyon Rd., Calabasas ✆ **818/222-3888.** www.saddlepeaklodge.com.

Spago $$$ CALIFORNIAN   There are no guarantees in life except death, taxes, and an A-list celebrity sighting at Spago in Beverly Hills. The food is guaranteed to be outstanding, too.

176 N Canon Dr., Beverly Hills. ✆ **310/385-0880.** www.wolfgangpuck.com/restaurant.

LOS ANGELES BY NIGHT

Hollywood Bowl   From spring to fall, world-class performers take to the famous stage at this amphitheater tucked in the Hollywood Hills. Bring a bottle of wine and a basket of provisions to any of the dozens of world-class summer evening concerts—including contemporary rock and jazz, as well as classical. The striking white bandshell was designed by Frank Lloyd Wright, and for first-timers, it's often as captivating as the music (though even the most jaded Los Angeleno may still gasp upon seeing it again). 2301 N. Highland Ave. ✆ **323/850-2000.** www.hollywoodbowl.com.

Live Theater   Head for the heart of old Hollywood and the gorgeous **Pantages Theater,** 6233 Hollywood Blvd. (✆ **800/982-2787** or 323/468-1770; http://hollywoodpantages.com), which you'll recognize from the many years it hosted the Academy Awards. Downtown L.A. is now culturally vibrant; before you come, check the concert line-ups at **Walt Disney Concert Hall,** 111 S. Grand Ave. (✆ **323/850-2000;** www.laphil.com), and the **Nokia Theater,** 777 Chick Hearn Ct. (✆ **213/763-6030;** www.nokiatheatrelalive.com), in the L.A. Live complex; opera and nationally touring plays go on stage at the **Dorothy Chandler Pavilion,** 135 N. Grand Ave. (✆ **213/972-0711;** www. musiccenter.org). If you don't want to spring for tickets, or plan ahead, for the price of a few cocktails as you explore the intriguing bar areas, you can catch the show and eye-candy hipster crowd at **The Edison** (see p. 36).

MIAMI
Sizzling, Semi-Tropical Escape

There may be no more exuberant city in the United States—if it really is in the U.S. (sometimes it feels like it isn't!). Miami is home to a fabulous collision of cultures all melding into a Cuban, Spanish, Southern, and international personality that is equal parts exciting and sexy.

THE art OF GETTING AWAY

If you're like us, brief getaways are a rare treat. They are contemplated for longer than the trip itself and dreamed about way more often than they are actually taken. Remember when we said that surprise, exceeding expectations, and maintaining a sense of wonder help create romance? Spoiler alert! Those moments rarely happen at home during your average month—or even year. Most couples know that they *should* take a getaway—a short weekend or even a single day to help remember to be lovers—but why don't more people do so? Sometimes it's money worries or long work weeks, but mostly it's inertia and a little laziness, too.

Planning a getaway takes less effort than you think. Keep your sights set close to home and you can take advantage of last-minute deals and be spontaneous. When you're driving, you don't have to give all that much thought to packing efficiently. Just throw a few things into a suitcase and go!

It's almost impossible to have a getaway here and not be affected by the city's erotic energy. Not just in the pulsating music of South Beach on a weekend night, but also on the beaches, in the shops, on the streets. Beautiful women of far-flung origins wearing tube tops, teeny skirts, and even teenier bikinis are almost anywhere any time. Downtown Miami may be slightly more discreet but, unlike most U.S. cities, Miami oozes sex appeal.

The beach walk in South Beach goes on forever, and it is a people-watching delight. You will see buff skaters, bikini-clad twenty-somethings, honeymooners, older Jewish couples—a bit of everything. The beach and ocean are beautiful, and you can peer into multiple beguiling hotels. Stop at a few for drinks at the lavish pool bars.

Miami is perfect for a romantic getaway. If it's adventure you crave, look no further. Miami says to the world: You've got a body, use it!

KEY ATTRACTIONS

The Everglades   This is one of the most unusual national parks in the United States, and among the most endangered. The alligators lounging around the edges may look like they are asleep, but don't fall for their act. You can, however, rent a kayak from **Everglades Adventures,** 107 Camellia St., Everglades City (② **877/567-0679** or 239/695-3299; www.evergladesadventures.com; kayak rental $55), and paddle safely through their mangrove forest habitat and grass-filled waterways. If that's more scary than romantic, take a tour on a fast boat through the sea grass channels and revel in this extraordinary water world. Contact **Speedy's Airboat Tours,** 621 Begonia St., Everglades City (② **800/998-4448** or 239/695-4448; www.speedysairboattours.com; $40 per person). You can take a short cruise through the "10,000 islands," and watch for birds of prey, sea birds, and dolphins. Try **Everglades National Park Boat Tours,** 815 Oyster Bar Lane, S.R. 29, Everglades City (✆ **866/NATPARK** or 239/695-2591; www.evergladesnationalparkboattours gulfcoast.com; $32). Bring mosquito repellent, especially at sunset.

Little Havana   Can't visit the real thing? Not to worry. You can pick up the vibe in this part of town at its cafes and street fairs. It's all Cuban coffee, cigars, food, and most of all, Cubans themselves conversing, arguing politics, and enacting a replica of life in the old country. Start at Calle Ocho, SW 8th St. to 27th Ave. (www.calleocho.com), the center of the community. Watch cigars being rolled at **El Credito Cigar Factory,** 1100 SW 8th St. (✆ **305/285-9154;** www.miamiandbeaches.com), and have authentic Cuban fare at **Versailles Cuban Restaurant,** 3555 SW 8th St. ($; ✆ **305/444-0240;** www.versaillesrestaurant.com).

Shipwreck Diving   The waters around Miami have had their storm victims and while they represent tragic historical events, the wrecks now provide at least 75 intriguing destinations for divers. Each attracts colorful marine life only a short boat ride from Miami's bustling downtown. One reputable outfitter is **South Beach Divers,** 850 Washington Ave. (✆ **305/531-6110;** www.southbeachdivers.com).

Vizcaya   This estate is authentic (in its own way). This industrialist's faux Italian Renaissance mansion has gardens so lush they are worth visiting even if you skip the mansion. But the interior offers a way to understand the lavishness of the famed Gilded Age. The place has hosted international meetings, presidents, queens, and popes and is available for wedding parties for us mere mortals.

3251 South Miami Ave. ✆ **305/250-9133.** www.vizcayamuseum.org. Admission $18 adult; $12 senior.

HOTELS WITH HEART
The Biltmore in Coral Gables $$$ If you like historic hotels emanating the glamor of the golden age of the Zelda and F. Scott Fitzgerald-crowd, this is a justly famous iconic representative of the genre. It is a National Historic Landmark, and thank goodness it's been preserved. The Spanish-inspired estate, modeled on buildings in Seville, plays on its origins with Moorish decoration throughout the public areas and rooms. It is famous for its huge pool, lavish suites, and beautiful golf course. A century ago, this was the U.S. elite's winter social center.

1200 Anastasia Ave., Coral Gables. ✆ **855/311-6903.** www.biltmorehotel.com.

Colony Hotel $ Built in the late 1930s as one of the first hotels designed by Miami Deco doyen Henry Hohauser, this is now an attractive deal both physically (conserving yet updating its distinctive period look in recent renovations) and fiscally. Behind the famous blue-neon Colony sign, you'll find 4-dozen spiffy little rooms with all the necessary modern conveniences (including nice big flatscreen TVs), a front-lobby bar, and the Columbus restaurant specializing in Italian. All in all, eminently worth colonizing.

736 Ocean Dr. (btw 7th and 8th Sts.), South Beach. ℘ **305/673-0088.** www.colony miami.com.

The Raleigh $ Yes, you can play Bogie and Bacall here—it's that Hollywood-glamorous, and the period is correct. These redone Collins Avenue hotels in South Beach have a patina and glitz all their own. The first-rate restaurant has a lush and seductive outdoor garden that sustains the '40s theme and a menu dishes made from locally grown food. Look for stone-crab salads, perfect grilled swordfish, and a divine key lime tart. The pool bar is next to a waterfall-fed pool, romantically lit by lanterns and punctuated by palms.

1775 Collins Ave. ℘ **305/534-6300** or 305/612-1148. www.raleighhotel.com. Discounted when booked at least 30 days in advance.

MOST ROMANTIC RESTAURANTS

Area 31 $$ SEAFOOD Miami glamor is paired with fine seafood at this gorgeous restaurant on the 16th floor of the elegant EPIC hotel. You can gaze on a terrific water and city skyline view from the sophisticated outdoor deck. Many of the preparations are deceptively simple—we are always amazed by what a talented chef can do with olive oil, lime juice, and chilies. Seafood is just off the line, or newly shucked—all sustainably fished from the local area 31 fishing region.

270 Biscayne Boulevard Way. ℘ **305/424-5234.** www.area31restaurant.com.

Azul $$ ASIAN/AMERICAN In one of Miami's most elegant hotels, the Mandarin Oriental, this lovely Asian fusion restaurant has a beautiful view of the city and Biscayne Bay. Azul's soaring ceiling, fine china, and refinement prepares you for their innovative cuisine. The Moroccan lamb is, without doubt, a signature dish worth the trip. Other specialties include unique Asian preparations of duck and tuna.

500 Brickell Key Drive. ℘ **305/913-8358.** www.mandarinoriental.com.

Casa Tua $$ NORTHERN ITALIAN Even in South Beach you can dine in an Italianate villa surrounded by tropical plants in glorious profusion. Totally private, the villa offers seating in a garden and romantic dining room. Several getaway nooks beckon, including an upstairs bar and deck.

1700 James Ave. ℘ **305/673-1010** or 305/673-0973. www.casatualifestyle.com.

Palacio de los Jugos $ CUBAN/AMERICAN You owe it to yourselves to explore this authentic Cuban Market—translated to "Juice Palace." The energy is fantastic, and the food is all perfectly rendered Cuban delicacies. You will find the real deal here: fresh juices, fresh fruit, and roast pig. You order at a counter and sit down at the joyfully chaotic picnic tables. Don't expect English-speaking waiters.

14300 SW 8th St. ℘ **305/226-3141.** www.elpalaciodelosjugos.com.

MIAMI BY NIGHT

Take in the glittering rooftop view from the **Townhouse Hotel's Bar,** 150 20th St. (℘ **305/534-3800;** www.townhousehotel.com), along with a sushi snack and chic cocktail on a chaise lounge. For another panoramic view, visit the bar at the **Lido Restaurant and Bayside Grill** at The Standard, 40 Island Ave. (℗ **305/673-1717;** www.standardhotels.com).

The glamorous **Setai Hotel,** 2001 Collins Ave. (℗ **305/520-6000;** www.thesetaihotel.com), is out of reach for most of us, but you can show up for cocktails on the beach, or in the courtyard near the hotel's entrance. Cozy sitting areas on high fashion couches grouped around the reflecting pools are a sophisticated and romantic way to experience the night. Order the signature passion fruit martini and toast each other.

MONTRÉAL
Flirting with French

To be in Montréal is to experience Europe in North America. Vieux-Montréal, the Old City, has the narrow streets, cobblestone sidewalks, and plazas that recall the 6th arrondisment in Paris or the historic center of Lisbon. On the streets of Montréal you hear many languages, and of course, the singular French accent of the Québécois.

Montréal has two personalities: summer and winter.

In summer, tourists pack the streets, congregating around Vieux-Montréal's central plaza, **Place Jacques-Cartier.** This wide promenade is rich in cafes spilling out onto the sidewalk, and shop after shop, some with tourist knick-knacks, others very chic. Amble down to the port, or get a lovely look-around by hiring a romantic and cheerfully decorated horse-drawn carriage.

The city has a plethora of things to do that you can walk or bike to. A nice route is the pathway right next to the **Lachine Canal.** The pathway leads you to the port, to the **Atwater Market** and then to the new urban beach, totally artificial, but very pleasing (www.quaysoftheoldport.com).

In winter, the hotel rooms are cozy, the city is gray, and people tend to stay inside, but the nearby mountains are snow white. Snowshoeing and skiing are only a short drive away.

KEY SUMMER ATTRACTIONS

Biking   The enormous number of bike paths and bike rental places makes it easy for the two of you to bike in an entirely new part of the city every day for weeks. You can plot your itinerary through **Vélo Québec,** 1251 Rachel St. E. Montréal (℗ **800/567-8356** or 514/521-8356; www.velo.qc.ca). Rent bikes from a fantastic inexpensive city program called **BIXI** (℗ **877/820-2453** or 514-789-2494; http://montreal.bixi.com; C$7 for 24-hr access), where you pick up bikes from one stand for the day and deposit them at other stands convenient to where you end up.

Cruising the River   Okay, this really will feel like Paris. These water tours along the Saint Lawrence River from mid-May to mid-October even have the same name as their Parisian antecedents: **Le Bateau-Mouche,** Quai

Jacques-Cartier, rue de la Commune Est Vieux- Port de Montréal (℗ **800/361-9952** or 514/849-9952; www.bateaumouche.ca; 1-hour cruise C$24 adult, C$22 senior). You will glide beneath bridges, see the islands, and take in the spectacular cityscapes. For an ultra-romantic experience, check out the three-hour dinner cruise (C$98–C$222) and coordinate with a night when the fireworks are scheduled to go off—during the International Fireworks Competition, that is.

Hiking Do as the locals do: Hike to **Mont Royal,** 1260 Chemin Remembrance (℗ **514/843-8240,** ext. 0; www.lemontroyal.qc.ca). The easy trails may feel familiar to people from New York, Chicago, St. Louis, and Seattle, since these tracks were also designed by Frederick Law Olmsted or his firm just as each other city's has their own Olmsted creation.

Ice Skating There is a place in Montréal where you can skate in any kind of weather. This is Canada, after all. **Atrium Le 1000,** 1000 De La Gauchetiere St. W. (℗ **514/3950555;** www.le1000.com; admission C$8 adults, C$7 seniors), is a fantastic skating venue in a downtown skyscraper. You can skate indoors for a few hours and then have a café au lait at one of the cafes surrounding the arena.

Jardin Botanique Montréal's Botanical Garden is a floriferous and fragrant haven all year long. It has a dazzling mix of plants, including a rainforest exhibition, an orchid greenhouse, impressive numbers of roses from spring through the fall, and an unusual collection of food-bearing plants. Perhaps most spectacular are the Asian gardens. The traditional Chinese Garden has Chinese indigenous plants and formal courtyards, while the Japanese Zen Garden is accompanied by a fine tearoom (where very correct ceremonies are demonstrated) and a captivating bonsai collection.

4101 Sherbrooke Est. ℗ **514/872-1400.** http://espacepourlavie.ca. admission C$19.

Kayaking If you want to do something on the water, stay near the Lachine Canal and rent a kayak at **H2O Adventures,** 2985B Saint-Patrick St. (℗ **514/842-1306;** www.h2oadventures.ca; 2-person kayak C$25 first hour, C$20 each additional hour).

KEY WINTER ATTRACTIONS

Carriage Rides Now you are thinking: This belongs under summer. Well, it works then, too, but we find being bundled together in a horse-drawn carriage surrounded by glinting snow is much more romantic than trotting around on a sweltering July day. Find the carriages in the Vieux Quartier at Place Jacques-Cartier and Place d'Armes.

Cross-country Skiing & Ice Skating Greater Montréal can be positively romantic in winter, especially at Christmas. Stay near town and go cross-country skiing on the Parc du Mont-Royal's lovely groomed course or drive an hour into the Laurentian Mountains. Multiple lakes turn into outdoor skating rinks throughout the area, and skate and ski rental shops are everywhere. Here are a few reliable operators: Parc-nature Bois-de-Liesse, 9432,

Bl. Gouin O. (© 514/280-6729; www.bonjourquebec.com; ski rentals C$9 for 1hr and C$3 for each additional hour); Bassin Bonsecours, Vieux-Port de Montréal (© 800/971-7678 or 514/496-7678; www.bonjourquebec.com; admission C$6; skate rentals C$7); Parc Jean-Drapeau, 1, circuit Gilles-Ville-neuve (© 514/872-6120 or 514/465-0594; www.parcjeandrapeau.com; ski rental C$19 for 2 hours, snowshoes C$9 for 2 hours); and Lac des Castors, Beaver Lake Parc du Mont Royal (© 514/280-8989 or 514/843-8240, ext. 0; skate rentals C$9 for 2 hours).

Mountain Excursion   The **Laurentians** (30 minutes to the north; http://laurentides.com/en) are a wonderful destination, particularly in the fall when the sugar maples turn hues of red and orange. But every season is wonderful: You can ski or snowboard **Mont-Tremblant,** Station Mont Tremblant 1000, Chemin des Voyageurs Mont-Tremblant (© **888/738-1777 or 514/764-7546;** www.tremblant.ca; lift ticket C$39), in the winter or hike and bike it in other seasons. The **Cantons-de-l'Est** region also has lovely farmland, charming inns, and the much-loved **Lake Massawippi.** In winter, the area offers skiing on **Bromont Mountain** (© **866/276-6668;** www.skibromont.com; lift ticket C$49); in summer there is kayaking, white-water rafting, and other water sports.

Musée des Beaux-Arts   If you are not on the slopes, you'll be looking for shelter. The Musée des Beaux-Arts is all about visual arts and popular culture. It is excitingly curated—look for the special exhibits from all over the world and in various media.

Pavillon Jean-Noel Desmarais 1380, rue Sherbrooke Ouest. © **800/899-6873** or 514/285-2000. www.mbam.qc.ca. Museum tickets free for ages 30 and under; 31 and up C$12; major exhibitions ages 13-30 C$12, ages 31 and up C$20.

HOTELS WITH HEART

Auberge Bonaparte $ If you like a chic, hospitable hotel, with staff who will remember your name and make you feel special, then this is the place. And, even better, it won't kill your budget. Some of the rooms are small, but everything is so well decorated you might not mind. Ask for a room with a whirlpool tub. Find time to have a drink on the rooftop overlooking the Basilica at twilight. Breakfast will be especially graceful in the quintessential Bonaparte Restaurant. Enjoying a delicious breakfast or coffee and gazing at the world from your window tables is a cozy experience to start your day.

447 rue Saint Francois Xavier. © **514/844-1448** or 514/844-0272. www.bonaparte. com.

Auberge du Vieux-Port $ This quite old and traditional hotel just sings romance. Ask for a room with a waterfront view, and you may spend many days here just enjoying the passing tableau. The spacious rooms have brick and stone walls, accented by massive beams. The lobby has a very civilized little wine bar, **Narcisse,** for a lovely end of the day.

97, de la Commune St. E. © **888/660-7678** or 514/876-0081. www.aubergedu vieuxport.com.

Hostellerie Pierre du Calvet $ We can't help but include this 18th-century building that has been turned into a charming and romantic hotel. With real antiques and original stone walls in some rooms, the interior is lavished with velvet and heavy brocades. Once a home, it is furnished as a wealthy owner might have put it together: four-poster beds, fireplaces, elegant gilded furniture, and fine paintings. The dining room, **Les Filles du Roy,** maintains the dramatic decor of a lodge of the period. In summer, the enclosed garden courtyard couldn't be more romantic.

405 rue Bonsecours Vieux-Montréal. ℂ **866/544-1725** or 514/282-1725. www.hotel-pierreducalvet.com.

Hôtel Le St-James $$ From the minute you walk in, the chandelier, the rich woods, and textures of materials let you know you are in the lap of exquisite luxury. Everything is opulent and the serious commitment to service is obvious. The hotel's **XO Le Restaurant** is in a great hall with tall Corinthian columns and gilded balconies. In another time, it was the stock exchange, and the hotel was a bank—hence the grand dimensions of the place. This is our pick for a honeymoon or anniversary celebration. It's expensive, but we think it delivers as much luxury and beauty as hotels in more expensive cities that would charge twice the price.

355 rue Saint-Jacques. ℂ **866/841-3111** or 514/841-3111. www.hotellestjames.com.

MOST ROMANTIC RESTAURANTS

Almost every restaurant in the Vieux Quartier has charm, but we've selected a few in and out of the quarter for special adulation.

Le Club Chasse et Pêche $ FRENCH When you ask Montrealers where to go for a romantic dinner, this is likely to be their suggestion. Choose from delicately fried oysters, wild boar, or venison, as the artistry of Chef Claude Pelletier is in every dish. Food is taken seriously here, and the mood is of sweet indulgence.

423 St. Claude St. ℂ **514/861-1112.** www.leclubchasseetpeche.com.

L'Express $ FRENCH Early or late, this is the place to feel as if the two of you are in Paris. Whether it's for dinner or a 2am nosh, the place is magic—and affordable. The high ceilings, gilded mirrors, and, of course, the black and white checkered floor contribute to the Parisian feel. Fish soup, onion soup, croque monsieur—do what you'd do in Paris or Provence.

3927 rue Saint-Denis. ℂ **514/845-5333.** http://restaurantlexpress.ca.

Toqué $$ FRENCH Chef/owner Normand Laprise has won Montréal's heart. Each dish here is an invention, and the chef keeps coming up with new tricks. If you want the meal to go on forever, choose the seven-course tasting menu with wine pairings. If you don't want the five-star treatment, go instead to the chef's reasonably priced **Brasserie T,** 1425 rue Jeanne-Mance (ℂ **514/282-0808;** www.brasserie-t.com), in the Musée d'Art, where the terrace is a romantic fair-weather spot. The indoor view is facilitated by floor-to-ceiling windows. Feast on French charcuterie and various delicious tartare selections.

If you haven't tried Coquille St.-Jacques, or haven't had it for a while, this would be the time to order it.

900 place Jean-Paul-Riopelle. ℭ **514/499-2084.** www.restaurant-toque.com. Reservations required.

MONTRÉAL BY NIGHT

Basilique Notre-Dame This glorious and awe-inspiring structure is worth visiting at any time, but is especially romantic at night. Every Tuesday and Saturday, the Basilica presents a sound-and-light show called "Et la Lumière Fut" ("And Then There Was Light"). *Fun fact:* If you are Catholic, you can get married here, the same place Celine Dion had her glamorous nuptials.

110 Notre Dame St. West. www.basiliquenddm.org. Et la Lumiere Fut ℭ **866/842-2925** or 514/842-2925, ext. 226. www.therewaslight.ca. C$10 adult, C$9 seniors.

Cirque du Soleil You've probably heard of Cirque du Soleil, as it now has companies touring all over the United States and is entrenched in Las Vegas. It started and remains based in Montréal. If you've seen one of its shows, you know how magical they can be. You can get lost in the wonder of the costumes, music, acrobatic artistry, and fantasia. If you are here in late spring or summer, shows are likely to be in session.

8400 2e Ave. ℭ **514-722-2324.** www.cirquedusoleil.com.

NEW ORLEANS
Loving Life in the Big Easy

The Big Easy has a sensual, party loving, musical soul. It practically has "Overindulge" engraved on the welcome mats. You *are* here to indulge your senses: to listen to vibrant music, drink regional cocktails (this city never was one for Sunday blue laws), and eat extraordinarily well. This is a place of stories, sordid and sexy, romantic, and sometimes flat-out debauched. That's why we love it.

But we are not here for the wild scenes of Mardi Gras. That may be New Orleans' most colorful time—but certainly not its most romantic. No, romance here is staying up late for good jazz and waking up early for perfect beignets, at **Café du Monde** (see below). Romantic is being laidback on a sultry day and nursing a Sazerac (the official drink of New Orleans) on your patio in the French Quarter. There are some less cheery (and bleary) aspects to New Orleans—some neighborhoods have scarcely recovered since Hurricane Katrina. But New Orleans wants to move forward and invites you to share in *le bon temps* (the good times).

KEY ATTRACTIONS

Café du Monde This is a must. Get up and smell the chicory coffee. Join the folks on the patios of Decatur Street and the Jackson Square people-watching people the "morning after." The signature beignets are delicious and not nutritious, but who cares on such a magical morning. These delectable treats were probably once inspired by the French donut, but now they have a powdered sugar presence that's all New Orleans. The cafe is open 24 hours, so you can't come too early or too late. Being there for the sunrise is a particularly only-in-New Orleans experience.

800 Decatur St. ☏ **800/772-2927** or 504/525-4544. www.cafedumonde.com.

Garden District This is an architecturally interesting neighborhood of mansions, some grand and some showing their age around the edges. Money from another time built these massive homes, and the years since have given each its own unique patina of Louisiana charm.

Preservation Hall Make sure you drop into one of the country's most time-honored jazz institutions. It's a happy, happening place to hear and feel the real *Basin Street Blues*.

726 St. Peter St. ☏ **504/522-2841.** www.preservationhall.com. Cover $15–$20.

HOTELS WITH HEART

Magnolia Mansion $ Lavish, lavish, lavish. Each room in this B&B has its own decor. The red entrance hall and antique-laden public rooms set the tone for the outrageous boudoir-style guest rooms.

2127 Prytania St. ☏ **504/412-9500.** www.magnoliamansion.com. Rates include continental breakfast.

Windsor Court Hotel $$ Here's what you need to know: The paintings by Reynolds and Gainsborough here are real. That tells you a lot. There is also a spacious spa that has couples services on the menu, a formal tea, and often, a jazz band in the background. The rooms are inspired by English gentry, and many have striking views of the skyline or river. It's one of the most opulent hotels in the French Quarter, but you don't have to own an estate to stay here.

300 Gravier St. ☏ **800/928-7898** or 504/523-6000. www.windsorcourthotel.com.

MOST ROMANTIC RESTAURANTS

New Orleans brags plenty about its remoulade sauce and most certainly its roux and gumbo, and for good reason. We can offer a few romantic choices of restaurants that serve them, but there are so many others. For maximum effect, we've concentrated on Creole cooking, that local mix of Louisianan and a number of world cuisines, most identifiably French and West Indian.

Cochon $ CAJUN This and its more casual sister restaurant **Cochon Butcher** are some of the best places to go for nouveau Cajun. The food is seriously good in a nice but no-frills atmosphere.

930 Tchoupitoulas St. ☏ **504/588-2123.** www.cochonrestaurant.com.

Commander's Palace $$ CREOLE This beloved and gracious restaurant is situated on a side street in the Garden District. Part of the charm is the area, easy to reach by old-fashioned street cars and populated by magnificent Southern-style mansions. The restaurant is across from an historic cemetery, replete with Civil War remembrances. Catering to tourists and locals, the

Commander's Palace is in a rambling old mansion. The main dining room has quiet corners to be tucked into, though the locals go to the second-floor discreet private dining rooms or to the closed-in porch with a lovely view of the gardens. Traditional delicacies include turtle soup and Creole bread pudding soufflé.

1403 Washington Ave. ✆ **504/899-8221.** www.commanderspalace.com.

Galatoire's $$ FRENCH   This restaurant has been around since 1905 and has had its ups and downs. But this is where high society still returns, and where food is still a lifestyle. You can get all the New Orleans favorites here. In our opinion, this is the place for gumbo—but competition is fierce, and you should try it in a lot of places

209 Bourbon St. ✆ **504/525-2021.** www.galatoires.com.

Upperline $$ CREOLE   It is here that the heavenly dish of fried green tomatoes topped with remoulade was invented. The eccentric and charming dining room sets the mood for perfect New Orleans cuisine like duck étouffée, turtle soup, and fried oysters with a spicy Creole sauce.

1413 Upperline St. ✆ **504/891-9822,** ext. 2. www.upperline.com.

NEW ORLEANS BY NIGHT

Nightlife here runs all night long and then some. You can go club-hopping in the French Quarter and just about every adjacent area (try going north a bit and experience one of the many clubs of Faubourg Marigny). Or you can dance to the Rebirth Brass Band. If it is playing anywhere in town, you should be there dancing! Besides the eponymous brass band, you are likely to hear great individual performers from vocal soloists to trumpet soloists a la Louis Armstrong.

The **Revolving Carousel,** at the Hotel Monteleone (214 Royal St.; (✆ **866/ 338-4684** or 504/523-3341; www.hotelmonteleone.com), has a platform beneath that turns the whole bar every 15 minutes. You may also enjoy the **Sazerac Bar,** at the Roosevelt New Orleans Hotel, 123 Baronne St. (✆ **504/ 648-1200;** www.rooseveltneworleans.com) and its wonderful Art Deco murals, perfect Ramos gin fizzes, and, of course, Sazerac cocktails (whiskey, absinthe, or sometimes Pernod, and bitters).

Maybe the most energetic place in the city to hear music any night of the week (or poetry readings every Sunday) is the **Maple Leaf Bar,** 8316 Oak St. (✆ **504/866-9359;** www.mapleleafbar.com), a real New Orleans institution. On nights with a popular band, the crowd is literally dancing in the streets.

NEW YORK CITY
Take a Bite

Ah, New York in springtime—when the flowers bloom and the cafes take over the sunny patches of sidewalk. Ah, New York in the fall—when the crisp air blows the autumnal leaves through the city's parks. Ah, New York at

Christmas—when it seems the whole city is decked in twinkling lights and the snow dusts the skyscrapers. Come to think of it, New York is spectacular any time of year, even summer (though the weather is rather sticky).

Granted, New York is an enormous city with some problems (though it's safer today than ever; recently the FBI ranked it the safest large city in the U.S.A.). But when you view it from the Statue of Liberty, or look at that icon from the shore, you can hardly stem the tide of powerful emotions that come up.

First trip to the Big Apple? We heartily recommend the two-hour **Circle Line Sightseeing Cruise,** Pier 83, West 42nd St. (© **212/563-3200;** www. circleline42.com; $39). It has shorter lines than the cruises to the Statue of Liberty and you pass the statue, as well as every major landmark, in the relaxing journey that takes in almost all of the Big Apple's highlights (the one exception is Yankee Stadium, which can be seen during the three-hour tour). For something more romantic, try the Harbor Light cruise and see how the skyline comes alive as the sun sets.

The energy of 8 million New Yorkers animates this dense concrete jungle of streets, shops, restaurants, theaters, and high-rises. Some of the energy of the city that never sleeps should rub off on you, too. Whether for a weekend or a week, New York City will be good for your relationship.

Two tips: First, you can get a pretty great (and free) view of the Manhattan skyline day or night on the return trip on the **Staten Island Ferry** (http://nyc. gov/statenislandferry). Hop on the ferry at Manhattan's southern tip (Whitehall Terminal) and when you reach Staten Island, just disembark and re-board for the return trip. Second, well worth the price of admission is the 360-degree view from **Top of the Rock,** 30 Rockefeller Plaza (© **877/692-7625** or 212/ 698-2000; www.topoftherocknyc.com; admission $27). You can skip the far bigger crowds atop the **Empire State Building,** 350 5th Ave. (© **212/736-3100;** www.esbnyc.com; admission $27).

KEY ATTRACTIONS

Broadway & Off-Broadway You can't go to New York and not see a play or musical. Ok, you can, but you shouldn't. Broadway's stars know how to pour on the razzle dazzle. Book tickets way in advance (perhaps with a discount from **BroadwayBox.com**) to see the show you want, or head to the **TKTS booth** in Times Square to view what's on when you're there.

Central Park New York's centerpiece park was designed by the famed 19th-century landscape architects Olmsted and Vaux, who believed that parks could be spiritual forces. Is that why a walk here is so stirring? You can go to the zoo, jog on the many paths, enjoy the water features, and people-watch. Most of all you can be alone together: Pack a lunch from one of Manhattan's delis and spread out your blanket for a picnic on **Sheep Meadow,** which is like a green beach come summer, thanks to all the sunbathers.

59th St. and 5th Ave. www.centralparknyc.org.

The Cloisters   No time or cash to go to Europe together? You'll get a taste of life "across the pond" at the Cloisters (at the north end of Manhattan). A recreated medieval monastery (several actual ones were brought over brick by brick to build this evocative museum), it was a gift to New York by the Rockefeller family. Serene gardens, beautiful Hudson River views, and the famed "Unicorn Tapestries" (which some think symbolize true love) make this a wonderful place for an afternoon date.

99 Margaret Corbin Dr. ℭ **212/923-3700.** www.metmuseum.org/visit/visit-the-cloisters. Admission $25, also gets you admission to the Met (and vice versa).

Grand Central Terminal   The main hall of Grand Central Terminal is, well, grand with its cerulean "sky" ceiling complete with sparkling stars. Head over to the **Campbell Apartment** (ℭ 212/953-0409), a soaring, old-fashioned bar on the Vanderbilt Hall side of the station (it was once the apartment of a Gilded Age tycoon; most nights a jazz trio plays). To feel like a New Yorker in the know, eat in either of the two fine restaurants in the west balcony, perched above the sprawling space. If you want a more casual experience, go to the main floor and chow down at the landmark **Grand Central Oyster Bar $$;** (ℭ **212/490-6650;** www.oysterbarny.com). Oysters are natural aphrodisiacs, didn't you know?

89 E 42nd St. ℭ **212/340-2583.** www.grandcentralterminal.com.

Greenwich Village & SoHo   When NYC was New Amsterdam, these two areas were farmlands where small "villages" grew up (hence the name of one; the other stands for "South of Houston street"). Today, thanks to their winding streets, old-fashioned brownstones and cast iron buildings, they still feel like places apart from the rest of Gotham. Darn nice places, actually, filled with trendy shops, and lots of art galleries and music clubs. The window-shopping is tops as is the people-watching. You won't even have to talk—just hang onto each other and enjoy the world that walks by! Experience old New York at **Ferrara Bakery & Café,** 195 Grand St. (**$;** ℭ **212/226-6150;** www. ferraracafe.com), little changed and at its same location since opening in 1892. The cafe makes for a delightful rest stop for cappuccino, pastry, or gelato.

The High Line   An abandoned elevated railroad track bed, 30 ft. above street level, is now a public park and lively promenade in Manhattan's Chelsea neighborhood. It has cozy loveseats for watching the ships in the Hudson River and the spectacular sunset.

Enter at 23rd St. just west of 10th Ave. www.thehighline.org.

Museum-hopping   You must see New York's great museums—at least once. Be awed by the actual Egyptian temple at the **Metropolitan Museum** (aka the Met; 1000 5th Ave.; ℭ 212/535-7710; www.metmuseum.org; admission $25), the massive dinosaurs at the **Museum of Natural History,** Central Park West and 79th St. (ℭ 212/769-5100; www.amnh.org), or the modern art at the **Guggenheim,** 1071 5th Ave. (℗ 212/423-3500; www.guggenheim.org; admission $22). The Guggenheim building itself is a treat, designed by Frank Lloyd Wright, with its spiraling ramp that looks like a conch. For sheer fun, hit the edgier **Museum of Modern Art** (MOMA; 11 W 53rd St.; ℗ 212/708-9400; www.moma.org; admission $5) and the nearby **Museum of Art and Design,** 2 Columbus Cir. (℗ 212/299-7777; madmuseum.org; admission $16). In the mood for something more risqué? Those under 13 aren't allowed into the **Neue Galerie** (1048 Fifth Ave.; ℗ 212/628-6200. www.neuegalerie. org), which has exquisite erotic art by the likes of Gustave Klimt. And there's always the **Museum of Sex** (233 Fifth Ave.; ℗ 212/689-6337; www.mosex. com) which has nothing artful about it . . . but can be a hoot!

HOTELS WITH HEART

Gramercy Park Hotel $$ The legendary 1925 hotel, set beside one of the city's most lovely pocket parks, used to be sweetly dowdy and full of chintz curtains. Not anymore. All rooms are painted in vibrant, old-fashioned jewel tones and are luxurious with mahogany English drink cabinets, velvet-covered beds, and overstuffed chairs. It's so romantic you may be tempted to stay in. If you do, the place to have a drink is the hotel's art-filled Rose Bar or dinner at Maialino, Danny's Meyer's upscale, and fabulous, trattoria.

2 Lexington Ave. ℗ **866/784-1300** or 212/920-3300. www.gramercyparkhotel.com.

The Inn at Irving Place $$ We love this 170-year-old inn because it has antique charm, spacious rooms, decorative fireplaces and is on a human scale. Each room is named for a notable 19th-century New Yorker, and you do feel like you are re-claiming a bit of old New York when you're lodging here. Add another touch of romance: Order breakfast in bed and in-room massages.

56 Irving Pl. ℗ **800/685-1447** or 212/533-4600. www.innatirving.com.

The Michelangelo $$ The only U.S. property of the Italian-based Star-hotel, the Michelangelo offers gracious Italian hospitality and decor. Coffee and cappuccino are served all day. The spacious rooms have marble foyers, cushy king beds, and two televisions (one in the bathroom). And those bathrooms have our mandatory romantic feature: deep whirlpool bathtubs.

152 W 51st St. ℗ **212/765-1900.** www.michelangelohotel.com. Rates include Italian breakfast.

The Pierre $$$ Some hotels are ultra expensive but offer an experience you'd want at least once in your life. The Pierre is one. The elegant white-glove service creates a mood of privilege, and your room—high ceilinged and sumptuous—continues the theme. Some feel like apartments and have Central Park views. All have up-to-the-minute sound systems and large plasma televisions. The marble bathrooms have glass-walled showers and some have tubs equipped with flat-panel televisions. If you can tear yourself away from your swank room, high tea and cocktails are served at **2E,** the lobby lounge off the hotel's 61st Street entrance.

2 E 61st St. ℗ **212/838-8000.** www.tajhotels.com/Pierre.

MOST ROMANTIC RESTAURANTS

What a dilemma! New York has enough romantic restaurants with superb cuisine to fill a book. Here are a few of our favorites, but it truly hurts to leave other favorites out.

Ai Fiori $$$ FRENCH/ITALIAN   With its Michelin star, this gorgeously understated restaurant resides on the second floor of the classy Setai Hotel. Huge vats of pink flowers—lilies, peonies, and aromatic flowers of the season—infuse the air with grace and perfume. The food is superb, and presented with a flourish. Tables for two are widely spaced so privacy is guaranteed.

400 5th Ave No. 2. ✆ **212/695 4005.** www.aifiorinyc.com.

The Dove Parlour $ The red brocade walls and dark wood furnishings make this place truly feel like a Victorian parlor. The tone is a bit less prim, of course, with lots of fun cocktails and a very fine soundtrack. The Dove's genteel settees tucked behind huge Victorian style plants are fertile scenes for flirtation. Good for a drink, a meal, or canoodling.

228 Thompson St. ✆ **212/254-1435.** http://thedoveparlour.com.

One if by Land, Two if by Sea $$$ NEW AMERICAN   In what was once Aaron Burr's carriage house, a couple can dine amid sumptuous flowers, two fireplaces, and the sounds of the resident pianist. The Beef Wellington is lovely, as is pretty much any choice at this restaurant, often described as one of the best in New York City.

17 Barrow St. ✆ **212/255-8649.** www.oneifbyland.com.

Per Se $$$ FRENCH   Thomas Keller, a chef we like for his French Laundry restaurant in Napa Valley (p. 133), operates this spot on the fourth floor of the Time Warner Center on Columbus Circle. Get ready for a feast! Keller's signature is multiple small courses (always cooked in a highly creative fashion, and crafted from the finest of ingredients), served by kindly waiters who know when to keep their distance and when to coddle you. The room in the Time Warner complex is opulent, but even it can't compete with the glittering views of Manhattan diners get through the massive plate glass windows.

10 Columbus Cir. No 4. ✆ **212/823-9335.** www.perseny.com.

River Café $$$ NEW AMERICAN   Grab a cab and cross over the Brooklyn Bridge for this riverside restaurant right at Fulton Landing. The River Café offers a spectacular view of Manhattan. The food is also wonderful; don't miss the chocolate desserts.

1 Water St. ✆ **718/522-5200.** www.rivercafe.com.

Skal $ Sometimes there's nothing more romantic than a culinary adventure, and that's what you'll have in this super-hip area of the Lower East Side (right next to Chinatown). The food is Icelandic (tasty and exotic, with lots of herbs and unusual fish dishes), the cocktails are creative and potent, and on summer nights, the restaurant sets tables on the sidewalk so that diners can watch the world go by.

37 Canal St. ✆ **212/777-7518.** http://skalnyc.com.

NEW YORK CITY BY NIGHT

New York is the U.S. nightlife capital, and you'll find much to do—for that reason especially, we think it's crucial to romance to reserve a quiet moment for a drink in a perfect setting.

Cafe Carlyle   The supper-club at the elegant Carlyle Hotel offers first-rate cabaret entertainment. Also here is the winsome Bemelmans Bar, named after the "Madeleine" books' illustrator who painted the bar's mural. It is a great spot to sink into a leather banquette with your partner and order something adventurous, perhaps inspired by the frolicking beasties in the mural. 35 E 76th St. ✆ **212/744-1600.** www.rosewoodhotels.com.

Ink48   Hands down, one of the absolute best places to see the New York skyline from the Manhattan side. The rooftop garden, covered in bad weather, has a panorama of New York that will thrill you. Sip your cocktails and hold each other close on the couches inside or push your chairs together on the terrace and drink in the intoxicating city view. 653 11th Ave. ✆ **877/843-8869** or 212/757-0088. www.ink48.com.

Swing 46   People of all ages come to this Theater District club to dance the night away. Don't know how to swing dance? No worries: The cost of your admission includes a class, taught at the beginning of the evening. This is truly one of the most joyous places in the city come nightfall. 349 W 46th St. ✆ **212/262-9554.** www.swing46.com.

SAN FRANCISCO
Come with Me to the Sea

Is there an American city with as many love songs sung to it? Is there another city so beguiling? We don't think so. This is our top romantic city in the United States.

San Francisco's iconic image is of the **Golden Gate Bridge,** shining over blue water filled with sailboats or half hidden in the fog with a ghostly and powerful presence. Crossing it on foot or bike is breathtaking. But equally iconic images proliferate: the "painted ladies" Victorian houses all proudly tarted up; the hills with cable cars slowly climbing up and down; and the wharves, jam-packed with restaurants and shops but also with fishing boats and other reminders of this city's relationship to the sea.

San Francisco has an ethos, a live-and-let-live gaity, and also a solid commitment to civil rights. It's a place where people can be themselves at home or in the streets. Any gathering will bring out men (especially) in humorous and clever costumes. The quirky sensibilities of the natives support a taste for both the outrageous and the highly civilized. It is a place you can be either or both, together.

KEY ATTRACTIONS

Cable Car   You may have to wait in line but, trust us, it's worth it to take the cable car down ($5) to Fisherman's Wharf on the Powell-Hyde line. Grab your camera when you reach the top of Nob Hill: This is one of the world's great photo-ops. The view of the bay will make you both start talking about why living in San Francisco might be a really good idea.

Day Tripping   Head across the bay to **Tiburon,** a cute town of vacationy shops and boutiques. **Sam's Anchor Cafe,** 27 Main St. (**$$;** ℂ **415/435-4527;** www.samscafe.com), one of the area's oldest restaurants, is perfect for a romantic brunch. Right on the water, it has a terrific view and a festive air.

A second day trip option is to take the ferry from the Ferry Building at the Embarcadero (a great looking building with a good selection of restaurants and shops) to the colorful **Sausalito** waterfront. The weekend brings too many tourists, and summer is just a hot mess, but during the week and in other seasons you'll find a perfect, quiet spot to look back at the city from and marvel at its beauty. **Scoma's,** Pier 47 on Al Scoma Way (**$$;** ℂ **800/644-5852** or 415/771-4383; www.scomas.com), on the waterfront has a lovely view and dependably good food.

Bird Watching

Walk around Telegraph Hill or Russian Hill, and you may hear squawking overhead. Look up—that's no ordinary flock of city pigeons. You may spot the city's famous flock of wild green parrots, which has grown from an accumulation of escaped household pets to a full-fledged flock now living free to the delight of most residents.

Another option is to head east. Enlarge your knowledge and please your senses when you gaze upon the 13,000 species of plants across 34 acres at the **University of California Botanical Garden,** 200 Centennial Dr. (ℂ **510/643-2755;** http://botanicalgarden.berkeley. edu; admission $12) in Berkeley. Are you there near a meal time? Then you're in luck. You're so close, why not make the pilgrimage to a foodies' mecca: **Chez Panisse,** 1517 Shattuck Ave. (**$$$;** ℂ **510/548-5525** or 510/548-5049; www.chezpanisse.com). In our opinion, it's where the free-range, grass-fed, local-cuisine revolution was hatched. The tables get booked fast. Even if you didn't reserve a table in advance, call anyway just in case there's an opening.

Golden Gate Park   As Central Park is to New York, so is Golden Gate Park to the City by the Bay. With nine lakes and thousands of trees, you'll find some very dreamy places to meander. Our favorite is the **Japanese Tea Garden,** 75 Hagiwara Tea Garden Dr. (ℂ **415/752-4227;** http://japaneseteagardensf. com; admission $7), designed to delight the senses and quiet the mind. If you want more excitement and less contemplation, go instead to the new **Natural Science Museum,** 55 Music Concourse Dr. (ℂ **415/379-8000;** www.calacademy.org; admission $30). At the dramatic **De Young Museum,** 50 Hagiwara Tea Garden Dr. (ℂ **415/750-3600;** http://deyoung.famsf.org; admission $10), new technology shows you the art from all angles. A nice added treat is the 144-ft. tower with a 360-degree view of the entire Bay Area from the top. Back on the ground, hike through the park to the ocean and park yourself in the **Cliff House,** 1090 Point Lobos (**$$**; ☏ **415/386-3330;** www.cliffhouse. com), for simply stunning views and fresh seafood.

North Beach   This is the old funky part of town with great Italian restaurants and neighborhoods with ethnic authenticity. Take a morning Tai Chi class on the green, where young and old practice their art beside Chinese experts, then afterward grab a cannoli at an Italian bakery. Walk down Columbus Avenue and be embraced by the intense aromas from coffee houses and Italian bistros. You will also pass the landmark **City Lights Bookstore,** 261 Columbus Ave. (☏ **415/362-8193;** www.citylights.com), known for its association with the beatnik poets of the 1950s.

HOTELS WITH HEART

The Argonaut $$ If you're going to play the role of tourist, there's no better stage than Fisherman's Wharf with its views of marina, Golden Gate Bridge, and Alcatraz. This vibrant nautically themed hotel in the middle of the tourist frenzy shares a restored 1907 warehouse with a free visitors' center for the **San Francisco Maritime National Historical Park** (www.nps.gov/safr).
495 Jefferson St. ☏ **800/790-1415** or 415/563-0800. www.argonauthotel.com.

Hotel Monaco $$ This hotel offers signature Kimpton hospitality in the heart of Union Square in a 1910 Beaux Arts building. Beyond the cozy robes and yoga mats in every room, they will pretty much get you anything you want, whether you forgot your phone charger or need a dog sitter (pets welcome) or a bike on loan. This hotel has colorfully painted rooms, a lovely small lobby, and complimentary wine hour. Massages are available in the spa or your room.
501 Geary St. ☏ **866/622-5284** or 415/292-0100. www.monaco-sf.com.

The Mandarin Oriental $$$ This hotel has a particularly gorgeous view (reason enough to go here), even though it is in the business district and quite expensive. It is perched so high above the city that the fog rolls in below you, and when it's sunny you can see forever.
222 Sansome St. ☏ **415/276-9888.** www.mandarinoriental.com.

Marina Inn $ Here's a great option for the traveler on a budget who doesn't mind a busy street. Set in a 1920s Victorian building, the floral wallpaper and heavy pine furniture give the place a cozy, cottagelike feel. Rooms are quaint, though a little noisy if close to busy Lombard Street (ask for a room in the back). With prices as low as $69 for a double, it's hard to find a better deal in the city, especially when you factor in the free continental breakfast.
3110 Octavia St. (at Lombard St.). ☏ **415/928-1000.** www.marinainn.com. Rates include continental breakfast.

White Swan Inn $$ This B&B near Nob Hill is a romantic prize. You are buzzed in, and instantly feel you are home. The marvelous rooms are large but cozy and warmly decorated. The decor is English upper class with Victorian furniture, real fireplaces, and complimentary wet bar and mini fridge. Afternoons bring offerings of hors d'oeuvres, sherry, wine, and homemade cookies.

845 Bush St. ✆ **800/999-9570** or 415/775-1755. www.whiteswaninnsf.com. Rates include breakfast.

MOST ROMANTIC RESTAURANTS

Grand Café $$ FRENCH   We don't usually suggest ballroom-size dining rooms but this one, with its soaring ceilings in a majestic Beaux Arts historic building off Union Square, is an exception to the rule. The impeccably prepared contemporary French cuisine is surprisingly reasonably priced. No wonder it's a favorite among shoppers, theater goers, and locals, who voted it as one of the city's best happy hour spots. If you make reservations early, you can request one of the more private plush booths.

501 Geary St. ✆ **415-292-0101.** www.grandcafe-sf.com.

Ideale Ristorante $$ ITALIAN   Most restaurants in North Beach serve red-sauce Italian-American food, but this homey spot lovingly presents authentic Italian dishes by Maurizio, a descendant of four generations of Roman chefs. All breads, pastas, and pastries are home-made.

1309 Grant Ave. ✆ **415/391-4129.** www.idealerestaurant.com.

La Folie $$$ FRENCH   This is as good as it gets, so come hungry. Chef-owner Roland Passot presides over the kitchen every night and is famous for his seared foie gras. Other swank treats on the menu include lobster with glazed blood oranges and venison with quince and huckleberry sauce. The surroundings are luscious, with wood paneling, elegant mirrors, rust-red drapes, and golden Venetian plaster. It's a temple to food, but not at all stuffy.

2316 Polk St. ✆ **415/776-5577.** www.lafolie.com.

Waterbar $$$ SEAFOOD   Looking for some bustle and a stupendous view of the city from your dining table? Waterbar ought to do it. Floor-to-ceiling aquariums dominate the dining room at this seafood restaurant and raw bar. (If you can't get a reservation, try for a seat at the raw bar.) In obliging weather, choose the patio and laze away some hours enjoying the waterfront views. If it's chilly out, try for a seat by the windows for a great night view.

399 Embarcadero South. ✆ **415/284-9922.** www.waterbarsf.com.

Yank Sing $ CHINESE   Sunday dim sum is a San Franciscan tradition, and this place has been serving it for what seems like forever. Yank Sing offers a seemingly endless array of choices in big, crowded, noisy, and joyful rooms. Afterward, take a walk around Chinatown and dive into the fascinating open-air food market. At Waverly Place, you can visit three Chinese temples: **Jeng Sen** (Buddhist and Taoist) at no. 146, **Tien Hou** (Buddhist) at no. 125, and **Norras** (Buddhist) at no. 109.

101 Spear St. ✆ **415/781-1111.** www.yanksing.com. Second location at 49 Stevenson St. ✆ 415/541-4949.

SAN FRANCISCO BY NIGHT

Beach Blanket Babylon   It's a San Francisco tradition: a silly, over-the-top musical with outrageous costumes and headdresses, sets, props, and gags. It is the perfect romp, filling the 400-seat Club Fugazi almost every performance. It's been playing for more than 30 years. Reserve weekend tickets at least three weeks in advance. We promise you, unless you are homophobic (in which case, what are you doing in San Francisco?), you will laugh a lot and thoroughly enjoy yourselves. 678 Beach Blanket Babylon Blvd. (Green St.). ℂ **415/421-4222.** www.beachblanketbabylon.com. Tickets $48–$85. General admission seating is first come, first served.

SANTA FE
Mystical Mountaintop Artist Retreat

Enter Santa Fe, and you enter a different world. You smell it in the air wafting from mesquite-burning fireplaces. You see it in the robin-egg blue skies that go on forever. You touch it in the native arts and crafts. You taste it in the local New Mexican and Mexican cuisines.

Santa Fe is different from other U.S. towns. Its artistic bent sometimes borders on and dives right into the spiritual. For eons, the adobe buildings (preserved through protective zoning) and high desert landscape have called to writers and artists. The most famous artist who found inspiration here was Georgia O'Keeffe, whose lush flower paintings have often been interpreted as highly sexualized. (It should be noted that when asked, she denied that her pistols and stamens had anything to do with the human anatomy, but we don't quite buy that.)

Santa Fe sits at 7,000 ft. above sea level, but you can go up from there. Skiing is a half hour away, and if you want another center for spiritual healing (and skiing), **Taos** is only another hour. But you can stay right in Santa Fe for everything you need in a romantic getaway: atmospheric hotels, world-class restaurants, and decadent spas (one of our two favorites in the United States) can settle you into sybaritic bliss.

KEY ATTRACTIONS

Exploring by Foot   Each street around **Old Town Plaza,** 201 W. Marcy St. (ℂ **800/777-2489;** http://santafe.org), not to mention the plaza itself, is intriguing. Walk along the historic 17th-century arcaded facade of the **Palace of the Governors,** 105 W. Palace Ave. (ℂ **505/476-5100;** www.palaceofthegovernors. org; admission $9), and look over the jewelry that local artisans have brought to town. Great shopping is literally everywhere. Bring money. Once a year, the whole plaza swells with the famous **Indian Market** (www.swaia.org) where, it seems, every artist in the state (and neighboring states) participates. Even the most discerning Indian jewelry lovers will find plenty to see. Complete

TEN THOUSAND waves

Twenty minutes from Santa Fe and 20 minutes from the ski slopes, this spa is perfectly positioned for going to or coming from skiing—or just going to and chucking the skiing. Nature's elegance is employed to full effect at Ten Thousand Waves, 3451 Hyde Park Rd. (© **505/982-9304;** www.tenthousandwaves.com; use of hot tubs $24–$53, massages from $112, spa treatments from $61), where the hot tubs look out at the vast starlit sky and mountains—snow-covered in winter. Various parts of the spa are single-sex or mixed. The mixed hot tub and cold plunge (if you dare) is clothing optional in the day, but bathing suits are mandatory at night. Your fellow tubbers may be a mixed group of locals, gays, lesbians, bikers, counter-culture drop-outs from long ago, honeymooners, and just about anyone else you can think of, all getting along very nicely. You can also reserve private hot tubs and pools. The perfection can be overwhelming: The mountains, the sky, the tub, the Japanese theme, the private-cottage massage rooms (or, heck, even the regular ones) all make this spa monumentally romantic. If you can't get your fill, you can also stay overnight in the hotel.

your shopping tour with a walk up to **Canyon Road** where you can browse through gallery after gallery after gallery of Native American art.

Georgia O'Keeffe   What a life this woman had! Here you can immerse yourselves in the lives of O'Keeffe and her fellow artists—sensualists every one. The **Georgia O'Keeffe Museum** in downtown (217 Johnson St.; © **505/ 946-1000;** www.okeeffemuseum.org; admission $12) is home to more than 1,000 pieces of her work. But to feel the essence of the woman, go beyond Santa Fe about 45 minutes to Abiquiu and visit the **Ghost Ranch,** 1708 Hwy 84, Abiquiu (© **877/804-4678** or 505/685-1000; www.ghostranch.org; tours $25–$85), where she lived the latter part of her life. Her adobe house and grounds are as she left them—serene, simple, and definitely spiritual.

The High Road   This is a region of incredibly interesting pueblos and ruins of ancient Native American cultures. The **Mountain Road** (or High Road) is the way to go. Head out for just a day, or go farther: One of the more fascinating national monuments in our country, **Chaco Culture National Historic Park,** 1808 County Rd. 7950, Nageezi (© **505/786-7014,** ext. 221; www.nps.gov/chcu/index.htm; admission $8), is within reach. You will pass farm country on your way to the village of Chimayo, a town of weavers. A famous restaurant there is **Rancho de Chimayó,** 300 Juan Medina Rd. (© **505/ 351-4444** or 505/984-2100; www.ranchodichimayo.com; main courses $10– $15), known for its heaping plates of classic Southwestern food. At the next stop, Cordova, admire the village, its renowned woodcarvings, and a number of very good galleries, including the **Castillo Gallery,** 181 County Rd. 80 (℡ **505/351-4067;** http://mulert.com/cg or www.paulacastilloart.com), which features the incredible welded metal sculptures of Paula Castillo and wood-carver Terry Enseñat Mulert. Four miles east are spectacular vistas of the imposing 13,101-ft. **Truchas Peak** and a good look at the **Rio Grande.** Nearby is the **High Road Marketplace,** 1642 Highway 76, Truchas (℡ **505/689-2689;** www.highroadmarketplace.com), an excellent artists' co-op gallery.

Santa Fe Opera   For some people, the beautiful performance hall 7 miles out of town is the focal point of their visit. Expect world-class performers in July and August. Plan ahead, as tickets do sell out.

301 Opera Dr. ℡ **800/280-4654** or 505-986-5900. www.santafeopera.org. Tickets $35–$260.

HOTELS WITH HEART

The Bishop's Lodge $ If you are just the two, or trying to find romance even with your family on the trip, this lodge can accommodate. The rustic mid-sized rooms use the work of local craftspeople to add charm. But the much more spacious new rooms are more to our taste: They have high ceilings and gas fireplaces, and most have either a balcony or a patio and splendid views. Better yet, go for the villas. These really luxurious two- and three-bedroom townhouses have kitchens, fireplaces, and relaxing outdoor spaces to take in the view. The Lodge has excellent babysitting services and a full-day children's program that can give you some privacy. In the summer you can share romantic moments on horseback, picnics, and nature walks. In winter, think of cozying in—you can get alone time here.

1297 Bishop's Lodge Rd. ℡ **888/272-9562** or 505/412-4067. www.bishopslodge.com.

The Inn at Loretto Downtown $ You can't get more centrally located than this rambling inn built in a Taos Pueblo style. The Navajo-themed rooms can have beamed ceilings, decorative fireplaces, and bathrooms with elegant amenities. The only problem: Everyone else likes to stay here, too, and sometimes in large groups (not our idea of romantic). Go in an off-season, and the big comfortable lobby is all yours.

211 Old Santa Fe Trail. ℡ **800/727-5531** or 866/582-1646. www.innatloretto.com.

Rosewood Inn of the Anasazi $$$ This is one of the coziest and best designed (and priciest) of the luxury hotels in town. With beamed ceilings and stone floors, most rooms have an authentic *chimenea* (fireplace). The special touches that enchant us are the small, very welcoming library and the splashes of color throughout the inn from Navajo artifacts, local art, and furniture made by New Mexican craftsmen.

113 Washington Ave. ℡ **888/767-3966** or 505/988-3030. www.innoftheanasazi.com.

MOST ROMANTIC RESTAURANTS

Café Pasqual's $$ MEXICAN   We admit it. We have had trips to Santa Fe where we ate at no other place. This unpretentious but colorful little restaurant in the core of Santa Fe is decorated with Mexican paper cutouts, paintings framed by white Christmas lights, and long strands of red chili peppers hanging from the ceiling. Don't let the informality fool you: This is amazing food by a celebrated chef. It's a local place, even if tourists come—you'll feel like an honorary Santa Fean.

121 Don Gaspar. ℂ **800/722-7672** or 505/983-9340. www.pasquals.com.

Geronimo $$ AMERICAN   Located in a restored 18th-century adobe Borrego House, Geronimo is a farm-to-table restaurant. Reserve a spot on the lovely porch to make it even more romantic.

724 Canyon Rd. ℂ **505/982-1500.** www.geronimorestaurant.com.

Santa Café $$ AMERICAN   When you arrive at this 18th-century house built by Father Padre Gallegos, you sense you are at the start of a special evening. Come during warmer months when you can sit in the romantically lit courtyard. Dinners are fantastic (a mix of Southwestern, Asian, and continental cooking), and the cafe also makes an amazing Sunday brunch.

231 Washington Ave. ℂ **505/984-1788.** www.santacafe.com.

SANTA FE BY NIGHT

El Farol   Driving down Canyon Road you could miss this funky restaurant-bar-dance club if you are not careful. It's crowded, friendly, and local. There will be kids, older people and hot young people dancing on any given weekend night. Various people will ask you to dance, and you'll find out somebody is an artist, and someone is a biker, and someone is at cooking school, and suddenly it's just one big happy dancing family. 808 Canyon Rd. ℂ **808/983-9912** or 505/983-9912. www.elfarolsf.com. $25–$40.

SEATTLE
Come Rain or Come Shine

Oddly enough, the romantic magic of the Northwest has become more widely known because of a family of vampires. Any fan of the "Twilight" trilogy knows the mysterious beauty of the Northwest coastline and Forks and Neah bays. We'd like to extend your repertoire of the romantic Northwest.

If you are lucky enough to be in Seattle on a clear sunny day, beat the crowds and start your day at the rotating **Space Needle,** 400 Broad St. (ℂ **800/937-9582** or 206/905-2100; www.spaceneedle.com; admission $11–$17) to see its 360-degree views. The ride up is fun: in one rotation, the views of Mt. Rainier (a dead-ringer for Mt. Fuji in Japan), the Cascades and the Olympic mountain ranges, Puget Sound, and Lake Washington. If there is a low cloud ceiling—forget it. Even if you miss the Needle, all is not lost. One of the most romantic things you can do at Seattle Center is visit the **Chihuly Glass Garden,** 305 Harrison St. (ℂ **407/956-3527** or 206/753-4940; www.chihulygarden

andglass.com; admission $19). You may have seen the work of this world-famous glass artist before, but certainly not like this. The fantastical creations in glass seem light as feathers and dainty as flowers. The additional indoor glass gardens, displayed in multiple large rooms, will cause your jaw to drop multiple times.

Next, head for the **Pike Place Market,** 1st Ave. and Pike St. (*②* **206/682-7453;** www.pikeplacemarket.org), one of the great farmers markets of the United States. Break for lunch at **Place Pigalle,** 81 Pike St. (**$$;** *②* **206/624-1756;** www.placepigalle-seattle.com), a charming small place with a few tables that look out at the Sound and the ferries passing by; or the **Pink Door**, 1919 Post Alley (**$$;** *②* **206/443-3241;** http://thepinkdoor.net), for great salads, fresh seafood, and the romantic deck in summer.

Head south on foot to the "old" part of the city, **Pioneer Square** for quite a few intimately sharable art galleries and restaurants. For dinner we recommend **Il Terrasso,** 411 1st Ave. S. (**$$;** *②* **206/467-7797;** http://ilterrazzocarmine. com), for its authentic and excellent Northern Italian cooking in a pretty courtyard with an architectural waterfall. If you are up for a game, depending on the season, Pioneer Square backs into the football and baseball stadiums. If not, Seattle's indoor delights can make your evening: jazz clubs, ballet, opera, and numerous professional theaters.

Tip: Unless you are coming to ski **Crystal Mountain** or **Alpental,** or head toward world-class cross-country skiing in the **Methow Valley** in eastern Washington, we have to say skip the winters in Seattle. This season is dark and dank and, as you may have gathered, really wet. The area starts to dry out in March and April (a trip to the tulip fields in **La Conner,** a great tourist town about an hour and a half away, will produce awesome vistas) but isn't predictably balmy until July through September.

KEY ATTRACTIONS

Leavenworth   Eastward lies this ersatz Bavarian village, but you don't go for the German hoopla; you go for **Run of the River Inn,** 9308 E. Leavenworth Rd., Leavenworth (**$$;** *②* **800/288-6491** or 509/548-7171; www.runof theriver.com) or **Sleeping Lady Resort,** 7375 Icicle Rd., Leavenworth (**$$;** *②* **800/574-2123** or 509/548-6344; www.sleepinglady.com; rates include dinner and breakfast). The Inn is cozy with big, satisfying breakfasts and a picturesque river site for a very reasonable sum. The Sleeping Lady offers an inviting rock pool in the summer, terrific cross-country skiing and sledding in the winter, and art and music festivals from spring to fall at Icicle Creek.

Outdoors In-town   You don't really need to leave Seattle if you are outdoors enthusiasts. The city is a great destination for hiking, skiing, or sailing.

Lake Washington has canoes in the summer for gliding on the lake or through the narrower waters of the estuary. You can also rent kayaks near the University of Washington medical complex and peer into the houseboat community nearby. **Greenlake** isn't far away, and it has a 3-mile walk around the lake and has paddle boats, canoes, and kayaks for rent.

better BIRTHDAYS

"Significant" birthdays (50th or 60th, for example) should be celebrated, and honored. A milestone birthday is a lot like a milestone anniversary (see p. 266)—we see it as an occasion to arrange to go somewhere your partner has longed to go. A gift of a trip shows you have given some thought, done some planning, and are invested in creating a shared experience and memory.

An ordinary birthday can be made memorable by traveling somewhere close to where you live. Check into a downtown hotel and then go to dinner and see a play or concert, or get in the car to go to the countryside within a few hours of your hometown.

As in this example for Seattleites shows, a great place can be a mere 45-minute drive, yet take you a world away. Celebrate in style at the **Salish Lodge & Spa** (see below). Book a romance package to have a bottle of chilled Veuve Clicquot Champagne and the Salish Lodge Signature Truffles waiting for you. You might splurge and book the Hidden Terrace, a tented room right next to the top of Snoqualmie Falls where the two of you can get a side-by-side Chocolate Moonlight Massage at 11pm. If that's outside your budget, talk to the concierge and reserve the gorgeous spa soaking pools and have them all to yourselves after 10pm.

For almost the same views with less effort, **Washington Park Arboretum,** 2300 Arboreteum Dr. E. (© **206/543-8800;** http://depts.washington.edu/wpa; admission), has nature trails that follow the estuary and go through the park itself. The park is at its most striking in the spring when its profusion of azaleas, rhododendrons, and blooming cherry trees.

Wine Country & Beyond   For wine lovers, one exciting excursion is a 45-minute drive to **Woodinville,** the suburban outpost for Eastern Washington's wine industry. At least 70 wineries are represented here (and more are appearing all the time), and almost all have tasting rooms, though some are open only to wine list members. We suggest visiting Delille, Isenhouer, Sleight of Hand, Alexandra Nicole, Mark Ryan, Pepperbridge, Januik, and Shah-Woodhouse. **Chateau St. Michele** (a spectacular campus that has big name outdoor concerts in the summer) has tours, private wine tastings, and a great gift shop. (See also "Walla Walla," p. 155.) Nearby is the acclaimed **Barking Frog Restaurant,** 14580 NE 145th St., Woodinville ($$; © **425/424-2999;** www.willowslodge.com), with a cozy room just across from St. Michelle Winery.

For more rustic pleasures, unbounded natural beauty is a mere couple hours away at the **Hoh Rainforest,** where a stay at the venerable **Lake Crescent Lodge,** 416 Lake Crescent Rd., Olympic National Park ($; © **888/723-7127** or 360/928-3211; www.olympicnationalparks.com), sets an exhilarating mood. This is one of the few temperate climate rainforests in the world—there is a very good chance you will be rained on. But you can almost predict that the walks past ancient mossy trees, bubbling streams, and the filtered light through tall evergreens will make for a romantic outing despite the rain.

HOTELS WITH HEART

Just 30 miles from Seattle is the **Salish Lodge,** 6501 Railroad Ave. SE., Snoqualmie (**$$; ℂ 800/272-5474** or 425/434-6111; www.salishlodge.com). The lodge is also about a half hour from skiing in the winter, 5 minutes away from golf and hiking in the summer, and next to the biggest tourist site in Washington, **Snoqualmie Falls.** Several of the attractive Northwest-Asian fusion rooms sit right beside the impressive falls, and all the rooms have soaking tubs and fireplaces. The wood-paneled dining room has a panoramic view of the falls, rivers, hills, and mountains, and carefully prepares local lamb, beef, and fish, often using honey from their own hives.

The area has two cute small towns, coffee shops, a golf course, a jazz club (**Boxleys**), and an adorable movie theater in North Bend. Ranger stations and local guidebooks can direct you to many hikes, which include going up **Mt. Si,** a 3,500-ft. peak near **Rattlesnake Ridge.** The Ridge itself is kind of a slog but rewards the effort with a huge view more than slightly reminiscent of Bavaria.

The Inn at the Market $ Right at the Pike Place Market in the heart of Seattle, this charming overnight spot has an excellent restaurant, but many restaurants are also within easy walking distance.

86 Pine St. ℂ **206/443-3600.** www.innatthemarket.com.

MOST ROMANTIC RESTAURANTS

Seattle is a foodie's city. The local trend seems to be to name the restaurants with short, singular names. Take for example, the highly recommendable: **Lark,** 926 12th Ave. (**$$;** ℂ 206/323-5275; http://larkseattle.com); **Lola,** 2000 4th Ave. (**$$;** ℂ 206/441-1430); **Pomegranate Bistro,** 18005 NE 68th St., Redmond (**$$;** ℂ 425/556-5972); **Tilth,** 1411 N. 45th St. (**$$;** ℂ 206/633-0801; http://tilthrestaurant.com; www.duparandcompany.com/pomegranate-bistro). You are also guaranteed great food if it is one of Tom Douglas's restaurants (http://tomdouglas.com), which include the **Palace Kitchen,** 2030 5th Ave. (**$$;** ℂ 206/448-2001), the **Dahlia Lounge,** 2001 4th Ave. (**$$;** ℂ 206/682-4142), and about six other great choices, each quite different from the other. Since Seattle is a center of appreciation for the extraordinary Washington wine industry, you can anticipate that many restaurants, like the **Purple Café & Wine Bar,** 1225 4th Ave. (**$$;** ℂ 206/829-2280; www.thepurplecafe.com), will have exciting wine lists.

SEATTLE BY NIGHT

Seattle lights up at night and seeing it all from the water is a rush. Line up a romantic cruise at **Argosy Evening Cruises,** 1101 Alaskan Way, Pier 55, Ste. 201 (ℂ **888/623-1445** or 206/622-8687; www.argosycruises.com; $76). The city teems with live music, and one place you can find it is the **Paragon Bar and Grill,** 2125 Queen Anne Ave. N. (**$;** ℂ **206/283-4548;** www.paragon

seattle.com), where funk, hip-hop, and soul combine with a decent wine list and well-prepared American food.

WASHINGTON, D.C. & ENVIRONS
More than Just Politics

We know, we know: What's romantic about dealing with the deficit, foreign wars, and political gridlock? But in all fairness, "The District" does have some very romantic restaurants, hotels, and experiences. The blooming cherry trees on the Mall in the spring easily qualify for this book. But we also love the numerous side trips and day trips while using D.C. as a base.

Washington, D.C.

It's been said power is an aphrodisiac, but most of us will happily rely on other aspects of our nation's capital for romance. A particular thrill is seeing famous monuments, such as the **Lincoln Memorial,** 2 Lincoln Memorial Circle (www.nps.gov/linc), at daybreak before the crowds arrive. The spacious terrace of the **Kennedy Center,** 2700 F St., NW (© **800/444-1324** or 202/416-8000; www.kennedy-center.org), offers a captivating view of the Potomac River, and you can spread a picnic blanket among the glorious blooms of the **National Arboretum,** 3501 New York Ave., NE (© **202/245-2726;** www.usna.usda.gov).

KEY ATTRACTIONS
The scenic **Capital Crescent Trail** (© **866/714-2250** or 202/234-4874; www.cctrail.org) lets you observe nature privately a stone's throw from the National Mall. On bikes, it's easy to cover the 11 miles between Georgetown and Silver Spring, MD. The trail was built in the 1990s on an abandoned B&O railway route. On wheels or on foot, you can share magnificent views together with dramatic backlighting at sunrise and sunset. Pack along a snack of goodies from **Cocova,** 1904 18th St., NW (© **202/903-0346;** www.cocova.com), an inspired chocolate maker in Dupont Circle that sells almost 100 types of chocolate truffles for $2 each.

HOTELS WITH HEART
Embassy Circle Guest House $$ Housed in a turn-of-the-20th-century mansion, this sophisticated option reflects its Embassy Row neighborhood of chancelleries and embassies and the artistic vibe of Dupont Circle, with its galleries and hip cafes. Guests are welcome to enjoy complimentary wine and snacks each evening in the elegant parlor, and an extensive complimentary breakfast, including a hot entrée, every morning in the dining room. Guest rooms take their decorative cues and their names from the antique Persian carpet displayed in each. So room no. 124, the Pearl Gazvin, presents the carpet of that name and a creamy, tranquil décor to complement it. The Red

Kashan carpet adds vivid color to its namesake, room no. 111, further enhanced by the room's brilliant paintings and furnishings.

2224 R St. NW (at Massachusetts Ave.). © **877/232-7744** or 202/232-7744. www. dcinns.com.

The Jefferson, Dupont Circle $$$ The elegantly decorated rooms are filled with artwork celebrating that great libertine and the hotel's namesake, Thomas Jefferson. Paintings depict his life in Washington, Virginia, and Paris. Even the bedcovers' toile designs show scenes of Monticello. Request front, corner rooms for a view of the Washington Monument a mile away. Other rooms open on the White House, down 16th Street. The rooms are quiet and well-insulated.

1200 16th St., NW. © **202/448-2300.** www.jeffersonDC.com.

The Normandy Hotel $$ This boutique hotel is charming, it's Parisian, it's pretty. The six-floor Normandy lies on a tree-shaded street lined with embassies, Macedonia's, Algeria's, and Senegal's among them; not surprisingly, the clientele is an international mix. You're a peaceful detour right off of busy Connecticut Avenue and only minutes away, by foot, from the heart of the Dupont Circle, Adams Morgan, and Woodley Park neighborhoods. The Normandy's 75 rooms are small, measuring between 220 and 270 square feet, but each makes good use of the space with cleverly designed and positioned furnishings: long, skinny desks, clever little reading lamps whose stems you can twist out of the walls just so; and compact Nespresso coffee machines and glass-fronted refrigerators placed out of the way. Front-facing rooms overlook tranquil Wyoming Avenue, while those at the back survey the courtyard. Three first-floor rooms open to a private garden terrace. Also on the first level is the parquet-floored lounge, with little sofas, armchairs, round tables, and a fireplace. Guests enjoy the $12 continental breakfast here or in the petite courtyard each morning and the complimentary wine and cheese hour held every evening.

2118 Wyoming Ave. NW. © **202/483-1350.** www.thenormandydc.com. Call or go online for best deals, which can fall well below the rack rate. Rates include evening wine and cheese hour and coffee and tea throughout the day.

The Willard Intercontinental Washington, D.C. $$$ A historic building close to the biggest D.C. attractions (the White House, ever heard of it?), this classy hotel with a grand lobby has a variety of lovely rooms, but sizes vary so ask if you prefer a spacious one. The oval suites overlooking Pennsylvania Avenue offer impressive views, but the courtyard-facing rooms are quieter. The Presidential suite is perfect for a wedding night. Multi-leveled, it has two bathrooms and a dining room (you could entertain, if you were so inclined), but the big attraction is its very large bathtub. It is positioned perfectly with a huge oval window that gives you a perfect picture of the city and the Washington Monument.

1401 Pennsylvania Ave., NW. © **800/496-7621** or 202/628-9100. https://washington. intercontinental.com.

MOST ROMANTIC RESTAURANTS

Blue Duck Tavern $$ AMERICAN This is a power restaurant—the President and First Lady have dined at the downtown spot. But the setting is sexy, with sleek slate floors and multiple rooms with glass walls. The lighting is soft, and everyone looks good in it. Memorable meals of soft-shell crab, Swiss-chard pie, sturgeon rillettes with caviar, and crispy sweetbreads are followed by changing dessert choices, always large enough to share.

24 & M St., NW. © **202/419-6755.** www.blueducktavern.com.

Gadsby's Tavern $$ AMERICAN Serving since 1770, Gadsby's has candlelit tables, ancient wood floors, and cozy corners to set the stage. Especially in the cooler seasons, we recommend huddling with your darling over a hot rum cider and ordering brie in puff pastry, dripping with raspberry coulis, for starters before moving on to steak.

138 N. Royal St., Alexandria, VA. © **703/548-1288.** www.gadsbystavernrestaurant.com.

The Shenandoah Valley

This Valley will grab your heart, with its expanses of beautiful farms and countryside manicured by cows munching their way along the hillsides. The broad vistas are unmarred by more than an occasional farmhouse, and it gets even more beautiful and rugged when you take the Skyline Drive of Shenandoah National Park.

KEY ATTRACTIONS

Charlottesville Here you are in the world that Thomas Jefferson helped build. The **University of Virginia** was designed by this exceptional Founding Father. It is immediately pleasing to the eye (undoubtedly in the top five of all university campuses for beauty and architecture) and has many historically interesting collections and buildings. The Blue Ridge region is wine country, and Charlottesville has several tour companies that will serve you some very good vintages and do the driving for you.

Riding at Bill Marriott's Hideaway The Marriott Hotels founder has preserved thousands of acres of pristine hills and valleys where the public is welcome to come and use its riding stable (© **877/278-4574** or 540/364-3741; 90-min. ride $45). Not a fancy hunt club kind of place, it's very informal and friendly. The well-behaved and well-fed horses will take you over the peaceful and lovely terrain.

Shenandoah National Park Follow the 105-mile **Skyline Drive** as it winds its way through the Blue Ridge Mountains of Virginia. Beautiful vistas, white-tailed deer, or even an occasional bear could emerge from the dazzling array of wildflowers (watch for the lush azaleas in June). Enter the park at Front Royal, about 70 miles west of D.C. along I-66.

© **540/999-3500.** www.nps.gov/shen. Dec–Feb $10 per vehicle; Mar–Nov $15 per vehicle.

HOTELS WITH HEART

The Inn at Fairfield Farm $ This is the centerpiece of Bill Marriott's hideaway Marriott Ranch. The inn is rather simple, though that is part its charm.

5305 Marriott Lane, Hume, VA. © **877/324-7344** or 540/364-2627. www.marriott ranch.com. Rates include full breakfast.

The Inn at Little Washington $$$ Chef and entrepreneur Patrick O'Connell has rejuvenated an old and charming town (laid out by George Washington—yes, that George Washington), creating a masterpiece from a refurbished old garage and several more homes and buildings. Each suite is grand, we mean *really grand,* and the non-deluxe rooms aren't small—except when compared to the capacious suites. Most rooms and suites are named after a famous chef, and we'd be honored to stay in any of them. The spacious Julia Child suite, with its French blue and white palate and tub for two, is perfect, and we adore the Thomas Keller suite, decorated with fine antiques and punctuated by precious Asian vases and bowls.

The kitchen is open 24 hours, and staff will prepare little packages, like dried fruit, to take with you while you are exploring the valley. You feel you are, indeed, the personal guests of the owner. It all adds up to the most romantic of weekends.

Middle and Main sts., Washington, VA. © **800/735-2478** or 540/675-3800. www. theinnatlittlewashington.com.

Red Fox Inn $ Stay at a place known as a former hang-out of Liz Taylor and Jacqueline Kennedy Onassis in the green fields of hunt country. We like breakfast and lunch at **Taverne,** its restaurant (main courses $6–$16).

2 East Washington St., Middleburg, VA. © **800/223-1728** or 540/687-6301. www. redfox.com.

MOST ROMANTIC RESTAURANTS

The Inn at Little Washington $$$ Chef O'Connell told us he wants his place to feel like a "wonderful country house that entertains a lot." And he succeeds. The gleaming kitchen, which opens on the outside gardens, has tables right in it, near a French fireplace. The cuisine has gotten all the awards the food industry has to give. You will have multiple courses, some traditional, some whimsical (such as an appetizer of truffle-dusted popcorn), all delicious. Little surprise "bites" pop up without ordering them—all kinds of extra goodies—just for the chef's pleasure.

Middle and Main St., Washington, VA. © **800/735-2478** or 540/675-3800. www. theinnatlittlewashington.com.

PASSIONATE CITIES: EUROPE

As we noted in chapter 3, cities can be, you'll excuse the pun, hotbeds of romance. That's particularly true in the transporting, dreamy metropolises of Europe. "Cross the pond" and you'll visit some of the most cultured, intriguing cities on Earth, places where the genders interact with a bit more old-fashioned gallantry and mystery and the nights are filled with adventure.

BARCELONA
Whimsy by the Sea

This Catalan capital of Northeastern Spain, with its beautiful palm-lined plazas and quaint narrow streets edged by flowers and cafes, is like no other city. It is romantic by nature, having long celebrated and supported projects that come from the heart, boggle the mind, and depend on intuition. Any city that would allow Gaudí, the famous eccentric architect, to create his whimsical, fantastical buildings and a grand cathedral has got a unique soul.

Of course Barcelona meets many of the requisites to be one of our top romantic cities: It is a port city and a food city and has a picturesque relationship to the sea, a sense of itself as a culture and a place, and its fair share of romantic streets. In fact, a charming section called **La Rambla** is full of twists, turns, restaurants and cafes, birds, flowers, and other surprises. Start your city explorations at the Canaletas fountain since a tradition proclaims that those who drink from it will always return to Barcelona. Trust us, we know you will want to—if for nothing else than the exquisite freshly baked croissants served early morning at the colorful and huge **Boqueria Market,** Rambla, 91 (✆ **93-318-25-84;** www.boqueria.info).

Barcelona has a positive, forward-thinking character. Unlike much of Spain, which reveres the past, Barcelona, with its history and tradition, still seems to look to the future; this center for art and literature always is inventing new ways to see the world and translating them for others. We think that is a good model for relationships as well: It is a pleasure experiencing both a traditional and experimental side.

KEY ATTRACTIONS

City Summit   You can get to the **Parc d'Attraccions del Tibidabo,** Barcelona's famous mountaintop amusement park (Plaça Tibidabo, 3-4; ℂ **93-211-79-42;** www.tibidabo.cat; admission 29€) by Blue Tram (Tramvia Blau) and then transferring to the Tibidabo funicular. Stop at the posh Sarrià district if you want, but to see splendid territorial views of the city, do continue on up via funicular as it climbs the mountainside.

Gaudí, Gaudí, Gaudí   Take a walking tour to find works by the highly inventive architect and Barcelona native son, Antoni Gaudí. Start at the center with his masterpiece, the **Cathedral Sagrada Familia,** Carrer de Mallorca, 401 (ℂ **93-513-20-60;** www.sagradafamilia.cat; admission 18.30€), a work in progress for 131 years, depending on on-again, off-again funding (not yet completed, though it now hosts religious services). Finished or not, the cathedral is an awesome sight, with soaring ceilings and whimsical detail. Next look at Gaudí's homes and apartment buildings—they are not hard to identify. Who else created buildings to look like they are melting? You can find houses by Gaudí along the main boulevard, Passeig de Gràcia: the over-the-top exterior of **Casa Batlló,** Passeig de Gràcia, 43 (ℂ **93-216-03-06;** www.casabatllo.es/ca; admission 21.50€), and **La Pedrera,** Provença, 261-265 (ℂ **90-220-21-38;** www.lapedrera.com; day tour 18€, night tour 30€), with its great view from the futuristic roof. Go down La Rambla to **Palau Güell,** Carrer Nou de la Rambla, 3-5 (ℂ **93-472-57-75;** www.palauguell.cat; admission 12€), another masterwork, a recently renovated mansion (much of Gaudí's work lingered in obscurity or disarray for years) that is now a museum and interpretive center. It will help you understand his genius: Only a person with a wildly romantic streak could concoct such projects.

Picasso and Miró   Go to the **Museu Picasso,** Carrer Montcada, 15-23 (ℂ **93-256-30-00;** www.museupicasso.bcn.cat; admission from 14€), home base of the father of cubism. Want to know more about the modern art of this region? You are near **Museu Europeu d'Art Modern,** Carrer de la Barra de Ferro, 5 (ℂ **93-319-56-93;** www.meam.es; admission 7€), in the 18th-century Palau Gomis. It's in El Born, the medieval quarter; once a labyrinth of earthy artisan workshops, its narrow, winding streets now lead to renovated old mansions that house chic shops, museums, and nightclubs.

HOTELS WITH HEART

Gran Hotel La Florida $$ This is a romantic must—at very least for dinner at the world-class **L'Orangerie,** and preferably for lodging. The hotel is removed from the downtown action, but its perch high on Tibidabo Hill gives almost every room a magnificent view. Don't miss the well-designed spa, infinity pool, and terraced gardens. Service is personalized and attentive, and you will be charmed by your greeting of glasses of rose-petal water upon arrival.

Ctra Vallvidrera al Tibidabo 83-93. ℂ **932-593-064.** www.hotellaflorida.com.

Hostel D'Uxelles $ These moderately priced rooms on the first floors of two adjacent buildings have artistic decor usually only found in higher priced places. The place is decked out in antique furniture, canopied beds, and elaborately tiled bathrooms.

Gran Via de les Corts Catalanes 688. ℂ **93-265-25-60.** www.hotelduxelles.com.

Hotel Arts $$ The preferred choice of celebrities, this waterfront hotel with a beachfront pool attracts the rich, famous, and their fellow travelers. Rooms are large and beautifully furnished, with pink marble bathrooms. Another plus: You are close to old Barcelona and beachy Barceloneta.

Carrer de la Marina 19-21. ℂ **93-221-10-00** or 93-551-30-00. www.hotelarts barcelona.com.

Hotel Casa Fuster $$ Long prized by architects, this hotel became an instant sensation when it took on its current ultra-deluxe incarnation. The opulent lobby is a prelude to the equally opulent bedrooms. The hotel aims to make you feel like a VIP so prepare to be pampered with impeccable, personalized service. This is the kind of hotel that not only delivers special amenities, such as fresh flowers by your bedside and first-rate toiletries, but also will try and satisfy just about any request you make.

Passeig de Gràcia, 132. ℂ **93-255-30-00.** www.hotelescenter.es/casafuster.

Hotel España $ This hotel, designed by a contemporary of Gaudí's, evokes his life and times. Think early 1900s, horses and carriages in the street, and ladies and gentlemen of leisure lingering over a long tea or an elegant lunch. The dining room has nice historical touches, such as highly polished brass fixtures and era-appropriate furniture. This is the perfect place for an Opera fan: Hotel España is right next to the Liceu Opera House.

Carrer Sant Pau, 9-11. ℂ **93-550-00-00.** www.hotelespanya.com.

MOST ROMANTIC RESTAURANTS

Café de L'Acadèmia $ CATALAN   We are suckers for a pretty setting, and this is one of the prettiest in town. Part of the charm is its location in Old Town, surrounded by Gothic buildings and near a fine old fountain. Sit across from each other in flattering candlelight and eat exceptional fare for reasonable prices.

Calle Lledo, 1, Barri Gòtic. ℂ **93-319-82-53.** Reservations required.

Can Majo $$$ CATALAN/SEAFOOD   You owe it to each other to have paella, and here you can have it right on the shore. The fine mélange of fish and mollusks is pricey, but it's truly the right recipe for feeding all your senses at once.

Almirante Aixada, 23, Barceloneta. ℂ **93-221-54-55.** www.canmajo.es.

Els Quatre Gats $$ CATALAN   The original bar here attracted Picasso and his cronies in their youth. The copies of famous artworks on the wall invoke memories of who has eaten and caroused in this space. There will be music and memories.

Carrer de Montsio, 3. ℂ **93-302-41-40.** www.4gats.com. Reservations required.

Via Veneto $$$ CATALAN   This restaurant is home to the to the best of Catalan cooking—and that is saying something. The tradition carries on in the fine decor of the room, the silver service, and the elegance of many of the clientele and all of the waiters.

Carrer de Ganduxer 10. ⓒ **93-200-72-44.** www.viaveneto.es.

BARCELONA BY NIGHT
Palau de la Música Catalana   The Palau de la Música Catalana is an Art Nouveau stunner, and the two of you won't regret taking the time to enjoy its good acoustics. Two sybaritic pleasures here for the price of one.

Carrer Palau de la Música, 4-6. ⓒ **93-295-72-00.** www.palaumusica.org.

Sunset Beach Cocktails   If you like the beach, and never get your fill, you might just be satiated by the 6km (4 miles) of Barcelona beach strolls. Do as the locals do: Stop at a few bars and enjoy a cocktail at the water's edge in the **Barceloneta** neighborhood. Toast each other as the sun sinking on the horizon casts an amazing golden glow.

ISTANBUL
Romance Spans Two Continents

Arriving in Istanbul by sea is a glorious sight. The skyline reflects its multi-cultural heritage and significance in history. Once Constantinople, Istanbul was a cultural center for Greeks, Romans, Byzantines, Ottomans, and Turks. Entering the famed Golden Horn harbor, an inlet of the Bosphorus Strait, you know you're in a global city. Its various tenants have left many wondrous souvenirs of their tenure here. In fact, this is the only city in the world strad-dling two continents, Europe on one side, Asia on the other, with beautiful suspension bridges strung between them.

One must-do in Istanbul is a ferry cruise down the Bosphorus to retrace the historical entry into the ancient city. In the Byzantine Era, a 6.5km (4-mile) wall (still visible in many places) was built from the Sea of Marmara to the Golden Horn as a defense against invaders from the East and was breached only at the city's grand entrances, which included imposing citadels that faced the Strait. The port is busy, and yours will not be the only ship in the harbor, but the industry is outshone by the hills and palaces, minarets and mosques that create a visually arresting tableau. The skyline has a certain quality, a golden haze, that is quintessentially Istanbul. A first glimpse reveals some very precious old buildings: the Blue Mosque, Ayasofya, and others. Istanbul's more modern charms lie in its cafe culture, commerce, and the diversity of its people.

Istanbul is a deeply romantic city, in the sense that its ancient beauty reso-nates with our gentler, more loving sides. At night, important buildings are dramatically lit up for a dazzling, glittering cityscape.

KEY ATTRACTIONS

Ayasofya   Once a cathedral, then a mosque, and now a museum and rare surviving example of Byzantine architecture, the Ayasofya (also referred to by its Greek spelling, Hagia Sophia) is truly an awesome building. Built in the 6th century, it kept its status as a church until the 15th century, when it was refitted as a mosque. The enormous main room with its soaring, glittering golden dome ceiling stops most visitors in their tracks.

Sultanahmet. © **0212/522-1750** or 0212/522-0989. www.ayasofyamuzesi.gov.tr. Admission 25TL.

Blue Mosque (Sultan Ahmet Camii)   Named for the 21,000 blue tiles that adorn the walls, this mosque is a 17th-century masterpiece. Still used as a mosque, it is also a tourist attraction. Women, please dress modestly or you'll be asked to cover up with a blue robe provided at the entrance, where visitors must also leave their shoes. A beautiful outdoor seating area between the mosque and the Ayasofya makes it easy to people-watch and contemplate the sublime architecture together.

Sultanahmet. © **0212/518-1319.** www.bluemosque.co. Free admission. Closed for 90 minutes at each prayer time.

Grand Bazaar   This is our favorite place on land in Istanbul. Started in the 16th century and now modernized with bright lights and air conditioning, the Grand Bazaar still retains its exotic allure. The high vaulted ceilings bestow elegance, and the stalls crammed with merchandise bring it all down to earth. We know it's just shopping, but there are more than 4,000 items to choose from. Just as fascinating as the goods, is the incredible mix of shoppers: women in black *abayas* with only their eyes revealed, chic Europeans, kids in backpacks from the world over, Turkish men with hookahs and tea. At times, it seems the whole world is here.

The selection is truly staggering (gold, silver, antique jewelry, leather goods, ceramics, and rugs, rugs, rugs) and the prices are enticing. Sure there is a lot of junk and probably a lot of counterfeits, but there are also treasures, and they can appear in a shop no bigger than a small closet; the size of a shop here tells you nothing about the quality of its goods. We have found fantastic antique prints from hundreds of years ago in the most modest of places. It is easy to get lost, but that is part of the fun.

Beyazıt. © **90/212-519-1248.** www.kapalicarsi.org.tr.

Spice Market   The smells of spices, food, and sweets waft over you at this 16th-century market. Its narrow lanes would induce claustrophobia if not for its vaulted ceilings and arched corridors. With the buzzing crowd and seemingly infinite choices, you will have no trouble clinging to each other. Keep an eye out for the vendors selling special merchandise for lovers. We kid you not: There are delicacies here shaped like penises. It is a phallic wonderland, all based on the idea of spices and food for potency.

Rüstem Paşa Mahallesi. © **0212/513-6597.** www.misircarsisi.org.

Topkapi Palace   The rooms and gardens at this massive palace are actually rather low key, considering how many Sultans have housed their harems here. Were it more likely that the women in the harem were pleased to be here, the harem section might be good for a few fantasies; but there are some unsettling hints of incarceration. Note the long, arched passageways, tiled baths, gloriously painted walls—and, rather chillingly, the barred windows. There are, however, other truly tantalizing exhibits: drop-dead gorgeous antique carpets and delicate Turkish dishware, some recent and some hundreds of years old.

What delights us are the jewels: the fist-sized uncut emeralds, the decorated swords, the bejeweled throne, and the almost gaudy Topkapi dagger, with a diamond-encrusted scabbard and a handle studded with gigantic emeralds. Take a peek at the 86-carat pear-shaped Spoonmaker's Diamond. Perhaps a good prelude to picking out a ring?

Sultanahmet. ✆ **0212/512-0480.** www.topkapisarayi.gov.tr. Admission 25TL.

Turkish Baths   What would a visit to Turkey be without a Turkish bath? But be warned: They are going to exfoliate the first several layers of your skin! Visit **Çemberlitaş Hamam,** Mollafenari Mh., Vezirhan Cad. No. 8 (✆ **0212/522-7974;** www.cemberlitashamami.com). For sheer thrill of the exotic, you can skip the massage and still use this 16th-century bath designed during the reign of the great Suleiman. As you would expect, there are only single-sex sections, with hot and cool rooms, big pools, and a variety of treatments. Also try the historic (built in 1741) **Cağaloğlu Hamami,** Yerebatan Cad. at Ankara Cad. (✆ **0212/522-2424;** www.cagalogluhamami.com.tr), a traditional Turkish bath but with a menu in English. Exfoliations and soap massage (including shampoo and head massage) in the traditional baths are about $50 including entry (tip 10%–15%); $35 entry to baths only.

HOTELS WITH HEART

The Ciragan Palace Kempinski in Istanbul $$$ This hotel is fabulous in every way. It might be reason enough to go to Istanbul. The former palace with white filigree is the go-to place for the price-is-no-object set. At Beşiktaş on the edge of the Bosphorus, it takes its name from the palace next door. You will be served like royalty, eat like a *paşa*, and enjoy a very elegant hamam.

Ciragan Cad. 32, Beşiktaş. ✆ **0212/326-4646.** www.kempinski.com.

Empress Zoe $ The hotel is well-located a few blocks from the major attractions of the Blue Mosque and the Ayasofya. Some of the rooms have particularly lovely touches, like hand-painted frescoes and Turkish rugs. Rooms are really reasonable and include a first-rate breakfast in the sweet garden. Because it is an exceptionally good buy, the Empress Zoe is quite popular and needs to be booked way in advance.

Istanbul University, Suleymaniye Mh. No. 1. ✆ **0212/518-2504.** www.emzoe.com.

The Green House Yeşil Ev $$ This hotel presents a great value for a very pleasant place with a romantic walled courtyard near the Blue Mosque.

Kabasakal Cad. No. 5, Sultanahmet. ℂ **0212/517-6785.** www.yesilev.com.tr.

W Istanbul $$ Very cleverly, the W has assembled a number of 19th-century row houses that, once updated, are no longer traditional, yet are not out of place. The townhouse facades have rooms and suites embellished with patios, terraces, or cabanas.

Suleyman Seba Cad. No. 22, Akaretler. ℂ **0212/381-2121.** www.wistanbul.com.tr.

MOST ROMANTIC RESTAURANTS

Food in Istanbul is generally very good but can be repetitive. You'd better like lamb and fresh fish. The fun selections are *mezes*—small plates or a variety of buffet choices of traditional Turkish foods—that are made to share. The international restaurants tend to offer them too, but count on the traditional places having a pretty good selection.

Hamdi Restaurant $$$ TURKISH   Good kabobs, Turkish meatballs, *mezes,* and a traditional menu, plus scenic views—Hamdi has long been an Istanbul mainstay.

Rüstem Paşa Mh., Kalcin Sk. No. 17, Faith. ℂ **0212/528-0390.** www.hamdi.com.tr.

Restaurant Lucca $ MEDITERRANEAN   Trendy Italian food is served in a pretty place—all light wood and cream colored chairs edged in black. This place is in the Bebek area of the city, a little further up the Bosphorus from the Old City.

Cevdetpaşa Cad. No. 51, Bebek. ℂ **0212/257-1255.** www.luccastyle.com.

ISTANBUL BY NIGHT

A great nightlife area centers around the mid-19th century **Ortaköy Mosque,** Mecidiye Mh. (www.greatistanbul.com/ortakoy.htm), clinging to the Bosphorus waterfront and romantically lit at night. In good weather, people spill out of busy nearby restaurants to sit under the trees and gaze upon the nearby water as it reflects and refracts the image of the mosque.

Beyolu is the city's official entertainment district. Pedestrian-only **Istiklal Caddesi** (Independence Street) is the long, huge street that goes on forever with restaurants and clubs on each side. When you get swept along with the friendly crowd, hang on to your sweetie.

Many Istanbul clubs feature skilled belly dancers. If you're staying up late, don't miss **Al Jamal,** Harbiye Mh. 34367 Şişli (ℂ **0212/231-0356;** www.capamarka.com.tr; summer only), a nightclub in the snazzy Maçka Democracy Park area. Decorated in rich indigo, purple, and gold, Al Jamal not only has belly dancers, but also drag queens and other sensuous live performers. A marble Turkish bath platform forms a centerpiece amid the tables under a tent-like ceiling.

A Bar with a View In this city of views—be it of the Bosphorus or Sea of Marmara or one of the seven hills dotted with turrets, minarets, and skyscrapers—the best views are from the city's rooftops. **360 Istanbul,** Istiklal Cad., Misir Apartments 8th floor No.163 (© **0212/251-1042;** www.360istanbul.com; reservations required), is a fine restaurant and bar on the roof of the century-old Misir Apartments with a view over busy Istiklal Caddesi. The chic crowd comes here for the good food and incredible city and sunset views through giant windows. The **Mikla Bar,** Mesrutiyet Cad. 15 (© **0212/293-5656;** www.miklarestaurant.com), on the roof of the Marmara Pera Hotel has truly fabulous views of the Golden Horn. **Bebek Balikci,** Bebek Mh., Cevdet Paşa Cad. No. 26 (© **0212/263-3447** or 0212/263-3669; www.bebekbalikci.net), feels like you are in the 1930s, but at a hideaway for watching boat traffic coming in and out of the harbor.

LISBON
Big European Heart, Small Euro Price

Lisbon is one of the most underrated cities in the world for tourism—thus, most people miss out on its romantic propensities. Not only is it charming and intriguing, but it offers great value for lodging, food, and wine. Budget-conscious romantics, this should be a choice destination to celebrate your relationship!

Lisbon is an easy city to negotiate. The Old Town neighborhoods have winding streets, but you end up where you want to be without much hassle—as with almost everything here. Lisbon has a light touch. It feels happy, and that's saying something for a town that that was wiped out by a disastrous earthquake and tsunami in 1775. Even now, every family has a story about the historic crisis. But that was long ago; today's relative prosperity, post-fascism and post-socialism, is the new way of life. The signature decorative Portuguese tiles are everywhere, both on the facades and insides of buildings. Boutiques are plentiful, and local restaurants serve fresh produce and ridiculously cheap wine (for the quality)—it's hard to find a bad meal. The people are friendly and casual in Lisbon, which is the doorway to a string of charming towns, north and south. You'll read about our favorite Lisbon getaway, Oporto, but we urge you to strike out in any direction: You'll very likely discover your own getaway place.

KEY ATTRACTIONS
Alfama You'll enjoy this picturesque Old Town more if you first take the tram to the Castelo da São Jorge gates and see the neighborhood from above. Then start walking, taking in the Moorish touches of the buildings and keeping an ear out for *fado*. Here and everywhere you go, you will see the traditional blue and white tiles on buildings and walls and in the parks, particularly the lovely Eduardo VII Park.

Bairro Alto (Upper City) This is where Lisbon's joyous party side lets loose. Lights get strung over alleys, and streets become makeshift patios for the night while people roam around looking for fun. This hilltop community preserves the quaint antiquity of old Lisbon, and buildings that survived the 1755 earthquake still stand here. It's also a lively place by day, with its old stone streets and bright colors illuminated by the sun glinting off the sea. You may see laundry hanging from clotheslines or hear exotic caged birds singing in weird harmony to the street sounds of fishmongers and other barkers. But if you can only come for a few hours, make it a night visit. That's when tourists and residents come out together in search of music, dancing, and dining. We're not sure what is more romantic than sipping drinks together at a *tasca*, a little bar, seemingly made for lovers. You can reach Bairro Alto's hilltop from the flat Baixa neighborhood via an elegant street elevator (created by the same guy, Gustav Eiffel, who designed that famous tower in Paris).

Fado Singers This soulful kind of singing with guitar is the national obsession and definitely a turn-on. A very famous *fado* club of the Bairro Alto (see above) is **Café Luso,** Travessa da Queimada, No. 10 (*©* **21/342-22-81;** www.cafeluso.pt). In a refashioned stables, Luso presents *fado* with a menu of very good regional food. Most nights, three shows are scheduled and often end after 2am. In some clubs, the *fado* plays until daybreak.

> ### Lisbon's Tram
>
> Yes, there is a whiff of San Francisco here, even beyond the cable car: The hills, aquatic vistas, tile rooftops, and flowers cascading down houses of varying heights can seem very familiar. Expand your comfort zone and hop on a tram (www.carris.pt) and see where it takes you—you'll find a colorful public plaza in every neighborhood.

Museu Calouste Gulbenkian This multi-million dollar museum, named for the Armenian oil magnate who once owned its treasures, houses a world-famous art collection, which includes Egyptian, Greek, and Roman antiquities; Middle Eastern and Asian art; medieval illuminated manuscripts; Renaissance tapestries and European sculpture; and paintings and Portuguese pottery from the 15th to 19th centuries. If you love art museums, don't miss this one.

Av. De Berna 45A. *©* **21/782-30-00.** www.museu.gulbenkian.pt. Admission 5€; free admission Sun.

National Tile Museum This baroque tribute to the history of *azulejos*, Portuguese for ceramic tiles, is housed in a former convent. See the impressive walls of the huge chapel, the Convent of the Mother of God. Its collection is the only of its kind in the world.

www.museudoazulejo.pt. Admission 5€ adults; 2.50€ seniors.

The Oceanario de Lisboa The second-biggest aquarium in the world (Osaka, Japan, hosts the largest), the Oceanario de Lisboa, features four ecosystems: one each for the Atlantic, Pacific, Indian, and Antarctic oceans. It's also home to a vast collection of water birds, sea mammals, and sea creatures of all kinds.

Parque das Nações. ✆ **21/891-70-00.** www.oceanario.pt. Admission 16€; seniors 11€.

Port Wine Institute   Well, this is what you are here for, no? Start with the experts at the Port Wine Institute (*Solar do Vinho do Porto*), lavishly ensconced at the Ludovic Palace in the Bairro Alto. This is the place to feel entitled to the amazing port you are about to learn about. By the end, you will be able to distinguish between different types (and ages) of tawny and ruby ports. Add a nice selection of bread and cheese and you have a delightful afternoon.

Rua de S. Pedro de Alcantara No. 45. ✆ **21/347-57-07.** www.ivdp.pt.

St. George's Castle (Castelo da São Jorge)   Said to be the cradle of Lisbon, this fortress is believed to predate the Romans. It's been occupied by Visigoths, Saracens, and the Moors, until Afonso Henriques, Portugal's first king, chased them out in the 12th century. All this history accounts for the castle's lovely hodgepodge of styles. It's called St. George's, after the patron saint of England, in honor of a historic pact with the Brits. Walk or take a cab or bus up the hill to the castle for good views of the harbor and Tagus River from the esplanades and ramparts. At the entrance is Castle Belvedere, an almost medieval structure that the Portuguese call their "ancient window." Stop there for a peek over the Alfama (the Old Town), the mountains of Monsanto, and the scenic Sintra area as a preview of what awaits you.

Rua de Santa Cruz do Castelo. ✆ **21/880-06-20.** www.castelodesaojorge.pt. Admission 7.50€ adults; seniors 4€.

HOTELS WITH HEART

The luxurious **Four Seasons Hotel Ritz ($$$;** Rua Rodrigo da Fonseca 88; ✆ **21/381-14-00;** www.fourseasons.com/lisbon) gives you some of the finest city and river views right from your balcony, which front the large and stylish rooms you'd expect from the Four Seasons. Its spa it a lovely place to be even if you're not staying there.

Altis Avenida Hotel $$ This sophisticated bargain is in a fine Art Deco building with retro mid-century decor. The location is terrific: amid Baixa, Alfama, and Bairro Alto, the areas you will visit the most. The rooftop restaurant, Brasserie Gourmet Rossio, offers romantic views of the city.

Rua 1 Dezembro 120. ✆ **21/044-00-00.** www.altishotels.com.

As Janelas Verdes $ Set in a small 18th-century palace, this cozy family-run inn, part of the Heritage Lisbon hotel group, is located in a lovely neighborhood and is right next to the National Art Museum. It's a convenient 20-minute bus ride from city center. The attentive staff refills your bottle with complimentary port every day and provides an excellent breakfast in its sunny courtyard. We think that sipping port on the library balcony overlooking the Tagus River is a particularly romantic way to end an afternoon of touring.

Rua das Janelas Verdes 47. ✆ **351/213-968-143.** www.heritage.pt/heritage-lisbon-hotels/as-janelas-verdes. Rates include breakfast.

Britania Hotel $ This popular boutique hotel in the historic center of Lisbon captures the romance of the 1940s with its stylish Art Deco interior, and it's located just one block off beautiful Avenida de Liberdade. A sister property to the As Janelas Verdes (above), the hotel offers spacious rooms with huge bathrooms and an excellent buffet breakfast.

Rua Rodriquez Sampaio 17. ✆ **351/218-200.** www.heritage.pt/heritage-lisbon-hotels/hotel-britania. Rates include breakfast.

Palácio Belmonte $$$ This romantic hideaway, taking its name from a Portuguese literary figure, is just outside Castelo de São Jorge. It's an undeniably cool place to hang your hats: It only offers suites and every one of them has deluxe furnishings. Priced from moderate to expensive, Palacio Belmonte lives up to its name, with a deluge of Portuguese tiles, antiques, and art, and it has a 4,000-book library. Its stunning swimming pool is lined in black marble.

Páteo Dom Fradique 14. ✆ **21/881-66-00.** www.palaciobelmonte.com.

MOST ROMANTIC RESTAURANTS

1300 Taberna $ PORTUGUESE The glass ceiling adds to the infectious and playful mood that prevails at this restaurant. Inventive design plays into every part of the place, including the great wine selection. The food—Portuguese with imaginative twists—is excellent.

Rua Rodrigues Faria No. 103. ✆ **21/364-91-70.** www.1300taberna.com.

Belcanto $$$ MODERN PORTUGUESE A "New York Times" reviewer said the meal he had here was the best he'd eaten in 2012. The classic restaurant in the Chiado district used to be a gentleman's club, but it's been reborn as a showcase for one of Portugal's hottest chefs, José Avillez. The menu offers impressive variations on lamb, beef, veal, crab, lobster, and salted cod. Be prepared for unusual signature dishes, including one splattered with sauces to resemble a Jackson Pollack painting.

Largo de São Carlos, 10. ✆ **21/342-06-07.** www.belcanto.pt.

Casa da Comida $$ PORTUGUESE/FRENCH Casa da Comida serves some of Lisbon's finest meals. Napoleonic touches decorate the dining room, and a romantic walled garden is a most natural site for flirtation. One house specialty is *faisão à convento de Alcântara*, pheasant stewed in port.

Travessa das Amoreiras, No. 1. ✆ **21/388-53-76.** www.casadacomida.pt.

Valle Flor $$ PORTUGUESE We cannot resist mentioning this one to lovers willing to pay the price of being in perhaps the most gorgeous,

Estremoz   Just 90 minutes away is one of Portugal's newer wine-growing regions. You will drive good roads through lovely fields and barely populated countryside. About 27km (17 miles) beyond Estremoz is the **Convento de São Paulo in Adeia da Serra ($; ℂ 351-266-989-160;** www.hotelconvento saopaulo.com). An imposing inn with traditional blue tiles and beautiful gardens and views, the Convento also has lovely hiking trails. The regional cuisine here at **O Ermita** is great and a good spot to start reviewing the local *quintas* (wine estates). Estremoz has good local markets and a gathering on Saturdays in the central square.

Follow the *Rota dos Vinhos do Alentejo* (the wine route) to get the best out of this region. The roads here can be tricky, winding through the many medieval villages so you might want to arrange the wine tour through your concierge.

Evora   A short drive from Estremoz, this town is less than two hours from Lisbon, and its archeological sites are as mysterious as Stonehenge. Majestic Roman ruins mingle with centuries of architecture in this walled town and UNESCO World Heritage site. The **Temple of Diana** is particularly inspiring for couples on a moonlit night, but beautiful any time. Baroque churches, palaces, and narrow streets are great backdrops for the numerous cafes and shops, mostly all concentrated at the town center. A 16th-century aqueduct runs 8km (5 miles) out to the farms and fields. Overnight at the **Evora Inn-ChiadoDesign,** Rua da República No. 11, near Giraldo Sq. **($; ℂ 26/674-45-00;** www.evorainn.com) an inexpensive and vibrantly decorated hostel.

Oporto   How could we not recommend a stop at the world center for port, a mere three hours from Lisbon? Oporto has great eating and lodging, hilly cobblestone streets, and high

over-the-top glamorous restaurant in Lisbon. Located in the Pestana Carlton Palace Hotel with squads of uniformed waiters and attendants, the Valle Flor is not only a restaurant—it's a national monument. It was originally part of a cocoa grower's 1907 villa, and it shows, with two dining rooms that remain exquisitely frescoed, gilded, and festooned with fine Romantic Revival accessories. Expect to be honored with old-style allure and etiquette—as well as with beautifully presented and carefully prepared dishes. We recommend virtually any of the seafood dishes, each with an imaginative sauce poured over the freshest catches.

In the Pestana Palace Hotel, Rua Jau 54. ℂ **21/361-56-00.** www.pestana.com.

window-shopping potential. You will likely walk downhill from your hotel and cross the bridge to the wharf area and the port tasting rooms, most of them in an area called *Vila Nova da Gaia*. You can have vertical tastings (different years of the same port) and tours of the port-making process here.

Warning: You can drive right into port country: Rent a car if you are brave enough to spend a day heading up the extremely steep hills along the Douro River that lead to the wineries.

The **Book Restaurant and Bar,** Rua de Aviz, No. 10 (**$;** © **91/795-33-87;** www.restaurante-book. com), is a popular restaurant with fish soup, great lamb dishes, and a fine house wine served by candle light in romantic environs with book-lined walls.

Foz Velha, Esplanada Castelo No. 141 (**$$;** © **22/615-41-78;** www.fozvelha.com), serves "don't miss" cuisine at a moderate set menu. If you want to taste the national Portuguese dish of cod, you'll find many variations here.

Toulouse-Lautrec could have loved the Belle Époque design of **Café Majestic,** Rua Santa Catarina (**$$;** © **22/200-38-87;** www. cafemajestic.com), with its huge mirrors and gilded cherubs. A particular thrill for JK Rowling fans: It is said she wrote most of "Harry Potter" here.

A 16th-century hotel on the Douro River in the Ribeira neighborhood, the **Pestana Porto Hotel,** Praça da Ribeira 1 (**$$;** © **22/340-23-00;** www.pestana. com), is classy with crisp lighting, high ceilings, and arched doorways that feel downright ritzy. The moderately priced group of townhouses offers rooms with a romantic river view. You can also get a room with a river view along the Douro at **Casa de Casal de Loivos,** Cabo da Rua (**$;** © **25/473-21-49;** www.casadecasaldeloivos.com), a 17th-century hilltop manor house with big traditional rooms loaded with chintz and family heirlooms.

LISBON BY NIGHT

Bairro Alto Hotel Rooftop Terrace   The sophisticated bar on this rooftop terrace can hardly compete with the scenic panorama, day or night. Praça Luis de Camoes No. 2. © **21/340-82-88.** www.bairroaltohotel.com.

Lisboa Regency Chiado   Take the elevator up to the Terrace Bar for a drink and a fine territorial view. Rua Nova do Almada 114. © **21/325-61-00.** www.lisboaregencychiado.com.

Sr. Vinho   This well-known club comes highly recommended for *fado*. It is nothing but a low-ceilinged room in a quiet neighborhood. But it books the most celebrated and romantic *fado* singers—just what you want to hear before you head back to your room. Rua do Meio a Lapa No.18. © **21/397-74-56.** www.srvinho.com.

PARIS
Amour at Every Turn

Paris is always our first thought for romance. No other city quite captures that ideal mix of intimacy and grandeur, of history and modernity, or of charm and grace. Of course, Paris is justly famous for passion and romance—could it be a cliché? If you count all the romantic movies set here and the number of teary-eyed love scenes on the Pont Neuf, we suppose romantic Paris could seem a little over-exposed. Yet a city with *magnifique* pastries within steps of wherever you are cannot easily be dismissed.

We say: Just go to Paris. The same alluring factors that inspired Hollywood still inspire real smitten lovers every day, and you can see them nuzzling each other, flirting at sidewalk cafes, and walking arm-in-arm.

KEY ATTRACTIONS

The Cruise   The **Bateaux-Mouche,** Port de la Conférence Pont de l'Alma, Rive droite (*©* **01-42-25-96-10;** www.bateaux-mouches.fr; cruise 13.5€; lunch cruise **$$**; dinner cruise **$$$**), are the tourist boats (some with restaurants and dance floors) that cruise the Seine. We recommend a night cruise for the thrill of gliding on the Seine while witnessing all of Paris lit up. **Bateau Parisiens** (www.bateauxparisiens.com; dinner cruise **$$$**) has a wonderful dinner cruise with unobstructed views of the major sights and a 3-course meal supervised by an Academie Culinaire de France trained chef. Ask for a private table for two, a bit more expensive but worth it. Otherwise you will be seated at a table of six or eight, and with bad luck, your new companions might speak English.

A lesser-known cruise, but *très romantique* for its breathtaking changes of scenery at every turn, is the 90-minute cruise on the **Canal St. Martin.** The trip starts on the Seine in front of the Musée d'Orsay, tunnels underground for a bit, and then resurfaces through a series of shaded neighborhoods, swinging bridges, and locks (about 15€ for a no-frills tour, but prices go up from there).

> ### Day Trips
>
> The romantic spirit of Paris spills over into the adjacent country-side. Plan a day trip out to **Giverny** (http://giverny.org), the famous home of Monet and the setting for his water lily paintings, or the **Roseraie de l'Hay,** rue Albert Watel, 94240 L'Haÿ-les-Roses (*©* **01-43-99-82-80;** www.roseraieduvaldemarne.fr; admission €3) in Val-du-Marne, one of the most extensive rose gardens in the world.

The Marais   Every *arrondisement* (neighborhood area) has its own charm, but for romance, we're partial to **the 3rd and 4th**, where you'll find the **Marais** (www.parismarais.com), with its cool shops, plazas, restaurants, and boutique hotels, many in or around the arcaded Place des Vosges park. This diverse neighborhood has long-established Jewish and Chinese communities and a growing gay population, and some of the city's top new art galleries and music spots. The Marais has a historic feel, with narrow streets and stately old buildings, including the **Musée Carnavalet,** 16 rue des Francs-Bourgeois (*©* **01-44-59-58-58**; http://carnavalet.paris.fr; free admission), now the repository of Paris's history, but formerly the home of an 18th-century widowed aristocrat who was famous for her many suitors.

Take a detour to the neighborhood's northern edge for a true aphrodisiac. **La Chocolaterie de Jacques Genin** (133 rue du Turenne; http://jacques genin.fr; *©* **01-45-77-29-01**) sells 40 different kinds of caramels. It might be a struggle to pick just one (or three); they appear in the morning and go quickly so you'd be wise to do the same. If you like your sweets with wine, pack up your treasures from Genin's and head to a very French wine bar nearby, **La Tartine,** 24 rue Rivoli (**$**; *©* **01-42-72-76-85**; www.tartine-et-chocolat.fr). The Art Nouveau fixtures here have not changed since the days of gas lamp lighting. The yellowish walls and antique mirrors help cozy up the place, and a discerning crowd of local artists and designers will provide good people-watching. Choose a sandwich (les Tartine) and a good red to wash it down.

The Walk   Night or day, a walk along the Seine, crossing the bridges and looking back at the city on either side, will heighten your awareness of your close bond and your gratitude to be sharing these romantic sights together. For a perfect, really long romantic walk, first pick up a good wine at **Nicolas,** SA, 2 rue du Courson (*©* **01-41-73-81-81**; www.nicolas.com), a few cheeses at **Christian Le Lann,** 1 rue du Retrait (*©* **01-43-66-64-60**), and a baguette at **Bakery Martin,** 34 rue Yves Toudic (*©* **01-42-40-44-52**). You can stop for a scoop of memorable ice cream at **Berthillon Glacier,** 31 rue Saint-Louis en l'Île (*©* **01-43-54-31-61**; www.berthillon.fr). Then stroll 4.8km (3 miles) along the Left Bank from the tip of the **Ile St. Louis** (Pont du Sully) and casually pass some of the most famous structures in the world: **the Notre Dame Cathedral, Musée d'Orsay,** and the **Eiffel Tower.** Then head down to the quai (the edge of the river walk) and **Pont des Arts** bridge for a perfect picnic on a bench or the grass. A sweet local custom is for lovers to pledge themselves to each other by attaching a padlock to the bridge's fence. It is a lovely symbol, but short-lived, because the city removes the locks every so often. Still, when in Paris, do as the French (and the Japanese, and the Germans, and the Spaniards, and just about everyone else) do.

HOTELS WITH HEART

Paris hotels are notoriously pricey so if you're on a budget, start hunting way in advance and consider private rental through www.airbnb.com or www. parisperfect.com.

You are going to have to pay for the privilege of a room with a view that has enough space for you two and your suitcases. Paris hotels have notoriously small rooms, so you generally have to go quite luxe to get the (even modest) honeymoon suite of your dreams. You may have better luck finding those hidden gems on the Right Bank. If you can afford it, two great splurges are **Le Bristol,** 112 rue du Faubourg Saint-Honoré ($$$; ✆ 01-53-43-43-00; www.lebristolparis.com), and the much-loved **Relais Christine,** 3 rue Christine ($$$; ✆ 01-40-51-60-80; www.relais-christine.com). The Christine, a restored 13th-century abbey, offers a 3-day romance package called "Fall in Love in Paris," which includes breakfast in bed, afternoon tea, and admission to the Rodin Museum.

Hotel Caron de Beaumarchais $

This romantic Marais hotel never varies in charm and hospitality. It looks like a movie set from the street, its bright blue sign and windows full of French antiques. The rooms are small but quaint, and some have double windows and a small balcony to open to the street. Price includes a lovely continental breakfast served in a well-decorated room, full of light and period furniture. (One warning: Some of the rooms require climbing some steep stairs.)

12 rue Vielle-du-Temple. ✆ **01-42-72-34-12.** www.hotelcarondebeaumarchais. com. Rates include continental breakfast. Watch for seasonally lower rates.

Hôtel Jeanne d'Arc le Marais $

Considering its prime location in the southern Marais, this cozy hotel is an incredible deal. Despite the low rates, rooms are comfortable, colorful, and nicely appointed, with pretty fabrics and furniture. Rooms book up months in advance, especially for fashion weeks (Feb, Mar, July, and Sept). *Note:* There is another hotel with the same name in the 13th arrondissement—make sure you are in contact with the hotel in the Marais when you reserve, or you will be in for an unpleasant surprise.

3 rue de Jarente. ✆ **01-48-87-62-11.** www.hoteljeannedarc.com.

Le Citizen Hotel du Canal Paris $$

This hotel has reasonable rooms with a captivating view of the adjacent canal and the colorful world that moves along it. The hotel has a more minimalist decor than traditional Paris hotels but its chic clean lines blend nicely into this locale, which is rapidly changing from modest restaurants and living spaces to a coveted neighborhood of the chic and fashionable.

> ### Parisian Flea Markets
>
> Two of our all-time favorite fleas are right in Paris: Cligancourt (18th arrondisement) and Porte de Vanves (14th arrondisement).

96 Quai de Jemmapes. ✆ **01-83-62-55-50.** www.lecitizenhotel.com.

MOST ROMANTIC RESTAURANTS

As love gestures go, fine dining in Paris speaks loud and in any language. Whatever your budget, you should splurge at least once for a meal, and **Le Meurice,** 228 rue de Rivoli ($$$; ✆ **44/581-055**; www.lemeurice.com), would be a good choice. It is very 15th century; in fact, it looks a bit like it had the same decorator who did Louis the 14th's apartments in Versailles. The view is special too: Expansive windows overlook the beautifully manicured Jardins des Tuileries.

Pepper's all-time favorite, however, is **Le Pre Catelan,** Bois de Boulogne, Route de Suresnes (**$$$;** ✆ **01-44-14-41-14;** www.precatelanparis.com/fr), in a beautiful setting within the Bois de Boulogne, only minutes from the Champs-Élysée. When you enter the very traditional and elegant white building you feel as if you've entered a private club. You are guided through a series of beautiful gilded, chandeliered dining rooms. In good weather, dine on the outdoor terrace that makes you feel you are in a Renoir painting. Everything on the *carte* is amazing. This is French food for the aristocracy, and you can play one (pre-revolution of course) for the evening.

Chez Nenesse $ TRADITIONAL BISTRO   This neighborhood haunt has stayed true to its proletarian roots in a frighteningly hip part of the northern Marais. At lunchtime, the chef sends out traditional bistro fare (like *blanquette de veau*, or rump steak) into the busy dining room, while dinner comes with a change in menus and ambience—the checked plastic tablecloths are traded for white linen, and *magret de canard au cassis* (duck breast with cassis liqueur) and filet *d'agneau a l'estragon* (lamb steak with tarragon) take center stage. Thursday is steak-frites day. Regulars crowd in at lunch for their weekly dose of the crispy house fries.

17 rue Saintonge. ✆ **01-42-78-46-49.**

La Coupole $$$ FRENCH   For a taste of the hustle and bustle of late 1920s Paris, don't miss this fantastic Art Deco dining room and gathering place of every important painter that lived at the same time as Matisse and Picasso (Chagall chose table 73 as his favorite). Every flamboyant dancer or musician from Josephine Baker to Patti Smith has made an appearance here. Order a huge platter of oysters or lobsters and top it all off with champagne.

102 Boulevard du Montparnasse. ✆ **01-43-20-14-20.** www.lacoupole-paris.com.

La Cuisine de Bar $ LIGHT LUNCH/SALADS   Making the most of its next-door neighbor, the legendary Poilâne bakery, this elegant lunch spot serves open-faced sandwiches (tartines) on its famous bread. There's no kitchen here, just toaster ovens. Arrive early for a light lunch as the sleek dining room fills up quickly with impeccably dressed locals lusting after the tartine of sardines with olive oil and sea salt, or chicken with garlic mayonnaise and capers. A *formule* including a tartine, a small salad or soup, a glass of wine, and coffee is 14€. There is a second location at 38 rue Debelleyme in the 3rd arrondissement (the Marais).

8 rue du Cherche-Midi. ✆ **01-45-48-45-69.** www.cuisinedebar.com.

Le Petit Canard $ FRENCH   Specializing in all things duck, this quirky restaurant cooks up the best fowl you have ever had. Don't miss the classic duck in orange sauce, or their duck with foie gras and balsamic vinegar.

19 rue Henri Monnier. ✆ **01-49-70-07-95.** www.lepetitcanard.com.

Restaurant du Terass Hotel $ BREAKFAST   For a romantic breakfast, on a warm spring or summer day, head to Montmartre, the hilltop neighborhood made famous by the Moulin Rouge and Toulouse-Lautrec. The food can vary from fair to great, but you cannot beat the ambience and the view from this restaurant.

12 rue Joseph de Maistre Terass Hotel. ℂ **01-44-92-34-00.** www.terrass-hotel. com. Open Apr–Sept.

PARIS BY NIGHT

Paris is a night city as well as a day city, and a perfect place to break your routines together. Your naughty little conspiracy may mean eating well, partying later, and eating again way after most people are sleeping it all off. If so, Paris is the ideal city for you.

Hungry at midnight? Walk over to the **Au Pied de Cochon,** 6 rue Coquillière (**$$;** ℂ **01-40-13-77-00;** www.pieddecochon.com) in Les Halles and feed each other oysters. Or go to the historic late night bistros like **Le Procope,** 13 rue de l'Ancienne Comédie (**$$;** ℂ **01-40-46-79-00**), in the 6th arrondissement that made the city famous for its artists' and writers' salons that continue late into the night. Stop by **L'Atelier Saint-Germain de Joel Robuchon,** 5 rue Montalembert (**$$$;** ℂ **01-42-22-56-56**; http://atelier-robuchon-saint-germain.com), an informal outpost of the famous chef open until midnight.

> ### Perfect Place to Kiss
>
> Kissing is *très bien* anywhere in Paris, but perfect? Try the **Rodin Museum,** 79 rue de Varenne (ℂ **01-44-18-61-10;** www.musee-rodin.fr; admission 9€), right in front of Auguste Rodin's famous sculpture, "The Kiss," in one of Paris' most charming gardens.

VENICE
Getting Lost Together

Here is a romantic experience everyone should have: being in St. Mark's Square (Piazza San Marco) in Venice with the orchestra playing a Venetian waltz, white-coated waiters fetching you food or coffee or wine, and the two of you watching the light change as the Venetian sun sets. Granted, this is happening to a multitude of people at the same time, but it is no less special for you.

Venice always mesmerizes. You are in a water world, temporarily perched on land. In the early morning or late at night, you can hear the water lap against the buildings and walls of the canals. The narrow streets invite and beguile. We think Venice is best in the fall or spring; the summer can be too hot and humid and the winter too rainy and gray. (Unless you are a film buff, avoid the first two weeks of September when the Venice International Film Festival sucks up every available hotel room.) One exception: Venice at Christmas. Holiday lights are everywhere, but the crowds are all gone. Some think the light is even more stunning during the holidays because the cold air collides with the sea and creates a kind of golden haze.

Explore by water taxi, so you can gape at the elaborate centuries-old palazzos, improbably settling just at the water line. Travel down the **Grand Canal,** the main water highway, and even if you can't stay in the most expensive palazzos (some cost more than a $1,000 a night), ogle the famous ones, like the 14th-century **Danieli** (see below), and go there at sunset for a cocktail just to see the magnificence of this ornate masterpiece with massive Venetian chandeliers and gleaming marble floors.

After you find your hotel, get out and walk. Use a map and find the **Bridge of Sighs** (one of 400 bridges in the city). The ornate small stone bridge was once less romantic in connotation (prisoners were transported across it). Then swing around to the beautiful **Piazza San Marco** (© **041-529-8711**), a big tourist stop, but who cares? It is full of cafes, orchestras, bars, and pigeons. Have a glass of wine, or an espresso. Then amble along the narrow streets and breathe in the life of this unique city.

KEY ATTRACTIONS

Churches   We suggest you stop in at any church you pass, since most are lovely and have noteworthy architecture and valuable paintings that have stirred hearts for centuries. Near the end of the Grand Canal, see **Santa Maria della Salute,** Fondamenta Salute 30123 (© **041-241-1018;** www.seminario venezia.it), a church built to thank God for the end of the plague, and now famous for its fantastic rotunda. The **Basilica di Santa Maria Gloriosa dei Frari,** San Polo 3072, 30125 (© **041-272-8611;** www.basilicadeifrari.it), has several masterpieces by Titian and Bellini. Or maybe you are interested in the restored paintings of Veronese in the **Church of San Sebastiano,** Dorsoduro Campo San Sebastiano (© **041-275-0462;** www2.patriarcatovenezia.it). Pick a theme for your church visits; we had fun looking for works by the great Renaissance architect Andrea Palladio. An easy Palladio to find is the 16th-century **Church of San Giorgio Maggiore,** Isola di S. Giorgio Maggiore 30133 (© **041-522-78-27**), on San Giorgio Island. You can spot it from the Hotel Danieli.

Gondola Ride   Yes, of course you should hire a gondola. Yes, of course they are pricey (29€ for 35 minutes and up). No, you cannot resist. Just pick wisely. At Santa Sofia station, you will find the most ornate gondolas. Pick a guy who is smiling and friendly—because some can be downright surly. You will want to snuggle and kiss, right? Well, some gondoliers are offended by this odd behavior, so you need someone who has a sweet spot for romance and doesn't mind the occasional nuzzle. You will have to read his face, though not his attire. They all wear the antique black and white costume of a former age as mandated by law. The gondoliers represent a prized tradition in this city. Chances are this gondola was handmade by a member of the gondolier's family long ago; if he speaks English, ask him about the history of his boat. He'd like that.

Museums   The **Galeria dell'Accademia,** Campo della Carità 1050, 30123 (© **041-520 0345;** www.gallerieaccademia.org; admission 15€), holds the largest collection of Venetian paintings but is not very famous, so it may be refreshingly uncrowded. Take a look at the **Peggy Guggenheim Collection,** 704 Dorsoduro 701-704, 30123 (© **041-240 5411;** www.guggenheim-venice. it; admission 15.50€), one of Europe's greatest modern art collections, from Cubism and Surrealism to Abstract Expressionism. It also tells the story of a fascinating American woman's infatuation with Venice and art.

Palazzo Ducale   The extraordinarily showy "house" of the Doges, once rulers of Venice, has many exhibits worth seeing, but the real draw for lovers is the cell of the famous Casanova. Not so surprisingly, there once were penalties for the seduction of young ladies, and even bigger penalties if you unrepentingly bragged about it. The 18th-century Lothario actually escaped his imprisonment and was never recaptured. Some characters are even larger in life than the ones in fiction

San Marco, 130135. ©**041-271-5911.** http://palazzoducale.visitmuve.it/en/home. Admission 16€.

Touring Nearby Islands   Here's how it goes: **Burano** for lace, **Murano** for glass, **Lido** for leisure. About a 40-minute ferry ride from Venice, Burano intrigues with its storybook houses and many lace-making studios. Murano, a quick boatride from Venice, has been a glassmaking center for centuries and its beautiful products are trademarked. You can get to both on a *vaporetto*—a public motorboat. Take a tour as it's hard to appreciate what you are seeing without a guide.

If you are in Venice in sunshine, a trip to the beaches and luxury of Lido is not a bad idea. Only about 20 minutes away from the center of Venice, it sets a totally different mood. Consider lunching on the veranda at the **Hotel Excelsior,** Lungomare Marconi 41 (**$$;** © **041-526-02-01;** www.hotelexcelsior venezia.com), and feel like you are at a grand hotel on the Riviera. If it's beach and sun you crave, you can stay here (**$$$**) and commute to Venice.

HOTELS WITH HEART
The Charming House $$$ A very modern, well-priced, and extremely well-located option, is just a few steps from the Peggy Guggenheim museum and the Dorsoduro, one of the gallery sections of Venice.

Dorsoduro 724, 30123. ©**041-277-02-62.** www.thecharminghouse.com.

Hotel Danieli $$$ One of the grand old palazzos on the Grand Canal, this Starwood hotel is expensive, but not astronomical, and the gorgeous public rooms and fine service justify the price. Ask for a room with a balcony.

Riva degli Schiavoni 4196, 30122. ©**800/325-3589** in the US and Canada or 041-520-02-08. www.danielihotelvenice.com.

Novecento $$ This is both a boutique hotel and a bit of an eccentric townhouse with frequent art exhibitions. The nine bedrooms display a mix of Venetian and Asian artifacts such as a low Thai bed and Asian sculptures. Near Piazza San Marco, the location is perfect for art lovers headed for galleries and exhibits.

San Marco, 2683, 30124. © **041-241-37-65.** www.novecento.biz.

Oltre Il Giardino $$ A charming break from the urban *metropoli* is a three-story villa with a mix of antiques and designer touches. Really a country house in the middle of the city, the six-bedroom retreat offers canal-side walks and a lovely garden. The largest rooms with canal views are expensive, but in the low season the smaller rooms are actually quite reasonable. The hotel is in a quiet historic area, but very near tourist magnets like the Rialto bridge.

San Polo, 2542. © **041-275-00-15.** www.oltreilgiardino-venezia.com.

Palazzo Abadessa $$ Secreted behind a walled garden, this well-placed hotel is part 16th-century grand palazzo and part updated hotel. It is a larger home with frescoed ceilings, marble floors, Venetian chandeliers, leaded glass windows that overlook the canal and features a grand old salon with a well-worn, homey look. The suites and junior suites are frayed elegance, but beware the rooms on the mezzanine floor above the breakfast room, which tend more toward shabby. This hotel is small, charming and reasonable, a welcome asset in Venice.

Calle Priuli Cannaregio, 4011, 30121. © **041-241-37-84.** www.abadessa.com.

MOST ROMANTIC RESTAURANTS

Venice is everything you would hope it would be in the romance department, but some of the most wonderful hotels are only for the extremely wealthy. Still, you can go to their restaurants and drink in the atmosphere.

You'll find good food at moderate prices at **Ristorante Riviera,** Fondamenta Zattere al Ponte Longo, 1473, 30123 (**$$$;** © **041-522-7621;** www.ristoranteriviera.it), just across the bridge from Giudecca Island, not far from **Gelateria Nico,** Fondamenta Zattere al Ponte Longo, 922, 30121 (© **041-522-5293;** www.gelaterianico.com), said to be the originator of caffe affogato, vanilla ice cream doused with espresso.

De Pisis $$$ MEDITERRANEAN The restaurant at the elegant Bauers II features beautiful glass and table settings. The food is classically Italian with Asian tastes and surprising experimentation. This gorgeous, extremely expensive hotel is right on the Grand Canal.

Palazzo S. Marco 1413/d 30124. © **041-520 7022.** www.ilpalazzovenezia.com.

L'Anice Stellato $$$ ITALIAN This small family-run restaurant on the Fondamenta de la Sensa near the old Jewish quarter is inexpensive (for Venice) and has tables right along the canal. Fish and shellfish are recommended, as is the wine selection. Everything is wonderful and cooked in traditional Venetian spices, with a special bow to anise. Reservations are recommended.

Sestiere Cannaregio, 30121. © **041-720-744.** www.osterianicestellato.com.

VENICE BY NIGHT

Venice is not a subtle city for hanging out—affable bars and lounges are everywhere, from famous watering holes like Harry's Bar to youth-oriented joints with ubiquitous DJs. **Harry's Bar,** Calle Vallaresso, 1323, 30124 San Marco (© **041-528-5777;** www.harrysbarvenezia.com; closes at 11pm), is best known for helping Ernest Hemingway through his dark nights. These days it's a tourist attraction, but still worth your time. It also supposedly was a favorite of Arturo Toscanini, Somerset Maughan, Noel Coward, Peggy Guggenheim, and Charlie Chaplin. The bar invented the Bellini, and it's just as clubby as you might think it would be. Avoid a daytime visit when the place is packed. Head downstairs for a nightcap instead.

VIENNA

4 | Decadence on the Danube

Vienna is a city of faded and real royalty. Its Hapsburg past created the most grand (and grandiose) of its architecture, but the living Vienna today offers some fantastic revivals of places to stay and be seen. This is also the city of classics and extravagant concert halls: Check out the **Volksoper,** Währinger Straße 78 (© **01/5144430;** www.volksoper.at), **Wiener-Konzerthaus,** Lothringerstraße 20 (© **01/242002;** http://konzerthaus.at), or **Musikverein,** Musikvereinsplatz 1 (© **01/5058190;** www.musikverein.at). If you want to participate in a bygone era, a good travel agent can get you into one of the famous holiday balls. If you just want to be lovers in one of the world's most elegant cities, Vienna is your town. The Austrian capital has ever-present delectable pastries and coffee shops; broad, elegant avenues; world-class museums; and gorgeous hotel rooms. One of the world's great rivers, the Danube, runs through Vienna.

We urge you to visit during the holidays if you can. December is a magical time when buildings are beautifully lit and ice-skating rinks pop up all over the city. An enormous one is at **Wiener Eislaufverein.** Lothringerstraße 22 (© **01/7136353;** www.wev.or.at), near the Intercontinenal Hotel.

KEY ATTRACTIONS

Austrian National Library   Located at the **Hofburg Palace,** Michaelerkuppel (© **01/5337570;** www.hofburg-wien.at), the historic bastion of the Hapsburg monarchs from 1276 to 1918, the Baroque library complex (Josephsplatz 1; © **01/53410252;** http://onb.ac.at/ev) are also incredibly ornate, with frescoed ceilings, beautiful bookcases, antique globes and books, artwork, and marble pillars everywhere.

Museums Quartier   The former Hapsburg stables-turned-cultural complex holds a range of exhibit centers (www.mqw.at). For starters is the huge **Leopold Museum** (© **01/525700;** www.leopoldmuseum.org; admission 12€, seniors 9€); the **MUMOK** (Museum of Modern Art; © **01/525000;** www.mumok.at;

admission 10€, seniors 8€); and the modern gallery **Kunsthalle Wien** (✆ **01/521890;** www.kunsthalle wien.at; admission 8€, seniors 6€).

Pastry und Kaffee At **Café Halle,** Museumsquartier 1 (✆ **01/ 5237001**; www.diehalle.at), sip your coffees in the Emperor's old digs. **Café Sperl,** at Gumpendorfer-straße 11 (✆ **01/5864158;** www. cafesperl.at) is what you dreamed a turn-of-the-century Viennese coffee house would be, with velvet upholstered booths and rich classical detailing. Ask for double cream (*doppelt schlag*) for coffee that feels like dessert.

The Spanish Riding School If you haven't seen the Lipizzans of the Spanish Riding School on tour, or even if you have, seeing them train in this gorgeous ring is thrilling. The white stallions are athletes with rippling muscles, and the fancy-uniformed trainers aren't bad either. The dressage moves are often described as a ballet done by horses and expert riders. Make reservations at least six to eight weeks in advance (Michaelerplatz 1; ✆ **01/5339031;** www.srs.at; tickets from 26€ and way up).

HOTELS WITH HEART

Alstadt Vienna $ In the Spittelberg quarter, this very atmospheric Belle Époque hotel, converted from a 19th-century townhouse, won't break the bank. Yet its period rooms are very romantic with damask wallpaper, elaborate chandeliers, and antique touches.

Kirchengasse 41. ✆ **01/5226666.** www.alstadt.at.

Hotel Imperial $$$ This is the fanciest hotel in Vienna—which is saying something. It's two blocks from the Vienna State Opera and a block from the Musikverein. Built in 1869 as the private residence of the Duke of Württemberg, like many older grand hotels, rooms vary. The fourth and fifth floors are where you want your love nest. Rooms on the mezzanine and first floors are lavishly baroque and get less elaborate the higher you go.

Kaerntner Ring 16. ✆ **800/325-3589** in the United States and Canada or 01/501100. www.luxurycollection.com/imperial.

MOST ROMANTIC RESTAURANTS

Pfarrwirt $$ VIENNESE   The ambience here is rustic inn, and it's very cozy and casual. Feast on woodsy views in the spacious enclosed veranda and order traditional food like goulash and wienerschnitzel.

Pfarrplatz 5. ✆ **01/3707373.** www.pfarrwirt.com.

Restaurant Korso $$$ VIENNESE   Planning a big Viennese celebration? Korso at the Bristol Hotel will serve nicely. This glittering restaurant has

4

PASSIONATE CITIES: EUROPE

Vienna

sparkling chandeliers, illuminating a baronial fireplace and two breathtaking baroque columns. You are right across from the Staatsoper, so get opera tickets, and you are set for the evening.

Mahlerstrasse 2. © **01/5151 6546.** www.restaurantkorso.at.

VIENNA BY NIGHT

Go to **Die Rote Bar,** Neustiftgasse 1 (© **699/15015014;** www.rotebar.at) if only to see the elaborate Volkstheater where it's located. This chill-out scene for theatergoers is turn-of-the-century opulence, with fantastic murals and flamboyant chandeliers, all covered and lit in unapologetic red.

Motto am Fluss, Franz-Josefs-Kai 2 (© **01/2525511;** www.motto.at/mottoamfluss), is a modern bar with views overlooking the Danube and the city. For jazz, **Porgy and Bess,** Riemergasse 11 (© **01/5128811;** www.porgy.at), is a club made from two boats on the Danube. It has a lively bar, restaurant, and a summer pool on the top deck.

If you can only visit one concert hall, choose the 19th-century **Staatsoper,** Opernring 2 (© **01/514447880;** www.wiener-staatsoper.at), to hear opera and the Vienna Philharmonic Orchestra. Ascending the grand marble staircase is exhilarating, and you can feel the musical history—Strauss and Mahler conducted here. However, even if you don't attend a concert or opera, you'll likely hear Mozart being played in cafes, restaurants, and church concerts.

PASSIONATE CITIES: EXOTIC LANDS

The cities in this chapter can be a bit more challenging—but in a good way. Buzzing with energy, filled with sights and smells that may be entirely new to you and your partner, they're ideal places for adventurers to head to. Also, these all are cities that stay up late, so get ready to explore the night together. Maybe you'll head out dancing one evening and to a bustling pub the next. Keep yourself open to all the world has to show you.

BANGKOK & CHIANG MAI
Steamy City, Soothing Mountains

5

Thailand is for lovers. Why? The country's beautiful physical assets are reason enough. But its people create an extraordinary atmosphere of good feeling, being extremely kind in their most quotidian gestures. The national greeting, *wai*, with palms together in prayer pose, like the Indian *namaste*, signals their respect for you. The higher the hands are held, the more respect or reverence.

Most trips to Thailand start in Bangkok, the fast-paced capital that will rev you up for the next stop, a relaxing trip to Chiang Mai and mountain country.

Bangkok

In this big, complex city, taxis, motorbikes, and crowds all parade past the humble doorsteps of small temples for everyday worship. Beyond the business quarter of the city are the gilded royal palace complex (best known to Americans for its debut in the 1956 film "The King and I") and huge markets where you can hunt down souvenirs. Perhaps because of the infernal racket of this gorgeous city, hotels and other tourist services make it their mission to protect you from the noise and chaos with glorious Thai hospitality and luxury.

KEY ATTRACTIONS
Chao Phraya River Urban honeymooners can enjoy Bangkok's river by either using it for transit (a river ferry ride at dusk is

about as romantic as it gets and costs less than a dollar), staying at one of the many hotels along its banks, taking a riverboat cruise, or dining at a river-view restaurant.

Grand Palace & Wat Phra Kaew   While in Bangkok you'll have many temples and cultural attractions to visit, but these two are absolute must-sees. Visit in the later part of the day to avoid the crowds and heat. Keep in mind that a dress code is enforced and that you cannot enter after 3:30pm.

Na Phra Lan Rd., Maharaj Pier. ✆ **2623-5500,** ext. 3100. www.grandpalace bangkok.com. Single admission gets you into both, 500B.

Thai Cooking Class   No need for a lot of cooking skills—just a love for Thai food. **Baipai Thai Cooking School,** 8/91 Ngam Wongwan Rd., Soi 54 Ladyao, Chatuchak (✆ **2561-1404** or 2561-1404; www.baipai.com; 2,000B per participant), gives a half-day cooking class that often starts with market shopping and learning about local spices and vegetables, followed by creating the basic dishes of Thai cuisine.

HOTELS WITH HEART

Arun Residence $ If you're looking for a real Thai experience in terms of views, room decor, and service, then this is your spot. This renovated Sino-Portuguese house on the riverfront has just a handful of lovely rooms and suites, all equipped with traditional Thai furnishings, with magnificent views of the soaring stupa of Wat Arun on the other side of the river. I particularly like the way deluxe rooms are designed on a split level, with the bed raised on an extended mezzanine, but given the choice I'd go for one of the suites, if only for their unforgettable views. It's on land owned by Wat Po, so it's easy to arrange a treatment by masseuses from its famed massage school.

36-38 Soi Prathu Nokyung, Maharaj Road. ✆ **02/221-9158-9.** www.arunresidence. com

The Four Seasons $$$ This is a big hotel with a boutique heart. The mahogany-trimmed rooms, with their green marbled bathrooms, set the stage for intimacy and luxury—the suites even have their own dressing rooms. The hotel's lovely courtyard is shaded by very tall trees and has a running stream with exquisite koi decorating the water. The expansive pool is similarly protected and relaxing. You could just throw out all sightseeing plans, and stay here and be happy.

155 Rajadamri Rd. ✆ **2126-8866.** www.fourseasons.com/bangkok.

Lebau Hotel $$$ If you worry about getting a great room, you can relax here: This hotel only has five-star expansive, luxury suites. Want a view? Relax again. You are in the Silom District in the State Tower of the two tallest towers in Bangkok. Want service? Ask for the chef to cook for you in your own digs. It doesn't get more luxurious or pampered than that.

1055 Silom Rd. ✆ **2624-9999.** www.lebua.com.

Mandarin Oriental $$$ This well-established and justly celebrated hotel remains a paragon of contemporary luxury. It has a rich history of making celebrity guests feel right at home, with discreet service and high-quality rooms. But fear not, you will not feel any less well treated.

48 Oriental Ave. © **2659-9000.** www.mandarinoriental.com.

Oriental Residence Bangkok $ This high-rise property, in the heart of Bangkok's shopping and embassy district, bills itself as an "apartment hotel" because its one-, two-, and three-bedroom suites have full kitchens, always a plus. It also offers stunning views, elegance, and luxury comfort for travelers. The hotel's sleek, international style appeals to the urban sophisticate who wants good prices without sacrificing amenities like spacious rooms, premium decor, fitness club, pool, and a fine on-site restaurant (where you can also go for high tea). The hotel offers free shuttle service to Bangkok Mass Transit System. Special deals are often available.

110 Wireless Rd., Lumpini. © **2125-9000.** www.oriental-residence.com.

Peninsula Bangkok $$$ This luxury hotel at the end of the Charoennakon Road beside the Chao Phraya River could really be its own self-contained universe, with its spacious rooms, wonderful spa, decorous restaurants with breezy terraces and glorious urban views, especially at night. The hotel provides a shuttle boat, just so you don't overlook visiting the eternal attractions of Bangkok.

333 Charoennakorn Rd. © **2861-2888.** www.peninsula.com.

MOST ROMANTIC RESTAURANTS

Cabbages and Condoms $ THAI   OK, so it's not romantic in the classic sense of the word—but it is worth a visit if you get a kick out of the restaurant's odd name and would enjoy ogling full-scale mannequins dressed entirely in condoms. We love it, firstly, because it was started by the hero of Thai population planning; secondly, because it is humorous and fun (they offer blue condoms for Democrats, red ones for Republicans); and thirdly, because the food is actually very good. Be prepared for a place unlike any other—and avoid it if you think being surrounded by condom messages is not what you came to Thailand for.

6 Sukhumvit Soi 12, Sukhumvit Rd. © **2229-4610.** www.pda.or.th/restaurant.

Celadon $$ THAI   Many people think Celadon vies for the honor of the best restaurant in the city. After being seated in your beautifully designed *sala*, you will be treated to expert service and a great deal of pampering as you dine from the authentic, and extensive, Thai menu representing different cooking traditions from across the country. Terraces overlooking a picturesque lotus-pond create a serene and tasteful ambience. One special experience you can reserve is a private dinner served in the romantic herb garden. The two of you will be attended by your own butler or have a private chef concentrate on only your table. Soft music on traditional instruments will play in the background. This might just be the perfect time to say something important to one another.

13/3 South Sathorn Rd. ☏ **2344-8888.** www.sukhothai.com.

The Deck $ THAI   The spacious "deck by the river" restaurant overlooks the Chao Praya River enabling you to enjoy the river activity against the sky-line of historically interesting buildings. The Deck will help you create your own special private experience for two with a variety of dinner choices.

36-38 Soi Pratu Nok Yung, Maharat Rd. ☏ **2221-9158.** www.arunresidence.com.

Salathip $$ THAI   Yet another wonderful restaurant overlooking the Chao Phraya River, the Salathip usually has traditional music wafting throughout the dining room, making it a great romantic pick. Take a table on the terrace and order from a good selection of Thai specialties. It does shellfish especially well.

89 Soi Wat Suan Plu, New Rd. ☏ **2236-7777.** www.shangri-la.com.

Vertigo and Moon Bar $$$ THAI FUSION   The entire city lies before you from this rooftop bar and grill. The vista is fascinating and bustling by day, sparkling at night. Whether the air is humid or balmy, this stylish place is a prime choice for a rendezvous and a cocktail, or even a full meal of grilled steak or fish.

21/100 South Sathon Rd. ☏ **2679-1200.** www.banyantree.com/en/bangkok.

BANGKOK BY NIGHT

The aptly named **Scirocco's Sky Bar,** 1055 State Tower, Silom Rd. (☏ **2624-9555;** www.lebua.com), is a good choice for an after-dinner cocktail. Open to the sky, this sophisticated magnet for lovers and tourists will give you an unbeatable view of the city and the Chao Phraya River. If you want to be high, this bar on the 63rd floor of The Dome at State Tower cannot be topped, at least in Bangkok.

But that shouldn't be the only bar you visit. The city is packed with inviting spots for a drink. A certain air of romance lingers over at the **Moon Bar** at the Banyan Tree Hotel, 21/100 South Sathon Rd., 61st floor (☏ **2679-1200;** www.banyantree.com), and the **Saxophone Pub,** 3/8 Phayathai Rd. Victory Monument (☏ **2236-5472;** www.saxophonepub.com).

Chinatown (the Old City's Thanon Thanao)   Here your delectable chop house meal or street snack is accompanied by some especially interesting people-watching. Scout around, and you may just discover the next "it" restaurant in Bangkok.

Cabaret   If you are looking for something beyond the mainstream tourist entertainment, seek out a Bangkok's Broadway-like cabaret shows featuring spellbinding performers in sequined costumes and larger-than-life hairdos. We recommend **Calypso Cabaret,** Warehouse No. 3, 2194 Charoenkrung 72-76 Rd. (☏ **2688-1415,** ext. 7; www.calypsocabaret.com; cover 900B; reservations required), and **Mambo Cabaret Show,** 59/28 Sathu-phararam 3 Rd. (www.bangkokcabaret.com; from 400B).

Chiang Mai

Chiang Mai is a mountain city with a wild side. It has historically intriguing temples and buildings and is surrounded by dense and mysterious mountains and forest, former trading routes once dominated by the drug trade. Today, increasingly modern Chiang Mai is a cultivated city without the tourism stigma of the "Golden Triangle," though it does attract more than 2 million foreign tourists annually. Each street can offer a window into the culture and history of this bustling, lively outpost in northern Thailand. Chiang Mai has hills to hike, mountains to explore, and *wats* (temples) of every size and age. We prefer the smaller ones to the famous (and crowded) one atop the mountain, **Doi Suthep.** Chiang Mai is close to Myanmar (Burma), and some of its famed jewels come from that country. However, if you were planning to buy your ring in Chiang Mai, be careful. The days of buying a fabulous ruby for a pittance here ended quite a while ago.

KEY ATTRACTIONS

Big Love   Unlike his African cousin, who is bigger, more arrogant, and less predictable, the Asian elephant can be a sweetheart. Still, humans have hardly always been kind to them; that's why places like **Patera Elephant Conservation Farm,** 299/22 Siwalee Rachapreuk Maettea, Chiang Mai (© **81992-2551** or 81671-0958; www.pataraelephantfarm.com), rescue and breed them and recruit you to make a hands-on effort. For a couple, it can be a day well spent. What could be more romantic than washing an elephant together? *Warning:* This camp requires you to be relatively fit. Riding elephants requires balance, pretty strong thighs, and flexibility—though riding is optional, it's certainly a big part of the fun, if the elephants are treated well.

An even more exciting choice of elephant thrills would be the **Four Seasons' Tented Camp Golden Triangle** ($$$; © **5391-0200;** www.fourseasons.com/goldentriangle), where you can spend several days in tented camps riding on and working with the elephants. Optional romantic evening: Arrange for your own private dinner and bonfire with the elephants posing as your backdrop.

Wat Phra Singh   This compound was built during the zenith of Chiang Mai's power and is one of the more venerated temples in the city. It is still the focus of many important religious ceremonies, particularly the Songkran Festival. More than 700 monks study here, and you will find them especially friendly with tourists, so pepper them with questions together. You'll have a lot of interesting topics to discuss over dinner if you do. Head to Samlarn and Ratchadamnoen roads.

HOTELS WITH HEART

Anantara Chiang Mai Resort and Spa $$ This wonderful, five-star resort is well-located close to the Night Bazaar and historic city center. A luxurious four-story bamboo structure located on the Mae Ping River, the resort is a mix of old Chiang Mai and the British Empire that once had a major presence here (see "The Restaurant," below where the British Raj atmosphere continues). Get a room with a balcony that faces the river or, even better, the pool that sits at the river's edge. The evening destinations, such as the Night Bazaar and Old Town, are only a 5- or 10-minute walk.

123 Charoen Prathet Rd. ✆ **5325-3333.** http://chiang-mai.anantara.com.

Baan Orapin $ Two-story Lanna-style buildings surround the 95-year-old mansion and attached gardens. While the rooms and suites are rustic in comparison with the larger resorts and hotels in the area, they are stylish and extremely clean, with sturdy teak-wood furniture, mosquito netting for the beds, and handicrafts that add wonderful local flavor. Large bathrooms are outfitted in beautifully polished, locally made green-and-blue tiling. And the staff will bend over backward to attend to your every need.

150 Charoenraj Rd. ✆ **05324-3677.** www.baanorapin.com.

Four Seasons Chiang Mai $$$ This resort is built as a Northern Thai village—but a luxury village that exists only in your dreams, and at the Four Seasons. As you look out from your own *sala* (deck) you might get a mountain, pond, or garden view. Your shower—in a gorgeous bathroom big as some bedrooms—is glassed in on one side to give the feeling of showering outdoors. If you want even more privacy and a more modern decor, the new villas with pools are gorgeous. Totally shielded from your neighbors, you can enjoy your own pool and hot tub, so no need to put on a swimsuit. If you choose to spend time in your elegant home (it feels like the perfect home: mostly bed, no kitchen), you will have a flatscreen TV and a Vinotemp wine bottle cooler. Additional special romantic touches? The infinity pool (and the excellent restaurant next to it) has a lovely view of the rice fields at the center of the resort. And we haven't even started talking about the spa. You can have an intimate steam room for two, and side-by-side massages followed by a rose-petal bath. One lucky couple a night can reserve the rice Barn, a small rustic platform on the lake near where the two resident water buffalo frolic. It comes with a multi-course dinner, glorious torch-lit views, and live Thai music. The food is to die for; the scene is unbeatable. If you have already proposed, do it again.

502 Moo 1, Mae Rim-Samoeng Old Rd. ✆ **800/819-5053** in the United States and Canada or 5329-8190. www.fourseasons.com/chiangmai.

The Mandarin Oriental $$$ An OMG kind of place, the Mandarin Oriental was designed to look like a 19th-century kingdom. You enter through a long portal of trees that opens on a vision of towering spires and an intricately carved roof. The resort spreads over 24-plus hectares (60 acres) of rice paddies, canals, lakes, and buildings in various Thai styles, from colonial periods to traditional teak houses. We love the Honeymoon Villas, with their own pools (for half the price you can get a similar place with just a plunge pool or Jacuzzi). All the rooms have teak walls, private balconies, and multiple relaxation areas usually spread over two floors. Splurge on the special barbeque where your private chef creates a gourmet feast in your room. It takes the staff two hours just to set up your pool or patio area, which becomes a bower of flowers with trails of rose petals and lit by dozens of candles. The two of you sit at a festooned table, and course after course is served. You will be treated and fed (and wowed) like royalty.

The Spa (✆ **02659-0444**), in a structure that looks like a palace, is world class. Sign up for the royal Thai treatment: two wonderful massages (and a couples dressing room) and Champagne, topped off by a short walk along a candlelit trail to your rose-petal Jacuzzi bath.

48 Oriental Ave. ✆ **2659-9000.** www.mandarinoriental.com/chiangmai.

Sukantara Cascade Resort and Spa $$
We can see why Angelina Jolie stayed here. This resort has only 16 lovely Lanna-Balinese-style suites and is rich in quiet comforts, such as breezy verandas near the stream with the sounds of the jungle wafting in. Guests can cross the river via the resort's swinging bridge and hike 1km (.6 miles) to the Tad Mok waterfall and 2km (1.25 miles) more to Karen village.

12/2 M.8 T. Maeram, A. Mae Rim. ✆ **81881-1444.** www.sukantara.com.

MOST ROMANTIC RESTAURANTS

Huen Huay Keaw Restaurant $ NORTHERN THAI/CENTRAL THAI
This rustic restaurant has personality that can only be achieved by simply aging into place. In the cool shadow of a waterfall not far from Do Suthep, Thai chefs provide superior food amid the sound of falling water in the cool mountain atmosphere adds even more texture. Don't miss the fish curry and spicy pork dishes.

3½ Moo 2 Huey Keaw Rd. ✆ **05389-2698** or 085/0485607. http://huenhuaykeaw-en.simdif.com.

The Restaurant $$$ INTERNATIONAL
The cuisines of many countries make this atmospheric restaurant a great pick for a special night out. The magic happens in a century-old building from the British colonial period, with ample romantic seating on an outside deck surrounded by trees. Think Thai curries, but also Korean barbeque and classic Indian dishes. Great for dinner, but also for a traditional English tea or a stop at the bar or Lobby, where the English vibe continues. A nice touch is the upstairs lounge where you can continue your cocktail, relaxing on a couch, looking at the Mae Ping River, and toasting each other's good luck to be in this fabulous place.

In the Antara Chiang Mai, 123 Charoen Prathet Rd. ✆ **5325-3333.** http://chiang-mai.anantara.com.

Thao Nam Restaurant $ THAI
Not far from the city center, this charming, traditional teak building overlooking the Mae Ping River will do nicely for a romantic evening. Eat outside right next to the water, underneath the protection of aged trees.

4313 Moo. 2, Changklan Rd. ✆ **5328-2988.** www.chiangmai.com/thanam_restaurant.html.

CHIANG MAI BY NIGHT

Riverside Jazz Cross the river from the Night Bazaar to explore the jazz, soul, and rock and roll clubs of **Charoenrat Road** (btw. Charoen Muang and Kaew Nawarat Rds.). You can choose from many small restaurants, with the river providing a backdrop for your meanderings.

Shopping at Night Join the locals on their nightly rounds of shopping, eating, drinking, and people-watching at the **Night Bazaar,** at the intersection of Chang Klan and Loy Kroh roads. What seems like an endless sea of sidewalk stalls spilling into the streets is actually a prime shopping destination where you can buy almost anything you can think of. The nightlife here is varied. Settle down at a sidewalk bar for a refreshing drink to rest a bit in the often hot and crowded setting.

Sundays on Ratchadamneon Road Wisely, the Thai officials have closed off Ratchadammeon Road and Tha Pae Gate on Sundays after midday. It's a great time to stroll more safely and sample the wares of the many vendors of this street fair. You will hear music and be tempted by local crafts at good prices.

BUENOS AIRES
South American Sophistication

Buenos Aires has had its economic ups and downs, and the downs have been very low indeed. But, today, it survives as one of the most beautiful cities in South America and the world. Glorious is its grand architecture, broad boulevards, and magnificent plazas.

Buenos Aires also has real street life, buzzing with energy. One of the few truly affordable and truly glamorous world capitals, it attracts an adventurous, often younger crowd to enjoy its sophisticated galleries, cafes, tango parlors, restaurants, and neighborhoods. Sometimes its mood is Latin, and other times it's European. Explore Microcentro, Recoleta, Palermo Viejo, Puerto Madero, and San Telmo; around the city, each neighborhood will show you how it merges its old world and new world vibes.

KEY ATTRACTIONS

Art & History Museums **MALBA** (Museo de Arte Latinamericano de Buenos Aires; 3415 Av. Pres. Figueroa Alcorta *©* **11/4808-6500;** www.malba. org.ar; admission $50, seniors $25; all admission on Wed is $25) is a beautiful modern building with a central atrium. At lunch, enjoy French-inspired cuisine at the museum's Café des Arts and on a nice day dine on the terrace. Another museum, continuing the mystique of the intriguing Eva Peron, is the **Museo-Evita,** Lafinur 2988 (*©* **11/4807-0306;** www.museoevita.org), which also has a nice cafe and lovely garden for a cup of coffee.

Avenida Exploration   This is a city full of grand architecture, and much of it is on boulevards with graceful trees all around to soften the picture. Start in the elegant **Recoleta,** and you will think you are in Paris. In **Puerto Madero,** don't miss the handsome Puente de la Mujer (Bridge of Women), inspired by the image of a couple dancing the tango. It swings open dramatically for boat traffic at the city's docks.

Coffee (or Hot Chocolate) Breaks   Coffee shops and the time you spend at them will give you a feel for Buenos Aires. **Cafe Tortoni,** Av. de Mayo 825 (✆ **11/4342-4328;** www.cafetortoni.com.ar), founded in 1858, is the oldest and seems straight from a Hollywood back-lot, with its dramatic, stained-glass high ceiling, dark wood moldings, and dense collection of framed portraits and other artwork.

San Telmo   One of the hipper neighborhoods, this area attracts a critical mass of people to its fashionable stores and is really a look at the newest version of Buenos Aires. If you enjoy art galleries, center your search on the **Calle Defensa** neighborhood (for great people-watching, too). Seek out the enjoyable antiques fair on Saturdays in the colonial district at **Plaza Dorrego** (✆ **11/4114-5724**). When the locals break out tango dancing, accept it as a gift.

Stay on an Estancia   Experience gaucho hospitality at an *estancia,* a rural ranching estate. Buenos Aires features a variety of perfect estancias to enjoy with a partner, especially on horseback. Styles range from luxury to historical, quaint, or traditional. Some are simple with campfires and barbeques. Others offer everything a major resort does, plus horses and golf. For a list of estancias around Buenos Aires and beyond, visit www.welcomeargentina.com.

Teatro Colón   This celebrated theater is on the Avenida 9 de Julio, which has seven lanes in each direction, plus parallel side streets that make it among the widest streets in the world. The Avenida's scale, plus the theater's extraordinary exterior, create quite a sight. The interior is even more grand. Acoustically impressive and gorgeously decorated in marble with French furniture and decor, the feeling is pan-European. The gold-leafed lobby and auditorium, with velvet chairs and painted and carved ceilings, are simply breathtaking. Sometimes chamber music concerts are in the Patron's room, modeled on the Palace of Versailles. This theater is a glorious space for hearing music, but if you can't get a ticket, take the tour.

✆ **11/4378-7100.** www.teatrocolon.org.ar.

HOTELS WITH HEART
Algodon Mansion $$$ A newer edition of luxury, this mansion has all the modern amenities plus pampering in a romantic Belle Époque cocoon. The rooms are spacious, and the suites' marble bathrooms are huge. With a wonderful combination of modern and traditional decor, this is a true boutique hotel. It sacrifices nothing, even though everything is on a smaller scale than the grand hotels. Peaceful and serious about service, it is perfect for lovers, if a bit pricey.

Montevideo Street 1647. ✆ **11/3530-7777.** www.algodonmansion.com.

Buenos Aires Park Hyatt $$$ This landmark unites contemporary design with the Palacio Duhau, the Duhau family mansion, for a compelling blend of old and new. The rooms in the old part of this neoclassical palace will make you feel like royalty. If you like more modern luxury, stay in the minimalist tower.

Av Alvear 1661. ℂ **800/633-7313** in the US and Canada, or 11/5171-1234. http://buenosaires.park.hyatt.com.

Casa Calma $ This is one of the few truly eco-friendly hotels in Buenos Aires, well-located and well-priced. Tropical in feel, light, airy, and spacious rooms have modern comfortable decor and romantic touches.

Suipacha 1015. ℂ **5411-4312-5000.** www.casacalmahotel.com.

MOST ROMANTIC RESTAURANTS

For your date night in Buenos Aires, don't just go to one restaurant, go to half a dozen! Popular food tours through such companies as Fuudis (www.fuudis.com) and Parrilla (www.parrillatour.com) will introduce you to a variety of wonderful dining experiences; the latter is particularly good for steak houses. Dining and wine-tasting courses run by the Argentine Experience (www.theargentineexperience.com; $85 per person) are also a savvy way for the two of you to learn more about the local culture and gastronomy.

But remember you are in the land of the Pampas, so steak is king. You'll want to indulge at least once, even if you don't usually eat red meat, because the quality here is extraordinary. The cuts will be wide, rather than thick, and generally overlap your plate—they're enormous, even by U.S. standards. You can split one easily, although that is not the Argentine way (neither is a doggie bag—but you can ask for a half portion). Fabulous steak places include the elegant Art Deco **Fervor,** Posadas 1519 ($$; ℂ **11/4804-4944;** www.fervor brasas.com.ar). **Miranda,** Costa Rica 5602 ($$; ℂ **11/5291-3333;** www.parrilla miranda.com), has thick steaks, a great wine list, and a fabulous specialty of grilled short ribs.

Bar Uriarte $ ITALIAN A floriferous, scented garden setting in the warm weather and a comfy one when it's cold, you can get cozy here next to the pizza ovens. Expect excellent contemporary food and fine pizzas in a romantic atmosphere and an inexpensive bill.

Uriarte 1572. ℂ **11/4834-6004.** www.baruriarte.com.

HG $$$ ARGENTINE This is a restaurant by a star chef, Hernan Gipponi, who has quite a few outposts in the city. Here the focus is on inventive and delicious seasonal menus. They serve big portions here so you might want the traditional digestive, *Fernet Branca*, which is, shall we say, an acquired taste.

Soler 5862, Palermo. ℂ **11/3220-6820.** www.fierrohotel.com.

Tomo1 $$ MEDITERRANEAN This elegant restaurant with delicious food is in the Pan Americano Hotel, so you get to walk through one of the more beautiful lobbies in the city to eat here. The two dreamy dining rooms are furnished in exotic woods and rough burlap and provide lovely intimacy for a special dinner for two. Be prepared for cuisine that soars as high as the ceilings—the food here has been celebrated since the 1970s. One superlative specialty is the Spanish octopus with pesto.

521, Carlos Pellegrini Mezzanine Floor South Tower. © **11/4326-6698.** www. tomo1.com.ar.

BUENOS AIRES BY NIGHT

How do you have a romantic life when dinner starts at 10pm? (It is considered ill bred, even scandalous, to dine as early as most Americans do. Sitting before 9 would be considered very odd indeed.) So go with the flow, which means observing a midday siesta. This is actually a wonderful tradition, a post late-lunch snooze that prepares you for a late-night dinner and perhaps is an opportunity for love in the afternoon.

Milion Follow the winding wrought-iron staircases into the glamorous rooms of the restaurant and bar. It's a dreamy place to linger, particularly the romantic patio.

Parana 1048. © **11/4815-9925.** www.milion.com.ar.

You Two Tango Tango is sexy, sensual, intricate, and very, very Latin. Try it, and it will likely add some heat to your visit. The shows for tourists are well worth seeing, but you don't have to limit yourselves to those. Heading to a local's tango parlor is a highlight of a trip to Buenos Aires. Many locals dance incredibly skillfully, and some will happily help you learn the dance yourself.

For an introduction to tango, see the history of the dance (through dance) at **El Querandi,** Peru 322 (© **11/5199-1770;** www.querandi.com.ar; show only 477ARS, dinner and show 1,034ARS). For a glitzed-up version, try **Señor Tango,** Vieytes 1655 (© **11/4303-0231;** www.senortango.com.ar; $450). Go to **El Caberet,** Martha Salotti 445 (© **11/4952-4111** or 11/4021-5580; www. faena.com), or **El Niño Bien,** Humberto Primo 1462 (© **11/4483-2588;** 40ARS–48ARS), to see serious tango dancers show you what they've got at the huge Belle Époque dance hall.

For lessons and a more low-key local vibe, try classes at **Confiteria Ideal,** Suipacha 384 (© **11/4328-7750** or 11/4328-0474: www.confiteriaideal.com; classes 50ARS), in an impressive 1912 mansion.

CAPE TOWN & THE SOUTH AFRICAN WINELANDS
It's Complicated

Nelson Mandela is gone now, but his example of courage, and his tireless efforts to improve life for the citizens of his country, have influenced this current generation of South Africans. We don't say this to sugar coat reality— South Africa faces major challenges. But that shouldn't put off the romantic traveler. It's a place to go and share in the future. This culturally and naturally rich country offers exciting frontiers to explore (and also treats visitors with uncommon courtesy and kindness).

Cape Town, in particular, is, simply put, gorgeous. Whether seen from the top of **Table Mountain,** the waterfront, or the coast highway, the semi-tropical views of palm and milkwood trees combined with water and mountains are entrancing. Cape Town joins Sydney, Vancouver, and San Francisco as the world's leading cities for watching water meet hills, mountains, and beaches in a blissful collaboration. Just outside the city are handsome suburbs, wide and clean beaches, and dramatic coastline.

You'll find several days' worth of activities here, some romantic, some sobering. We love the downtown markets (the **Green Market**); **Bo Kaap,** Schotsche Kloof (✆ **021/481-3939;** www.bokaap-capetown.co.za), the center of Cape Malay life; and the **South African National Art Gallery,** which is part of the **Iziko South African Museum,** 25 Queen Victoria St. (✆ **21/481-3800;** www.iziko.org; admission R30, seniors R15). If you are garden enthusiasts, don't even think of skipping the **Kirstenbosch Botanical Gardens,** Rhodes Drive, Cape Town 7735 (✆ **21/799-8783** or 21/799-8782; www.sanbi.org; admission R45).

KEY ATTRACTIONS

Robben Island   The skiff ride out is a wondrously beautiful trip, but the visit to the site of Mandela's incarceration will be sobering. Coming here is essential to understanding what native Africans experienced to achieve their hard won equality of citizenship; it is best experienced with a soulmate, someone you trust at important moments.

www.capetown.travel or www.robben-island.org.za.

Table Mountain   The view is terrific, with rocky outcroppings above and Cape Town below. The hike up is recommended for the ridiculously fit. Or, do as we did: Drive up to the parking area at the funicular. Buy a ticket (round trip R215, one-way R110) for the ride that takes you almost straight up the cliff. If you have trouble with enclosed spaces or vertigo, this is not for you, although the ride is mercifully quick. Some people take the funicular and walk down, but that is only for the athletic. Wild nature paths at the top are rich in natural specimens and reveal incredible scenery not viewable any other way. The restaurant up there is comfy, especially since the weather can be pretty cold and windy.

Tafelberg Rd. ✆ **21/424 8181.** www.tablemountain.net.

The Winelands   Many tourists err in heading to the wine country (just 90 minutes from Cape Town) for just one day. They—and you!—deserve a longer visit. Take at least 2 days (3, if you both are serious about wine) and make the lovely village of **Franschhoek** (tourism office: 62 Huguenot Rd., Franschhoek; ✆ **21/876-2861;** www.franschhoek.org.za) your base for tasting some excellent wine in one of the most (if not the most) gorgeous wine regions on earth. If you want to live like a star (like former guests Elton John or Richard Gere), book a room at **La Residence,** Elandskloof Rd., Franschhoek (**$$$;** ℘ **21/876-4100;** www.laresidence.co.za), a beautiful boutique hotel with a pool, themed rooms decorated in antiques and views of the vineyards from most of them. **Le Quartier Français Hotel,** 9 Wilhelmina St. (**$$;** ℘ **21/876-2151;** www.lqf.co.za), is another option, a charming, somewhat quirky, hotel with a noted restaurant and outdoor eating area that is *trés sympatique.* Good wine tours are available at the lovely rural **Vrede en Lust,** Intersection R45 and Klapmuts Rd., Simondium (℘ **21/874-1611;** www.vnl. co.za; reservations required), and **Warwick Wine Estate,** between Stellenbosch and Klapmuts roads, R44, Stellenbosch (℘ **21/884-4410** or 21/884-3144; www.warwickwine.com). Warwick has good food and wine and offers a clever Wine Safari. You'll go to the hills to find the "Big Five Grapes" the way the wildlife safaris help you find the "Big Five" game animals. Afterwards, you have a gourmet lunch. Romantic touch: A goblet here has a love story. Supposedly, a king nixed his daughter's marriage to a common goldsmith, unless the goldsmith could create a wine goblet both lovers could drink from together without spilling a drop. The Goldsmith solved the problem, married the princess, and now lovers here can drink from his clever invention. For help planning a trip, contact the winelands' regional tourism board (℘ **76/807-5181;** www.winelands.co.za).

HOTELS WITH HEART

Cape Town is a big city, but your visit will mostly focus on its bustling waterfront, which has several delightful hotels walking distance from fine restaurants and shops.

An African Villa $ A series of adjoining two-level Victorian houses was converted into this chic little guesthouse by a group of friends. They decorated it with good-quality African art, crafts, and fabrics, ensuring it comes across feeling perfectly homey and comfortable, while not being cluttered. The small pool and sun loungers there are perfect for the recovery interval between the beach and a night on the town. Excellent value and a great central location that's a little out of the fray make An African Villa a stand-out.

19 Carstens Street. ℘ **27 83 900 7894.** www.capetowncity.co.za.

Twelve Apostles $$$ This absolutely luxe choice faces the coast and the churning sea. It is very expensive, and if you're not doing a very high-end visit, it might be worth visiting just for tea and the view.

Victoria Rd., Camps Bay. ℘ **21/437-9000** or 21/437-9255. www.12apostleshotel.com.

Victoria and Alfred Hotel $ Upgraded from its humble motel-ish beginnings, the Victoria and Alfred is a good value in a perfect location. Shops filled with authentic African baskets, textiles, and masks are only two minutes from the hotel.

Waterfront Pierhead. ℘ **21/419-6677.** www.newmarkhotels.com.

NATURAL LUXURY IN safari CAMPS

South Africa has many superb game camps. One of the most stunning is **&Beyond Phinda Private Game Reserve in Kwazulu-Natal ($$$; ⓒ 11/809-4313;** www.phinda.com or andbeyond. com). The reserve has six different locations in the large park. We like the Forest Camp best because of its modern glass buildings that integrate you right into the trees and animal habitat. We also like the bonus of flying over the Drakenberg Mountains to land in **Nyala ($$$; ⓒ 11/809-4313;** www.nyala.com). When we were at a camp in Nyala, the biggest elephant anyone had ever seen walked in and owned the place for a while. As the camp is located around an active watering hole, we saw troops of elephants and other animals every evening.

Kruger National Park, Skukuza Camp Rd., Skukuza (ⓒ **12/426-5000;** www.krugerpark.com), is bigger than some nations. Lodges in the camps tend to be luxurious, but with a natural "bush" feel. **Dulini Lodge,** Sabi Sands Wildertuin, Skukuza (**$$$; ⓒ 11/784-6830;** www.dulini.com; rates include 3 meals a day, safari activities, house wines, and local spirits), is a lodge in the **Sabi Sand Game Reserve** (www.sabisand. co.za), a private reserve bordering Kruger Park. The lions here can roar so loudly it seems as though they are lying on your doormat. Have no fear—you can snuggle up, safe and sound in your substantial cottage with elevated

MOST ROMANTIC RESTAURANTS

Emily's Restaurant and Cooking School $ AMERICAN   Our favorite city restaurant in South Africa (we could eat here every night) is across a small, transcendent bridge on the wharf, not far from the Victoria and Alfred Hotel. The food is modern and tasty, and the service warm and reliable.

55 Kloof Street Gardens. ⓒ **21/424-0882** or 21/761-7631. www.emily-s.com.

Koi $ CONTEMPORARY ASIAN   Commanding a breathtaking position in Bantry Bay, the windows at this restaurant unfold to help you experience the seaside atmosphere more intimately. The incredible view and atmosphere is matched by excellent service and dependably good food. Romance, cuisine, and nature all fit together beautifully.

In the Ambassador Hotel, 34 Victoria Rd. ⓒ **21/439-7258.**

CAPE TOWN BY NIGHT

There are wonderful and safe places to go at night in Cape Town (but be careful of petty crime in the street). We've had a peak moment dancing on tables at **Mama Africa's,** 178 Long St. (ⓒ **21/424-8634;** www.mamaafricarestaurant.co.za), plunge pool. &Beyond has two fantastic, but very expensive camps in Kruger, **Exeter River Lodge,** with modern and sophisticated villas (**$$$**; ⓒ **11/809-4313**; www.andbeyond.com) and the lavish **Leadwood Lodge ($$$)**, which has only six villas and a communal dinner table.

The camps all offer romantic touches: surprise candlelit dinners in your room; baths drawn and covered with rose petals; or singing and dancing by the staff at feast dinners lit by the fire inside the Boma (an outdoor enclosure that keeps you safe from predators).

One way to make safaris more affordable is to join a group tour. The best variety and prices that we have seen for trips all over Africa can be found at **Grand Circle Travel** (www.gct.com). For example, Kruger and other places for R$2,295 for 19 days including meals, excluding airfare; for a little more money, you can join a much smaller group—never more than 10–16 people—with its sister agency **Overseas Adventure Travel** (www.oattravel.com).

Or check out the safaris offered by Lion World Travel (www.lion worldtravel), a company run by South African ex-pats. It's usually the price leader when it comes to affordable safaris. A final suggestion: Consult with Adventure Center (www.adventurecenter.com), which serves as a clearinghouse for smaller (but vetted) safari and adventure tour companies, many of which are run by Brits, Aussies, and South Africans.

while members of a band, mixing African and rock and roll music, played their hearts out on a rotating stage.

MARRAKECH
Oasis Getaway in the Maghreb

Marrakech has the perfect ambience for exotic romance: With the high Atlas Mountains as its distant backdrop, the city is a riot of colored tiles, intricate and abundant gardens, tribal rugs, ornate palaces, and mysterious labyrinthine streets. The Old City has a wealth of exotic goods to buy and appetizing foods you will eat with your hands (and if that's not sexy, I don't know what is). Most visitors find themselves returning over and over to the central square, Jemaa el Fna, the famous gateway to vast *souks* (outdoor markets). Here entrepreneurial retailers set up their food and craft tents beside the covered *souks* that radiate off the square. Add snake charmers, herbalists, henna hand-painters, acrobats, fortune-tellers, and jugglers to the tableau, and you get a sense of the wild commotion that sparks the pulse of Marrakech—and may spark yours, too.

In a country of artists and artisans, fancy and humble shops alike offer enticing merchandise. Brace yourself for haggling (while being served mint tea, a civilizing touch). You'll want to explore the **Souk Semmarine,** the main shopping avenue for textiles, carpets, and souvenirs. The carpet places here are sumptuous, with stacks of vibrant tribal and other Oriental rugs, couches, and inlaid tables. **La Porte d'Or,** 115 Souk Semmarine (℗ **212/0524-445454**), in particular, is a respected store; **Mustapha Blaoui,** 142-144 Bab Doukkala (℗ **212/0524-385240**) is another good choice. Visit the **Place des Ferblantiers,** rue de Berrima, where tinsmiths make filigree lanterns, and wander among the **Kasbah's Spice Souk** where you can get deals on saffron and **Rahba Kedima** for Berber whiskey (aka mint tea). Or just enjoy being lost and let Marrakech's winding alleys and streets lead the way to new discoveries.

KEY ATTRACTIONS

Hamams   Rejuvenate with steam and a massage in a domed hamam. These are wonderful experiences to be had alone, as none of the Old City's hamams are co-ed. Think of the stories you'll have to tell each other! The ritual: You enter the steam room in hamam attire (underpants and a towel), find an empty bucket and scoop, sit down, and as you begin to sweat, douse yourself alternately with hot and cold water from a communal tap. The **Medina Spa,** Quartier Kennaria Derb Zaari, No. 27 (℗ **212/0524-385059**; www.medina-spa-marrakech.com; 150dh), is a newer hamam with a more luxurious and modern approach. It has two steam areas, eight private massage rooms, a beauty treatment room, and a post-steam room for unwinding. You can head up to the roof for a Jacuzzi and a place to sun. The elegant **Les Secrets Hammam & Spa,** 62 rue de la Liberte, Gueliz (℗ **212/0524-434848**; 60dh–1,400dh), offers an assortment of modern and ancient massages, beauty treatments, body wraps, and more.

Majorelle Garden   Begun in the 1920s, this carefully planned tropical wonderland on rue Yves Saint Laurent (℗ **212/0524-301894**; www.jardin marjorelle.com; museum 25dh; garden 50dh) has passed through the hands of the rich and famous; in fact its savior was Yves St. Laurent, who rescued it from development and donated objects of beauty to the **Musée de Marrakech,** Place Ben Youssef (℗ **212/0524-441893**; www.museedemarrakech. ma; admission 30dh), next door.

Mosques & Palaces   Marrakech's most prominent landmark is **Koutoubia Mosque,** a towering minaret just west of Djemaa el Fna, visible for miles in all directions. The romance comes in when it's illuminated by floodlights at night. To be further awestruck, visit the 16th-century **Koranic Ben Youssef Medersa,** Kaat Benahid (℗ **212/6613-50878**; www.medersa-ben-youssef. com; admission 60dh). One of Marrakech's most important Islamic monuments, it is also an extraordinarily peaceful place that can transport you to another era. Similarly, the sultan's splendor at **Bahia Palace**, 5,6 Derb El Arsa Riad Zitoun Jdid (℡ **212/0524-389615**; www.gharnata.com), flashes back to an age of pashas and concubines with exquisite examples of Moroccan carving and decoration.

Ouarzazate   The scenic four-hour drive from Marrakech to this mountain desert tourist town ascends the Atlas Mountains to a windy, foggy pass and then descends into another world. The tableau of red mountains, traditional Berber dwellings, and the village of Ouarzazate, location for "Lawrence of Arabia," combine for a romantic image from the past.

To overnight in Ouarzazate, try the **Amanjena,** Route de Ouarzazate, Kilometer 12 (**$$$**; ℡ **0212/5243-99000**; www.amanresorts.com), another fine creation of the dependable Aman luxury hotel brand. This one is a fantastic Moorish-themed riff on palace life and the royal treatment. A half hour beyond Ouarzazate in Skoura is **Dar Ahlam** (**$$$**; ℡ **800/735-2478** in the United States or Canada or 0212/5248-52239; www.darahlam.com), an updated adobe palace. Surprises are on the menu at this luxurious and mysterious resort. Dinner locations are not known in advance and change regularly. Candles and rose petals create sudden romantic dining locations beside the pool or in the gardens or special salons.

Ourika Valley   Not everyone has the time or stamina to climb Mt. Toubkal, the tallest peak in North Africa—but plenty of other sights make good day trips. Especially in the torrid summer, driving up to the **Ourika Valley** in the Atlas Mountains can be a great escape. Check out the ski resort, **Oukaïmeden** for swell spring and summer hiking just 90 minutes from Marrakech, and the village of **Setti Fatma** with its seven waterfalls.

HOTELS WITH HEART

Dar Ayniwen $$$ It's only a 10-minute ride from Djemaa el Fna, but Dar Ayniwen feels like a luxurious Moorish villa in an oasis. Sit by your fireplace in your lavish suite, or have an in-room massage or perhaps transfer to the more exotic hamam or be pampered poolside.

Tafrata–Palmeraie de Marrakech. ℡ **0212/5243-29684.** www.dar-ayniwen.com.

Dar Kantzaro $ This elegant two-story guesthouse in the Palmeraie sits amid olive groves at the end of a long driveway, lit by candles at night. Spacious public rooms radiate from a glorious marble central patio. The luxuriousness continues in the dining room, with its inlaid mother-of-pearl decor and in several stylish salons. Up the marble and cedar staircase are two suites with private terraces and views of the Atlas Mountains. The three double rooms and one-bedroom house in the garden also have private terraces. The swimming pool and hamam gives a taste of spa luxury.

Route de Fès, Km 10. ℡ **0212/5243-28912.** www.darkantzaro.com.

Riad Kniza $$ This 18th-century *riad* (courtyard home) has been in the same family for almost 200 years. Its traditional architecture and Moroccan furnishings create a gracious feel that is reinforced by the friendly and attentive service. The two-story residence surrounds two garden courtyards, one with a hamam and swimming pool. Off the other are common rooms, furnished in Oriental antiques and each with a fireplace. The charming rooms and suites combine traditional style and modern conveniences. The large roof terrace, with sun canopies and lounges, is a romantic place to share breakfast or dinner by candlelight.

34 Derb l'Hotel, Bab Doukala. ℂ **212/0524-376942.** www.riadkniza.com.

MOST ROMANTIC RESTAURANTS

Dar Yacout $$$ NORTH AFRICAN   The shimmering candlelit rooms, cut-metal lanterns, and mosaics reference Morocco, but this splurge restaurant has a modern flamboyance all its own. It's untraditional, but it works. It is hard to get a reservation, so you might want to book before you leave home.

79 rue Sidi Ahmed Soussi. ℂ **212/0524-382929.**

Ksar Char-Bagh $$$ FRENCH   In the lush Palmeraie neighborhood on the outskirts of Marrakech, this restaurant is in a replica of a Kasbah hotel and fortress. It is worth seeing and particularly worth dining on its Mediterranean and North African specialties. Don't miss the tagine of lamb and apricots or the dessert soufflé.

Palmeraie de Marrakech. ℂ **800/735-2478** in the United States or Canada or 212/0524-329244. www.ksarcharbagh.com.

Terrasses des Epices $ EUROPEAN/MOROCCAN   This inexpensive but atmospheric rooftop escape offers traditional food as well as international offerings. *Note:* No alcohol or credit cards.

15, souk Cherifia. Sidi Abdelaziz. ℂ **212/0524-375904.** www.terrassedesepices.com.

MARRAKECH BY NIGHT

Le Bar Churchill   This is just what it should be: old world clubby, with lots of leather chairs and animal skins. It may be a touch politically incorrect now, but in Winston Churchill's time animal skins were the height of class. Churchill and Franklin D. Roosevelt stayed at the La Mamounia Hotel during World War II. In the La Mamounia Hotel, Avenue Bab Jdid. ℂ **212/0524-388600.** www.mamounia.com.

Le Comptoir Darna   Enjoy superb belly-dancing while dining on good French-Moroccan food. This show is a little wild and definitely fun to watch. It is also a pretty sexy place: The lighting is intentionally dim from aromatic candles and Moroccan lamps theatrically placed for romantic effect. You can sit at low tables under the Berber tent or inside the charcoal-colored dining room. For a more casual evening, lounge in the lovely little garden. A broad staircase leads up to the bar, all decked out in harem-chic veils, where DJs play dance music. Avenue Echouada. ℂ **212/0524-437702.** www.comptoirdarna.com.

Palais Soleiman   This is a romantic rendition of a 19th-century palace at moderate prices. The food is good enough, but you are here for the concerts and music in the huge palace courtyard. Dar Layadi, Kaa machraa. ℂ **212/0524-378962.** www.palais-soleiman.com.

RIO DE JANEIRO
Celebrating Life Together

Rio will dazzle you with its natural assets—and that includes the "assets" the locals like to show off in their bathing suits. With sun-kissed complexions, men as well as women, young and old, all wear bathing suits that could be described as itsy bitsy—but that's still an understatement. The action on the famous beaches of **Ipanema** and **Copacabana** is extraordinary. Whether you're watching incredibly fit men play beach volleyball or admiring the women strutting their stuff along the sand, sexuality and fun are the order of the day. Small spontaneous parties form at various parts of the beach during the day, then in the late evening (nothing starts before 10pm or so), the party moves on to crowded restaurants, sidewalk cafes, and hot nightclubs with live music and shows. If you want to dance the night away in an uninhibited fashion, this is your destination.

But even if you don't stay up until the dawn, there is the pleasure of watching the people who do, seeing the verve of their colorful shirts and skirts, the omnipresent vendors selling exotic fruits and juices, and most of all feeling the warmth and energy of the Brazilian people.

This city wedged between mountains is as eye-popping as its people. Great views are everywhere: whether you look out from the 130-foot tall statue of **Christ the Redeemer** (named one of the wonders of the world and a World Heritage site in 2007) or hop the cable car up, up, up to **Sugar Loaf Peak** to watch the sunset. It's hard not to fall in love with Rio—and to fall more deeply in love with your partner when you're there.

KEY ATTRACTIONS

From on High   Travel up through the Tijuca Rain Forest to **Corcovado Peak** and the iconic **Christ the Redeemer** statue at the top for the best view of Rio. Go by bus, taxi, car, or train (which ascend every 30 minutes), but don't go up too late because tourists can be a target for pickpockets, especially after dark. Another option: After seeing famed **Sugar Loaf Mountain** from every angle the city offers, take the cable car to the peak (www.bondinho.com. br; ✆ **021/2546-8400; R62**). It leaves every half hour from 8am to 10pm and offers a 360-degree view of Rio along the way.

Samba School   All that fancy dancing you see at Carnaval takes nearly a year of practice. Many neighborhoods have samba schools where you can watch local teams rehearse for the big event. If you feel inspired to try some of those sexy, swaying moves yourself, we think the best place is **Carioca da Gema** (see "Rio by Night," below), which is all samba, all the time.

Soccer   Soccer—err, sorry—*fútbol* is the national religion. You can worship with the passionate fans waving their giant flags and playing noisy percussion instruments (if you're lucky you'll be there during a local Flamengo

carnaval IN RIO

People party like there's no tomorrow during Carnaval (Mardi Gras) in Rio. The costumes are outrageous (and skimpy), dancing is frenzied, and the drinking is out of control. The party is during the four days before Ash Wednesday. The city stops and everyone, regardless of age, celebrates together, in clubs and on the streets. You'd better like crowds if you go—a more vivid spectacle probably doesn't exist. Carnaval is during the height of the very hot Brazilian summer, so prepare to sweat. Seeing the many samba schools compete on Sunday and Monday from 9pm to dawn at the **Sambadromo,** Rua Marquês de Sapucaí (℃ **021/2976-7310;** www. sambadrome.com) is well worth the price of tickets (only about $50). They sell out quickly, so be sure you arrange tickets through your hotel long before your trip.

Each neighborhood's samba school has between 3,000 to 5,000 dancers and will be judged on its theme, costumes, songs, harmony, percussion band, floats, flags, and props. Each school's cast breaks down into several clusters of about 200 dancers, each wearing the same distinctive and imaginative plumed costume, dancing between the school's colorful floats bedecked with male and female beauties, wearing mostly body paint and glitter. If you're brave and willing to fork out between $300 to $700 for a costume, you can actually join one of the schools in the parade. Here's just one of the websites where you can join in the fun: www.rio-carnival.net.

Tip: **BACC Travel** (℃ **800/ BACC-RIO**) is a travel consolidator that offers discounted tickets on major airlines from numerous U.S. cities; it can arrange Carnaval packages that include hotel and parade tickets. The company recommends you do this by September for the best prices.

vs. Fluminense game—think "poor" vs. "rich"). Leave your valuables at the hotel and ask the concierge how to use public transportation to get to humongous **Maracanã Stadium,** Rua Professor Eurico Rabelo (www.maracana. com), one of the largest in the world. A moat surrounds the field to protect players and referees from potentially angry fans. Games played in the smaller and closer **Sao Januario,** Rua General Almério de Moura (℃ **021/2176-7373**) are also fun; players who merge samba rhythm with their soccer moves give quite a show.

HOTELS WITH HEART

Copacabana Palace $$$ This very famous hotel has been around a very long time—it used to be the place where the movie stars stayed in the 1940s—and still retains its glamor. The spa is elaborate as are the rooms. It is worth asking for a room with a view here, as the views are killer. The hotel has the biggest pool in town. Do be careful in the neighborhood though—pickpockets know this is tourist central.

Avenida Atlântica 1702. ℭ **800/237-1236** in the United States and Canada or 021/2548-7070. www.copacabanapalace.com.br.

Hotel Fasano $$$ This is a slick and stylish Philippe Starck beach hotel in Ipanema with an amazing rooftop infinity pool and a wonderful, close-up view of the ocean. If you want to be among the beautiful people, this is it.

Avenida Vieira Souto, 80 Ipanema. ℭ **800/745-8883** in the United States and Canada or 021/3202-4000. www.lhw.com.

Hotel Gavea Tropica $ A small 6-suite hotel in the hills that gives you a fabulous view of Christ the Redeemer and Sugar Loaf, this boutique hotel couldn't be any more romantic. Rooms are painted in yellows and golds and many have four-poster beds. The balconies beckon with their views, and the beds bring you back at night when the city lights up beyond you. All this and a spa, pool, and sweet place to eat, too (a delicious breakfast comes with the room).

Rua Sergio Porto 85. ℭ **800/260 2700** in the United States. http://gaveatropical. com. Rates include breakfast.

MOST ROMANTIC RESTAURANTS

Brazil has a cuisine all its own. *Feijoada,* a kind of a slow-cooked spiced cassoulet of rice and black beans with chunks of pork, is the national dish. For drinks, order a *caipirinha* cocktail, made of lime and *cachaça*—a distilled sugar cane juice liquor—which can get you drunk remarkably quickly. Brazil is well known for its barbeque, and you can sample it at most restaurants and small cafes, but it is best experienced in a genuine *churrascaria* where waiters parade by your tables with skewers of various meats, slicing off cuts for your plate until you just can't eat any more.

Casa da Feijoada $ BRAZILIAN   The Brazilian tradition is to serve a full *feijoada* only on Saturday, though this place serves it every day. Start with a *batida de limão* (lime cocktail) then bring on the main dish, made with all kinds of meats, mostly pork. Side dishes include white rice, *farofa* (roasted manioc flour), and the traditional orange slices. You add malagueta peppers to make it as spicy as you'd like—have a Brazilian beer handy if you underestimate the heat.

Rua Prudente de Moraes 10 Ipanema. ℭ **021/2523-4994.** www.cozinhatipica. com.br.

Churrascaria Carretão $$ CHURRASCARIA   With locations in both Rio and Ipanema, this outfit provides you with a *churrascaria* meal in a festive, but not fancy, atmosphere at reasonable prices. Ask your concierge to find out which location is closest to your hotel.

Siqueira Campos Street, 23, Copacabana. ℭ **21/2236-3435** or Visconde de Pirajá Street, 112, Ipanema. 21/2267-3965. www.carretaochurrascaria.com.br.

Confeitaria Columbo $ TEA ROOM   With a lovely stained-glass dome and Belgian framed mirrors, this romantic Victorian tearoom looks much like it did when it opened in 1894. You can buy delicious sweets at a front counter, or go inside for tea, sandwiches, and sweets served on fine china in the elegant tearoom. On Saturdays the upstairs dining room serves a full *feijoada*. A location serving a slightly smaller menu but with fabulous ocean views is inside the Forte Copacabana, Praça Coronel Eugênio Franco 1 (✆ **021/2521-1032;** www.fortedecopacabana.com), a military fort turned into a cultural center.

Rua Gonçalves Dias 32. ✆ **021/2505-1500**. www.confeitariacolombo.com.br.

Gero $ ITALIAN   You'll watch the beautiful people and eat authentic Italian food in sophisticated style here. Specialties include rack of lamb and *osso buco*. Avoid the overpriced Brazilian wines in favor of the mid-priced Chilean and Argentine vintages.

Rua Aníbal de Mendonça 157 Ipanema. ✆ **021/2239-8158.** www.fasano.com.br.

Restaurante Gabbiano Al Mare $$ INTERNATIONAL   This restaurant overlooks the glorious beach that introduced topless sunbathing to the Americas. It serves a wide range of memorable Brazilian and international cuisine a la carte for lunch and dinner.

In the Sol Ipanema Hotel, Avenida Vieira Souto 320. ✆ **021/2521-6464** or 021/2525-2020. www.solipanema.com.br.

RIO DE JANEIRO BY NIGHT

Rio more than makes up for all of the destinations in this book that have no nightlife. This is the capital of sybaritic living. Do be careful, though. Rio has a lot of petty crime and some rough neighborhoods. Know where you are going and don't wear your jewels (even your pretend ones).

Beach Area Clubs   The most affluent area of Rio, Leblon has the hip, stylish **Black Bar,** Av. General San Martin 1219 (✆ **021/3079-9581**; www.blackbarleblon.com.br) for live Latin sounds. If you're a jazz aficionado, you know Rio is the place to hear world-class Latin jazz and Bossa Nova. For the latter, go to the source: **Garota Ipanema,** Rua Vinicius de Morais 49 (✆ **021/2523-3787;** www.bargarotadeipanema.com; main courses R49–R66), where the song "Girl from Ipanema" was written, as they proudly tell you all over the walls. For smooth jazz and great food in an intimate Ipanema Beach setting, try **Lounge Boox Ipanema,** Rua Barão da Torre 368 (✆ **021/2522-3730;** lounge only R66.50 for women; R133 for men).

Lapa   A historic area full of music and dance clubs, Lapa's key landmark is an 18th-century aqueduct. Sure, there are noisy American style clubs here with deafening music, but there are also intimate places where you can hear touchingly romantic guitar music. Try **Rio Scenarium,** Rua do Lavradio 20 (✆ *021/3147-9000;* www.rioscenarium.com.br; snacks R19–R45), a samba club and restaurant. **Carioca da Gema,** Avenida Mem de Sá 79 (✆ **021/2221-0043;** barcariocadagema.com.br; cover R21–R25), is the most famous Lapa club that makes you feel like you're at Carnaval any time of year with authentic bands and floor shows.

SYDNEY
Sun-kissed Romance

This is a gorgeous city, and almost everyone knows its iconic topography, at least from photos: the Opera House that looks like it can take wing at any minute, the Harbor Bridge span that people climb almost every day (as a doable but challenging adventure), and the beaches that seem as if San Francisco and Miami had a lovechild.

Sydney's personality is bright, sexy, and raucous, yet casual, comfortable, and easy going. It is in harmony with beauty and nature, and almost every short excursion offers up something amazing to see. Even a trip to the **Sydney Zoo,** Bradleys Head Rd. (© **02/9969 2777;** http://taronga.org.au/taronga-zoo; admission A$44), a short ferry ride from Circular Quai at Wharf Four, will have you looking back on the dominating spectacle of the Opera House.

Sydney's bouncy tone sets the romantic mood, and its variety—gorgeous harbor sunsets, world-class sophistication in the arts, and glorious natural getaways—make Sydney a place for unbridled discovery.

KEY ATTRACTIONS
Darling Harbour hosts Sydney's main tourist center and a waterfront promenade with museums, shops, and exhibitions, but we most enjoy the funky restaurants of Cockle Bay Wharf and King Street Wharf.

Beach Bumming **Bondi Beach** (www.bondivillage.com) remains a model for urban beaches, with its wide sweeping shore, interesting restaurants and bars, and plenty of attitude and beautiful bodies. Quieter beaches are in outlying areas, like **Tamarama** with its wild surf, and the picturesque **Bronte Beach.** A view-rich elevated walk, popular with locals, takes you between the cliffs from Bondi to Bronte.

Bike Rides Rent bikes (by the hour or day) on Sunday morning when traffic is light and pedal together all over the city. From The Rocks area (Sydney's original central city), cross the bridge for breakfast at a sidewalk table at **Garfish,** 2/21 Broughton St. Kirribilli NSW 2061 (**$;** © **02/9922 4322;** http://garfish.com.au). Afterward, follow the coast at your leisure or cruise the urban throughways.

Boat Tours Hop on a passenger ferry at Circular Quay for a cheap and absolutely splendid way to understand how the city is situated; fare is A$5.80 per adult. For a thrill, **Harbour Jet** (© **1300/887 373** or 02/9212 3555; www.harbourjet.com) offers 35-, 50-, and 80-minute jet-blast adventures, starting at A$80 for an adult.

Harbor Bridge Climbs Want to do something together that's a little demanding and a lot of fun? Climbing the Sydney Harbor Bridge might qualify. (Queasy about heights? Guides here are trained to help you enjoy the climb.) The 134m (440-ft.) ascent typically takes 3½ hours to the top, and the tour vendor provides the guide, safety wear and equipment, and a photo of you at the top. **BridgeClimb,** 3 Cumberland St., The Rocks (© **02/8274 7777;** www.bridgeclimb.com) offers a variety of options. The adult fee is A$235 to A$348 and a little higher at peak times after Christmas through early January. Every 10 minutes, small groups leave from the **Sydney Harbour Bridge Visitor Centre.** In your "bridge suit" harnessed to a line, you may not bring anything with you—not even your camera. Catch the last daylight tour, and you'll be at the summit for a romantic sunset and descend as the city lights come on all around you.

Wharf Outing A variety of amusements await you at wharf after wharf. At the **Jones Bay Wharf,** just beyond the Harbor Bridge, you can fantasize about the super-yachts and eyeball the magnificent views of the city skyline and bridge. A good place to do that is the fabulous **Flying Fish Restaurant,** 19-21 Pirrama Rd., Pyrmont ($$$; © **02/9518-6677;** http://flyingfish.com.au). In an exuberant airy space on Pier 21, it serves sophisticated seafood. This wharf is a good starting point for cruising the shops at **Darling Harbour** (© **02/9240 8500;** www.darlingharbour.com) or **Pyrmont Village's** (http://pyrmontvillage.com.au) cafes, studios, and art galleries.

Wine Excursions & Tastings Two hours from Sydney, **Hunter Valley** invites comparisons to the best winelands of the world. The area is well known for its Shiraz, Chardonnay, and Semillion grapes and wines. Multiple tasting rooms are in and around **Pokolbin** (for example, the well-reviewed Tower Estate, Brokenwood, Capercaillie, and Rothbury Estate are in beautiful eucalyptus flatlands backed up by the Brokenback Mountains). For a really romantic excursion, reserve ahead and overnight at the exquisite **Tower Lodge,** 6 Halls Rd., Pokolbin ($$$; © **02/4948 7022**; www.towerlodge.com. au). The carved doors at the entrance prepare you for a heady experience: enormous public rooms and extravagant bedrooms with high ceilings, and touches of French, Malaysian, and Moroccan design. **Robert's Circa 1876,** 64 Halls Rd., Pokolbin ($$; © **02/4998 7330;** http://robertscirca1876.com) restaurant offers a pretty garden, a romantic dining room with a French feel, and three cozy private rooms that can be requested for special evenings.

HOTELS WITH HEART

Establishment Hotel $$$ A very cool hotel with a split personality. Some rooms are sleek and modern with black floorboards and flashes of color; others are bathed in pastels. All bathrooms are large with marble or bluestone tubs. A couple of trendy bars, and the popular **Tank** nightclub are fun, in addition to the fine restaurant, **Est.** The building is a hip translation of an historic Sydney warehouse.

5 Bridge Lane. © **02/9240 3100.** www.merivale.com.

Pullman Quay $$$ With luxurious views of The Rocks, the bridge, and harbor, this hotel is a few doors away from the Opera House. Best thing: You can sit outside on your terrace and watch the ferries and cruise ships come and go. The view's not bad from the indoor pool and spa either.

61 Macquarie St. © **02/9256 4000**. www.pullmanquaygrandsydneyharbour.com.

Regents Court $ With cool design touches and elegant studios, this moderately priced boutique hotel lies in Potts Point, a great spot for exploring good restaurants, bars, and Sydney's club scene. Reminiscent of New York brownstone buildings, it has a lovely rooftop garden for lingering together to view the world from on high.

18 Springfield Ave., Potts Point. © **02/9331 2099.** www.8hotels.com/Sydney.

Shangri-La Hotel $$ On the 20th floor or above, large windows show off one of the greatest views of the harbor without breaking your budget—a view repeated in many of the rooms. A peaceful Asian theme suffuses this conveniently located hotel complete with a spa, sundeck, pool, and gym.

176 Cumberland Street, The Rocks. © **866/565-5050** or 02/9250 6000. www.shangri-la.com.

MOST ROMANTIC RESTAURANTS

Aria $$$ MODERN AUSTRALIAN   With huge windows and views of the bridge and Opera House, the elegant Aria is arguably the best situated restaurant in the city. Dining here, you'll feel like Sydney has been laid out at your feet, a gift just for you and your honey.

19/1 Macquarie St. © **02-9240-2255.** www.ariarestaurant.com.

Icebergs $$ MEDITERRANEAN   This old swim club complex that overlooks Bondi Beach is now a haven of relaxed elegance. Floor-to-ceiling windows, a perfect clifftop setting, and a bar view that spans beach and water, near and far? Bottom line: In a city of fabulous views, this one is probably the best.

One Notts Avenue, Bondi Beach. © **02/9365 9000.** www.idrb.com.

Takumi $ SUSHI   With his unmistakeable grin, Tokyo-born Papa San (Hatsushiro Muraoka) is the near-cult personality behind Takumi, one of the best sushi restaurants in Cape Town, and certainly one of the better values. He'll make your feel coddled, as will the food: ultra-fresh, rather addictive, and often somewhat experimental sushi, served in robust portions. *Note:* No children under 10 are allowed, which keeps the atmosphere sophisticated and adult.

3 Park Road. © **27 21 424 8879.** www.takumi.co.za

SYDNEY BY NIGHT

Bluesalt Bar   Passion is made of moments, and this is the kind of place that makes moments. Gazing upon the panorama, you can sip your drinks or nibble on a light meal (or an ear); you'll find moments to savor here. At the Crowne Plaza Coogee Beach Hotel, 242 Arden St., Coogee. © **02/9315-7600** or 02/9315-9130. www.crowneplazacoogee.com.au.

St. George Open Air Cinema   This outdoor movie theater has a truly romantic setting overlooking the harbor. The Opera House and Harbor Bridge are across the water, but it's also worth going just to see the three-story high screen rise silently from the ocean. The movies tend to be from independent producers plus some blockbusters. Fleet Steps, Mrs. Macquaries Point. www. stgeorgeopenair.com.au. A$31–A$33, plus a small booking fee.

Natural Romance

6 Earthy Delights: U.S.
7 Earthy Delights: Canada & Mexico
8 Earthy Delights: Europe

EARTHY DELIGHTS: U.S.

I f your heart grows warmer when you are surrounded by the majesty of natural wonders, then this chapter is for you. Many feel that life gets put in proportion when they see magnificent settings like the Tetons, Banff, Uluru in Australia, or Sedona's red rocks. They are then more likely to bring that sense of humility, gratitude, and awe back to their partner to create a beautiful state of being together. It's easier to get over past issues or create new beginnings looking at the glory that is this Earth we live on. Seeing the best of these wonders, indeed, brings out the best of what is within us for each other.

ASPEN, COLORADO
Rocky Mountain Highs

The magnificence of the U.S. Rocky Mountains is something no true romantic should miss, and their blessings are vast in Colorado. We could mention many areas, but for the overall provision of year-round gorgeous scenery and romantic things to do, why not do what the "beautiful people" do? Go to Aspen for outdoor and indoor fun and dreamy possibilities. From Denver, you can fly there or drive the 4 hours. If you're driving at ski season, interesting detours pop up along the way.

Aspen is popular in every season, and it's not your cheapest romantic getaway, but if you plan your visit for late fall (before ski season) or early spring (before the summer sports take hold), you can get some real deals. Renting in Snowmass Village rather than Aspen also can bring costs way down.

KEY ATTRACTIONS (WINTER)
Dog Sledding On first blush, this might not sound romantic, but it is—especially at twilight. Dinner trips offered through Krabloonik restaurant (see later listing), start late in the afternoon to catch the falling sun. You cuddle up on the sled, and the dogs (a 10-dog sled team), thrilled to be going out on a run, connect you to this pristine environment in a new way. After your adventure, you are taken to a private, log cabin dining room for a four-course

dinner. The price for the 90-minute sled ride in Snowmass backcountry plus dinner is $340 dollars ($285 for lunch) per person. For more information, call © 970/923-3953 or visit www.krabloonik.com.

Skiing   This is the main deal here. Powder breeds passion among skiers—and there is plenty of both in Aspen. Make a date to ride the ski lift together, and you'll have privacy and great views! Of the four mountains here, Aspen is the main one, and since one company, **Aspen Snowmass** (© 800/525-6200; www.aspensnowmass.com), manages all of them, a single lift ticket admits you to all four. Aspen's slopes range from hair-raising runs to Buttermilk, a mellow ride for beginners and tentative intermediates. **Snowmass**, a very large resort with a renowned ski school, is a kinder, gentler mountain with many easy and intermediate runs but just enough really challenging slopes, including Hanging Valley Wall, the steepest in the whole area. **Aspen Highlands** goes from easy to extreme, plus some particularly beautiful views. **Aspen Mountain** is right downtown, but just because it is easy to get to doesn't make it easy. The mountain has 23 double diamond runs and a significant proportion is un-groomed. Expert skiers love it, but less experienced people should go to the other slopes.

Cross-country skiing is a beautiful way to experience Mother Nature together. With more than 60 miles of free cross-country and snowshoe trails that connect Aspen, Snowmass, and Basalt, both expert and novice skiers will be satisfied. For details, contact the **Aspen Cross Country Center,** 39551 W. Hwy. 82, (© 970/925-2145; www.utemountaineer.com), or **Snowmass Cross Country Center,** 0446 Clubhouse Drive, Snowmass Village (© 970/923-5700; www.utemountaineer.com).

Spas   The two most popular après-ski activities are soaking your weary body in a hot tub and then getting someone to pound your aching flesh back to normal or better. (Drinking is right up there with them; we will get to that later). In a town filled with fine spa services, we like **Remède Spa** at the St. Regis Aspen Resort (© 970/429-9038; www.stregisaspen.com), **Aspen Club Spa** (© 970/925-8900; www.aspenclub.com), and **The Spa at Viceroy**, Snowmass (© 970/923-8007; www.viceroyhotels.com).

KEY ATTRACTIONS (SUMMER)

Biking   Aspen is etched with wonderful bike trails. An easy one (if you cycle one-way) is the **Rio Grande Trail** that begins in Aspen, crosses babbling brooks and follows a river on a fairly flat trail that, ever so slightly, but irreversibly, goes downhill. After seven lovely miles, you arrive at Woody Creek and the **Woody Creek Tavern** (© 970/923-4585; www.woodycreek tavern.com), where you and everyone else stops for lunch or a beer. It's an authentic hang out and a lot of fun. Plus, there is taxi service there that can stow your bikes if you want to cab it back rather than do the uphill return ride. Rent your bikes downtown from one of Aspen's many bike shops.

Festivals   Every season in Aspen has a festival worth planning for. June is **jazz festival** month (© 970/920-4996; www.jazzaspensnowmass.org), with fantastic music every day by top musicians in the shadow of the mountain. The **Aspen Music Festival** (© **970/925-9042;** aspenmusicfestival.com) features international classical stars like Yo Yo Ma. The music is everywhere: outdoors at night, at the **Victorian Opera House,** at the library, and also in the form of free classes and lectures. *A tip:* Bring a picnic to the evening concerts at the music festival campus. Paid seats are in the tent, but you can hear it all on the lawn for free with your bottle of wine, loaf of bread, hunk of cheese, and each other. June also ushers in "Food & Wine" magazine's **Classic in Aspen** (© **877-900-WINE** [9463]; www.foodandwine.com/classic), which brings in the industry superstars. For some mental stimulation, find out what the **Aspen Institute** (© **970/925-7010;** www.aspeninstitute.org) has on deck; world-class speakers and events are slated year-round.

Horseback Riding   Even if riding isn't your thing, this country is so lovely it deserves to be seen slowly and astride a horse. Some stables will arrange a trip with gourmet meals and even Western poetry readings or sing-alongs. (Bonus or a deal breaker? You decide.) Riding among the peaks and wildflowers can be breathtaking and romantic, and most outfitters have mild horses that are, as they say, "dead broke." If you haven't ridden or haven't ridden in a long time, opt for the shorter 2-hour ride. Otherwise you might be hurting later in the wrong places—which is decidedly unromantic. **Aspen Wilderness Outfitters** (© **970/928/0723;** www.aspenwilderness.com) can get you in the saddle.

River Running   By kayak or paddleboard, you can spend an exciting day on the Roaring Fork, the Arkansas, or the Colorado rivers; your experience will depend on the season. You will get plenty of an adrenaline rush from these class 3 rivers, and thrills are good for romance—but terror is not! Check with an outfitter for an appropriate adventure: **Blazing Adventures** (© **800/ 282-7238;** www.blazingadventures.com) or **Up tha Creek Expeditions** (© **877/ 982-7335;** www.upthacreek.com).

A SIDE TRIP FROM ASPEN

If possible, we suggest you work a day or two into your trip to visit **Vail** and **Beaver Creek,** both under a 2-hour drive from Aspen and about a 15-minute drive from each other. The stunning **Ritz Carlton at Bachelor Gulch,** 0130 Daybreak Ridge, Avon (**$$$;** © **970/748-6200;** www.ritzcarlton.com), here is modeled after the grand Western lodges we profile elsewhere in this book and offers an outstanding spa and the Rockies edition of **Wolfgang Puck's Spago.** Nearby, the luxurious **Lodge and Spa at the Cordillera,** 2205 Cordillera Way, Edwards (**$$;** © **800/877-3529;** www.cordilleralodge.com), has great couples activities such as snowshoeing, sleigh rides (cuddled together sipping hot chocolate, or something stronger) and miles of groomed cross-country trails through woods. In summer, try horseback riding or the celebrated golf course.

HOTELS WITH HEART

The Hotel Jerome $$$

This historic 19th-century hotel is very expensive, but there are some deals to be had in summer. The property has been totally remodeled but there is some controversy about whether or not it maintains its luxe Western personality. There's a big spa onsite, and some rooms are very luxurious—with marble tubs for two—while other rooms are just cute and comfortable, but none is less than 500 square feet. You are well located here.

330 E. Main St. ✆ **855/331-7213.** http://hoteljerome.com.

Hotel Lenado $$

Tucked away from the hustle, bustle, and glitz in a quiet neighborhood, the Hotel Lenado is also not going to induce sticker shock; the rates are quite reasonable for Aspen (and they include a full breakfast). The lodging melds the intimacy and style of a boutique hotel with the comfort and service of a B&B, and the results are inviting. Accommodations are bright and cheery, with light woods and checkered comforters, including the larger Smuggler rooms and the slightly smaller Larkspur rooms. The vibe is sociable, and the rooftop hot tub is one of the best places to see Aspen while not being seen yourself.

200 S. Aspen St. ✆ **800/321-3457** or 970/925-6246. www.hotellenado.com. Higher holiday rates; lower rates spring and fall.

Limelight Hotel $$

This small hotel, a renovated ski lodge with a pool and mountain views, has been completely redone into a stylish sister of the glamour hotels that surround it downtown. Now under the same management as The Little Nell (see following listing), they are doing their best to keep the rates reasonable (well, reasonable for Aspen). The **Terrace** and **Penthouse** suites look back at Aspen Mountain, so you can have the same views as the Little Nell for a much lower tariff.

355 S. Monarch St. ✆ **855/925-3025.** www.limelighthotel.com.

The Little Nell $$$

Right at the base of the Silver Queen Gondola at Aspen Mountain, this is the elegant choice for ski-in, ski-out access. The theme is intimate-sophisticated, but the service (and the price) is pure Ritz. Rooms differ, but each has a gas fireplace, big comfy chairs or a sofa, and a luxury bathroom. (Some lovely rooms are wheelchair accessible.) Ask for a suite with a Jacuzzi and steam shower; try for a room or suite with a mountain view and a balcony. The hotel restaurant is a very romantic venue with expansive views of the hotel courtyard and Aspen Mountain. The Ajax Tavern is a cozy hangout in the shadow of the ski lift. *Note:* The very active concierge service here is eager to conspire with you and will do just about anything to help people pop the question or have an extraordinary honeymoon or wedding.

675 E. Durant Ave. ✆ **855/920-4600.** www.thelittlenell.com.

MOST ROMANTIC RESTAURANTS

Justice Snow's $ GASTROPUB   Replacing the venerable Bentley's as the resident eatery and watering hole at the historic Wheeler Opera House (below), this is one of the best new restaurants and cocktail bars in the West. Named for the local justice of the peace in the late 1800s, the copper-topped bar and rough, ornate woodwork prove a nice backdrop for the inventive fare, ranging from a burger to a Colorado bass. But the thick, leather-bound cocktail list with 100-plus offerings organized by liquor, including a bit of history on each drink, is a showstopper, as is the cocktail-making, verging on performance art.

328 E. Hyman Ave. in the Wheeler Opera House. ✆ **970/429-8192.** www.justice snows.com.

Krabloonik $$$ INTERNATIONAL   This restaurant is part of a dog-sledding adventure (see previous information)—but you can have an adventure at the restaurant without the dogs, too. It's a really romantic experience that should bring out the mountain man (and woman) in you. You will be in a log cabin, watching the sled dogs come and go, and hunkering down on a tender elk loin or a wild boar chop. (Non–meat eaters will find fish and vegetable dishes.) Taking in the huge mountain views and sitting around a sunken fireplace, this is a wonderful rustic vision of Colorado.

4250 Divide Rd., Snowmass Village. ✆ **970/923-3953.** www.krabloonik.com.

Piñons $$ CONTEMPORARY REGIONAL   The famous Piñons has seen other restaurants come and go, but it maintains its place as the best restaurant in town. The interior is casually elegant, and the large windows make Aspen Mountain your focus. The wine list is excellent, and your food splurge should include the crushed macadamia nut trout and the tender Colorado lamb. As an alternate, you can snag a two-course prix-fixe dinner at the bar for $30.

105 S. Mill St. ✆ **970/920-2021.** www.pinons.net.

ASPEN BY NIGHT

39 Degrees   Inside the ultra-hip Sky Hotel, the decor is a bit much for us for a hotel, but just right for a bar. There are striped sofas and log walls and some hysterical names for cocktails (try the Botox Martini). It's frequented by a rich young crowd, but if you want to absorb some pulsating hormones, drop by. A major attraction is the slope-side pool, which you can use even if you are merely a bar customer. 709 E. Durant Ave. ✆ **970/925-6760.** www.theskyhotel.com.

The J-Bar   A sophisticated, quiet bar in the historic Hotel Jerome, and a great way to spend time in the super-pricey hotel. 330 E. Main St. ✆ **970/920-1000.** http://hoteljerome.com.

The Wheeler Opera House   This beautiful, 19th-century performing arts venue has a revolving program of music, theater, dance, film, and lectures. The elaborate decor—crystal chandeliers, polished wood, red carpeting, and red velvet seats—makes it a romantic venue for an evening out. 320 E. Hyman Ave. ℂ**970/920-5770.** www.wheeleroperahouse.com.

BUCKS COUNTY, PENNSYLVANIA
Antiquers' Paradise

Much of the East Coast and especially Philadelphia are blessed with easy access to this lovely countryside with sophisticated touches for weekend getaways. It is jam-packed with B&Bs, one more romantic than the next, and while we normally don't recommend B&Bs, because they often lack privacy (and bathrooms), we make an exception here. This area has made a high art of the B&B, the main kind of lodging in a place so lovely it really shouldn't be missed.

Bucks County is too close to major cities and too beautiful and full of attractions not to crowd up in summer. But here, in a few turns you can be away from the crowds and out in the most peaceful, bucolic farmland, blessed with gorgeous old farmhouses, magnificent estates, and sweet little villages, reminders of the Dutch and Amish people who once streamed here to set up a productive way of life.

Bucks County's physical setting is truly lovely, with the Delaware River bordering on the east and Montgomery County on the west. Because of the proximity to Philadelphia, most the "new" people here tend to be lapsed urbanites. But go further into the countryside, and you meet the small town inhabitants whose families have been here for several hundred years.

KEY ATTRACTIONS

Active Pursuits The **Delaware Canal** once hauled coal and now makes for a nice meandering walk. It parallels the nearby Delaware River, and the path along the Pennsylvania side is especially lovely, taking you to Lumberville's historic **Black Bass Hotel,** 3774 River Rd. (ℂ **215/297-9260;** www.blackbasshotel.com), for breakfast, lunch, or dinner. Some hotels and shops will rent you a tandem bicycle; ask at your hotel. **Bucks County River Country** in Point Pleasant (ℂ **215/297-5000;** www.rivercountry.net) will help you drift down the Delaware River together on tubes, kayaks, or canoes.

Antiquing Bucks County may have the largest concentration of **antique shops** in the United States. If that steps up your pulse, the Saturday auctions (**Brown's Brothers auctions;** ℂ **215/794-7630;** www.brownbrosauction.com) and the great shops in the towns and countryside will excite you! Take US Route 202 to Durham Road (Route 413) and Swamp Road (Route 313), and you will find some good browsing spots. Fans of "The Bridges of Madison County" might like the romance of the **12 covered bridges** of Buck's County! All of them use the Town Truss design, and you can drive through ten of them; two cannot bear the weight of cars. Pennsylvania has more than 200 covered bridges, the most of any state.

The Fireworks at New Hope   This town can get flooded with tourists, but there are good reasons for it: a multitude of fun bars and shops and extraordinary people-watching. And at 9:30pm come Friday night, from Memorial Day through Labor Day, it turns quite romantic with the weekly fireworks display. Fireworks are always on our romantic must-do list! Here, they team nicely with other fun, such as the late-June canal festival and "Canal Crawl," a chance to sample local restaurants and support Delaware Canal clean-up efforts. www.newhopelambertvillefireworks.com.

A Mad Castle   Doylestown's **Mercer Museum,** 84 S. Pine St., and **Fonthill Castle**, at East Court Street and Route 313, are the legacy of historian (and scion of the Mercer Tiles company) Henry C. Mercer, who amassed a huge collection of pre-Industrial Age craftwork to preserve the passing era. In 1916 he built a whimsical six-story castle to house it. Yes, it delivers an education on early American life, but don't miss the five-story atrium that dangles, among other things, a Conestoga wagon and sleigh. The place is a bit mad—which makes it all the more interesting for mad lovers!

© **215/345-0210** for both museums. www.mercermuseum.org. Admission to each $12 adults, $10 seniors 65+.

Polo   From spring through fall, the **Tinicum Park Polo Club** (© **908/996-3321;** www.tinicumpolo.org) holds exhibition games in Erwinna. For you, it's a drive-in affair: Pack a picnic, cuddle up together, and watch from your car on the sidelines.

Rice's Market   Get to this 30-acre country market early. It has a bit of everything: Amish furniture, textiles, and antiques, plus all kinds of fresh produce, local cheeses, and crafts from local artisans. Tour the main building and then get lost among the hundreds of outdoor vendors. There are ATMs onsite and paved walkways for wheelchairs and unsteady walkers. The market runs every Tuesday and on Saturday in the summer.

6326 Greenhill Rd., New Hope. © **215/297-5993.** www.ricesmarket.com.

HOTELS WITH HEART

Bridgeton House on the Delaware $ Twenty minutes north of New Hope in Upper Black Eddy and not far from Lambertville, this postcard-ready

---

Perfect Place to Propose

Bowman's Hill Wildflower Preserve, 1635 River Rd. (© **215/862-2924;** www.bhwp.org; admission $5 for adults, $3 for seniors 62+), a 134-acre nature preserve and botanical garden near New Hope contains nearly 1,000 plant species native to Pennsylvania in a lovely setting of woodlands and meadows with a pond, creek, and 2½ miles of trails. In spring the blooms can prove irresistible to thoughts of matrimony!

inn on the banks of the Delaware pampers you with feather beds, fine linens, and Jacuzzis. French-inspired details have translated an ordinary 19th-century building into a place where you could hold a small wedding or a restorative retreat. Ask, and they can make it extra romantic with a candlelight dinner just for two, surrounded by lights at the end of a pier. Or you can hire a private chef for an evening and dine fireside in the lobby or on your porch (with a river view) in the warmer months. Stays can include a spa package, premium rooms and suites with lovely river views, or the wonderful boathouse or penthouse rooms with forever views of the river. Special picnic baskets are available for romantic dining in your room or at a beautiful spot near the water. This is an ultra-romantic getaway!

1525 River Rd., Upper Black Eddy. ✆ **610/982-5856.** www.bridgetonhouse.com. Rates include breakfast.

Inn at Barley Sheaf Farm $$ Playwright George S. Kaufman once lived here, and it still feels like someone's home. There are wonderful collected fine pieces in each suite. It's a delightful aesthetic throughout with original Mercer tiles, stained glass windows, hand-painted murals, and wood beams in the 19th-century barn. The Manor House itself has sections dating from several periods, the earliest has visible stone walls. The 16 suites (some with kitchens) are each individually decorated and have gas fireplaces and Jacuzzi tubs. A very good spa is on premises. Hospitality is the idea here, and nice little unexpected touches keep appearing: a wine and cheese gift upon arrival and breakfast served in the glass-walled conservatory dining room, which grows even more romantic when dinner is served with gentle lighting.

5281 York Rd., New Hope. ✆ **215/794-5104.** www.barleysheaf.com. Rates include breakfast.

Inn at Bowman's Hill $$$ This amazing country estate has meticulously groomed gardens and grounds for walking hand in hand. All the amenities— the pool, the terrace, and more—are magnificently arranged. You can choose between the main building or the carriage house. Decorations are deluxe, and the elegant rooms have king-sized feather beds, flatscreen TVs, gas fireplaces, and romantic tiled bathrooms with Jacuzzi and shower. A lovely place for a proposal or recommitment ceremony is the Orchid Room conservatory. This place is geared for romance and will oblige any reasonable creative ideas for a romantic stay, including couples massages or private dinners and picnics. Breakfasts are an event.

518 Lurgan Rd., New Hope. ✆ **215/862-8090.** www.theinnatbowmanshill.com. Rates include breakfast.

MOST ROMANTIC RESTAURANTS

Lambertville, located across the river from New Hope, has been the site of a fine dining boom in recent years. In addition to Hamilton (see later listing) consider **Lilly's on the Canal,** 2 Canal St. ($$$; ✆ **609/397-6242;** www.lillys gourmet.com), on the canal path off Bridge Street, with its hip vibe and eclectic menu—don't miss the eggplant fries and peanut butter pie!

The Freight House $$ NEW AMERICAN   This old barn has been refitted as a very stylish restaurant and bar. The curvy bar, private booths, leather seats, and original modern artwork create an intimate, sensual experience with a contemporary sensibility. Come here for good American food, especially fresh fish and steaks. Or come just for the original cocktails and signature martinis and mojitos. On the weekend, the bar turns into a cabaret, and summer nights you can dance, Thursday through Saturday.

194 W. Ashland St., Doylestown. ✆**215/340-1003.** www.thefreighthouse.net.

Hamilton's Grill Room $$ AMERICAN   This seems to be where the locals go, even though it's in the heart of the tourist bustle in Lambertville. It's a bit hard to find, down a small street near the canal in what used to be a boathouse. Bring your own wine and prepare for great regional cuisine that concentrates on grilled meats. The decor is contemporary inside with a nice outdoor courtyard in the summer. It's very popular, so make reservations way ahead.

8 Coryell St., Lambertville. ✆**609/397-4343.** www.hamiltonsgrillroom.com.

Honey Restaurant $$ NEW AMERICAN   A small place with a nice patio, the soft lighting inside is romantic. Come here for wonderful seasonal menus such as wild salmon tartar with apple, cured olives, and honey; salads with fried goat cheese over greens with berries; and Meyer lemon pieces mixed with jicama and black tea–glazed spareribs. The menu is always changing and, philosophically, is perfect for couples: There's something for everyone, whether your partner is a fussy eater or open to experimentation.

42 Shewell Ave., Doylestown. ✆**215/489-4200.** www.honeyrestaurant.com.

BUCKS COUNTY BY NIGHT

Bucks County Playhouse   This old renovated gristmill is the center of New Hope entertainment and the site of local plays, Broadway reviews, and just about anything that can be done on a stage. It's a fun time to enjoy together.

70 S. Main St., New Hope. ✆**215/862-2121.** www.bcptheater.org.

THE CALIFORNIA WINELAND: SONOMA & NAPA VALLEY
Food & Wine Wonderland

Just about an hour from San Francisco, you will find some of the loveliest landscapes in the world, textured by some of the world's most famous wineries. Wine, and the vineyards that produce it, have long been interwoven with romance. Here, so many ventures are trying to perfect the art of romantic hospitality, fine food, superlative wines, and luxurious living that books could—and have—been written about where to go and what restaurants and wineries to visit. We give you our personal picks for romance, but we are only scratching the surface. Do not think about a trip here: Think about many trips here.

Sonoma County: Sonoma & Healdsburg

Sonoma County is twice the size of neighboring Napa, and some people think twice as beautiful (which is saying something!). We crave both areas, but we give Sonoma the edge for its quieter demeanor and rolling hills. Wine country itself, however, has a beauty all its own that covers all areas. Wine producing is, after all, farming, and the carefully cultivated fields and fresh farm-to-table restaurants hearken back to very deep agrarian roots and sensibilities for many of us. It speaks to an earlier time—slower, more intentional, and grateful for a good harvest. We think it brings out the best in people. We might mention it's kind of nice to get intimate back in your room with a little bit of a buzz on, too.

The two hubs for wine touring in Sonoma County are **Sonoma** and **Healdsburg,** both sophisticated towns that retain their small town feel. Each has an inviting square, although here we'd give the nod to Sonoma, because of how much fun that square is to walk and window shop. Both regions are just plain fun for getting lost, driving around back roads, and happening upon a winery. Of course, if you plan to drink rather than just taste, a better idea is to hire a limo (there are a lot of good companies; ask at your hotel) or name one of you the designated driver (or sacrificial lamb, depending on how you see it).

Starting from Sonoma, you can wind your way through Santa Rosa and the Russian River Valley and continue to Healdsburg and maybe onward to the even more laid-back Alexander Valley. It depends on how much time you have. If you're attaching this jaunt to your urban romance adventure in San Francisco (see p. 54) and only want to do a half-day excursion, make Sonoma your destination.

KEY ATTRACTIONS

There are hundreds of great wineries; here are a few that have great wine *and* make you feel romantic when you are there.

Benziger Family Winery   The winery sits handsomely on the side of Sonoma Mountain. You take a tram up, and the territorial views are wonderful.

1883 London Ranch Rd., Glen Ellen. ℂ **888/490-2739.** www.benziger.com.

Chateau St. Jean   This very romantic spot has manicured grounds graced with bubbling fountains, fruit trees, and a vineyard. You can get what you need for a lunch at the tasting room—and the wines are excellent.

8555 Sonoma Hwy., Kenwood. ℂ **707/833-4134.** www.chateaustjean.com.

Dry Creek Vineyard   This vineyard is from a Hollywood set; it looks the way you'd hope a traditional vineyard and tasting room would. The

Thirsting for Your Loved One

Shakespeare wrote that alcohol "provokes the desire but takes away the performance." Although it's hard to resist, don't overdrink. Not only is it dangerous if you're driving, but you will squander all the romantic currency you've built up if you fall into bed and fall asleep immediately. It's nice to do some of the in-town tasting rooms so you can walk back to your room. Another romantic option is to rent a limo (some of the upscale places provide their own pick-up services free), and cuddle in between wineries.

ivy-covered stone building is surrounded by lush landscaping, tall trees, and a groomed lawn that invite picnic lovers to linger.

3770 Lambert Bridge Rd., Healdsburg. ℂ **707/433-1000.** www.drycreekvineyard.com.

HOTELS WITH HEART

The Kenwood Inn and Spa $$$ This intimate Tuscan-style villa is romantic from the moment you turn into the driveway. It has earned awards in every category, for its extensive wine list, its impressive chef, and its luxurious spa, but it also seems to garner quite a few overall Reader's Choice awards, too. Most important for maximizing romantic potential, this is a "no kids and no TV" zone. Fruit trees and landscaping surround the arcaded building in Kenwood, and the rooms offer mountain or garden views, each with fireplace, feather beds, with Italian linens, large candles by the oversize tub, and turn-down service that has you return to romantic music playing and a fire already glowing for you. At night the outdoor areas, including the garden dining courtyard, are romantically lit; by day you can enjoy the large, very quiet pool area. The Inn is located in a particularly pretty area of Sonoma, near Benziger and Chateau St. Jean wineries, and about a 10-minute drive from downtown Sonoma.

10400 Sonoma Hwy, Kenwood. ℂ **800/353-6966.** www.kenwoodinn.com. Call about up to 30% discounts off season and midweek; price includes delectable cooked-to-order full breakfast.

The Sonoma Mission Inn $$$ This is Sonoma's premier hotel; with a fine restaurant **(Sante)**, it is not far from the plaza and has great curb appeal. Built in 1927, it is referential to early missions but in reality is a full-scale resort, with a significant 18-hole golf course. Still, it has warm dark wood appointments and, somewhat incongruously, French country rooms and large, luxurious marble bathrooms. For privacy, and for a higher price, separate buildings house the elegant suites that have truly romantic getaway features such as fireplaces and two-person Jacuzzi tubs. The stand-out attraction? The hot mineral springs, utilized by the spa and the three pools and fed by an underground thermal mineral stream.

100 Boyes Blvd. ℂ **707/938-9000.** www.fairmont.com/sonoma.

Sonoma's Best Guest Cottages $ These adorable little houses were once grubby workmen's cottages for field hands. Today, they've been upgraded to become terrific mini-homes for tourists. Candy colored and sweet, they're equipped with kitchens (BBQ grills on request), living rooms, big bathrooms, wide-plank wood floors, and outdoor sitting areas. Their location 2 miles east of Sonoma town makes for an ideal home base to explore both Sonoma and Napa. *Bonus:* Their small on-premise market cafe offers local cheeses, wines, coffee, and sandwiches and salads.

1190 East Napa St., Sonoma. ℂ **800/291-8962** or 707/933-0340. www.sonomas bestcottages.com.

MOST ROMANTIC RESTAURANTS

Fremont Diner $ DINER This adorable, roadside diner with an old-fashioned aesthetic and homey, hearty cooking has Bay Area foodies making a special trip. Come here for fluffy omelets, serious coffee, brisket hash, fried chicken, pies, and milkshakes so thick they need a spoon. When the weather's nice, people eat outside, though the real character is indoors here.

2660 Fremont Dr., Sonoma. ℂ **707/938-7370.** www.thefremontdiner.com. Mon–Wed 8am–3pm, Thurs–Sun 8am–9pm.

The Girl & the Fig $ COUNTRY FRENCH This small, adorable restaurant right on the square in Sonoma is crowded at lunch and dinner, and reservations are almost essential. They do accept drop-ins and provide a small sitting area that, if free, is a cozy spot to sit and have some cheese and wine while you wait. They make a variety of fig spreads and olive oils to taste, which is a lot of fun. The menu food is well-done country French. They have a few rooms to let upstairs if you want to be right in the middle of town.

110 West Spain St. ℂ **707/938-3634.** www.thegirlandthefig.com.

Madrona Manor $$$ NEW CALIFORNIA We love a really fine Victorian house in all its gingerbread glory. This outstanding 1881 example, furnished in antiques, commands attention from its hillside position, and its mature gardens invite you in. Many of the vegetables you eat grew just seconds away from your table. There are four-, five-, or six-course prix fixe menus and an extraordinary wine list with suggested tastings and pairings. It's a perfect wine country stop for lovers.

1001 Westside Rd., Healdsburg. ℂ **800/258-4003.** www.madronamanor.com.

Napa Valley: Yountville & St. Helena

People can disagree over which is the heartbeat of Napa, Yountville or St. Helena. These towns are about an hour apart and quite different. Yountville is a laid-back place that has more recently been exploding with culinary arts and vintages, and cool boutique hotels and galleries, although it has long been on the winery map—Napa's first grapes were planted here. St. Helena is the valley's most attractive town. Main Street is charming, and the compact downtown has pricey but interesting shops; the leafy neighborhoods are fun to walk or bike.

6

The California Wineland: Sonoma & Napa Valley | EARTHY DELIGHTS: U.S.

One special plus for couples could be signing up for a class (or just lunch) at the **Culinary Institute of America at Greystone,** St. Helena (© **800/888-7850;** www.ciachef.edu/california). Classes range from single sessions to week-long master courses on food and wine, with private tours to wineries and the best restaurants. If you two are foodies, this could be your haven, and heaven.

If you were exploring the area solely to create a nice itinerary for lovers, you might start in Yountville for a day or two, then go to St. Helena and then cross the valley and head back into Sonoma wine country (or vice versa). In a languid fashion, it could take a week; but if you really just wanted to scope out the area, you could do it in 3 days.

KEY ATTRACTIONS

Here are a few of our favorite wineries, from Yountville to beyond St. Helena.

Artesa Vineyards & Winery   On your way to Yountville and beyond, you may pass through Napa. If you do, we urge you to stop here for what may be the most rapture-inducing view of your trip. The winery owns the most expansive horizon imaginable: the valley, the bay, and on a clear day, San Francisco. The winery itself is simply designed but is surrounded by gentle waterfalls and reflecting pools. The wine selection is wide—taste them but also drink in the view.

1345 Henry Rd., Napa. © **707/224-1668.** www.artesawinery.com.

Chappellet   Chappellet's views rival its extremely fine Cabernet. You are high on a hill with a gorgeous view of Lake Hennessy and the valley. There is an excellent tour of the wine caves, but indulge yourselves: Call first for a private tasting and ask for the extended tour and luncheon.

1581 Sage Canyon Rd., St. Helena. © **707/963-7136.** www.chappellet.com.

Jessup Cellars   We love this small, simple tasting room, which is a hop, skip, and jump from the Bardesonno hotel (so you can walk there and stagger back without worrying about driving or hiring a limo!). Great eats, excellent red wines, and a friendly young staff.

6740 Washington St., Yountville. © **888/537-7879.** http://jessupcellars.com.

Schramsberg Vineyards   This is a bit further afield, but it's such a romantic place we can't help ourselves. Schedule a tour to their very mysterious, moss-covered caves. The atmosphere is thick with allure. Top it off later with a sparkling wine tasting, which can be paired with some really delicious tidbits like salmon and caviar. Honestly, can anyone ever drink an excellent bubbly without feeling romantic?

1400 Schramsberg Rd., Calistoga. © **707/942-4558.** www.schramsberg.com.

MOST ROMANTIC RESTAURANTS

When you just can't stomach another precious salad or truffle-covered something, head to **BarBersQ** ($; 3900 D Bel Aire Plaza, Napa; © **707/224-6600;** www.barbersq.com) for down-home, genuine Memphis-style BBQ. Ribs, brisket, beans and ham, fried chicken—yup, it's a carnivores paradise, though this being Napa, anything that once grew in the ground will be locally sourced. Top it all off with addictive chocolate bourbon pecan pie or Key lime pie—if you can.

St. Helena

Auberge du Soleil $$$ WINE COUNTRY CUISINE   You could pass this French-inspired place, and the inn that goes with it, on your way from Yountville to St. Helena and miss it—except for the single small sign on the Silverado Trail. Stop for any meal, but especially lunch. From its large deck, Auberge has the best view in the valley, over the vineyards and as far as the Mayacamas Mountains. The kitchen is well known and well loved. Lunch offers entirely satisfying entrée salads and perfectly cooked fish, and it's also the best value here (though you should consider drinks or dinner, since the terrace is a great place to watch the sunset). The inside dining room is beautiful and far more formal, with a subdued color palate and an impressive French hearth and lavish vases of flowers. We had one of the best dinners of our lives there. Ooh-la-la.

180 Rutherford Hill Rd., Rutherford.© **800/348-5406.** www.aubergedusoleil.com.

Yountville

Ad Hoc $$ INTERNATIONAL   For those who'd like to try star chef Thomas Keller's cuisine (see French Laundry review, below), but also pay rent this month, Ad Hoc is the solution. Most famous for its fried chicken dinners (served only on Mon.), the restaurant offers a daily changing, prix fixe menu, which is served family style and ranges across the globe for its inspirations. One day you might get jambalaya, and on another day the menu will feature falafel, the one constant being the high quality of both the ingredients and the cooking. (Also on Washington Ave., Keller's **Bouchon Bakery** is famous for its chocolate croissants).

6475 Washington St.© **707/944-2487.** www.adhocrestaurant.com.

Etoile at Domaine Chandon $$ FRENCH   This very chic restaurant has a gracefully curved ceiling and wine country views from its terrace, plus a prix fixe menu (expensive, but not in the realm of French Laundry) and a very extensive wine list. Domaine Chandon makes a variety of sparkling wines, so you might want to toast each other before dinner in the tasting room.

1 California Dr.© **888/242-6366.** www.chandon.com/etoile-restaurant.html.

The French Laundry $$$ CLASSIC AMERICAN/FRENCH   Here is the world-famous French Laundry, created by Thomas Keller. If you want to eat, make your reservation way in advance. Founded in 1992, this place changed the face of Yountville and launched the town's reputation as the gourmet hub of the valley. It's in a charming old home, and the service and food are a bit self-important, but it seems deservedly so. The cuisine is extravagantly creative and delicious and likely to stir more than one of your senses. Be prepared to pay *a lot* for your dinner. The wine list is an event all by itself.

6640 Washington St.© **707/944-2380.** www.frenchlaundry.com.

Mustards Grill $$ CALIFORNIAN   If the two of you need a respite from expensive fancy dining, go here for wonderful American food. This friendly, intimate, and informal place can make it easy to connect over tasty meals at decent prices for this area. That's comfort food!

7399 St. Helena Hwy. ℂ **707/944-2424.** http://mustardsgrill.com.

HOTELS WITH HEART

St. Helena

Dr. Wilkinson's Hot Springs Resort $ OK, this place isn't going to win any romance awards, but it's an institution among the Calistoga spas, and your money here buys you a simple, immaculately clean, and comfy room (some with kitchenettes) along with access to multiple hot-spring pools. Buildings are distinctly 1950s motel (standard room sizes, walls made of era brick tile, and an Americana-style neon sign out front), but the resort has gone to extra lengths to renovate the rooms to a more refreshed standard (think flatscreen TVs, iPod docking stations, nice textiles). The patios and outdoor courtyards are well-groomed, fitting places to unwind before exploring the shops and food along Lincoln Avenue. If you stay here, you can avail yourself of a standard pool plus a pair (indoor and outdoor) of pools fed by mineral water. Then, of course, there's Dr. Wilkinson's famous medicinal mud bath spa.

1507 Lincoln Ave. (Calif. 29, btw. Fairway and Stevenson aves.), Calistoga. ℂ **707/942-4102.** www.drwilkinson.com.

Meadowood $$$ This is an elegant resort sprawled over 250 acres with a nine-hole golf course and a country club feel. Its good-looking rooms and suites with vaulted ceilings and working stone fireplaces are worth the hefty tariff. But if you prefer only a taste of elegance, try the restaurant. Swanky but relaxed, it is acclaimed not only for its cooking, but also for the serious attention it gives the wine and fresh produce of the region.

900 Meadowood Lane, St. Helena. ℂ **877/963-3646.** www.meadowood.com.

Napa & Yountville

Bardessonno $$ Honored as one of only three LEED Platinum-certified hotels in the United States for its leadership in energy-efficient and environmental design, you will immediately feel relaxed as you step in and see the calming colors, natural wood furniture milled from salvaged trees, and gorgeous artwork (that happens to be for sale). Greeting you with a glass of wine, the friendly staff lets you know it will do anything to make your stay perfect. Each commodious suite has a private little patio and an outdoor shower, plus a flatscreen TV, high-tech shower, and a deep tub in a bathroom that's already equipped for in-room couple's massage. The property's second story linear pool with private cabanas is a perfect place to watch the setting sun (and perhaps propose). **Lucy's** is a stylish and worthy restaurant that is open to the public; its outdoor bar has a happy hour famous with the locals where anyone can enjoy the field-to-fork cuisine around unique high-tech fire pits.

6526 Yount St., Yountville. ℂ **877/932-5333** or 707/204-6000. www.bardessono. com.

Best Western Plus Elm House Inn $ One of the best values in Napa, this bargain escape's rooms are spacious and attractive, the service gracious, and there are all sorts of extras, including a good breakfast, lovely landscaping, a hot tub on the patio, and experts behind the desk (they're helpful in setting up wine-tasting itineraries for first timers). The hotel is within walking distance of Napa's downtown center and close to Hwy. 29, the region's thoroughfare; wineries are mere minutes away.

800 California Blvd., Napa. ⓒ **888/849-1997** or 707/255-1831. www.bestwestern. com.

Maison Fleurie $ This charming inn comprises three ivy-covered houses, so the digs vary greatly depending on whether you're in the Provencal-style main house, in the carriage house, or the bakery-turned-guesthouse. If having a private balcony, patio, or Jacuzzi tub is important, be sure to read the website descriptions carefully; what all rooms have in common is their cozy looks, comfortable beds, and private bathrooms. The lovingly tended grounds include a pool and a hot tub. A generous breakfast starts the day; end it in style with afternoon hors d'oeuvres and wine (also complimentary).

6529 Yount St. (btw. Washington St. and Yountville Cross Rd.), Yountville. ⓒ **800/ 788-0369** or 707/944-2056. www.maisonfleurienapa.com.

JACKSON HOLE, WYOMING
Back in the Saddle

Depending on your view, this town is either on its way to becoming a world-class destination or on its way out and totally inauthentic to the real Western experience. It already has very good restaurants, tempting high-end stores and galleries, smashing lodgings and majestic scenery that makes your heart stop. Look with awe at the jagged granite Tetons and the Cottonwood-framed Snake River! Even if you see a lot of cowboy wannabe's who mostly ride Range Rovers, you also see the real thing: handsome or grizzled, old or young, scarred and worn from working horses and cattle and the occasional rodeo. The glitz ends at the town line. After that it's a world that belongs mostly to the trout, eagles, elk, moose, and bears.

The town is delightfully schizophrenic: part ski village, part Santa Fe artsy, part watering hole for ranchers, nirvana for sportsmen and women, and glitzy second home for princes of industry and Hollywood, relaxing in jeans but living like royalty. Plus, there are fun cowboy touches everyone; some are pure kitsch, others reminders that this actually is cowboy country. The **Million Dollar Cowboy Bar** (see below), near the main square, is a hodgepodge of mementos and bar seats made from saddles. **The Silver Dollar Bar** (p. 140) is a classic wood bar, just like in the movies, but embedded with thousands of silver dollars.

KEY ATTRACTIONS (SUMMER)

Champagne & Ballooning   We like the **Wyoming Balloon Company** (℗ **307/739-0900;** www.wyomingballoon.com; 1-hr. trip $325 per adult) because they add a bit of romantic flair to their send off. They start early while the air is predictably calm and float along for an hour above gorgeous ranch lands angling toward the most romantic views of the Tetons possible. At the end of this breath-taking jaunt they pop a cork and serve you good champagne. You are done with the day still ahead of you, but we think it might be nice if you went back to bed.

Golfing   **Teton Pines,** 3450 N. Clubhouse Dr., Wilson (℗ **307/733-1005;** www.tetonpines.com; greens fees $65–$160, depending on season), is an Arnold Palmer–designed course about 7 miles from Jackson, and your hotel concierge can usually get you into the Robert Trent Jones, Jr.–designed **Jackson Hole Golf and Tennis** club, 5000 Spring Gulch Rd. (℗ **307/733-3111;** www.jhgtc.com; greens fees $65–$185, depending on season), if you are staying at some place relatively tony.

Hiking   Fall is the best time to hike here, when the orange and yellow Aspens are at their most striking. But any time of year is beautiful, and most people's first hike is in Grand Teton Park. Further afield is Bridger-Teton National (℗ **307/739-5500** or 307/739-5010; www.fs.usda.gov/btnf), just east of Jackson, and **Shoshone National Forest** (℗ **307/527-6241;** www.fs.usda.gov/shoshone), northeast of Bridger-Teton. All around you are magnificent specimens of nature: crystalline alpine lakes and huge, glacial peaks, still jagged as if newly risen to their 13,000 feet. If the two of you love to hike or fish, you might have found your paradise.

Horseback Riding   If you want to get in the saddle, outfitters can take you out for several hours, a half-day, or even an overnight trip. Take a longer ride to see the most scenic country. Horseback riding can be a serene experience, with casual cookouts, square dancing, hiking, wildlife viewing, and photo op's not to mention constant ogling of the dramatic Grand Tetons. Ask your concierge to set you up.

River-rafting & Float Trips   The earlier in the summer season, the more whitewater you get on the Snake River. This is the place you are most likely to see abundant large four-hoofed wildlife. The thrills of whitewater rafting can get those endorphins and other hormones working to your advantage. Contact **Will Dornan's SRA Scenic River Float Trips** (℗ **307/733-3699;** www.jacksonholefloattrips.com; 2-hr. guided trips $65 per adult) or **Solitude Float Trips** (℗ **888/704-2800;** www.grand-teton-scenic-floats.com; 10- to 13-mile trips $70 per adult).

Taking a Romantic Drive   The 130-mile drive from the city of **Riverton** to **Grand Teton National Park** will knock your woolen socks off. Route 26 takes you past magnificent scenery, which, of course, we find romantic. Then Route 191 travels the length of Grand Teton Park, passing Jackson Lake and the Snake River and ends within 6 miles of **Yellowstone National Park**'s entrance. Yellowstone is theoretically possible as a day's excursion, but many hours pass before you even get to the park, and Yellowstone, unlike Teton, is vast—more than 2 million acres. You might want to make Yellowstone another trip altogether, or stay the night. But whatever you do, make sure you see a sunset against those magnificent mountains, an array of Rocky Mountain ranges.

KEY ATTRACTIONS (WINTER)

You don't have to ski to love winter in Jackson Hole.

Dog Sledding Get mushy! If you are visiting in the winter and want a mutual adrenaline rush, then don your ski jackets and get behind a pack of scrambling dogs that can't wait to take you on a tour of the mountains. Several companies in Jackson Hole offer half-, full-, or multi-day dogsledding excursions; ask your concierge for a recommendation.

National Elk Refuge Sleigh Rides Sleigh rides are almost by definition romantic. But add an enormous elk herd (we are talking thousands here) and the experience might overwhelm. If you're traveling between mid-December and early April, book far in advance with Double H Bar, Inc., outfitters (*Ⓒ* **888/734-6101** or 307/734-6101; www.bart.com.) For more information on the Elk Refuge, visit ww.fws.gov/refuge/national_elk_refuge.

Skiing In the winter, Jackson Hole becomes a ski town with world-class runs at **Jackson Hole Mountain Resort,** 3395 Cody Lane, in Teton Village (*Ⓒ* **888/333-7766** or 307/733-2292; www.jacksonhole.com), which claims the highest vertical rise of ski areas in North America. The complex also includes the welcoming **Snow King Hotel,** 400 E. Snow King Ave., Jackson (*Ⓒ* **307/733-5200;** www.snowking.com), a quick walk to shops and cafes in town. Cross-country skiing is our winter pick for romance, especially in the light-powder snow here. It is so tranquil and allows you to stop, take in the forest, and count your blessings. **Grand Targhee Resort,** 3300 Ski Hill Rd., in nearby Alta (*Ⓒ* **800/827-4433** or 307/353-2300; www.grandtarghee.com), is in one of the most beautiful cross-country sites in the United States, with the added possibility of seeing wildlife.

Snowmobiling Here's another exhilarating couples experience: riding the roaring power of a motored sled and exploring areas you couldn't see otherwise. **High Country Snowmobile Tours, Wyoming Adventures**, and **Rocky Mountain Snowmobile Tours** offering guided trips in Jackson Hole and Yellowstone all share a reservation service (*Ⓒ* **800/647-2561** or 307/733-2237; www.snowmobiletours.net). Operators will also outfit you with the proper clothing and helmets.

HOTELS WITH HEART

A stay in Jackson can be truly rustic—or beyond elegant. Or, you might opt for a mix of the two.

Campers, note: **Jenny Lake Campground,** with 51 tent-only sites, is in a quiet, wooded area near the lake and is one of the loveliest places imaginable to see the sun set or rise. It's worth it to arrive first thing in the morning to get a site.

Guest Ranches

For some, the cowboy experience is the height of erotic imagery! Think about the roughneck romance of riding into the mountains, a chuck-wagon cookout, a blazing campfire, or landing on the bank of a class 4 river and catching trout for lunch. But maybe you'd prefer to rest your head on 500-thread-count sheets. Here are our two favorite romantic ranch destinations.

Lost Creek Ranch & Spa $$$ It's expensive, only open in summer, and you must stay a week—but this is a special place. Directly opposite the Grand Tetons in Moose, this lodge is small and exclusive, plush, and very beautiful—and your hosts will pamper you. Fortunately, your considerable rate includes gourmet meals and all the activities you'd expect at a guest ranch (great fly-fishing, unlimited horseback riding, guided hikes), all of which are good bonding activities. Your luscious spa treatments, however, are extra. The cabins, especially the duplexes, are truly elegant, and the cuisine is exceptional.

1 Lost Creek Ranch Rd, Moose. ✆ **307/733 3435.** www.lostcreek.com.

Spring Creek Ranch $$ On elevated open grassland, this ranch has nine buildings with cabin-like exteriors. Some rooms have a panoramic view of the Grand Tetons, others just a peek-a-boo mountain view, but all have a wood-burning fireplace (a major romantic plus). The price of your room will depend on your view; if you can, we recommend you kick in a few more dollars for the view. Lavish condos with kitchens are also for rent. And one more reason we love this place: A resident naturalist takes guests on wildlife "safaris."

800 Spirit Dance Rd., Jackson. ✆ **800/443-6139** or 307/733-8833. www.spring creekranch.com.

Hotels

A stay at **Amangani** (1535 NE Butte Rd., Jackson; ✆ **877/734-7333** or 307/734-7333; www.amanresorts.com), cut into the side of East Gro Ventre Butte and providing all sorts of private romantic opportunities, offers one of those unforgettable experiences; but you'll not soon forget the price tag, either. In the off-season, a double at the **Four Seasons Jackson Hole** (7680 Granite Loop Rd., Teton Village; ✆ **307/732-5000;** www.fourseasons.com/jacksonhole) might be doable at $219 to $319 a night (in season tack on another $500 per night).

The Jenny Lake Lodge $$$ These rustic but beautiful atmospheric cabins are set in a handsome secluded landscape and the lodge offers great horseback riding that takes in the views. Two meals come with your daily rate and you'll be thrilled to have them here (see later).

In Grand Teton National Park. ✆ **307/733-4647.** www.gtlc.com.

The Rusty Parrot Lodge $$$ In town, you can't do better than this country lodge and (full-service) spa, with an outstanding restaurant serving regional cuisine right in the center of Jackson across from a quiet park. The stylish Western decorating with peeled logs, swanky furnishings, and river-rock fireplaces doesn't come cheap—so try to grab a room in the off season. Rooms are spacious, and some have private balconies.

175 N. Jackson St., Jackson. ⓒ **800/458-2004** or 307/733-2000. www.rustyparrot. com. Rates include breakfast.

A Teton Tree House $ For more than 40 years, innkeeper Denny Becker has been building and tweaking and rebuilding his B&B, literally located in the treetops in Wilson, about 10 minutes from Jackson at the foot of Teton Pass. From the road, it is almost 100 steps up to the front door, and the curious design is a perfect fit for the surroundings, and an ideal spot for bird watching—no, it is not an actual treehouse, but an architectural marvel that melds the best of a treehouse with a real home. Most rooms have decks and views of Jackson Hole; some can accommodate up to 4 guests. Heart-healthy breakfasts with no eggs or meat include breakfast banana splits with yogurt, and Denny is an awesome resource for exploring Grand Teton National Park.

6175 Heck of a Hill Rd., Wilson. ⓒ **307/733-3233.** www.atetontreehouse-jackson hole.com. 3-night minimum. Rates include full breakfast.

Wyoming Inn $ Renovated to the nines in 2013, the Wyoming Inn is a cut above most of its mid-priced competitors in Jackson proper and our mid-priced pick in a relatively expensive market. The subtle "New West" design in both the rooms and public areas pleases the eye, and there are nice perks like free laundry machines and in-room fireplaces in premium units. The hotel is a walkable mile to Town Square.

930 W. Broadway, Jackson. ⓒ **800/844-0035** or 307/734-0035. www.wyominginn. com.

MOST ROMANTIC RESTAURANTS

Jenny Lake Lodge Dining Room $$$ CONTINENTAL   Open in summer only, the lodge is in Grand Teton park itself and famous for its excellent dinners. You will be surrounded by beautiful scenery and, of course, this is also a really nice place to stay. But plan ahead if you want to eat or sleep (see later listing) here: Reservations are essential and hard to get. Specialties include trout, with a menu ranging from escargot to buffalo!

At the Jenny Lake Lodge, in Grand Teton National Park. ⓒ **307/733-4647.** www. gtlc.com.

Snake River Grill $$ NEW AMERICAN   Request a table in the romantic room tucked away in the back and tuck into local fish and game prepared with imaginative touches.

On the town square, Jackson. ⓒ **307/733-0557.** www.snakerivergrill.com.

Trio $$ NEW AMERICAN   Three chefs, who already had a great reputation in the valley, started this venture, and it was an immediate success when it opened in 2005. It's dimly lit with an open kitchen and is comfortable for romance or just plain comfortable. The one-of-a-kind fossil-rock bar sets the tone for the uniquely delish fine cuisine. The seasonal menu includes elk, of course, and the regional specialty, Idaho rainbow trout. Don't miss the killer fries and an addictive blue cheese fondue.

45 S. Glenwood Dr., Jackson.☎ **307/734-8038.** http://bistrotrio.com.

JACKSON HOLE BY NIGHT
The Mangy Moose at 1 W. Village Dr, Teton Village (☎ 307/733-4913; mangymoose.com), might put you in the mood: big steaks and ribs and lots of fun with live music all year long. Nearby at the **Million Dollar Cowboy Bar** (25 N. Cache St., Jackson (☎ **307/733-2207;** www.milliondollarcowboybar. com) two-steppers can dance to live bands.

Nikai   The fish is flown in daily at this popular sushi spot, which is also great for sake or unique cocktails. Fridays have a DJ, and you can dance or just mix with the locals who get friendlier and friendlier as the evening goes into the morning. 225 N. Cache, Jackson.☎ **307/734-6490.** www.nikaisushi.com.

The Silver Dollar Bar and Grille   If you are into history, visit this touristy but genuinely atmospheric Silver Dollar in the Wort Hotel. Around since the 1920s, the place feels like the old west; it's funky but with many authentic western touches including good western paintings, bronze statues and murals, and of course thousands of 1921 Silver dollars preserved in the extensive bar top. The joint is particularly fun on Bluegrass Tuesday nights (and hold on to your hats on weekends). Be friendly, and you might meet an artist, cowboy, ranch owner, or a folksy politician. 50 N. Glenwood St., Jackson.☎ **307/733-2190.** www.worthotel.com/dining-entertainment.

KENTUCKY HORSE COUNTRY
Just Horsing Around

They call it Bluegrass Country because the fields of the hardy grass the Kentucky horse farms grow have a bluish tinge. Bluegrass signals the romance of the horse world, of graceful animals—the best of the best—living the glamorous lives entitled by their breeding at stately farms with grand traditions. Driving around the horse farms and colorful towns between Lexington and Louisville and going to the Kentucky Derby and ogling the famous horse flesh generates an appealing romantic rush, especially for horse lovers and, surprisingly, for people who don't know horses at all. To us, just seeing all that bluegrass feels rejuvenating.

After horses, bourbon is the region's biggest product. But don't go to Bourbon County for a drink—it's dry! But no worries; we've found a few favorite spots to sip bourbon (see later listings).

KEY ATTRACTIONS
Bourbon Tasting Tour   It's pretty dreamy to take a day to leisurely sample fine bourbons and bourbon-spiked chocolates. Several distilleries near

Lexington offer tours, and visiting their hometowns can be fun, too. The **Kentucky Distillers Association's Kentucky Bourbon Trail** (© **502/875-9351;** www.kybourbontrail.com) can help guide your tour. Kentucky's oldest operating distillery is **Woodford Reserve Distillery,** 7855 McCracken Pike, Versailles (© **859/879-1812;** www.woodfordreserve.com; discovery tour $7 per person), located among the lush, rolling horse farms. An onsite lunch cafe offers alfresco seating and lovely views.

Churchill Downs This track has hosted the Kentucky Derby from the start, in 1875. You can buy general admission tickets on race day (the first Sat in May) and watch the race on monitors in the garden over your mint juleps. Grandstand tickets are awarded by lottery (unless you are running a horse), and current holders get first pick. Another option: Party with 80,000 fans on the grass inside the oval, where there is no shade and being tall is a serious advantage. We're thinking that's not too romantic. But the Derby scene is fun. Women compete in a contest to wear the most glamorous or outrageous hat. This is people- and horse-watching at their finest. Get tickets, plan your outfits, and have a ball together!

700 Central Ave., Louisville. © **502/636-4400.** www.churchilldowns.com. Admission $14 for adults, $13 for seniors 55+.

Claiborne Farm The birthplace of Seabiscuit and the place where Thoroughbred royalty, Secretariat, spent his years at stud, and is now buried. Many make the pilgrimage to visit Secretariat's grave so call of in advance for a tour.

Paris. © **859/233-4252.** www.claibornefarm.com. Free guided walking tours, by appointment only.

Keeneland No doubt about it: This is one gorgeous race course. For a thrill, attend the Keeneland Sales, when the big money from around the world arrives to bid on yearlings and other horses. (You will know you are among the heavy hitters when you see the Sultan of Brunei's jet at the airport).

4201 Versailles Rd., Lexington. © **800/456-3412** or 859/254-3412. www.keeneland.com. Free self-guided walking tours.

Kentucky Artisan Center Located about 40 miles south of Lexington, this center features exhibits, folk arts and crafts, and a fine gift shop featuring Appalachian pottery, textiles, furniture, jewelry, basketry, and local music.

200 Artisan Way, Berea. © **859/985-5448.** www.kentuckyartisancenter.ky.gov. Free admission.

Kentucky Horse Park Both a museum and an equestrian arena, this state-run horse park draws almost a million visitors a year. The museum is quite informative about racing and horses, past and present, and Man o' War, one of the greatest racehorses of all time, is buried here. Get here early, especially in race season, and you'll see horses doing a morning gallop in the grey light of dawn. It's thrilling, and usually it's just you, the riders, and the horses. During your visit, you can book tours for off-site horse farms, and from March to October you can explore the magnificent grounds and see an array of equine breeds.

4089 Iron Works Pkwy., Lexington. ℂ **800/678-8813** or 859/233-4303. www. kyhorsepark.com. Admission $10–$16 adults, depending on season.

Paris, Kentucky This pretty little town is about 17 miles northeast of Lexington. Immerse yourselves in truly cool old places, such as the beautiful Bourbon County Courthouse; Duncan Tavern, a pub that Daniel Boone supposedly frequented; and the 1877 Colville bridge, one of only 13 covered bridges left in Kentucky (at Road 1893 and Colville Rd.). "The Bridges of Madison County?" Ha! Create your own love story on this quiet rural corner.

See Derby Winners & Other Horse Athletes Drive down Old Frankfort Pike, and you can see the horses from the road. Some barns will accept drops-ins during visitor hours; some require appointments. You can't visit Calumet Farms (www.calumetfarm.com), the big-shot winningest breeder around here, but you can visit the following farms:

Shaker Village of Pleasant Hill Now, here's a break in your tourist routine! Shakers were the longest lasting commune in America, dating from just after the American Revolution. They believed in equality of race and sex and freedom from prejudice. They were celibate and didn't marry or bear children and were known for their unbridled dancing—hence the name. We're not sure what impact that had on romance—hey, different strokes. Maybe it's not surprising there are no more Kentucky Shakers. But their legacy lies in the 33 buildings and beautiful craftwork they left behind here. There is plenty to do at the village, including horseback riding in the picturesque area. You could even take a trip to the late 18th century and hop aboard a riverboat excursion. There are also self-guided tours, plus hotels and restaurants in the village.

3501 Lexington Rd., Harrodsburg. ℂ **800/734-5611.** www.shakervillageky.org. Admission $7–$15 for adults, depending on season.

Three Chimneys Farm See where Triple Crown winner Seattle Slew and his son Big Brown stood at stud. The octagonal barn for stallions is so spacious and beautifully appointed that city dwellers may view their own abodes as cramped forever after.

Versailles. ℂ **859/873-7053.** www.threechimneys.com. Public tour $10 but book at least 6 months in advance.

HOTELS WITH HEART

Snug Hollow Farm Bed & Breakfast $ This organic farm is a perfect romantic getaway from Lexington. The main farmhouse shelters you with its comfortable furniture and handpicked antiques, but for extra privacy there is a rustic (but not too rustic) log cabin. You won't go hungry here: The farm breakfasts are generous, and vegetarians will be especially pleased with the availability of gourmet meatless meals.

790 McSwain Branch, Irvine. ℂ **606/723-4786.** www.snughollow.com.

A Storybook Inn $$ Just like you'd hope it would look: lavishly decorated with original paintings, antique furnishings, and beds you can sink into, and loaded with charm.

277 Rose Hill Ave., Versailles. ℂ **877/279-2563** or 859/879-9993. www.storybook-inn.com.

Swann's Nest Inn $ This horse farm mansion was turned into a romantic B&B and maintains its authenticity. It's not far from Keeneland, so if you want to mingle with local horse people, this is the place to do it.

3463 Rosalie Rd., Lexington. ℂ **859/226-0095.** www.swannsnest.com.

MOST ROMANTIC RESTAURANTS

Sadly, really excellent restaurants are scarce in horse country. But, in addition to the cuisine at Snug Hollow Farm B&B (above), we have a couple favorites.

Lilly's $ BISTRO/FARM-TO-TABLE Chef-owner Kathy Cary was an early advocate of the farm-to-table movement; her restaurant is a lovely combination of elegance and coziness. Don't miss the Bourbon tastings. Everyone raves about the tomato salad and crème brûlée, but we especially love the fried oysters and her take on southern Louisiana style cooking. A steal for the prices she charges.

1147 Bardstown Rd., Louisville. ℂ **502/451-0447.** www.lillyslapeche.com.

The Oakroom $$ CLASSIC AMERICAN This is a dressy restaurant with local delicacies like river sturgeon, frogs legs, and bluegrass bouillabaisse.

At the Seelbach Hilton, 500 S. 4th St., Louisville. ℂ **800/333-3399.** http://theoakroomlouisville.com.

MONTANA: GLACIER NATIONAL PARK & WHITEFISH
Embracing Big Nature

Less than 50 miles north of Kalispell, Montana, are Flathead Lake, Glacier Park, and the town of Whitefish, which combined are a bit of heaven for nature lovers. Whether you start at Flathead and drive to Glacier, or fly to Kalispell and enter the park after exploring Whitefish, you can ride a horse, river-raft the middle fork of the Flathead River and boat on the lake all in one day—and on the next day, you can hike and explore true wilderness.

The Queen of this paradise is **Glacier National Park** (named for its terrain carved from Ice Age glaciers), which spans more than 1.4 million acres of wilderness, alpine lakes, meadows, and mountains and abuts her Canadian neighbor, **Waterton Lakes National Park.** Vestiges of ancient seas, thrusting rock, and the undulations of the earth's crust have produced some of the greatest scenery on the planet here. Only a handful of the original glaciers remain and climate experts say they may be gone in the next 20 years. So, go now. But even when the ice is gone, the romantic vistas and opportunities for the heart will survive. This includes rustic lodges (that require booking way, way in advance) and what may be the most glorious drive in the West (or anywhere), the **Going to the Sun Road,** whose awesome climb up to Logan Pass offers breathtaking viewpoints all along the way. *Warning:* This road is fully open only 3 months a year, and spring comes late to the Rockies, so check ahead. If you are traveling in the summer, plan to take this drive. In peak summer months, a free shuttle takes people up to popular trailheads and views. Some of the jagged peaks, glacial ice, and cascading waterfalls can be seen from the highway; others are reserved for hikers.

You can start your journey in Whitefish, a charming town that has Big Mountain, a great (and well-priced) ski resort in winter, and plenty of attractions when the snow is gone. We suggest ending at Flathead Lake or one of the Glacier Lodges. It will be one of the most beautiful trips of your lives.

KEY ATTRACTIONS

Hiking   There are short, uncomplicated hikes for people who simply want to enjoy each other and this gorgeous country up close. The 2.3-mile **Avalanche Lake trail** is pretty simple and beautiful. Go through Avalanche gorge and see an amazing glacier field and a serene alpine lake. The inbound hike to **Hidden Lake**, close to the Logan Pass visitor center, is easy (partly on a boardwalk), and the jagged mountains present dramatic contrast to the quiet, pristine lakefront, covered with wildflowers in the summer. But it's steep on the return and a bit taxing. The chance of seeing bighorn sheep makes it a worthy trip. Along the **Garden Wall Hiking Trail** (at Logan's Pass), sheer cliffs spout waterfalls for non-stop visual thrills. Be prepared for stunning scenery, acres of wildflowers in the summer, and good views of the Continental Divide. Unless you are an expert hiker, a guide would be advised. Contact **Glacier Guides** (ⓒ **800/521-7238;** www.glacierguides.com), an operator within the park. *Warning:* Grizzlies are seen here, but usually far enough away not to be dangerous.

Kayaking   Gentle kayaking—a perfect activity for two—can be done on Whitefish Lake and the Whitefish River, but start early unless what you really want to do is rent Jet Skis, which start up later in the day.

Rafting the Flathead River   The middle fork offers serious whitewater rafting in the spring (June in Montana!) on rapids whose names forecast their intention—Bone-crusher, Jaws, and Pinball—or more of a lazy affair in late summer. Still you can tip a boat almost any time, so be prepared to get wet. Much of the river is shallow, but occasional swimming holes let you stop and enjoy the water; that is, if you don't mind the freezing glacial melt. A number of raft operators in West Glacier can hook you up.

Visiting Bigfork   This darling little tourist town has a great marina (Jet Skis, kayaks, and other rentals available) on 30-mile long **Flathead Lake** (the largest freshwater lake west of the Mississippi) and many excellent nearby restaurants you can drive or boat to. We like **Many Springs,** 24377 Montana Highway 35 (✆ **406/982-3900;** www.manysprings.com), a classy motel on the lake with excellent food and world-class sunset views, and the **Laughing Horse,** 22360 Montana Highway 83 (✆ **406/886-2080;** www.laughinghorse lodge.com), a cozy restaurant with a limited but well-done menu and charming, reasonable cabins near Swan Lake. Bigfork itself has some worthwhile art galleries, and the summer-stock theater is fun; you can get there by boat, or go there in late summer and gently float down the Swan River in an inner tube. It will be slow enough and warm enough for a lazy afternoon in July or August—but be prepared for the shock of glacial runoff).

Visiting a Ski Resort (in Summer or Winter)   At **Whitefish Mountain Resort,** 3889 Big Mountain Rd., Whitefish (✆ **800/858-3930;** http:// skiwhitefish.com), you will find a big mountain and extensive downhill ski runs. In the summer, you can take the lift up to 6,000 feet-plus for gorgeous views of peaks all around and the Flathead valley below. Share sandwiches on the deck and enjoy the view. We don't know if it's the altitude or Mother Nature's grand horizon, but couples have been known to experience some mutual euphoria up here.

Watching Wildlife   Follow the Middle Fork of the Flathead River to the Izak Walton Inn, which is a piece of railroad history and a great place to consume some calories before you explore further. The inn has a lot of train memorabilia and is set up for winter and summer tourism. Next head to the natural Salt Lick in the park along the river, where you'll see mountain goats show up to satisfy their need for salt.

HOTELS WITH HEART
The Bar W Guest Ranch $$ A few minutes outside Whitefish, this ranch on Spencer Lake is in a gorgeous valley of timbered hills, the lake, and pastures. This is a perfect option if you want to ride all day but your sweetie wants to hang out in town. The lodge is more Western suburban than rustic. There is one big honeymoon suite—grab it if you can. Otherwise, there are tents with large western pole beds that are quite romantic (and a short walk to shared toilet and bath facilities) and a separate duplex with much larger accommodations and nice views. The best scenery will come during the wonderful rides and cookouts in the mountains. If you are interested in Western horsemanship, the ranch starts where your skills start, and when you are ready, gives you lessons in sorting cattle or rodeo sports like pole bending. Other activities (archery, fly-fishing, and skeet shooting) are there for people with sore butts and partners who relish relaxation more than riding. Winters offer backcountry skiing, sleigh rides, and even dog-sledding. *Note:* Most lodges require a week stay, but this ranch has 3-day packages (except high season July–Aug), and your rates include meals and activities.

2875 Hwy. 93 W, Whitefish. ✆ **866/828-2900.** www.thebarw.com.

Glacier Park Lodge $$ Just inside the southeast entrance at East Glacier, this is the park's flagship inn. The imposing timbered lodge marks the early days of the park when the Great Northern Railroad brought tourists to Glacier. The inexpensive lodge is attractive with huge log pillars and, like most the other Glacier lodges, simply furnished a la 1950s rustic. But you are not here for life inside a lodge; your romantic moments will be on the lodge's beautiful groomed lawn, viewing wildflowers, having a cocktail on the deck of the lounge area, or even getting up early to catch a mesmerizing sunrise.

1 Midvale Creek Rd., East Glacier Park Village. © **406/226-5600.** www.glacier parkinc.com.

Kandahar Lodge $ This is a nice alpine lodge and a great value. Big comfy chairs for après ski and soaking tubs to renew your tired body. It's slope-side location on Big Mountain is terribly romantic.

3824 Big Mountain Rd., Whitefish. © **406/862-6098.** www.kandaharlodge.com.

Lake McDonald Lodges & Cabins $ This historic, intimate lodge, built in 1914, is on the park's largest lake. You quickly pass through the atmospheric lobby to the expansive porch facing the lake, which is edged by impressive peaks. The common rooms are iconic lodge style—big, worn couches and chairs for rocking and reading around the large stone fireplace. No one has fancied up the rooms, but they also have a traditional feel to them. Beware the second- and third-floor rooms if climbing stairs isn't easy for you (there's no elevators). We can't recommend the motel units even though some of them have a nice relationship to the lake; they are just too modest to be romantic. The cottages in the woods have a nicer feel to them, a little bit like being back in summer camp. The food here is excellent. And the beach is flat and good for walking, but often busy: This place gets a lot of families and large groups. The entire lake is a center for boating activity; a neat thing to do (that will also remove you from family hub-bub), is to get a canoe and a guide to take you to see wildlife. There are also daily cruises around the lake.

Inside Glacier National Park. © **406/888-5431.** www.glacierparkinc.com. May–Sept.

The Lodge at Whitefish Lake $$ If you start or end up in Whitefish on the Going to the Sun Highway, a stay at this lodge, built in the style of the historic park lodges, would be a romantic getaway. Using local stone and wood, the feel of a classic lodge is intact even with modern and luxurious touches like picture windows and slate floors. Some of the suites are spectacular duplexes with full kitchens and balconies with expansive lake views. The views of the lake from the excellent restaurant are wonderful, and in the cold months when you can't use the lake for water sports, a couple can ice skate, bundle up for a romantic dinner on the ice (!), or just have a perfect port or hot toddy in the two-story lobby before a blazing fire (watched over by a major moose head). Courtesy shuttles to and from the ski lifts, a mere 6 miles away, make this luxury property a veritable bargain, compared to the rates charged up the mountain during peak winter months. Connected by a sky bridge is the less expensive **Viking Lodge,** run by same management.

1380 Wisconsin Ave., Whitefish. © **877/887-4026.** www.lodgeatwhitefishlake.com.

Many Glacier Hotel $ This 1914 lakefront hotel is what we think a great lodge ought to look like. It is a huge, sprawling four-story building and the most popular place to stay in the park—so get your reservation far in advance. The rooms are forest-service simple, but the view is grand—say goodnight to each other still gazing at the lake and the multi-colored mountains. A wide range of activities starts here: boating, hiking, and bird-watching, among them. Rooms have an historic feel, and are adequately sized, but not luxurious. You have two choices: rooms in the main lodge with balconies overlooking the lobby, or lakeside rooms. We vote for the latter because of their views of Swiftcurrent Lake. If you go during berry season, be prepared to see bears wandering around the lodge, greedily eating the succulent huckleberries.

64 Grinnell Dr., Babb. © **406/892-2525.** www.glacierparkinc.com.

Prince of Wales Lodge $$ This lodge is the farthest from the concentration of the park around Whitefish, Flathead Lake, and Big Fork. It is actually over the border in British Columbia and part of the Waterton Lakes National Park in Canada (and more remote than most), but what a scene it is. An imaginative old lodge, kind of a fantasy really, it looks over the lake surrounded by mountains in a spiritual way. It is indescribably romantic. The lodge was built in 1927 as part of the Great Northern Railway lodge-building program, but its gingerbread look makes you think you are in the Swiss Alps. The rooms are small but charming. The most romantic rooms are lakeside; if you can, splurge for one of the suites, which face the lake. Mountain views are also quite nice and less expensive. Even if you don't stay here, it's worth stopping by for the afternoon tea in the lobby.

In Waterton Lakes National Park, British Columbia. © **403/859-2231.** www.glacierparkinc.com.

MOST ROMANTIC RESTAURANTS

Echo Lake Café $ CAFE A charming local wood cabin sort of hang-out where breakfast hooks people in, but lunch is special too (closed for dinner). Breakfast is especially lavish with big portions of several kinds of Eggs Benedict (the hollandaise is exquisite) and good renditions of old classics, like Joe's Special with fresh spinach, onions, and sautéed ground beef. The coffee is excellent, and so are the prices.

1195 Swan Hwy. 83, near Bigfork. © **406/837-4252.** www.echolakecafe.com.

Heaven's Peak Dining and Spirits $$ AMERICAN Housed in a massive log building, this restaurant is framed by gorgeous gardens and lawns. The roadside location makes it a bit noisy, but the dynamic view of the Glacier wilderness holds your attention. This is not to say the gorgeous setting is the only reason to come here: The chef's talent shines in the fresh fish dishes, plus all the Montana favorites (buffalo, beef, and our pick, huckleberry chicken). This is comfort food, done well.

12130 Hwy. 2 E, West Glacier. © **406/387-4754.** http://heavenspeakresort.com.

Serrano's $ MEXICAN/SOUTHWEST   Serrano's does a great mix of Mexican, Californian, and Southwestern cuisines. Be mindful of the margaritas: They are justly famous, but if you're not careful you will be too looped to taste the fine enchiladas and other classic dishes. Come early; the place gets packed.

29 Dawson Ave., East Glacier Park. ℭ **406/226-9392.** http://serranosmexican. com.

Tupelo Grille $$ CAJUN/SOUTHERN   It's not exactly Western ambience, but this restaurant has excellent Creole cooking, which just may strike you as romantic after you've had one too many buffalo burgers from local hang-outs.

17 Central Ave., Whitefish. ℭ**406/862-6136.** www.tupelogrille.com.

GLACIER NATIONAL PARK BY NIGHT

The only nightlife inside the park is wildlife hunting prey—so maybe you should be tucked in your tent or lodge when it turns dark. If you are in Whitefish, though, try the **Great Northern Bar and Grill,** 27 Central Ave. (ℭ **406/ 862-2816;** www.greatnorthernbar.com) downtown for live music and dancing. The **Alpine Theater Project at the Whitefish Performing Arts Center,** 600 E. 2nd St. (ℭ **406/862-7469;** www.alpinetheatreproject.org), offers way-off Broadway summer productions that are very good, with purloined East Coast talent.

SEDONA, ARIZONA
Hiking the Glorious Red Rocks

Whether you fly into Phoenix and drive north to Sedona on state highway 174 or you fly into Flagstaff and drive south on 89A, you are going to see mind-boggling, strikingly beautiful scenery. You probably will have to pull off the road to absorb the startling ochre of the rocks, their mammoth size and the spiritual gravitas that they impart. If you happen to get there at sunset when the rocks start to glow, you will arrive at your hotel in a state of awe that may not lift until you depart. Sedona's vistas from any direction are among the most dramatic that you can find anywhere.

This is called red rock country: One red behemoth after another challenges you to decide which is more gorgeous, more touching, more grand. The mountains surround numerous canyons, rivers, creeks, and swimming holes providing unending new ways to take in their majesty and mystery. The mountains make everything else—except love, except each other—look small and passing, and their impact on a couple can be significant. You begin to talk about what's important in life: Do you really want to stay in a big city, or do you need to spend more time together? Nature here puts on its most spectacular tableaus, eroded canyon walls and buttes, and mesas of extraordinary size and shapes, and she asks you to examine the passage of time and use it wisely. Add this extraordinary backdrop to some wonderful outdoor adventures and several sumptuous places to stay or eat, and you have the ingredients for a stay that is beyond romantic.

There is a caveat, however. Downtown Sedona has not been managed well, and while the scenery is sublime, the town center is strip malls with a tiny nod to a western theme. You can avoid it most the time, and, fortunately, most the places we recommend are hidden from this vulgar side of paradise.

KEY ATTRACTIONS

Unlike Phoenix, Tucson, and many other desert areas, Sedona has four seasons. The summers are hot, but the area has abundant woods, canyons, and creeks where the heat drops precipitously; in fact, it can be downright cool at night. The summer has a "monsoon," but the storms pass quickly; personally, we find the thunder and occasional lightshow quite romantic. Much closes in winter, but you'll still find snowshoeing, Nordic (cross-country) skiing, and, about an hour and a half northwest toward the Grand Canyon, significant downhill runs.

Most people come here during warmer weather for the red rocks and the national forests. You can busy yourself with them within close range of downtown Sedona.

Cliff Castle Casino Hotel   Sedona is a pretty quiet place, and we like it that way, but if it suddenly feels eerie, here's the antidote: lounges, bowling, music, and gambling at the local casino-with-a-view.

555 Middle Verde Rd, Camp Verde. ✆**800/381-7568**. www.cliffcastlecasinohotel. com.

Excursions   Several ancient Indian ruins, including **Tuzigoot** and **Montezuma Castle**, are an easy trip and worth visiting. We think that going up into the mountains to see the quirky town of **Jerome** is also romantic. While you are on the roam consider the 4-hour tour aboard the **Verde Canyon Railroad** (300 N Broadway, Clarkdale; ✆ **800/582-7245**; verdecanyonrr.com; $35–$55 for coach, $80–$120 first class, $600 private caboose). And, if you have never given the **Grand Canyon** the time it deserves, this might be a really great overnight trip. The Grand Canyon really should be seen from the bottom as well as the top but even a cursory look over the canyon is awesome. Check out www.gatewaytosedona.com for details.

Hiking   The city disappears quickly, and you immediately enter a wilderness area where trailheads are everywhere. (If it looks familiar, it's because Hollywood discovered the easy access to this spectacular scenery early on and immortalized it in cowboy movies.) It's heaven for hikers, but beware of the trails that have easy access because you will encounter a lot of other hikers. If your dream of a hike is being alone in the wilderness, avoid the trails that start right off Arizona 179 or 89A because all the newbies and novices (like us) will be starting off from there. That said, a good introduction to the hikes is the 4-mile trail that starts at **Bell Rock Pathway,** which is right near the Village of Oak Creek. A trail less traveled is the **Cathedral Rock Trail**, through its trailhead in a housing development (which is marked before you get to the Village of Oak Creek). We are also fans of the **Boynton Canyon Hike** (pick it up off Boynton Canyon Rd.) and the **Mystic Trail,** which has an unmarked parking pull-off on Chapel Road, not too far from the Chapel of the Holy Cross. This undemanding stroll also takes you past a few home developments, but get on the trail, and you'll feel nicely isolated. Finally, for a rewarding 3½-mile loop that includes fabulous views, go to the **Airport Mesa Trail.** It's an easy hike that starts about halfway up Airport Mesa on Airport Road. Start early in the day to avoid crowds in the parking lot.

Horseback Riding   Even if you're not a rider, just taking the horse for a walking tour of the scenery will give you a whole new perspective of this fascinating environment. **Day in the West**, 252 N. Hwy. 89A (🕿 **800/973-3662** or 🕿 928/282-4320; www.adayinthewest.com; $95 per person), can find you the right horse.

Mountain Biking   As you might expect, red rock mountain biking can be a challenge. Couples may want to head to the base of Bell Rock, where there are both easy and hard biking paths; choose one that you both can enjoy. You can rent bikes and get advice at **Mountain Bike Heaven** (1695 West Hwy 89A; 🕿 **928/282-1312;** www.mountainbikeheaven.com) and **Sedona Bike & Bean**, Village of Oak Creek (75 Bell Rock Plaza; 🕿 **928/284-0210**; www. bike-bean.com), which also sells coffee. If it all gets too hot for you in the summer here, you can push your peddles towards Flagstaff where its cooler temperatures might suit you better.

New-Age Events   Perhaps you've heard of the Vortex: It is the way people describe what they feel is a special energy that Sedona puts out. New Agers flock here to get zapped with it, and you might find that you feel it, too, even if you usually smirk at the suggestion of such things. If you are interested in exploring this more, there is no end to the classes and meditations offering the experience. Look for opportunities on local billboards.

Picnicking with a View   There are plenty of good spots for a scenic picnic in Sedona but our favorite is at the top of **Schnebly Hill Road,** amid the red rocks with views of the sculptural rocks cascading into the distance. This dirt road is best driven in a high-clearance vehicle (Jeeps can be rented in Sedona). To get there, head south on SR 179, cross the bridge over Oak Creek (at the Tlaquepaque shopping center), and turn left on a road that starts out paved but soon turns to dirt. Follow the scenic switchbacks and cliff-edged curves right up to the Schnebly Hill overlook. That's where you spread your blanket, take out your wine bottle and edibles, and open your hearts.

River Splashing & Tubing   **Oak Creek** is a surprisingly long and deep stretch of water. It's not far out of town, and its right off Highway 89A in the state park, so you can't miss it. *Heads up:* On weekends its family time so you won't have solitude, but it's beautiful, and feels awfully good when the summer heat closes in. Have fun at the famous **Slide Rock.**

HOTELS WITH HEART

Canyon Villa Bed and Breakfast Inn of Sedona $

This award-winning owner-operated B&B was designed to showcase views of Bell Rock and Courthouse Butte, two famous Red Rock icons of Sedona. A three-course breakfast with homemade cinnamon buns is included, as are late afternoon appetizers and evening dessert trays. The solar-heated pool has spectacular red rock views. Although designed for a romantic couple experience, children age 11+ are welcome.

40 Canyon Circle Dr., village of Oak Creek. © **800/453-1166.** www.canyonvilla.com. Multi-night discounts.

El Portal Sedona $$

Built of hand-cast adobe, El Portal looks like an old hacienda and is filled with Arts and Crafts period antiques. Each large room has a distinct character, from Arts and Crafts to cowboy chic. Whirlpool tubs, private balconies, and red-rock views are available in many room. For a few extra dollars, you can enjoy a superb breakfast in your room.

95 Portal Lane. © **800/313-0017** or 928/203-9405. www.elportalsedona.com.

Enchantment $$

At the opening of Boynton Canyon, this resort has a breathtaking setting, and the pueblo-style architecture almost disappears into the landscape. You are not only in one of the top hostelries in Sedona, but also at a perfect place to start your hikes. Glimpse some ancient petroglyphs and ruins, and end your days in reverie. Trails can get crowded, so go early in the day. If you can, spring for one of the one-bedroom casitas, or better yet, a suite so that you can have one of their wonderful sitting areas with high ceilings, wood beams, and authentic southwestern fireplaces. You will be able to sit on your patio and take in the amazing views of this box canyon. In fact, the views will follow you everywhere: at the wonderful Yavapai restaurant (where you can dine even if you don't stay here) or at **Mi amo**, the resort's destination spa designed as a modern Native American–style pueblo. Shaded by cottonwood trees, the spa backs up to the red-rock cliffs of Boynton Canyon, while indoor and outdoor pools and outdoor massage cabanas are at the foot of the cliffs. You might consider the boldly designed and gorgeously tricked out guest rooms that are here, near the spa; each has a private patio and a gas fireplace.

525 Boynton Canyon Rd. © **800/826-4180** or 928/282-2900. www.enchantmentresort.com.

L'Auberge de Sedona $$$

Along Oak Creek under towering sycamore trees, this deluxe boutique resort is inspired by the rushing water that defines its boundary. Some of the hotel's cabins and cottages are gathered here by the water, while others are away from it all on a hill, with a gorgeous red rock view. Their rustic exteriors belie elegant French country interiors, complete with wood-burning fireplaces. Units closest to the babbling brook are surrounded by private, lushly landscaped grounds, and all of them have romantic outdoor showers with enough hot water to last for over an hour. The

THE healing POWER OF TRAVEL

Relationships can hit the rocks for many reasons and when they do, they need a time and place for nurturing and strengthening—a place to heal. A partner might have been sick for a while and needs to recover from both the illness itself and the fear that comes with surviving a major illness. The other partner needs to get out of the caretaker role and back to feeling like a lover again. Other times it's the loss of a job or a parent, the antics of a wayward teenage child, a big move, or other painful ordeals that put you both through emotional trauma that unbalances you. And perhaps there is nothing wrong in your relationship that can be named but still something seems off— you've been arguing or more critical than usual—and you are both recognizing that it's been ages since you've been intimate.

That's when it's time to re-center. Places of majesty can help you to remember that life is much bigger and grander than what you've been through or are going through. Destinations of awesome beauty—especially mountains and canyons that took millions of years to form—help you put things into perspective. Other places, like Sedona, get known for their aura or "vortex" or other characteristics that suggest they are spiritually endowed. This type of travel venue yields many shared spiritual moments that will support your psyche as well as your romantic connection. Throughout this book we recommend several are places to meditate and just to communicate a little better with the universe.

Because life is so stressful and distracting, sometimes just going to a place where you can feel strong again in mind and body can help you heal. We're not sure how spas got to be so focused on women; we believe that spas are an underutilized resource by men and couples, too. Many spa retreats, if they offer enough physical activities and stimulating evening programs, can be perfect places to go together.

We recognize that trying to bring back romance after very difficult periods of life is no small challenge. We are not advocating

more modern residences on the high side of property are in their own neighborhood, but are an easy walk to the creekside restaurant. These are among the largest and most luxurious accommodations in Sedona.

The restaurant is excellent (with an extra fine wine list) and is probably the most romantic place to eat in Sedona. All the tables have a beautiful view of Oak Creek, and the small whirls and waterfalls keep you entertained. And the inventive American menu has strong Mediterranean influences.

conventional counseling while you're traveling, but we do think that professionals in healing environments can help get you back on your feet and help you begin to heal your connection to each other.

Here is one such place, not too far from Sedona, that helps couples rebuild happy, healthy, and balanced lives, while enjoying vacation fun. It includes couples workshops and skills-building activities that create emotional magic, which carries over when you return to "real life."

One of the world's top destination spa resorts, **Miraval** is less than 2 hours south of the Phoenix airport (where you would fly to get to Sedona) and located on 400 acres near the Santa Catalina mountains of northern Tucson. Guest rooms range from casual but spacious doubles that may be upgraded with an outdoor patio or shower or a soaking tub to splendid private villas with stunning vistas, full kitchens, and infinity pools, but what sets Miraval apart from other spas is the array of activities designed to boost confidence and bring couples closer by taking on the challenges together (see the website for full list of classes and programming). A team of first-rate therapists and specialists offer activities and programs that are dedicated to relationship-building and sexual health. Among the fascinating ways to heal (all optional, of course), couples move together across a cable 30 feet, an exercise that forces collaboration. Another option is the Equine Experience, a horse-handling program (that's really about YOU), guided by Wyatt Webb, a renowned Miraval specialist and "cowboy psychologist," as a way for people to get some insight into their emotions and relationships. Famous guest speakers address various aspects of wellness, including celebrity chefs who share secrets of food that is both fabulous and healthy. There is a holistic doctor on staff, too.

5000 E. Via Estancia Miraval, Catalina. ℂ **800/232-3969.** www.miravalresorts. com. $870–$2,400 per night. Rates include all meals and many activities and lectures, plus resort credit toward activities and spa treatments. Multinight and seasonal packages available.

L'Auberge oozes romance and to help you along they offer, among other options, a "proposal package" that includes breakfast; a four-course intimate dinner with creek-side views; a couples massage; turndown service with rose petals, champagne, and strawberries; and a private hiking trip to a picturesque location.

301 L'Auberge Lane. ℂ **800/905-5745.** www.lauberge.com.

MOST ROMANTIC RESTAURANTS

We love the excellent, if pricey, restaurants at L'Auberge and Enchantment (previous listing), but here are a few more dining experiences.

Cucina Rústica $ MEDITERRANEAN   Give yourself a bit of luxury after your days of hiking and biking. The restaurant's central dome is illuminated by would-be stars but you can sit on the patio for the real thing. The menu shares some credits with Dahl & DiLuca, its sister property (following), but Cucina cooks up some of the world's best grilled prawns, wrapped in radicchio and prosciutto.

Tequa Plaza in Oakcreek Village, 7000 Rte. 179. ✆ **928/284-3010.** www.cucina rustica.com.

Dahl & DiLuca $$ ITALIAN   You're in Tuscany here, and its colors and grotto makes it very high on the romance-o-meter (we might call it a tie with L'Auberge for the most romantic restaurant in Sedona). Even if it weren't so romantic, the excellent Italian food would make it worth your visit. Pasta is the main thing, and portions are big. The calamari is divine, and the veal and seafood dishes are also excellent. Vegetarians have good options: Pick anything with eggplant here, and you won't go wrong.

2321 West Highway 89A. ✆ **928/282-5219.** www.dahlanddiluca.com.

The Heartline Café $$ NEW AMERICAN   The restaurant's logo is the Zuni heart line, a symbol of health and longevity and just right for the healthful, creative food served here. Winning flavor combinations—tea-smoked chicken dumplings with spicy peanut sauce or warm red-cabbage salad—spark the senses. The Heartline's most famous dish is the pecan-crusted local trout with Dijon cream sauce, and the vegetarian selections are sublime. The lovely courtyard is a pleasure to enjoy together, and the traditionally elegant interior makes for a romantic setting. Visit the adjacent **Heartline Gourmet Take-Out & Market** for the makings of a fine picnic lunch.

1610 West State Route 89A. ✆ **928/282-0785.** www.heartlinecafe.com.

SEDONA BY NIGHT

Evening Sky Tours   If you weren't an ardent stargazer before, Sedona's brilliant starry sky may convert you. If you want to know what you are looking for, go on a sky tour, guided by a professional astronomer. Village of Oak Creek. ✆ **928/203-0006** or 928/853-9778. www.eveningskytours.com. $60 adult, $50 seniors.

Rene at Tlaquepaque   A local landmark at the charming Tlaquepaque Arts and Crafts Village, this French restaurant and bar has a casual warmth that is great for sipping a margarita after sunset or indulging in fine American and Continental cuisine. 336 Arizona Rte. 179. ✆ **928/282-9225.** www.rene-sedona. com.

Canyon Moon Theatre   This small theater presents eclectic fare, including classic plays, light comedies, or edgier stuff—and does it well. 66001 Rte. 179, Village of Oak Creek. ✆ **928/282-6212.** www.canyonmoontheatre.org.

WALLA WALLA WINELANDS (WASHINGTON STATE)

Holding on to Small Town Charm

Of all the wine country areas we mention in this book, this is probably the least known, and like other travel writers, we have a shiver of regret sharing a somewhat secret place with the rest of the world. But it deserves your attention for a romantic getaway, particularly if you loved Napa about 40 years ago and would like to taste the flavor of first-rate wineries before the vintners became celebrities and billionaires took over the area.

Walla Walla is still a small picturesque town that's about a 5-hour drive or 45-minute flight from Seattle. You might want to drive it, though: There are great wineries along the way, starting about 2 hours outside of Seattle in the Yakima valley and continuing pretty much all the way up to Walla Walla. Lowden, just 15 miles west of Walla Walla on Highway 12, should not be missed, namely **Woodward Canyon Winery** (11920 W. Hwy. 12; © **509/525-4129;** www.woodwardcanyon.com); **L'Ecole No 41** (41 Lowden School Rd.; © **509/525-0940;** www.lecole.com), whose tasting room is in an old schoolhouse; and on arriving in Walla Walla, you might want to visit the incredibly welcoming **Reininger Winery** (5858 Old Hwy. 12; © **509/522-1994;** www. reiningerwinery.com).

Walla Walla seems to reinvent itself every so often. At one time it was the center of banking in the state, and there are still some significant old bank buildings in town (now mostly used for other things) that show the town's initial aspirations. It is still the center of wheat farming, and there are many prosperous and productive wheat fields in the area. However, the wine industry has started to nudge some of those fields into vineyards, causing a bit of bad blood between wheat and grape growers. But there is plenty of land for both, and a string of little towns in the area also beckon with new industries such as weekend summer markets and gourmet food production (see below for a destination fromagerie!). Still, these days in Walla Walla it is the romance of wine that has renewed Main Street, which now offers significant restaurants, cozy inns, and charming tasting rooms in and out of town, all set against the gorgeous Blue Hills (they actually do turn a deep blue in certain light) and rolling hills of wheat or vineyards in every direction.

KEY ATTRACTIONS
Wine Tasting

Wine is romantic to think about: red and luscious, white and crisp, tantalizing your taste buds and opening your heart to love and, let's face it, lust. Walla Walla has many tasting rooms, some with a fee, many without, certainly enough to get very inebriated, very quickly. A designated driver is a must unless you are tasting only downtown (where tasting rooms are within a block or two of each other). If you choose to swallow rather than spit (and most people do), you might want to find a place to stay nearby.

There are special weekends (Spring Barrel, Fall Barrel, Cayuse, and Leonetti Weekend—where cult wines Cayuse, Reynvann, and Leonetti host their club members) when seldom-open tasting rooms open their new vintages and sometimes their library wines. But because most Washington wine growers and vintners are small producers, some of the boutique-tasting rooms are open to only wine club members. But fear not: More wine tasting rooms are open than you will be able to visit in 3 days of serious quaffing. Following are our picks for the most romantic tasting rooms.

Castillo de Feliciana   This tasting room has a Spanish theme, and its wines have a Spanish heart. Feed each other little tapas or bring your own charcuterie since there are heartwarming spots to picnic looking out at the vineyards. Their red blends are what you want, and we are partial to their Malbec and Tempranillo.

85728 Telephone Pole Rd., Milton-Freewater, Oregon. © **541/558-3656.** www.castillodefeliciana.com. Tasting room open Fri–Sun.

DaMa Wines   This woman-owned business has a classy tasting room and a nicely sassy attitude. It is located in the pulsating heart of historic Walla Walla and the exceptional red wines are complimented by the colorful personalities of the owners, who are often found pouring for their patrons. We love the Cowgirl Cab, but we'd probably buy it for the label alone. Get some Walla Walla lore here and buy a bottle for a picnic.

51 E. Main St. © **509/525-2299.** www.damawines.com. Tasting room open Thurs–Mon; call for private tastings.

Garrison Creek   One of the more beautiful tasting rooms is about 20 minutes outside of Walla Walla, housed in a beautiful new barn that's based on a classic design, with vaulted ceilings and a pristine barrel room, and sweeping views of the Blue Mountains. Its syrahs and cabernet sauvignons are wonderful.

4153 Hood Rd. © **509/525-7377.** www.garrisoncreekcellars.com. Tastings by appointment only.

More Wines to Explore   Castillo de Feliciana (above) is situated in a beautiful area of the valley with rolling hills and wineries here and there surrounded by vineyards. While you are driving around, you might want to visit **Sleight of Hand Cellars,** 1959 J. B. George Rd. (© **509/525-3661;** www.sofhcellars.com; tasting room open Thurs–Sat, or by appointment); **Waters Winery,** 1825 J. B. George Rd. (© **509/525-1590;** www.waterswinery.com; tasting room open Fri–Sun; $10 tasting fee refundable with purchase); **Va Piano Vineyards,** 1793 J. B. George Rd. (© **509/529-0900;** www.vapianovineyards.com; tasting room open daily); and **Pepper Bridge Winery,** 1704 J. B. George Rd. (© **509/525-6502;** www.pepperbridge.com; tasting room open daily; $10 tasting fee refundable with purchase). These are terrific wineries within minutes of each other, close to the Oregon border. All are friendly places, and Waters has a gorgeous modern tasting room with a picnic spot in the back.

Beyond the Wineries

Bicycling   Rent a bike at **Allegro Cyclery,** 200 E. Main St., Walla Walla (© **509/525-4949;** www.allegrocyclery.com), and head toward the Blue Mountains or the wineries at the Airport or the intense number of wineries near Stateline (the road that divides Washington and Oregon). There are lots of flat paths, tree-covered neighborhoods, and small wineries to visit. Bring a corkscrew and a picnic basket and celebrate your relationship by uncorking a treasured bottle at a pretty place.

Cheese-tasting   Located about 30 minutes from Walla Walla, **Monteillet Fromagerie** (109 Ward Rd., Dayton; © **509/382-1917;** www.monteillet cheese.com; tasting room open Fri–Sat, Sun by appointment only), is an authentic French *fromagerie*, complete with East Friesen-Lacaune lambs, French Alpine goats, and Great Pyrenees dogs. Young people come from around the world to intern here.

Hiking   The trail at **Palouse Falls State Park** (© **360/902-8844;** www. parks.wa.gov) runs along the rim above the falls. For your trouble, you get a terrific view of the 185-foot falls splashing down on the Palouse River against a dramatic basalt background. Just try to resist embracing with this background. Nearby is Waitsberg, a cute town where you can stop for fantastic burgers at the **Whoopemup Hollow Café** (120 Main St.; © **509/337-9000).**

Walking   The **Bennington Lake & Mill Creek Trail** (© **509/527-4527**) is a walkers' walk and a people-watchers' place; it's an easy ramble and full of birds, river mammals, and some humans that enjoy them.

HOTELS WITH HEART

The Inn at Abeja $$$ A few miles outside of town, this picture-perfect inn is surrounded by vineyards, beautiful auxiliary buildings, and an elegant barn amid green lawns, flowers, and big shade trees. Guest rooms are in a collection of converted outbuildings, and while each suite is different from the next, each has plenty of room and romantic personality. The Edison room is our current favorite: Facing a wooded gully with a stream running through it, the room has modern stylish lines and a fantastic shower—it's instant motivation to open the excellent wine Abeja has placed in your room and forget about the rest of the world. It has its own winery, but you will also be in strolling distance of **K Winery** and **Walla Walla Vintners**. Reserve far in advance. 2014 Mill Creek Rd. © **509/522-1234.** www.abeja.net.

The Marcus Whitman $ This is the largest hotel in town and the grand dame of the area. She has toughed out hard times to emerge as a quite wonderful destination. The dining room has an ambitious and creative chef, and the rooms have been fluffed up, especially the tower suites. They are quite large, with big gleaming white bathrooms and comfortably large sitting rooms. The old world charm here is quite romantic. Downstairs are paneled dining rooms and a paneled bar where the winery people often gather to sample each other's wares. Breakfast is included with your room and is an abundant buffet. The management can't do enough for you.

6 W. Rose St. ⓒ **866/826-9422** or 509/525-2200. www.marcuswhitmanhotel.com.

Walla Faces $$ Several large, sophisticated downtown Walla Walla apartments are available to rent. Dine in and create your own candlelight dinner here. For romantic views, however, we like their country property about 10 minutes outside of Walla Walla in a beautifully situated home on a hill looking at vineyards or territorial views. ⓒ **877/301-1181.** www.wallafaces.com.

MOST ROMANTIC RESTAURANTS

The Marc Restaurant $$ NORTHWEST   The Marcus Whitman Hotel has invested in a serious chef, and its menu is now among the most sophisticated in town. Cuddle into a booth and share a really great steak here, or get braver and try some of the fine game offerings. If you stay at the Marcus Whitman, you can order up room service and make it even more romantic.

6 W. Rose St. ⓒ **866/826-9422** or 509/525-2200. www.marcuswhitmanhotel.com.

Saffron Mediterranean Kitchen $$ MEDITERRANEAN   This is an intimate place with major achievements. Always an ambitious menu and excellent food, it's a treat to eat here. The chef combines unusual ingredients together, but they always seem to feel inventive rather than just odd. You need to reserve early here because just about everyone adores this downtown restaurant. See if you can get the romantic corner table next to the window.

125 W. Alder St. ⓒ **509/525-2112.** www.saffronmediterraneankitchen.com.

Whitehouse-Crawford Restaurant $$ NORTHWEST   This lovely space, formerly a woodworking mill, is now a spacious and sophisticated restaurant with brick walls, white cloth table settings, a sweet little bar (which we think is wonderful for a romantic moment before dinner) and an extensive wine list. The menu is always intriguing, with careful selection of the best sources for produce and meat.

55 W. Cherry St. ⓒ **509/525-2222.** www.whitehousecrawford.com.

WALLA WALLA BY NIGHT

Wine towns don't generally have much nightlife. The bar at the **Marcus Whitman** is always a nice place for, um, another glass of wine. Some of the Main Street restaurants and bars have live music on the weekends and visiting performers often play at Whitman College, a pretty little campus adjacent to downtown that also offers a safe romantic place to stroll. Sometimes there is music at the **Whoopemup Café** in Waitsberg, about a half-hour away. If an exciting nightlife is what you seek, you are likely to be a little disappointed here. Better to dine late, drink well, sleep in and in the morning head to **Olive's** (21 East Main St.; ⓒ **509/526-0200**) for a perfectly executed latté.

WILLAMETTE VALLEY (OREGON)
Tuscany in Oregon

You are sitting on your balcony at a golden stucco inn. Beyond the red-tiled roof to your west and as far as your eyes can see are rolling hills, densely covered with vineyards. The mist is settling over the valley, but in the distance you see two giant balloons floating above the bucolic scene. Are you honeymooning in Tuscany? No, you haven't even used your passports. This is Oregon's Willamette Valley, and it's a stunner.

Oregon's wine industry now produces some of the finest Pinot Noir on Earth, and more than 200 boutique and large wineries reside in this enclave only 45 minutes from Portland, which itself deserves a romantic nod. The scale of Portland is European. A river city, its walking and bicycling paths run for 318 miles, serving as a seductive backdrop for some extremely well priced boutique hotels and fine restaurants. Stay a few days in Portland when you come for the nearby wine country. You can use it as your quite wonderful base for a coastal visit, but in late spring, summer, or fall, the wine country is your romantic destination. It ranks in beauty and infrastructure with the other romantic winelands in this book, surpassed in beauty perhaps only by the Winelands outside Cape Town (p. 104)

The Valley is linked by a series of smallish towns. With Newburg and Dundee—just 2 miles apart—arguably at the center, the Valley is linked by a string of towns from about 20 miles west of Portland to McMinnville that is full of wineries. To do this area justice, you need 3 days, but you probably won't want to leave after that. We think this is the perfect road trip for lovers: beautiful scenery, award-wining vintages, and off the beaten path. Quite a few people hire a limo service familiar with the area (several offer wine tours; try www.winecountrycarservice.com or www.insiderswinetour.com) to steer them through wine country, and that's not a bad idea. The charm of the area, like Tuscany, is its winding roads, high hills, and arresting vistas, but those features can be both tricky and distracting, and you don't want to add alcohol in the mix. Drivers need to focus on their driving. Ah, but passengers here can concentrate on romance!

KEY ATTRACTIONS

What can we say? We love a good wine. Below, some memorable wineries and other attractions that are worth your time.

Wine Tasting

Anderson Family Vineyard Here's what we mean by passion. Cliff Anderson left his job in the geek world to form a wine partnership with his wife as soon as they could afford to do it. They found a magical hill (with a stunning, almost 360-degree view) that had exceptional sun exposure and soil.

Cliff is a charming host, and his pride in his small, handcrafted wines is inspirational. Pinot Gris, Chardonnay, and Pinot Noir from several different parts of his property reap the praise of everyone you meet, including us.

20120 NE Herring Lane, Newberg. ☎ **503/554-5541.** www.andersonfamilyvineyard. com. Free tasting for scheduled visits of groups smaller than 8.

Archery Summit   This winery perches, as you might imagine from the name, on high, amid beautiful grounds. In good weather, tastings are outside and in. We suggest inside because the tasting room is very small and intimate, and you get a lot of attention that can add up to a special shared experience. And wait until you taste the wines: deep rich Pinots (to be truthful, our favorite Pinot from anywhere, ever!) and not too buttery or oaky chardonnays.

18599 NE Archery Summit Rd., Dayton. ☎ **503/864-4300.** www.archerysummit. com. Tasting fee $15 per person.

Argyle Winery   Yes, you can have too much Pinot Noir. We craved champagne and got its sublime American equivalent right in downtown Dundee. Argyle is a big wine distributer, but also makes wines in small quantity sold only at the Winery. (Grab the Blanc de Blanc!) In a cute house with a nice specimen garden and, in the spring, masses of rhododendrons, it is a tasting experience that pleasures all of the senses.

691 Hwy. 99W, Dundee. ☎ **888/427-4953,** ext. 233, www.argylewinery.com. "Backstage Pass" tour and tasting $25 per person (with 15% off purchase after tour).

Domaine Serene   A Tuscan–style winery with a gorgeous approach and vistas to match. The large beautiful tasting room with tables is a perfect place to sip away the afternoon. Right across the road is the excellent **Domain Drouhin Oregon**, owned by a French family of some winemaking renown that has vineyards in Burgundy and with a fine deck, set before a gorgeous view that can leave you speechless.

6555 NE Hilltop Lane, Dayton. ☎ **866/864-6555.** www.domaineserene.com. Tasting fee $20 per person.

Winderlea Vineyard & Winery   Here's a break from the Tuscan or farmhouse theme. This place is all steel and glass and high-concept modern. Hey, couples thrive on new experiences! It is handicapped accessible at the entry and in the bathrooms, and it looks like something you might see in a chic neighborhood of architected homes—all the more surprising because it is the work of the same architect, Ernie Munch, who did the Tuscan-themed Domain Serene and Domain Drouhin (and quite a few other wineries in the area). Sit and enjoy a yummy rosé or a pinot noir.

8905 NE Worden Hill Rd., Dundee. ☎ **503/554-5900.** http://winderlea.com. Tasting fees $20 per person.

Beyond the Wineries
Ballooning   Romance and passion are the mother of invention—or is it the other way around? Anyway, to keep love alive, be inventive. When's the last

time you rode in a hot-air balloon? Let this be the first! Ballooning here has the added magic of beautiful views (typically at sunrise) of the Willamette Valley combined with the visceral thrill of being aloft. A chase crew follows you on land to scoop you up for champagne wherever you descend an hour or so later. Talk about casting your fate to the wind! Fun ballooning outfits are **Portland Rose Balloons** (℗ **877/934-6359;** www.portlandroseballoons.com) and **Vista Balloon Adventures** (℗ **800/622-2309;** www.vistaballoon.com). They both offer special packages for airborne weddings and proposals.

Bicycling   Biking Dundee and the Red Hills would require you to be very fit, but you can bicycle with ease through the relatively flat and gloriously green farmland that makes up much of the Willamette Valley. Pick up a gourmet sandwich at the slick **Red Hills Market,** 155 SW 7th St., Dundee (℗ **971/832-8414;** http://redhillsmarket.com)—don't stint on the macaroons—and take a ride out to one of the many nearby parks. Champoeg Park is near Heirloom Roses (below) and is rather an heirloom itself. With hills gently sloping to the Willamette River, Champoeg is the place where Oregonians decided to join the American Revolution and separate from England. Nicely shaded areas along the river make great places to spread a blanket and open a bottle of wine.

Evergreen Aviation and Space Museum   Has your guy had enough fine dining, wine, and roses? Take him to the space museum (and water park and Imax) just outside McMinnville. These huge glass buildings house a full-scale Titan II missile, dozens of antique and modern planes, and the amazing Spruce Goose, the odd invention of the even odder Howard Hughes. This thing was flown once for under an hour and now it sits perfectly unscathed inside a building that rivals the air and space museum in Washington D.C. Seriously, you will both be blown away by this place.

500 NE Captain Michael King Smith Way, McMinnville. ℗ **503/434-4185.** www.evergreenmuseum.org. Admission $25 for adults, $24 for seniors $65+.

Heirloom Roses   The colors. The aroma. The fragile beauty of the official bloom of love. If you love roses, or even sort of like them, here is a wonderful place to stop. This famous breeder and importer of old, rare, and English roses invites you to its 5-acre gardens of thousands of roses. Grab a Pinot at the nearby Anderson Family Vineyard (see above) and some vittles at Sandwiches Express (homemade bread!), also in Newberg, and have a picnic. See whether your love is like the Scottish poet's: Like a red, red rose, of course! It's about 25 miles from Portland (which has its own amazing rose garden) in St. Paul, near Newberg and Dundee.

24062 NE Riverside Dr., St. Paul. ℗ **503/538-1576.** www.heirloomroses.com. Free admission.

HOTELS WITH HEART
Portland
The Benson $ This is perhaps the most elegant Portland hotel, with an excellent continental restaurant and a superior wine cellar. Major renovations were done in 2007, so the old hotel has some new zip. The spacious rooms

and suites with brass and velvet fittings remind you that this is the kind of hotel presidents have stayed in.

309 SW Broadway. ℭ **503/228-2000.** www.bensonhotel.com.

The Heathman $$ This luxury hotel is located near the Symphony and Performing Arts Center. But more to the point: It was the backdrop for much of the naughty "Fifty Shades of Gray"—it's up to you what to do with that information. The large, genteel rooms and suites are equipped with nice amenities like French press coffee makers. The paneled Tea Court lobby is kind of a happening place with Jazz concerts and afternoon teas.

1001 SW Broadway. ℭ **800/551-0011** or 503/241-4100. www.heathmanhotel.com.

Hotel Lucia $$ This centrally located hotel is chic and modern in every way, with cool muted tones in the stylishly comfortable the rooms. Here's a nod to couples who like to work out together: It has a 24-hour fitness center.

400 SW Broadway. ℭ **866/986-8086.** www.hotellucia.com.

The Willamette Valley

The Allison Inn and Spa $$ The premier Willamette Valley hotel has every service imaginable and is marred only by its location in a neighborhood, rather than the scenic wonderland at the Black Walnut Inn (below). But the Allison compensates with extensive acreage, gardens, and abundant sophistication. You are welcomed under a dramatic stone and glass *porte cochere,* as if at an exclusive country club. The rooms, especially the suites, are large and luxe, with gas fireplaces, soaking tubs, and window seats. Dining at the restaurant, Jory, is extremely fine, with a fabled wine list. You'll find amenities galore, like the large spa, indoor pool, and men's, women's, *and* co-ed lounges. We like the latter a lot. We hate that so many places forget that men and women who have just had a wonderful massage might be in a mood to be together afterward.

2525 Allison Lane, Newberg. ℭ **877/294-2525.** www.theallison.com.

Black Walnut Inn $$$ This all-suite Dundee hotel has done a good job of impersonating a Tuscan villa. You drive up a hill on a long, winding, wooded lane, then through a carriage house and into a lovely courtyard and the soothing sounds of a fountain and birds singing. The substantial main building is informal inside. You'll find a medium-sized dining room (where you will have a delicious breakfast). The living room windows yield a spectacular view beyond a grand lawn. Not all of the suites have the extraordinary views, but many do and almost all of them have something—a small garden, a terrace—to recommend them. Lavish bathrooms with soaking tubs are not uncommon. One extremely beautiful suite (Vista) is fully handicapped accessible and has a special tub. There are plenty of outdoor sitting areas to enjoy the incredible view.

9600 NE Worden Hill Rd., Dundee. ℭ **503/538-8663.** www.blackwalnut-inn.com.

Le Puy Inn $$ For this pricey valley, we can call this place reasonable. Le Puy is an eight-room inn in a peaceful setting that was once a private home. Set in a beautiful valley near amazing scenery and very fine wines, it is a lovely, unpretentious but classy place to stay, especially if you plan to spend more time together outside than in.

20300 NE Hwy. 240, Newberg. © **503/554-9528.** http://lepuy-inn.com.

MOST ROMANTIC RESTAURANTS
Portland
Andina in Portland $$ NEW PERUVIAN This little jewel of a restaurant gives you a genuine taste of Peruvian culture, with aromas, flavors, and musical performances that hit the spot. It specializes in one of our favorite genres of couples food: tapas, the little bits of Hispanic culture the world over that are best served with each other's forks or fingers, or nuzzled over. This lively cafe has dozens of choices, and it's located in the chic and easy to navigate Pearl District.

1314 NW Glisan St. © **503/228-9535.** www.andinarestaurant.com.

Cocotte $$ FRENCH It means casserole, but this little French bistro has a far more romantic personality. You can cuddle together here on the comfortable banquette seats, and the servers will let you order at your own pace, as leisurely as you want. The food is an imaginative interpretation of country French, focusing a lot on fish, chicken, and rabbit, and Cocotte offers a wide choice of historical cocktails. It's quite informal, but gracious.

2930 NE Killingsworth St. © **503/227-2669.** http://cocottepdx.com.

Le Pigeon $$ FRENCH This restaurant is run by Chef Gabriel Rucker, winner of the James Beard Rising Star Award, who is also famous for his offbeat takes on classic French foods like pâté, veal cheeks, and beef tongue, as well as serving cowboy steaks on truffles and magnificent hamburgers. His food is universally praised, but so is the romantic setting, with muted lighting and comfortable modern decor. Tables for two are available outside when the weather permits.

738 E. Burnside St. © **503/546-8796.** www.lepigeon.com.

Willamette Valley
The Painted Lady $$$ FRENCH This glorious restaurant resides just off Dundee's main street in an adorable turn-of-the-19th-century house. It rolls out its special fare with the kind of expertly calculated perfection that deftly lures two hearts to the brink of romance. Its glistening white and cream walls, servers in white shirts and black pants and ties, fancy china on dazzling white tablecloths, crystal chandeliers and candles strategically placed tell you about the restaurant's ambitions (plus the fact that you must reserve quite a bit in advance). The five-to-seven course tasting menu (with optional paired wines and an optional artisan cheese plate) is finely conceived and executed. Each course is imaginative, and small surprises arrive between courses, such as candied nuts, a scrumptious cheese puff, and chef's whims, such as a

salmon tartar, cucumber "caviar" or a small but fantastic taste of homemade pasta that has divine but not always recognizable ingredients. Our dinner ended with a perfectly done Grand Marnier soufflé and the signature chevre cheesecake, this time with fresh rhubarb topping. In a wine-tasting room, we overheard someone declare this restaurant the "best in Oregon." It may be.

201 S. College St., Newberg. ℘ **503/538-3850.** http://thepaintedladyrestaurant. com.

The Red Hills Provincial Dining $$ CONTINENTAL/NORTHWEST The homey feeling, good wine list, and wonderful food make a comfy combination in this tidy restaurant tucked into a restored Craftsman bungalow in Dundee. It's a great place for ruminating on the day's pleasures and mapping tomorrow's. Truth is, you'll want to keep talking and eating all night. The food is non-trendy, even traditional, and flawlessly prepared, relying on the herbs, fruits, and vegetables grown in the organic gardens on the grounds. Things are so copacetic here the only argument we can imagine arising is whether the wine complements the food or the food the wine.

276 N Hwy 99W, Dundee. ℘ **503/538-8224.** http://redhills-dining.com.

ZION & BRYCE CANYON NATIONAL PARKS (SOUTHWEST UTAH)
Monumentally Awesome Canyons

We think much of the American West is enchanting, and Utah plays a large role in our thinking, with five incredible national parks. For us, Utah's Zion and Bryce Canyon parks are romantic way beyond expectation! Both are sites of unparalleled natural beauty and, because they are close together, you can visit them both in one trip. If you don't live in the region, plan to fly to Las Vegas and rent a car or take a shuttle to St. George, Utah, and rent one there.

Zion National Park

Zion National Park (℘ **435/772-3256;** www.nps.gov/zion) tops our list of romantic Western parks. Zion has it all: spirituality, beauty, rugged challenges and, when you want it, pampering for your body and pure relaxation for your mind. Entering Zion is one of the most magnificent mountain experiences on earth—especially at daybreak and sunset, when it's almost unbearably beautiful and the red rocks light up with incandescent inner life. On Utah's high Colorado Plateau, massive sandstone monoliths contrasting with the big blue sky are mesmerizing like nowhere else.

The mountain highway that runs down to the bottom of Zion Canyon has occasional gaps in the rock that let you glimpse the canyon walls before you reach the floor. It's like a slice of heaven, and you can't wait to get the whole panorama. (Note that the national park controls descent into the canyon, and in spring and summer you must go in by shuttle; however, some tours will stop for views). At the bottom, the sheer cliffs rising from the canyon floor are massive and breathtaking, and if you have our reaction, you probably won't be able to say more than "Wow," and give your partner a hug.

The region is full of iron, so at sunrise and sunset the canyon glows brilliant red, orange, or pink, and sometimes, all three. Of course, we also love Bryce Canyon and other nearby parks (Canyonlands and Arches, for sure), but for sheer romanticism and expansion of the soul, it is Zion we recommend not only heartily, but absolutely. Do your life a favor: Put Zion on your list.

KEY ATTRACTIONS

Pleasure Hiking & Scenic Lookouts   Many day hikes within Utah's **National Parks** (© **800/200-1160;** www.utah.com/hike) are stunning. Fortunately, Zion has many short walks for people who want the views but not the tougher climbs. **Riverside Walk** is good for novices and lovely in the spring when native flowers cover the rocks. **Weeping Rock** has some steep parts, but it is a short excursion. If you are up for a challenge (and don't mind high ridges with over a thousand foot drop below) the summit of **Angels Landing** is worth the climb. For less heart-pounding tours, there is a lovely paved road along the river called the **Pa'rus Trail,** and it's good for a bike ride or just a nice walk.

There are iconic things to see as well. A striking and major sandstone monolith called **The Great White Throne** is a must see for park visitors. Happily, you don't have to be a hiker to see it: It is visible from the park's drive as well as from Angels Landing and various other places, including **Observation Point, Deertrap Mountain,** and **Emerald Pools Trails.** Sharing an awe-inspiring moment in front of something so magnificent will make you feel closer to each other and intensify this shared experience.

The Narrow is an unusually dramatic stone canyon—extremely narrow, but 1,000-feet deep! A rainstorm can show you the might of the river, which flows peacefully along in fair weather. But beware: Flash floods are common for the Narrows, so check weather forecasts before heading out.

HOTELS WITH HEART

Flanigan's Inn $ Just outside Zion park, this complex of rustic rock and timber buildings creates a lodge atmosphere, and the setting, among trees and landscaped lawns and flowers, is very pretty.

428 Zion Park Blvd., Springdale. © **800/765-7787.** www.flanigans.com.

Harvest House Bed & Breakfast $ This B&B has plenty of western atmosphere. It was built only a few decades ago, but it feels like a charming 19th-century Victorian. You can view the signature red rocks of Zion from the garden and from various parts of the lovely, landscaped grounds, including the decks of some of the rooms. The rooms themselves have a sweet, winsome quality, and you will not hear your fellow travelers every move. It's homey great breakfasts prepared with care and decorations reflecting the owners taste in local art. Ask for a west-facing room that offers that famous Zion sunset or the two with porches that give you a full on view of the Zion cliffs.

29 Canyon View Dr., Springdale. © **800/719-7493** or 435/772-3880. www.harvest house.net.

Zion Lodge $ Zion Lodge looks old and authentic but actually what you see is a replica of its original style, re-created after a terrible fire in 1966 destroyed the older structure. It's not fancy, but it has the prime Zion location, right at the bottom of the valley floor, and it's surrounded by the forest and magnificent slabs and peaks of pink sandstone. There is a range of rooms, a motel-like building that has basic comforts, and cuter cabins with wood beams and stone fireplaces that fulfill your yearnings for lodge-like charm. Most fetching are the sweet, small porches where you can sit and watch the changing light illuminate the cliffs.

1640 W Redstone Center Dr., in the park. © **435/772-7700.** www.zionlodge.com.

MOST ROMANTIC RESTAURANTS

Red Rock Grill in Zion Lodge $ AMERICAN   This is the view you came for. You can see the amazing rock formations through the Grill's huge window and never have to hike a foot. Plus you won't have to sacrifice taste, and this is the place to try the region's famed mountain trout.

At Zion National Park Lodge, 1640 W Redstone Center Dr., in the park. © **435/772-7760.** www.zionlodge.com.

The Spotted Dog Cafe $ AMERICAN/REGIONAL   The large windows and spacious patio help keep your eyes on the spectacular scenery. This is a great place to greet the day: Breakfasts are big and fresh. For dinner, we love the seasonal menu here, but the trout is always a good choice. This restaurant will tempt you with other local favorites like lamb and beef, all hormone-free and from ranches and farms that observe environmentally sensitive practices. The wine cellar and microbrews on draft are something to howl about.

At Flanigan's Inn, 428 Zion Park Blvd., Springdale. © **435/772-3244.** www. flanigans.com.

Bryce Canyon National Park

Drive about an hour and a half from Zion and you will discover another awesome park, and it is completely different from what you've seen. What you will notice first at **Bryce Canyon National Park** (© **435/834-5322;** www. nps.gov/brca) are the "hoodoos," twisted limestone spires shaped by millions of years of erosion that make you feel you are on another planet. They exist in an enormous natural amphitheater that you can hike to see these amazing structures from every angle, or you can see the gorgeous rock formations from the scenic drive and selected viewpoints. A nice thing about this park is that it offers a paved canyon-view trail and accessible in-park lodging for those who use a wheelchair or have limited mobility in any way.

KEY ATTRACTIONS

Serious hikers have plenty to choose from, but there are also some fairly easy trails that will take you to many of the park's most majestic spots. However, almost anywhere you look you will see the **hoodoos.** A good place to see them is on the undemanding **Queen's Garden trail,** where there is a famous hoodoo labeled **Queen Victoria** because the top of it looks quite like a crown. Trails are rated for difficulty, and if you are ambitious, you can pick the **Navajo Trail,** which begins at **Sunrise Point.** Wherever you go, keep your eyes focused both far and near because the chances of seeing wildlife is really good. Prairie dogs are common, but you could also see a coyote, bald or golden eagles, or if you are really lucky, the occasional shy mountain lion that comes out to hunt, often after the big supply of rabbits that cover Bryce. You don't have to hike far to see the park's wonders; in fact, you don't have to hike at all. You can rent bikes or just drive the 18-mile scenic paved road that traverses the park.

Scenic Adventures   See this magical world from the air, and enlist **Skywalker Balloon Company** (© **866/366-8824;** www.skywalker.at) to arrange it for you (you can do a private ride, too).

Pepper thinks that the best way to see anything is on the back of a horse (or in this case, it could be a mule), and Bryce Canyon is a unique place to do it. **Bryce Canyon Rides** (© **435/679-8665;** www.canyonrides.com; trail rides $60–$80 per person), located within Bryce Lodge, can guide you privately or in a group. The rides go slow, but you should know that there are some rather narrow passages. Your steed brings you close to the rock formations, and your guide will tell you what their shapes bring to mind. If you are up for a longer time in the saddle, companies located in Red Canyon (just outside the park) offer customized half-day excursions.

HOTELS WITH HEART

The Lodge at Bryce Canyon $ Great curb appeal here. This handsome 1924 ponderosa pine lodge has been updated, but it's lost none of its charm. We like the cabins for romance. They whisper tales of the old west, and in the cooler months, you can hold hands and cuddle in front of the stone fireplaces, which are sort of authentic except they are gas rather than wood burning. Less authentic, but with more modern conveniences are the suites within the main lodge. They have a nice light feel to them, and if you are the kind of couple that wants a bit of private space, you will like the fact that they have a sitting area that is separate from the bedroom.

Hwy. 63, in the park. © **435/834-8700.** www.brycecanyonforever.com.

Majestic View Lodge $ In the land of stunning views, this two-story rustic stucco and log place competes well. Every room we have seen is oriented to the fabulous bluffs and changing light on the cliffs. Guest rooms are furnished with rustic aspen decor, and you can choose your outdoor space—a terrace, a patio, or a balcony; the deluxe suites have kitchenettes. This is cattle country, so mosey up to **Majestic Lodge Steakhouse** and have a significantly large steak, or visit **The Lady in Red Saloon** or the **Zion Canyon Brewing Company** where you can drink in the view as well as have a quality beer. Your visit should include a fun exploration of the Lodge's trading post and wildlife museum.

2400 Zion Park Blvd., Springdale. ℂ **866/772-0665.** www.majesticviewlodge.com.

Stone Canyon Inn $ This is the get-away-from-it-all favorite, a place for lovers to be alone. The inn is charming, romantic, and anchored by the kind of views you come for when you visit these parks. Here, however, you get the added perk of pampering with all the attention to details that high end hosting requires. Each of the six guest rooms has that Aspen look, with wood paneling and fine western furniture. We particularly like the cottages, although they are really designed for families or two couples since they have two bedrooms and two bathrooms.

1380 W. Stone Canyon Lane, Tropic. ℂ **866/489-4680.** www.stonecanyoninn.com.

MOST ROMANTIC RESTAURANTS

Ebenezer's Barn & Grill $$ AMERICAN Live large, live western. You can soak up cowboy culture, music, and food here and just have a great old time.

110 E. Center St., Bryce Canyon City. ℂ **435/834-8003.** www.ebenezersbarnand grill.com.

The Lodge at Bryce Canyon Restaurant $ AMERICAN This historic lodge is a bit rough around the edges, but that's part of its charm. Don't come here looking for a celebrity chef, but you will find good food (first rate steaks and salmon, and yummy berry bread pudding) and a cozy lodge vibe. Like all atmospheric park lodges, the restaurant includes large stone fireplaces, and in this case, large windows looking out at the scenery.

At the Lodge at Bryce Canyon, Hwy. 63, in the park. ℂ **435/834-8700.** www.bryce canyonforever.com.

BRYCE CANYON BY NIGHT

Astronomy Talks A black night with a sky emblazoned with stars is one of the most awesome sights in nature. We don't know why, but the stars talk to us and beg us to think of worlds beyond our imagination. Looking up into stars that twinkled many millions of years ago is a romantic experience, but astronomy lectures from park rangers can make it a mind-expanding one, as well. The unpolluted skies of Bryce Canyon, far from city lights, allow more stars to dazzle us. Listen to experts explain the heavens on Wednesday and Friday evenings from spring to fall. For extra romance, go on the night hikes that are given on a full moon. ℂ **435/834-5322.** www.brycecanyoncountry.com.

EARTHY DELIGHTS: CANADA & MEXICO

To the north are sky-high mountains and pristine lakes, forests, and critter-filled meadows. To the south are more mountains and deserts and beaches and other national wonders. We who live in the United States are geographically blessed, to be sure. This chapter covers some of the greatest natural wonders—romance-inducing ones—in Canada and Mexico.

BANFF & LAKE LOUISE (CANADIAN ROCKIES)
Love on the Rockies

No mountains or lakes are more beautiful. If sharp-edged peaks with glacial ice tinted by sunset and nature, displayed in infinite varieties, get to your hearts, make reservations for this Rocky Mountain paradise.

For a good, 1-week itinerary, fly or drive to Calgary and then drive the 129km (80 miles) west to Banff. Stay for a few days and move on to Lake Louise and then return to Calgary. A truly romantic alternative is **The Rocky Mountaineer** (✆ **877/460-3200**; www.rockymountaineer.com). The luxury train starts in Vancouver, toddles along the coast and through the mountains for a day, and stops for one night in the beautiful Kamloops area before arriving in Banff the next day, while some itineraries include stops at Lake Louise and Jasper. Prices vary according to hotel accommodations and whether you go for 3 or 4 nights (approximately $1,143–$1,351, per person including meals and hotel accommodations); 7-day packages ($2,173) include Banff and Lake Louise and can include helicopter tours of the glaciers. The train is all windows, service, great food, and luxury, and you get vistas of the Rockies usually reserved only for expert hikers who have several weeks available. In fact, you could spend many weeks in the Canadian Rockies, winter or summer, and never be bored by the scenery or the action. Each season has its offerings.

Banff

A huge Canadian national park in Alberta's Rockies along the Trans-Canada Highway, Banff is also the name of the resort town at the park's center, known for its mountains and hot springs. The park is expansive, more than 5,180 sq. km (2,000 sq. miles) of dramatic peaks and valleys with enough beautiful lakes and hikes to easily accommodate the huge international population that comes to ski, hike, or fish in just about every season. It is undoubtedly among the most beautiful and striking locations on the planet. That said, the town of Banff can get stretched a little thin: The streets and sidewalks can be crowded in both winter and summer. Some shops close in the winter and shoulder seasons, but when high season returns shops galore and trendy restaurants announce that tourism has returned. Golfers flock here in the spring and summer, many of them to one of the most famous courses in Canada, the 27-hole **Fairmont Banff Springs Golf Course** (② **403/762-6801;** www.fairmont. com/BanffSprings; greens fees C$155–C$230, depending on season). If golf is something the two of you share, this course would be a double eagle.

After your more civilized pursuits, the magnificent Rocky Mountain wilderness will be waiting. It is a great destination for outdoor sports of all kinds and at all levels: hiking, biking, camping, mountain climbing, skiing, and more. And, of course, the sightseeing is incomparable.

KEY ATTRACTIONS

Biking   Serious biking couples, fear not! There is an ambitious, but highly doable biking tradition here: the 286km (178-mile) trip between Banff and Jasper. Travel along the Icefields Parkway accompanied most of the way by astounding views of mountains and glaciers. Make sure you both are experienced at this kind of cycling: It's all at high elevation and considered a demanding ride (www.rockymountaincycle.com).

Hiking   Banff is also a hiking paradise, with more than 80 good-to-go trails at last count, with more always being added. Some are easy strolls, but others are only for people who know how to hike the back country and are prepared to encounter wildlife. You will need a permit if you opt for exploring the back country.

Caution: Remember, this is Grizzly country, and all kinds of precautions have to be taken so you don't end up mauled. Check with park rangers.

Almost anyone can enjoy the **Johnston Canyon hiking trail** with its wooden bridges, tunnels, wide paths, and sheer cliff faces. Its upper and lower falls are glorious in summer and dramatically frozen in winter. It's a workout to negotiate the six other cascades to get to the upper falls, but not too much of a sweat. You will have a lot of company if you stop at the Upper Falls. However, it will be more private beyond the Falls, where the trail gets steep as it heads to the Inkpots, a series of deep-green pools slotted into a beautiful alpine meadow. This additional (and worthwhile) excursion takes 4 hours round-trip. Not ambitious enough? Bourgerau Lake is a 14.5km (9-mile) hike that takes about 5 hours to complete; it starts off the TransCanada Highway,

15 minutes west of Banff. Be on the lookout for wildlife—both for your enjoyment and your safety.

Horseback Riding   **Warner Guiding and Outfitting** (© 800/661-8352 or 403/762-4551; www.horseback.com) offers short day trips with a meal (breakfast or dinner) for C$218 to C$400 per person. Some rides travel between backcountry lodges, while others make a loop from their base.

Rafting & Canoeing   There is rafting, and then there is RAFTING. Easy floats can be had on the Bow River, while tougher ones happen on the gorgeous Kicking Horse River. **Canadian Rockies Rafting** (© 877/226-7625; www.rafting.ca) will tell you how the rivers are running at the time of year you visit and explain the various levels of rating—from easy to experts only— that each river experience presents. For serious white water (not to mention seriously frigid water) the Kicking Horse River is the real deal, with Class IV rapids. **Hydra River Guides** (© 800/644-8888; www.raftbanff.com) will pick you up in Banff or Lake Louise for a 2½-hour run down there, but remember: This is an adventure river.

Riding the Gondola   Take the **Sulphur Mountain gondola;** it's 8 minutes up to the 2,281m (7,486-ft.) peak, with an altitude gain of 698m (2,292 ft.). (There's a restaurant here, if you are starving.) Below, the Bow River Valley spreads out in a vista of rushing water and jagged peaks. Now you are parallel with the peaks you've been straining your neck to see from below. There are gentle trails here, and you can follow a boardwalk to neighboring Sanson's Peak, where you'll find the **Cosmic Ray Station and Observatory**, a historic weather station. If you're feeling up to it, hike back down—it's not difficult.

Seeing the Icefields   If you have never seen a true glacier, here is your chance. The Icefields Parkway will take you there, and this is also the Highway 1 that will take you to Jasper, the other famous resort area in the vicinity. Less ambitious hikers can take the Peyto Lake trail (and still get awesome views) for about a half-hour walk from the sign announcing the first Icefields stop on the Parkway after Banff. You don't need a guide: There are explanatory displays along the mile-long loop. If, however, you just want to hop on a bus and be driven to the icefields (especially the massive Athabasca Glacier), there are specially equipped snow buses that leave every half-hour from the **Columbia Icefield Glacier Discovery Centre** (located just off Hwy. 93); reservations are not required, and the cost for the 80-minute adventure is C$49.95. But if you don't want to take the time to get up close and personal, don't worry: You can see glaciers almost all the way to Jasper.

Skiing   Ski season here lasts into late May. The two principal ski areas in the Park (**Mount Norquay** and **Sunshine Village**) pool their business interests with the third area, **Lake Louise Mountain Resort.** Contact Ski Banff Lake Louise Sunshine (© 844/762-7190; www.skibig3.com) for all information and bookings.

Trout Fishing   This region is trout-fishing central. If you feel out of it because you don't know how, or if your interest in the sport is now piqued, learn something new together! For couples that would like a guide, **Hawgwild Flyfishing** (✆ **403/678-7980;** www.flyfishingbanff.com) will give you fly-fishing lessons and guarantee a catch or your money back! Tours start at C$449 for two people.

HOTELS WITH HEART

The Fairmont Banff Springs Hotel $$$ The views from this historic spot just might draw as many visitors to it as all of its other features combined. If you took a room here without a view you'd be cheating yourself big time, though once inside you may never want to leave. Views *of* the hotel are also pretty amazing. The Fairmont looks like a Bavarian castle when seen from another hill peeking grandly out of the trees; it was quite the event when it opened in 1888. The property has been renovated many times, and it now has a fabulous spa (a less-expensive way in—just go for the view from the sky-lit hot pool if nothing else). Guest rooms vary in size; some have quite modest square footage, but they are all attractively decorated and offer fine personal bathroom amenities. For the most privacy, request one of the honeymoon suites; located in the quiet turrets of the castle, they come with a Jacuzzi and the requisite stunning views. Wandering through the hotel is fun, though, even if your own room is viewless. There are grand party rooms, a small and lovely wine bar to eat or drink in, and more than one posh restaurant (plus a deli where it is easy to grab a bite in when you are too tired to walk down to the village, or too maxed out on multicourse dining).

405 Spray Ave. ✆ **800/441-1414** or 403/762-2211. www.fairmont.com/banff-springs.

Rimrock Resort Hotel $$ A local classic, Rimrock is outside of town just above the Banff Springs Hotel on a mountain slope, and most every room has a knock-out view of the Bow Valley. (Ours just stunned us!) The towering lounge, with its floor-to-ceiling windows and huge fireplace, is the best place to experience it all. The understated opulence—unpolished marble floors and traditional but cushy/comfy sofas and chairs—are in complete harmony with the excellent service. Room prices are gauged to the view; suites are large and have cozy couches (request one on the 4th floor), plus full patios to relax on and take in the splendid view. In the winter, Rimrock serves hot cider and cocoa beside the outdoor ice rink and fire pit. There are also three restaurants (at every price and formality level) so if you just want to cozy in, you can. In the summer, the gondola is a short walk away. One romantic promotion we just loved was a specialty martini that could be ordered with either crystal or diamond earrings for her.

300 Mountain Ave. ✆ **888/746-7625** or 403/762-3356. www.rimrockresort.com.

The Storm Mountain Lodge $$ This is a rustic and romantic alternative to the bigger, fancier lodges. The main log lodge has a lovely outdoor veranda in a peaceful setting with stunning mountain views; most of the accommodations are log cabins with big stone fireplaces. There is an excellent restaurant on site, which is important since the lodge is 20 minutes from much busier Banff and Lake Louise. Here, the wilderness is right outside your door.

Banff Windermere Parkway. © **403/762-4155.** www.stormmountainlodge.com.

MOST ROMANTIC RESTAURANTS

The Bison Restaurant and Terrace $$ AMERICAN   The Bison's casual blend of tradition, innovation, and elegance is tucked into a relaxing dining room. Its "Rocky Mountain Comfort Food" makes it the best restaurant in the area. We liked the elk and the venison, which was tender and plentiful, but the bison burger was also delicious! Other excellent choices were the bison short ribs and macadamia-crusted lamb sirloin. The decor is modern minimalist made stylish by wood floors and vaulted wood ceilings.

211 Bear St. © **403/762-5550.** www.thebison.ca.

Bow Valley Grill $$ CANADIAN   The famed dining room in the Banff Springs Hotel is pricey, but the majestic views of the Fairholme Mountain Range and the Bow River are worth it—and the food is first rate. Fine local offerings, such as pan-fried Bow River trout and Alberta beef steaks make up for somewhat unimaginative sides (baked potatoes). This restaurant lives up to its popularity.

In the Fairmont Banff Springs, 405 Spray Ave. © **403/762-6860.** www.fairmont. com/banff-springs.

BANFF BY NIGHT

Aurora   How about martinis on the Rockies? Aurora is Banff's convincing version of a cool cocktail lounge—with assorted martinis and DJs.

110 Banff Ave. © **403/760-5300.**

Soaking at Upper Hot Springs   The hot springs, just up Mountain Avenue, stays open until 11pm. The huge outdoor pools have undergone renovations and can handle a good-sized crowd (the waters are usually around 90°F, so it's most popular in winter). You can sit comfortably on a sunken bench that circles the pool. The 1931 building is a perfectly preserved example of mountain architecture of the era. But inside it's contemporary and the home of **Pleiades Massage and Spa** (© **403/760-2500;** www.pleiadesmassage. com), complete with steam room, massage, and aromatherapy.

At the top of Mountain Ave., 4km S of the center of Banff. © **800/767-1611** or 403/762-1515. www.hotsprings.ca.

Lake Louise

The small town of Lake Louise is 56km (35 miles) northwest of Banff and feels less touristy than its neighbor. It's nestled in trees and has no main street. Across the lake you'll see the Victoria glacier over blue-green waters. The town also has some of the most amazing skiing and—whatever the season—trekking in Banff National Park.

KEY ATTRACTIONS

Exploring the Glaciers   The Victoria Glacier is an easy hour's walk on the **Lakeshore Trail** from town. If you are fit enough, you can continue toward the aptly name **Big Beehive** along the **Plain of Six Glaciers Trail**, which as you might imagine, leads you to permanently snow-covered rock faces and at one point, the fantastic sight of the six glaciers for which the trail is named. If you have made the trek, you will certainly deserve your lunch or perfect cup of tea at the **Plain of the Six Glaciers Teahouse (© 403/667-4663)**, where the view is otherworldly.

Hiking Paradise Valley/Larch Valley   This hike, near Lake Louise, is for serious hikers. This 17km (10.5-mile) hike covers diverse elevations and delivers a gorgeous array of sights. If you are experienced hikers—we mean it; you should both be in very good physical condition to do this hike—you will not want to miss the romantic views of major waterfalls, peaks, and passes that this trail provides. Your reward at the end of your approximately 8-hour hike is the spectacular Moraine Lake, which some people think it is even more impressive than Lake Louise.

Horseback Riding   A mountain breeze and the rhythmic thud of horse hoofs are the only sounds on **Timberline Tours (© 888/858-3388** or 403/522-3743; www.timberlinetours.ca), an outfitter that runs single- and multiple-day horseback trips from Lake Louise. Think of the easy backcountry ogling of scenery a couple can do if they don't have to hike there! These outfitters know what they are doing and keep a quiet string of horses; all you have to think about is each other. Eating lunch or a dreamy dinner along a wilderness trail can be very romantic.

Winter Sports   With 113 ski runs, Lake Louise is among the largest ski resorts in North America. (For information, see Banff, previously.) But romance in winter can also mean simple fun, like ice-skating right on Lake Louise, romantically framed by an ice castle in front of Chateau Lake Louise hotel. Or go sledding on the toboggan run behind the Fairmont Banff Springs hotel or on the great sledding hill next to Bow Falls, with a nearby ice rink where a bonfire pit is usually blazing. Tobogganing is a major adrenaline rush—all you have to do is hold on to each other!

HOTELS WITH HEART

The Fairmont Chateau Lake Louise $$$ Perhaps the most picturesque Alpine-like hotel in the country—at first sight, it looks like a fairytale chateau—set before the improbably turquoise waters of Lake Louise and its glacier mountain backdrop. Inside, the massive turreted Edwardian hotel is part lodge, part elegant hotel, and 100% luxurious and expensive. Some guest rooms are small, but all are elegant and comfortable, with luxurious feather duvets and walls decorated in soft tones. Rooms on the Fairmont Floor offer top-notch concierge services and pampering. But whatever you do, angle for a room with a view down the lake. It is mesmerizing. If romantic bathrooms are important to you, all of them here are well appointed and commodious. The staff is extremely helpful and pleasant.

111 Lake Louise Dr. ☏ **866/540-4413.** www.fairmont.com.

The Post Hotel & Spa $$ Gracious hospitality is the hallmark here. The 1940s log dining room and bar are now joined by a hotel wing, which is graced with beautifully furnished rooms. This posh Lake Louise landmark doesn't have a lakeside setting, but it is close to the river and has plenty of charm with a rustic touch. Most rooms have stone fireplaces; the "F" suites are considered the best. Comfort is key, with roomy balconies and comfy furniture. In fact, the lobby and the library are particularly cozy and inviting. The former is full of big chairs and sofas that feel just right, especially in winter when there is almost always a fire blazing away, and the latter is wood paneled and very clubby in the nicest sort of way.

In Banff National Park. ☏ **800/661-1586** or 403/522-3989. www.posthotel.com.

MOST ROMANTIC RESTAURANTS
Baker Creek Bistro $$ CANADIAN This simple, cozy restaurant serves some of the best cuisine around, featuring mostly local ingredients.

At Baker Creek Mountain Resort, in Banff National Park. ☏ **403/522-2182.** www. bakercreek.com.

The Post Hotel Dining Room $$$ INTERNATIONAL This is one of the most famous restaurants in Canada. The Austrian-themed wood paneled dining room has offered destination dining for years, dating back to when its esteemed host was a mere motel. The restaurant has earned countless awards for both its food and wine—it has a wonderful 30,000-bottle wine cellar. Have a meal in the original log building near the romantic roaring fireplace. Service is impeccable, and the food is sublime. Top menu items are the meat and seafood choices, but save room for the impressive desserts. It would be a mistake to pass up the opportunity to dine at the Post Hotel while you are here, though it will cost you. One more piece of advice: The food is so good, and the wine is so tempting that driving home might not be the best idea. You can order a cab for round-trip service from your hotel.

At the Post Hotel & Spa, in Banff National Park. ☏ **800/661-1586** or 403/522-3989. www.posthotel.com.

JASPER (CANADIAN ROCKIES)
Thrills, Not Frills, in the Wilderness

Jasper National Park (☏ **780/852-6236;** www.jasper.travel) is Canada's largest mountain park and offers visitors a more laid-back, less urbane, mountain experience than Banff, but with equal options for adventure, discovery, and relaxation. Think of the park and the town of Jasper (in the park) as a great escape from urban life and, above all, a place to connect with nature. The park has the largest Dark Sky Preserve in the world, and its visitors focus more on what lies outside of town than what's in it. They come for the hiking, biking, climbing, horseback riding, and rafting.

There is one proviso in naming Jasper a romance capital: It is uniquely for lovers who strongly identify "rustic" with romance. Shopping and fancy dinners? Not so much.

A good introduction to the area is aboard the **Jasper Tramway** (© **780/852-3093;** www.jaspertramway.com; $35 adults, tram only; $46 tram plus meal). From the foot of Whistler's Mountain, passengers ride up to the peak (7,283 ft.), where you step onto an alpine picnic area carpeted by mountain grass or dine at the upper terminal's romantic **Treeline Restaurant**. Surveying the vast park below you, you'll feel you are both far away—and close together.

KEY ATTRACTIONS

Jasper may be wild country, but it offers some of the diversions more "civilized" resorts do. You can go trout fishing on your own, but you can also opt for full-on planned excursions, with an outfit like **Jasper Adventure Centre** (© **800/565-7547;** www.jasperadventurecentre.com), a local favorite for customized jaunts and memorable experiences. Our favorite was the tour of Maligne Lake (© **866/625-4463;** www.malignelake.com). Golfers can hit the Jasper Park Lodge's 18-hole course (1 Lodge Rd.; © **780/852-6090;** www.fairmont.com/jasper/golf; greens fees C$145–C$185, depending on season), just east of town. But the rest of your romantic fun will be a bit more rustic!

Hiking The 8km (5-mile) **Jasper Discovery Trail** (© **613/860-1251),** which circles the town of Jasper, is good for novices or strollers, but it does provide some challenges . You can do it in a leisurely 2 (or so) hours, but you can certainly explore off trail if you like; plus there are plenty of exits along the way that lead back to town. Other easy hikes are **Cavell Meadows,** often picturesquely dotted with wildflowers, and the **Valley of the Five Lakes** hike, which passes through a lodge pole pine forest and a creek with beavers to a lakeside picnic spot. It's 6km (3.7-miles) round-trip. For a challenge, try **Maligne Canyon**, a breathtaking gorge whose view is most spectacular looking up from the depths of the gorge itself. The hike is 7.4km (4.6 miles) round-trip. For more information, check out the local nonprofit website **Hikejasper. com**; for guided hikes, try **Walks and Talks Jasper** (© **888/242-3343** or 780/852-4994; www.walksntalks.com).

Horseback Riding Trail horseback riding is a fantastic way to see more of the backcountry than you might on foot. Options range from a quick few-hour jaunt to a 3-day tour that will take you to a remote but well-appointed lodge. Ask your hotel for details.

Miette Hot Springs They aren't kidding: These are *hot* springs. Get in slowly; you will be poached in about 104°F water. Take the waters in an expansive swimming pool or two soaker pools surrounded by trees and a sublime mountain skyline. The hot springs are reason enough to make the trip, but there's a bonus: spotting elk, deer, coyotes, and moose in their natural habitat along the drive to Miette, making it one of the best places in the park to view wildlife.

Jasper National Park. ℂ **800/767-1611** or 780/866-3939. www.hotsprings.ca.

Rafting Being on water makes us feel romantic, and the scenery here makes it even more transfixing than usual. Jasper has a number of beautiful, but sometimes demanding, rivers. Depending on the time of year and the river, you can get a lazy float or white water thrills. Check out the Athabasca, Fraser, and Sunwapta. Outfitters tell us that the Athabasca River is usually the river of choice for people who just want to float calmly down the river, with just a few little rapids to jazz up the experience. The other rivers offer more adventure. Your concierge can tell you which outfitter is running which rivers. Or, contact **Maligne Rafting Adventures** (ℂ **780/852-3370;** www.mra.ab.ca).

Skiing Jasper's exciting, underrated downhill ski area, **Marmot Basin** (ℂ **780/852-3816;** www.skimarmot.com), is just as much fun to ski as Banff, but not nearly as crowded. The Basin, 19km (12 miles) from Jasper on Highway 93, is skiing as it used to be: few lines, plenty of lifts, plus more than 50 runs.

HOTELS WITH HEART

Becker's Chalets $ We love resorts that are next to rivers, and this one is a nostalgic nod to the time when log cabins were the likely lodging of a trip to the woods. But these cabins are a modern take on the old favorite and light and comfortable inside. The kitchen will help you stick to a budget (or make your life easier if this is a family vacation), but Becker's dining room is among Jasper's best (see following). For romance, we appreciate the large bedrooms and the river rock fireplaces for getting cozy, lulled by the sounds of the nearby Athabasca River.

Highway 93 South, Icefields Parkway. ℂ **780-852-3779.** www.beckerschalets.com. Family cabins available with up to 4 beds.

The Fairmont Jasper Park Lodge $$$ Here's another of the magnificent lodges built by the Canadian Pacific Railroad. Its vibe is 19th-century woodsy gentility, and it's Jasper's most exclusive hotel. The Fairmont boasts 900 acres of wooded and elk-inhabited lakefront grounds, and the main lodge defines the Western lodge aesthetic: lofty ceilings, huge fireplaces, and rustic decor. Choose from cabins, lodge rooms, chalets, and cottages, all decorated in different historical styles. The full-service resort has a heated pool, tennis courts, fine golf course, a health club, afternoon tea (2–4pm daily), horseback riding, canoes, and bike rentals. Service is at your fingertips.

Old Lodge Rd. ℂ **866/540-4454** or 780/852-3301. www.fairmont.com/jasper.

MOST ROMANTIC RESTAURANTS

Becker's Gourmet Restaurant $ CANADIAN/FRENCH The specialty here is a rich assortment of fresh local cuisine—and gourmet it is. Begin with starters from the seasonal menu, such as venison carpaccio or butternut squash ravioli, and move on to entrees that can include apricot-glazed rack of lamb and a pinto bean *mole* chili. This lovely country dining room is a good place to relax as you catch the gorgeous sunset reflected in the Athabasca River.

At Becker's Chalets, Highway 93 South, Icefields Parkway. © **780/852-3535.** www.beckerschalets.com.

Cavell's Restaurant & Terrace $$ CANADIAN   Situated in the Fairmont Jasper, Cavell's is a good choice for a special meal. The steep prices might be mitigated by the luscious setting: unobstructed views of the majestic Mount Edith Cavell with Lac Beauvert in the foreground. The vast and interesting wine list coupled with the well-prepared elegant dishes are splurge-worthy. We liked the fresh seared tuna and local wildfowl. Of course, this is the west, so you can't go wrong with a steak, either.

At the Fairmont Jasper Park Lodge, on Old Lodge Rd. © **780/852-6052.** www.fairmont.com/jasper.

Tekarra Lodge Restaurant $$ INTERNATIONAL   This is a western gem: peace and quiet and a welcoming fireplace. It offers a terrific menu of globetrotting cuisine, and a quiet place to enjoy each other's company. The chef is imaginative and often injects Asian items like sushi into the more expected menu items like buffalo and elk.

In Tekarra Lodge. © **780/852-4624.** www.tekarrarestaurant.com.

JASPER BY NIGHT

Idling at the Emerald Lounge and Patio in the Fairmont Jasper Park Lodge   We love the Fairmont's homey lobby, certainly for its huge windows and great views, but also for its comfy couches and large fireplace. It's a grand place to have a drink (there is a very good wine selection) and a few munchies. The hotel's **Tent City Pub** is the area's most popular hangout for 20-somethings, but it's also a good place to relax after an active day. Have some pub food and maybe just shoot a game of pool. Old Lodge Rd. © **866/540-4454** or 780/852-3301. www.fairmont.com/jasper.

Listening to Live Music   Check out the town's pubs to see who's playing: **The Whistle Stop Pub,** 1050 Miette Ave. (© **800/282-9919;** www.whistlersinn.com); **O'Shea's Lounge,** 510 Patricia St. (© **877/542-8422;** www.athabascahotel.com); and **Downstream Lounge,** 620 Connaught Dr. (© **780/852-9449**).

RANCHO LA PUERTA (TECATE, MEXICO)

Connecting through Wellness

This famed wellness resort was created by Deborah and Edmund Szekely in 1940, and today, it boasts one of the most loyal fan bases in the world. People don't just come to the ranch, they make a pilgrimage, and Rancho La Puerta has become the go-to place for restoring energy, health, and peace of mind; in 2013 it was voted the "World's Best Overall Top Destination Spa" by *Travel & Leisure* readers.

What few people know is how romantic it can be for couples, which account for about 20% of the Ranch's customers. You'll see a lot of women here, traveling solo or with friends or daughters. But when couples come, they find what romance needs: a beautiful place to explore together that seems to put the world and the relationship in perspective.

The ranch is a bit east of San Diego, just beyond the Mexican border in the sleepy town of Tecate. It's set on more than 3,800 private acres in the shadow of Mount Kuchumaa. Groomed lawns stretch between undulating banks of flowers, timed to give a show of color in all seasons, and life-size sculptures of beautiful indigenous women dot the landscape.

Because violence in Mexico has gotten so much press, we want to stress that this area of Mexico is considered safe. Also, the Ranch picks you up at the San Diego airport in staggered-timed buses and returns you there; while in Mexico you are in a gated enclave just 3 miles from the U.S. border. For those who choose to drive the short distance themselves, it's an easy drive, but you need to stop before the border to buy inexpensive Mexican auto insurance for your few days there. If you prefer, there are safe places to leave your car in Tecate, California (about $8/day); the ranch will arrange for pick up and drop off there as well.

KEY ATTRACTIONS

It is a tranquil world here and yet a busy one. Every hour offers something exciting or educational: swimming, all kinds of exercise, a full range of massages and other spa treatments, art classes, dance, meditation, and varied and supportive weekly lectures (from visiting experts) about diet, the arts, and other ways to promote personal happiness. It can be described alternately as a luxury retreat, a healing place for medical and/or physical challenges, or a camp for grown-ups.

Guests enter the gated community into a haven of superbly landscaped grounds in contrast to the ominous boulders in the hardscrabble Baja desert surrounding the retreat. The guest casitas range from rather elegant Mexican-modern suites to simple, nicely decorated one-bedroom rancheros, all with bathrooms decorated in cheerful Mexican tiles. Most have fireplaces. The main dining room looks like a hacienda from the outside, with trees and terraces all around, flowers trailing from every nook, and fountains creating the gentle sounds of falling water.

Many who come here especially treasure the **early-morning hikes** through mountains and meadows. In the winter, the hikes start in the dark, and in the summer even earlier, to escape the intense heat of the day. Hikers share an uncommon light as the sun comes up and hits the meadows, trees, and mountain and gives a glow to the distant mountains and valleys. Hikes are available to suit your fitness level, so if you and your honey split up for the hike you can meet up for a breakfast date afterward. Breakfast is a lavish affair and served in the dining room or poolside in the Villas Sol section of the resort, or it can be delivered to your room. Breakfast and lunch are served buffet style, but dinner is served in multiple courses. Daily menus are keyed to calories and nutrition, but you won't go hungry, and you can always order more. For those for whom a vacation is not a vacation without a few of their usual libations, there's a wine bar on site.

Couples learn to relax and soften as they share experiences, whether it be walking a few miles before breakfast or taking a yoga class in a beautiful studio with sliding-glass windows that yield breezes and scenic views or trying to sculpt or paint for the first time or taking a cooking class together. But couples don't have to *do* anything. They can hold hands over dinner at a table for two, or join others. They can socialize or just wander back to their casita or take in an evening lecture. But what almost every couple will find is that time slows down, talk increases, and conversations tend to pass easily beyond the mundane and into deeper territory.

ⓒ **800/443-7586** (in U.S.) or 858/764-5500. www.rancholapuerta.com. Rates vary by season, number in room, and length of stay (7 days or more is the usual stay but there are 3 and 4 day specials.) $ 3,840–$4,050 per person double occupancy for week. Rates include all meals, classes, hikes, and educational and entertainment programs plus Saturday transportation to and from the San Diego airport. (Weekday taxis cost approximately $100.) Guests staying in Mexico longer than 72 hours need visas (US$35). Rates are heavily discounted from June to September and can be as low as $2,500 per person for the week for a couple sharing a casita. Discounts of 20% are often offered to those who book early.

EARTHY DELIGHTS: EUROPE

I f you thought that Europe's glories all reside in its cities, think again. Some of the most soul-stirring spots in the UK, Ireland, Italy, France, and the other countries of Europe are rural and not only that, wonderfully serene. Which makes them perfect places to head to when you and your honey want to have a vacation that's both wonderfully relaxing and often intellectually stimulating.

COTSWOLDS, ENGLAND
Strolling through Storybook England

This is quintessential rural and village England. It is totally charming—but you could have a lot of company, particularly in summer and early fall. For romance, that makes a shoulder-season visit a great idea. High season is July through August. Aim for spring or late fall to avoid having your sentimental journey to the Cotswolds run over by tour buses.

One of the best ways to see the adorable villages, quaint inns, and gentle landscape is on foot. Numerous tour operators can take you on short or long hikes to famous towns as well as tiny villages off the tourist path. **Walk the Landscape** (www.walkthelandscape. co.uk) and **Compass Holidays** (www.compass-holidays.com) organize guided and self-guided hikes in the Cotswolds.

The Cotswolds are rich in romantic imagery: beautiful yellow limestone houses, rolling green hills, meandering rivers, surprise discoveries of ancient Roman habitations, and little markets, shops, and pubs. The lure of a simpler and less-developed world somehow persists. In the cold, it is the right place to snuggle, and in good weather, simply walking about can be glorious. In fact, there are literally a few thousand miles of moderate walking paths that meander through the Cotswolds. Pack the right shoes and, later, exchange foot rubs!

KEY ATTRACTIONS
Antiquing This is antiques central. Even if you don't want to buy anything, view the furniture and luxury items of past centuries

ROMANTIC walks

Trails tend to be clearly marked, as "Footpath" or " Public Bridle-way." Each area is appealing, and all paths are free. Some go through private property, so proper etiquette is to close all gates as you proceed.

- **The Cotswold Way** (www. nationaltrail.co.uk/cotswold-way). The most celebrated route, this sensational 102-mile national trail marks the western boundary. Starting at Chipping Campden, the usual route meanders through Broadway, Winch-combe, and Painswick. Some folks take it all the way to Bath. The trail takes you through pastures and forests, small villages, and even Roman ruins. You can make a 3-, 7- or 10-day loop, or do a quick loop between Chipping Camp-den and Broadway.

- **The Heart of England Way** (www.heartofenglandway.org)

runs 104 miles. You start from Bourton-on-the-Water and work your way north to Chipping Camden.

- **The Warden's Way** and **The Windrush Way** The War-den's way (13 miles) starts at Winchcombe and passes through many charming small towns. You can also start the Windrush Way at Winchcombe and go round-trip to Bourton-on-the-Water; this walk is bounded by a river (very romantic) and includes a worthy view of Sudeley Castle.

- **The Colne Valley Walk** (www.colnevalleypark.org. uk). If you only have time for one walk, do this one. Starting at Bibury (and end-ing there), it is definitely one of the most scenic and varied ambles in the Cots-wolds, traveling about 6 miles along the River Coln.

as a museum walk! Serious antiques (the kind that get auctioned for hundreds of thousands of dollars) and more common items like pottery or glass are here for impulsive buys. The center of it all is **Stow-on-the-Wold** but, trust us, good shops are everywhere.

Arts and Crafts Movement William Morris (1834–1896), the famous artist, is credited with helping found the Arts and Crafts movement here to herald the handwork of artisans over mass production. A Guild of Handicrafts was instituted in Chipping Campden in the early 20th century, and this tradi-tion lives on nearby in the **Cheltenham Art Gallery & Museum,** Clarence Street, Cheltenham (© **44/1242-237431;** www.artsandcraftsmuseum.org.uk; free admission [donations welcome]).

Exploring the Towns Almost every town has a market day with a profusion of crafts and produce. Local cheeses and juices are tasty purchases and great for a picnic. It's fun to wander amid the wares and explore these enchanting towns. **Cirencester,** a hub from Roman times, boasts 17th- and 18th-century stone buildings and the **Corinium Museum,** Park Street (✆ 44/1285-655611; coriniummuseum.org; admission £4.95 adults, £4.10 seniors 60+), with local Roman artifacts. Visit **Bibury** for great Roman remains, including the **Chedworth Roman Villa** (✆ 44/1242-890256; www.national trust.org.uk/chedworth-roman-villa; admission £9 adults); it doesn't get the big buses, and that alone makes Bibury a treat. A bridge over the Windrush River makes a charming entry to **Burford,** a former wool center that is now a bucolic escape for urbanites. Stroll along the Windrush and stop at an inn for a glass of wine, a loaf of bread, and each other. The Friday market here dates from the 12th century. Two miles south at the **Cotswold Wildlife Park** (✆ 44/1993-823006; www.cotswoldwildlifepark.co.uk; admission £15 adults, £10 seniors 65+), large mammals cavort around a Victorian manor house. **Broadway**, in the heart of the Cotswolds, has the same problem as its New York namesake: too much success. In summer tourists rightfully flock here to see the 1,000-year-old **St. Eadburgha's Church**, the picture-perfect High Street and the **Vale of Evesham**, a verdant panorama you've probably seen in movies. Go to **Broadway Tower Country Park,** just outside town, and climb the tower for a stunning view.

Less visited are **Painswick** and **Owlpen Manor**. See Painswick for its 14th-century gray stone houses and lavish **Painswick Rococo Garden** (✆ 44/1452-813204; www.rococogarden.co.uk; admission £6.50 for adults, £5.50 for seniors 60+). Owlpen Manor is a lovely hamlet Hansel and Gretel could inhabit. Its central manor house is open from spring to fall. A romantic idea: Rent a darling cottage on the estate (✆ 44/1453-860261; www.owlpen.com; from £168 cottage [3- to 7-night minimum stay]). At **Stow On the Wold** don't miss Chastleton House, a Jacobean home from the early 1600s; it's a bit ramshackle (part of its considerable charm) and has wonderful antiques and gardens (✆ 44/1494-755560; www.nationaltrust.org.uk/chastleton-house; admission to garden £3 adults, to entire property £8.50 adults). Other dreamy towns romantics will visit without regret: **Chipping Campden**, **Bourton-on-the-Water, Swinbrook,** and **Moreton-in-Marsh.**

Touring the Gardens The English are passionate about their gardens, and that's just fine with us. Gardens are romantic, and the more profuse and individualized they are, the better. Many here are world class; our hands-down fave is Hidcote (see following) but all are worth the price of admission if beautiful gardens delight you.

○ **Hidcote Manor Garden** (✆ 44/1386-438333; www.nationaltrust.org.uk/hidcote; admission £10 adults) is a symphony of distinct garden rooms near Chipping Campden and close to Stratford on Avon. Narrow paths open to beautiful vistas, and many contemplative places and stone-thatched cottages are all part of the estate.

- **Kiftsgate Court Gardens** (℅ **44/1386-438777;** www.kiftsgate.co.uk; admission £7.50 adults) has a light touch with white gardens, its very own rose, and beautiful vistas.
- **Painswick Rococo Garden** (℅ **44/1452-813204;** www.rococogarden.org.uk; admission £6.50 adults, £5.50 seniors 60+) was created in the formal English tradition; it's famous for its snowdrop plants that cascade over hillsides and fields.
- **Rodmarton Manor** (℅ **44/1285-841442;** www.rodmarton-manor.co.uk; admission to garden only £5 adults, admission to house and garden £8 adults) is a beautiful garden with perfect herbaceous borders, particularly in summer. We also like its well-restored country mansion.
- **Sezincote** (℅ **44/1386-700444;** www.sezincote.co.uk; admission £5 for adults), in its Mogul style, is something of a wonderment, and the gardens have enchanting ponds and architectural embellishments. It's exotic and fun.
- **Sudeley Castle** (℅ **44/1242-604244;** www.sudeleycastle.co.uk; admission £15 for adults) is a treat for rose lovers.
- **Westonbirt National Arboretum** (℅ **44/1666-880220;** www.forestry.gov.uk/westonbirt; admission £5–£8 adults, depending on season) features wonderful lanes of trees that are particularly spectacular in autumn yet a perfect setting for concerts in summer.

HOTELS WITH HEART

Barnsely House $$$ If you are looking for stylish glamour and have been disappointed in the Cotswolds, cheer up. You are now among the beautiful people in this trendy and tasteful Georgian mansion. The grounds are fabulously landscaped and the summer's flowers bloom lavishly. Yes, you will pay for the privilege, but you will get big bedrooms that are exquisite and yet playful, with current technology in every room, including your large bathroom (with a shower and tub). You will also eat extremely well, but no nouvelle cuisine here; you can chow down on copious plates of fresh produce and well-done meat, fish, and fowl.

Barnsley, Cirencester. ℅ **44/1285-740000.** www.barnsleyhouse.com.

Charingworth Manor $$ Luxurious and romantic, this Tudor-Jacobean house, in typical Cotswold stone with a slate roof, resides on extensive groomed grounds. It's the perfect country house getaway, and each bedroom is comfortable, stocked with antiques and covered in romantic fabrics. Some rooms are quite modern, while others are period rooms with four-poster beds. Choose your room according to your taste and budget. You also have a good restaurant and bar on premises and an indoor pool.

Near Chipping Campden. ℅ **44/8446-932961.** www.classiclodges.co.uk.

Lord of the Manor Hotel $$ Would you like to feel like you are rich—really, really rich? Like your driver just dropped you off at your Cotswolds club in your Bentley rich? If you can get into that (at least for a night) plus a beautiful setting, elegantly modern public rooms and guest rooms, and

Top: Colonial-style house in Charleston, SC. *Bottom left:* Old Montréal.
Bottom right: Strolling in Paris.

Top: View of Golden Horn from Galata Tower, Istanbul.
Middle: Aerial view of Cape Town, with Green Point and Sea Point, Table Mountain, Lion's Head, Signal Hill, and Devil's Peak.
Bottom: The Cathedral Basilica of Saint Francis of Assisi.

Top: Tuscany.
Middle: Chateau de Saumur, Loire Valley, France. Grand Tetons near Jackson Hole.
Bottom: Hiking in Glacier National Park, Montana.

Top: Walla Walla Valley. *Middle:* Lake Moraine, Banff National Park. *Bottom:* View of the famous Lake Louise from Fairmont Chateau Lake Louise hotel.

Top: Quivertree Forest in Namibia.
Middle: Angkor Wat Temple, Siem Reap, Cambodia.
Bottom: Uluru Kata Tjuta National Park, Northern Territory, Australia.

Top: Watching a group of lionesses during a safari in Ngorongoro Conservation Area, Tanzania. *Middle right:* Elephant sighting on a safari. *Middle left:* Sunset on the deck at Serengeti Migration Camp. *Bottom:* Okavango Delta, Botswana.

Top: Old Walled City in Dubrovnik, Croatia. *Middle left:* Tour on Okavango Delta in Botswana. *Middle right:* Luxury tent at Paws Up resort, Montana. *Bottom:* Villa at Amandari resort in Bali.

Top: Koh Samui Island. *Middle left:* Four Seasons Koh Samui. *Middle right:* Time out on a Florida beach. *Bottom:* Vineyard in Santa Ynez Valley.

first-rate cuisine, this might be your choice. Just driving up to this expansive 17th-century manor house located in an archetypal Cotswold village is a thrill. You have your choice in accommodations: a room in the main house or in a re-purposed granary and barn. All have classic English country house chintz, antiques, and comfortable chairs. You can walk the grounds together, taking in the fields, the lake, and a stream that can be fished. We would recommend, however, letting the excellent restaurant do the work for you—choose the prix-fixe menu. If it all sounds too snooty and expensive, you can work on the latter issue during off-season when some genuine bargain rates apply.

Upper Slaughter. ✆ **44/1451-820243.** www.lordsofthemanor.com.

The Lygon Arms $$ This famous 16th-century inn, in the thick of town, has a striking facade with gables and mullioned windows. It also offers polished service as befitting an inn of such long distinction. Many historically important figures have laid their head to troubled rest here, and for the most part, the inn has kept their rooms as period pieces. (The annex, however, does not.) The front is urban, but the back is pure English estate with three acres of groomed lawns and gardens with stone walls and many private little areas for lovers to be alone. It has all the modern conveniences, too, plus two good restaurants, a bar, a health club, and an indoor pool and spa.

High St., Broadway. ✆ **44/1386-852255.** www.pumahotels.co.uk.

The Swan Hotel $$ Way back in the 14th century, this was a small riverside cottage, but like other old properties it prospered and grew. The Swan now has the proportions of a stately home with the decor to match. Guest rooms have a certain gravitas, but the antique furniture is just plain comfy. The beds are romantic, and if you ask, one of the four-poster rooms may be available. The most romantic choice would be one of the three luxurious and more modern suites that just a short walk from the main inn.

Bibury. ✆ **44/1285-740695.** www.cotswold-inns-hotels.co.uk.

MOST ROMANTIC RESTAURANTS

Russell's of Broadway $$ MODERN BRITISH   Lots of romantic possibilities: Choose either the patio in the front of the restaurant, or the courtyard at the back. The mood is chic, sunny, and contemporary, and the food is regional (think local lamb with rosemary or prime beef topped with yummy fruit soufflés). The cheese plate is especially good.

20 High St., Broadway. ✆ **44/1386-853555.** www.russellsofbroadway.co.uk.

Wesley House $$ MODERN EUROPEAN   Romantic inns just make us all tingly. This 15th-century half-timber building of exposed beams and stone walls keeps romance alive with its red-carpeted dining room! The seasonal menu may include oak-roasted salmon, roasted guinea fowl, and other classic English dishes. For something less formal, try the bar and grill. Sitting on bar stools together sharing cheeses and charcuterie and a good wine or beer sounds like a pretty romantic alternative.

High St., Winchcombe. ✆ **44/1242/602366.** www.wesleyhouse.co.uk.

IRELAND
Giving Romance the Green Light

All we have to do is hear an Irish brogue, and we are charmed. An Irish brogue in an Irish pub? Pure pleasure.

This small country has a charm that is infused in its green hills, coasts, plush pastures dotted with sheep, and its perfect little villages of stone cottages. It is physically diverse to be sure: from a gently sloping walkable terrain to some of the starkest, most brutal cliffs that will ever transfix you. Furthermore, if fantasy is romantic to you, it is a country of fairytale castles and cottages, which mean both grandiosity and simplicity. If you are looking for a country that spans the romantic universe, this one should do.

There are always unexpected towns to explore, effortless or demanding walks, and conversations to be had with locals. There's only one problem: too much success. Crowds can truly influence your experience. We advise you to think really hard about how to encounter Ireland up close and personal. You may have to visit in a shoulder season; avoid the roads, trails, and horseback rides; or stay put and absorb the feeling of a particular locale rather than roam around.

Whatever strategy you choose, here is a list of perfect romantic places that call to us in this world of green (the hills and golf courses, of course!), great storytellers, and aristocratic dwellings. County Clare, County Kerry, and County Mayo, all in the West, are most in our hearts.

County Clare

County Clare is nothing if not diverse. There are the postcard pictures of green pastures and rolling fields, dotted with enchanting cottages and farmhouses. But it also has one of Ireland's most dramatic coastlines, and that's saying something. Follow the coastline and take time to investigate its charming and friendly small towns along the way.

KEY ATTRACTIONS

The Burren This is basically a vast land of limestone, with stones catawampus throughout its grasslands. Its romantic touches: long spans of wildflowers and butterflies everywhere in the right season, and evocative guided tours of ancient sites, forts, and castles. Visit the Burren Center in the village of Kilfenora (or at www.theburrencentre.ie) for information.

Castles & Great Houses Part of Ireland's mystique is its enchanting castles and manor houses, and there are some amazing ones to visit, or even spend the night, including the 5th-century **Dromoland Castle** (see later listing).

Exploring the Cliffs of Moher These dramatic cliffs, rising vertically out of the Atlantic, look like someone hacked them off across the top. They stretch along the coast as far as the eye can see and frame views of the Aran Islands. It is a bit unsettling to inch out to the unfenced edge; we like standing back a bit. As you can imagine, a walk along the cliff at sunset can spur your ardor, but the monster crowds can defeat you. Go early or late, or try our following suggestions to elude them: You can also see the cliffs by air or sea. For a grand gesture, charter a helicopter, or take a day trip to the Aran Islands. Several helicopter services are in Galway. Check with your hotel for a boat to the Aran Islands. Visit www.cliffsofmoher.ie for more information.

Hearing Traditional Music   County Clare is known for its music scene. You can usually hear classic Irish tunes, modern jazz, or folk singing in the small villages, especially in **Doolin** (it holds a festival every Feb) and **Miltown Malbay**, where many pubs feature impromptu sessions of traditional music. The mood is infectious—why not participate?

Medieval Banquets   These events recreate the period in actual Medieval castles with authentic food and drink with staff attired in period costumes, while musicians perform period madrigals. Yes, some of the events are beyond touristy, but are a lot of fun. The most famous one, at the **Bunratty Castle & Folk Park** (© **353/61-360-788**; www.shannonheritage.com/BunrattyCastle AndFolkPark), is quite well done—if you want to use it as a proposal site, the organizers will help you bring it off. (You have to call them and plan it ahead of time, of course). Possibilities include having a medieval instrument serenade, a ring, or token of love delivered by a "knight" etc.

Seeing the Towns   A bustling seaside resort, **Lahinch** is known for its long beach, golf links, and **Seaworld** (www.lahinchseaworld.com). **Kilkee**, with its Victorian dwellings, presides over a mile-long horseshoe bay and has a wonderful sandy beach that is protected by a reef. On the left bank of the Shannon River is **Killaloe** and its quaint narrow streets lined by old shops and houses that rise along the steep hillside that affords a romantic view of its 13th century cathedral.

HOTELS WITH HEART

Dromoland Castle Hotel and Country Estate $$ This 19th-century indulgence is now a storybook place to stay. Seeing the magnificent towers and picturesque castle beside the lake is one of those memories couples will want to share. Walking, jogging, or cycling the 178 hectares (440 acres) makes you feel like landed gentry, and happily, this is not one of those places that are all facade. The interior is plush, with paneled walls, oil paintings, elegant chandeliers, and Irish antiques. Guest rooms are mostly suites; newer rooms are less historic in feel (some bedrooms are small, so be careful when reserving). This will cost you, but if you can, go all the way: Reserve a bedroom in the main house, with a four-poster or canopied bed and a view of the lake. For optimal romantic ambience, dine here in the **Earl of Thomond Restaurant** (it offers special feast dinners, too). Don't skip the spa, or the golf and tennis, if that's important to you and your honey.

Newmarket-on-Fergus. © **800/346-7007** or 353/61-368-144. www.dromoland.ie.

Gregans Castle Hotel $$ It's not really a castle, but a gorgeous manor house. It has great views of The Burren and Galway Bay and historic decor aplenty. The main rooms have antiques and important paintings; the bedrooms are also filled with antiques and are elegantly laid out to make you feel special. The rooms have perfect views of the splendid countryside, and the dinners are true gourmet feasts, featuring local specialties such as Clare Island salmon and roast Burren lamb.

5km south of Ballyvaughan village on N67, Ballyvaughan. ☏ **353/65-707-7005.** www.gregans.ie.

Moy House $$ On a windswept hill overlooking the sea, this beautiful 18th-century Italianate home's estate covers 6 sloping hectare (15 acres). Bedrooms have Irish linen and are decorated with original paintings, period antiques, lavish window dressings, velvet furniture, oriental carpets, and marble fireplaces. Modern conveniences and elements of the building's old architecture are beautifully combined in the bathrooms; some of them have freestanding old-fashioned bathtubs. Pick a room with a sea view (there are six) or over the cloistered garden. Downstairs is an elegant drawing room where you can pour yourself a drink and the small, attractive dining room with good food and a swell sea view over Lahinch Bay. Cozy, warm, and friendly, this charmer is only a few minutes from the busy seaside town of Lahinch.

Lahinch. ☏ **353/65-708-2800.** www.moyhouse.com.

MOST ROMANTIC RESTAURANTS

In addition to lively pubs (which also provide your best nightlife options), with their tasty stews and other fine traditional dishes, your best dining choices in this area will usually be at your hotel. Following is a fabulous exception.

Cullinan's Restaurant & Guesthouse $$ SEAFOOD   This small, charming restaurant is housed in a farmhouse with very romantic floor-to-ceiling windows overlooking the Aille River. It specializes in seafood and wonderful fresh local ingredients—among them regional goat cheese, smoked salmon, Doolin-caught crab, and rack of Burren lamb, followed by homemade desserts. A few inexpensive cottage-type rooms are for rent.

Doolin. ☏ **353/65-707-4183.** www.cullinansdoolin.com.

County Kerry

County Kerry is famous, and you know what happens then. You'll have to fight for your romantic moment; otherwise, traffic jams and blocked views will ruin it. If you come here in high season, consider yourself warned. Still, how could you miss some of the famous sites here? No way. So, be smart about how you go about seeing them. Think shoulder season, or stop at the more overlooked villages along the **Ring of Kerry,** the tourist trail that leads through many of the best attractions in Kerry. Most of our destinations here are on the Ring.

KEY ATTRACTIONS

Dingle Peninsula   The Ring of Kerry is the area's headliner. The stunning scenery covers Kenmare and Killarney and countless towns, churches, castles, and beautiful nature preserves; we recommend you give yourselves 3 days here. But the busses are a buzz killer. Especially in season, you may prefer the nearby **Dingle Loop**, a more rustic and Gaelic romp through working towns closer to the sea. The mountainous peninsula, which stretches 48km (30 miles) into the Atlantic, teems with sheep, lovely villages, and historic markers and signs noting the arrivals of Bronze Age settlers, Medieval monks, English gentry, and Hollywood filmmakers ("Ryan's Daughter" and "Far and Away").

Exploring the Towns   **Dingle Town/An Daingean** (the town's Gaelic name) offers delightful stone buildings climbing up hills and down dales with abundant charm, Medieval history, and panoramic views; its pubs reach out warmly to visitors. But you could fall in love with any of the small villages here. One glorious way to see them is via an organized bike ride in the hills. The views from Conor Pass, the main road from Tralee to Dingle Town, are awesome. Kenmare is also famous. People flock to admire its stone cottages on their way to see the Ring of Kerry. In summer, it's quite adorable with overflowing flower boxes and abundant gardens just about everywhere. One fine way to avoid the crowd is a Kenmare Bay romantic cruise—contact **Seafari** (℃ **353/64-664-2059;** www.seafariireland.com) or **Star Outdoors** (℃ **353/ 64-664-1222;** www.staroutdoors.ie). The bay is beautiful, and you'll get a nice taste of the scenery from the water, and even see the local seal population up close.

Muckross House   The **Kerry Folklife Center** dwells at this 19th-century Elizabethan house and features traditional Irish crafts and music. Enjoy the elegant period rooms and an informal garden lunch.

℃ **353/64-663-0804.** www.muckross-house.ie; admission 7.50€ for adults.

Taking a Buggy Ride   In high season, **Killarney** is overcrowded, and the buggy drivers will pressure you to hire them for a ride around the lake. But talk to a driver and negotiate a couple's jaunt: The driver picks you up at your hotel or B&B early in the morning and is your guide for the day, exploring the lakeside in **Killarney National Park** or other points. The guide may offer a prepacked picnic basket of traditional goodies and wine. Plan also to take the 40-mile drive to **Dunmore Head,** the rocky westernmost point of mainland Ireland. A magnificent Atlantic sunset here is a sure way to increase your mutual attraction.

HOTELS WITH HEART

Carrig Country House $ Relax in the lovely public rooms or stroll the gardens at this restored Victorian residence. Or jump into sports such as golf and fishing—or the lake for swimming and other water activities. It's also a great location for horseback riding, hiking, and scenic drives. The guest rooms are luxurious and close enough to the water to hear it lapping at the edges of the shore. The lakeside restaurant with locally sourced food, an imaginative menu, and fetching lake views is a romantic place to end the day.

On Caragh Lake. ℂ **353/66-976-9100.** www.carrighouse.com.

Iskeroon $ The setting here is lavishly beautiful. You look over sailboats in Derrynane Harbour and the Skelligs beyond, and pretty Derrynane Beach is a 15-minute walk down the scenic coastal "Mass Path." The tidy building—with three affordable suites—is familiar to anyone who has seen a Cape Cod seaside cottage. You make your own breakfasts here, but staff will help you get the fixings.

Caherdaniel. ℂ **353/66-947-5119.** http://iskeroon.com.

Park Hotel Kenmare $ This wonderfully romantic 19th-century hideaway near Kenmare Bay has high ceilings, formal sitting rooms, and a woodburning fireplace. An honest-to-God set of armor presides over a classic staircase, and all the rooms have antiques, Georgian and Victorian furnishings, balconies, and views of the water or mountains. A romantic plus is the full-service spa with well-trained therapists, in addition to all kinds of feel-good programs including yoga and meditation. Perk up your hormones at the pool, tennis courts, and 18-hole golf course.

Kenmare. ℂ **353/64-664-1200.** www.parkkenmare.com.

MOST ROMANTIC RESTAURANTS

The Chart House $$ SEAFOOD This is a great place for traditional Irish comfort food with some imaginative twists and warm and friendly service.

The Mall, Dingle. ℂ **353/66-915-2255.** www.thecharthousedingle.com.

Lord Baker's $$ PUB FARE/SEAFOOD This pub has good pub food and excellent coziness. Sit in a private alcove around a stone fireplace or in the bright and light conservatory. Grab the oysters and steaks, lobster, or rack of lamb.

Main St., Dingle. ℂ **353/66-915-1277.** www.lordbakers.ie.

The Tankard $$ SEAFOOD Head here for loads of romantic ambience. You are seated behind huge picture windows showing fantastic views of the sea and waterfront. The decor and menu are very contemporary, especially in the preparation of the excellent seafood. They do well with meat, too, and you will enjoy the rack of lamb, duck, and quail. Be there at sunset for the perfect moment.

R558, Tralee. ℂ **353/66-713-6349.**

County Mayo

In some ways, Mayo lives in the shadow of the better-known Galway. They share the gorgeous rugged coastal scenery, but in County Mayo, you will have it more to yourselves. The beautiful miles of extremely vertical cliffs will share your hearts with some incredibly loveable farms and seaside villages.

This is also the county of ancient mysteries and early civilizations worth exploring.

KEY ATTRACTIONS

Ancient Stones & Ancestral Places   If you like mystery with your romance, visit **Céide Fields** (✆ **353/96-43325;** www.museumsofmayo.com/ceide.htm; admission 4€ adults, 3€ seniors), an ancient setting with breathtaking views. Exhibits as the visitor center explain the random rocks strewn about the megalithic tombs buried under the local pastures, and the early foundations of a 5,000-year-old village.

Exploring the Towns   Located on the edge of a river, **Westport** personifies the charming Irish seaside village. This is the Ireland of our dreams: gentle landscapes, sensational small towns colonizing the shore, and, occasionally, a darker mountainous presence. There is an open, almost contemplative feeling among these landscapes.

Fishing   This is the land of rivers that deliver freshwater salmon and trout. **Cloonamoyne Fishery** (✆ **353/963-1928** or 8776-97193 [mobile]; www.cloonamoynefishery.com) can take care of all of your needs from tackle to casting rod. If you want to get really serious, sign up together for the **County Mayo Pontoon Bridge Hotel Fly Fishing School** in Pontoon (✆ **353/94-925-6120;** www.pontoonbridge.com).

Golfing   County Mayo's lovely 18-hole golf courses are open to visitors year-round. **Castlebar Golf Club**, Rocklands, Castlebar (✆ **353/94-902-1649;** www.castlebargolfclub.ie; greens fees 20€ Oct–Mar, 25€ Apr–Sept), has a family-run bar and restaurant with home-cooking. Scenic **Westport Golf Club** (✆ **353/98-28262;** www.westportgolfclub.ie; greens fees 25€ Jan–Feb, 35€ Mar and Oct, 45€ Apr–Sept) hosts international tournaments.

Walking   Most major walking tour companies list this region for good reason. The walks vary from easy to "you better know what you're doing!" They can be unmarked and quite dangerous in bad weather (slippery rocks, bogs, and so on) so going with a tour guide is a very good idea. In addition to the famous miles of sheer cliffs are other fine attractions, such as the white-sand beach at **Portacloy** on the R314, a trailhead for a lovely walk. You traverse the beach and fairly steep pastoral hills and end at a sheer cliff. Not a walk for inclement weather or children, but pretty romantic for two reasonably fit people.

HOTELS WITH HEART

Ashford Castle $$ A former fortress built in 1228, the Ashford has a high tea every day, just one of the reasons guests love this posh place. Other reasons: the turrets, towers, and drawbridge outside, and inside, the elegant oak drawing rooms, antique furniture and paintings, and the lovable views of Lough Corrib. Looking for a romantic place to get married? Actor Pierce Brosnan and his bride chose to wed here, perhaps for the castle's reflection in the lake, its groomed gardens, and the sumptuous period guest rooms and big, luxurious beds. The restaurant is formal—one of the few places in the country that requires men to wear jackets and ties after 7pm. **The Prince of Wales Cocktail Bar** has a clubby feel that is warm and cozy after a long day of hiking or fishing.

Castle View, Cong. ✆ **800/346-7007** or 353/94-9546003. www.ashford.ie.

The Bervie $ Feel like you are in someone else's romantic view, with the thrill of staying in a former coast guard station. Your wild and windy views of the sea aren't too shabby either. You will most likely have a sea view from your well-priced room, and definitely will from the lovely sitting rooms and breakfast room. Before you are the roiling sea and the jagged cliffs across the bay. Breakfasts are exceptional; dinners are first rate, but have to be reserved ahead.

The Strand, Keel, Achill. ✆ **353/98-43114.** www.bervieachill.com.

Enniscoe House $ Escape your world and snuggle into this expansive Georgian country estate. It has everything: views over water and woods with wonderful paths (some guided by a naturalist). The grand interior has wonderful details, fireplaces fit for a manor house, and, of course, a presentational staircase. It's expensive, but deserving. Guest rooms are each very different. Ask for a larger one in the front of the house; they have more elaborate furniture, including canopy beds. Still, you can't go wrong, since all the rooms have lovely park or lake views. You will dine well on lake or farmed fish and homegrown produce.

Castlehill Ballina. ✆ **800/223-6510** or 353/96-31112. www.enniscoe.com.

MOST ROMANTIC RESTAURANTS

Achill Cliff House $$ SEAFOOD If you have ventured out to the county island of Achille, make sure you go to the hotel restaurant in Keel. Perched by the sea, it delivers awesome views of the bay and nearby cliffs. Seafood is the menu's main theme—lobster, oysters, mussels, and grilled fish. This is a friendly, casual place—you can breathe the sea air deeply and just enjoy yourself. There are inexpensive comfortable rooms here as well.

Keel, Achill Island. ✆ **353/98-43400.** www.achillcliff.com.

An Port Mor $$ MODERN IRISH/SEAFOOD If you don't believe us, believe the awards: This romantic little place with Mediterranean flair has a lot of admirers. It is primarily a casual regional seafood restaurant, and everything is beautifully cooked and presented. Try the local crab and cheese tart, the trout, or Clew Bay scallops with lemon and fennel.

1 Brewery Place, Westport. ✆ **353/98-26730.** www.anportmor.com.

Newport House Hotel Restaurant $$$ CONTINENTAL The destination restaurant at this fine Georgian mansion is a very romantic place to dine. Food lovers make a beeline for its lavish and imaginative meals; fish entrees—wild salmon, turbot, or hake—are superb, as is the six-course meal. The hotel's long central staircase will impress you upon entering, and the very high ceilings, antique furniture, and ancestral oil paintings make everything feel quite grand. If you choose to stay here, too, you won't be disappointed. Sophisticated, spacious guest rooms in the main house and two historic court-yard buildings are quite atmospheric.

Newport. ℰ **353/98-41222.** www.newporthouse.ie.

LOIRE VALLEY (FRANCE)
Once Upon a Time

What's more romantic than a valley of castles, kings, and royal gardens? The great castles of this area are second to none in the world and, for some of us, represent fantasy desires to live the life of a prince or princess. A stay in the Loire can pretty much satisfy them for you! And it is something couples can experience together in a number of ways: seeing many castles by car, explor-ing an area by bicycle for a day from Paris or for weeks with extended stays near palaces that are even better than what our imaginations devise.

This is a fairytale land, good for the soul and the imagination. The castles have had many incarnations, but most started in the Renaissance when turrets and towers were in vogue. Most of them have lost the thousands of acres they once presided over, but the estates are still extensive, and the countryside—with its vineyards, rolling hills, forests, and rivers—are divine, as luscious as the meals you will enjoy in this region. This is a place of bounty, of beautiful places to stay, wander, eat, and sleep.

KEY ATTRACTIONS

Biking   Even if you explore mostly by car, try to rent bikes and ride the bike paths along the Loire that the French government has thoughtfully laid out for you, the **Loire à Vélo** (www.cycling-loire.com). Use the website—it's in English—to plan your ride. A regional train line (TER) runs along the river, and you can get on with your bikes and get off wherever you want to ride. It's not hard: Shops along the way can prepare a picnic for you, and the Loire Valley is pretty flat, so you have big views and easy going most of the way. Don't be afraid to stop at a winery or two and pick up a bottle for your picnic! You can rent bikes from your hotel or any company in a nearby town, but if you want a guided tour (self-guided or with a tour guide) you might want to book ahead with a company like **BikeToursDirect** (ℰ **877/462-2423;** www. biketours.com), which conducts trips and generally has extremely competitive prices compared to other U.S. companies.

Hot Air Ballooning   If you are up early, you will see hot-air balloons aloft. Sometimes that's enough to put you in a romantic mood. But balloons do give a perspective all their own. The countryside becomes an undulating palette for the chateaux, rivers, and towns. Several companies boast aerial adventures over the Loire Valley. Ask at your hotel.

ENCHANTING castles

The romantic châteaux are the main event here. If you can only do a day trip or an overnight, we suggest that you start at Valençay and visit Chambord and Cheverny, but we really recommend that you stay a bit longer, embracing your role as romantic travelers and giving this region this time it deserves. A starter list follows.

Note: On summer nights, many of the châteaux host *son et lumiere* (sound and light) shows.

Château d'Amboise (℡ **33/2-47-57-00-98;** www.chateau-amboise.com; admission 11€–15€ adults). This huge 15th-century château rests against a rock face along the valley and river. The unusual, elaborate ramps—one winds up to a terrace overlooking the river and countryside and another leads to a tower—were an express route for knights and royalty on horseback. Although the entire original château has not endured, an arresting Gothic chapel, Chapelle de St-Hubert, and the elegant royal living apartments have.

Château de Blois, 9 place Saint Louis, Blois (℡ **33/2-54-44-50-50;** www.chateaudeblois.fr; admission 10€). Started in the 13th century and tweaked by various kings over the years, the château looks like a place of intrigue and is: Its history is a soap opera of nefarious acts. Your guide will describe the murders and treacheries that have happened here, including the demise of Duc de Guise at the hands of King Henry III's henchmen. Inside are architectural masterpieces: Don't miss the Hall of the Estates-General, the Charles d'Orléans gallery, the Louis XII wing, and the wonderful François I wing, with its splendid staircase.

Château de Chambord (℡ **33/2-54-50-40-00;** www.chambord.org; admission 11€ adults). You can hire a horse at a nearby stable and approach this château on horseback. Marked by four towers, its most famous architectural detail is a marble double-spiral staircase that two people can use at the same time and not encounter each other. (Some conjecture it was invented in part by the king's advisor, one Leonardo da Vinci.) The magnificent and confusing roof terrace with its complicated composition of towers, turrets, and cupolas is a must-see.

Château de Chaumont (℡ **33/2-54-20-99-22;** www.domaine-chaumont.fr; admission 11€ adults). Diane D'Poiters lost her first chateau to her lover's widow (see Chenonceau, below) and this was her next, which she didn't much like. But to our eyes, it's not too shabby. Overlooking the Loire, it's nicely accented by a tree-lined park. The impressive facade is graced with twin turrets that frame a double drawbridge.

Château de Chenonceau

(☎ **33/2-47-23-90-07;** www.chenonceau.com; admission 11€–16€ adults). Spanning the Loire, this château, in our opinion, is the most beautiful in the valley, and its history is equally remarkable. It involves two women—a queen and a mistress—and one not very politic king. In 1547, Henri II gave Chenonceau to his beautiful mistress, Diane de Poitiers, which, as you might imagine, deeply angered his less physically blessed legal wife, Catherine de Médici. When Henri died, Catherine got it and built the gallery across the bridge— actually, a lovely addition.

Château de Cheverny

(☎ **33/2-54-79-96-29;** www.chateau-cheverny.fr; admission 9€–19€ adults). This 17th-century château has a bloody history of kingly cuckoldry, revenge, and other deadly royal temper tantrums, but things seem to have settled down these days (it's still a private home). The outside is not as impressive as some, but the interiors are sumptuous with fine exhibits and exquisite Gobelin tapestries.

Château de Valençay, 2 rue de

Blois, Valençay (☎ **33/2-54-00-10-66;** www.chateau-valencay.fr; admission 12€ adults). Talleyrand bought Napoleon's minister of foreign affairs this 16th-century Renaissance château, one of the closest to Paris, in 1803 in order to wow state visitors and foreign dignitaries. He added various flourishes, which make it a bit over the top. Have a nice picnic in the garden and deer park.

Le Château de Villandry

(☎ **33/2-47-50-02-09;** www.chateauvillandry.com; admission 10€ adults). This 16th-century Renaissance château offers the most elegant formal French garden we've even seen, with rose beds, other perennials, and gorgeously arranged vegetables. Much is geometrically framed with boxwood and bordered by miles and miles of perfectly cut hedge. The garden's theme involves Medieval chivalry and love—so you mustn't miss it, right? Best in June and the summer months when everything is in bloom!

That said, visit on the 1st weekend of July during the "Nights of a Thousand Lights," when paths lighted by lanterns lead vistors to entertainments of music and dance. The on-site restaurant (☎ **33/2-47-50-02-10**) has a lovely view from the terrace. This chateau is a bike ride from Tours (about 17km/11 miles), along an easy and scenic path partly along the Cher River.

HOTELS WITH HEART

This is a large area that offers many tempting places. Therefore, we offer just a few selections that are especially romantic.

Auberge du Bon Laboureur $ This stylish inn has many rooms with courtyards, patios, flowers, and birds to complement the indoor comforts. Accented by lovely French fabrics in light and cheerful pastels, most rooms in the main house are spacious (avoid the ones overlooking the street); those in the former stables are more agreeable and private. The best are in the patio house near the terrace.

6 rue Bretonneau, Chenonceaux. ✆ **33/2-47-23-90-02.** www.bonlaboureur.com.

Château de Pray $$ Long and deservedly famous, this château starts earning points for romanticism as soon as you see its twin towers near the Loire River. The ambience is elegant and peaceful, and guest rooms are all lovely, including the ones in the Pavilion Renaissance. Dining is a pleasure, and if you don't stay here, you should eat here at least. (Reserve well in advance.) Chef Frédéric Brisset's Michelin-starred restaurant has two romantic salons, one in gold tones, the other warmed by tapestries and a sculpted-wood fireplace.

Rue du Cèdre, Amboise. ✆ **33/2-47-57-23-67.** http://praycastel.online.fr.

Domaine des Hauts-de-Loire $$ Right near Chateau de Chaumont, this lovely 18th-century, vine-covered hunting lodge has fantastic public rooms with timbered and exposed brick walls, a wonderful pool, tennis courts, jogging and walking trails, and a lake with swans for you romantics out there. Guest rooms vary from modern to classical French, and the bathrooms are luxurious. This place also has Wi-Fi and is air-conditioned, which is not an automatic amenity in the area, especially in historical buildings. The terribly romantic restaurant, filled with flowers grown onsite, provides very tempting but costly formal French cooking. If money is no object, you will be happy to know there is a helipad for your 'copter.

79 rue Gilbert Navard, Chaumont sur Loire. ✆ **33/2-54-20-72-57.** www.domaine hautsloire.com.

Hôtel Diderot $ This rambling elegant 17th-century house is a wonderful, affordable hideaway from the more-touristed parts of the valley. The house's main rooms and some guest rooms have exposed beams; a Renaissance-period fireplace is in the dining room, used for both breakfast and dinner. In good weather you can take tea in the private garden and patio. The staff is extremely hospitable, and the rooms are large and charming. All have hardwood floors, antiques, and modern bathrooms. Ask for one with both a tub and shower. An additional romantic plus: Chinon is a lovely place to wander before and after dinner.

4 rue de Buffon, Chinon. ✆ **33/2-47-93-18-87.** www.hoteldiderot.com.

Le Fleuray $ One of the most appealing hotels in the region is this well-maintained ivy-covered manor house, run by a family of English expatriates, a short drive from Amboise. Guest rooms have been recently renovated and evoke an elegant but not terribly formal English country house; several have private terraces. With peaceful surroundings and plenty to do on the extensive grounds, this is an excellent base for château touring and unwinding. The hotel also has an excellent restaurant serving food infused with regional and international flavors.

Route D74, near Amboise. www.lefleurayhotel.com. ℂ **02-47-56-09-25.**

MOST ROMANTIC RESTAURANTS

Auberge du Bon Laboureur $$$ TOURAINE   This is exquisite food in a very romantic environment. The langoustine, foie gras, and rabbit are specialties, and the chefs make wonderful homemade ice creams for dessert. Try to be seated in the older room of the restaurant, so you might sit in 16th-century reproduction chairs under old wood-beam ceilings. The food is a delight, whatever the room. You can order the turbot or cod with confidence.

6 rue Bretonneau, Chenonceaux. ℂ **33/2-47-23-90-02.** www.bonlaboureur.com.

Côté Jardin Restaurant $$ FRENCH   This is in a very romantic location, near the Chenonceau Chateau. Try to get a table on the terrace by the large windows with the lovely view of the peaceful chateau gardens. The food is carefully prepared, the decor is lovely, and the service is thoughtful. There is often a little starter treat (an *amuse-bouche*) and the set menu is wonderful for lunch. There are usually creative elements to each dish with varied and good selections of regional wines. Desserts, such as a raspberry sorbet in a meringue, are delicious.

14 route de Bourges, Gien. ℂ **33/2-38-38-24-67.** http://cote-jardin-restaurant.com.

Les Délices du Château $$ FRENCH   Set in a restored 12th-century house on the grounds of the chateau in Saumur, Les Délices has atmosphere to spare and the view from the dining terrace is amazing; the city and Loire river are before you, and you are surrounded by flowers. Service is excellent, and the traditional French cooking with wine-infused sauces is delicious. French classics, such as beef with foie gras or truffles and sautéed sweetbreads, are beautifully executed and totally satisfying.

Les Feuquières, Saumur. ℂ **33/2-41-67-65-60.**

Les Gueules Noires $$$ TRADITIONAL FRENCH   This is a casual restaurant with lots of charm, fresh, locally sourced ingredients, and delicious local wine. It is right in the middle of vineyards, and it feels authentic and unpretentious. The menu is not extensive but everything, along with the service, is excellent. A little gem of a place.

66 rue de la Vallée Coquette, Vouvray. ℂ **33/2-47-52-62-18.**

L'Orangerie du Chateau $$$ TOURAINE   This place has the most romantic setting a restaurant could have: on a stone terrace, facing a French chateau (in this case, Chateau du Blois). The 15th-century orangerie is surrounded by beautiful gardens and offers seasonal menus and excellent wines. Favorites: Filet mignon with truffles and a shellfish sampler. Local wines include excellent variations of the fine wine of the region, Sauvignon de Touraine. To our taste, the desserts to order are the extraordinary soufflés. There is nothing touristy about this restaurant, even though it is next to a tourist attraction. But make reservations, even for lunch.

1 av. Jean-Laigret, Blois. ℗ **33/2-54-78-05-36.** www.orangerie-du-chateau.fr.

LOIRE VALLEY BY NIGHT

In chateau country, you may be living on the land—and perhaps lingering over your evening meals, but save an evening to visit one of the very old cities in the region, **Orleans,** or the smaller **Blois,** which is right in the chateau area and has its own chateau. Each has historic distinction—and a few nice jazz and rock clubs. If you're visiting in the summer, don't forget the son et lumiere shows at the chateaux.

PROVENCE (FRANCE)
Lavender Fields Forever

Some places stay in your heart because of the pictures they plant in your mind. When we long for Provence, we think of the blazing sun on the fields that van Gogh immortalized or the rows of lavender filling the landscape as far as the eye can see. Provence itself is actually far more diverse than these images. Its five sub-regions include canyons, the Riviera, forests, and even the Alps. But for us, the most romantic destinations are the famous hill towns of the Luberon in the Vaucluse, like **Roussillion, Bonnieux** and **L'isle sur la Sorgue,** and the cities of **Arles** and **Aix-en-Provence.** Here sidewalk cafes spill into the streets, flowers are everywhere, and colorful village markets offer local produce, fine soaps, art, and crafts.

Provence offers quintessentially summer visions—huge sunflowers, aged olive groves, and cypresses lining the avenues. People are out and about taking afternoon promenades that enliven the street scene. They sit and chat and shop at the fresh markets, looking for treasures such as the highly prized local truffles. They may not eat dessert (well maybe one nougat, for which they are famous), but they would never have a meal without the cheese course. And the summer is dedicated to outdoor dining at lunch or under the stars at dinner.

You can take the high-speed TGV train from Paris to Aix-en-Provence in 3 hours, but consider driving to explore the many appealing towns and hidden gems to explore along the way. If you have time, take the TVG there and explore the countryside on rented bicycles. It's a sensual way to enjoy the countryside, but be aware that the roads to some of the hill towns are steep and will require serious effort. Sightseeing on foot is also a delight, as you pass sheep on the hillsides, abundant wildflowers, and paths that provide shortcuts through the woods to terraced hills of olive trees, villages, and vistas so romantic you'll feel a mutual sense of wonder.

AIX-EN-PROVENCE

Full of fountains and shops (from lingerie to wine to antique shops), this lovely city (often abbreviated to "Aix") is the cultural capital of Provence, though Marseilles is the actual capital. Aix has ties to ancient Rome and is also the territory of Cézanne; you may recognize the houses and landscapes from his paintings. The local tourist office (en.aixenprovencetourism.com) can help you locate Cézanne's studio and its garden cafe, among other destinations. The atmospheric neo-classical **Mazarin** quarter offers a beautiful setting and many historic buildings to explore. The city has a major music festival midsummer that draws an international crowd of classical music lovers.

ARLES

Van Gogh did much of his work here, including "The Starry Night," "The Bridge at Arles," and "Sunflowers." This ancient Roman city of fabulous relics and ruins also boasts good hotels and food. A perfectly preserved Roman aqueduct (at **Barbegal**) is in the neighborhood and looks particularly fetching by moonlight. It crosses the Gardon River, and you can rent kayaks and paddle under it. The view from the water is spectacular.

KEY ATTRACTIONS

Bull "Dancing" in Arles   Inside Arles' genuine Roman arena, the action transpires in traditional fashion. The fight is exciting—but in Arles you can maintain your playful romantic feelings because the bull lives! Instead, you'll see bull dancing, where men of valor tie ribbons to the bull's horns (not an easy task, for sure) and the bull ends up with his head, if not his pride, intact.

Exploring Montagne Ste.-Victoire   This mountain (© **33/4-42-64-60-90;** www.grandsitesaintevictoire.com), a limestone backdrop for much of Provence, provides a wonderful nature tour, and its hiking paths are rich in olive groves, cicadas, cypress, and local blooms. Dozens of Cézanne's paintings immortalized this stony facade and its abundance, and so it all looks wonderfully familiar. A good finish is a stop at **Thermes Sextius,** 55 av. des Thermes (© **33/4-42-23-81-82;** www.thermes-sextius.com), in Aix's central city. This natural spa will soak out what ails you, as it has done for others for millennia.

Summer Concerts at the Théâtre Antique   What could be more romantic than an open-air concert in an imposing first-century B.C. ruin with Corinthian columns intact?

Rue du Cloître, Arles. © **33/4-90-96-93-30.**

Shopping in L'isle Sur la-Sorgue   With 300 antique shops, the charming Sorgue River town is the undisputed antiques center of Provence. It also has a lively produce market on Thursday and Sunday mornings. The romantic old city is picturesque and often unknown to those who don't buy antiques. Think about coming here on Easter and Assumption for big annual sales. The collectables amid the aged surroundings can transport your romance to another era, at least for a few minutes.

ⓒ **33/4-90-38-04-78.** www.oti-delasorgue.fr.

Visiting Carpentras The center of a fantastic wine-producing region next to the Vaucluse (notably Chateau neuf du Pape), Carpentras (ⓒ **33/4-90-63-00-78;** www.carpentras-ventoux.com) is not a conventionally pretty town, but it offers a different focus. A center of commerce since antiquity, it is loaded with old commercial architecture along shady narrow streets and surrounded by ruins and forts that fire up the imagination. It also has a reputation for truffles and a highly esteemed *chèvre*—so expect to see lots of goats. If you are there in strawberry season, do not miss the incredibly sweet berries; they don't travel well, so feed them to each other very carefully. **Maison Trévier,** 36 place du Docteur Cavaillon (ⓒ **33/4-90-51-99-98;** www.maisont revier.com), is a lovely 18th-century inn here.

HOTELS WITH HEART

Grand Hotel Nord-Pinus $$ Bullfighters, writers, and artists have adopted this elegant but cozy hotel in Pont du Forum. Its romantic rooms are adorned with terracotta and wrought iron and have pleasant views of tiled roofs and ivied walls. The bar is a romantic retreat decorated in black and white photography, paintings, chandeliers, and simple furnishings for the ages. The restaurant's curved archways, soft yellow walls, and leather chairs make for a charming environment that extends into a lovely outdoor dining area.

Place du Forum, Arles. ⓒ **33/4-90-93-44-44.** www.nord-pinus.com.

Le Manoir $ Located near the center of old Aix-en-Provence, this former abbey's own private garden makes it feel sheltered and apart from city doings. Originating in the 14th century, the abbey was converted into this tidy and evocative hotel in the 1980s. The rooms are historically correct, with true antiques dating from the time of Louis XIV and Louis XV, plus the Napoleanic era. That means lots of gold touches. If you have an Empire style room, expect a quieter decor that hearkens back to a more pastoral theme. The hotel's veranda, under a vaulted cloister, is a construction that never fails to impress, and you can eat your breakfast there.

8 rue d'Entrecasteaux, Aix-en-Provence. ⓒ **33/4-42-26-27-20.** www.hotelmanoir. com.

Rent a Cottage in Bonnieux, in the Luberon We have spent many wonderful days near this village in a renovated 18th-century stone "cottage." It's wonderful in both the hot summers and cool fall. Once inhabited by poor farmers, the cottages here have been refitted into very chic residences. Many are second homes for wealthy and/or famous sun-seeking Parisians and are spectacular inside while retaining their more humble facades. A good place to start looking is **Auberge de L'Aiguebrun,** Domaine de la Tour, Route Departementale 943 ($$; ⓒ **33/4-90-04-47-00;** www.aubergedelaiguebrun. com), a country inn outside of town with lovely cottages and a pool. In the same area is the extravagant **Le Domaine de Capelongue,** Domaine de Capelongue, Les Claparèdes, Chemin des Cabanes (**$$**; ✆ **33/4-90-75-98-52;** www.capelongue.com), a renovated farmhouse and outbuildings transformed into luxurious rooms with kitchens on 15 acres with a huge pool, spa services, cooking classes and a gourmet restaurant. A less expensive option is **Les Trois Sources,** Chemin de la Chaîne (**$**; ✆ **33/4-90-75-95-58;** www.lestroissources. com), a boutique hotel with romantic views over vineyards and orchards and a lovely courtyard where you can have breakfast alfresco at classic French cafe tables. Perfect.

Villa Gallici $$$ Each of the 22 rooms and suites in this chic inn has different decor, and some have a private terrace or garden; all overlook an aromatic lavender garden and are draped with magnificent textiles and sunny embroidered materials. It is close to an excellent restaurant, **Le Clos de la Violette** (✆ **33/4-42-23-30-71;** www.closdelaviolette.fr), and a short walk from the town center. A place where famous people bask in sybaritic anonymity, it's expensive and requires advance reservations.

18 Avenue de la Violette, Aix-en-Provence. ✆ **33/4-42-23-29-33.** http://villa gallici.com.

MOST ROMANTIC RESTAURANTS
Aix-en-Provence

This is the dining center for Provence. There are more formal options below, but you could always seat yourselves at a cafe on the tree-lined **Cours Mirabeau** for a meal, or just flirt between sips of a cafe Français and watch the world go by.

Le Bistro Latin $ PROVENÇAL   Come here for a quintessential Provence bistro experience. Choose between two cozy rooms: one on the ground floor, the other in a colorfully decorated cellar. The youthful staff takes pleasure in acquainting you with the menu. The menu is fixed-price, so try everything! This place does wonderful French things with sauces for entrees from seafood to rack of lamb in an herbed crust.

18 rue de la Couronne. ✆ **33/4-42-38-22-88.**

Pierre Reboul $$$ MODERN FRENCH   In Aix's old town, this signature spot of master chef Pierre Reboul has a modern feel. Whether nibbling on pan-seared foie gras, goat cheese, and profiteroles of herring with rocket sorbet, or lamb under a cheesy crust, it's the right mix of tradition and invention for a lovely evening, albeit a pricey one.

11 petite rue Saint Jean. ✆ **33/4-42-20-58-26.** www.restaurant-pierre-reboul.com.

Arles

Many good restaurants lie close to the central Place du Forum in Arles.

La Charcuterie $$ DELI   This former charcuterie survived World War II and has become a regional treasure. It strives for romance, with intriguing little figurines and personal touches with lavishly red velvet banquettes to make sure you know you have permission to cuddle here. The affordable menu is small (like the restaurant) and its specialties include Charolaise beef and tender rack of lamb. We also like their signature charcuterie dish: the *assiette anglais,* a delicious spread befitting serious beef and sausage lovers.

51 rue des Arènes. ℂ **33/4-90-96-56-96.** www.lacharcuterie.camarque.fr.

La Gueule du Loup $$ FRENCH/PROVENÇAL   Set in an atmospheric 17th-century stone house near the ancient Roman arena, this fine choice specializes in regional cuisine with hearty meat and fish entrees. Reservations are essential, as the room seats only 30. In romance, cozy can be good.

39 rue des Arènes. ℂ **33/4-90-96-96-69.**

L'Atelier de Jean Luc Rabanel $$$ MEDITERRANEAN   This restaurant is a textbook, albeit a romantic one, on the most wonderful tastes in Provence. Chef Jean Luc Rabanel grows many of the ingredients in his organic garden and picks them shortly before you encounter them. The menu changes daily, but you can count on a fabulous meal with tastes that reflect the chef's personal obsession with coaxing out different flavors from myriad varieties of the same vegetable. So prepare to taste some anew.

7 rue des Carmes. ℂ **33/4-90-91-07-69.** www.rabanel.com.

PROVENCE BY NIGHT

Café Le Grillion Brasserie, 49 cours Mirabeau (ℂ **33/4-42-27-58-81;** http://cafelegrillon.free.fr), is located amid the nightlife of **Aix-en-Provence**. The rambling cafe, with terraces and two indoor levels decorated in 19th-century wrought iron adornments and intriguing period portraits, sets a definite romantic tone. Whether you are seeking a movie, dancing, music, shops, or piano bars, first find Le Grillion for a Provence-style meal of fresh local cuisine and then head out for your entertainment.

The scene in **Arles** is quieter, probably due to its relatively small population (50,000). An appealing diversion is their music hall **Le Cargo de Nuit,** 7 av. Sadi Carnot (ℂ **33/4-90-49-55-99;** www.cargodenuit.com), where you'll find live music Wednesday through Saturday night. The cover varies, depending on the evening (8€–25€). Another place to kick up your heels, **Le Café van Gogh,** 11 place du Forum (ℂ **33/4-90-96-44-56**), a hip place that has live bands most nights.

TUSCANY & UMBRIA (ITALY)
Luscious Hill Towns with Wines to Match

Every time we consider an exciting new romantic destination, we rank it against our perpetual favorites. Tuscany and Umbria always remain near the top of our list. These adjacent Italian regions share a sense of slowing down time, exultation in beauty, and meals created as works of art and acts of friendship. The good life is pursued relentlessly here with small gestures that make every man and woman feel as rich as any aristocrat. These sibling Italian hills and valleys share a border and a sensibility. Their cuisines are more localized and their wines have a specific *terroir*, or sense of place, but they share a family resemblance. Even so, the regions have been sparring for most of history as bitter enemies at worst and, at best, fierce competitors. That said, Italy tells you how to live—and Tuscany and Umbria tell you where to do it.

Note: **Florence** is the capital of Tuscany and is full of extraordinary cultural gifts with romantic places, and it certainly qualifies as a perfect place for romance and may deserve its own chapter next time, but for now we'll concentrate on the smaller romantic hill towns of the region.

Here are some tips for letting romance happen in Tuscany and Umbria:

- **Walk the walk**. Like most of Italy, the hill towns partake in *passeggiata*, an evening stroll where romance is openly displayed, so feel free to express yourselves!
- **Forget your diet**. Eating in Italy is a social occasion, a blessing, and a compliment to the chef. Savor every meal and don't cheat yourself out of experiencing the Italian way of life.
- **Get lost**. Let serendipity be your guide. Forget about the destination sometimes and just wander. Stop at little farm venues selling their wine, fruit, honey, or olive oil and sample it—another shared experience.
- **Forget time**. Relax, have a simple agenda and talk to each other about life and living well. Have more wine over a longer period and don't rush anything.
- **Stop for sudden festivals**. In summer cultural festivals are everywhere. Think of them as a gift, not an interruption. Plan for them if you can, but if you stumble into them, enjoy. With the right attitude, you'll be ready for the time of your lives. *Avanti!*

KEY ATTRACTIONS

Ballooning over Tuscany   This fantastic landscape of vineyards, farmland, and medieval estates should be seen from every angle—how romantic to float over it on your way to a champagne breakfast. Ask your hotel concierge about available tours and possible romantic add-ons.

Il Palio   There's nothing quite like the horse races held each July 2 and August 16 in Siena. Horses and bareback riders thunder around the Piazza del Campo at breakneck speed on bricks temporarily paved with dirt. Thousands of excited citizens attend to bet on the horses, the riders, and their own clan flag—or just for the party. Amid the vibrant racing colors and jockey's silks is competition between clans and ancient families that is more than just historic custom. It's been happening since the 17th century and perhaps is just as serious and life-threatening now as it was then. Get there early, or you won't be able to see anything—the crowd density is matched only by its intensity. Even if you don't fancy the race, you will find the pageantry romantic: There is much waving of family crests, beating of drums, and playing medieval music and songs. At night, the bars fill with supporters and participants—it's an amazing show.

www.ilpalio.org.

National Gallery of Umbria   Yes, go to Italy for the food, the wine, the joy of life—but don't skip the art. It is the wellspring of passion and part and parcel of Italian patrimony and culture! So drink it in here like wine.

Corso Pietro Vannucci 19, Perugia. ℂ **39/075-586-68410.** gallerianazionaleumbria.it.

Pack a Picnic   This is home to fantastic cheeses and charcuterie. Buy yourself some pecorino (in fact, bring home some of that fabulous cheese) and some Parma ham, or prosciutto, and colonize some particularly beautiful plot of countryside. If wine is your thing, take a drive between Florence and Siena to **Brolio Castle** and the **Barone Ricasoli Winery** (ℂ **39/0577-7301;** www. ricasoli.it), the oldest winery in Italy, where Chianti Classico was invented.

Hills Towns We Love

There are so many glorious destinations in Tuscany and Umbria that are worthy of exploration. Following are just a few of our favorites.

Tuscany

SIENA

This town has a special feel, bestowed in part by its medieval towers, piazzas, and buildings. Traditionally a rival of Florence in politics and business, Siena still lives its history through restaurants, streets, museums, and traditions, such as the Palio horse race (see previous). But Siena is more about daily life with excellent wines from local vineyards and lots of dinners and drinks with family and friends that go on for hours of conversation and enjoyment of the moment. Do your own version!

Siena Adventures   There's a lot to see on foot: Pass the **Piazza del Campo** (ℂ **0577/292-230**) and look at tall Medieval campanile of the **Palazzo Pubblico** (ℂ **0577/292-111**); the majestic steeple rises 320 feet. You can have fun trying to locate the Moorish, Roman, and Gothic touches on various buildings, and it's almost breathtaking to see the **Duomo**'s black-and-white striped marble. The 16th-century **Fort Medicea** in Terza di Camollia (Siena's northern third) has been transformed into a place with all kinds of romantic options. There is an open-air theater, dramatic ramparts, and a bar at Italy's national wine museum, **Enoteca Italiana** (Piazza Libertà 1; www.enoteca-italiana.it; ℂ **0577/228-811** or 0577/288-497). At small tables in bricked halls or on summer terraces, you can taste a vast selection of Tuscan and Italian wines. It might take you years to sample all of them, but we think that's a noble goal. You've got to love a country that has an official state-mandated museo del vino. At night, wander here to sample the region's full-bodied Chianti.

Romantic Dining   Meals here are hearty and delicious, with incredible roasted meats, bruschetta, herb-flavored vegetable dishes, and Pici, a thick, chewy spaghetti. **Osteria le Logge** ($$$; Via del Porrione 33; www.osteriale logge.it; ℂ **0577/48-013**) serves the lively and pungent traditional food of Tuscany in a quiet atmosphere with plenty of homemade pasta, local produce, and creative adaptations of fish, steak, and roasted chicken. Locals come here for special dinners. **Antico Osteria da Divo** ($$; Via Franciosa, 25; www.

osteriadadivo.it; © **0577/286-054**) has a more contemporary approach, with a creative menu, soft jazz, and a main dining room of stone, wood, brick, and rock. Superb are the pasta dishes, hand cut and hand rolled. Specialties include gnocchi with chives and duck breast with saffron mashed potatoes. The rooms in back are Etruscan tombs—a nice quiet place for a romantic repast. **La Chiacchera** (**$**; Costa di Sant'Antonio 4; © **0577–280–631.** www.osterialachi acchera.it) is best described as a hole in the wall, one tiny, rustically decorated room tucked about halfway along a steep alleyway that serves great Sienese food such as *ribollita*, a hearty bread and vegetable soup; *salsicce e fagioli* (sausage and white beans*); or *tegamata di maiale*, a Sienese pork casserole.

MONTERIGGIONI

Twelve miles northwest of Siena, this lesser known village is one of the most perfectly preserved fortified villages in all of Italy (call © **0577/304-810** for information). All 14 observation towers remain intact and are almost a storybook vision. The town remains kind of dozy—it only has a couple of restaurants—but its beautiful gardens testify that someone is busy. If you want to stay here, a four-star inn, **Hotel Monteriggioni** (**$$**; Via 1 Maggio 4; hotelmonteriggioni. net; © **0577/305-009**) is in one of the old fortress buildings. There is not much else in the village—so prepare to contemplate each other, a lot.

SAN GIMIGNANO

Down the road from Monteriggioni, this is a larger medieval town with even more towers, each so different, it is a bit of a hodge-podge. But the ultimate effect is charming, and Gimignano's skyline at night, lit electrically or by moonlight, makes it an especially romantic hill town. The colorful center of town—Piazza della Cisterna and Piazza del Duomo—adjoins **Collegiata** (San Gimignano Siena; © **0577/940-316**), the town's generously frescoed historic church, and the civic buildings. Here's the bad news: San Gimignano is a crowd favorite, so put in your romantic time early in the morning or later after the buses leave and the town exhales.

Romantic Dining Our favorite special-occasion eatery, **Ristorante Dorando** (**$$$**; Vicolo dell'Oro 2; www.ristorantedorando.it; © **0577/941-862**) is near the Piazza Duomo, and its classic stone walls, beautiful place settings, and attentive waiters set just the right tone for lovers who happen to be hungry! Students of cooking will appreciate that the menu describes the history of every traditional and ancient Etruscan recipe. The seasonal menu changes often. For hearty meals enjoyed by the locals, try **Ristorante Latini** (**$$$**; Via Dei Platani 1; www.ristorantelatini.com; © **0577/945-019**) just outside of town. Favorites include homemade sausages and traditional recipes. It's also an inn with modest prices. This tiny vaulted cellar of **Chiribiri** (**$**; Piazzetta della Madonna 1; © **0577-941-948**) almost next to the city walls seems more serious about what it sends out of the kitchen than many of the more expensive places closer to the center of town do. Ravioli with pumpkin, white beans and sage, beef in Chianti, wild boar stew, and other Tuscan classics are done well and served without fuss.

Umbria
TODI

You'll want to walk the winding streets and climb lots of steps to fully absorb the town's charm. Todi was first inhabited in the 2nd century B.C., and the medieval character of its walkways, steps, and alleys are enchanting. The town is so attractive that houses on the way into town are being snatched up by ex-pats or vacation-home buyers.

The town's walls follow three different traditions: Umbrian, Etruscan, and Roman. From each gate, all roads lead to the big rectangular square, **Piazza del Popolo,** one of the few flat surfaces here! The buildings surrounding the plaza are rather forbidding, but the ubiquitous flowers and arcades soften the effect, and the cafes tucked under the arcades are quite romantic. The **Duomo** is worth visiting for the paintings inside and its sweeping medieval staircases; it looks like a grand stage or movie set. Nearby is **San Fortunato**, a large church with poignant art and design touches from the 13th and 14th centuries; the upper half of the facade has never been completed, which may be a record for procrastination. Also, find the domed **Temple of Santa Maria della Consolazione** on Viale Consolazione (*©* **075/894-3395**), which is lovely, particularly on the outside.

Romantic Dining   Try **Ristorante Umbria** (**$;** Via S. Bonaventura, 13; www.ristoranteumbria.it; *©* **075/894-2737**), a beautiful restaurant that sets its tables under 15th-century beamed ceilings and rustic chandeliers. Umbrian traditions of roasting and grilling boar, steak, duck, and trout are wildly successful, and the pastas are homemade. Fresh wild and cultivated produce—truffles, wild mushrooms, wild asparagus—pop up in every meal. Order the mozzarella, olive, and artichoke appetizer if it's on the menu. For romance, good weather encourages dining under the vines on the terrace overlooking the hills; in cooler weather, go inside, warm up by the big fireplace, and watch the cooks grill over an open fire.

ORVIETO

This walled city on a plateau a thousand feet high has a long, continuing history of fine wine. The ancient Romans showed up to get access to Orvieto's famous wines, which we understand: We, too, are big fans of Orvieto Classico. The wonderful white wine goes far to warm up this city, whose stone walls give it a grim appearance at first. The Duomo, with its beautiful mosaic facade, seen for miles glinting in the sun, makes the town more inviting.

Romantic Dining   The tasty cuisine at **Trattoria del'Orso** (**$$;** Via I della Misericordia 18; *©* **0763/341-642**) is an enchanting mix of the regional style and the pungent Abruzzo origins of the chef. The tiny place has an intimate and romantic feel. The homemade pasta is served with the cheeses, mushrooms, truffles, and tomatoes of the region. The specialties, chicken with olives and game hen with truffles, are magnificent. A delicious and less expensive alternative is **Tipica Trattoria Etrusca** (**$;** Via Lorenzo Maitani 10, Orvieto Terni; www.tipicatrattoriaetrusca.com; *©* **0763/344-016**), in a setting with vaulted ceilings and graceful arches beneath a 15th-century palace. The gravitas of age is offset by the modern art on the walls. A similar balance exists in the food: homemade gnocchi, rabbit in a delicate herbed sauce, and marvelous lamb.

ASSISI

We love this town. Its tiers step down the hill, showing off its pale pink and grayness, and it is surrounded by lovely countryside stretching to the captivating slopes of Mt. Subasio. Assisi can seem like a postage stamp of a place when you find yourself in its narrow streets or in a perfect little chapel or a tiny shop reading, sipping coffee, and chatting with your seatmate. Then there is the grander part, like the huge Basilica of St. Francis of Assisi.

Basilica Di San Francesco Assisi   Damaged in 1997 during a tragic earthquake, the basilica and other historic buildings have been restored to the extent they could be. Paintings by Italian masters survived, including extensive works by Giotto, as well as the tomb of St. Francis, the patron saint of Italy. To get the most out of the huge edifice and chapels, take a tour. You can wander even further back in time at the **Roman Temple Portico.** Remarkable and intact, on the main square of Assisi, this archeological treasure is difficult to miss. Such wonders produce a lot of tourism—but Assisi can be quiet in the morning and evening, which is when you can walk down the Via Giorgetti to the antiquities and maintain a contemplative mood.

Piazza San Francesco 2. www.sanfrancescoassisi.org. © **075/819-001.**

Romantic Dining   At **La Stalla** ($; Via Santuario delle Carceri 24;© **075/812-317**), a wonderful countryside trattoria (and inn) just outside of town, guests are seated at long wooden communal tables beneath ceilings darkened by open-fire grilling, and down big platters of homemade pasta and the house red. A few steps from the main piazza, **La Fortezza** ($; Vicolo della Fortezza 2b; www.lafortezzaristorante.it; © **075/812-993**) serves inspired cannelloni, veal Parmigiana, gnocchi with tomato, mushrooms, and garden vegetables plus a fine wine list in a lovely stone-walled dining room. For something beyond local cuisine, try **Medio Evo** ($; Via Arco dei Priori 4; www.ristorantemedioevoassisi.it; © **075/813-068**), a romantic spot bedecked with flowers under stunning vaulted ceilings, that dishes up northern European specialties like grilled or poached salmon with vodka and tomatoes, in addition to the wonderful local mainstays.

PERUGIA

Perugia is a city and university town, full of life and an international population. It is equidistant from Florence and Rome and at least a drive-in stop on most tours. It received a black eye from the Amanda Knox murder trial a few years ago, but the city's estimable gifts will certainly survive the scandal. This gorgeous city overlooking the Tiber has a vibrant spirit, evident in its delicious chocolate, wonderful summer jazz festival, and great restaurants and hotels.

At some point, best in the evening, make your way to **Il Punto di Vista** (Vis Indipendenza 2; © **339/662-0326**), which is just what it sounds like: the place with the view. This outdoor bar has a heavenly view of Umbrian hills. Here your nightly stroll will be on the **Corso Vannucci**, the ancient Etruscan road that is Perugia's main street. You may want to precede your walk with a jump in Lake Trasimeno, a short ride outside of town. Less famous than those in the Italian Lake country, this lake offers similar joys. Circle it by car or scooter (rent one from **Umbria in Vespa, $;** Via Case Sparse 42, San Savino; ✆ **075/843-062**; www.umbriainvespa.com) or rent a canoe. Plan a romantic picnic on the bank with the wonderful bread and cheese and Prosciutto you brought for the occasion!

Besides the ubiquitous art museums and galleries here, we also recommend putting your mouths on a big chunk of **chocolate**. Perugia makes a lot of chocolate and brags about it. No argument there—it is of the highest quality, and chocolate shops abound. The biggest brand is Perugina, purveyor of the famous Baci chocolates.

Perugia is well located for day trips. You can head to **Torgiano,** about 10 miles to the south, whose wines are the stars of Umbria—this is where Rubesco was born. Visit **Fondazione Lungarotti** (✆ **075/988-661;** www.lungarotti.it), the winery whose owner founded Enoteca Italiana (see above). The estate's hotel/restaurant complex **Tre Vaselle** (Via Giuseppe Garibaldi 48, Foligno, Perugia; ✆ **075/988-0447;** www.3vaselle.it) offers outstanding food and upscale rooms in a 17th century building with pool and grounds.

Three miles south of Perugia, is the **Ipogeo dei Volumni** (Via Assisana, Ponte San Giovanni Perugia; ✆ **075/575-961;** www.archeopg.arti.beniculturali.it), one of the finest Italian **Etruscan tombs**. Three miles further lies **Deruta**, the center for Italy's fine ceramics since the 13th century. You may see cheaper imitations in the shops in Perugia, but when you see the Majolica pottery here—hand-painted and hand-wheeled, exquisite and expensive—you know it is the real thing. Visit the **Museo Regionale della Ceramica di Deruta** (Regional Museum of Ceramics; ✆ **075/971-1000;** www.comunederuta.gov.it/cultura-e-territorio/museo-regionale-della-ceramica) on Largo San Francesco to get a better sense of what you are looking at.

Romantic Dining   You could just eat your way through Perugia and be happy. Start with breakfast at **Pasticceria Sandri** (Corso Vanucci 32; ✆ **075/572-4112**), a romantic pastry shop that's been around since 1860, in an elegant domed dining room with painted ceilings and a chandelier. With lovely cappuccino, it's a perfect place to pop something delicious into each other's mouths. For a blissful lunch or dinner, try **Osteria a Priori** (**$$$;** Via dei Priori 39; www.osteriaapriori.it; ✆ **075/572-7098;**), the perfect place for shellfish, charcuterie, cheeses, and a good wine selection. Hand-made pasta is always on hand, and pork and other dishes with truffles, in season. For your splurge dinner: **Il Postale** (**$$$;** Strada Montevile 3, Famiglia Capaccioni; ristoranteilpostale.it; ✆ **075/572-4214**), which not only earned a Michelin star, but it has a tiny magical dining room inside a castle! This over-the-top romanticism is matched only by the effort that goes into the food. Reserve way ahead. Back on Earth, **Il Falchetto** (**$$;** Strada Fontana La Trinità 2/d; www.

ilfalchetto.it; © **075/573-1775**) is where locals go for a fine meal. On the edge of town, it serves great homemade pasta, and the specialty is a divine casserole of spinach-and-ricotta gnocchi.

HOTELS WITH HEART
Tuscany

SIENNA The lovely **Antica Torre** (**$**; Via Fiera Vecchia 7; www.anticatorresiena.it; © **0577/222-255**) dates from the 16th century. The bedrooms are small but cozy with elegant marble floors, iron beds, and sexy curtains. Ask for a room on the highest level for the view over rooftops to the hills. This family-run place has warm hospitality and soul, which helps make a stay special. Owned by the same family is **Palazzo di Valli** (**$$**; Via Enea Silvio Piccolomini 135; © **0577/226-102**; www.palazzodivalli.it), a 17th-century 12-room country hotel with lovely grounds. A few miles outside of Sienna, **Castello Delle Quattro Torra** (**$**; Strada di Pieve al Bozzone 36; © **333/466 3208**; www.quattrotorra.it) was once a fortress but now is a photogenic B&B. One apartment overlooks olive groves and vineyards and another looks out on Siena's Mangia Tower. The five-star **Grand Hotel Continental** (**$$$**; Banchi di Sopra 85; © **0577/56011**; www.ghcs.it), in the heart of medieval Siena, specializes in romantic weddings. Once a wedding gift from Pope Alexander VII to his niece, this palace is an architectural jewel with beautiful frescoes that make romance irresistible.

PIENZA About 45 minutes away from Siena are two charmers. At **Hotel Il Chiostro di Pienza** (**$**; Corso Il Rossellino 26; © **0578/748-129**; www.relaisilchiostrodipienza.com), a transformed Franciscan convent, some rooms have frescoes and others, stone walls. The restaurant, on a terrace with a stunning view in summer, is excellent. **Terre di Nano Monticchiello Pienza** (**$**; Localita Il Nano Monticchiello; © **0578/070-115**; www.terredinano.com) has two apartments and three houses to rent, all with the same luscious views that the sculptor Cellini enjoyed here. This area, called the Val D'Orcia, has been immortalized by Italian artists, so it may look familiar, plus it's a UNESCO World Heritage site.

SAN GIMIGNANO **L'Antico Pozzo** (**$$$**; Via San Matteo 87; © **0577/942-014**; www.anticopozzo), the premier hotel here, is in a 15th-century palace where Dante stayed. The junior suites are fantastic, with canopy beds or perhaps a frescoed or wood ceiling. Some top floor rooms have city views, but all have artistic touches and plush beds. Breakfast is served on a nice terrace in good weather. This place is elegant without being stuffy.

HOTELS WITH HEART
Umbria

ASSISI Ancient Roman ruins make up part of the foundation of **Hotel Umbra** (**$**; Via degli Archi 6; www.hotelumbra.it; © **075/812-240**). This 13th-century building offers lovely views over the rooftops and valley; room have antique appointments and some have balconies or terraces with views. Great Umbrian food here is a bonus, with special emphasis on truffles and al fresco dining in summer. **Hotel Subasio** (Via Frate Elia, 2; ⓒ 075/812-353), a 16th-century palace beside the Basilica of St. Francis of Assisi, has antiques everywhere. Some rooms have pleasing views of the valley or the basilica, and the restaurant charms with original vaulted ceilings.

ORVIETO   **Hotel La Badia** ($$; Località La Badia 8; www.labadiahotel.it; ⓒ 0763/301-959) is not far from town, but the former abbey (built in the 8th and rebuilt in the 14th century) is a peaceful haven from tourism. Some rooms are luxurious and decorated with medieval sensibilities, but a few are quite small. The loft spaces are commodious. The surrounding property is lovely, and the suites in the outbuildings have good views of the city across the valley. The 16th-century **Palazzo Piccolomini** ($; Piazza Ranieri 36; www.palazzo piccolomini.it; ⓒ 0763/341-743) is a great choice for budget-conscious travelers with romance in mind. It's not a five-star, but has lovely salons and several old frescoes to remind you of its past. Rooms and bathrooms are simple but still elegant. Ask for a luxurious suite with a canopy bed. As usual in these antique palazzos, the ground-floor rooms have higher ceilings and feel grander, and the upper floors have better views. Breakfast is included in the rates.

PERUGIA   **Hotel Brufani Palace** ($$; Piazza Italia 12; brufanipalace.com; ⓒ 075/573-2541) offers romantic views, and the elegant rooms enhance them. This large hilltop hotel has a wonderful basement pool with a glass bottom that lets you see the Etruscan ruins below while you swim. For a splurge, consider **Castello di Monterone** ($$$; Strada Montevile, 3; castellomonterone.com; ⓒ 075/572-4214), an actual castle, and so romantic. Just a few miles from town, it has lovely grounds with rose gardens, enchanting courtyards, and two excellent restaurants, especially Il Postale (see above). The pool, with a stunning view, is just made for sipping your cocktail poolside. **Villa Monte Solare** ($; Via Montali 7, Tavernelle di Panicale; www.villamontesolare.com; ⓒ 075/832-376) is 25 minutes outside of Perugia, but you will be well rewarded for rambling along rural gravel roads to find it. The chapel with painted ceilings, glorious garden, and the formal (you have to dress for dinner) gourmet restaurant are perfect. In summer, the chapel hosts classical music concerts every night—a romantic moment that alone would justify your trip. The concierge here gladly organizes your vacation, if you wish, offering a walking tour, cycling excursion, and cooking classes. Most rooms are in the farm buildings and are very modern and convenient, but you may gravitate to the pool in the summer or on cooler days, to the main house's top-floor reading room for its panoramic views of Lake Trasimeno.

TODI   In the historic center, **Fonte Cesia** ($$; Via Lorenzo Leonj 3; www. fontecesia.it; ⓒ 075/894-3737 or 075/894-4677) combines 13th-century palazzo architecture with modern decor, convenience, and wonderful service. Public rooms have vaulted ceilings, and the expansive terrace is studded with greenery. Breakfast is dreamy in a spot near the hotel's namesake fountain. Suites have either a patio or a balcony.

Beach Romance

9 Sultry Shores: U.S.
10 Sultry Shores: Caribbean & Mexico
11 Sultry Shores: Europe
12 Sultry Shores: Exotic Lands

SULTRY SHORES: U.S.

T his is the scenario that beach lovers dream about: a perfect white sand cove, adjacent to a great bar (with an inventive and interesting, but discreet, bartender). Attached to the bar is an open-air restaurant where the couple can eat while barefooted. A cooling breeze wafts through the air as they look at the dramatic star-studded sky, brilliant because it is unimpeded by city lights.

Yes, there are variations on this theme: Some people like their beach to be near a happening town; others want it so isolated that they see no one else during their stay except the guy who flies in their food. But whatever the variation on the surf-and-sand theme, for beach lovers, the word vacation means nothing more than a lovely beach, and the very best of those in the United States are in this chapter (often with other attractions in case a partner needs a few more fun distractions).

9

CARMEL-BY-THE-SEA, MONTEREY & BIG SUR
Inland Sun & Coastal Fog

This sun- and fog-kissed coast has about every possible climate. You can do all of them in an extended weekend and have a variety of romantic experiences. Monterey and Carmel have the moody fog, artsy B&Bs, and a romantic rugged coast; Carmel Valley is all sunlight and winding rural roads with expansive resorts; and Big Sur is something else entirely. It all works, and it is among the most romantic of getaways.

Carmel-by-the-Sea
This coastline is awesome under all weather conditions. It can be cold here, and you will still want to wander the coast and look at the trees twisted by the elements as if they were giant Japanese

bonsai. Even Carmel proper, whose actual name is Carmel-by-the-Sea, is town enough to charm without the coast: Downtown is home to more than 500 boutiques and numerous thriving art galleries. It's fun to hunt for unusual crafts or discover intimate restaurants and small quaint hotels and B&Bs. Or, you can leave town and go higher into the Carmel Highlands for expansive views. Sure, this is a tourist town, but it is also eccentric; there are still non-franchised shops, and there are many romantic vistas and walks to enjoy.

KEY ATTRACTIONS

Pretty Strolls Start at romantic **Carmel Beach City Park,** where cypress trees frame the silky white stretch of sand (that also makes for quite good people watching). Farther south is lovely **Carmel River State Beach,** which offers more privacy but the same white sand plus dunes. It is a bird sanctuary with brown pelicans, gulls, and much more exotic species. Off the beach, **Carmel Walks** (✆ 831/642-2700; www.carmelwalks.com; $25 per person) offers 2-hour guided tours that explore gardens, homes of famous writers and artists, and lovely cottages, delivered with a dose of juicy gossip about Carmel's past. You also can explore the romantic home and gardens of the **Tor House,** on Carmel Point, 26304 Ocean View Ave. (✆ 831/624-1813; www.torhouse.org; tours Fri–Sat only, $10 per person), which was built for the poet Robinson Jeffers, using stones from around the world, including some from the Great Wall of China.

17-Mile Drive Pack a picnic, head to one of the five entry gates, and then get ready to see some of California's most romantic views and poshest real estate. The most convenient entrance is at Hwy. 1 at the Holman Highway exit, but traffic may be lighter if you enter at the Carmel Gate. Your $9 admission fee includes a map with 26 points of interest including Seal and Bird Rocks and Cypress Point Lookout, with its 20-mile view up to the Big Sur Lighthouse. You will see the famous Lone Cypress tree that has inspired many photographers. The drive also traverses the Del Monte Forest, where you might see some black-tailed deer. *Note:* If you like to bike, that's an even better way to see the memorable drive. For more information, visit www.pebble beach.com/activities/explore-the-monterey-peninsula/17-mile-drive.

HOTELS WITH HEART

The Carriage House Inn $$ Whether you choose a room on the first floor (wood-burning fireplace, whirlpool tub) or the second (sunken tub, vaulted beam ceiling), you will be surrounded by a cozy kind of luxury and impeccable service, just 1 block south of the beach. Breakfast comes to your room, and complimentary wine flows twice a day.

Junipero, between 7th and 8th aves. ✆ **800/433-4732** or 831/625-2585. www. carriagehouseinncarmel.com.

The Cypress Inn $$ Each room in this landmark boutique property (co-owned by Doris Day) has a different decor and personality, and while the rooms can be small, the romance is not lost. You can even bring your pets.

Corner of Lincoln and 7th. ✆ **800/443-7443** or 831-624-3871. www.cypress-inn.com.

The Hyatt Carmel Highlands $$$ A few miles outside Carmel on a cliff above Point Lobos, this is a perfect destination for honeymooners and anyone who wants to recharge a relationship. With just the right shadings of rustic and luxurious touches, the place is abloom in wildflowers—a good atmosphere for lovers. Your view: crashing waves against jagged rocks and the ocean's horizon. Your room's deck will call to you, sometimes rewarding you with distant views of migrating whales or just an unforgettable sunset. Choose carefully—each room is different (some have two levels), and the spa rooms have separate living areas, but all have a fireplace and can accommodate an in-room massage. The restaurant is excellent, with splendid views of the turbulent ocean and (sometimes) live music.

120 Highlands Dr. ✆ **831/620-1234.** www.highlandsinn.hyatt.com.

MOST ROMANTIC RESTAURANTS

Aubergine $$$ FRENCH Dining here is a lingering affair, so budget at least 3 hours for the full effect. The restaurant excels with exotic dishes like kumquat and almond soup; the potato, truffle, and onion foie gras; and duck breast ravioli. Local produce is used when possible. Wine offerings (or suggested pairings) are as exceptional as the food, and with just 12 tables you are guaranteed an intimate experience.

Monte Verde, at 7th Ave. ✆ **831/624-8578.** www.laubergecarmel.com.

Club Jalapeño $ MEXICAN Go to Club J for enchiladas in rich mole sauce—and give your wallet a reprieve. Take your taste buds to Tijuana via the fried and battered Baja fish tacos with lime-cilantro dressing or the coconut-encrusted fried fish. The two of you can share the spicy shrimp fajitas with a side of fresh fruit salsa. The decor is rustic with exposed beams and iron furnishings, and after dinner you can retire to the sexy corner bar to share a pure agave tequila.

San Carlos St., between 5th and 6th aves. ✆ **831/626-1997.** www.clubjalapeno.com.

Flying Fish Grill $$ PACIFIC RIM/SEAFOOD Asian influenced, this 40-seat dining room has a dark, intimate atmosphere with redwood booths and cuisine featuring fresh seafood with exquisite Japanese accents. Shabu-shabu, sushi, and tempura are excellent as is the peppered ahi tuna and pan-fried almond sea bass.

Mission St., between Ocean and 7th Ave. ✆ **831/625-1962.** www.flyingfishgrill.com.

CARMEL BY NIGHT

Carmel beds down early, so don't plan on rousing entertainment—at least not beyond your hotel room. However, you can count on good cocktails with captivating views of Big Sur at the **Sunset Lounge** in the Hyatt Carmel Highlands, 120 Highlands Dr. (✆ **831/622-5445;** www.highlandsinn.hyatt.com), served up with appetizers and music by local performers. Or check out the piano bar in **The Restaurant** at Mission Ranch, 26270 Dolores St. (✆ **831/625-9040;** www.missionranchcarmel.com), Clint Eastwood's resort.

Carmel Valley

Carmel Valley lies just east of Carmel; the sun shines more here, so it is where folks retreat from the coastal dampness. Many go for the famous golf courses, but everyone enjoys this scenic valley of rolling hills.

KEY ATTRACTIONS

The Great Outdoors   **Garland Ranch Regional Park** (about 8 miles east of Carmel on 700 W. Carmel Valley Rd.; www.mprpd.org) offers many scenic hiking trails; be sure to carry plenty of water to combat the glorious sunshine. The climate is alluring, and the scenery stunning for golf at several great locations, notably **Quail Lodge,** 8205 Valley Greens Dr. (℗ **831/624-2888;** www.quaillodge.com; greens fees $125–$150 for guests) and **Rancho Cañada Golf Club,** 4860 Carmel Valley Rd. (℗ **800/536-9459** or 831/624-0111; www.ranchocanada.com; greens fees $40–$70).

Wine Tasting   Small wine-tasting rooms are everywhere! We like the selection of wines at the **Château Julien Winery,** 8940 Carmel Valley Rd. (℗ **831/624-2600;** www.chateaujulien.com; tasting fee $15 per person) and also at **Bernardus Winery,** 5 W. Carmel Valley Rd. (℗ **800/223-2533** or 831/298-8021; www.bernardus.com; tasting fee $12 per person). You also will find many smaller, mom-and-pop tasting rooms that offer easy casual hospitality and very good wine.

HOTELS WITH HEART

Bernardus Lodge $$$ This ultra romantic spot is a dead ringer for a stay in Provence. The 57-room luxury boutique hotel has a lovely main lodge and dining room, two restaurants, spacious romantic rooms (and posh adobe-style guesthouses), an excellent winery, a gorgeous spa you will want to hit every day, and a vineyard. Activities include a meditation garden, bocce and tennis courts, and a pool. The main lodge has the look of a French country home, with rural touches such as wood beams, antique wrought iron, and limestone fireplaces. Your room likely will have a wood-burning fireplace, a feather bed, and French doors opening to your private deck. Carmel is just a 15-minute drive, but you won't want to leave. We love the fine dining at Marinus.

415 W. Carmel Valley Rd. ℗ **888/648-9463** or 831/658-3400. www.bernardus lodge.com.

Stonepine Ranch $$ This 330-acre resort amid lush meadows, ponds, and waterfalls is tucked deep into the valley and is as secluded as it can be in this part of the world. Built in 1928, the once-private estate was the biggest thoroughbred breeding farm in the West, and the expansive equestrian center remains in operation. While the rooms are very nice, the activities—horticulture, archery, horseback riding, and more—are the main appeal. Meals are served in a variety of charming sites around the property.

150 E. Carmel Valley Rd. ℗ **831/659-2245.** www.stonepineestate.com.

PLANNING A destination WEDDING

Destination weddings can be a wonderful gift to your family because everyone gets to share in an especially exotic or gorgeous place. Couples celebrating their second marriage often decide to make the event smaller and more intimate, which makes a far-flung destination wedding easier to do than a hometown celebration, where it may be difficult to exclude friends and extended family that may expect to be invited.

Any wedding can be harrowing to plan, but going away poses some special challenges: namely, the expense of getting there (or paying for family members to get there), the dangers of flight delays or cancellations, and the potential complications of planning in another time zone. You can expect that the farther away and more expensive the place, the fewer people can come.

We strongly suggest you hire a wedding planner for the job, but if your budget demands a DIY event, enlist the help of your hotel's concierge. If your wedding is in the United States, we recommend you visit a wedding-planning site like www.weddings.com or www.weddingwire.com. These sites have listings for all kinds of vendors—musicians, DJs, florists, photographers, tuxedo rental shops, wedding cake bakers, and more—throughout the States. We believe it "takes a vil-lage" to bring off perfect destination weddings.

Some questions to consider:

1. **Would your nearest and dearest *want* to visit this place?** Your close friends and family will want to be there for you, but will the destination add to or subtract from their fun?

2. **How much is this going to cost your guests?** Be sure to consider the cost of your event to your guests and, if their attendance matters to you, then this consideration may guide just how far flung your destination wedding will be. If your chosen hotel is pricey, how far away will guests need to go for more affordable lodging if they want it? A relatively easy and inexpensive idea for nature lovers is having your wedding near or in a national park. Most of America's great parks feature venerable old inns and resorts. For example, Aspen's hotels are pricey, but not too far from the Denver airport. **The Estes Park** (1700 Big Thompson Ave. ℓ **855-377-3778** or 970/577-6400; www.theestes parkresort.com; $179–$290 double) is now courting wedding business with its multimillion-dollar renovations and reasonable rates. It's the only venue where you can take your vows on the banks of the

grand Lake Estes with its majestic Rocky Mountain backdrop.

3. **Is it difficult to get to your destination?** Is there a likelihood of transfer snafus in places without direct flights from major cities? If so, you might consider changing to a location you can count on. For example, to get that European feeling in America, you can experience Provence in California if you hold your wedding in the Carmel Valley. (Then you can head to the Big Sur coastline for your honeymoon.)

4. **Is the hotel the right size?** The size of the property can really affect the ambience of your wedding. At a smaller place, you may have the opportunity to fill the entire place with friends and family. If you like the Pacific Northwest, we recommend a place like the **Black Walnut Inn** in Oregon's Willamette Valley (p. 162), or if you prefer northern California's wine country, the **Kenwood Inn and Spa** (p. 130) allows you to do whatever you wish with the entire premises. (*Note:* It's an adult-only inn.) A larger hotel might have many other functions going on at the same time, and your celebration might feel less special. Inquire about how they stagger weddings to be sure you won't be hearing

someone else's music while your ceremony is going on.

5. **Could the weather become a factor?** If you are luring your friends and family to Bora Bora (p. 308), it would be a shame if the great hotel deal you got was because it was the rainy season, and you wound up doing everything indoors!

6. **Is the place accessible for you or others who have health or mobility issues?** Some places are designed for people who have different kinds of physical ability; some would be very hard on anyone with a physical limitation.

7. **Is the venue experienced at doing weddings?** If you go with an experienced venue, you can usually trust it to handle all the details. Consider the **Kahala Hotel** and resort (p. 242), for example: Nestled in a prestigious neighborhood not far from Waikiki, the Kahala offers two wedding gazebos (one with a view of the Koko Head volcano in the distance; the other keeps the endless blue waters of Kahala Bay in sight), plus an "Orchid Wall" that winds down a huge staircase—perfect for your wedding photos. The Kahala prides itself on being multicultural and welcomes same-sex union ceremonies as well as all others who want a Hawaiian-style wedding.

Monterey

A mere 5 miles up Highway 1 from Carmel is this bustling, hustling tourist town. The wharf is schlock central, but you should brave the flim-flam shops to visit one of the country's marvels, **Monterey Bay Aquarium** (see later listing), a unique center for oceanic research and conservation. To see something truly heartwarming, look no further than the sea otter exhibit here, where the otters romp, tumble and wrestle as though they were the ones on a romantic holiday! This is obviously a place to get in touch with nature, too.

KEY ATTRACTIONS

The Great Outdoors   You can take a sea kayak tour of placid Monterey Bay and get up close and personal with the sea otters outside the aquarium. Tour operators will take you to the otters and more, even at sunrise. Or rent some bikes and do the 29-mile **Coastal Bike Trail,** along the Fort Ord Sand Dunes, and be on lookout for sea lions, dolphins, and whales. Your hotel can help you arrange these tours.

Monterey Bay Aquarium   At the edge of one of the largest underwater canyons on Earth, the aquarium features incredibly diverse marine life. A clear three-story tank houses everything from leopard sharks to anchovies, all swimming through a thick kelp forest. The Outer Bay tank houses open-ocean life, including large green sea turtles, barracuda, sharks, and schools of bonito. Don't miss the Giant Octopus exhibit.

886 Cannery Row. ⓒ **831/648-4800.** www.montereybayaquarium.org. Admission $40 for adults, $35 for seniors 65+.

HOTELS WITH HEART

Old Monterey Inn $$ This is as good as a B&B can be! It's nowhere near the ocean, but its three vine-covered stories, bubbling brook, and rose gardens make it prime for romance. All rooms have plush feather beds and down duvets, but make sure yours also has a private bath and a wood-burning fireplace (our faves are the book-lined Library and the Stoneleigh, with the fireplace facing the bed and its own private entrance). Breakfasts are stellar and are included in your rate—and can be served in your room. In the afternoon, enjoy fireside wine.

500 Martin St. ⓒ **800/350-2344** or 831/375-8284. www.oldmontereyinn.com.

The Spindrift Inn $$ First, the bad news: The Spindrift is right in honkytonk central on the waterfront. Better news: It's just a short walk to the aquarium. Best news: This four-story hotel is lovely after you come in off the street. It's romantic and elegant, with down feather beds, wood-burning fireplaces, and cushioned window seats or private balconies. Enjoy afternoon wine tastings. The ocean-view and corner rooms are worth the splurge.

652 Cannery Row. ⓒ **800/841-1879** or 831/646-8900. www.spindriftinn.com.

MOST ROMANTIC RESTAURANTS

Montrio Bistro $$ AMERICAN BISTRO   With a touch of urban élan, this fine coastal eatery is in a converted 1910 firehouse. The dining room is spacious with a fun decor that includes clouds suspended from the ceiling and curvy walls. The open kitchen's oak-fired rotisserie grill is the star, producing such delicacies as crispy Dungeness crab cakes with spicy rémoulade and a fine roasted portobello mushroom with polenta and ragout of vegetables. The award-winning wine list includes numerous fine vintages by the glass.

414 Calle Principal. ℗ **831/648-8880.** www.montrio.com.

MONTEREY BY NIGHT

Monterey hosts the world's longest-running jazz festival every September. **Cibo Ristorante Italiano,** 301 Alvarado St. (℗ **831/649-8151;** www.cibo. com), is a popular, artsy restaurant (good for a complete meal or a great pizza) that serves up live jazz (Sun and Tues–Thurs 7–10pm) alongside its famed 9-ounce martinis.

Big Sur

One of the most dramatic coastlines on Earth, Big Sur leaves every visitor awestruck, fixated on how the cliffs, rocks, and trees are positioned against the ocean. This gorgeous juxtaposition of land and sea always stays arresting; in fact, just looking at these amazing views is reason enough to be here. Everything you'll want to do or see is right off of Highway 1, which hugs the entire Big Sur coastline. Head south from Carmel, and the visuals will knock you out the whole way: Point Lobos State Reserve, Bixby Bridge, Point Sur Lighthouse, Pfeiffer Beach, Sand Dollar Beach, and Jade Cove.

HOTELS WITH HEART

The Post Ranch Inn $$$ Clinging to cliffs 1,200 feet above the ocean, this romantic resort has been widely praised ever since is opening in 1992. The charming guest cottages—each with its own fireplace, digital music system, and private deck—are built around existing trees; the secluded Ocean and Coast cottages seem nearly in the clouds (especially as viewed from your private spa tub), but the woodland cottages are equally impressive. The inn's infinity pool and sun decks are also spectacular. If the cost of the hotel proves prohibitive, consider a magnificent consolation prize: Go enjoy the floor-to-ceiling ocean views from the **Sierra Mar** restaurant and bar.

47900 Hwy. 1. ℗ **888/524-4787** or 831/667-2200. www.postranchinn.com.

MOST ROMANTIC RESTAURANTS

The restaurants and hotels of Big Sur are easy to spot: Most are situated directly on or just off the highway. A must-stop along the way, if for nothing but to look down from the cliffs and admire the celestial view of the ocean, is **Nepenthe**, 48510 Hwy. 1 ($$$; ℗ **831/667-2345;** www.nepenthebigsur.com). In good weather, take in the sun on the terrace and have an expensive, but heavenly, hamburger (lunch is definitely a better deal than dinner). If it's cool, take advantage of the redwood and adobe restaurant with its wood-burning fireplace. There's also a terrific gift shop with beautiful original art.

For romance, nothing tops the view at **Sierra Mar** restaurant at the Post Ranch Inn, 47900 Hwy. 1 ($$$; ℗ **831/667-2800**).

FLORIDA KEYS
Sun, Fun & Fish

We won't deny that Miami is sexy, particularly South Beach, with its high-concept restaurants and international set. In fact, we recommend you go there (see p. 39). But then head to the Florida Keys, where nature still has a foothold, and life is quirky and unpredictable. It will take you 3 or 4 hours to drive the full length of the Keys, and pretty quickly you'll get the impression that you aren't in the United States. Some of the Keys house funky fishing operations and even funkier roadside attractions, but there are also fine resorts. Furthest down you'll find Key West, where the artists and writers who have claimed it have created an alternate universe of hedonism, with a "party 'til the end of the world" feeling. Whatever else it is, it is a whole world oriented to water, sand, diving, snorkeling, fishing, and flip-flops. You either like the mood, or you don't—but we think it's very romantic.

There are many Keys, more than 800 islands, and they string out over 113 miles. Entrepreneur/railroad man/land baron Henry Flagler had mad plans to connect the Keys by railroad, but it didn't quite work out as planned. Instead, what remains are fingers of land jutting out from the connecting causeway and bridges that have made the Florida Keys penetrable. These beautiful and sometimes wild places are usually referred to as the upper, middle, and lower Keys, and they are usually quieter and less visited than the rest—until you get to Key West. We can't cover them all, but discovering an intricate landscape like this would be a romantic journey. We offer some favorite stops, and if you want some audio with these suggestions, we suggest the Beach Boys or Jimmy Buffett. Then head to Key West.

Key Largo (Upper Keys)

This is the largest, northernmost key. It's a coral wonderland with a huge protected marine life park, surrounded by numerous islands with barely rooted trees densely dotting them. To get to this protected habitat for crocodiles and water birds from afar, travel along the Card Sound Bridge, the northern entry to the Keys and a momentary deviation from U.S. Route 1. You travel over many bridges, surrounded by different shades of blue water, surrendering to the sole route linking the keys together.

KEY ATTRACTIONS

Diving Lessons Islamorada's **Chesapeake Resort**, 83409 Overseas Hwy. (© **800/338-3395** or 305/664-4662; www.chesapeake-resort.com), gives lessons and certifications. But it isn't a 1-day instant process. It takes lessons, exams, and test dives. But if you both are up for it, being dive partners is an intimate experience. You absolutely need to be responsible for each other's safety. There are many people who think the most romantic and wondrous sights to be seen are far below sea level.

Snorkeling & Kayaking   It's romantic to explore an explosion of colorful reef fish in your underwater world together. The **John Pennekamp Coral Reef Park,** 102601 Overseas Hwy. (© **305/451-6300;** www.pennekamppark.com), is the only living coral reef in the continental United States, meaning you are at the Grand Central Station of fish. Check in at **Tavernier Dive Center,** 90451 Old Hwy. (© **800/433-8946** or 305/852-4599; www.tavernierdivecenter.com), or **Quiescence Diving Services,** 103680 Overseas Hwy. (© **305/451-2440;** www.keylargodiving.com), and competent guides will show you around.

Kayaking is an especially great way to see nature up close. Marathon is not a romantic town, but **Marathon Kayak** (© **305/395-0355;** www.marathonkayak. com) gives a uniquely romantic tour of the mangroves, exploring this mystical environment and helping you understand the symbiotic relationship between the flora, sea, and fish. You might see turtles, sting rays, or nurse sharks, or one of the world's oddest and seemingly best-tempered sea mammals, the manatee. More than a thousand pounds each, whiskered like walruses, they are endangered by motorized boats accidentally hitting them in their feeding waters.

Sport Fishing   This is beach and sport fishing central, and we suggest you head to Islamorada to try your hand. It's almost hard not to catch anything! **Holiday Isle Resort,** 84001 Overseas Hwy. (© **305/433-9941** or 305/433-9942; www.holidayisle.com), will charter a sport fishing day for you from its marina. Get expert help at **Bud and Mary's Fishing Marina,** 79851 Overseas Hwy. (© **305/664-2461;** http://budnmarys.com), or **Robbies,** 77522 Overseas Hwy. (© **888/316-7754** or 305/664-8070; robbies.com), where you can feed the tarpon as they jump out of the water to grab bait from your hand! Sport fishing can encourage togetherness—you may need teamwork to reel in a big fish! *Caution:* Think twice if you tend at all to get seasick. Feeling nauseated on a boat is among the most unsexy things in the world.

HOTELS WITH HEART

Azul del Mar $ This Art Deco boutique hotel has six stylish guest suites with kitchenettes, and it's close to John Pennekamp Coral Reef State Park.

104300 Overseas Hwy. © **888/253-2985** or 305/451-0337. www.azulkeylargo.com.

Casa Morada $$$ This boutique hotel has stylish white interiors and a romance-friendly adults-only policy—and you get a view of the bay from every suite.

136 Madeira Rd., Islamorada. © **888/881-3030** or 305/664-0044. www.casa morada.com.

The Cheeca Lodge $$$ The luxurious rooms can be pricey, but the more expensive bungalows right on the beach are worth the extra investment. The lodge organizes golf, tennis, windsurfing, and fishing trips for you and keeps your kids or grandchildren busy, should you bring them. The large spa has many options for lavish treatments.

81801 Overseas Hwy., Islamorada. © **800/327-2888** or 305/664-4651. www. cheeca.com.

Kona Kai Resort and Gallery $$ This is the romantic choice in Key Largo, with a no-kids policy, great privacy, and a nod to both the artistic present and past of Key West. Lush vegetation surrounds the traditional Caribbean tin roof buildings. The rooms have cool tile floors and rattan furniture; hibiscus, hydrangea, and palms surround the pool. The fragrance is intoxicating.

97802 Overseas Hwy., Key Largo. ☏ **800/365-7829** or 305/852-7200. http://konakairesort.com.

The Moorings Village $$$ Expect atmospheric private cottages on an old coconut plantation, right next door to Cheeca (see previous listing). You are pretty much left alone, with kitchens to provide your daily coffee, breakfasts, or other meals. The cottages are small and provide large romantic soaking tubs and a splendid beach.

123 Beach Rd., Islamorada. ☏ **305/664-4708.** www.themooringsvillage.com.

MOST ROMANTIC RESTAURANTS

Atlantic's Edge $$ SEAFOOD   Cheeca Lodge's stylish restaurant features fresh seafood caught locally, prime steaks, and organically grown local produce prepared imaginatively at a more reasonable price than you would expect. Part of the thrill is the Tiki Bar, located between the restaurant's outdoor deck and the pool; the entire complex is on the beach, and the Atlantic views are incomparable.

81801 Overseas Hwy., Islamorada. ☏ **800/327-2888** or 305/664-4651. www.cheeca.com.

Green Turtle Inn $ SEAFOOD   The inn is famous for fantastic breakfasts, especially the coconut French toast. Expect lots of atmosphere for your early morning coffee in a 1940s diner.

81219 Overseas Hwy., Islamorada. ☏ **305/664-2006.** www.greenturtlekeys.com. Closed Mon.

Morada Bay Beach Café $$ SEAFOOD   This is it, just what we romantics want: fresh seafood, grilled and sauced perfectly, and served beside a beautiful beach, positioned well for the dazzling sunset and lit by torchlight.

81600 Overseas Hwy., Islamorada. ☏ **305/664-0604.** www.moradabay-restaurant.com.

THE UPPER KEYS BY NIGHT

For a subdued atmosphere, try **Zane Grey Lounge,** 81532 Overseas Hwy., Islamorada (☏ **305/664-9271;** restaurants.basspro.com/ZaneGreyLounge), a handsome stained-glass and mahogany-wood bar and club on the second floor of the World Wide Sportsman shop. Enjoy a view of the bay's calm waters, watch the sunset, and soak up the history of longtime anglers. Have a cocktail, and stick around for casual dishes of local seafood. Another great place for sunsets, cocktails, and seafood is **Lorelei Cabana Bar**, Mile Marker 82, Islamorada (☏ **305/664-2692;** www.loreleicabanabar.com). Locals and tourists mingle at this outdoor cabana bar after 5pm. On the huge deck, you'll find local bands playing—mainly mellow rock, reggae, or blues—under a thatched-roof.

Key West

Think Tennessee Williams, Hemingway (definitely visit his home), Truman Capote, and Jimmy Buffett; think extremely gay-friendly. Key West is many things to many people, and tolerance breeds a happy liberation here. Nature has also helped Key West be a world apart. If you want to drive, there is just one long causeway that goes there, the Florida Overseas Highway. If there is an accident, well, bring a book with you. Otherwise, it's water, water everywhere, and don't the two of you want to enjoy it?

KEY ATTRACTIONS

Budding Artists Many artists find their inspiration in Key West, which means there are plenty of art galleries and art happenings to peruse. If this sounds like fun to you, don't skip the Armory, a 1903 space that is now called **Studios of Key West,** 600 White St. (✆ **305/296-0458;** www.tskw.org). There is always something new, whether it's an exhibition or a concert.

The Neighborhoods Key West isn't only the bars on Duval Street (thank goodness). There are lovely neighborhoods just off the main drag with many elegant and quite romantic Victorian homes. It's a different world with leafy trees and quiet walkways—a nice place to hold hands.

Yoga on the Beach We think it's romantic to start the day together with mindful but not excessive exercise. Every morning about 8am people gather and face the sea together (modest fee; yoga mats provided) at Zachary Taylor State Park for Yoga on the Beach (✆ **305/296-7352;** www.yogaonbeach.com).

HOTELS WITH HEART

Alexander's Guesthouse $$ By all means, stay if you're gay, and they'll let you in if you're not (but do have the right spirit). Rooms are furnished in keeping with the lovely 1901 house. It's a deal, so reserve well ahead.
1118 Fleming St. ✆ **800/654-9919** or 305/294-9919. www.alexanderskeywest.com.

Casa Marina, A Waldorf Astoria Resort $$ Built in the 1920s and renovated recently, Casa Marina has the classic Henry Flagler look (he's the developer who brought art deco to south Florida's luxury destinations). Visit the **Sun Sun Beach Bar** and just drink it all in.
1500 Reynolds St. ✆ **888/303-5717.** http://casamarinaresort.com.

Paradise Inn $ Classy and pricey, with a lovely pool and many luxurious amenities.
819 Simonton St. ✆ **305/293-8007.** http://theparadiseinn.com.

MOST ROMANTIC RESTAURANTS

Louie's Backyard $$ CARIBBEAN The island casual atmosphere adds to the better-than-casual cooking, priced from moderate to expensive. We like the ambience here, and this is another candidate for sensationally good lime pie (gingerbread crust with a raspberry sauce!).

700 Waddell Ave. © **305/294-1061.** www.louiesbackyard.com.

nine one five $$ ECLECTIC   Duval Street can be a bit much, but this restaurant is low-key and has excellent Asian fusion cuisine. As the night wears on, a lounge on the second floor turns into a romantic, fun space with a mixed crowd (age, sexual orientation) dancing with verve and, sometimes, abandon!

915 Duval St. © **305/296-0669.** www.915duval.com.

KEY WEST BY NIGHT

You have to do Key West at sunset. The place? **Mallory Square,** the center of Key West's historic waterfront, and it's often a packed house. Next stop? Duval Street and **Orchid Key Inn,** 1004 Duval St. (© **305/296-9915;** http://orchidkeyinn.com), a tiny bar with an art deco style overlooking an illuminated pool and a more sophisticated vibe than most of the bars in Key West. Depend on the bartenders to mix virtually any concoction you can think of—or let them suggest something, such as the French 75 (Hendrick's gin, St. Germain, lemon juice, and Champagne). Just around the corner is **Captain Tony's Saloon** (428 Greene St.; © **305/294-1838;** www.capttonyssaloon. com), where regulars at this smoky old bar can recall the island when they say Hemingway drank and caroused here.

HAWAII (THE BIG ISLAND)

Volcanic Romance

Flying into the Hawaiian islands is always breathtaking. You travel thousands of miles over the deep blue sea and then—land ho!—miles and miles of beach and rugged coastline with waves lapping at the edges. If you've seen Oahu, Maui, or Kauai, your first look at the Big Island is kind of a shock. It is volcanic; parts of it are very dry; and many of the beaches are of black sand. When you drive around (you will need a car unless you plunk yourself down some place wonderful and never explore), you will see the topography is extremely diverse: desert, red clay, black soil, hills, flats, ranch lands, and dense tropical foliage with flowering acacia trees, orchids hanging on rocks, and then suddenly back to desert. Within minutes of each other are vastly different climate zones. The longer you stay, the more you wonder: Is this the best island of all?

The commercial center, **Kailua-Kona,** is close to some elegant resorts and retains charming seaside restaurants, shaved ice, excellent coffee, a few atmospheric buildings, a walkable in-town waterfront—and too many T-shirt shops. Lovers don't come here for the town—on the Big Island you head to where the wild things are: an active volcano, caves, reef dives, cowboys, and coffee groves. There, you'll find Hawaii untamed if you try.

This is The Big Island, so it can take a while to get someplace. Getting to **Kilauea volcano** is a significant commitment, as is going to **Hilo,** an older non-touristy town on the Kohala coast, the opposite side of the island from the luxury hotels and popular beaches. We think the Kohala coast is the most tastefully developed beach area on the island and glorious for its sunsets and ancient sacred ruins, lush gardens, and aquatic wildlife. Visit the ancient places here, and you'll feel the spiritual energy.

KEY ATTRACTIONS

Hawaii Volcanoes National Park   Want to see how the world was made? See it here. This park is reason enough to visit the Big Island. **Kilauea** is a live volcano, and it smokes most days, though lava viewing conditions change daily. Some days, molten red-hot lava spews down the mountainside and into the sea. But even on a quiet day, walking around here is fascinating. Investigate the Halemaumau Crater, an active pit of steam and sulfur; the Lava Tube trail (destroyed by lava); and the Chain of Craters Road, where lava spills across the blacktop. You can also tour the other volcano, **Mauna Kea,** and the biggest telescope in the world. Usually it's all very safe, but occasionally, not so much. The very good information center can tell you about the times Kilauea has been a bad boy, wiping out beaches, historic temples, and houses, instead of a well-behaved tourist attraction. All that said, it is thrilling to see an active volcano and if she is acting up within acceptable boundaries while you are there, go up the mountain and see Mother Nature at her most awesome and powerful.

The Parker Ranch   If you're like us, cowboy country invigorates you, but the Parker Ranch, dating from the mid-19th century, is an extraordinary sight even if it doesn't. Thousands of acres of cattle ranching that a couple can explore together await you, glad that this magnificent expanse is preserved. Just driving through it stimulates your senses, connecting you viscerally to a bygone era on the islands.

66 Mamalahoa Hwy., Kamuela. ℂ **808/885-7311.** http://parkerranch.com. Self-guides tours are free.

Underwater Weddings

Looking for an unusual way to get married or renew your vows? **The Sheraton Keauhou Bay,** 78-128 Ehukai St., Kailua-Kona (ℂ **808/930-4900;** www.sheraton keauhou.com), has a special manta ray viewing point just off shore, and you can dive or snorkel at night with the rays, the odd-shaped creatures whose wings span up to 20 feet. If both of you are like fish in water, you can take this one step further and, if you are certified, get married under water with the help of a dive master who can legally officiate at an underwater ceremony.

Pololu Valley Lookout Here is that iconic romantic view of Hawaii. Just drive to the end of the island (literally). Head northwest to the village of Hawi, near the birthplace of King Kamehameha (the warrior King who united the islands). Where the road ends, you walk to the lookout. You may recognize the long sweep of sea and land from travel posters, but seeing it will feel overwhelmingly personal and satisfying to you both. The mountain is to your right, the bluest of seas below flailing against a black sand beach. With green velour-coated rocks, native flowers, and birds all around you, this is a very good place to feel grateful for being able to experience this stirring view together.

Snorkeling & Diving On the West Coast, the water is calm, warm, and clear—and perfect for diving and snorkeling. The island's countless inlets and reefs harbor the bright little fish that look like aquatic jewels and move you to gesticulate madly at your underwater companion. Snorkeling at **Hapuna Beach Cove**, you'll be among schools of yellow tangs, needlefish, and green sea turtles. Or swim with fast-moving game fish at **Ulua Cave** at the north end of the **Kohala Coast**. Dozens of reputable dive shops provide instruction and trips.

HOTELS WITH HEART

The **Four Seasons at Hualalai** ($$$; 72-100 Ka`upulehu Dr., Kailua-Kona; ℂ **808/325-8000;** www.fourseasons.com/hualalai) is as expensive as you'd think, but we think it's worth considering if you feel like splurging.

Holualoa Inn $$ Want to feel like a native Hawaiian? Go up country to Holualoa, and you just might get the Aloha spirit—at moderate prices (for Hawaii). This town has become a bit of an arts center, but is not so rarified that you feel like you are in a resort. At the inn, located on a Kona coffee estate, you trade the typical oceanfront view for fabulous territorial views from 1350 feet above the sea. You can swim in the inn's huge pool overlooking a glowing green world. This is an adult world with only six suites and ideal for honeymoons and small weddings. How's this for authenticity: Your gourmet breakfast each morning includes the estate's homegrown Kona coffee. At night, grill your own dinner by the pool and use the high-powered inn telescope to marvel at the stars. It's only 20 minutes to the beach, but you may prefer to just hold hands and drink in the view of Kailua Kona and the endless blue ocean below.

76-5932 Mamalahoa Hwy., Holualoa. ℂ **800/392-1812.** www.holualoainn.com.

Mauna Lani Bay Hotel $$$ This is a blessed piece of geography on the Kohala Coast. A long sinuous sandy beach outlines the property, and ancient canals and tide pools here teem with sea life. At some pools, signs warn you to take care because endangered baby sea turtles are being raised in them. Signs also guide you to the ancient petroglyph areas next to the resort. At the new moon, the Mauna Lani hosts a storytelling night (see "The Big Island by Night," later). Other pluses: spacious, ocean-view rooms with lanais; bungalows for families; and great kids programs.

68-1400 Mauna Lani Dr., Kohala Coast. ℂ **800/367-2323.** www.maunalani.com.

Palms Cliff House Inn $$ A traditional Hawaiian set of handsome white wood buildings and verandas, with a slightly southern personality and your own lanai to sit on and watch the waves crash. Let the breezes caress you together. Each of the eight oceanfront rooms has a private entrance that makes it easy to get lost in your own world. It's informal, hospitable, and relaxing.

28-3514 Mamalahoa Hwy., Honomu. ℂ **866/963-6076.** www.palmscliffhouse.com.

Silver Oaks Guest Ranch $ The real deal: two cottages on a 10-acre working ranch. It's not a dude ranch, so you don't play cowboy, but you get one heck of a place for a very reasonable tariff. You will see endless ocean views, and while you fantasize you are in a distant private world, you are very close to both the airport and Kailua-Kona. The rooms are lovely, there is a pool, and you will welcome the cool night air when you come back to your cozy hideaway from the very hot beach.

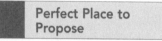

> ### Perfect Place to Propose
>
> Hire a helicopter in Hilo to fly over the steamy black expanses and red-glowing flows of Pu'u O'o volcano (of course, your partner may not be able to hear you because of the noisy blades, but it will still be romantic and thrilling).

73-4570 Mamalahoa Hwy., Kailua-Kona. ℂ **877/325-2300.** www.silveroaksranch.com.

MOST ROMANTIC RESTAURANTS

Brown's Beach House $$$ BIG ISLAND CUISINE   When you dream of a romantic tropical setting, this is what it looks like: open-air dining beside a lagoon facing the ocean and the sunset. Afterward in the darkness, tiki torches are lit and cast long shadows of the coconut trees. The tables are elegantly dressy, and their candlelight reflects off the lagoon. Magically, the food—particularly freshly caught seafood in Pacific Rim, Hawaiian, and Big Island styles—is as good as the setting. It's here, at the Fairmont Orchid resort.

1 North Kaniku Dr., Kohala Coast. ℂ **808/887-7368.** www.fairmont.com/orchid-hawaii/dining.

Canoehouse at the Mauna Lani Bay Resort $$$ HAWAII REGIONAL   Have a cocktail in the gazebo! And then wander to your outdoor table just in time for the sunset. The Hawaii Island Shellfish Bowl with fresh shrimp, scallops, clams, mussels, and Kaffir lime coconut broth argues forcefully for passion unleashed.

68-1400 Mauna Lani Dr., Kohala Coast. ℂ **808-881-7911.** www.maunalani.com.

Kamuela Provision Company at the Hilton Waikoloa $$$ STEAK & SEAFOOD   You sit above the edge of the lava fields, beneath the stars with the ocean lit up and lapping a few yards beyond your table. The steaks and seafood are excellent, and the cocktails (and first-rate wine list) at the Blue Lagoon bar have that same amazing view for you to drink in. For an over-the-top romantic experience, you can make a special reservation at

Buddha point, just for the two of you, surrounded by lanterns and tiki torches and the crashing ocean. Most any list of romantic restaurants on the big island lists this spot in the top three.

69-425 Waikoloa Beach Drive. ☏ **808/886-1234.** www.hiltonwaikoloavillage.com.

'Ulu Ocean Grill and Sushi Lounge $$$ CONTEMPORARY PACIFIC RIM   Any closer to the water and you would need a snorkel. You get to this charming restaurant (the name means "aquarium") by going over a bridge of natural logs. Ocean views are on three sides, and everything underlines the aquatic theme. The sushi and seafood is fresh, of course, some farmed by the establishment; signature dishes are lobster won ton soup and whole oven-roasted fish. Open for breakfast, lunch, and dinner.

72-100 Ka`upulehu Dr., Kailua-Kona. Four Seasons ☏ **808/325-8000.**

THE BIG ISLAND BY NIGHT

Want a little old-style Hawaiian entertainment? Flirt with each other at one of the friendly pubs in **Kailua-Kona** or at any resort; you'll usually find a veranda with a gasp-worthy view. The wild side of The Big Island makes your evenings seductive without even trying. A sizzling orange sun sinks into cobalt waters, and the majestic mountain, Mauna Kea, glows fiery red in a hazy purple sky. That sets the stage for romance, but you can augment it. **Twilight at Kalahuipua'a,** a monthly Hawaiian cultural celebration held on the Saturday closest to the full moon, begins with the evocative bugling of a conch, calling people together. The evening proceeds dramatically with traditional storytelling, singing, and authentic hula dancing on the oceanside lawn at the Mauna Lani Bay Hotel. Locals and visitors alike bring a picnic and spread their blankets. Catered meals are available, too. For more information, call ☏ **808/881-7911** or visit www.maunalani.com.

MARTHA'S VINEYARD & NANTUCKET
An East Coast Tradition

In the summer it seems the whole East Coast empties to these secluded islands just minutes away from Cape Cod, and with good reason. The islands have long been treasured as luxurious yet no-frills havens for vacations or weekend escapes. With virtually no gimmicks or tourist traps, privacy is a prized commodity here that translates into incredibly intimate retreats for lovers. Maybe most of us can't afford a home in these transcendent Atlantic isles, but we can still live the life of the lucky locals and wealthy summer people—if for just a short time.

Places this romantic are expensive in summer, but good deals are available in the "shoulder seasons," before or after summer. That's great, because

Martha's Vineyard and Nantucket can be extremely romantic during the extended fall when the waters around Nantucket Sound are warmest, and the days remain sunny while nights cool down for cuddling. These are great destinations any time, but we recommend the off-seasons, even winter, when you can have the beaches at their lonesome, most glorious, best.

Nantucket

The smaller of the two islands, Nantucket still shows its rustic origins as one of the world's busiest whaling ports, but now this 14-mile long island is primarily a tourist destination. It still defines itself, in part, by its isolation.

You arrive here in 2 hours by one of the most romantic watercraft ever invented, a ferry, or in half the time by high-speed catamaran (both from Hyannis on Cape Cod). Small as it is, the island offers more than 80 miles of shoreline—no wonder you can still find moments alone on the beach. The island's one town, Nantucket, rings a yacht-filled harbor and bursts with sophisticated shops, galleries, quaint inns, restaurants, cobblestone streets, historic sites, and pristine beaches. But town is not what romance on this island is about. It's about beachcombing, enjoying the beach at dusk, and reading books together on a porch with an ocean view. Here are a few more romantic things couples can do to make this a warm and intimate vacation, weekend, or—who knows?—maybe a whole summer or fall!

KEY ATTRACTIONS

Art & Artists   In town are numerous art galleries and festivals where artists show their work, including weekend and holiday markets and a 10-day Fall Arts Festival in October, plus a concert series in the spring with local chamber groups and some well-known entertainers.

Biking & Hiking   Many on this island travel by bike, and if not, they are covering the windy island trails on foot. On the coast are the dunes and windswept beaches you have seen on postcards. One of the nicest features of these idyllic paths is that many of them are flat and easy on problem knees or other conditions that make you wobbly. We recommend the rustic, but flat, 8-mile **Siasconset path** to the island's east end. For more ambitious bikers or hikers is the hillier 6-mile **Madaket path** or bike routes like **Surfside**, which is exactly that.

Exploring the Bogs   Some natural flora are quintessentially specific to a certain environment. In this ecosystem, its cranberry bogs, which come to harvest in the fall and offer startlingly lovely crimson vistas (www.nantucket conservation.org).

Great Point Lighthouse   For a robust romantic adventure, visit this iconic lighthouse on the northern tip of the island. You walk in from the road, but it's worth it. The remote lighthouse is at the end of a spit, with anglers casting off in the shallows for striped bass on both sides. Perhaps it is the isolation that makes it so romantic, suggesting a tale of a lonely outpost where a love story took place . . .

Picnicking   What says summer romance more than a picnic on the beach? You can also do it in the fall here, until the chill. For a luxe experience, order a steamed seafood feast or lobster lunch (you must eat lobster on this island unless you are allergic) from several restaurants, including the **Lobster Trap** (**$$;** 23 Washington St.; ℭ **508/228-4200;** www.nantucketlobstertrap.com; lobster dinners $30–$92), which will deliver it to your beach.

Sailing   In the summer, consider a 90-minute island tour aboard the 31-foot replica sloop *Endeavor* (ℭ **508/228-5585;** www.endeavorsailing.com; $40 for 90-min. tour, $50 at sunset), or at least enjoy the beautiful sight of sails billowed by the wind and colorful spinnakers making the sea a gallery of modern art. In late May a serious race, **the Figawi,** kicks off the summer season with a run from Hyannis to Nantucket that makes for a festive day and later at the bars an even more festive night.

HOTELS WITH HEART

Cliffside Beach Club $$$ This is the Nantucket experience you always imagined. It's on the beach and a short walk (about a mile) to town. The clubhouse, decorated in antique wicker, adds colorful blue, yellow, and green umbrellas along its beachside. Its renovated **Galley Beach** restaurant is one of the island's finest.

46 Jefferson Ave. ℭ **800/932-9645** or 508/228-0618. www.cliffsidebeach.com.

Wauwinet Inn $$$ Stay in this Cape Cod–style hotel (the only Relais & Chateau property on the island) and you may want to don white pants and a blue blazer, but you don't *have* to look nautical. You are in your own ultra-deluxe romantic hideaway—dress any way you want! The inn is at the tip of a wildlife sanctuary nestled between the Atlantic Ocean and Nantucket Bay. All the rooms—some smallish—have pine armoires, Audubon prints, and an array of antique accessories. If you order breakfast in your room, the steward sets it up with a white tablecloth and fine china. Don't miss the Wauwinet's **Toppers**. The 1850 restaurant has cozy banquettes and in the fall, a chill-chasing fireplace. The menu features fine regional cuisine: Lobster is a major event. Desserts are also fabulous. Consider eating here even if you don't stay at the Wauwinet. For a romantic touch, the hotel runs a complimentary boat service between town and the restaurant for lunch and dinner from late June to mid-September.

120 Wauwinet Rd. ℭ **800/426-8718.** www.wauwinet.com. Closed Nov–Apr.

MOST ROMANTIC RESTAURANTS

American Seasons $$$ REGIONAL AMERICAN   This spot features a sustainable menu, but we also like it because it's just a nice little romantic spot. Here you'll find flavors from New England (naturally the Pacific Coast, cowboy country, and Down South, plus produce from local farms). We like the Nantucket fluke with creamed local corn, chorizo (spicy Portuguese sausage), littleneck clams, and squash blossoms. Throughout the evening you can order from the lighter *tapas* menu.

80 Center St. ℭ **508/228 7111.** www.americanseasons.com.

Centre Street Bistro $$ NEW AMERICAN   This exquisite BYOB restaurant in the center of town has about eight tables and features wonderful, creative cuisine that includes such delicacies as warm goat-cheese tart to start, followed by Long Island duck breast with pumpkin and butternut-squash risotto. Of course we wouldn't turn up our noses at the sautéed Nantucket Bay scallops, either.

29 Centre St. © **508/228-8470.** www.nantucketbistro.com.

Company of the Cauldron $$ CONTINENTAL   One of the island's most romantic restaurants offers one fixed-price meal nightly; check ahead for best results. But whatever the dish, you'll dine by candlelight; if you're lucky, you'll nosh on the soft-shell crab appetizer and be able to choose among swordfish, rack of lamb, or beef Wellington. Desserts are great. Try the chocolate soufflé cake. Because the portions are large, this restaurant is actually a fine-dining bargain. In season, a harpist serenades diners most nights.

5 India St. © **508/228-4016.** www.companyofthecauldron.com.

NANTUCKET BY NIGHT

Nantucket town usually has an attractive crowd of bar-hoppers. **The Pearl Bar,** 12 Federal St. (© **508/228-9701;** www.thepearlnantucket.com), part of a fine seafood restaurant, crafts imaginative cocktails and pours rosé bubbly by the glass. After dinner, a late-night lounge scene arises with a cool soundtrack and a vibrant mix of visitors and locals. You'll also find good cocktails at **Slip 14,** 14 Old South Wharf (© **508/228-2033;** www.slip14.com). Meanwhile, it may be Reggae Night at **The Chicken Box,** 16 Dave St. (© **508/228-9717;** www.thechickenbox.com), when the median age of this rocking venue rises by a decade or two.

Martha's Vineyard

Called "The Vineyard" by locals, this island is much larger than Nantucket and similarly is best savored in the off-season to avoid crowds, the need for restaurant reservations, and very high prices. Named by a 17th-century English explorer for his daughter and the island's wild grapes, this New England beachhead boasts wonderful historic areas as well as fine resorts. Visit the six towns here, and you can see hundreds of gingerbread Victorians, historic relics, posh shops, and amazing natural sites to explore. The many romantic restaurants, sea vistas, towns, and hotels make the Vineyard worthy of at least a 4-day trip—it will justify the wait time at the jammed ferry (in summer). You'll see 18th-century sea captains' houses, dramatic lighthouses, shops that sell more than fudge (think scrimshaw), and authentic fishing villages. Romance? Just wait 'til you experience the many miles of pristine beaches and the plentiful walking paths rolling past farmland and picturesque bogs!

KEY ATTRACTIONS

Aquinnah   Drive, bike, or take a shuttle bus to the island's west side Native American community to see the majestic red-clay Aquinnah Cliffs and picturesque Gay Head Lighthouse, 65 State Rd. (© **508/645-2300;**

http://gayheadlight.org; admission $5 for adults). A long path leads down to a pristine beach. In the off-season, some of the private beaches open up here.

Bird-watching **Felix Neck Wildlife Sanctuary,** 100 Felix Neck Dr., Edgartown (*C* **508/627-4850;** www.massaudubon.org; admission $4 for adults, $3 for seniors 65+), is a Massachusetts Audubon property and easy 2-mile bike ride from Edgartown. The visitor center is staffed by naturalists who can help you sight osprey and other wildlife. The Waterfowl Pond has a big observation deck so a couple can ogle together. By bike you can visit **Wasque Reservation** (www.thetrustees.org) on **Chappaquiddick** Island, a sanctuary on the easternmost reaches of the island with flocks of nesting shorebirds, including egrets, herons, terns, and Piping Plovers.

Chilmark Visit the fishing village of **Menemsha** and in the afternoon watch the fishing boats unload the catch of the day. At day's end, watching the sunset over a picnic dinner at Menemsha Beach' is a Vineyard tradition. Get a lobster dinner to go at the famous **Home Port** restaurant, 512 North Rd. (**$$;** *C* **508/645-2679;** www.homeportmv.com), right next to the beach.

Edgartown & Beyond See the old sea captains' houses and white picket fences up close. Shopping and galleries are in the center of town. Bike along South Beach on the Atlantic Ocean (it's clamming central). Stop at the **Martha's Vineyard Museum** (*C* **508/627-4441;** www.mvmuseum.org; admission $7 summer/$6 fall through spring for adults, $7 summer/$6 fall through spring for seniors) for cool exhibits on historic whaling.

Hiking & Biking Almost a third of this island is natural open space. Most of the conservation areas have marked biking and hiking trails; find them at the 300-acre **Cedar Tree Neck Wildlife Sanctuary** in West Tisbury and Vineyard Haven's almost 90 acres at **West Chop Woods**. For information on both, visit www.sheriffsmeadow.org.

Just email **marthasbikerentals.com** or **vineyardbicycles.com,** and they will deliver a bike to you anywhere you are! A bike for one will set you back $25 to $35 per day (depending on the kind of bike you want). For $40, you can get a bicycle built for two! You can also just ask your hotel manager. Many of the Vineyard hotels and Inns keep a few bikes around for guests.

Nude Beaches This summer pleasure has sparked local consternation periodically since the 1970s. The only existing "clothing optional" beaches are at **Aquinnah** and **Lucy Vincent Beach** in Chilmark, where nudists are reserved and seem intent mostly on avoiding a tan line.

Oak Bluffs See the 19th-century "gingerbread cottages" in the island's first summer community (www.mvcma.org). Ride the **Flying Horses Carousel,** 33 Circuit Ave. (*C* **508/693-9481;** $2.50 per ride) and duck into **Mad Martha's,** 12 Circuit Ave. (*C* **508/693-9151**) for ice cream, and then enjoy the people watching on Circuit Avenue. At night catch a play at the **Vineyard Playhouse.**

Polly Hill Arboretum Horticulturist Polly Hill developed this 20-acre garden in West Tisbury over the past 40 years and lets the public wander the grounds daily from sunrise to sunset. The vibe is magically romantic, particularly mid-June to July when Dogwood Lane is in bloom. Walk along the rustic old stone walls to the Tunnel of Love and see the lush carpet of witch hazel, camellias, magnolias, and rhododendrons.

809 State Rd., West Tisbury. ✆ **508/693-9426.** www.pollyhillarboretum.org.

Watching the Stars You get surprisingly good views of the heavens at the beaches here. Why not have a romantic dinner at the beach? Pick up some lobster rolls from Grace Church on a late Friday afternoon (www.grace-churchmv.com), and observe a tasty island tradition at their picnic tables overlooking the Vineyard haven marina for less than $15. Or, have a clam bake. If you don't know how to do that, no problem: Contact **www.myclam bake.com**, and you can get an experienced caterer to find you just the right beach and give you the classic New England beach dinner of clams and corn on the cob. Or you could look at the stars from the deck of the **Aquinnah Shop** restaurant, 27 Aquinnah Circle (**$$**; ✆ **508/645-3867**; www.theaquinnah shop.com) with a 360-degree view of the sea.

HOTELS WITH HEART

Beach Plum Inn $$ Close to the harbor, this place has a rural feel and offers a croquet course, a synthetic grass tennis court, and rental bikes. Rooms are in the main inn or in four cottages, but they all feel private, with a certain elegance, along with top-quality linens and, in some, whirlpool baths. Expect a deck or patio, and perhaps a view of Menemsha Harbor. Guests receive passes to private up-island beaches. We love the hotel's fine-dining spot; enjoy the international menu in the simple but elegant dining room or outside on the tiled patio.

50 Beach Plum Lane, Menemsha. ✆ **508/645-9454.** www.beachpluminn.com.

Harbor View Hotel $$$ This grand Gilded Age waterfront hotel includes an impressive pool and 13 luxury suites, some with private gardens and outdoor showers. It is actually two former Gilded Age hotels now joined by a 300-foot veranda that overlooks Edgartown Harbor and the lighthouse. It's just far enough from "downtown" to avoid traffic, but close enough for pleasant walks past regal captains' houses. The elegant **Water Street** restaurant serves lunch and dinner; and **Henry's** is a cozy barroom.

131 North Water St., Edgartown. ✆ **800/225-6005** or 508/627-7000. www.harbor-view.com.

The Outermost Inn $$ This grey-shingled New England house overlooking the Gay Head cliffs is your perfect rural hideaway with a wonderful swimming beach. The marvelous vegetable and herb gardens are used for the excellent restaurant. Rooms are simple and attractive, with Shaker furniture and high-thread-count linens and duvets. Guests tend to come once and become regulars.

81 Lighthouse Rd., Aquinnah. ✆ **508/645-3511.** www.outermostinn.com.

MOST ROMANTIC RESTAURANTS

The Beach Plum Inn Restaurant $$$ INTERNATIONAL   If views set the stage for romance—and we think they do—visit this place above the colorful old fishing village of Menemsha. Sit in the simple but elegant dining room or outside on the tiled patio. You'll enjoy the sunset views of the harbor from either site. The hazelnut-crusted halibut with Marsala wine beurre-blanc sauce is a winner. Follow up with the chocolate quadruple-layer cake made with white and dark chocolate mousse and Chambord.

50 Beach Plum Lane. ✆ **508/645-9454.** www.beachplumrestaurant.com.

Le Grenier $$ FRENCH   Steak au poivre, calf's brains Grenobloise with beurre noir and capers, and lobster Normande flambéed with Calvados, apples, and cream are staples. Le Grenier means attic, and that's where it's located. Very romantic and lit by hurricane lamps.

96 Main St., Vineyard Haven. ✆ **508/693-4906.** www.legrenierrestaurant.com.

L'etoile $$$ CONTEMPORARY FRENCH   This spot offers the freshest and most varied local produce and fresh-caught seafood, such as the étouffée of lobster with cognac and chervil sauce combined with littlenecks, bay scallops, and roasted corn fritters. But non-seafood dishes are equally tasty. This chef does wonders with roasted pheasant breast in cider and apple brandy.

22 N. Water St., Edgartown. ✆ **508/627-5187.** www.letoile.net.

MARTHA'S VINEYARD BY NIGHT

Try **Hooked** (15 Island Inn Rd., Oak Bluffs; ✆ **508/693-6093;** hookedmv.com), an inland seafood restaurant with dancing and musical performances nightly.

Old Whaling Church   Once a church, this 1843 Greek Revival masterpiece is now a 500-seat performing-arts center. Check what's playing and go—the surroundings are cozy and evocative of simpler times. 89 Main St., Edgartown. ✆ **508/627-4442.** www.mvpreservation.org.

The Ritz Café   Couples looking for higher-octane fun should seek out this funkified club on the dock at Oak Bluffs. 4 Circuit Ave., Oak Bluffs. ✆ **508/693-9851.**

Trinity Park Tabernacle   Couples can time travel together at this old-fashioned community sing. Concerts are held Wednesdays at 8pm and irregularly on weekends. Typically the acts are less well-known locals, but celebs like James Taylor and Bonnie Raitt have been known to show up. Open July through August. Oak Bluffs, on camp meeting grounds. ✆ **508/693-0525.**

MAUI, KAUAI & OAHU
Beaches, Breezes & Natural Wonders

Choosing which is more romantic, Kauai or Maui, is not easy. The two islands are as different as Champagne and chocolate, yet both are equally romantic.

Oahu, the most visited Hawaiian island, can also be very romantic and unique, if you know where to go and what to do.

But they all share that wonderful Hawaiian breeze. As soon as you land, the fresh, fragrant air tells you where you are. Even if it's hot, a light breeze helps you adjust quickly to being in Paradise. If you are lucky, a friend or tour guide will put a frangipani or plumeria lei around your neck. If not, buy one for your honey (and one for yourself!) at the airport. These tropical flowers aren't just for the tourists; Hawaiians give them to each other all the time—for birthdays, anniversaries, promotions, hello, goodbye—you name it. Breathe in that fragrance and become a little more Hawaiian.

Maui

Everyone will agree: The best beaches, and winter whale watching, are on Maui. It is the second largest island (after The Big Island) and has incredible biodiversity, with rainforests and deserts, mountains, and beaches that go on forever. And it may be one of the world's great laidback locales.

People also may tell you that Maui is overdeveloped, but we could argue that it is only intensely developed in a few places, and much of the island has as much privacy and wildly flamboyant nature as you could possibly desire. If the two of you really want to be alone with one another on this island, take the drive to Hana. The 55-mile ride takes a long time with curvy and twisting roads that require concentration. Slow, sure, but you will be rewarded with glorious views of the ocean, a constant tangle of tropical flowers and forest, and a smug feeling that you have left the high-rise district far behind. This is a drive to take Maui style—without a watch. You are now officially celebrating the journey and not the destination. Stop and kiss at waterfalls or ocean vistas. When you get to Hana, pack a lunch, and take a longer hike to the 400-foot Waimoku waterfall. Or stop a half-mile after mile marker 10 and visit the glorious Garden of Eden Arboretum and see the cascading waterfalls there. Not had enough? Go beyond Hana and walk through the unearthly bamboo forest in Ohe'o Gulch and see the Waimoku Falls spilling down a high cliff. We don't exactly know why sitting at a magnificent waterfall is romantic, but it just is—so do it.

KEY ATTRACTIONS

Lahaina   It's been a long time since this was an active whaling community, but the town, while wildly commercial, still has a lot to offer. At one end of town the largest banyan tree in Hawaii dominates a public square near the beach and historical buildings. During the day, it shelters local artists selling their work, or tired tourists. Some good restaurants hang over the water and the stretch of shops (some alarmingly similar) but it's is still fun to stroll together.

Lanai   Take a day trip, or a 2-day trip (much better) to this secluded island, just a 50-minute ferry ride from Maui's Lahaina Harbor. If you've done your homework right, you can get picked up by one of the two luxury places to stay on the island: the **Four Seasons Lodge at Koele,** 1 Keomoku Hwy.

($$; © **808/565-4000;** www.fourseasons.com/koele) or the **Four Seasons Inn at Manele Bay,** 1 Manele Bay Rd. ($$$; © **808/565-2000;** www.fourseasons.com/manelebay). You can also just reserve a jeep, pick it up at the ferry, and drive to **Lanai City** and settle in at the inexpensive **Hotel Lanai,** 828 Lanaʻi Ave. ($; © **808/565-7211;** www.hotellanai.com), for the rare experience of feeling you were in the Hawaii of the 1940s.

While the Four Seasons resorts are gorgeous (and now undergoing renovations by new owner Larry Ellison, the Oracle founder, who bought the entire island), the island's romance stems from Lanai City's not having been developed. The Lanai Hotel, although a gourmet destination, remains simple, authentic, and charming (alas, we must report it has thin walls).

Whether you stay simple or luxe, Lanai is special. It is a place to go off-roading to deserted beaches, eat breakfast at local places, and perhaps hire a ride through the Lodge at Koele to explore a few views by horseback. The Four Seasons are world-class places (Bill Gates reserved them both for his wedding), but it is the ungroomed nature of Lanai and the Hawaiian feel of the Hotel Lanai that make this place, well, irreplaceable.

Makena Beach This enormous golden crescent is located just past the luxe resorts of Wailea on the south side of the island. The views are beautiful, and it is rarely crowded. Its dramatic crashing waves are breathtaking, but can be dangerous, so it's not the easiest swimming beach, and it's best to stay close to shore. It is refreshingly non-commercial, which means you should pack a picnic and boogie boards for two.

Paia People either dislike Paia's hippie/surfer vibe, or they love it for the very same reason. It's a fun walk for two to check out the town's galleries, surf shops, and nice restaurants (but real restaurant romance lies outside of town at Mama's Fish House [see later listing]).

HOTELS WITH HEART

The Grand Wailea Resort and Spa $$$ The Grand Wailea specializes in Hawaiian-themed weddings and provides the kind of lush tropical setting you might dream about, including a delightful, open-air chapel. If you want the works, your wedding will be announced by torchbearers, conch blowers, and drummers. Pretty nifty. Think about it for a recommitment ceremony, too.

3850 Wailea Alanui Dr., Wailea. © **800/888-6100.** www.grandwailea.com. (Rates lower in May and Nov–Dec.)

Lumeria Maui $$$ This place is a beautiful blend of Yoga retreat, wellness center, and old Hawaiian and Asian luxury. A Los Angeles yoga lover has recreated the old Baldwin estate, about a half- hour from Paia, into a romantic and serenely simple but sophisticated Hawaiian getaway. The buildings encircle a broad lawn that is used for some of the hotel's signature yoga classes. Massages are given in a cabana looking out at the ocean. There are also a yoga studio, dining room, and a beautiful rendition of the Baldwin house (unlike any in its former life) for evening entertainment, discussion, or just quiet moments. The rooms are old Hawaii with new-age bathrooms that often can accommodate two in the tubs and slate showers. If you want a romantic getaway that is organized around wellness and serenity, this is the place for you.

1813 Baldwin Ave., Makawao. ✆ **855/579-8877.** www.lumeriamaui.com.

MOST ROMANTIC RESTAURANTS

Hali'Malie General Store $$ AMERICAN/HAWAII REGIONAL   Up Hali'imaile Road in Makawao, you will find a foodie destination in a converted turn-of-the-19th century store. You are in cool and breezy cowboy country, called up-country by the locals. But the people at Hali'Malie are not ranch hands. This place is known far and wide for its imaginative menu (burgers to cherish, ribs so good you could weep with gratitude) and bread pudding and other dishes Chef Beverly Gannon has published in her celebrated cookbooks. It's a fun trip out there—it's got its own kind of romance. Best to make a reservation.

900 Haliimaile Rd., Makawao. ✆ **808/572-2666.** http://bevgannonrestaurants. com/haliimaile.

Mama's Fish House $$$ SEAFOOD   This is a Maui institution, and what a pretty, rambling, multiple-roomed landmark it is. The grounds are green and groomed, punctuated by palm trees and expansive ocean views. It has that romantic "let's just lie under this palm tree together and watch the world go by" feeling, and that's a good thing, because, without a reservation, you'll be admiring the view for quite a while. If you haven't booked Sunday brunch long in advance, don't even think about it.

799 Poho Place, Paia. ✆ **808/579-8488.** www.mamasfishhouse.com.

Merriman's $$$ PACIFIC RIM   This may be the most romantic place to eat or drink near the famed **Kaanapali Beach.** The restaurant is located on a large parcel of land in Napili that winnows down to the point that gives it its name. From the point, the expansive view of the water deepens your blissful mood, even as night makes the ocean disappear, and the tiki torches and fire pit come alive. Drinks run about $10 to $12 at the bar, but the lovely dining room is unrelentingly high priced. The food, a mix of Hawaiian and Mainland classics, is excellent, however, and worthy of a special occasion.

1 Bay Club Place, Lahaina. ✆ **808/669-6400.**

The Terrace $$$ HAWAIIAN/INTERNATIONAL   Planning to pop the question? This could be the place. Located at the Ritz-Carlton, Kapalua, the Terrace offers seasonal, organic, and locally sourced Hawaiian specialties and serves it oceanside on an elegant covered terrace illuminated by tiki and candlelight, with stirring views of Moloka'i and the Pailolo Channel. Yes, yes, the only possible answer is yes.

1 Ritz-Carlton Dr., Kapalua. ✆ **808/669-6200.** www.ritzcarlton.com.

MAUI BY NIGHT

Sunsets never get old. You can get a great sunset pretty much anywhere from Kapalua to Lahaina, and some of our favorites are from Merriman's in Lahaina, the outdoor bar at the Hyatt Regency in Kanapali or, if you want to be away from hotels and just communing with nature, the Kapalua coastal trail or the Big Beach in Makena State Park. (The Little Beach is also great, and the Sunday drumming circle is an awesome accompaniment to the sunset, but, and here's a big but, you better feel comfortable on a nude beach cause that's what happens there.)

Another option: Board a sunset cruise with **Pacific Whale Foundation** (© **800/942-5311;** www.pacificwhale.org; about $55 per person) and you can pair that view with a fine meal and a whale-watching tour, all while supporting this great foundation. You board a smooth-riding catamaran from Lahaina Harbor. Seated on deck, you see glorious views of the horizon, ocean, green mountains, and neighboring islands. The evening begins with cocktails and live island music, followed by a gourmet dinner (the local catch of the day or an expertly grilled local steak). *Romance alert:* Upgrade your ticket for a private table for two on the bow or upper deck. From mid-December through April, you can almost count on seeing whales, although they appear after April, too.

Kauai

Our take: Kauai is the most scenic, the lushest, the trickiest weatherwise, and the most dramatic of the islands (except for the live volcano on the Big Island). To see the Na Pali coastline by air or sea is to be hushed into reverence by such verdant and rugged beauty. To walk it is to be part of an elite community blessed by the coastline's special gifts. Kauai is a place where your beauty meter is always racing.

KEY ATTRACTIONS

Hanalei Beach   This is one of those perfect beaches that always gets on the world's 10 best beaches list. Hanalei also turned up on the list of much-loved songs, in this case "Puff the Magic Dragon," by Peter, Paul, and Mary. Viewed from the bluffs overlooking the bay and watching the nearby brutal cliffs carved by rivulets to significant waterfalls, this north shore beach is perfectly formed in a graceful crescent. It goes on and on, and it's easy, once you leave the bluffs, to pull right up to it and dig your toes in the soft white sand and have it all to yourselves.

The Kalalau Trail, Na Pali Coast   This is a long dramatic trail, but you can get the romantic hit even if you are not fit enough for the entire 11 miles. Go just a half-mile in and you'll pass waterfalls, step over streams, and see vertiginous views of the water and hills that are almost unimaginably vivid. You can hike far enough to share a mutual sense of wonder and then hightail it back to the beach and relax. Stay on the trail another 90 minutes, and you'll reach the beautiful and beguiling run-off from Hanakapiai Falls. The danger sign warns that the water here can pull you under, and that would be it. But not to worry: You don't have to take any chances. Take an alternative: Plenty of sunset sails and other boat trips can take you along this gorgeous coast and let you feel its power from the comfort of your boat, with a tropical drink in your hand. Nothing wrong with that.

Waimea Canyon   The size of this extraordinarily beautiful canyon will startle you. You can drive up to its edge most of the way; then you have to leave your car in the parking lot and ascend some ramps and steps to get the best view. Occasionally the effort is rewarded with a perfect sight of a vast canyon of many geological stripes and colors, soaring birds, and the flash of touring planes catching the sunlight. Pay attention on your way down. When you get off the cliffs and a bit closer to the valley, the most wonderful panoramic view opens up. Pull over and savor it together.

Note: The breathtaking views can be totally subverted and lost on a cloudy, rainy, or foggy day.

HOTELS WITH HEART

Sharing the same oceanfront property as the Castle Kiahuna Plantation (later listing) but operated by a different owner, the **Outrigger Kiahuna Plantation** (*$;* © **866/733-0587;** www.outriggerkiahunaplantationcondo.com) offers very nice oceanfront double at much better rates.

Castle Kiahuna Plantation $$$ We just love this slightly funky resort in Poipu, and we adore its special senior rates. There's a choice of rooms but all share the same comfortable Hawaiian decor, nothing fancy. First floor units get less of an ocean view but open satisfyingly on the expansive lush grounds. The beachfront units are best—at night it's just the two of you and the ocean, although people walk there during the day.

Uber romantic here is the old plantation house restaurant at the resort's center; when you walk in you pass orchids growing in profusion over lava rocks. Nicely scaled dining rooms open on a great veranda overlooking the lawn, dense foliage, and flowers, creating an atmosphere that appeals to the senses, and all is right with the world. There is often a guitarist playing softly in the evening. The food is very good, and relatively straightforward; figure on some very fresh fish and good quality beef.

2253-B Poipu Rd., Koloa. © **808/742-2200**. www.castleresorts.com. Reasonable senior rates are available.

The Grand Hyatt Kauai $$$ Sure, they have big groups here, but it doesn't feel corporate. This resort is in the high-end resort column, with a beautiful lobby that looks out on the ocean (as does at least one bar) and extensive manicured grounds with man-made waterfalls and a sinuous walking path that follows the ocean. A full program for kids and a junior water park can safeguard private time for parents. For purely adult pleasure, dine at the Tidepools (discussed previously) and follow with late-night hot lava stone massages at Anara spa (or in your room, four-handed) together. Guaranteed romantic outcomes.

1571 Poipu Rd., Koloa. © **808/742-1234.** http://kauai.hyatt.com.

Marjorie's Kauai Inn $ The advantage of this quiet property overlooking the lush Lawai valley is that it is not really suitable for kids since it is organized around honeymooners and people who want quiet and privacy. So chances are, you can have quiet adult time around its huge pool. Perfect if you're on a budget, since the three units feature kitchenettes. Stunning views and only 10 minutes from Poipu Beach, the inn sits adjacent to the National Topical Botanical Garden and is in the same part of the island where "Pirates of the Carribean" (and "Jurassic Park") were filmed.

P.O. Box 866 (off Hailima Road). ℂ **800/717-8838** or 808/332-8838. www.marjories kauaiinn.com.

Waimea Plantation Cottages $$ A 27-acre grove of coconut palms and ironwood trees places you suddenly in old Hawaii. The cottages used to be workers housing on an old sugar plantation, but now they are just charming, and reasonably priced, guest lodgings with nicely equipped kitchens should you just want to settle in and cook with each other. You are very near the canyon and right on the water, too. There is a very old-fashioned feel and a simplicity here that encourages you to take advantage of the quiet and the privacy together.

9400 Kaumualii Hwy., Waimea. ℂ **866/774-2924** or 808/338-1625. www.waimea-plantation.com.

MOST ROMANTIC RESTAURANTS
The Beach House Restaurant $$ HAWAIIAN REGIONAL   This is *the* restaurant for watching romantic sunsets, and reservations for sunset can be scarce. But fear not; a public beach is directly in front, so come here for the great Pacific Rim dishes any time, but come again, hand-in-hand for the sunset and find a spot on the nearby grass or rocks.

5022 Lawai Rd., Koloa. ℂ **808/742-1424.** www.the-beach-house.com.

Tidepools $$ SEAFOOD   Atmosphere counts, and while the contemporary Hawaiian cuisine here is very good, the ambience is even more seductive. Open to the breeze and positioned perfectly to take in the beach and the ocean, this extremely romantic open-air restaurant is surrounded by waterfalls and seems to float above tropical lagoons filled with exhibition size koi. When the sun goes down, the torches and candles are lit for a romantic tour de force.

1571 Poipu Rd., Koloa. ℂ **808/742-1234.** http://kauai.hyatt.com.

KAUAI BY NIGHT
Kauai is not known for its nightlife, but there is one enchanting natural phenomenon that may become a shared moment you'll always remember. The marvel is a green flash that happens just after sunset, which locals say comes when the sun kisses the ocean good night. The scientific version is based on light bending as it curves around the Earth, casting a laser beam of green just at the moment the sun drops into the sea. Watch for it.

Oahu

Sure, Waikiki Beach is too busy and Honolulu is too business-oriented, but that's just a small part of spectacular Oahu. Just a stone throws from Waikiki is **Diamond Head Crater**, the iconic marker of this island and an area of beautiful beaches and classy hotels and homes. And remember that beautiful untouched world where herbivore dinosaurs existed in a primal green world in the movie *Jurassic Park*? It was filmed on location in Oahu at **Kualoa Ranch,** 49-560 Kamehameha Hwy., Kāneʻohe (© **808/237-7321;** www. kualoa.com).

KEY ATTRACTIONS

Kailua Beach About half an hour from Waikiki on the windward side of the island is one of the world's best beaches. (It regularly appears on top ten lists.) Rent a car to get there; it is separated from Honolulu by some significant mountains with tunnels between and through them. Turn onto the Pali Highway exit ramp, and your journey will give you a mesmerizing view of green peaks and the bay. (Stop for the **Nuuanu Pali Lookout**, for sure.) You will travel on to Kailua to find one of the few extensive crescent beaches on the south side of the island that has absolutely no high-rise development. It is the perfect beach to walk, swim with turtles, and watch locals practice longboat racing.

Shaved Ice Every islander thinks he or she knows the best place to get this frozen Hawaiian treat. Some locals swear by **Matsumoto,** 66-087 Kamehameha Hwy., Haleiwa (© **808/637-4827;** http://matsumotoshaveice.com), in the surfing town of Haleiwa. Others follow President Obama's lead and go to **Island Snow,** 130 Kailua Rd. Kailua (© **808/263-6339;** www.islandsnow. com). Try the coconut and passion fruit for a sensual and addictive experience.

Swimming with Dolphins We think communicating across species is magical—and that means romantic. There are several tour operators, and of them, **Dolphin Excursions** (www.dolphinexcursions.com) comes recommended. Having a guide will help you find the dolphins in their shallow bays on the west side of the island.

Waimea Valley This is Oahu's garden valley, about an hour from Honolulu in distance, but light years away in spirit. Here you can view thousands of different specimens of jungle plants, including wild coffee plants, lowhanging guavas, and plenty of hibiscus and other native flowers, all packed into over 1,800 acres of tropical rain forest. There are some steep climbs to get to archaeological sites, temples, and burial caves, but there are also some easy hiking trails. Hire a guide (a bargain at just an extra $10 or $15), who will lead you through this rugged valley and explain the sights. Top it off with a swim at famous Waimea Falls. But make reservations to visit: This valley's beauty is no secret. And if it looks vaguely familiar, that's because you may have seen this exact location on "Lost" or in *Journey to the Center of the Earth*. Visit www.waimeavalley.net for more.

Watching Surfers at Waimea Bay in Winter   This bay, on the north side of the island, has a split personality. In the summer it's truly peaceful, but in winter, it becomes a surfer's dream. The towering waves (30- to 40-feet high) look impossible to ride, but serious surfers do it. It's an amazing athletic spectacle and you can get a front row seat.

MOST ROMANTIC RESTAURANTS & HOTELS

Many of the island's best restaurants are in hotels, so here we combine dining with lodging recommendations.

Halekulani $$$ This is a much-celebrated hotel and no wonder. Its awesome location, overlooking Diamond Head and Waikiki Beach, would be reason enough to stay here. It is a supremely beautiful setting for weddings, often done on the terrace overlooking the sea. **Orchids,** the restaurant, makes yummy banana-macadamia pancakes for breakfast. You have to dress up a bit for dinner. The high-end restaurant, **La Mer,** has won international acclaim.

2199 Kalia Rd., Honolulu. ☏ **808/367-2343.** www.halekulani.com.

Kahala Hotel $$$ For our money, this is the best luxury hotel on the island. The sophisticated rooms are elegantly cream-colored with black accents and have some Hawaiian touches and wood floors. With a lovely beach and sunset views, this hotel is close enough to the ocean for you to hear the roar and see the lagoons with their own resident dolphin population. The restaurants are very romantic; we like the beachfront **Seaside Grill** for lunch, and for dinner, **The Veranda** overlooking the dolphin lagoons. By the way, you can swim with them here!

5000 Kahala Ave, Honolulu. ☏ **800/367-2525** or 808/739-8888. www.kahalaresort.com.

The Moana Surfrider $$$ An older, impeccably rennovated Westin hotel with a perfect position on the beach. The lobby and rooms have been recently redone and brought back to their stylish Hawaiian grandeur. The public rooms are extremely classy, and the best rooms turn toward Diamond Head (a 2½-mile run, if you'd like). The hotel is known for its fine restaurants,

---

Perfect Place for a Wedding

With perfect weather practically guaranteed year round, and your choice of a wedding gazebo with a view of the Koko Head volcano or one with the endless blue waters of Kahala Bay, the **Kahala Hotel** (see above) prides itself on being multicultural and welcomes ceremonies for same-sex couples as well as all others who want a Hawaiian-style wedding. An "Orchid Wall" winding down a huge staircase is perfect for your wedding photos.

and **The Veranda** is particularly romantic for lunch or high tea, and not to be confused with the excellent restaurant of the same name at the Kahala Hotel (see previous listing). **The Banyan Courtyard** is a wonderful escape for dinner, with its Hawaiian steel guitar ensemble and hula dancers.

2365 Kalakaua Ave., Honolulu. ℂ **808/922-3111.** www.moana-surfrider.com.

Turtle Bay Resort $ There are 410 renovated spacious rooms, suites, and cottages in this hotel, the only one in a prized location on the lovely North Shore—and all of them have ocean views. We're fond of this remote area because it's away from the hustle and bustle of Waikiki, so far more relaxing and romantic in our minds. In fact, this place is a favorite among honeymooners. Dine right on the beach and enjoy the stunning views. Good spa, too. The staff gets high marks for being friendly and helpful. Given the lack of shuttle service to the airport, this hotel best suits those who have rented a car.

57-091 Kamehameha Hwy., Kahuku. ℂ **866/475-2569** or 808/293-6000.

OREGON COAST
Moody Rugged Beauty

A 90-minute drive from Portland takes you to one of the world's most dramatic, yet accommodating, coastlines. (Fly into Portland or Eugene, Oregon, to get here.) The diversity of this coast is staggering, with haystack mountains emerging from the sea, miles of dunes, craggy promontories, quaint fishing villages, lumber towns, luxury resorts, and long stretches of thick forest. You are also likely to see lounging seals, sea lions, and in season, not too far off, migrating gray whales.

The weather can be misty, foggy, and rainy or, especially in the early fall, bright sunshine, and sparkling ocean. Northwesterners tend to like the grayer months for what writer Tom Robbins called oyster light; it can have a mystical and romantic resonance in these pearly gray months.

The sheer variety makes for an incredible journey—and there are many truly romantic stops. Regrettably, some (for example, Lincoln City and Newport, where development has been harsh and fast food restaurants and uninspired tourist attractions dominate) don't seem very romantic. Yet even these places offer fantastic views, exciting fishing expeditions, and older attractive neighborhoods. Here we concentrate on the Oregon coast's most romantic stops, traveling from north to south.

Astoria

Astoria has a commanding site near the mouth of the Columbia River. This port city has some age on it, visible in the many attractively restored Victorians that add charm to the town. Across the bridge lies southwestern

Washington—this community benefits from being a center of fishing and entertainment for both states. Astoria's working waterfront is romantic to browse through and offers fantastically atmospheric places to eat.

Just a half-hour away in Washington is the Long Beach Peninsula, which brags that it is the longest beach in the world. There is a really first-rate museum there that will fill you in on the area's connections to Lewis and Clark's expedition. The view from the Lewis and Clark Interpretive Center at Cape Disappointment is amazing; it is the only place you can see the Columbia River and the Ocean meet.

KEY ATTRACTIONS

The Confluence Project   Mostly on the Washington side of the river are seven installations, under various stages of construction, by the artist Maya Lin (designer of the Vietnam Veterans Memorial in Washington, DC) that celebrate Lewis and Clark's journey and explore the intersection of environment, differing cultures, and a regional history. Visit www.confluenceproject. org for more info (**℃ 360/693-0123**).

Lewis and Clark National Historical Park   This historic park (www. nps.gov/lewi; admission $3 for adults), where explorers Meriwether Lewis and William Clark built a fort and encampment in 1805–1806, spans parts of both Oregon and Washington. The encampment is long gone, but a recent replica helps you imagine what life along the Columbia River was like at that time (through actors and craftspeople in the summer). It has a very cool trail system to explore, too.

HOTELS WITH HEART

Cannery Pier Hotel $$ This hotel is built 600 feet out on a pier on the Columbia, for a dreamy, super-romantic feel. The rooms are full of romantic details like window seats and balconies. A nice festive touch: The claw-footed tubs in the bathrooms are positioned so you can bathe, pop champagne, and still see all the activity on the river.

10 Basin St. **℃ 888/325-4996** or 503/325-4996. www.cannerypierhotel.com.

China Beach Retreat $ In Ilwaco, Washington, near Long Beach, and owned by the Sherburn Inn, this beachfront getaway on Bakers Bay is only a half-hour from Astoria, and is seriously romantic. The Craftsman cottage has been divided into two rooms and a suite in the main house (sharing the extensive waterview and living room), and there is also a private, adorable cottage on the property. Rates include a gourmet breakfast at the Sherburne Inn, which is minutes away (as is the Lewis and Clark Interpretive Center and Cape Dissapointment exhibits.)

222 Robert Gray Drive, Iwaco, Washington. **℃ 360/642-2442.** www.chinabeachretreat.com.

Hotel Elliott $$ This lovely, historic hotel is a wonderful blend of modern conveniences and period decor. Guest rooms are modern, but decorated with regional crafts and art. For romance we love those comfy feather-top beds! Top off a day of exploration on the Elliott's rooftop, either warming up near the fire pits or just taking in the expansive view.

357 12th St. ℂ **877/378-1924** or 503/325-2222. www.hotelelliott.com.

MOST ROMANTIC RESTAURANTS

Baked Alaska $$ NORTHWEST   Located on a pier right over the water, you can't help but be in a romantic mood. The sea views are spectacular and often include marine mammals like seals and sea lions. This moderately priced restaurant specializes in American comfort food with excellent soups, steaks, tuna, and salmon. Of course, dessert would have to be baked Alaska.

1 12th St. ℂ **503/325-7414.** www.bakedak.com.

Bridgewater Bistro $$ NORTHWEST   This romantic restaurant is located across the water from the Cannery Pier Hotel in an old cannery building. Seeing the Astoria-Megler Bridge arching overhead can be liberating to the romantic spirit! The historic building elements play nicely against modern design, and the overall impact is invigorating. The menu offers many small plates, which we think is a romantic way to have dinner together. You are in Dungeness crab country, so you won't want to miss it if it's in season (Dec 1–Aug 15). In summer, wild berries decorate the excellent fragrant duck. If you are in the mood, the Flying Dutchman Winery tasting room is part of the complex.

20 Basin St. ℂ **503/325-6777.** www.bridgewaterbistro.com.

The Depot Restaurant $$ AMERICAN   Just off the main drag in Seaview on the Long Beach peninsula, this charming gem of a restaurant is lodged in an old railroad depot. It is small, adorable with an atmospheric small bar/counter, many private tables, and great attention to everything on the menu. Chef-owner Michael Lalewicz sources everything locally: Don't miss the filet, lamb, and the oysters. It is extremely popular; book well ahead.

1206 38th Place, Seaview, Washington. ℂ **360-642-7880.** http://depotrestaurant dining.com.

The Shelburne Inn $$ NORTHWEST   Listed in the National Register of Historic Places, the Shelburne's 1896 New England cottage demeanor is cozy and authentic with its original stained glass windows intact. Located on the main street through town, nonetheless, it is a haven from the Honky Tonk of this popular summer beach area. The food is gourmet and ambitious (their use of wild mushrooms is fantastic), and the seasonal menus change regularly. There is an atmospheric pub, too, where you can hang out with the locals, and if you are not up to whiskey, or seduced by the fine wine list, you can warm yourself with a latte. Book way ahead in season.

4415 Pacific Way, Seaview, Washington. ℂ **360-642-4150.** www.shelburneinn.com.

ASTORIA BY NIGHT

Check out the **Liberty Theater,** 1203 Commercial St. (ℂ **503/325-5922;** www.liberty-theater.org). The lovingly restored 1920s movie palace hosts theater productions, readings, concerts, visiting pop musicians and dance presentations, as well as the Astoria International Film Festival (in Oct).

Gearhart

One of the closer towns to Portland, Gearhart is really not oriented to tourists. It's more like a New England seaside town: quiet and quaint with not much to do except walk the beach. But it is a wonderful stretch of beach, with grasslands between you and the sparse houses along your beach walk, and quietude as a dominant theme. If you want to situate yourself in a slower, gentler world, this is your stop.

Gearhart isn't a "dining out" kind of town, but **Pacific Way Café and Bakery**, 601 Pacific Way (**$;** ✆ **503/738-0245;** www.pacificwaybakery-cafe.com) fits in and is a local favorite. The feel is east coast beach cafe, circa 1930, with American salads and sandwiches at lunch and more gourmet seafood fare (try the scallops) at dinner. The next door bakery (open 7am–1pm, closed Tues–Wed) is a great place to pick up yummy bread and cookies.

Gearhart Ocean Inn, 67 N. Cottage Ave. (**$;** ✆ **800/352-8034** or 503/738-7373; www.gearhartoceaninn.com), with its motel-style buildings, is a throwback to the days before travel became so design and luxury oriented. But these rooms have been groomed nicely, with roses and greenery tucked into little pocket places, and fireplaces or charming kitchenettes in some. There's not much to choose from in Gearhart, but this inn earns romantic points and is well priced. Don't expect Martha Stewart, but it's comfortable and, best of all, in Gearhart.

Cannon Beach

Cannon Beach is a fun town to browse and an area arts center with a crowded but cute main street, several excellent restaurants and first-rate lodgings. The wide beach here, with its opportunities for kite flying, strolling, beachcombing and campfires, is where many Portlanders go for romantic or family getaways.

KEY ATTRACTIONS

Browsing the Galleries   There is something particularly sweet about strolling downtown Cannon Beach and looking at art together. **Cannon Beach Gallery,** 1064 S. Hemlock (✆ **503/436-0744;** www.cannonbeacharts.org), is run by a local arts organization. A lot of area artists are represented here, so you can stop and do a little gallery viewing here and be satisfied or seek out the numerous other galleries to explore; many are on Hemlock Street.

Massages   We always think massages are romantic. And here they are well priced—so what's not to love? Couples packages are available at the **Cannon Beach Spa,** 232 N. Spruce St. (✆ **888/577-8772** or 503/436-8772; www.cannonbeachspa.com).

Hiking & Wildlife Viewing   A natural gem is the **Jewell Meadows Wildlife Area** (✆ **503/755-2264;** www.dfw.state.or.us), 37 miles east of Cannon Beach on U.S. 26. It hosts a big herd of Roosevelt elk in the fall at mating season (Sept–Oct). At that time, you'll be treated to the bulls' bugling—an arresting, almost haunting sound. Sit and watch, and you'll see the maneuvering that elk-lust engenders; happily, the males usually outsmart each other for the female elks' favor, as opposed to actually locking horns. If you visit in June, you may see the outcome of all this romance: the elk cows with their calves. In winter, the elk are fed hay to get them through the season. You can help feed them—but you have to call the morning of December 1 to reserve your day.

Saddle Mountain State Natural Area   A day hike here, about 25 miles west of Cannon Beach on US 26, gives fantastic views of the coastline, but you will have to work for it: The 2½-mile trek to the mountaintop is steep and rough. Ideally, go in spring when the wildflowers are in bloom.

HOTELS WITH HEART

Arch Cape Inn $ Located between Cannon Beach and Manzanita just off Highway 101 is a shockingly French manor house. It is not on the beach, but if you really want to live in the lap of luxury and play Louis XIV and Madame du Barry, this would be your destination. It mimics a French chateau on the outside, and inside are antiques, tapestries, and French bedspreads and fabrics. This place was designed for intimate getaways, and each room amply supports the romantic theme. You can sequester your honey up in the Tower Room, or perhaps overwhelm her artistic sensibilities in the Tapestry Room. Many rooms have soaking tubs, and all have elegant furnishings. Over-the-top breakfasts are served in the conservatory.

31970 E. Ocean Lane. ℰ **800/436-2848.** www.archcapeinn.com.

The Ocean Lodge $$ This Northwest deluxe hotel, nestled beside the Stephanie Inn, ups the cozy ante. Inside is an abundance of wood and sturdy beams; the pleasing vibe is local and authentic. The rooms are really big with sitting areas, jetted tubs, fireplaces, and decks. We think the best are the ones with views of famous Haystack Rock; first floor rooms open up to the beach.

2864 South Pacific St. ℰ **888/777-4047** or 503/436-2241. www.theoceanlodge.com.

Stephanie Inn $$$ Stephanie Inn is genuinely romantic and a favorite getaway for Seattleites and Portlanders celebrating their relationships and willing to splurge. The theme is charming New England, with manicured gardens and cozy rooms, and you are right on the beach. From the moment you step into the lobby—with its river-rock fireplace, beamed ceiling, and wood posts, it feels right. The guest rooms reflect the touch of an interior designer, and most have gas fireplaces and luxurious bathrooms. Request a third-floor room for the view and bigger balconies. Breakfast is special, and the inn hosts an afternoon glass of wine and in the evening a bit of port before bed (even better, you can book massages here). The elegantly furnished dining room is all about romance and offers a sophisticated prix fixe dinner. Reserve both inn and restaurant way ahead.

2740 South Pacific St. ℰ **800/633-3466** or 503/436-2221. www.stephanieinn.com.

MOST ROMANTIC RESTAURANTS

Bistro $ NORTHWEST   We give this place the nod for its romantic French country atmosphere, starting with the beguiling entryway behind a garden and down a narrow brick walkway. Then there is the intimate dining space with French prints and fresh flowers on the tables. The food is also well done with special attention to seafood, halibut, scallops, or trout, often made with fruit, or tomatoes, capers, parsley, and white wine in the French manner.

263 N. Hemlock St. ✆ **503/436-2661.**

Newman's at 988 $$ FRENCH   Chef/owner John Newman, respected for his work at the Stephanie Inn (see previous listing), now practices his art here. This cottage restaurant is intimate, dimly lit, and flush with romance. The ambitious French-Italian cuisine uses local delicacies like wild mushrooms, fresh caviar, and lobster in creative ways, such as lobster ravioli with hazelnuts and Marsala cream sauce.

988 Hemlock St. ✆ **503/436-1151.** www.newmansat988.com.

Gleneden Beach (near Lincoln City)

Lincoln City has a huge sweep of beach, but we don't recommend it because it has a lot of ugly development. On the other hand, it has this wonderful stretch of nature, the simple antidote to excessive progress.

Your hotel here is the **Salishan Spa & Golf Resort,** 7760 Hwy. 101 N. (**$$;** ✆ **800/452-2300** or 541/764-3600; www.salishan.com). It shows its age a bit, but the 700-acre property is still a handsome place to stay (with a very good golf course). It's *the* destination resort on the coast, located at the southern end of Siletz Bay. The hotel lies about a half-mile from the beach, close enough to walk or bike over. Inside its groomed walkways and weathering wood buildings you might run into a lot of families. But if you choose a second-floor deluxe or premier room, you will get fantastic views, lofty ceilings, and a stone fireplace—in other words, all the romantic backdrop you need. The restaurant is worth staying in for as well; it has a sophisticated menu and wine list.

Yachats

The village of Yachats has an artistic as well as a fishing community. That makes it interesting, but isn't all that necessary, since the town, on the north side of Cape Perpetua, is really in a gorgeous location. The rugged coastline here offers many coves and tide pools with uncrowded beaches. It feels like a place that has yet to be discovered by tourists and may be just right for your getaway.

Take in the views here. **Cape Perpetua's tide pools** are arresting, and there are so many of them you could just go from one to the next and become totally captivated. But you'd probably snap out of it when you saw the dramatic waves smashing against the rocks. A good way to see the waves is to follow the short ocean-side trail to **Devil's Churn,** a spouting horn formed by waves crashing into a narrow opening in the basalt rocks. The pressure sends plumes of water into the air, while waves tumble around flamboyantly through narrow fissures in the rocks. Gray whales come close here. In the spring, look for them from Cape Perpetua; they summer at the mouth of the Yachats River. **Neptune State Scenic Viewpoint** is also a good place to see them, and you usually can find sea lions sunning on the rocks at the **Strawberry Hill** wayside there.

The restaurants in Yachats don't entirely fulfill our romance requirements, but hang out at **Green Salmon,** 220 Hwy. 101 N. ($; ℂ **541/547-3077;** www. thegreensalmon.com), for good organic coffee, dreamy baked goods, and light meals.

HOTELS WITH HEART

Overleaf Lodge & Spa $$
The lodge overlooks a brutally beautiful shoreline that immediately summons romance. You will feel like you are in a luxurious Victorian beach cottage, and happily, one that orients itself to couples and romance rather than families. You can stay inside and drink in the ocean view or sun on your balcony or patio. The Restless Waters rooms have whirlpool tubs overlooking the churning waves below, and the luxurious spa has special treatment packages for couples. If you visit in the winter, request a room with a fireplace. For even more seclusion, ask for one of the separate cottages next to the lodge.

280 Overleaf Lodge Lane. ℂ **800/338-0507** or 541/547-4880. www.overleaflodge. com.

Sea Quest Inn Bed and Breakfast $
This modern and luxurious inn has a terrific setting on a bluff above the beach near the mouth of Ten Mile Creek. Surrounded by miles and miles of beach, you will feel particularly secluded, and your romantic solitude will be enhanced by your private guest room entrance. Each room has an ocean view and a whirlpool tub for two. If you want more sociability, a gathering room on the second floor offers huge views and a very big deck.

95354 Highway 101 S. ℂ **800/341-4878** or 541/547-3782. www.seaquestinn.com.

Florence

A 45-minute drive from Eugene, Florence offers some of the greatest coastal sights: miles and miles of gorgeous—sometimes awesome—dunes and the Sea Lion caves, populated by dozens of the entertaining animals. On the Siuslaw River, Florence itself is a satisfying place to wander because of its historic character. Many of the buildings in its historic downtown have been renovated and now house comely restaurants and shops.

Florence and the **Oregon Dunes National Recreation Area,** which stretches south of town for almost 50 miles, provide one amazing sight after another. The dunes keep coming and coming—some are more than 500 feet tall. They are, in fact, a natural wonder—the largest sand dunes on the West Coast. For better and for worse, the area is highly discovered, and Oregon law allows all kinds of activities here including riding off-road vehicles through the dunes. There are several attractive towns in this long sweep of coast, including the 19th-century town of **Gardiner,** which was a prosperous mill town and has many renovated Victorians.

Trekking the Oregon Dunes The park area is a mix of forests, lakes, parks, and the magnificent dunes themselves. Some parts are packed with people, others almost deserted. You can start at the **Jessie M. Honeyman Memorial State Park,** 84505 Hwy. 101 S. (✆ 503/986-0707; www.oregon. gov/oprd/parks), 3 miles south of Florence; it has a beautiful lake surrounded by trees and some of the biggest dunes. You can picnic, camp, or hike here and also get access to **Cleawox and Woahink lakes.** Cleawox Lake has a swimming venue and boat rentals. The dunes at Cleawox Lake can be used by off-road vehicles. You can rent a dune buggy or ATV from **Sand Dunes Frontier,** 83960 Hwy. 101 S. (✆ 541/997-3544; www.sanddunesfrontier.com). If motorized vehicles ruin rather than enhance your enjoyment of the dunes, stay away from the South Jetty area (just south of Florence) and Siltcoos Lake.

For quick entry to the Dunes, go to the **Taylor Dunes Viewing Platform** off Highway 101. The beach is a 15-minute walk from the viewing platform, and you walk through dunes for most of that trek. To see the most dramatic dunes, take the **John Dellenback Dunes Trail,** which begins a half-mile south of **Eel Creek Campground,** 72044 Hwy. 101, Lakeside (11 miles south of Reedsport).

For a cozy spot to warm your souls together, try the **Waterfront Depot Restaurant & Bar,** 1252 Bay St. ($; ✆ 541/902-9100; www.thewaterfrontdepot. com). Walk into this dimly lit, cozy waterfront restaurant, look at the menu on the blackboard, and be charmed. In a 1913 railroad depot in historic Old Florence, it has wood floors, older furniture, and a particularly romantic small bar. The chef does amazing things with local shellfish, especially the oyster stew, and at reasonable prices. You also can get delectable grilled salmon here and very good lamb.

The luxurious **Edwin K Bed & Breakfast,** 1155 Bay St. ($; ✆ 800/833-9465 or 541/997-8360; www.edwink.com), is located in Old Town Florence. None of the rooms are terribly expensive, but go for one of the four rooms upstairs: Each has a lovely view of the Siuslaw River across the street. Two rooms have claw-foot tubs; another has a Jacuzzi and shower for two. Then again, downstairs is an attractive room with private entry to the backyard and a 30-foot waterfall. Breakfasts are serious five-course presentations. You will both feel pampered here mornings and afternoons (when tea, sherry, and cookies appear in the shared public room).

Bandon

Bandon's beach has probably been photographed by every photographer that ever traveled the coast: In the sea here are all kinds of large monoliths and haystack rocks. Bandon is another charming seaside town. Particularly inviting is the boardwalk that connects to the Coquille River. This is a great vantage point December through February to watch gray whale migrations that come close to shore. Very romantic . . .

KEY ATTRACTIONS

Bird-watching & Scenery Ogling   This is one of the best places in Oregon for bird-watching. More than 300 bird species, including wonderful tufted puffins, have been spotted here. The puffins, with their immediately recognizable vividly colored large beaks, are protected along with other wildlife in the **Oregon Islands National Wildlife Refuge,** which includes reefs and islands off the coast and views of the famous ocean monoliths of Bandon.

Bullards Beach State Park   Located just across the river from downtown, at 52470 Hwy. 101 N. (© **541/347-2209;** www.oregon.gov/oprd/parks), this park has a lot to recommend a visit: beaches, marshes, hiking, and horseback-riding trails (**Bandon Beach Riding Stables,** 54629 Beach Loop Rd.; © **541/347-3423**). You can picnic or camp here or lower your boat into the water and find good fishing and crabbing. This is also where you can see the city's landmark: the 1896 **Coquille River Lighthouse.**

World-Class Golf   Bandon Dunes Golf Resort, 57744 Round Lake Dr. (© **888/345-6008;** www.bandondunesgolf.com; greens fees $100–$295 for golf-only guests, depending on season), has been compared to Pebble Beach and St. Andrews. It's right on the ocean, and if you are avid golfers, this may be a heavenly destination. Be prepared for challenging winds, however. The Oregon coast can get some serious weather.

HOTELS WITH HEART

Bandon Dunes Golf Resort $$ Even if golf isn't your mating game, this resort offers plentiful romance, starting with the absolutely breathtaking coastline views at sunset. The wild Old World style golf course along the rocky shore sets a romantic mood. The beautiful lodging choices range from spacious single rooms to multi-bedroom suites and private cottages, with choices of ocean, forest, and links (or combination) views. Restaurant choices are all good, from elegant fine dining to a fun pub. Plus, there is a series of trails, a fitness center, and a world-class spa.

57744 Round Lake Dr. © **888/345-6008.** www.bandondunesgolf.com.

Bandon Inn $ Located on a hill with arresting views of town and the Pacific, this brown-shingled inn has a traditional New England feel. You experience a sense of great privacy, yet you can walk down the stairs into town. These inexpensive rooms are comfortable and tastefully decorated.

355 Hwy. 101. © **800/526-0209** or 541/347-4417. www.bandoninn.com.

MOST ROMANTIC RESTAURANTS

Alloro Wine Bar $$ ITALIAN   This sophisticated bar and restaurant serves excellent and authentic Italian food that guarantees a crowd almost every night. Traditional favorites like prosciutto-wrapped asparagus or zucchini blossoms stuffed with ricotta and basil are almost always on the menu and served in quiet elegance at this jewel box-sized ristorante. Given its ocean-side location, however, the specialties (moderate to expensive) always include crab and halibut and other seaside delicacies. Meat-eaters, relax: There is a tasty steak Florentine. The wine list is excellent and boasts good local and Italian vintages.

375 2nd St. SE. ℭ **541/347-1850.** www.allorowinebar.com.

Wild Rose $$ MEDITERRANEAN   This cottage houses the most romantic restaurant in town. The roses in the garden last all summer, and while the menu is Mediterranean, the English cottage effect still works. The kitchen excels in crab dishes, and the excellent pistachio-crusted halibut is memorable. The homemade pasta is a good bet here, too (try the fresh crab ravioli, and handmade gnocchi).

130 Chicago Ave., SE. ℭ **541/347-4428.**

SAN JUAN ISLANDS (WASHINGTON STATE)
Just a Ferry Ride Away

If you love the wind- and sea-shaped pines of the California coast near Monterey and Carmel, imagine islands with the same coastline and then add a mountain here and there. The San Juans are all different, but we nominate three of them as the most stirringly romantic spots, and they are only short ferry rides apart. Lopez Island is mostly an agricultural community and not hilly, so it's the best for bike-riding together. Orcas is an island with a very fashionable and lively center, an accessible mountain to climb, and a vibrant art scene. San Juan is where you go for whale watching (primarily June–Oct, but you could be lucky any time of year; a pod near San Juan sticks around most the time). The three isles share some characteristics: They can be reached by ferry from either Seattle or Vancouver (ℭ **206/464-6400**); they are incredibly beautiful; and they all are packed in summer. If you want to enjoy these islands, go before June or after September—or plan ahead!

> ### Hurry to the Ferry
>
> *Heads up:* Islands can have crowded ferry schedules; you can easily be in line for hours, which is no fun at any time, but especially when it's only a weekend getaway. Think about leaving early in the day to avoid stress or taking a midweek vacation day.

Lopez Island

This is bike and camping central, without a lot of tourist development. Places to stay are small and can best be found on VRBO (www.vrbo.com) or other websites with home and room rentals. There is a wonderful state park on the northeast part of the island where you can camp. **Spencer Spit State Park** (_©_ **360/468-2251;** www.parks.wa.gov) has 44 campsites on a wooded hillside right above a picturesque beach. Very romantic. For a touch of civilization, bike into the small but nice Lopez Village and get meals at the dozen or so cafes and delis there, or follow the ads on the bulletin boards to the many farms that sell their produce in summer. It's a bike-friendly, green island with many coves to explore, and most importantly, where motorists take care and give right of way to you, engendering an all-over sense of well-being for both of you.

Orcas Island

Here is a mountain worth exploring, plus many beaches, a ring road with continuing views of small islands, and here and there a marina, if you want to explore these isles by boat. There are also plenty of places for short or extended hikes, many with amazing views. **Eastsound** is the very sophisticated big town on this island—more New England than West Coast—with many shops, a couple of first-rate restaurants, plenty of very good art right on Main Street, and a highly browsable **Darvill's Bookstore,** 296 Main St. (_©_ **360/376-2135;** www.darvillsbookstore.com). If you'd like a glass of wine after a satisfying day trying on clothes and trinkets in the many excellent village stores, there are several places nearby with good wine lists (see later suggestions). You won't want for cultural opportunities, either: The island has first-rate music festivals during the summer that can add an appealing soundtrack to your romance. You wouldn't be the first couple to visit here and figure out a way to stay for good or book a place for the summer.

KEY ATTRACTIONS

Arts & Crafts Tour   We think it's sexy—maybe miraculous—to turn dirt into art, and so we suggest a pottery tour! Just outside of Eastsound, right off Enchanted Forest Road (don't you just love an island that could have a road with that name?) is **Orcas Island Pottery,** 338 Old Pottery Rd. (_©_ **360/376-2813;** www.orcasislandpottery.com), the oldest pottery studio in the Northwest. We also like **Crow Valley Pottery,** 2274 Orcas Rd. (_©_ **877/512-8184** or 360/376-4260; www.crowvalley.com), which has two locations on the island, one in a rambling cabin in the center of the island, another in a rambling shop on Main Street in Eastsound. While you are there check out the work by island artists at **Orcas Island Artworks,** 215 Main St. (_©_ **360/376-4408;** www.orcasisland.com/artworks).

HOTELS WITH HEART

The Inn on Orcas Island $ We like the juxtaposition of this New England–themed inn with neighboring Deer Harbor (where sea planes fly in and out and we ogle boats and the view.) But even though the marina is fascinating, it's not the only environmental attraction: There are staggeringly gorgeous and very simple strolls nearby. The inn is an interior decorator's dream: formal fabrics in the downstairs sitting room and decorated throughout with the owners' oil paintings, antiques, and knick-knacks. The main and auxiliary buildings look out on a lovely meadow with an inlet that fills deeply enough with the tide to float the small rowboat the inn provides to row around in, and then all but disappears when the tide goes out. You enter what feels like a friend's elegant home, with an opulent living room to your left and a pretty breakfast room to your right (where you will be served truly sumptuous breakfasts—woe to you if you are on a diet). The main house offers individually decorated, bright, large and very attractive bedrooms. Most have water views. The suites have jetted tubs, and all of them feel luxurious, but we think the perfect getaway place is a cozy one-bedroom cottage with a gas fireplace slightly separated from the main house. If, however, you want to cook for each other, choose the carriage house, which has a full kitchen available for guests' use.

114 Channel Rd. ✆ **888/886-1661.** www.theinnonorcasisland.com.

Turtleback Farm Inn $ This charmer boasts a peaceful, pastoral view that looks over some of the 80 acres of farmland at the foot of Turtleback Mountain (which has easy to hard, well-marked hikes). Each room has a different flavor, but all spacious and cheery and filled with antiques. A favorite room is the Mountain View room with a deck and old-fashioned iron claw-foot tub. However, the four rooms in the Orchard House are the largest and most luxurious and rate high on the romance meter with their gas fireplaces, claw-foot tubs, balconies, and refrigerators that can hold a bottle of champagne. A special treat: big farm-fresh breakfasts with elegant table settings. (Breakfast also may be delivered to your room at the Orchard House).

Crow Valley Rd. ✆ **800/376-4914.** www.turtlebackinn.com.

MOST ROMANTIC RESTAURANTS

We also like **Roses ($;** 382 Prune Alley; ✆ **360/376-4292**) in Eastsound for a lovely lunch on a nice summer day; the food is great, and the setting is charming.

Inn at Ship Bay $$ NORTHWEST This is *the* romantic restaurant on the island, and we go for both the atmosphere and the food. It's on the way to the biggest resort on the island (the historic Rosario, more a family place than a romantic one) and is in a pretty cluster of yellow country houses set perfectly in a field above the water. The kitchen excels at local seafood, and you really can't go wrong with anything on the menu. For romance, reserve a window table looking out at the water. If you fall in love—with each other or the place—you may want to stay; the rooms are simple but very nice, and then there's that shore view. Many people prefer this inn to any other on the island.

326 Olga Rd. ✆ **877/276-7296** or 360/376-5886. www.innatshipbay.com.

San Juan Island

This is the only island where you can walk to town right from the ferry landing. Maybe that is why it is the most visited of the three major tourist islands. Another reason: It is a center for whale watching, which is really spectacular in this part of the world. We hate to brag, but we were once there late fall, the last boat of the season really, when (we were the recommended distance away from the pods) all three pods turned and swam right up to the boat. Every passenger was stunned and lapsed into reverential silence; the skipper and our tour guide were so surprised and touched that they cried.

KEY ATTRACTIONS

Nature-watching   This is bald eagle country. You can see them at any of the islands, but there are a lot of venues, like American Camp, an old garrison on Cattle Point Road, where a nesting pair has been for many years. American Camp has bluffs with views near and far, so it is also a good place (from spring to fall) to view sea creatures such as seals, porpoises, and otters. The otters are especially adorable, floating on their backs and plucking mussels and oysters from the bays. Hard to imagine *not* holding hands here.

Whale-watching   These awesome black and white leviathans are a marvel—enjoy the thrill of seeing them together! There are three resident pods, and you can find out a lot about them at the Whale Watching museum in town. There are also many good tour companies, all easily reachable. But if you don't want to go on a boat, visit **San Juan County Park** (© **360/378-8420;** www.co.san-juan.wa.us/parks), where you can see the Haro Strait, a whale hangout. There are romantic campsites at the park, too, sheltered under windswept trees, with fine views of the sometimes calm, sometimes turbulent ocean. (Call way ahead, as demand far outstrips availability.) **Lime Kiln Point State Park** (© **888/226-7688;** www.parks.wa.gov) is also a likely place to see whales.

HOTELS WITH HEART

Friday Harbor House $$ Northwest style at its purest. This boutique hotel is right in town, and its casual elegance is spare but comfy. The hotel is right on a bluff, so if you request a view when booking, you will have a treat. Right below lies the ferry landing, the marina, and, in the distance, Orcas Island. The rooms have fireplaces and large Jacuzzi tubs, and some have balconies, so it has all the romantic equipment needed. In some rooms you can cuddle in your tub together and still see the view and the fireplace. How thoughtful of the architect! It's convenient, too: Nearby you can visit the small but well-done whale museum and "adopt" a whale. (We did.)

130 West St., Friday Harbor. © **866/722-7356.** www.fridayharborhouse.com.

Lakedale Resort at Three Lakes $ If you aren't after Northwest sophistication, how about romantic tents and a great Log Cabin Room? Wrapped around several lakes, this is an ultra-romantic venue. (The downside:

It's also a family spot, so unless you have teenagers or older children, this might not be your getaway dream.) Still, there are very cool and affordable two- and three-bedroom cabins with kitchens, gas fireplaces, and large cedar porches that overlook the forest; luxurious rooms in the big lodge and deluxe tents that are not at all like real camping. The 82-acre resort supplies canoes for the lakes (also good for swimming and fishing), and there are extensive walking trails.

4313 Roche Harbor Rd., Friday Harbor. ✆ **800/617-2267** or 360/378-2350. www.lakedale.com.

Roche Harbor $$$ We must mention this venerable destination. The big complex is constructed around the historic Hotel de Haro, built in 1886. Some parts of the old hotel are creaky, but the setting—right on a harbor you can sail or motor into—is glorious. The restaurants are excellent, and the new buildings (pick the McMillin or Quarryman suites or one of the carriage houses or cottages) are luxurious and some have splendid views. Yes, there are tourists who come just to see the place, and, yes, there are families here, but it remains a wonderful place to dine and a quiet resort at night. They are full-service as well and can set you up with sea kayaking, whale-watching, or boating excursions.

248 Reuben Memorial Dr., Roche Harbor. ✆ **800/451-8910.** www.rocheharbor.com.

MOST ROMANTIC RESTAURANTS

Note: Many restaurants in the islands are open only during the tourist.

Backdoor Kitchen $ ECLECTIC/INTERNATIONAL This place will charm your eyes, your stomach, and your heart. It is hidden in the back of an industrial building in Friday Harbor, and you walk in through a very Zen kind of garden to find a cozy place that spills into the patio. The food is fantastic, featuring mostly local produce, fish, and lamb.

400b A St., Friday Harbor. ✆ **360/378-9540.** www.backdoorkitchen.com.

Duck Soup Inn $$ INTERNATIONAL/NORTHWEST This is such a romantic place. You have to have directions at night, but when you drive in, the old house is lit up with twinkling lights and is nothing but welcoming. It serves creative and excellent multi-course meals, but the mood is wood-walls rustic and fieldstone-fireplace casual.

50 Duck Soup Lane, Friday Harbor. ✆ **360/378-4878.** www.ducksoupinn.com.

The Place $$ ASIAN/CONTINENTAL Right after you exit the ferry, you might notice this waterfront restaurant. The name is so pretentious you might ignore the opportunity to eat there. But to many, this is the best fish on the island—and we are suckers for a view of the harbor. You will need reservations, and it is only open during the tourist season.

1 Spring St., Friday Harbor. ✆ **360/378-8707.** www.theplacesanjuan.com.

SANTA BARBARA & THE SANTA YNEZ VALLEY
First the Beach, Then the Wine

It's hard to think of a better weekend getaway than Santa Barbara. This enchanting city is wedged between wonderful ranches, winelands, the Santa Ynez mountains, and beautiful sandy Pacific beaches. The colorful 18th-century **Old Mission Santa Barbara** (www.santabarbaramission.org) is still home to a community of Franciscan friars. The weather is almost always perfect and, while hotels right on the water are scarce, places near the water are plentiful, and the beach is always easy to reach. Romantic accommodations here run the gamut from lavish beachfront hotels to Victorian B&Bs.

Is that Oprah? It could be. A lot of wealthy celebrities have homes or getaway places in Santa Barbara or its even ritzier neighbor, Montecito. The clusters of small, chic restaurants on the main streets of each town are likely to contain a face you've seen before. If it's romantic to you to walk the hills where Oprah may have trained, by all means do so!

Santa Barbara is just the right scale and the Santa Ynez valley is just the right kind of casual for romance. For Westerners, booking here for Valentine's Day might be just the right idea; more distant lovers could come for a week and not be bored.

KEY ATTRACTIONS

The Beaches   East Santa Barbara congregates at East Beach, a long slope of land that stretches from the Zoological Gardens to the wharf. But lovers may prefer wilder destinations northward, such as **Leadbetter Beach**, less sheltered and more popular with surfers (just follow Cabrillo Blvd. after it turns into Shoreline Dr.).

Country Wine Tasting   You needn't go to Napa. The Santa Ynez Valley in Santa Barbara County produces fine wines in beautiful countryside. Many of the more than 40 wineries have intimate tasting rooms and beautiful surroundings of rolling hills, oak groves, and the very cute towns of Los Olivos, Buellton, Santa Ynez, and Ballard. Especially romantic is **Sunstone Winery,** 125 Refugio Rd. (© **800/313-9463;** www.sunstonewinery.com), which is patterned after Provence. It's easy to behave like lovebirds in the French countryside here. The beautiful setting is the perfect place for a picnic with one of Sunstone's big red wines. **The Gainey Vineyards,** 3950 E. Hwy. 246 (© **805/688-0558;** www.gaineyvineyard.com), has a serene setting, an elaborate tasting room and vineyard views with a dramatic mountain backdrop. The picnic area takes full advantage of the view. It's an ideal place to buy a bottle, spread a blanket, and unpack the cheese, prosciutto, and fruit you picked up at **Los Olivos Grocery,** 2621 Hwy. 154 (© **805/688-5155;** www.losolivosgrocery.com), in nearby Santa Ynez—what happens next is up to you! Sometimes this winery has concerts, so time your visit appropriately.

Horse Sense   Monty Roberts may not be the original Horse Whisperer, but the Santa Barbara horseman has popularized the magic of training horses without invoking fear or physical punishment. His famous ranch, **Flag is Up Farms** (✆ 805/688-4382; www.montyroberts.com) is not far from Santa Barbara in Solvang. You can visit almost any time (Roberts is usually gone, touring and teaching); the gate is usually open. The beautiful animals will likely be in training, and it's fascinating to see them in action.

Santa Barbara Museum of Art   Spend a few hours with some 20th-century artistic masters. The rich collections of early-20th-century American and French paintings here include major works by Matisse, whose lush colors and joyful themes, for us, invoke the romantic side of our natures.

1130 State St. ✆ **805/963-4364.** www.sbmuseart.org. Admission $10 adults, $6 seniors 65+.

Surfing, Kayaking, Biking, & Boating   If you are a surfer, you've probably already heard about Arroyo Burro County Park, well-known for its great wave action and opportunities for bodysurfing. A palm-lined path hugs the coast and provides a view-rich, easy trail for a bike ride for two. If you want a more urban experience (and access to some serious window shopping) use the bike lanes that cut through town. If boating strikes you as romantic (as it does us) go to the **Santa Barbara Harbor** (✆ 805/962-2826; www.sbsail.com), where you can rent kayaks, take a sailing class, or charter a sailboat or motorboat for an hour (or the whole day).

Urban Wine Tasting   You will want to drive to the Santa Ynez valley wineries, but first, follow an urban wine trail where the two of you can get mellow, relaxed, and maybe more than ordinarily titillated, knowing you don't have to stay sober enough to drive! For 15 solid suggestions, consult **www.urbanwinetrailsb.com**. We think Anacapa Street provides some good stops including Pinot Noir at the **Santa Barbara Winery,** 202 Anacapa St. (✆ 805/963-3633; www.sbwinery.com), and excellent Sauvignon Blanc at **Kunin Wines,** 28 Anacapa St. (✆ 805/963-9633; www.kuninwines.com). Since you're only a block from the beach, have a romantic escapade: Buy a bottle and watch the sun go down from a beach blanket.

Wandering   This is a place to slow down to foot speed and wander. The foothill trails in the **Santa Ynez Mountains** can keep you busy all day and yet probably won't over-tax you. Get a trail map at **Traffic Solutions** (✆ 805/963-7283; www.trafficsolutions.info). Another gentle trek is the **Seven Falls/Inspiration Point Trail,** a ramble down Tunnel Road past the mission that borders on Santa Barbara's Botanic Garden, where you'll find even more paths to explore. An easy and beautiful spot to walk together with an ocean view is the Douglas Family Preserve above Arroyo Burro Beach.

Whale-watching & Sunset Tours   December through March is whale-watching season, and there are a number of cruises that will take you out to see the Pacific Grays on their migratory path. **Captain Don's Harbor Tours,** on Stearns Wharf (© **847/526-2576;** www.captdon.com), and **Condor Express** (© **888/779-4253** or 805/882-0088; www.condorexpress.com) both have good reputations.

HOTELS WITH HEART

The Four Seasons Biltmore, 1260 Channel Dr. ($$$; © **805/969-2261;** www.fourseasons.com/santabarbara) is gorgeous and elegant and truly a beach-lover's paradise. If you can't swing the tab (few can!), be sure to have a sunset drink on the romantic beachfront patio.

The Canary Hotel $$ This gem's artful blending of Moroccan and Spanish decor lets you know you are in for something special. And it's a perfect fit with the classy casualness of this community, with such details as four-poster beds with fine linens and modern touches like flatscreen TVs, yoga DVDs, and mats in every room. There's no on-premises spa, but that hardly matters when you can easily order up massages and facials in your room. Hot tub and heated pool on the roof are the best places ever to enjoy the famed views of the Santa Ynez Mountains, the seacoast, and downtown. If you love your dog as much as you love each other (we would understand that), you might want to stay here since they have a welcome mat out (including treats and a special dog bed) for the four-legged members of your family.

31 West Carrillo. © **866/999-5401** or 805/884-0300. www.canarysantabarbara.com.

Hotel Oceana $ Directly across the street from the beach, this Spanish style boutique hotel near downtown has mid-century pastel decor and rooms located in six buildings with garden courtyards and two pools. The use of beach-cruiser bicycles comes with the room.

202 W. Cabrillo Blvd. © **800/965-9776** or 805/965-4577. www.hoteloceana santabarbara.com.

The Simpson House Inn $$$ Here's where you can live out a Jane Austen romance! Filled with Victoriana, this traditional B&B provides an acre of verdant gardens for arm-in-arm walks and captivating views. Stay either in an elegant cottage for privacy or in one of the invitingly decorated rooms in the main house or in the big old barn. Fireplaces, claw-foot tubs, and cushy quilts and bedding come with the territory. Not to mention in-room massages and other spa services. They do not skimp on amenities here, starting with the scrumptious gourmet breakfast. Afternoons signal the Mediterranean appetizers and regional fine wines in the impossibly atmospheric parlor. What you have here is a perfect blend of luxury and privacy.

121 E. Arrellaga St. © **800/676-1280** or 805/963-7067. www.simpsonhouseinn.com.

MOST ROMANTIC RESTAURANTS

Bouchon $$ CALIFORNIA   This romantic restaurant is all about the wine. Its name is French for "wine cork," and it digs deep into 50 wonderful vintages in the restaurant's immediate vicinity. For each course, you can turn to a different glass (or half glass); ask you servers to help you match each course to the perfect wine. The menu changes with the seasons. You may get to taste smoked Santa Barbara albacore "carpaccio" or local venison sliced "Parmesan" with spaetzle in peppercorn-Madeira. In addition to the fabulous vittles (desserts are not to be ignored!), you may dine al fresco on the heated front patio, if you request it.

9 W. Victoria St. ✆ **805/730-1160.** www.bouchonsantabarbara.com.

Brophy Bros. Clam Bar and Restaurant $$ SEAFOOD   Settle in to this informal and very popular place to watch the marina and water view and order some very fresh grilled fish. You won't even have to take off your flip-flops. *Tip:* Keep in mind that people come for the view, and the lines can be discouraging—it's best to have a plan B.

119 Harbor Way. ✆ **805/966-4418.** www.brophybros.com.

Stella Mare $$ FRENCH COUNTRY   With a beautiful house of Victorian and French decor, a lovely garden room, attentive service, and really fine food—Stella Mare is perfect for a Valentine's dinner, anniversary, you name it. (For us it was Valentine's Day.) Try the garden conservatory or the larger dining room, but we found every room softly lit and romantic.

3302 McCaw Ave. ✆ **805/969-6705.** www.stellamares.com.

Wine Cask $$ ITALIAN   This 1920s wine shop with its massive stone fireplace and romantic dining patio has morphed into an outstanding Italian restaurant, beloved by the local population. The chef works his magic on fish, fowl, and meat, but we were especially impressed with the sesame-crusted hamachi served with edamame and sea bean salad. Even very picky wine lovers will feel at home here: The restaurant cellars more than 2,000 wines.

813 Anacapa St. ✆ **805/966-9463.** www.winecask.com.

SANTA BARBARA BY NIGHT

Santa Barbara is a small town with an amazing array of cultural institutions given its size. There are musical imports from Broadway and excellent opera and symphony performances housed in the elaborate **Granada Theatre.** Before or afterward, scope out **Lower State Street** (try **Cielito Restaurant,** at 1114 State St.; ✆ **805-/965-4770;** http://cielitorestaurant.com), or relax with live jazz downtown at **Soho** (1221 State St.; ✆ **805/962-7776;** www.sohosb.com) and a glass of something chilled.

SULTRY SHORES: CARIBBEAN & MEXICO

Just a two- to three-hour flight from most gateways in the United States are these idyllic beach vacation spots. If what you want is an umbrella-ed drink, talcum-soft sand, and wonderfully intimate experiences, head to one of the convenient choices in this chapter.

BERMUDA
Easy East Coast Getaway

Bermuda is a perfect, hassle-free spot for a quick but glamorous getaway from U.S. East Coast locations. Yet, Bermuda is a misunderstood jewel. A mere 568 miles east of the Carolinas, the island is not tropical in the winter, so it draws less traffic than it should, given its palm trees, green golf courses, and lush vegetation in all seasons. The Gulf Stream provides a remarkably mild climate—between 75°F and 85°F degrees in the summer—and no consistent rainy season.

Land at the small airport, less than 2 hours from its East Coast satellites (Atlanta, Philadelphia, New York), and you are surrounded by blue water and distant hills dotted by pastel homes. Your cab (only locals are allowed to drive a car here) will take you to the main tourist areas via a causeway and narrow winding roads through carefully groomed hedges.

Come often and get to know your driver. There are not so many on the island, and they are great guys, full of opinions, island knowledge, and personal charisma. People in Bermuda are friendly and make it clear that you are welcome in their green, civilized, and well-tended home. The island's English ancestry remains very much intact and goes beyond just driving on the left side of the road. The dress is rather formal dress at dinner (our favorite is the Bermudian jacket, tie, and Bermuda shorts combo); the island is blessed with many pubs (and great pub food); there's a very British passion for gardening here (hence splendid rose gardens and English plants combined with the tropicals); and yes, you will be offered afternoon tea.

Rental scooters can be extremely tricky on the winding streets (we don't recommend them) but, as we said before, you can rely on cabs, plus a very good and cheap bus service, and an efficient ferry system that comes with romantic vistas, comfortable boats, and a regular schedule. Take a ferry to downtown Hamilton or one of the old forts that dot Bermuda. The view on the ride dazzles: great estates on the water and colorful neighborhoods (especially on the local ferries, rather than the resort ferries). Travel in the sunshine topside or cuddle comfortably, sheltered from the wind, in the boat's main salon. Bermuda will take care of you.

KEY ATTRACTIONS

Bermuda's Lovely Pink Beaches Bermuda is known for its pink beaches, a mixture of sand and crushed coral. (Is that why Bermudians have a penchant for pink broadcloth shirts?) Many private little coves are easily accessible, as are the long strands that crowd up in the hot summer months. Still, no matter how many people are out, lots of remote beaches never have crowds. **Cove Park** is tucked away in the steep cliffs in Warwick Parish, and hillside tables overlook a sandy cove at West Whale Bay. You can even rent horses at **Spicelands,** 50 Middle Rd. in Warwick (© **441/238-8212;** www.spicelands riding.com; private trail ride $180) and ride on trails above spectacular **South Shore beach**. The wind in your hair and the water lapping or crashing—depending on the weather—on the rocks achieves romantic perfection.

Golfing Bermuda is also a paradise for golfers, but keep in mind the reason for your visit—romance. So, if golf is not a shared passion, consider other activities on the island. But if it is, you are in for a treat. There are both public and private courses, and your hotel may get you into the private ones. If you stay, for example, at the posh **Tucker's Point Resort & Spa** (see later listing; greens fees are $260 for nonmembers, $130–$230 for hotel guests) you can not only play its elegant and demanding course, but they can set you up elsewhere. We are partial to the **Ocean View Golf Course, 2 Barkers Hill Rd., Devonshire** (© **441/295-9022;** www.oceanviewgolfbermuda.com; greens fees $77 for nonmembers, $50 for seniors). Even if you are not ambitious players, the scenery and walk are worth it, and the crowning romantic glory will come after the 18th hole with a dramatic sunset view of the North Shore.

Kayaking & Sailing Most hotels have kayaks to rent, and this is the perfect island for taking to the water, with many quiet bays for the novice kayaker or the experienced one who wants to explore the tiny islands or probe the neighborhoods along the water. You can also rent a sailboat with or without a captain and go for a smashing sunset tour for a couple of hours. This is a sea-faring island (regattas are numerous, and the island frequently hosts fleets of Tall Ships, the traditionally three-masted vessels with full rigging a la "Mutiny on the Bounty"), so your captain will know a lot about the sea and the wrecks below. Bermuda's deceptive shore has a hidden shelf that has been the ruin of many a ship. Visit Hamilton's **Bermuda Underwater Exploration Institute,** Crow Lane (© **441/292-7219;** www.buei.org; admission $15 adults,

$12 seniors 65+), to view a map that shows the history of the tragic miscalculations that created a dive paradise here.

Snorkeling & Diving   Usually it's too cool to snorkel in winter, but the other seasons offer sheltered bays (like **Church Bay** in Southampton) with impressively varied marine life. Extra special here are the shipwreck and coral reef dives. Among the many ships to find: "The Constellation," a 197-foot four-masted schooner, wrecked in 1943 and about 30 feet down on the northwest side of the island; the "Cristobal Colon," a 472-foot Spanish luxury ship that ran aground in 1936, lying 30 to 56 feet underwater. The "North Carolina," dating from the 1800s, is well preserved, and if you are both expert divers, the masses of brightly colored fish that gather there could make it a thrilling afternoon. Contact **Dive Bermuda** (© **441/238-2332;** www.bermudascuba.com) or **Snorkel Bermuda** (© **441/705-5555;** www.snorkel bermuda.com).

Wandering the Island   Ferries or buses can get you anywhere, and, with minimal planning, you'll bump into some remarkable experiences, starting in Hamilton, with its unique shops and occasional troupes of costumed Gombey dancers, who perform a kind of Afro-Caribbean athletic dancing seen only here. If you want to walk or bike together, the 18-mile **Bermuda Railway Trail** reclaims a retired railroad line across the island, and it's a safe alternative to the narrow roads that rarely have a paved lane for walkers or bicyclists. Pick up a free railway trail guide at the **Visitors Service Bureau,** at 8 Front St. in Hamilton (© **441/295-1480**).

Most romantic, we think, is the underground **Crystal Cave** and the deeper **Fantasy Cave** in Bailey's Bay. The illuminated stalactites, stalagmites, and crystal-clear pools of the caves are awesome. It's a bit chilly down there, so besides your love, you might want to take a sweater to keep you warm. Start your visit at the Crystal Caves Information Center, 8 Crystal Caves Rd. in Hamilton (© **441/293-0640;** www.caves.bm; $22 per cave or $30 for both).

Another nice outing (on a bike if you are athletic) is a trip to **St. George,** site of the island's original settlement and statehouse, built in 1620. At this cute seaside village, you can visit a replica of an old sailing ship. Drop in at the 19th-century **Commissioner's House** at the **Royal Naval Dockyard** in the Bermuda Maritime Museum (1 The Keep, Sandys; © **441/234-1418;** www.bmm.bm; admission $10 for adults, $8 for seniors 60+). It has historical exhibits and is a good place to buy the local perfumes we love so much! At the dolphin experience here (© **441/234-4464;** www.dolphinquest.com), a couple can swim and commune with the friendly sea mammals.

HOTELS WITH HEART
Cambridge Beaches Resort & Spa $$$ This is our hands-down favorite on the island but, alas, it doesn't come cheap (although you should check their website and travel booking sites for frequent online deals). Here, a traditional historic house is at the center of a group of cottages, each looking out toward the sea or the bay. Graced with the most romantic setting on the

island, it is on a private peninsula with its own marina and several beaches including a private little cove (where you can have a private dinner) and a long strand bordered by mature tropical gardens.

While the spacious and handsome rooms have been updated, the place still feels like old Bermuda, and we love it for that. The main house has updated its pool and terrace area, complemented by a spiffy infinity pool, a "waterfall," and a set of decks overlooking a small cove. If you want a totally private dip, you can spring for one of the newer cottages that have their own ocean-view plunge pools. For sunning au natural, there is a European-style private deck above the pool area. Both restaurants are excellent and have killer views. The Tamarisk dining room (main courses $25–$35) offers wine tastings and other events, but we think its most romantic contribution, besides the view, is the scrumptious nightly soufflé. To us, a soufflé is the most sensual of all the food groups.

30 Kings Point, Sandys. © **800/468-7300** or 441/234-0331. www.cambridgebeaches. com/Bermuda-getaway. Bargains can be had in the winter months.

Oxford House $ If you want to plug into middle-Atlantic urban life (and spend less money), this is one of the top guesthouses in Bermuda, and the family that runs it provides first-rate personal service. Oddly enough, the 12 spacious rooms in this elegant townhouse have a French feel even though it has an English name. No matter, it's an ideal base for exploring Hamilton's very good restaurants and shops on Front Street, a fine place to pick up a surprise gift for your honey without going broke.

Woodbourne Ave., Pembroke. © **800/548-7758** or 441/295-0503. www.oxford house.bm.

The Reefs $$$ The Reefs underwent a dazzling renovation, making it hard to pick a more dramatic setting or more beautiful beach. The units trail down the cliffs to the sea and a private powdery pink beach with jagged cliffs for a backdrop. The hotel lies across a busy street (something to think about if you're traveling with young kids or bad knees), with immediate access to the old railway trail for walking and biking. This is a place for lovers, but the two- and three-bedroom condos with private infinity pools attract a good number of families (who also come for the kid-friendly beach and children's menus). For a romantic adult experience, great seafood, and a view of the beach, try the restaurant, **Coconuts** (main courses $18–$24 at lunch, $24–$36 at dinner); call ahead to reserve a six-course, private torch-lit dinner at the water's edge.

56 South Shore Rd., Southampton. © **441/238-0222.** www.thereefs.com.

Tucker's Point Hotel and Spa $$$ This might be the best choice for a golfing couple. It is the most luxurious resort on the island, and spread across its 200 acres is a respected and beautiful golf course, an 88-room main hotel, and a lovely private beach with a fine restaurant. It has a country-club feel and a glamorous setting that has witnessed many perfect weddings and honeymoons.

60 Tucker's Point Dr., Hamilton. © **800/532-5075** or 441/298-4000. www.tuckers point.com.

MOST ROMANTIC RESTAURANTS

All the hotels mentioned above have restaurants with terrific views; we especially love the ones at Cambridge Beaches Resort and The Reefs Hotel.

The Harbourfront Restaurant & Komodaru Sushi Lounge $$

ASIAN/MEDITERRANEAN/SEAFOOD/SUSHI   Have lunch here on the ground floor of the Underwater Exploration Institute; it combines people-watching and serious cuisine, served inside or out. We prefer to be outside looking across the bay and playing footsie.

Pembroke Hall, 40 Crow Lane, Pembroke.✆ **441/295-4207.** www.harbourfront.bm.

Tom Moore's Tavern $$ CONTINENTAL/FRENCH   Love this place!

You can't see it from the road, but you drive in through dense tropical foliage and discover this historic building that dates from 1652, perched beside Walsingham Bay. Split a Bermudian lobster or just have great drinks later in the evening. The age of the place and the intimacy of the rooms make this a unique and romantic experience.

On Walsingham Bay, near the Crystal Cave.✆ **441/293-8020.** www.tommoores. com.

Tribe Road Kitchen $ BAKERY/CAFE   A healthful and sweetly inti-

mate choice for lunch (not open for dinner), Tribe Road offers a casual menu with great salads, seafood, and sandwiches, served inside or out in a lovely little garden. The local wahoo (a type of fish), marinated and grilled, is a star attraction.

87 Reid St., Hamilton.✆ **441/734-1637.** www.triberoadkitchen.com.

The Waterlot Inn $$$ STEAK & SEAFOOD   Lots of romantic ambi-

ence and consistently fine food characterizes this historic inn and warehouse that's part of the Fairmont Southampton Princess. Another eatery on the Fairmont's grounds, Windows on the Sounds, offers a lovely, lavish Sunday brunch.

101 South Shore Rd., Southampton.✆ **441/238-8000.** www.fairmont.com.

BERMUDA BY NIGHT

Bermuda has nightlife, but mainly in the summer. In winter we suggest you content yourself with drinks on **Front Street** in Hamilton or at your hotel—many have bars with inspiring views in genteel surroundings that can jump-start your libidos. In summer, try activity floats from hotel to hotel with steel drum or calypso performances and dancing—even beach parties. Many pubs feature sing-alongs at the piano, a common entertainment in Bermuda. The little **Port of St. George** and nearby **St. David's Island** have some of the most convivial pubs, where you can also find good eats. The service is friendly, if plodding, but as long as you have a glass of something and each other, you'll be fine. We like **Black Horse Tavern,** 101 St. David's Rd. (✆ **441/297-1991**) on St. David's Island, which immediately adjoins St. George, where you'll find the **White Horse Tavern,** 8 King's Square (✆ **441/297-1838**), jammed most

CELEBRATING milestone ANNIVERSARIES

Let's face it: Some milestones in life demand a certain amount of respect and, often, a spectacular gesture. We can't let anniversaries in general (big ones in particular) just slide by unnoticed. In fact, it is the rare happy couple that doesn't want to do something special for an anniversary. Coupling a big trip and the occasion together will almost certainly make the occasion—and the trip—that much more memorable.

Bermuda is a great example to illustrate what we think would make for a splendid *romantic* celebration of love. It's so close, yet so foreign in feel, filled with English gardens and other holdovers from centuries as a former British colony. And you get the full island experience, even if you just go for a weekend getaway! If you can, reserve one of the gorgeous cottages facing the ocean or marina at Cambridges Beaches. Have the concierge arrange a picnic basket and take it to one of the secret little beaches, like the ones at Astwood Cove and Jobson's Cove, or go underground into the Crystal and Fantasy Caves for a romantic and spectacular visual afternoon trip. Then, for our money, there isn't anything more romantic than having a white-tablecloth gourmet dinner in your own private cove with the waves lapping gently just a few feet away; this resort will serve you a meal in a number of places near the water and far from anyone else.

Going away for an important event in your life together makes great vacation memories that don't quickly fade. We believe observing these occasions is not a trivial celebration. There are few enough times that are clearly delineated as times to lavish affection and attention on each other. Why not grab them and let them help you be your best as a partner and lover?

evenings with a mix of locals and visitors. We especially like the location of this one: at the water's edge overlooking the harbor. Just add moonlight.

CABO SAN LUCAS
Romance Among the Dunes

You may have heard that this is "Arizona by the Sea," and there is something to that, but Cabo San Lucas, Mexico, and the nearby area of San José del Cabo, are much more than desert climate and blue water. This may be party central during spring break, but otherwise, it is an ethereal place of beauty, endless dunes and beaches, and excursions that are hardly touristy. Of course,

Cabo offers wonderfully scenic places to sport fish, snorkel, boat, and just sunbathe overlooking Los Arcos, the famous rocks that mark the end of the Baja peninsula and the place where the Pacific meets the Sea of Cortez.

KEY ATTRACTIONS

ATV Rides   Feeling adventurous? Rent an ATV and ride it together to **La Candelaria,** a remote Indian village about 25 miles north of Cabo. The village is fascinating and so different from Cabo; it's more like an oasis, with its lush foliage (even palms!) and tropical fruit trees fed by an underground river. **Another ride:** You may prefer the excitement of renting a dune buggy and taking on the scenic dunes by the sea. Check with your concierge for recommended vendors.

The Beaches   Cabo is pretty much about beach life. **Playa El Medano** is a strip of cute bars and cafes, safe swimming, and lots of water sports. But no one will mind if you just kick back and sip your margarita or read your book, occasionally taking in the great views of **Land's End Beach** and the rocks trailing into the ocean. Snorkelers can also visit **Playa Chileno, Santa María,** and **Pelican Rock.** Each has great places to observe fish, and you can start at the beach rather than being dropped off by a boat. The most famous beach is **Playa del Amor** (Lovers Beach). This is the image you have in your head about Cabo: picturesque cliffs and swimming and kayaking around the giant arch of El Arco. It defines lovely and romantic.

Excursions   You can book inexpensive day trips to the city of **La Paz** and the surrounding countryside along the way, through your concierge. You can purchase superior rugs and weavings at the famous **Fortunato Silva** shop. Or visit **Todos Santos,** where you can enjoy the low-key atmosphere and tour museums, a fine mission, and a cathedral; linger at sidewalk cafes; or tour artists' studios (art walks are 5–9pm Thurs). Guided by a naturalist, you can see rare leatherback turtles here. Surfers tend to like the waves at the town's beaches.

Having a Spa Day   With so many hotels, there are some amazing places to pamper your bodies. One that offers the most unusual kinds of treatments is the **One & Only Palmilla,** Carretera Transpeninsular, Km 7.5, San José del Cabo (✆ **866/829-2977** or 52/624-146-7000; http://palmilla.oneandonly resorts.com), where thirteen private villas each face a garden—to keep your experience private. Walking through the adobe halls and archways and gardens with gently bubbling fountains amid bougainvillea-draped tile roofs, you feel someone is working hard just to please the two of you! Relax on the shaded day beds after your spice body wraps, hydrotherapy, or Balinese massages and enjoy life in the slow lane. Another luscious option is the **PAZ Spa at Cabo Azul** (✆ **52/624-163-5100;** www.caboazulresort.com/paz); with its rooftop treatment rooms and beachside pavilion, it's the perfect respite for body and mind.

Horseback Riding in the Surf   We think it is extremely romantic to ride a horse along the beach, but you have to be realistic about your level of expertise. Some beaches are crowded with people who won't make allowances for a nervous horse. So, if you are able to control your horse rather than just sit on him, call **Rancho Colín** (© **52/624-143-3652**). They will rent you a horse and take you on a magnificent ride to the mountains, desert, or the beach at sunset.

Sunset Cruises/Whale-watching   Some sunset cruises are cheesy, drunken affairs, to be avoided at all costs, but some are truly romantic. On the ocean here, watching the rocks at sunset can be mesmerizing. From January to March you can combine your cruise with a whale-watching tour and add a sense of awe to your romantic excursion. Your hotel can recommend sunset and whale-watching cruises.

HOTELS WITH HEART

The most luxurious hotels are clustered in San José del Cabo near Cabo San Lucas. It's a short distance from Cabo San Lucas, but the level of exclusivity—and expense—is considerably higher.

The Cabo Surf Hotel $$ This appealing boutique hotel near downtown is on one of Cabo's best surfing beaches. It's a favorite breakfast place, even for people who are not staying here. The 36 rooms all face the sea, as do the excellent, seafood restaurant (**7 Seas Seafood Grille**) and the day spa. The view includes an ocean cove and sand beach with rock formations and jade green waters. The look is Malibu beach house with white stucco walls and red tile roofs, and the grounds are verdant.

Playa Acapulquito, Km 28, Cabo San Lucas. © **52/624-142-2676.** www.cabosurf hotel.com.

One&Only Palmilla $$$ This gorgeously landscaped hotel, one of the most elite destinations in the world, is arranged on a seaside cliff, and each room has a marvelous view of the Sea of Cortez. Each of the rooms has its own terrace and Jacuzzi and oozes with restrained elegance; suites get their own pools, but there are beaches and pools for all guests to share. Romance is easy in the open-air Aqua Restaurant. (The Market restaurant, though not as lovely, demonstrates the talented hand of its famous chef, Jean-Georges Vongerichten). Lovers will appreciate romantic touches such as hanging lanterns and candle-lit pathways. Golf fanatics will love the championship course. This is, however, a very expensive hotel, so trying for off-season or shoulder season is a good idea.

Carretera Transpeninsular Km 7.5, San José del Cabo. © **866/829-2877** or 52/ 624-146-7000. http://palmilla.oneandonlyresorts.com.

Sunset Beach Resort & Spa $$$ This luxury all-suite hotel sits on a private coastal bluff. Privacy and peace reign and when you arrive, you are greeted with a glass of champagne and chocolate-covered strawberries—hints of the pampering to come. Marble floors lead to private balconies so you and your fab view are never separated for long. If you don't want to eat out every meal, not to worry: You have a fully equipped kitchen, or you can opt for the meal plan. The resort is beautifully landscaped; there are waterfalls, swim-up bars, and six pools from which to choose. In lieu of an onsite swimming beach, there is a shuttle to the hotel's sister property, **Pueblo Bonita Rose**, where you can swim and use their other facilities. **La Frida**, the Sunset's most elegant restaurant, has sweeping ocean views, and the Spa is highly rated. An extra romantic plus: swimming with the dolphins at the nearby Aquatic Center.

<table>
<tr><td>

Perfect Place to Honeymoon

The Sunset Beach's luxury and a bluff-top position on the coast make it a glorious place to celebrate your union—and get the privacy and peace you want. We could lounge all day in its turquoise infinity pool. But be sure to avoid spring break.

</td></tr>
</table>

Predio Paraíso Escondido, Cabo San Lucas. © **800/990-8250** or 52/624-142-9999. www.pueblobonitosunset beach.com.

The Westin $$$ This striking modern design is romantic from the moment you enter the lobby. Festive colors buoy spirits and celebrate the sun; long pathways are full of flowering plants and strategically placed fountains. We like it for additional reasons: Each room contains a "heavenly bed," a walk-in shower, and an ocean view. If you're traveling with children, this hotel is a good choice; the Westin Kids Club will keep the kids happily engaged in fun, leaving parents to find some time for each other.

Carretera Transpeninsular, Km 22.5, San José del Cabo. © **800/228-3000** or 52/624-142-9000. www.westin.com/loscabos.

MOST ROMANTIC RESTAURANTS

Edith's Restaurant $$ MEXICAN/SEAFOOD   Flickering lanterns and aromatic bouquets of fresh flowers add to the romantic ambience here. Great drinks, a fine wine cellar, and a hearty menu at prices that won't make you cringe. Expect comfort food made elegant—classic steaks, lobster, and fresh fish—plus inspired traditional Mexican dishes with the same sure touch.

Camino a Playa El Medano s/n. © **52/624-143-0801.** www.edithscabo.com.

El Farallón $$$ TRADITIONAL BAJA   This may be one of the all-time romantic entrances to a restaurant: You drive through a torch-lit tunnel to get to it. The payoff is even greater when you see the ocean view from your table at this cliff-top retreat. Fortunately, the food is nearly as good as the setting.

In the Capella Pedregal Resort, Camino Del Mar 1. © **52/624-163-4300.** www. capellahotels.com.

Flora Farms $$ NEW AMERICAN   A unique destination: Flora Farms is an organic farm with an accompanying restaurant that serves fresh produce and fantastic breads and baked goods from their farm and bakery. Everything they serve is kind of inspiring—seasonal, sustainable, and reasonably priced! This is a new concept for Cabo, and it's a satisfying place to go for a drink, dinner, brunch—or just to explore the grounds.

Las Animas Bajas, San José del Cabo. © **52/624-355-4564.** www.flora-farms.com.

CABO BY NIGHT

Nikki Beach (© **52/624-145-7800;** www.nikkibeachcabo.com) is probably the best-known club/lounge in Cabo, located on the sand off Medano Beach at the Me Cabo Hotel. It often features live music or a guest DJ for dancing and a club experience later in the night. It's great for a sunset drink, but if you want a long evening, you can have it here.

If you want to stay up late and not be surrounded by 20-somethings, consider **Two for the Road,** Hotel Tesoro Local A-15, on Marina Blvd. (© **52/624-143-7759**); the restaurant on the Marina side of the Wyndham Hotel is a mellow place, featuring live jazz.

In San José del Cabo, the colonial-themed **Tropicana Inn Restaurant** (© **52/624-142-4146;** www.tropicanainn.com) has traditional Mexican live music during the week and Salsa dancing on Saturday nights. Also in San José del Cabo, **Deckman's,** Carretera Transpeninsular (© **52/624-172-6269;** www.deckmans.com), is a music mecca. It's a restaurant (don't miss the twice-cooked octopus), but with legit live music (blues, jazz, blue grass), and sometimes a good jam session can make it a late night.

MAYAN RIVIERA COAST, CANCUN TO TULUM
Beach and Jungle and Ruins—Oh My!

This area, which follows the Caribbean coastline of the Mexican state of Quintana Roo on the Yucatán Peninsula, is a romantic bonanza. Amazing hotels, powdery beaches, great restaurants, wonderful scenery, and entertainment stretch out along coastal Highway 307 for miles. The romantic settings and options in this part of the world seem endless.

The varieties of ambience—the water's edge, the enchanted starry nights, the jungle pathways blessed with exotically plumed birds and lush vegetation—almost guarantee romance will be on the agenda.

The destinations listed provide tantalizing choices: Lavish beach resorts with plenty of activities in Cancún, ecotourism and archeology on the Mayan coast, and a historic and peaceful beachfront retreat at Tulum. But feel free to consider the whole area your oyster, and you will be rewarded with more than one pearl.

Cancún

The most prosperous city on the Yucatán Peninsula is also a huge tourist attraction, but the sheer size of Cancún's coastal resort area ensures that you can have a serene visit and the privacy you need. You can relax together at any of dozens of world-class spas (some with luscious outdoor treatments), go off through the jungle to visit Mexico's largest and most famous ruins at Chichen Itza, or take a snorkeling or scuba expedition.

Cancún has gotten some negative publicity concerning personal safety here, but the U.S. State Department says violent crime is not a concern here, although petty theft can be. Naturally you need to be aware of your surroundings—don't flash jewelry or wads of cash, and don't leave anything valuable in your car if you are sightseeing. The good news is some resorts create such a seductive and secure oasis that you may never want to leave the property!

KEY ATTRACTIONS

Chichén Itzá   Visit this ancient capital of the Mayan Empire on a day trip from Cancún. Many consider this archaeological zone to be one of the wonders of the world. You can no longer climb the stairs of its famed pyramid but it is a magical sight, as is the equally famous early observatory, the sacred cenote, the mysterious ball court, and exquisite Temple of Kukulcan, the plumed serpent God, and many more sets of ruins built over several eras. There are dozens of ways to get here, from cheap buses that let you wander on your own to guided tours. We felt it was worth the extra money and paid a private taxi driver to get us there early, before the crowds from the slower buses filled the place and before the hottest part of the day in the jungle would sap our energy.

Isla Mujeres   A romantic day trip from Cancún, this island is an 8-mile float via the ferry or water taxi. The island is bounded by El Garrafón Natural Park (great for snorkeling) and a picturesque village with good shopping, small restaurants offering a variety of world cuisines, and Playa Norte, a beautiful "swept-away" beach. Our favorite underwater part is the fish ladder, where thousands of fish gather and linger, basking in the current. You will feel like lingering, too; Isla Mujeres is an uncrowded, laid-back place to wander around, see the views, and find a nice spot to enjoy your margaritas—and each other.

Jet Ski Jungle Cruises   There are two ways to cruise Cancún's lagoons and mangrove estuaries: either drive a *lancha* (a small speedboat) or a Wave-Runner jet ski. We like the speedboats. Otherwise the two of you can't sit beside one another—and that takes away romance points. Ask your concierge to book a trip.

Reef Diving   Cancún, with its diverse sea life, is one of the world's best places to take up scuba diving. The Punta Nizuc reef is the largest reef in the Western Hemisphere and offers dazzling colors and several sunken boats among the dive or snorkel options.

Submarine Trip   Here's a way to observe sea-life without diving, snorkeling, or swimming. For this adventurous alternative, you use personal "breathing observation bubble" (BOB) submarines. You boat from the Embarcadero to a reef close by, where you and your BOBs lower into the water. Traveling by mini-subs, you can descend 6m (20 ft.) below the surface of the Caribbean, cruising along with your heads safely contained in big air bubbles connected to oxygen tanks. Ask your concierge to recommend a company.

HOTELS WITH HEART

Fiesta Americana Grand Coral Beach Cancún Resort & Spa $$$

The feel here is classic elegance. Think Mexican Waldorf or St. Regis. Decorated mostly in neutral tones (beige and off whites) with pops of bright colors, all rooms are junior suites and have a large sitting area, decorative Mexican touches, and a balcony—some are oceanfront while others are ocean view. It's a good place to get married and has an on-site wedding planner and room enough for a big wedding. As with most large resorts, you never have to leave to try new restaurants. The beachside **Villa Del Mar** is a romantic option and lets you pick your catch of the day (sweet Caribbean lobster is an excellent choice). The hotel's **Gem Spa** (✆ **52/998-881-32-00;** www.gemspacancun. com/en) will profoundly recharge your romance! Book a treatment at this 40,000-square-foot marvel even if you aren't staying here. We adore the co-ed "sensations" pool, which is modeled after Roman baths, and delivers multiple bubbling sensations: mini-waterfalls, cervical neck jets, and floor geysers, and the couple's massage, "Romantic Escapes."

Bulevar Kukulcán Km 9.5. ✆ **52/998-881-3200.** www.fiestamericanagrand.com/en.

Live Aqua $$$

Live Aqua is an all-inclusive that does not feel like one as it provides a true luxury experience with phenomenal service and a Zen spa ambience. Opt for an Aqua suite with a sun deck and sea view (it comes with its own beach cabana, luxurious reclining chairs and free 20-minute foot massages). You will hear the waves crashing on the beach, and we don't think there is a more romantic sound in the world. Another romantic plus is the large circular Jacuzzi tub near your bed—you can lounge there and take in the view.

If you are honeymooning or celebrating an anniversary, let the concierge know and voila! They will provide all kinds of special touches—bougainvillea petals on your bed, dessert surprises.

Bulevar Kukulkán Km 12.5. ✆ **52/998-881-7600.** www.feel-aqua.com/en.

Villa del Parmar Cancún $$

This place will put you about 20 to 30 minutes away from all the action in downtown Cancún, but we think this value-priced hotel is the better for it. Its gourmet restaurants and refreshing pools will keep you busy, plus all the rooms have a view of the ocean and many have Jacuzzis and balconies. They offer an all-inclusive price but unlike some all inclusive hotels, it doesn't feel like quantity over quality on the buffets or dinner menus. A great touch is that the car ferry to the romantic Isla Mujeres island is right at the hotel, and this will take you to wonderful snorkeling adventures and the beautiful Playa Norte beach.

Carreterra a Punta Sam. Km 5, 2 Playa Mujeras. ✆ **52/998-193-2600.** www.villa parpar.com. Rates include all meals.

MOST ROMANTIC RESTAURANTS

Inlaa'Kech Lobster & Grill $$ STEAK & SEAFOOD

This is the place for lobster, steak, and veal, and you can watch and interact with the chef preparing your meal. Inlaa'Kech has a Hemingwayesque feel to its décor of white draping, warmed by candlelight to create a private romantic cocoon.

At Live Aqua hotel, Bulevar Kukulkán Km 12.5. ℂ **800/343-7821.** www.feel-aqua. com/en.

Le Basilic $$$ FRENCH/MEDITERRANEAN   Le Basilic is the only AAA 5-diamond restaurant in Cancún. It has sinfully delicious French and Mediterranean infusion food. Innovative touches include live jazz and a resident artist who paints while you eat and makes it an interactive event.

At the Fiesta Americana, Bulevar Kukulcán Km 9.5. ℂ **52/998-881-3200.** www. lebasiliccancun.com.

Thai $$ THAI   How could we include a Thai restaurant in Mexico and in a shopping plaza, of all places? Trust us, the food—with dishes like roasted duck breast in coconut red curry—is amazing and so romantic and authentic you'd think you were in Thailand. You'll dine in your personal palapa, a breezy private hut built over the lagoon and equipped with a table, sofa, and candlelight.

Bulevar Kukulcán Km 12.5. ℂ **52/998-176-8070.** www.thai.com.mx.

CANCUN BY NIGHT

Consider leaving the hotel zone and go salsa dancing at **Mambo Café,** Plaza Hong Kong (ℂ **52/998-884-4536;** www.mambocafe.com.mx). It feels like an old-school Mambo club. The huge salsa band plays amazing music for dancing or just listening and watching. You could also stop next door at the bar and do Spanish karaoke.

The Mayan Coast

The Yucatán's northern coast, from Cancún to Tulum, is known as the Riviera Maya for its amazing beaches and perfect water. Its most impressive natural asset, the Great Mesoamerican Reef, protects most of the coast from harsh currents. Tulum's long beaches and its small hotels make it ideal for getting away from the crowds and strolling on the sand.

KEY ATTRACTIONS

Caving at Aktun Chen   A few miles south of Akumal and down a dirt road off Route 307, Aktun Chen has a forest of stalactites and stalagmites that lead you to a deep pool. The 1-hour excursion, led by a knowledgeable guide (included in the fee), is compellingly other-wordly and delivers you to an open-air cafe at tour's end.

The Cenotes   A series of mysterious jungle pools, part of a collapsed cave system, appears throughout the Mayan empire. If you love adventure and mystery and beauty, explore these caves—but you need to go with a guide. The sinkholes can be vast or small, and these freshwater openings can be seen as doors to a watery underworld. The Mayans saw them as spiritual places, links between the living and the dead. If you go down the coast far enough to the **Sian Ka'an Biosphere Reserve** (ℂ **52/984-87-12499;** www.cesiak.org), this protected area contains the **Lagoon of Chunyaxche,** a very large and lovely pool that is actually a cenote. Enjoy magical exploration of this unusual and beautiful place. Closer to Tulum, you will see road signs for the **Gran Cenote,** which is definitely worth a dip, especially for divers.

Mayan Archaeology   Take some days to share the beauty and majesty of ancient civilizations in Cobá or Tulum, the only Mayan ruin at the sea. Less-visited ruins are **Palenque,** a jungle adventure, and **Uxmal,** with its astounding carved details and remarkably well-preserved multilevel structures. If you go really early to avoid crowds, these can be magical and romantic excursions.

River Float   We find **Xel-Há National Park,** Carretera Chetumal-Puerto Juárez Km 240, Xel-Há (℃ **888/922-7381** or 52/998-251-6560; www.xelha. com) surprisingly romantic, even though it is crowded and has many families. But you can escape by floating down the river in tubes here and jumping into pools —it brings out the kid in both of you. Admission is $89 for adults and includes continental breakfast, buffet lunch, and snorkeling equipment rental; online discounts are available.

Playa del Carmen

Playa del Carmen's beaches, such as Playa El Faro, are among the riviera's most beautiful, with soft sand and minimal surf. Playa del Carmen's Quinta Avenida offers the best shopping, from Brazilian bikinis to traditional embroidered dresses. In the same neighborhood, you'll find terrific local cooking.

HOTELS WITH HEART

Playa's many affordable small hotels allow you to explore this fun town rather than staying in one of the resorts in Playacar. There are reasonably priced inns if you don't mind being off the beach; for example, the **Hotel Lunata ($;** ℃ **52/984-873-0884;** www.lunata.com) is quite lovely, with beamed ceilings, bright colors, colonial furniture, and charming walkways that make you feel you are staying in a hacienda. It's very atmospheric and only a few minutes away from the beach or shops. **La Tortuga Hotel & Spa ($;** ℃ **866/550-6878** or 52/984-873-1484; www.hotellatortuga.com) in the Playa is also well priced. However, if you want luxury and the beach, read on.

Esencia Estate $$$ A white stucco villa that once was the private residence of a duchess has enough space for 29 classy guest rooms. Guests stay in individual Palapas, which are very modern inside and privately ensconced beneath trees and lush native foliage. Most of them have plunge pools and terraces, where breakfast is served every morning.

Carretera Cancún-Tulum Km 265. ℃ **877/528-3490** or 52/984-873-4835. www. hotelesencia.com.

Royal Hideaway Playacar $$ This grand, adults-only beachfront resort's colonial architecture sets a sophisticated mood. Suites are subsumed into villa units and surround a central courtyard. Two-story suites with decks on the ocean could easily become passion pits! The complex is acclaimed as an idyllic wedding and honeymoon setting.

Lote Hotelero Mz 6, Playacar. ✆ **52-984-873-4500.** www.royalhideaway.com. Rates include meals, water sports, taxes, and gratuities.

MOST ROMANTIC RESTAURANTS

Yaxché $ MAYAN   The chef uses mostly native products and spices for a menu of regional fare beyond that of other Yucatán restaurants. Try the cream of chaya (something like spinach).

Av. 5ta and Calle 22. ✆ **52/984-873-3011.** www.mayacuisine.com.

Tulum

Tulum has many stretches of beautiful beaches, but its outstanding attraction is the only waterfront Mayan ruin in existence. That being said, the town and area itself have intriguing romantic possibilities. The stunning walkable beach off Boca Paila Road offers a lot of simpler places than the big resorts, and it encourages privacy.

HOTELS WITH HEART

Coqui Coqui, Carretera Tulum Boca Paila Km 7.5 (**$$;** ✆ **52/1-984-100-1400;** www.coquicoquispa.com), is located near the ruins, but it's worth staying here for other reasons as well: It has a beautiful beach where a hammock for the day would seem perfect, and the rooms offer romantic sensual stone bathtubs to luxuriate in.

Closer to the ruins at Uxmal, the **Hacienda Temozón,** Carretera Mérida-Uxmal Km 182 (**$$;** ✆ **52/999-923-8089;** www.starwoodhotels.com), a luxury hotel with lush jungle gardens, will knock you out. It's an elegant place to gather by the pool and recover from, or get ready for, this impressive destination.

NEGRIL, JAMAICA
Tropical Getaway with a Beat

Legendary reggae singer-songwriter Bob Marley made Jamaica, his homeland, the most famous island paradise in the Caribbean. Legions of fans all over the world think about making pilgrimages to Jamaica. If you're among them, go! A trip to the island is great anytime (except hurricane season), especially around February 6 when tribute music festivals honoring Marley's birthday erupt all over the island. We recommend Negril, the serene beach town on the west tip of the island and one of the most romantic places in the world. A Marley celebration may be a once-in-a-lifetime event, but here nightly reggae parties go all year long, so go anytime. You'll feel sexy, seeing your partner discover his or her sensual self, as you sway together to the soulful tunes.

"Everytin' irie, mon," is the greeting all over Jamaica. It means being at total peace with your situation, no worries—and nowhere is it more true than in Negril. It's perfect for honeymoons and memorable birthday or anniversary celebrations or as a place for healing. Negril features reasonably priced boutique hotels, restaurants, shops, and nightclubs all along its famed Seven-Mile beach, celebrated as one of the world's best beaches for its fine, white sugar sands and pristine turquoise water (no pesky rocks or shells under foot)—not too warm, not at all cold. You can hang on a raft there for hours. Nearby reefs and the water's crystal clarity make it a snorkeler's paradise. The term "laid-back" is a gross understatement.

You've no doubt read about the crime in Jamaica, but it rarely affects tourists. Just use common sense and go to the right places (we strongly recommend you avoid the city of Kingston and some sections of Montego Bay and don't leave valuables on the beach while you swim). We return to Negril year after year and never feel threatened. Every hotel on Seven-Mile Beach has security guards to ensure your safety. You can stay in any number of world-class all-inclusive resorts and still enjoy Negril's natural beauty and vibe without leaving the secured premises. We prefer being a part of the local culture, so we hang at Seven-Mile Beach. But one more caveat: Jamaica is not a gay-friendly destination.

Tip: We go during "shoulder season" (after Thanksgiving but before Christmas) when the rates are still quite low. Fly to Montego Bay, rent a car, and then take a leisurely hour-long drive to Negril (or have the hotel arrange a taxi or tour bus from the airport).

KEY ATTRACTIONS

Appleton Rum Factory   The Appleton Estate (www.appletonestate. com) has been blending rums since 1749. A trip to the factory makes for a great day trip as it is also on the Black River in one of the most beautiful valleys in Jamaica, south of Negril.

Golfing at Negril Hills   Negril Hills (© 876/957-4240; www.negrilhills golfclub.com) is a fun round of golf. The fairways are not long, but there are certainly many challenges: target shots, sloping greens, hilly lies, four par-five holes where you can let it fly, and usually a gentle ocean breeze.

Horseback Riding   There are several stables in Negril. Let your concierge guide you to the ones that allow you to ride their horses along the beach or the stables that lead rides into the mountains and to old plantations.

Snorkeling   We recommend doing a day snorkel trip to the reef. Lots of boat owners will approach you on the beach and make you a good deal, but you can also check in with your concierge about arranging a trip. This physical activity will rev up your hormones!

Taking a Sunset Cruise on a Catamaran   Along the beach you'll see reps from competing catamaran companies trying to get you to sign up for a sunset cruise (you can join other couples until they fill the boat, or go alone if you're on a family trip). They all take you to the western end of the island, with two stops, one for snorkeling near the reef and the other for a swim through turquoise colored **Pirates Caves,** where a James Bond movie was shot. Typically, they offer an open bar of Red Stripe beer and jerk chicken dinner included for one low price (depends on number of passengers but we paid about $20 per person). You can inquire at the front desk about which companies they recommend.

Visiting the Waterfalls   Waterfalls are refreshing and sensual (why is Niagara Falls a traditional honeymoon destination?), and Negril has two inspiring cascades. **YS Falls,** along the Black River in Cornwall, makes a great day trip; it's about a 2-hour drive, including a quick stop at reggae pioneer **Peter Tosh's Monument,** just south of Negril. For **Dunn's River Falls,** take a tour bus and climb the terraced 600-foot-high falls on foot!

HOTELS WITH HEART

If you prefer the seclusion, convenience, and amenities (and extreme security) of an all-inclusive, check out the frequent special deals at **Sandals Negril** (✆ **888/SANDALS** [786-9851] or 876/957-5216; www.sandals.com), a romantic adult couples–only resort.

Azul Sensatori Jamaica $$ This place is a find, whether you're traveling with kids or as a couple. This property will be undergoing renovations over the next few years to bring it up to the impeccable 5-star standards of Karisma Resorts, a collection of Gourmet Inclusive resorts in the Riviera Maya and now Negril. When you book, ask for a room away from any construction. There are plenty of supervised activities for kids of all ages, but the real stars of this property are the stellar chef and picture-perfect beach location. Especially good for romance is the adult-only section, the beachfront honeymoon swim-up suite, and ocean-view family loft suites that puts kids upstairs. Fit for a king and queen, at steeply discounted prices during renovations.

Norman Manley Blvd. ✆ **888/280-8810.** www.karismahotels.com/hotelsresorts.

Coco La Palm $ Coco La Palm's open courtyards, lush gardens, and native architecture embrace you as though you've found a paradisiacal home away from home. This small hotel sits right on the famous Seven Mile Beach and is perfect for honeymooners. If that's the purpose of your trip, by all means book its honeymoon suite with a beach view of a lifetime; otherwise, go for a reasonable junior suite king, or pay slightly more for an oceanside suite, both with private decks (if you need grab bars to get in/out of the shower, ask for a room that is equipped). Breakfast in its open-air restaurant starts you with fresh baked banana bread while you wait for your order.

Unlike the cloistered big resorts, you actually will see and meet friendly Jamaicans on the beach here, some strumming instruments to serenade you and offering to braid your hair. In the evening, you don't need a car. Just idle along the beach in flip-flops to casual restaurants and reggae clubs nearby. We go during "shoulder season" (after Thanksgiving but before Christmas) when the rates are still quite low.

Norman Manley Blvd. ✆ **800/320-8821** or 876/957-4227. www.cocolapalm.com.

The Rockhouse Hotel $ If you feel cloistered at an all-inclusive resort but don't want to be in the path of the beach souvenir hawkers, we recommend this remote hotel that stretches across the cliffs of Pristine Cove within 8 acres of tropical lush gardens. Its exotic thatched roofed villas perch on the water's edge; your hedonistic potential jumps exponentially when you shower together among the rugged rocks outdoors on your private terrace. Guests swim in the 60-foot horizon pool or use the stairs carved into the rocks down to the cove for snorkeling on the reef.

West End Rd. ✆ **876/618-1533.** www.rockhousehotel.com.

MOST ROMANTIC RESTAURANTS

Beachside lunches are a delight. Get true local flavor by crossing the street at Coco La Palm resort on Norman Manley Boulevard for a to-go jerk chicken lunch at **Best in the West**. Then bring it back to the shaded beach tables at your hotel for an easy-going meal. Two doors up from the hotel find the friendly staff of **Sun Beach Restaurant and Bar** (✆ **876/957-9118**) where the local fish sandwich is delicious (as is the curry chicken platter and other inexpensive Jamaican cuisine). The next day, grab lunch in tiny downtown Negril at **Juici Patties** (just ask a local to point it out), or just wait until a "patty mon" walks his bike (with cardboard box full of goodies) past your beach chair, and then let one of the women fruit vendors slice up pineapple or mango pieces for a sensual dessert.

Ivan's Bar $$ JAMAICAN This impressive, terraced oceanfront restaurant has a clifftop setting with amazing romantic sunset views. Try the succulent Lobster Thermidor for a treat.

In Catcha Falling Star on West End Rd. ✆ **876/957-0390.** www.catchajamaica.com/ivans.htm.

The Rockhouse Restaurant and Bar $ INTERNATIONAL This is another romantic place in Negril to watch the sun go down from the wood-hewn terraced restaurant while eating some of the best food in Negril, prepared by one of Jamaica's most honored chefs, Warren Rowe.

In the Rockhouse Hotel on West End Rd. ✆ 876/618-1533. www.rockhousehotel.com/eat.

NEGRIL BY NIGHT

The most romantic way to kick off your evening is to view the sunset at the famous **Rick's Café,** on West End Road (✆ **876/957-0380;** www.rickscafejamaica.com), with the West End Cliffs being the perfect site to share a moment of awe, beholding both the setting sun and Negril's death-defying cliff divers. You'll feel like locals as you listen to Rick's house band **Dollyman** jammin' true Jamaican reggae; try a banana daiquiri.

Some of the best reggae bands in Jamaica show up in Negril. Most of the small clubs are on Norman Manley Boulevard and set directly on Seven Mile Beach for dancing; they take turns hosting, and guys on the beach hand out invitations so you know where to go that night (local bands start around 9:30pm;

headliners show up later). These places are really informal so show up in your flip-flops. Give a listen at the makeshift beach fence before paying admission.

If you want to crank up the heat several notches, head for **Hedonism II** (© **631/588-4336;** www.hedonism.com), the most pleasure-focused all-inclusive in Jamaica. A night pass (around $75) gets you in and includes all the food, drink, and entertainment you can handle. You'll see the resort's guests are in thong bikinis in one of the hottest discos in all of Jamaica.

ST. LUCIA
Peaks, Beaches & Verdant Views

The word verdant was invented for St. Lucia. Or it should have been. St. Lucia is a sea of green juxtaposed against an equally compelling sea of blue. Vibrant energy pulsates from the forests and hills of this beautiful Caribbean island, closer to South America than to the United States. It has some of the most awesome scenery in the Caribbean, plus the usual pleasures of hibiscus flowers everywhere and mango trees begging to be plucked. The island is only 27 miles long and 14 miles wide and, because it has a perimeter road, it is easy to see it all. Many side roads are serpentine, narrow, and a bit perilous, so be alert if you go off the main highway.

St. Lucia is a pleasing combination of great luxury and inspiring natural resources. The **Edmund Rainforest,** which covers the island, could consume your days if you wanted it to. It's a natural set for a romantic movie with pooling waterfalls, streams running through picturesque ravines and valleys, and hills that interrupt the skyline in interesting and dramatic shapes. From time to time, parrots flit into view, so vividly colored that they seem unreal. Mountains like the famous Pitons (a UNESCO World Heritage site) are so steep that they seem carved by a knife, and inside the jungle, you actually can swing on the hanging vines—again something out of a movie, except that it is real. This is a place for lovers, adventurers, and people who are a bit of both.

KEY ATTRACTIONS

Cas-en Bas Beach   The beautiful mile-long beach at Gros Inlet on the Atlantic is a romantic setting for a picnic, or a restaurant meal on the beach—right after your romantic bareback pony rides! Also, plan to walk, swim, and windsurf. Your hotel can rent you windsurfing or kite-boarding equipment (or recommend a place that will) or rent horses for a splash in the surf or a trailride.

Diamond Falls Botanical Gardens & Mineral Baths   This six-acre garden is all that remains from a huge, 18th-century estate, but this lovely landscape near Soufriere feels expansive and offers many indigenous tropical flowering plants. By their nature, flowers are romantic; you could share an intimate moment among them.

© **758/459-7155.** http://diamondstlucia.com. Admission $5.50 adults.

Fond Doux Estate   This 35-acre cocoa plantation in the Soufriere Valley has a cool tour and a small number of cottages for rent (inexpensive for this island). Restaurants here serve delicious fresh fish and vegetables grown on the estate, which supplies cocoa to the United States (specifically for Hershey chocolates). You can buy some special products that don't make it out of the country in their gift shop. Cocoa and chocolate, you may remember, have aphrodisiac qualities.

© **758/459-7545.** http://fonddouxestate.com.

Hiking   **En Bas Saute** is a 3-mile loop that includes a picnic area that will make you want to linger and a bonus waterfall. You can take an easy stroll along the **Doree River** in the southern part of the island or, for something more demanding, partner along the **Des Cartiers Rain Forest Trail** in La Sociere Mountains. If you want to climb **Gros Piton**, you will need permission in advance by the Forest and Lands Department. But think twice: It is demanding, often slippery terrain, and minor injuries are not unlikely (*©* **758/ 450-2078**). Even if you are experienced, we recommend you forget about climbing Petit Piton; it's considered dangerous. If you'd like an easy excursion, hike to **Fort Rodney** on Pigeon Island, which is connected by a causeway to the mainland. Take a break at the **Pigeon Island Museum and Interpretive Center** (*©* 758/452-5005; admission $2 adults). Rodney Bay, an area of shops and restaurants, isn't far away if you want to end the day catering to your more sybaritic sides.

La Soufriere Volcano   La Soufriere is known as "the world's only drive-in volcano," meaning, you can drive up to the dormant volcano and visit springs that still issue steam and other signs of geothermal life. The hot springs draw many visitors to **Sulphur Spring Park** (*©* 758/459-5726; http:///soufriere-foundation.org), who come to soak in the springs and mud baths. You won't stand the heat for long (or the heavy sulphur odor, for that matter) but many visitors say that their skin thanks them after a quick dip. It's a short drive to Soufriere, a tourist town on the West Coast; it's best to visit later in the day when the traffic is lighter.

The Pietons   The **Gros** and **Petit Pieton Mountains** are the triangular peaks that help distinguish St. Lucia from other Caribbean islands. These are the mountains that you will see in most advertisements for the island, and you can see them from all over the island. If you are driving, each new turn opens up another angle on the trademark peaks, and each stands alone when viewed from the beach. If you are not intimidated by the switchback roads that take you up the mountains, your drive will open up a gorgeous territorial view, punctuated by waterfalls and exotic forest plants.

Snorkeling   Of the many wonderful snorkeling spots, some are only accessible by boat. One of the best is the unfortunately named Bay of Pigs (Anse Cochon). So if you can get past the unfortunate name, you will find the reef in in great shape with a shipwreck nearby. (We think exploring shipwrecks is oddly romantic.) To visit, you'll need to purchase a day pass at **Ti Kaye Village Resort** (☏ **758/456-8101**; www.tikaye.com); your passes cover renting all the gear for your excursion, plus massages for each of you.

Taking a Day Cruise   Various tour operators will take you to bays around the island to swim, snorkel, or just luxuriate on the boat, taking in scenery and sun. Two we like: **Endless Summer Cruises** (☏ **758/450-8651**; http://stlucia boattours.com) and **Sail Oasis** (☏ **800/263-4202**; www.sail-caribbean.com).

HOTELS WITH HEART

For ultimate, lavish privacy with unique accommodations (rooms only have three walls, completely open to a view of the Pietons and the weather [hence, the heavily-netted beds]), Jade Mountain **($$$; ☏ 800/223-1108;** www.jade-mountainstlucia.com) *is* a magical resort, located at the highest point of the Anse Chastanet resort.

The Jalousie Plantation $$$ On the entrancing Sugar Beach, this deluxe hideaway shines with service, views, and charm. Roomy villas and bungalows have infinity pools and drop-dead gorgeous views of the Pitons. The Rainforest Spa is excellent and has unusual treatments (for example, massages using bamboo sticks) in lovely thatched-roof rooms on stilts in a lush forested setting. Even if you don't stay here, you can buy a day pass to use the picture-perfect beach, restaurant, and bar. Consider upping your restaurant budget a bit to enjoy the excellent Great Room, specializing in innovative Caribbean dishes.

Val des Pitons. ☏ **758/456-8000.** www.jalousieplantation.com.

Ladera $$$ Stacked 1,000 feet high on a mountainside, this luxurious resort has won many popularity polls. Its villas and open-sided suites offer magnificent views of the Pitons, the sea, and the sunset, as well as private pools, of course. The view of the bay and the two peaks really is stunning, but if you can't afford to stay here, the budget view is available at the **T'Cholit Bar** at sunset.

☏ **866/290-0978** or 758/459-6618. www.ladera.com.

Stonefield Resort and Estates $$$ These lovely one- to three-bedroom villas, some with private pools and all with porches, hammocks, and expansive views is the perfect hideaway for lovers. The centerpiece of the tree-framed resort is the **Mango Tree** restaurant, which faces the sea and is a romantic place for drinks or dinner.

☏ **800/420-5731** or 758/459-7037. www.stonefieldresort.com.

MOST ROMANTIC RESTAURANTS

The restaurant at the ultra-luxe **Jade Mountain ($$$; ☏ 758/459-4000;** www. jademountainstlucia.com) is wrapped around an infinity pool and worth the splurge.

Apsara at Trou Au Diable Soufriere $$ CARIBBEAN/EAST INDIAN Excellent Indian-Caribbean dining on the beach, priced from moderate to expensive. A steep set of stairs takes you down to the beach. This 500-acre resort also has fantastic views of the Pitons.

At the Anse Chastanet Resort. ☏ **800/223-1103** or 758/459-7000. www.anse chastanet.com/dining.

Boucan in the Hotel Chocolat $$ INTERNATIONAL The restaurant is on a cacao plantation, and the food quite naturally is cacao inspired, making for innovative flavors. Dinner is served at a lush tropical patio under the romantic light of tiki torches.

The Rabot Estate. ☏ **758/572-9600.** www.thehotelchocolat.com.

Dasheene at Ladera $$ WEST INDIAN Dramatic cliff side dining with a view of the Caribbean and the Pitons that could almost, but not quite, make you forget how delicious the West Indian food is on the plate in front of you (try the blackened tuna with papaya). It's a great place for lunch and dinner; reserve the terrace (by the way, this might be a very good place to declare your love).

☏ **758/459-6623.** www.ladera.com.

ST. LUCIA BY NIGHT

On Friday evenings, locals gather at **Anse La Raye** for fresh grilled fish, and reggae fills the restaurants and bars on Front Street. There is also the **Gros Islet Street Party** on Daphne Street. On Saturday nights, the town of **Dennery** on the East Coast hosts the party. And people here party in a happy and relaxed way. You can let out your inner Caribbean here. On Sunday evenings there is usually jazz at the charming and inexpensive **Jambe de Bois** (☏ **758/450-8166**) on Pigeon Island—a mellow, soulful kind of evening.

We suggest you have dinner one night at the affordable **Chateau Mygo House of Seafood,** Marigot Bay (☏ **758/721-7007;** www.chateaumygo.com), and dance the night away to their spirited Creole live music. At the **Fire Grill and Lounge Bar,** Reduit Beach Ave., Rodney Bay Village (**$$$;** ☏ **758/451-4745;** www.firegrillstlucia.com), you can taste drinks made from the largest rum selection on the island. It's a great place to relax and have a casual dinner, or you can just come for the weekly jazz and blues bands.

SULTRY SHORES: EUROPE

The beaches of Europe often aren't as powdery or as white as those of the Caribbean or Mexico. But there's something about the communities that have grown up around these strands that make them as appealing, if not more, than those places where you can dig your toes deep into fluffy sand. These centuries-old towns have a certain elán about them, a sophistication that goes well beyond "fun in the sun." Head to the coast of Europe with your sweetheart and you'll experience areas that are rich in both natural beauty and culture, places where stylishness is a habit and "amour" is respected as one of the rewards of a life well lived. There are few better places in the world to rekindle romance.

AMALFI COAST
Curve Your Enthusiasm

The site of dozens of romantic movies and untold romantic fantasies, Italy's Amalfi Coast exudes pure glamour. The 25 miles of twisting and turning highway that runs along the cliff-flanked coast—a drive that takes you through a sparkling set of exquisite towns and long stretches of sheer cliffs, green hills, and seascapes—is reason enough to visit. It's the type of landscape that will make you want to hug, kiss, make love, and explore this blue and mountainous world all the more. But on the practical side, we'd suggest you either hire a driver or take the bus (Amalfi–Salerno line) as the hairpin turns on these mountainous roads can be hair-raising. With someone else doing the driving, all you have to do is hold hands, and soak it all in.

Your journey starts at Ravello and Amalfi, meanders through colorful Positano, and then continues on to the less well-known Nerano and off to the island of Capri—but we urge you to explore even more on your own. You might want to head back to Sorrento and fly out of nearby Naples, possibly stopping at the famous ruins and reconstructions of Pompeii. (Pompeii is usually a must-see, but given your romantic goals, its tragic themes may not hit the right note.)

Amalfi

Amalfi is the main hub on the coast, with a sweet central plaza, a cathedral, charming outdoor cafes, and, in season, lots of tourists. Cute shops sell marine antiques, lemon products (limoncello, a lemon liqueur, is the regional drink), and other pricey items, but not the chic international brands you will see in Positano or Capri. The town dates back at least to the 6th century and over the centuries became a port for spices and other exotic goods. A 12th-century earthquake wiped out Amalfi's ancient buildings, and its modern identity is as a picturesque cliffside fishing village.

KEY ATTRACTIONS

Boating the Coast Amalfi isn't a beach town, though some small, mostly rocky beaches are attached to the coastal hotels. Hire a boat at the Marina Grande and explore the coastline from the water. You also can visit lovely coves and nearby beaches such as Duoglio and Santa Croce this way. Other options: During the summer months, for just a few euro, you can take a local boat service that runs all day from the town of Amalfi.

Exploring the Land A bus from Amalfi travels along the coast; you can alight at the town of your choice and then descend about 400 steps to the beach.

Hiking This is primo territory for those who love to walk, and we particularly recommend the easy and wonderful hike through the valley of the Torrente-Canneto, known as **Valle dei Mulini** (Valley of the Mills), a World Heritage Site noted for its picturesque and unspoiled environment. Start in town and, about an hour later, arrive at the Mulino Rovinato (Ruined Mill). For a more demanding trail, continue through the Vallone delle Ferriere (Ironworks Gorge) and see very old iron mills operated from medieval times into the 19th century. If you are really fit, continue up the steep ascent to view the waterfalls. It's a 2-hour walk if you do just the first leg of the hike, but 6 hours if you go to the falls. Another famous scenic hike, parts of it quite challenging, is the **Via degli Incanti** (Trail of Charms), which connects Amalfi to Positano through the countryside. Most people do just a section of this trail or camp out and do the hike in several days.

The Duomo This striking building, begun sometime in the 9th century, has an intricate, geometric facade and a remarkable 11th-century bronze door. Every century since has added decoration or architectural interest, including a baroque interior and a magnificent staircase leading to a lovely black and white marble atrium. The adjacent 13th-century cloister has Moorish arches and is alone worth visiting. In summer, concerts are held here on Friday nights.

Via Duca Mansone 1. ℭ 39/**089-871-059.** www.amalfitouristoffice.it.

HOTELS WITH HEART

Hotel Lido Mare $ One of Amalfi's few bargains is set on a small square just beyond the main street fray, and provides a lot of pleasant, old-fashioned ambience in a 13th-century palazzo. Some of the large, high-ceilinged, tile-floored rooms have sea views, and all are furnished with a scattering of antiques. Amalfi's beach is just steps away.

Largo Piccolomini 9. ℂ **39/089-871332.** www.lidomare.it.

Hotel Luna Convento $$ This hotel, a former 13th-century convent, has taken over Amalfi's 6th-century watchtower overlooking the harbor. In the midst of a garden, with terraces and a large seawater swimming pool at the edge of a cliff, Hotel Luna has two restaurants, one with terrific sea views. If you want someplace to go after dinner, this is your place—with a disco and a piano bar. Guest rooms vary but all are good-sized, are cheerful, and—most important—have excellent views. Ask for a room with a private terrace. The staff also can organize speedboat tours of the area if you wish.

Via Pantaleone Comite 33. ℂ **39/089-871-002.** www.lunahotel.it. Closed Jan 8–Feb 28.

Hotel Marina Riviera $$$ Close to both the harbor and historic center, the Hotel Marina Riviera fulfills that all-important romantic consideration: It has exquisite views. All the rooms have water views, and some have terraces or balconies. Furnishings are simple, but handsome. Not all bathrooms have a tub, however, so ask! The hotel restaurant offers romantic views of the bay and hillside, and it specializes in fine, fresh fish creations and an elaborate wine list.

Via Pantaleone Comite 19. ℂ **39/089-871-104.** www.marinariviera.it.

Hotel Santa Caterina $$$ This is the top of the line in Amalfi. The romance is in the cliffside dining, private beach, and wonderful gardens and citrus groves. There is also a very nice saltwater pool. Guest rooms are spacious and charming with antique furnishings and decorative ceramic tiles. The bathrooms are luxurious but if you, like us, want a bathtub as part of your romantic sojourn, make sure your room has one. All rooms have a balcony or patio and a sea view. Suites are a big step up: Some have a private garden and snuggle into the lemon trees, and a few have a small pool.

S.S. Amalfitana 9. ℂ **39/089-871-012.** www.hotelsantacaterina.it.

MOST ROMANTIC RESTAURANTS

La Caravella $$$ MODERN AMALFITAN   La Caravella, set in a grand dining room in a 12th-century *palazzo,* has been romancing diners since 1959, becoming a Mecca to many gourmets. It has no view but inside is quite elegant, with ornate table settings and formal service. The seasonal tasting menus, graced with wonderful pasta and seafood dishes, are a worthy splurge.

Via Matteo Camera 12. ℂ **39/089-871029.** www.ristorantelacaravella.it.

Lido Azzurro $$ AMALFITAN   The views are smashing from this pasta and seafood restaurant, located right on the town's seaside promenade. The menu includes variations of clams, mussels, and fish (a specialty is fish baked in a potato crust).

Via Lungomare dei Cavalieri 5. ✆ **39/089-871-384.** www.ristorantelidoazzurro.it.

Ristorante Santa Caterina $$$ CREATIVE AMALFITAN   This spot is on many a "best" list for European travelers and is among the most prized restaurants on this cuisine-gifted coast. In the beautiful Hotel Santa Caterina, it enjoys an elegant setting and offers innovative pastas and first-rate steaks.

Via Mauro Comite 9. ✆ **39/089-871-012.** www.hotelsantacaterina.it.

AMALFI BY NIGHT

Being a tourist town for a few centuries has its advantages. In the evening, Amalfi teems with open-air cafes, and dining is a celebration. On warm evenings, the **Marina Grande** restaurant, Viale della Regione 4 (**$$;** ✆ **39/089-871-129;** www.ristorantemarinagrande.com), opens a candlelit lounge on the beach with party decor—all for a good time, or *tempo felice*! Nightclubs are hard to find here, but drive to Praiano for the cavernous and outrageous **Africana Famous Club,** Via Terramare 2 (✆ **39/089-874-858;** www.africanafamousclub.com), where you enter on an artsy walkway down to the sea and then dance the night away.

Ravello

This picturesque clifftop village overlooks the sea, and you can see other villages (Minori and Maiori) from town. Ravello is also a ceramics center, and the plates and bowls arranged outside and inside the shops are delightful to look at even if you don't buy (but resisting them is tough). The town always has had its celebrity contingent—Greta Garbo, Pierce Brosnan—and can be crowded in high season.

The internationally famous **Festival di Ravello** (✆ **39/089-858-422;** www.ravellofestival.com) runs July through September and features classical, jazz, and dance performances. The festival makes creative use of Ravello settings, including the Piazza Duomo, Villa Rufolo, and Villa Cimbrone. The **Concerti del l'Aurora**, concerts, performed at dawn, are incredibly romantic.

KEY ATTRACTIONS

Walks   The Monastero di San Nicola makes for a pleasant, easy hike. From the center of Ravello, walk to the village of Sambuco, less than a quarter-mile away, and then climb about 500 feet to the Monastery of Saint Nicholas. To hike to Minori, follow the marked path near the Villa Rufolo fountain; it takes you over steps and through valleys to the town of Torello. Continue on past the olive trees and on to the Minori seashore. It's a pretty and easy half-hour walk, but the return trip is harder, traveling uphill from the sea.

Villa Rufolo   This beautiful 13th-century villa and its romantic gardens are situated on a crest that puts its architectural highlights on grand display. The entrance arches, courtyard, and tree-lined paths grace the way to a handsome inner court; they are all worth exploration. In summer, classical concerts are held in the garden.

Piazza Duomo. ✆ **39/089-857-621.** www.villarufolo.it. Admission 5€ adults, 3€ seniors 65+.

HOTELS WITH HEART

Hotel Graal $$ This family-owned inn offers spacious rooms with sea views at a more moderate price than most of the hotels in this area. The on-site restaurant creates delightful lemon-inspired dishes of the region.

Via della Repubblica 8.. ✆ **39/089-857-222.** www.hotelgraal.it.

Palazzo Avino $$$ Here's a romantic dream: an elegant 12th-century palace on the side of a steep mountain. If you can afford it, this is a world-class destination, a honeymoon haven. Rooms are full of antiques, lovely textiles, and flooring created by local tile-makers. Not all the rooms have views, but they are all expansive, and some of the suites are huge. (Try for room numbers 1, 201, 204, 301, and suite 304.) The bathrooms are gorgeous, with Italian marble and large tubs, perfect for two. The restaurant Sasso, a short shuttle ride away on a terrace above the sea, is equally romantic.

Via San Giovanni del Toro 28. ✆ **39/089-818-181.** www.palazzoavino.com. Closed Oct 27–Mar 31.

Villa Maria Hotel $$ The gardens of the lovely Villa Maria overlook the sea, and the large, sun-filled guest rooms are accented by colorful tiled floors and bathrooms. **Ristorante Villa Maria** inspires romance on a terrace draped with greenery—it's worth dining here even if you aren't a guest—and the menu features food from the hotel's organic garden. If you are a pair of traveling foodies, consider signing up for a class at their well-respected cooking school.

Via Santa Chiara 2. ✆ **39/089-857-255.** www.villamaria.it.

MOST ROMANTIC RESTAURANTS

Da Salvatore $$ AMALFITAN   Da Salvatore's water views from its dining room and garden terrace are beyond delicious—and the food is pretty good, too. Here, a friendly staff serves up well-prepared Italian comfort food in an atmosphere of casual ambience. Grilled fish and pasta choices are excellent, and the homemade breads are a standout.

Via della Repubblica 2. ✆ **39/089-857-227.** www.salvatoreravello.com.

Rosellinis $$$ CREATIVE AMALFITAN   Chef Pino Lavarra's elegant restaurant has been recognized by two Michelin stars. He struts his stuff on his tasting menu with large ravioli filled with crab and a liberal use of local olives. As you might have suspected, this restaurant is very expensive and should be reserved for a special night out.

Via San Giovanni del Toro 28. ✆ **39/089-818-181.** www.palazzoavino.com. Closed Nov–Mar.

The Restaurant at Villa Maria Hotel $$ AMALFITAN   This is one of our favorites; their pastas are exceptional, as are the *grigliata mista* (grilled fish or meats).

Via Santa Chiara 2. ✆ **39/089-857-255.** www.villamaria.it

RAVELLO BY NIGHT

Ravello is a quiet town, so don't expect razzle-dazzle. What passes for evening antics takes place around the main square, where folks congregate at the *tavernas* and pizzerias to talk and sip on something. **Bar Calce,** Via Roma 2 (✆ **39/089-857-152**), near the Duomo, won't disappoint. Of course, in summer, you could pick up tickets for a performance at the **Festival di Ravello** (see above).

Nerano

This is the closest town on the mainland to Capri, and the last town on the Amalfi Coast before you hit Sorrento. Nerano is an inspired place to have lunch before you take a hydrofoil to Capri. (You can kayak there, too, but it's a demanding 8 miles, so make sure you know what you are doing.) Feel the love at Nerano's fine dining spot, **Quattro Passi,** on Via Vespucci (**$$;** ✆ **39/081-8082-800**; www.ristorantequattropassi.com); enjoy the embrace of the floriferous patio.

Capri

Capri's reputation as a romantic getaway seems unshakable. No wonder. The town is so charming it looks like a movie set for a love story. The streets unravel here along narrow pathways; we suggest you abandon any goals and see where the streets take you. As you walk—tall pines, cypress, and palms are everywhere—the street will ultimately lead to a plaza somewhere. If you actually need to get somewhere specific, take a taxi, but try to grab a convertible one (and up the romance quotient)! Sure, Capri has become commercialized, and every high-end designer has set up shop here—but in the evening, when the streets are quiet, the charm of the flowers and cute little houses overwhelms whatever changes its popularity has wrought.

KEY ATTRACTIONS

Capri's Famous Rocks   Take a taxi to the crest of the island to get a beautiful view of the **Faraglioni rocks** coming out of the water like giant sculptures. You can also get close and personal with these dramatic spires on a tour boat that goes through the rocky archway. It might sound hokey, but it's wonderful. Try **Capri Guide Services** at Via Aiano di Sopra 10 (✆ **39/081-8377-878**; www.capriguideservices.com).

The View From the Top   The romance of this area is closely linked to its splendid views. Take a taxi to the top of the island, and your reward will be an endless view of Sorrento, the Gulf of Naples, Naples, and even Vesuvius, the volcano that razed Pompeii in A.D. 79. The **Chairlift to Monte Solaro** (✆ **39/081-8371438**; www.capriseggiovia.it; 7.50€ one-way, 10€ round-trip) offers fabulous views of dramatic cliffs and the sea; you can board the lift in Anacapri, a short walk along a very easy trail.

   Note: It's a sheer drop, so take a pass if you suffer from vertigo.

Walks   Just a few minutes' walk from the Piazzetta, near the Via Krupp, the **Gardens of Augustus** make for very romantic walks and knockout views of the Mediterranean.

HOTELS WITH HEART

Caesar Augustus $$$ It doesn't get much more spectacular than this villa. In the front, beautiful gardens, and in the back, terraces perched above a sheer 1,000-foot cliff. If you can swing it, this is a serene place for your romantic getaway, and losing yourselves in the two-tier infinity pool could make your afternoon. Rooms are subtle (especially compared to the canary yellow front of the villa), floors are tiled, beds are wrought iron, and you will have your own balcony or terrace cliffside. The spa is an added bonus.

Via G.Orlandi 4. ℭ **39/081-8373395.** www.caesar-augustus.com.

Capri Palace $$$ The pick of the glittery litter is the elegant Capri Palace, surrounded by manicured gardens and decorated with antiques, while still maintaining a modern feel. We love it especially for its outstanding restaurant, **L'Olivo** (see below).

Via Capodimonte 14; ℭ **39/081-9780-111;** www.capripalace.com

La Guardia Bed & Breakfast $ This two-bedroom B&B near the Punta Carena lighthouse is outside the town of Capri but worth the 10-minute commute. It is an exception to our usual aversion to B&Bs for romance, because it is so hospitable that you feel like you're one of the locals and no longer a tourist. Both bedrooms have a sea view, and there is a pool and terrace with a gorgeous 180-degree view.

Via la Guardia 47. ℭ **39/081-8372-667.** bblaguardia@virgilio.it.

Luna Hotel $$$ We like the Luna because it's modern, has luxurious rooms, and also boasts a wonderful cliff-top location. The elegant rooms have a panorama of the cliffs or the gardens, and the bathrooms are large. Some bathrooms have a shower only, so if you want a tub, like we do, ask when booking. The restaurant is excellent and has a charming and romantic setting.

Viale Matteotti 3. ℭ **39/081-8370-433.** www.lunahotel.com.

MOST ROMANTIC RESTAURANTS

Lido del Faro $$ CAPRESE   This moderately priced spot is in a striking, secluded seaside setting in the southwestern corner of the island, tucked into the spiky rocks below the lighthouse. A destination in itself, it also has a beach club and a place for special events. Regional seafood is the main event here, but there are other good choices. Reserve well ahead for dinner. Lunch is a simpler affair: You can go to Lido's beach and swim in the saltwater pool or in a sheltered cove of the Mediterranean. Then eat lunch or have an early dinner when the patrons thin out a bit.

Località Punta Carena. ℭ **39/081-8371798.** www.lidofaro.com.

L'Olivo $$$ CREATIVE CAPRESE   This is the place to splurge for a meal on Capri. When you are skillfully escorted to your table and look at the place settings of silver, delicate glasses and lovely cloth, you remember that truly fine restaurants do not miss a detail. Considered one of the best restaurants of the region, it was created by German Chef Oliver Glowig, who makes symphonies with fresh fish and tasting menus.

Via Capodimonte 14. ℗ **39/081-9780-111.** www.capripalace.com.

CAPRI BY NIGHT

The hotels on Capri have wonderful cocktail bars, some with entertainment. One of the most romantic is **Quisi Bar e Terrazza**, Grand Hotel Quisisana Capri, Via Camerelle 2 (℗ **39/081-8370-788**; www.quisisana.com), a classy bar on the terrace of the elegant Quisi restaurant, which is also great for a candlelight dinner. The famed **La Lanterna Verde Club,** Via G. Orlandi 1 (℗ **39/081-8371427**; www.lanternaverdecapri.it), at the Hotel San Michele is built into a white rock with windows facing the sea and Vesuvius!

DALMATIAN COAST: DUBROVNIK, SPLIT, HVAR & KORČULA

Ancient Cities, Arresting Coastline

The Adriatic coastline in Croatia is so fantastical that sometimes it feels like a Disney creation. Most tackle it as a road trip, and so should you, as this is a wildly romantic drive through historic and eye poppingly lovely coastal villages and cities. But the coast also can be explored by sailboat, ship, or ferry. And the dramatic views rival those of Italy's Amalfi Coast. Your itinerary should include at least two or three cities besides Dubrovnik, and perhaps an island or two (choose from thousands!). We are partial to the cities described here for their mesmerizing landscapes and rich architectural traditions.

Dubrovnik

Lord Byron called it "the pearl of the Adriatic," and it is a jewel of a city in an irresistible setting: surrounded on three sides by the Adriatic Sea and on the fourth by the limestone Srđ Mountain. Dubrovnik was imperiled by an earthquake in 1979 and bombings in the early 1990s during Croatia's war for independence, but it has come back strong.

A UNESCO conservation site and World Heritage site, Dubrovnik has beautiful weather and beaches and draws a crowd in summer, but it's never really empty. Your best chance of getting the feel of the city is in the early morning, especially in spring or fall. Get there before the cruise ships do!

KEY ATTRACTIONS

Walk, Walk, Walk   Feel the city, visit the historic churches, and admire the architecture. The walk into the Old Town through the Ploce Gate on the Placa is a walk through time: The arched entry opens on a perfectly preserved late-Medieval walled city. To the left, just past the gates, you'll see a pharmacy that claims to be the oldest in the world; a great souvenir is the divine face cream still made by the Franciscan monks who have produced the formula since the 1300s. The grand wide boulevards, like the highly buffed limestone Stradun (the Placa) (*caution:* It's slippery when wet), are busy with outdoor cafes and stores selling local products like lace, oils, and lavender. All of this is located near beautiful Baroque churches, Renaissance palaces, and a historic synagogue. Sightsee first and then go to an open-air market where you can stock a picnic basket to unpack later at the beach or harbor.

Luza Square   Luza is the crossroads of the city, day and night. Explore the exhibits in **Sponza Palace,** visit the city bell tower (which rings each hour), see the 12th–century **Gradska Kavana** community center, and take a break on the steps of **St. Blaise Church.** You can act like locals and cool off with water from the square's 15th–century **Onofrio's Little Fountain.** Luza marks the start of Dubrovnik's Summer Festival and the place where many religious processions end.

The Ramparts   Climb the irregular steps to traverse the entire old city wall; it takes about 90 minutes. You not only get terrific views of the seascape and landscape, but you get to peer into the courtyards and alleys and see how people live now in this ancient fairytale city. Of course, there are also plenty of nooks that provide private places to kiss. This would be one of those perfect places to propose.

HOTELS WITH HEART

Hilton Imperial Dubrovnik $$$ This hotel couldn't be more centrally situated, and it has the romance of old elegant 19th-century hotels. Many of the rooms provide captivating views over the Old Town and the Adriatic.

Marijana Blažića 2. ✆ **385/20-320-320.** www.hilton.com.

The Hotel Excelsior $$ This elegant art deco hotel, reconstructed in 2008, provides guest rooms that are sunny and classy and have views of the sea and the port. Bathrooms have broad windows that let in the sea air. The service is gracious, and you can have drinks at the romantic Abakus piano bar; then have fine sushi at Satu.

Frana Supila 12. ✆ **385/20-430-830.** www.hotel-excelsior.hr.

Villa Dubrovnik $$$ This smallish hotel closes for the winter, but is romantically viable in other seasons because of its decent off-season rates and its guest-room balconies that overlook gardens and a secluded beach. You are on the cliffs over Dubrovnik, which naturally afford great views, and you can also use the hotel's boat service to take you to Old Town.

Vlaha Bukovca 6. ✆ **385/20-500-300.** www.villa-dubrovnik.hr.

MOST ROMANTIC RESTAURANTS

Konoba Lokanda Peskarija $ DALMATIAN   A charming cafe, it's next to the harbor on a terrace that lets you breath in the ocean air and smooch a bit while you watch the boats and enjoy superb local fish, shrimp, and oysters (not to mention the fab risotto).

Na Ponti bb. ✆ **385/20-324-750.** www.mea-culpa.hr.

More $$ MODERN DALMATIAN Located in the Hotel More, this imaginative and reasonably priced restaurant offers breathtaking views of the Adriatic by day and night, alongside its creative, mostly Dalmation cuisine. You'll work up an appetite for your meal by climbing a significant hill to get here. For romance we'd opt for a table on the terrace, but true foodies may prefer a table in the dining room with a view of the chef in the open kitchen.

Kardinala Stepinca 33. ✆ **385/20-494-200.** www.hotel-more.hr.

Proto $ SEAFOOD Proto has a sidewalk cafe and a rooftop terrace; both offer traditional, freshly grilled fish, but the primo setting is on the upstairs terrace, where the breezes and the view are sublime. Glass panels make it possible to dine in an intimate nook with stone walls and dark wood while enjoying a winter garden.

Široka ulica 1. ✆ **385/20-323-234**.

DUBROVNIK BY NIGHT

D'vino Wine Bar This lovely Old Town bar near the Stradun is perfect after shopping or sightseeing, or after dinner when you want to relax together. It offers dozens of wines by the glass, but they are not limited to regional fare—D'vino's cellar stows vintages from the world's great wine regions and offers wine flights for tasting. It's open to midnight daily. Palmoticeva 4a. ✆ **385/20-321-130.** http://dvino.net.

Trubadur Hard Jazz Cafe This is a well-known jazz club, with extras. You can get close to the live performers inside, or snuggle up on cushy seating outdoors under umbrellas and still hear the jam—and if your love for music exceeds your love for fine dining, you can grab a sandwich here. *A practical note:* It's a Hotspot zone, so you can catch up on your email. Bunićeva poljana 2. ✆ **385/20-323-476.**

Split

With one of the area's two major airports, Split is often a first stop on the Dalmation Coast tour. But even if there were no airport, you would want to see what's left of the 4th-century retirement palace of the Roman emperor Diocletian. The glorious palace ruins now support restaurants, shops, and private homes. Beyond the ruins, Split's beaches are an equally magnetic draw. The waterfront, called the **Riva**, is one of Croatia's busiest promenades, with excellent shopping (best bets: jewelry and olive oil) and people watching. In the morning, after the market or before their days begin, folks linger over coffee at sidewalk tables—and the tables remain busy all day. The Riva is never deserted, but it's at its busiest in the evening when people dine, stroll its length, or arrive and depart on the evening ferries.

HOTELS WITH HEART

Hotel Vestibul Palace $ This boutique hotel, on a site adjacent to what was once Diocletian's bedroom, was renovated brilliantly. Artisans took care to expose original Roman stone walls and brickwork but then carefully blended the antiquities with modern glasswork and other design details. Each room incorporates some detail of the palace with modern amenities such as flatscreen TVs.

Ulica Iza Vestibula 4. ℂ **385/21-329-329.** www.vestibulpalace.com.

MOST ROMANTIC RESTAURANTS

Restoran Boban $ DALMATIAN   One of Split's top restaurants, Boban is moderately priced nonetheless. The menu covers a wide range of seafood, meats, and traditional Croatian specialties, all excellent. The very good wine list favors mostly regional vintages. You'll find the mood is right for romance both in the dining room and on the charming outdoor terrace. A good choice for a late dinner, this place stays open until midnight.

Hektorovićeva 49. ℂ **385/21-543-300.** www.restaurant-boban.com.

Restoran Sumica $$$ SEAFOOD   This is an expensive choice, but one you won't regret. The romantic atmosphere and incredible seafood make this an almost required stop. We strongly recommend the house specialty, tagliatelle with scampi and salmon. Waiters can pair your choices with fine selections from Sumica's great wine list. Dinner . . . on the terrace . . . amid a little pine grove is the perfect romantic spot, but the dining room is airy and lovely, if a bit more formal and public.

Put Firula 6. ℂ **385/21-389-897.**

Hvar

An old Roman city, Hvar has historical sites from the 5th to the 15th centuries. Hvar Town and Stari Grad are the most popular areas, although Hvar Town has become Croatia's Monaco, a glamorous playground of the very wealthy. The bars keep multiplying and are populated by the young and fashionable. All ages are drawn to the almost continually sunny climate. Along with lovely beaches, vineyards cover the deeply alluring grey-green hills, and beautiful fields of lavender are abundant. Unfortunately, the glitz factor has driven up the cost of the hotels and restaurants.

HOTELS WITH HEART

Adriana $$$ Adriana's rooftop terrace is worth a visit, even if you don't stay there (but you can enjoy it a lot more if you do). It has a heated indoor-outdoor seawater pool and a relaxing bar and lounge area. Should you ever leave the rooftop haven to go to your room, you will not be disappointed. The sizeable and bright guest rooms have big bathrooms, and the cheery ambience is quite romantic. The Sensori Spa is another place to go to get lost; you can opt for a couples massage on the spa terrace overlooking the sea.

Obala Fabrika 28. ℂ **385/21-750-555.** www.suncanihvar.com.

Riva $ Historic buildings are wonderful, but they can be stuffy. The charm of this painstakingly renovated hotel is its whimsical and light mood. You may not have a luxury yacht to pull up to the pier, but you can watch others do so from your perch on the grand terrace, which is bordered by a fine pizzeria and a sushi bar. The guest rooms, restricted by historical preservation rules, are small but stylish, with cool modern bathrooms and nice patios.

Obala Riva 27. ✆ **385/21-750-555.** www.suncanihvar.com/riva.

MOST ROMANTIC RESTAURANTS

Dordota Vartal $$ DALMATIAN This romantic terrace restaurant sits on an elevated stone porch that transports you to your own private world. The canopy draped with vines and the pots of refreshing lavender plants create a seductive mood! The menu is 100% Dalmatian, so immerse yourselves in the excellent pastas, grilled meats, and seafood, including, of course, lobster.

Krizna Luka 8. ✆ **385/21-743-077.**

Konoba Menego $ CROATIAN Inexpensive and delicious Croatian food served at long wooden tables in an atmospheric grotto tavern. Go native!

Groda bb. ✆ **385/21-742-036.** www.menego.hr.

Palaca Paladini $ DALMATIAN Gardens are romantic, but the stone-walled, Renaissance-style garden here is one for the ages. Dine among the orange trees that afford a certain privacy. This charming bi-level restaurant specializes in seafood and offers incredible vegetarian meals, too. The specialty is *hvarska gregada*, fish stew with glorious flavors defined by aromatic local herbs.

Trg Tv. Petra Hektorovića 4. ✆ **385/21-742-104.** www.tihi-hvar.com/paladinis.

Korčula Island

Korčula has had its allure for centuries. Its pine-covered hills drew the Romans early on, and they created the stunning walled city of Korčula Town. But modern inhabitants have been busy, too, tending their impressive vineyards, olive groves, and wineries. The island is a great place to hike and visit sleepy towns like Lumbarda and Blato. It's less than 50km (30 miles) across, but still has "hidden" beaches that are worth finding. Take a moment to admire the red-tiled roofs that contrast with the blue Adriatic and don't miss the adjacent Venetian Gothic and Renaissance city palaces. A 3-hour ferry ride from Dubrovnik, the island can be kind of crazy with summer tourists mobbing the ferry terminals. But don't give up. After you climb the 19th-century Grand Staircase with its 15th-century tower and stroll through the 14th-century gate, you will leave the press of tourists.

Behind the wall, Old Town is crisscrossed with picturesque houses, museums, restaurants, and churches—all built with local stone. A profusion of inclined, dark, and narrow streets branch off from the major north-south thoroughfare (Korčulaskog Statuta). One added attraction: Korčula is the birthplace of legendary explorer Marco Polo, and you can tour his house. The city also hosts the annual Moreska Sword Dance, a spectacle about a battle between Christians and "infidels" that was fought over a woman. So the island has a romantic past—you can give it a romantic present!

HOTELS WITH HEART

Hotel Korčula $ The Hotel Korčula is a former waterfront villa on Korčula Town's west side. You'll quickly notice the place has character: You'll want to hang back and have another cup of coffee with breakfast to more fully take in its romantic veranda and expansive terrace. This old treasure has more romantic bravado than any other hotel on Korčula. And even better news: It's pretty reasonably priced. The rooms are small, but lovely, and while they don't have air-conditioning, each room has a fan. You should insist on an ocean view (the small surcharge is worth it).

Obala dr. Franje Tuđmana 5. ℂ **385/20-711-078** or 20-711-732. www.korcula-hotels.com. Additional 10% for sea view.

Lešić Dimitri Palace $$$ This 18th-century bishop's palace, which has been transformed into a luxurious boutique property, is the definition of "the royal treatment." There are only six residences (ranging from 1–4 bedrooms) and each is furnished in the style of a global destination: Arabia, Ceylon, India, China, Venice, and Korčula. All have elegant modern kitchens and over-the-top bathrooms; personalized service comes with every residence. Best of all, they are all just a short walk to the sea. It's super luxe—and priced accordingly.

Don Pavla Poše 1–6. ℂ **385/20-715-560.** www.lesic-dimitri.com.

MOST ROMANTIC RESTAURANTS

Konoba Adio Mare $$ DALMATIAN It's touristy and noisy, but the fresh grilled fish, octopus, and other seafood at this Old Town restaurant are well prepared, reasonably priced, and served with very good wines.

Marka Pola 2 ℂ **385/20-711-253.** www.konobaadiomare.hr.

KORČULA BY NIGHT

Cocktail Bar Massimo Nightlife in Korčula is low key. Still, this Old Town bar in a turret with killer views has a pretty good "wow" factor. Setaliste Petra Karnevelica. ℂ **385/21-715-073.**

GREEK ISLES CRUISE
Sparkling Turquoise Water and Opa!

What couple hasn't thought about visiting the Greek islands? Seeing the whitewashed houses cascading down the cliffsides toward that true-blue sea, people can go weak in the knees. We know we do. And we think the best way to see the Greek islands for the first time is by ship.

A big sailboat or small yacht may be the swanky way, but that's not affordable for most folks. Besides, even yachts don't have the perks of a good-sized cruise ship: restaurant choices, entertainment, naturalists, and a spa. Those options can provide a lot of material for your romantic script.

Cruise ships loop through the 140 inhabited Greek islands in dozens of routes. Most start in **Athens** (or Rome or another close port), stop at **Naupalion** on the mainland, and then visit a variety of islands and possibly parts of **Turkey**. Ships vary from the humongous (1,000+ passengers) to smallish ships or boats with 100 to 300 on board.

We know there are many itineraries available, but in this section we look at one fabulous itinerary that includes some of the best ports you will find on your cruise. We experienced this one aboard the magnificent *Azamara Quest,* which carries about 700 lucky travelers to the mainlands of Greece (**Nauplion**) and Turkey (**Istanbul** and **Bodrum**, see p. 72) and to the islands of **Mykonos**, **Santorini**, and **Rhodes. Azamara Club Cruises** (✆ **877/999-9553;** www.azamaraclubcruises.com; all-inclusive from $2,699 per person) is a luxury line (but not the most expensive), and like all top cruise lines that also have Greek and Mediterranean itineraries, Azamara knows how to pamper its clients in a multitude of ways. On arrival aboard the *Azamara Quest,* for example, you are met with an icy towel, chilled champagne, and assurances that your luggage will magically appear in your room—and it does.

Also plying these waters is the *Oceania Riviera* (✆ **800/386-9283;** www.cruiseoceania.com), which consistently gets raves for service, food, and offshore offerings; it's an elegant choice with five restaurants. Oceania is also one of the more reasonably priced companies and has cabins including meals and some alcohol, starting at $270 a night. For such big ships, Oceania is able to offer intimate excursions, such as visits to small family wineries or businesses that help couples feel special as opposed to herded.

Shopping Around for the Best Cruise Deals

It's a well-known fact that steep discounts are available on many cruise lines. There's a lot of competition for your cruise dollars, and since cruises offer similar itineraries, it pays to shop around. Naturally, you can do this yourself, but there are plenty of travel agents out there who specialize in cruises and can help you navigate the sometimes complex system.

First, check directly with the cruise lines for pricing, and then go to an online consolidators— cruiseguy.com, cruisesonly.com, cruisestar.com, icruise.com, vacationstogo.com, and vca-travel.com, to name a few—and see what kind of discounts they are offering. Some consolidators throw in free airfare, a cabin upgrade, or other valuable lures. Check all your options!

For a small-ship experience, **Seabourn** (② **877/301-2174;** www.seabourn. com) has a line of six smaller ships, which accommodate 200 to 450 passengers, all of them in suites. Everything is included in the initial tariff: tipping, wine, etc., which means you don't have to sweat the small stuff (or worry that the small stuff is accumulating into large stuff). This luxury alternative has a relaxed but elegant atmosphere. Seabourn also has great itineraries sometimes going to less-visited Greek, Turkish, and Middle Eastern stops on their different journeys. Their weekly rates start at $2,800 and go way up from there.

And such mass-volume lines as **Celebrity Cruises** (② **866/592-7225;** www.celebritycruises.com), **Costa Cruises** (② **800/247-7320;** www.costa cruises.com), and **Holland America** (② **877/932-4259;** www.hollandamerica. com) hit the Greek Islands, too (often for as little as $150 a night), though many times visits to Greece will be mixed in with port stops in Turkey and Italy—not necessarily a bad thing.

KEY ATTRACTIONS

Shipboard Romance   We'll set the stage on the model itinerary of the *Azmara Quest.* The ship looks like a luxury hotel inside: elegant dark wood, curving staircases. Room sizes vary, and you get what you pay for. But what you should pay for is an **outside room**—preferably a suite—with a balcony. A suite gets you the balcony, plus space enough for two to dine and lounge and use the bathroom without elbowing each other in a territorial power grab for sink space. Most important for romance: The tub and shower are large enough for two—if you are inclined to soak or spritz together. On many ships, suites come with nice perks: butler service for high tea, snacks, and meals set up for two on your balcony or in your room. We think the romantic settings prepare you for even more intimacy. Ironically, a huge ship can feel intimate. Fares that cover all meals, drinks, and tips are great—on a romantic vacation, it's liberating not to quibble every 10 minutes over whether you can afford another glass of wine or how much to tip!

Perhaps unique to cruises are the opportunities for extraordinary romantic touches. Want a marriage or recommitment ceremony? A special evening out? A room bedecked with rose petals and fresh flowers? It's all possible—just ask. For best results, ask at the beginning of the cruise.

If cruises have a drawback, it is that your stops are brief, and your appetite is only whetted for more. Following are some fabulous stops from the Greek Isle cruise.

Athens

Athens has had a tough time of it lately because of the devastated Greek economy. But we are hopeful it will weather the challenge and remain an inspiring destination. How could you not be awestruck? Athens has one of the great wonders of the world: the Acropolis and Pantheon, which dominates part of its skyline, night or day.

KEY ATTRACTIONS

The Plaka **The Old City.** Full of romantic shops and restaurants with outdoor patios, the **Plaka** has wonderful museums and antiquities along its narrow winding streets. **Adrianou Street** beckons you with its aromatic restaurants, and you'll discover a major ruin, **Hadrian's Library,** along the way. Most of the restaurants here have a gorgeous view of the **Acropolis** (which you'll want to climb up to for a close-up view).

Museums The **National Archeological Museum of Athens,** 44 Patission St. (℃ **30/213-214-4890** or 30/213-214-4800; www.namuseum.gr; admission 7€), lets you walk over a series of glass floors that reveal fascinating archeological finds and ongoing digs below, but the **Acropolis Museum,** 15 Dionysiou Areopagitou St. (℃ **30/210-900-0900;** www.theacropolismuseum.gr; admission 5€; closed Mon), has the antiquities you came to see. The sculptures are glorious, with romantic themes and vision—and some seem to have contemporary sensibilities. You can spend hours here. Best to see both, but if you see only one, make it the Acropolis museum.

HOTELS WITH HEART

You'll need to arrive in Athens at least 1 night before your cruise departs.

Divani Apollon Palace & Spa $$ Well-located on Kavouri beach, this gorgeous resort is surrounded by towering palm trees, lovely gardens, and two large swimming pools. It has an amazingly isolated feeling, for a hotel in a big city. Each room boasts an ocean view with roomy balconies and luxurious marble baths. With its picturesque private beach, this is the most romantic hotel in Athens. Some rooms are quite affordable—which will help you justify a meal in the resort's esteemed seafood eatery, **Mythos of the Sea.** Ask for an oceanside table.

Agiou Nikolaou 10. ℃ **30/210-891-1100.** www.divanis.com/apollon.

Grande Bretagne $$ This iconic hotel is among Athens's most distinguished 19th-century structures and has emerged from a $70-million renovation with aplomb. The incredible Beaux Arts lobby was saved, indoor and outdoor swimming pools were added, and the old faded rooms have been reborn as cheerful sybaritic locations for lovers—guest rooms with balconies overlooking Syntagma Square, the Parliament building, and the Acropolis are especially inspirational. Famous people stay here, so you can expect extraordinary service—and pricey rates.

Syntagma Square. ℃ **30/210-333-0000.** www.grandebretagne.gr.

MOST ROMANTIC RESTAURANTS

Very good affordable dining is available in most neighborhoods at the many romantic outdoor restaurants and little indoor *ouzeries* (cafes that serve small dishes—*mezes*—with ouzo).

Matsuhisa Athens $$$ JAPANESE *Matsu* in Japanese means "pines," and they surround this lovely eatery in the Astir Palace Hotel Complex. The sea views are beautiful, and the food is a wonderful hybrid of traditional and modern Japanese and Greek cuisines. With great confidence, we recommend the black codfish with sweet miso, and the sushi. This place is a splurge, especially if you opt for the seven-course Omakase menu, a meal featuring Chef Nobu Matsuhisa's most famous dishes.

40 Apollonos St., in Astir Palace Resort. ℭ **30/210-896-0510.** www.matsuhisa athens.com.

Milos $$$ SEAFOOD Milos has views of ancient ruins, an ambience that makes you feel like you have "come home," and seafood that is soul food for lovers. Easy to find at the Hilton hotel, it's the place for all serious seafood fanciers. The fresh ingredients that come from all over Greece meet up with the fresh catches of the fishing boats, and the fusion is remarkable!

Vas. Sofias 46. ℭ **30/210-724-4400.** www.milos.ca/restaurants/athens.

Varoulko $$$ INTERNATIONAL/SEAFOOD Dinner is served on a romantic rooftop terrace with an Acropolis view and a personalized/customized menu for each guest. Many Athenians believe chef/owner Lefteris Lazarou serves some of the best dishes in Greece.

80 Piraeus St. ℭ **30/210-522-8400.** www.varoulko.gr.

ATHENS BY NIGHT

Take a stroll through the old **Plaka** and **Monastiraki** neighborhoods and **Exarchia** and **Syntagma** Squares. Here, you'll find hundreds of shops vending kitschy tourist curios as well as really fine art, plus outdoor plaza restaurants. Another zone as cool as you'll find in any European city or North America is **Gazi** and **Psiri,** which came of age during the 2004 Olympics. The area has endless cafes, ouzeries, bars, theaters, and galleries and is especially lively during Apokreas, Greece's Carnival (the period preceding Greek Easter). We recommend a night stroll up Arditos Hill to admire the view of **Panathenaic Stadium's** track and stadium in all their illuminated beauty, accompanied by the soundtrack of smooth jazz pumping from a nearby club in the quiet night.

Outdoor Movies Athens's summertime open-air cinemas are a real treat. The **Riviera**, in Exarhia at Valtetsiou 46 (ℭ **30/210-3844-827**), is like going to the movies in a garden. The **Aigli Village Cool,** at Zappeion Gardens (ℭ **30/210-3369-369**), has balconies and tables. At the roof-top **Cine Paris,** Kidathineon 22, Plaka (ℭ **30/210-3222-071**), you watch the movie beneath the lit walls of the Acropolis; it can make for a very romantic evening—if it's the right movie!

Clubs **Duende,** Tziraion 2, Makrigianni (ℭ **30/210-924-7069**), is a small brasserie, featuring old-fashioned, romantic cocktail music for background but where you can hear each other talk. If it's jazz that stirs your emotions, try the **Half Note Jazz Club,** Trivonianou 17 (ℭ **30/210-9213-310**).

Most Romantic Cruise Stops

Cruise ship excursions vary, but these are some of our favorites.

Nauplion The most popular postcard image for this town on the Peloponnesian Peninsula is the charming 15th-century **Bouts Island Fortress.** Take a tour of the flower-bedecked ruins of the supposed castle of **Agamemnon,** and up the 999 steps to the 17th–century **Palamidi Castle:** You will be rewarded with a beautiful view. Rent a car or bike for a short ride to the ruins of **Mycenae,** including its lions gate, which is impressive even though the two beautiful lions are missing their heads. Or go to the ancient **Theater of Epidaurus** in Epidavros, about a half-hour from town. **Karathona beach** is sandy and quiet with a couple of *tavernas* at the far end. The water is shallow and warmer than some other beaches with less gradual drop-offs. The privacy and simplicity puts Karathona high up on the romance index.

Mykonos The white houses are trimmed in primary colors, and bougainvillea crawls over everything on this gorgeous isle. Some of the winding streets are so narrow only an average-size person can pass through them. The countless shops offer clothing and jewelry—you'll find whimsical well-priced jewelry alongside investment gems and 18- and 24-carat gold pieces. The feel of Mykonos by day or night is young, carefree, and sensual, and the island is known for its beaches and liberal attitudes. **Paradise Beach** in particular is very gay friendly. The beaches form hubs of activity, and several cater to nudists. **Super Paradise** is a nude beach that can be a little too hectic and fleshy to be romantic. A romantic walk can lead anywhere, from a restaurant to an ancient ruin, or to one of the 400 churches here, some about as big as a one-car garage. The most commonly photographed is the beautiful Byzantine **Panagia Paraportiani.** We recommend dining at casually elegant **N'Ammos ($$;** ✆ **30/228-9022-440;** www.nammos.gr) on fun and trendy **Psarou Beach.** It attracts well-to-do locals who stop in for wonderful risottos and other spicy Mykonian delicacies. For a quiet meal, try **Sea Satin Market ($$;** ✆ **30/228-9024-676;** www.caprice.gr), where the closing scene of *The Bourne Identity* was filmed. The open kitchen gives you a good look at the catch of the day sizzle on the grill. Or, you can head to the Alefkandra quarter for the serene, seaside **Aqua Taverna ($$;** ✆ **30/228-9026-083;** www.caprice.gr). The menu is outstanding with specials based on what the fishermen caught that morning. The Italian kitchen offers delicious pasta and seafood dishes. Come early and ask for a table on the terrace—this is the place to dine at sunset.

In the evening, **"Little Venice"** (the nickname for the **Alefkandra quarter** because the homes here hang over the sea) is a great place to watch the sunset, especially on the beach just below the windmills. Look for Nightlife in the same area, where fashionable bars are prized for their sunset views. You can sip an ouzo and listen to Mozart most nights at the **Montparnasse,** Agiou Anargyron 24 (✆ **30/694-662-0273;** www.thepianobar.com), or at the very gay-friendly **Kastro Bar,** Agion Anargyron (✆ **30/2289-023-072;** www.kastrobar.com). If you want to stay up late, hit **Caprice** (✆ **30/22890-23541;** www.caprice.gr).

Santorini   Sailing at night into the Santorini Caldera (a depression caused by an ancient volcano) and seeing the sheer cliff illuminated is an unparalleled romantic sight. Santorini is the largest island in a string of islands of the same name. It's marked by its volcanic mountains and loved for its white-washed buildings that crawl up the steep hills.

You get up from the shore in two ways—by cable car or donkey—but it will be hard to leave the beach! The towns of **Perissa** and **Kamari** have black sand beaches, and people swear the water is warmer there because the black sand absorbs more heat. Worthy destinations are the **Megaro Gyzi Museum** in Fira (✆ **30/22860-23077;** www.megarogyzi.gr; admission 3€; closed Sun), the **Archaeological Museum** (✆ **30/22860-22217**; www.santorini.com/museums/archaeological_museum.htm; closed Mon), and the **Agiou Mina church**, an 18th-century church with the familiar blue dome and white bell tower you may have seen in postcards. Take a bus to the seaside town of **Oia** for mind-boggling sunsets and cute shops. The cobblestone streets are attractive but can be treacherous for unsteady walkers.

Have a meal in Oia at **Strogili ($; ✆ 30/228-6072-367)**, which might include perfectly grilled whole fish, heaping helpings of lamb and vegetables, and other traditional Greek dishes at reasonable prices. Hidden from the street, you can locate it by climbing up a stairway full of geraniums just off the main drag. The eggplant is fit for immortals, and the grilled grouper is as perfect as the sea view. The terrace looks out at what seems to be an endless sea, and it goes on our list of best places to propose. In fact, some people have gotten married against this transfixing background. The **1800 Restaurant ($$; ✆ 30/228-6071-485;** www.oia-1800.com) in Oia offers another great sea view and an excellent wine cellar featuring Santorini and other Greek vintages. Have a meal there (the lamb chops are amazing), but just make sure you have it on the rooftop terrace. **Selene,** in Pyrgos village **($$; ✆ 30/228-6022-249;** www.selene.gr), the finest restaurant on the island, has elegant style and a captivating view of the Caldera from the terrace.

Rhodes   With more of a central city than the other islands, Rhodes has a darker, moodier presence, but it also has fine beaches and jagged cliffs. It's home base for the Knights Templar, romanticized by the Indiana Jones movies, and related old buildings are scattered around. In **Rhodes Town,** see the **Palace of the Grand Master (Byzantine Museum),** on Street of the Knights in the Medieval City (✆ **30/22413-65270;** admission 6€ for adults, 3€ for seniors 65+), with its elaborate moats and drawbridges, towers, and battlements—real fantasy material. A half-hour away is **Lindos,** a picturesque town with winding, narrow streets, abundant flower gardens, and a well-preserved acropolis. It's definitely worth a visit.

Rhodes boasts a large number of the family restaurants that are the stock-and-trade of urban areas in this part of the world.

MOST ROMANTIC RESTAURANTS

Diafani Garden $$ GREEK   This *taverna* offers fine traditional Greek meals in a pretty setting punctuated by tables set under a spreading walnut tree in a vine-laced courtyard, For a typical Greek dish, we suggest the *papoutsaki,* stuffed eggplant with béchamel sauce and chopped meat.

3 Plateiaac Arionos. ℭ **30/224-1026-053.**

Manolis Dinoris Fish Taverna $$$ GREEK/SEAFOOD   This eatery is housed in the former stables of the 13th-century **Knights of St. John's Inn**—talk about atmosphere! Its quiet garden and old stone hearth provide a romantic setting all year long.

14A Museum Sq. ℭ **30/224-1025-824.**

Mavrikos $$ GREEK/FRENCH   This 70-year-old family restaurant serves some of the most elegant and innovative dishes in all of Greece.

Main Square, Lindos. ℭ **30/224-4031-232.**

RHODES BY NIGHT

Younger travelers usually gravitate to the **New Town,** with its lively cafe scenes at the harbor, or on Galias near **New Market,** along Diakonou. In the **Old Town,** the bars are along Miltiadhou.

A **sound-and-light** show at the lush gardens of Odos Papagou, south of Plateia Rimini (ℭ **30/224-1021-922**), reenacts the life of a young man who joins a monastery in 1522, just before Rhodes falls to the Turks. The **Traditional Folk Dance Theater,** in Old Town (ℭ **30/224-1020-157**), will stir your senses with 20 male and female traditionally dressed dancers moving with wild (choreographed) abandon to live music. They demonstrate dances from all over Greece.

SULTRY SHORES: EXOTIC LANDS

Beyond the time you'll spend lolling on the gorgeous sands, a trip to Bali, Tahiti, the Maldive Islands, and Thailand will introduce you—and your very significant other—to cultures where having "me" (and "us") time is considered essential to a well-rounded life. It seems to us that no Puritan work ethic pushes the people here to toil all day. Instead, locals seem to be raised with the understanding that meditation and contemplation are important practices; that spending time with the one (or ones) you love is more important than climbing the career ladder. So relax and spend all afternoon gazing into one another's eyes. In these places, that's considered a very appropriate way to spend the day.

12

BALI
Peace, Passion, Perfection

Bali is one of the world's great romance capitals, with white-sand beaches, crystalline waters, electric green rice paddies, and lush jungles. Before that passion-perfect background, romance really comes down to something very simple—exquisite attention to detail.

Balinese hoteliers understand that unique touches can make a blissful experience transcendent: a basket of fruit decorated with flowers waiting in your villa; a private dinner overlooking the water as a server waits on you attentively, yet discreetly. And nearly every resort's beach furnishings include *bales,* exotic four-poster beds with gauzy drapes for privacy.

Bali helps you put body and soul together. It is an island of daily spiritual activity, where every morning local men and women carry fruit and flowers to a temple or sanctuary for blessings from the gods. Each village has a specialized art form, which means that driving (or, as we recommend, being driven) from village to village yields artistic discoveries of sculpture, music, dance, basketry, and painting. The island is almost always celebrating something; plan your trip around a full or new moon, and you will witness particularly inspiring ceremonies. But do take care when booking in March: This is the season for their "silent holiday," Nyepi, which happens several days during the month. It is widely observed, and during this time, restaurant and hotel staff will not perform any outdoor activities.

Worried about what you've read in the newspapers? Bali is a peaceful island, but quite a few years ago some terrorist incidents occurred. We can't say it will never happen again, but avoid the heavily trafficked areas (like Kuta), check the U.S. State Department warnings, and you should feel, and be, secure. And if you're worried about a tsunami, relax: Bali is not in as vulnerable an area as other Indonesian islands (such as Java). In addition, some sides of the island (Nusa Dua) have a sea shelf that makes large wave action almost impossible.

KEY ATTRACTIONS

Biking Through Ancient Rural Villages   Bike tour companies pick you up early in the morning, and some will stop for breakfast overlooking an active volcano! A 2½-hour gentle bike ride will take you through lovely scenery where you can take photographs, talk to farmers, visit a local temple, or spend the afternoon in a traditional Balinese home and enjoy a multicourse lunch. River rafting excursions are also possible.

Private Beaches   They're everywhere, but you'll need help finding the best, most secluded, ones. A worthy concierge will not only find the cove, but pack a picnic and offer to send someone with you to serve, clean up, and magically disappear until requested again.

House Blessings & Temple Ceremonies   Here again, a good concierge can arrange such an experience and guide you with your attire (formal dress, with a sarong, sash, and head scarf) and what to bring (small gifts of fruit and flowers). Depending on what is being celebrated in the ceremony, the event could start early or late—or go all night. Participants are dressed beautifully, and you'll enjoy a night filled with dancing, music, and sometimes, ancient stories of good versus evil spirits or love triumphant over mysticism. We find the traditional music of the gamelan orchestra stirring—even magical—and one of our ingredients for romance.

Find a Rice Paddy Hideaway   There are sweet little places rentable for a night or longer, amidst terraced hills and rice paddies. They are usually basic, but in astoundingly beautiful and scenic locations.

Go Shopping   Shopping in Bali can be an adventure that takes you from downtown Ubud to nearby villages, each with its own specialized craft. One village specializes in basketry, while another has jewelry and silver. Try to visit artist studios in Ubud and all through the island. Many have fine carving, painting, textiles, or other handcrafted items. You can shop the island with a personal guide; there's no fee for the tour, but guides add 15% to whatever you purchase. Ask your concierge for a reputable guide.

Tip: Resist visiting the **Monkey Park**: The monkeys can be aggressive and give you a bad day. Don't go. We also don't like **Kuta Beach** and downtown **Denpasar**, touristy spots full of sellers and hangers on. They may be good for

sensual MASSAGE, BALI STYLE

Couple massages here are so affordable ($35–$85), you can have a lot of them! Most massage rooms are enclosed on three sides with the fourth opening onto a stream or fountain. Here are some of our favorite romantic spa experiences in Bali:

- **Antique Villa Spa,** Jalan Dukuh Indah, Seminyak (℅ **62/361-739-840;** www.antiquebali.com). A 10-minute drive from Seminyak, Antique Villa serves both a gay and straight clientele. We recommend the rose bath. Your masseur soaps you up all over, and we mean all over. Then you lie on a slab and are hand rinsed. This treatment is offered for couples, too. Pretty erotic.

- **Jari Menari (Dancing Fingers),** Jalan Raya Legian, Seminyak (℅ **62/361-736-740;** www.jarimenari.com). Clean, safe, and pretty, Jari Menari features an all-male staff. The highlight is the four-handed massage done by two people. You can arrange to do this massage together.

- **The Spa at the Four Seasons—Jimbaran Bay,** Kuta Selatan; (℅ **62/361-701-010;** www.fourseasons. com/jimbaranbay). Pricier, but the elegant surroundings

make it special, and you can buy something sensual to slather on your partner's body later.

- **Spa on the Rocks** (at Ayana Resort & Spa, Jalan Karang Mas Sejahtera, Jimbaran; ℅ **62/361-702-222;** www.ayanaresort.com). Built on rocks overlooking the Indian Ocean, this spa incorporates natural ingredients in a luxurious setting. In a cottage facing the ocean, couples can soak together and then get massaged side-by-side, as sea breezes waft over their bodies. A memorable choice is the Rose Petal couple massage. Soak in a private pool strewn with rose petals and then clean each other off in an outdoor shower—before two lovely masseuses rub you down, side by side. Mmmm.

- **The Spa at Como Shambhala Estate,** Banjar-Begawan, Desa-Melinggih-Kelod, Payangan ℅ **62/361-978-888;** www.comohotels.com/comoshambhalaestate). The view will mesmerize you, while the personally calibrated programs will destress and detoxify you. Nestled beside a waterfall, this spa oozes romance.

people-watching or a late-night party, but if you desire pristine, romantic Bali, this isn't it.

Tanah Lot Temple This rock formation is a natural ancient Balinese Hindu worshiping spot, and one of the world's most beautifully situated temples. At low tide you can walk to it; at high tide you can view it from the shore. It can get crowded but has nooks and crannies where you can lose yourselves in the romance. It's most dramatic at sunrise and sunset.

✆ **62/361-880-361.** www.tanahlot.net.

HOTELS WITH HEART

Amandari Ubud $$$ Part of the ultra-exclusive Aman chain, this getaway is situated among verdant terraced rice fields and a deep, beautiful valley. Paths to your room wind past shrines and intricately carved doorways that make you feel like you are in an actual village. The entrance to each villa looks old and venerable, as if many centuries of Balinese had lived behind these doors. In some villas you walk on stepping stones in a koi pond to enter your villa. Suites are large with a 20-foot ceiling of native reeds and woods. Many include a large private pool (think: moonlit skinny-dipping) in addition to a sunken tub and private outside shower.

Jalan Raya Kedewatan, Ubud. ✆ **62/361-975-333.** www.amanresorts.com.

Amankila at Nusa Dua $$$ The story is water here—a dramatic vista stretches down beyond a series of lap pools to the bluest seas. The villas themselves begin with an outdoor room facing the sea. The interior, where a vase of tuber roses fills the air with the sweetest scents, is graced with marble floors and fine teak furniture. Some rooms have their own pools with striking views of the bay, and others turn inward toward the jungle. You can reserve the palm-shrouded resort pool near the beach just for the two of you and follow your swim with a torch-lit multicourse feast at the sea's edge.

Manggis, Nusa Dua. ✆ **62/363-41333.** www.amanresorts.com.

The Conrad at Nusa Dua $$$ This top-of-the-line Hilton is right on the beach. The entry lobby is grand but warm, with beautiful wood rafters and expansive ocean views. The rooms are large, bright, and quite beautiful and feature a two-person tub hidden behind a shuttered glass window that has a view of the water. This is perfect place for families as there are many huge, kid-friendly pools and an all-day kid program that can give you some free time on your own; if you want a kid-free environment, Conrad Suites has a private pool, even more luxurious rooms and a "no child under twelve" policy.

Jalan Pratama 168, Nusa Dua. ✆ **62/361-778-788.** www.conradbali.com.

Desa Seni—A Village Resort $$ If you crave historical authenticity and a meditative experience, try Desa Seni, where an entire village has been re-created. Each villa is different: some quite simple, others, true houses. It is all warm and artistic. Yoga enthusiasts will love the outdoor yoga pavilion. Beautiful objects, furniture, and shrines dot the landscape; villas face the pool or are private, surrounded by greenery.

JL Kayu Puth No. 13 Pantai Berawa, Canggu. ℭ **62/361-944-639**. www.desaseni.com.

Four Seasons at Sayan $$$

A great choice in the artistic Ubud area. Only a few minutes from town, this lovely river valley will make you will feel hidden away. Rooms are a chic mix of modern and classic Balinese woods and materials. The Terrace restaurant at the edge of Ayung river is truly romantic, and the property itself offers many rambles for lovers.

Jalan Raua Sayan. ℭ **62/361-977577.** www.fourseasons.com.

Matahari Beach Resort & Spa $$

This is an unpretentious and ecologically sensitive place where the rooms are traditional and lovely, the food is excellent, and the sea beckons. On the seldom visited west side of the island (prepare for a 3-hour ride from the airport), the vibe is laid back, but there are lots of activities to keep you busy including tennis, horseback riding, and excellent snorkeling around nearby Menjangan Island.

JL Serinit Gilimanuk, Pemutera. ℭ **62/36292312.** http://matahari-beach-resort.com. Rates include airport transportation & all meals.

Shanti Natural Panorama View Hotel $

On the unspoiled north coast in the hills with mountain views, Shanti is a well-hidden romantic escape tucked into a small traditional village—pure "Old Bali." Six inexpensive villas are adorned with netting, gorgeous carved beds, and lovely porches; many of them are just a few feet away from a large infinity pool that overlooks the hills, mountains, and waterfalls. You can even take a short walk to a hidden waterfall.

Sambangan Village, North of Bali. ℭ **62-362-001331.** www.shanti-northbali.com. Rates include airport transportation & breakfast.

Tandjung Sari $

The large bedrooms and villas feel warm and authentic, and the grounds are beautiful here in "Old Bali." You feel the culture so vividly that the more contemporary clutter of Sanur beach will not penetrate the mood. You will be treated like an honored guest and perhaps become part of the many regulars who come here year after year.

Danau Tamblingon, No 41, Sanur. ℭ **866/599-6674.** www.tangdungsari.com.

MOST ROMANTIC RESTAURANTS

Floating Dinner $$$ The **Kayumanis at Jimbaran Bay** is a resort that offers many pleasures, but for sheer romantic splendor, it's hard to beat its Floating Dinner. Here, the staff creates a unique experience for you at their lovely pool—under the stars, surrounded by candles and flowers . . . the effect is magical.

Jalan Yoga Perkanthi. ℭ **62/361-765777.** experience@kayumanis.com.

The Hotel Tugu Bali's Javanese Cooking Experience $$$ JAVANESE

The Hotel Tugu Bali is as much a museum as a place to stay and eat. Set on Canggu Beach, it's a treasure trove of Balinese antiques, sculptures, and statues. For a special romantic experience, a master Javanese cook will take you to the market and then teach the two of you how to create Balinese and Javanese cuisine, culminating in a sumptuous dinner together.

Jalan Pantai Batu Bolong, Canggu Beach. ℰ **62/361-4731701.** www.hoteltugu bali.com.

Sunrise Buffet $ BREAKFAST

At the Maya Ubud Resort & Spa, the resort's award-winning design of massive stone walls, recycled timber, and a mix of modern and traditional elements sets the stage for its sunrise buffet, a sumptuous repast set in the midst of a tropical jungle with the sound of the Petanu River rushing below.

Maya Sari Mas, Ubud. ℰ **62/361-977888.** www.mayaubud.com.

Tapa at The Bale Resort $ TAPAS

This ultra-stylish, colorfully lit restaurant oozes energy in an outdoor setting. With live guitar music in the background, the party heats up with acoustic music on Wednesday and Friday nights. Foods are grouped by texture (crispy, smooth, crunchy, etc.), and the specialty is a delicious barbequed young pig. The food is served in small tapas fashion, great for sharing, and service is amazing.

Jalan Nusa Dua Selaton. Nusa Dua. ℰ **62/361-775111.** www.fun@tapabistro.com.

BALI BY NIGHT

If you are looking for performances and cultural life, this is your island. Because Ubud is a center for the arts, dances and rituals are often done by torchlight. Holding each other while absorbing the sensuous and intricate dances and musical intonations is sure to inspire a little romance.

Sky Garden Lounge   Party the night away with other revelers at this rooftop lounge and bar. Sip generously poured exotic fruit cocktails and martinis. If you tire of the crowds, sneak away to the secret couch under the stairs. If it's vacant, it's yours! Jalan Legian, Kuta. ℰ **62/361-755-423.** http://61legian.com.

BORA BORA
The Ultimate Getaway

In addition to Tahiti, Bora Bora is one of the few South Sea destinations most people have heard of. And no wonder: It is dramatic and devastatingly beautiful. But it is farther away and smaller than you might imagine—230 miles northwest of Tahiti in the Pacific. It is less than 17 sq. miles in area. Packed onto that speck of an island are dazzling beaches, verdant peaks, and breathtaking views. People who know the islands well would agree that it has the most beautiful lagoon and coral reef in the southern Pacific. There are also a great number of *motus* (small sandy isles), so if you dream of seclusion, you can find it here (particularly if you have a sailboat or charter one). This is the island of honeymoons, weddings, and anniversary celebrations. You'd be hard pressed to do better.

But be aware that Bora Bora is one of the most expensive vacation destinations in the world. We suggest some of our favorite places to stay and dine for those lucky enough where budget is not a concern, but for others who wish to go, we'd recommend you investigate renting out private properties via Airbnb. com or VRBO.com. We have seen several properties on those sites that are affordable in high season.

KEY ATTRACTIONS

The Beaches   **Matira Beach** is widely hailed as the most beautiful beach in French Polynesia. Two miles long and sheltered by tall palms, it gives entrance to a lagoon with a soft sandy bottom. You can pretty much walk through the clear turquoise waters to snorkel along the coral reef—or get around on outrigger or paddle canoes, glass-bottom boats, catamarans, Hobie Cats, jet skis, kayaks, or anything that floats! The lagoons protect you, and this gorgeous idyll is a must for lovers. Sunset is best, but any time is good. You can even parasail here. For rentals, contact **Bora Bora Activity Center** (© **689/21-69-36;** www. boraboraisland.com); **Bora Bora Parasailing** (© **689/78-27-10**); **Bora Bora Kayaks** (© **689/70-77-99**); or **RoHoTu Fare** (© **689/70-77-99;** www.rohotu farelodge.com).

Snorkeling & Diving   Novice divers can start out near the **Bora Bora Lagoonarium** (© **689/67-71-34;** $110 per person for full-day, $70–$83 per person for half-day). Among the best snorkeling spots is the aptly named Aquarium, near Motu Piti Uuuta, home of the Sofitel Motu (Nunue; © **689/ 60-56-00;** www.sofitel.com). You can also snorkel off **Matira Beach** south of the Hotel Bora Bora and paddle near the overwater bungalows where a reef attracts many fish. Beginning divers there often are directed to **Anau**, a site where manta rays congregate. **Topdive Bora Bora** (© **689/60-50-50;** www. topdive.com) and **Bora Diving** (© **689/67-77-85;** www.boradiving.com) can outfit you and direct you to the right spot. **Aqua Safari** (© **689/28-87-77;** www.aquasafaribora.com) offers diving helmets for people who do not want to dive but love the idea of walking on the bottom to view the fish.

Four-wheel-drive Treks   These Jeeps and vans offer some fun tours. You can stop and get a fresh pineapple off a tree, see sarong prints being designed and printed, visit old U.S. military artillery sites (this feels quite weird), and take in killer views of ocean and lush valleys. Several tour operators can take you to places to feed exotic but generally harmless sea creatures, such as black-tip reef sharks, moray eels, green turtles, and extremely large manta rays. Ask your concierge for a recommendation.

Pearls   When you come by air, you will land in **Vaitape**, and its main street is lined with pearl shops. You may initially resist them, but their beauty grows on you, and soon you'll develop an eye for quality—it's only a matter of time until you are forking over serious bucks.

Ancient Temples & Sites of Sacrifice & Worship   Only the stone configurations are left, but these places have a hallowed feel. See the **Aehautai Marae**, with outstanding views of Mount Otemanu, and the **Marotetini Marae**, both restored temples. It's best to get a guide: Try **Bora Bora Tours** (✆ **689/67-70-31**), **Bora Bora Safari Land** (✆ **689/67-71-32**), or **Otemanu Tours** (✆ **689/67-70-49**).

HOTELS WITH HEART

Four Seasons Resort Bora Bora $$$ Pure luxury, starting with the boat ride and chilled towel even before your arrival. You'll be taken on a golf cart through the gorgeous grounds to your room, where champagne and tropical fruit await. All the amenities you'd expect are here (a living room, work space, and flatscreen TV) and perhaps some you would not (a bathroom view of the lagoon). Your bedroom will also have great views of the mountain and lagoon, and naturally, there is a lovely deck—especially so if you opted for an over-water bungalow.

Other perks: an onsite marine biologist and an excellent spa (pre-order spa packages for savings). In a treatment room with translucent floor panels, your body can be soothed while you watch fish swim below. A romantic plus: Book at night for the two of you and watch the stars together during your treatments.

Motu Tehotu. ✆ **689/60-31-30.** www.fourseasons.com/borabora.

InterContinental Resort and Thalasso Spa Bora Bora $$$ This luxury resort is on Motu Piti Aau, a narrow, 6-mile-long island shared with Le Meridien Bora Bora. The spa is renowned, and you should use it, even if you don't stay here. Try a couple's massage in one of the three rooms that extend over the lagoon and watch the fish swim beneath. There's also a wedding chapel with a glass floor and a stylish Asian fusion suite over the lagoon. Top that off with fine views of Mount Otemanu from the restaurants, bars, and infinity swimming pool. Guests here can use the facilities at the InterContinental Le Moana Resort.

Matira Point, 8 km from Vaitape. ✆ **800/327-0200.** www.tahiti.interconti.com.

Rohutu Fare Lodge $$ This lush lodge is tucked into thick mountainside gardens above Povai Bay and is one of Bora Bora's more affordable properties. The beautiful bungalows seem designed with love in mind. Between the teak floors and natural thatched roofs are four-poster beds, sexy paintings, statues, and other exotica in the bedrooms, and faucets that sometimes resemble body parts in the baths. The two bungalows with views of the lagoon are especially charming, and all have ceiling fans, kitchens, and decks with lounge furniture and lovely views. (Complimentary bicycles and shuttles can take you to restaurants and the nearby beach and the airport.)

Vaitape. ✆ **689/70-77-99.** www.rohotufarelodge.com.

MOST ROMANTIC RESTAURANTS

Most resorts host some form of a **Tamaaraa,** a traditional evening feast coupled with a Polynesian dancing performance—definitely touristy, but fun, too. See "Bora Bora by Night" for details.

Bloody Mary's Restaurant & Bar $$$ SEAFOOD/STEAKS   Yes, it's a tourist magnet—so what? It's a wonderful place: charming and light-hearted and a must-do. Dig your toes into the white-sand floor—the rest is kind of brilliantly catawampus: the thatched roof, chairs made from palm tree trunks, and scattered butcher-block tables. Go for the barbecued- or charbroiled-to-order fish that you choose raw from a bed of ice.

Povai Bay, 1 km (½ mile) north of Hotel Bora Bora. ✆ **689/67-72-86.** www.bloody marys.com.

La Villa Mahana $$$ INTERNATIONAL   In the only big town on the island, this tiny Mediterranean cafe is on every gourmet's agenda (you need to reserve well in advance). It's romantic, with a charming patio and seductive lighting. Significant use of lobster, prawns, and caviar contributes to heavenly salads, and the zesty sauces and marinades accent Ahi tuna and mahi mahi. Coconut curries and perfectly cooked steak are other mouthwatering options. The prix-fixe tasting menu, while pricey, is superb.

Vaitape. ✆ **689/67-50-63.** www.villamahana.com. Closed Sun.

Restaurant Fare Manuia $$$ FRENCH   Polynesian allure under a thatched roof and casual French cuisine create a romantic ambience—and a satisfying restaurant. Go here for big portions of prime rib and beef with an array of French sauces. Fresh fish is served simply, planked and grilled. The fish soup is delicious.

Matira, between InterContinental le Moana Resort and Hotel Maitai Polynesia. ✆ **689/67-68-08.**

BORA BORA BY NIGHT

The **Tamaaraa** traditional evening feast is typically accompanied by Polynesian dancing performed by male and female entertainers in dazzling costumes. Most resorts have this kind of "Polynesian Night" and, if touristy, these events are fun and an awe-inspiring demonstration of what human hips can do. Check with your concierge.

For a quieter night, consider the truly romantic **Bubbles Bar** (✆ **689/60-76-00;** www.tahiti.interconti.com) and keep the lagoon and Mount Otemanu in your sights.

If you just want to be with your honey, you are in the perfect place for **star gazing.** Take a short walk on a beach at night or just go outside your room and look up at the carpet of millions of shining stars in the sky.

MALDIVES
A Private World of Water

This is honeymoon country. Absolute privacy is possible in this Indian Ocean republic of 1,190 idyllic islands, each with a slightly different ambiance. Most of the islands are undeveloped, and if you want to get lost, here is the place to start.

You'll find elegant dining by starlight and candles, plus spas to pamper you. You can steal away to a nearby uninhabited island all by yourselves for a day, partake in a diving excursion, go fishing at night, or just hang around a magical resort watching the beautiful aquamarine sea. It's quite likely you will see dolphins swimming just offshore, displaying the same carefree spirit you are feeling!

Yes, getting here can be hard work—it's not on the way to anyplace else, and it's more than 30 hours from the U.S. East Coast. Pick your season carefully—the monsoon can create soggy conditions from May to early fall. But complete your long journey at the right season, arrive at your resort, and then you can exhale and start concentrating on each other—and maybe on how many white sand beaches you can visit.

KEY ATTRACTIONS

This area is all about the water, watersports, and water contemplation—you can add spa treatments to that list, too. But if you are looking for nightspots, this may be the wrong destination. They exist in the capital city, Malé, but on the atolls, evening entertainment is mainly star-gazing, perhaps a movie, a random lecture here or there, and whatever activities your resort cooks up. You do not come to the Maldives for nightlife, unless, of course, you include love-making in that category. Then you have certainly picked the right place!

HOTELS WITH HEART

All hotels listed here, and most others in the Maldives, are all-inclusive resorts meaning that the rates include all meals, non-alcoholic beverages, and some activities. Expect to pay extra for alcohol, spa treatments, and special excursions.

Banyan Tree Maldives Vabbinfaru $$$ You are on an atoll just big enough for your resort. You will feel like you've gone native—and indeed you have, albeit luxuriously so. The digs are superb: round Indonesian houses with thatched roofs and outdoor baths, shielded by private gardens from any eyes but each other's. Some huts are particularly private; all are oriented to the sea and beach. You will have extremely romantic dinners among the palms, and scheduled activities occur on an enchanting outdoor pavilion with a lofty thatched roof. The excellent spa has treatments and massages from various cultures, some performed outdoors.

Vabbinfaru Island. © **866/822-6926.** www.banyantree.com. Rates include all meals.

Embudu Village $$ On the small island of Embudu, near the Malé airport, you can enjoy living, even walking, on the water—the bungalows have glass floor panels over the sea. The hotel is surrounded by a beautiful lagoon and is only 100 yards or so from a snorkeling reef; it's also close to major diving sites. The hotel, which has a good restaurant and bar, also has the fine Serena Spa.

Embudu village. ✆ **960/664-0063.** www.embudu.com. Rates include all meals.

The Four Seasons at Kuda Huraa $$$ This is not one resort—it is a collection of them, with sites on two private islands and a luxury catamaran you can overnight on (for up to 3 nights). You get your own stretch of the famous white sands, excellent service, and meals are included. In the evening, retreat to your villa for a **Bath Ritual** poured by the resort's Bath Butler (it involves essential oils and aromatherapy). Perfect for two! The thatched beachside and overwater bungalows are bright and airy with white stone walls and four-poster beds. The picturesque and secluded spa (which has night treatments as well as day) is on a separate island in the lagoon, only accessible by wooden sailing *dhoni*.

On North Malé Atoll. ✆ **960/66-44-888.** www.fourseasons.com/maldiveskh. Rates include all meals.

MOST ROMANTIC RESTAURANTS

In the Maldives, you typically eat where you stay, mainly because so many resorts are all-inclusive. But you can visit other eateries via a short cruise between atolls.

By the Sea Restaurant $$$ JAPANESE/PERUVIAN   In the Gili Lankanfushi Maldives hotel on North Malé Atoll, this tree-shaded spot is on two levels beside the sea. The intimate setting accommodates 26 guests on comfy daybeds. The open kitchen helps create closer interaction with the chef. The menu, with Peruvian and Japanese offerings, features freshly picked organic produce direct from the chef's own garden.

Lankanfushi Island. ✆ **960/664-0304.** www.gili-lankanfushi.com/by-the-sea.

Dr. Ali's $$$ CHINESE/INDIAN/MIDDLE EASTERN/VIETNAMESE
Oceanside restaurants get the romantic nod based on location alone. This one, at the Shangri-La Villingili Resort & Spa on Addu Atoll, explores Indian tandoori, Cantonese, and Arabian menus in separate dining rooms. The South China Sea room delivers the Chinese flavors plus dim sum; the Indian Ocean lounge specializes in spicy curries and tandoori roasts; and exotic Middle Eastern fare is on the menu is the colorful Arabian Gulf room. Imaginative desserts explore both Arabian and Chinese tastes.

Villingili Island. ✆ **960/689-788-8.** www.shangri-la.com.

Salt $$$ SEAFOOD   This is a great place for a late-night nosh, and it stays open until no customers are left. But it's open for lunch, too, and has a lovely lagoon view, particularly at sunset. Located at the Huvafen Fushi Resort on North Malé Atoll, it's a 30-minute speedboat ride from Malé.

In Huvafen Fushi Resort. ✆ **960/664-181-8.** http://huvafenfushi.peraquum.com.

ROMANCE ON A family HOLIDAY

Do we hear our readers laughing? We think it's possible to cultivate a romantic mood on a family holiday. Is it easy? No. Is it our first choice for a romantic getaway? No way. But raising kids, wonderful as that is, takes a long time, and we don't think you should be romance-less that long. Also, when your kids grow up and leave the house, some move far away, so a family vacation may be one of the few opportunities you get to be together with them. If you can afford to take only one vacation a year, then you may need to construct one that allows for some romance for the two of you while you're visiting with the kids and grandkids. You have to look for the right features when choosing your destination and accommodations. For starters, look for places where the staff supervises and entertains kids of all ages leaving you with hours, days, or even overnights that remind you that you are lovers as well as parents.

For families, we like the time-share villas that are associated with some of these hotels; they have kitchens to make life less expensive and usually have optimal room arrangements for privacy. Units tend to have one big master bedroom, a kitchen, and a living room layout, which is paired with a "lock off," a connected studio that can be locked for privacy at night. Nice for Mommy and Daddy.

We also like cruises because, if your kids are old enough, they can stay in their own room close by yours, and the butler has to deal with their demands, not you. Guest ranches (formerly known as

MOOREA & TAHITI
Swooning for Lagoons

Many people think of this part of the South Pacific as the ultimate honeymoon getaway, and you will get no argument from us. We suggest you sample more than one island (for geographic diversity alone) and Moorea and Tahiti are great places to start. But they wouldn't necessarily be your first choice if you longed to be stranded on a truly deserted *motu*, a tiny island or strip of sand, in the Pacific. If you don't really want to get away from it all, this is paradise.

Moorea

The 9-mile ferry trip to Moorea is an enjoyable 30 minutes from Tahiti. It is odd that this island is not as well known as Bora Bora, because it is closer to Tahiti and a major airport. Maybe it's because the name Bora Bora is so much dude ranches) are great because there are always so many activities. For example, The Resort at Paws Up in Montana (p. 349) has skeet shooting, ballooning, fly-fishing lessons, horseback riding, cattle drives, river rafting, and archery. Pack the day with activities, but the trick will be to tire your children out without overdoing it yourselves, so you leave some prime time for each other.

Best of all, we like the all-inclusives that truly entertain—and often teach—your kids while you play. The best of these include meals as well as water sports and other activities. Club Meds that are geared toward families—like the one at Cancún Yucatan (℃ 52/998-881-82-00; www.clubmed.com) are great for this.

In the Maldives, we suggest the **Lux Resort** ($$$; ℃ **960/668-0901;** www.luxresorts.com) in the South Ari Atoll. Activities go on all day for kids 3–12, but we especially love that the teen club (ages 12–17) takes your kids on an overnight camping trip! With seven restaurants, even when the kids are around, they will be happy (and safe) going to the Italian restaurant on their own to share a pizza while you choose from the melting pot of cuisines—Maldivian, Indian, Thai, Indian, and Japanese—for a romantic dinner for two. By day, everyone enjoys the 4 kilometers of pristine beaches and watersports.

See p. 396 of our Romantic Interest Index for more top picks for family vacation spots with romantic oppportunities.

---

fun to say—and it is a gorgeous island. Still, we actually are a bit sweeter on Moorea. To us, it is the ultimate South Pacific stunner. The jagged mountains are strikingly exotic, and the greener-than-green valleys are particularly friendly for hikers. The lagoons are sparkling, and the beaches wide and clean, and there are romantic coves at every turn. The island is even heart-shaped! Mount Mouaroa, the "Bali Hai mountain," is the iconic backdrop that tells you where you are. Every bay presents a picture as well, and the views down Cook's Bay and Opunohu Bay are as awesome as scenery ever gets.

Every tour will take you up the destroyed wall of an early volcanic crater to the Belvédère Lookout. But if you are not on a cruise or part of a tour, by all means go yourselves. The stupendous view at the top shows you both Cook's and Opunohu Bays, and the contrast of mountains, blue sea, and green botanical walls is a never-to-be-forgotten sight. One caution here: The heavy mist and cloud cover can descend, and you might find yourself looking at an impenetrable veil instead of one of the world's most romantic sights. Going early in the morning makes it more likely you'll have a clear view.

KEY ATTRACTIONS

The Beaches An offshore coral reef forms a vast lagoon here, and a coastal road makes this the accessible blue lagoon of your dreams and safe watersports of every kind. Wonderful white sand beaches are on almost every part of the island. **Mareto Plage Publique** (Mareto Public Beach) is particularly picturesque, backed by a coconut grove between two bays. The lagoons on the northwest side have very romantic *motus* to visit, but beware of tricky currents. To boat over safely, go to **Moorea Locaboat** (☏ **689/78-13-39;** www.moorealocaboat.com), next to Hotel Les Tipaniers.

Snorkeling The **Temae Plage Publique** (Tamae Public Beach) is gorgeous, easy to navigate, and has teeming fish populations. **Pianapo (Pineapple) Beach** (☏ **689/74-96-96;** www.painapo.com) requires a small fee but that includes equipment. **Tip Nautic,** on Hotel Tipanier's beach (☏ **689/78-76-73**; www.tipnautic.com), rents snorkel gear and offers kayaks, waterskiing, and dolphin-watching trips.

Scuba Diving Moorea's outer reef is good for viewing whitetip and blacktip reef sharks. The lagoon's coral reef has been damaged, and so much of it is dead, that in order to see a healthy reef, dives need to be relatively deep. Many companies "salt" the waters by having shark feedings. **Opunohu Canyons** is a popular place to see them. Coral roses are at a much lower depth, between Opunohu and Cook's Bays. There is an old ship that was purposely sunk inside the lagoon to attract fish, which it does, wonderfully. There are a number of reliable dive operators: **TOPDIVE,** at the InterContinental Moorea Resort & Spa and the Hilton Moorea Lagoon Resort & Spa (☏ **689/56-31-44;** www.topdive.com); **Moorea Blue Diving,** at Moorea Pearl Resort & Spa Center (☏ **689/55-17-04;** www.mooreabluediving.com); and **Moorea Fun Dive** (☏ **689/56-40-38;** www.moorea-fundive.com). On the northwest coast, contact **Scubapiti Moorea,** at Hotel Tipaniers (☏ **689/56-20-38;** www.scuba piti.com).

Stingray World Located near the InterContinental Resort Moorea, you can come here to see the stingrays, just lingering in the water or doing shallow dives. Couples who have petted these amazingly tolerant, and even friendly, creatures rave about the experience. We are a bit squeamish, but all reports have been good.

Lagoon Picnics We think being deposited on a *motu* in the lagoon is very romantic. Your hotel will arrange it for you, packing a lunch, or catching a fish to grill during the trip. Go as a couple for romance "points" and snorkel together. Larger tours incorporate shark and/or ray feeding.

Hiking We think the archaeological hikes are the most fascinating, revealing the remains of ancient villages. If you are up for a half-day hike, go to the Opunohu Valley with **Tahiti Evasion** (☏ **689/56-48-77;** www.tahitievasion. com; half-day hike $52 per person).

Horseback Riding   If you like riding, what could be more romantic than riding a good horse along the beach or into a tropical jungle? Try **Ranch Opunohu Valley** (✆ 689/56-28-55), which offers several tours each day.

Interior Trips   Hike up to **Atiraa Waterfall** and have a swim; many tours include a funky juice stop at **Jus de Fruits de Moorea**, which we like a lot. **Albert Tours** (✆ 689/55-21-10; www.albert-transport.net), and **Haamatea-rii's Inner Island Safari Tours** (✆ 689/56-20-09; inner-saf@mail.pf) have interior trips. For a four-wheeler trip into the interior, **Mahana ATV Tours** (✆ 689/56-20-44; www.mooreamahanatours.com) takes you on all-terrain vehicles into the Opunohu Valley.

Sunday Church Services   If you find yourself near the town (Maha-repa), or choose to make a special trip, one of the loveliest experiences we've had here was at the local church on Sunday; you will hear the most amazing multipart harmonies imaginable from the audience. The scene is a mix of artistic hats and guitar-playing locals that produces a feast for both the eyes and ears.

HOTELS WITH HEART

Hilton Moorea Lagoon & Spa $$$ The location is divine—a white sand beach with views of green mountains behind and the lagoon in front. The many over-water bungalows are luxurious with vaulted ceilings, private decks, and the requisite transparent section of the floor to watch the fish swim by. The garden bungalows have private plunge pools and terraces. There are extensive gardens and awesome ocean views in the **Eimeo Bar** above the pool. Grab a casual waterfront lunch at the **Rotui Bar and Grill,** a warm, wood-paneled, and breezy spot that sometimes opens for dinner. The stunning view adds to the charm of the lagoon-side **Arii Vahine** restaurant, with a mixed Polynesian and international menu. A Polynesian dance show plays here twice a week. For a romantic drink, or crepe snack, you can't beat the over-water thatched-roof **Toatea Bar.**

✆ **689/55-11-11.** www3.hilton.com.

InterContinental Resort & Spa $$$ This luxury resort is for lovers who want to be active. Its lagoon is not too enticing, but it offers the widest range of watersports activities on the island (also available to non-guests): scuba diving, parasailing, water-skiing, wake-boarding, jet skis, glass bottom boats for viewing coral and fish, plus exploring the lagoon in diving helmets. You also can fish and rent boats. Most of the guest bungalows extend partly over the water on man-made islands. This is not the most atmospheric place, but the rooms have tropical ambience. The Tahitian dance show on the beach is very good.

✆ **888/IC-HOTELS** or 689/55-19-19. www.ihg.com.

Sofitel Moorea la Ora Beach Resort $$$ This big resort is positioned just south of Moorea's No. 1 public beach and lagoon (Temae Public Beach), and it has a downright mystical view of the mountains of Tahiti, beyond the sea. The bungalows are luxurious, and there are a large number of over-water places to choose from. Honeymooners might like the ultra-deluxe and ultra-private accommodations that also have great views on the south side of the resort. You can eat very romantic meals in the colorful gourmet restaurant, which has a sand floor and thatched roof.

ⓒ **689/55-12-12.** www.sofitel.com.

MOST ROMANTIC RESTAURANTS

La Plantation $$ CAJUN/FRENCH   You may not have come to Moorea for Louisiana gumbo or Cajun style jambalaya, but somehow it fits in at this big restaurant with a plantation feel. It's romantic to eat out on the veranda amid soft and heartwarming lighting; the prix-fixe menu can keep costs down.

ⓒ **689/56-45-10.** www.laplantationmoorea.com.

Painapo (Pineapple) Beach $$ TAHITIAN   The Sunday lunch and brunch and the early suppers any day are served at tables on a sand floor and under a natural thatched-roof or under the shade of a beachside tree—this is paradise. The traditional Sunday buffet of Tahitian foods is not to be missed. Monday to Thursday, Pineapple Beach is open from 9am to 3pm. (cash only).

ⓒ **689/74-96-96.** www.painapo.com.

Te Honu Iti $$$ CLASSIC FRENCH   With its great views of Cook's Bay and the shark-toothed mountain, "The Little Turtle" is one of the best restaurants on the island. The chef will flambé your lobster or crêpes suzette at your table. It's a night you will remember (and there's free shuttle transportation to/from your hotel).

ⓒ **689/56-19-84.**

MOOREA BY NIGHT

Sunset Cruises   You owe it to yourselves every night to find the sunset, which is best seen by sea. For a party atmosphere, try **Hiro's Tours** (ⓒ **689/78-70-10** or 689/56-57-66; www.hirotour.com), whose 2-hour affair floats on a catamaran, with a Tahitian band playing Polynesian songs. Rum punch, beer, wine, and soft drinks are included. **Manu Catamaran** (ⓒ **689/56-28-04**) operates out of the Nautical Center at the Intercontinental Moorea; its 90-minute sunset cruise requires at least four passengers; drinks are included. **Tuaini Activities Moorea** (ⓒ **689/74-32-500**) delivers a 2-hour sunset cruise aboard a glass bottom boat on the lagoon in Haapiti; the trip includes a Mai Tai cocktail.

Tiki Theatre Village   The traditional dance show here is really fun and enlightening. And ooh, those Polynesian men and women! The best show in this whole area is here at Tiki Theatre Village, which looks like an ancient

Tahitian village, with huts where craft workers demonstrate tapa-cloth making, carving, tattooing, painting, weaving, cooking, and musical instruments, and they do the most exquisite flower arrangements. A pearl demonstration shows how black pearls are cultured. It's open Tuesday through Saturday.

Make sure to reserve for the Tahitian dance show. You'll be picked up at your hotel and delivered to start your evening on a nice stretch of beach near the theater. After a drink at sunset, comes a tour of the village and a plentiful buffet. The dance part of the show follows, and the costumes are dramatic and authentic. It's really fun, and if the costumes move you, you can go whole hog and arrange for a Polynesian wedding ceremony on the beach for you! They will bedeck you in flowers and traditional clothing.

© **689/55-02-50.** www.tikivillage.fr. Admission $17 adults; dinner & show $99 adults; show only $49. Tues–Sat.

Tahiti

You will hear that Tahiti is not worth visiting—but that's not fair. True, the busy and crowded Papeete is not what you came to the South Pacific to see. Yet the island still has abundant charms, and its black sand beaches and rain forests are alluring. If you go to Tahiti Iti on the eastern peninsula of Tahiti, you'll find an old Polynesia that you can't find anywhere else (an isthmus cuts across the entire island of Tahiti).

KEY ATTRACTIONS

Sunset over Moorea You'll see incredible views of Moorea from Tahiti's west coast. If you are ending or beginning a cruise, you may dock at the InterContinental Resort Tahiti, whose beach and Restaurant Pink Coconut are splendid spots to witness the sun's nightly decent.

The Marché Municipale (Municipal Market) This Papeete market is so much fun. It's open daily (Mon–Fri 5am–6pm, Sat 5am–1pm, Sun 4–8am) but go very early because it's picked over by 8am. It's a perfect breakfast stop. There are stacks and stacks of produce, baked goods, handicrafts, pareo sarongs, aloha shirts, blankets, fish, and meat. Sunday mornings are particularly hectic and colorful.

Central Papeete. Free admission.

Museums Tahiti is the only island in the Pacific with museums dedicated French Polynesia's fascinating culture. Among the best is **Musée Tahiti,** Puna'auia PK 15, Pointe des pêcheurs (© **689/54-84-35;** www.museetahiti.pf; admission $7 for adults); set in a grove of coconut palms beside a lagoon, it has exhibits on island culture, history and crafts, marine life, plants, and geology of the region. The **Paul Gauguin Museum,** PK 51, 2 Papeari (© **689/57-10-58**) covers the famed Impressionist's life and times, though it does not exhibit his art. The nice **Restaurant Musée Gauguin** (© **689/57-13-80**) is nearby. While there, take a romantic stroll at the nearby **Harrison W. Smith**

Jardin Botanique (℡ **689/57-10-58**), a beautiful botanical garden in Arue. Also on the museum circuit is the home of the eccentric **James Norman Hall** (Arue, East of Papeete Km5.5; ℡ **689/50-01-61;** www.jamesnormanhall home.pf), co-author of *Mutiny on the Bounty* and other books on the South Seas—the home is full of Hollywood memorabilia and the **Robert Wan Pearl Museum** (beside the Paofai Temple, Papeete; ℡ **689/46-15-55**). Stop at this repository of pearl knowledge *before* you go pearl shopping.

Natural Wonders The **Arahoho Blowholes** and the **Cascades de Tefaarumai Blowholes** are always fascinating. The holes result from pounding surf eating away an opening in the rock face overhanging the water. Waves are forced through the holes, and huge and powerful fountains erupt. Nearby is another wonder: Follow a marked road to the **Cascades de Faarumai,** a lovely waterfall. Of course, there is a romantic legend that goes with it, which you'll read on the signs near the parking area. In Taravao is the **Taravao Plateau Overlook**, with its spectacular view of the entire isthmus. On the south side at **Teahupoo** is a world-famous surfing village near the enormous waves at **Havaa Pass**.

Watersports Based at the InterContinental Resort Tahiti, **Aquatica Dive Centre and Nautical Activities** (℡ **689/53-34-96**) offers a comprehensive list of watersports activities, for both guests and visitors. Also contact them about dolphin- and whale-watching tours. For scuba diving, other islands in the area have the rays and sharks, but you are likely to see smaller, more colorful fish here. Popular dive sites are on the west coast of Tahiti Nui. Equipment and guidance are available from **Aquatica Dive Centre** (above) and **TOPDIVE Tahiti** (℡ **689/53-34-96;** www.topdive.com), also at the InterContinental.

Swimming & Snorkeling Most beaches on Tahiti have black volcanic sand. The one beach here that rivals those we have described on the other islands is **Plage de Maui** on Tahiti Iti. It's far away from everything else, but its white sands and translucent lagoon are enchanting. There is also a snack bar, so you won't starve.

Surfing If you are a surfer you have probably heard of the Billabong Pro championships that are held at Teahupoo every May. Riding these waves is quite dangerous, and only for world-class surfers. Even then, the waves crash near jagged rocks—only a romantic picture if you are not in the water. Tahiti does have an advantage over Bora Bora and Moorea: The surf here more typically breaks on sandy beaches. If you want to give it a try, contact Ecole de Surf Tura'i Mataare, otherwise known as the **Tahiti Surf School** (℡ **689/77-27-69;** www.tahitisurfschool.info).

HOTELS WITH HEART

InterContinental Resort Tahiti $$$ This is your best choice on Tahiti. It has a variety of luxurious rooms, with canopy beds, elegant bathrooms, and private patios or balconies, but the best ones in our opinion are the newer and larger overwater bungalows with perfect views of Moorea. The resort is quite big so it doesn't have that tropical "castaway" feeling, but it has great amenities including two pools—the smaller one is especially romantic. It is also close to the romantic **Le Lotus** (see later listing). There is a sophisticated all-night lobby bar and more activities than you can ever have time enough to try.

📞 **689/86-51-10.** www.tahiti.interconti.com.

Le Meridien Tahiti $$$ This luxury resort is far away from Papeete and on one of the island's few white sand beaches. It has stunning regional architecture, a more authentic feel, and is much simpler than many of the more fanciful resorts. The over-water bungalows do not have transparent panels for fish-watching, and not all are air-conditioned. But the hotel rooms have balconies; you want the ones that face the view of Moorea, if possible. Its restaurant, **Le Carré,** is easily one of the best in Polynesia.

📞 **800/543-4300** or 689/47-07-07. www.lemeridientahiti.com.

MOST ROMANTIC RESTAURANTS

For a change of pace, walk along the western end of the waterfront near Papeete, along Place Toata, where little cafes, formerly *roulottes*—mobile trucks that serve excellent food at bargain prices—still serve excellent food in their more permanent spots. They're open for lunch, Monday through Saturday, and dinner Friday and Saturday.

La Plage de Maui Restaurant $$ POLYNESIAN   Near the beach of the same name, it has absolutely gorgeous views and is a romantic stop for lunch: Think burgers, steaks, and fish. Cash only.

📞 **689/74-71-74.**

Le Belvédère $$$ FRENCH   Get ready for a jaw-dropping view of the city of Papeete and the island of Moorea. The food is French inspired, but really it's the view you want, so get there early for the sunset.

📞 **689/42-73-44.**

Le Carré $$ FRENCH   Le Meridien Tahiti's fine-dining is under a round thatched roof and set romantically on a deck beside the beach and the resort's wade-in swimming pool. The cuisine mixes French and island sauces and flavors. Fixed-price dinners offer up to three courses.

At Le Meridien Tahiti, PK 15, Punaauia. 📞 **689/47-07-07.** www.lemeridientahiti.com/en/lecarre.

Le Lotus $$$ CONTINENTAL/FRENCH   Now this is really romantic. You sit in one of two thatched-roof rooms that extend over the water and look straight at the gorgeous spires of Moorea. All the tables are at the water's edge, and the lagoon is backlit, just to make it swoon worthy. Fish are attracted to the light, but this is one time you will probably just pay attention to each other and the elaborate menu. The perfect cuisine usually has a French flavor, but they have visiting chefs so the menu might change for your visit.

In the InterContinental Resort Tahiti, Faaa (7km/4 miles west of Papeete). ☎ **689/86-51-10**, ext. 5512. www.tahiti.intercontinental.com.

L'O à la Bouche $$$ INTERNATIONAL   This excellent and celebrated Papeete restaurant has a charming French bistro ambience; however, it hardly serves bistro food or prices. Fish is dressed with elegant fruit sauces; ginger is used imaginatively; and the shellfish salads are delicious.

Passage Cardella, Papeete. ☎ **689/45-29-76.**

TAHITI BY NIGHT

Tahitian Dance Shows   Like Moorea's, Tahiti's big resorts have shows at least 1 night a week (tickets usually run about $100 apiece). See the **Grande Danse de Tahiti troupe** at the Tiare Restaurant at InterContinental Resort Tahiti (☎ **689/86-51-10**—call the resort and ask which show reenacts the dance that seduced the crew of HMS *Bounty!*). For another good show: **Captain Bligh Restaurant and Bar** (☎ **689/43-62-90**), usually at 8:30pm Fridays and Saturdays. Expect to pay about $63 for the show plus a seafood buffet at Captain Bligh's and $106 for the shows at the big resorts.

Pub-Crawling   Papeete has pubs and clubs for everyone's taste, from upscale private (*privé*) discothèques to dance halls where Tahitians play guitars while drinking Hinano beer. If you look like a tourist, you get entry into the private clubs where things really get going after 9pm (except on Sunday, when most pubs are closed). None of the clubs are inexpensive.

The **Piano Bar** (☎ **689/42-88-24**) is the most popular of the "sexy clubs" along the narrow **Rue des Écoles** in Papeete's *mahu* district, where strip shows feature female impersonators. It's open daily from 3pm to 3am. For a tamer evening, head to **Hotel Le Royal Tahitien,** in Pirae (☎ **689/50-40-40**), where on Fridays a live band plays Tahitian music and Wednesdays feature jazz jams. This seaside place has good food at reasonable prices.

PHUKET & KOH SAMUI
Exotic Luxury & Amazing Hospitality

Phuket and Koh Samui are among Thailand's largest islands, and their natural beauty, incredible beaches, and cultural offerings make them uniquely conducive to romance. With relatively small populations compared to Bangkok, a casual attitude prevails on each of these southern Thai isles. Spend a week, spend a month—your passion quotient is bound to rise the longer you linger amid this natural splendor.

Phuket

You will hear two things about Phuket: "It's wonderful" and "it's awful." Our feeling: It's both, but the wonderful is preponderant. Phuket is crowded but has some of the most amazing topography anywhere. The rock formations, especially at the sea, as you approach this Indian Ocean island (which, by the way, is the size of Singapore) are transfixing; it is as if some king-sized dice thrower took the mammoth rocks and scattered them at random. The effect is breathtaking.

It can also be exciting to explore Old Phuket, following the preserved narrow streets of the old Sino-Portugese town. The historic sector was founded when Phuket's main activity was tin mining, but now it has many chic shops, restaurants, and antique galleries. It's delightful to get lost in its winding lanes.

KEY ATTRACTIONS

Nature Excursions   The good news about Phuket is that glorious vistas are everywhere: long sweeps of tropical beaches, hidden coves by the hundreds or maybe thousands, and magnificent hotels. The not-so-good news is that the popularity of this place threatens the romance quotient with extreme overcrowding. Case in point: We took a tour to the Phi Phi island group, whose sights are so gorgeous they ended up in James Bond movies. Now everyone wants to see them, so when you go, say, to the part of the Phi Phi islands where they filmed *The Man with the Golden Gun*, you get 30 other boats and hundreds of people. The beach is smothered—and so are your romantic feelings.

On the other hand, we took a tour to Phang Nga Bay with **John Gray's Sea Canoe,** 124 Soi 1 Yaowarat Rd., Taladyai, Muang (© **66/76-254-5057;** www.johngray-seacanoe.com), and it was a whole different experience and one that we would highly recommend. We were taken to the national park there and witnessed one of the most fantastic sights we have ever seen. The bay has a strong tide, and when it's low, you get into the small kayaks that Gray designed for exploring the low caves (you lie down not to get scraped by hanging stalactites) and discovering the interior rooms of the limestone mountains that rise from the water in this bay. It is hard to describe how beautiful, mysterious, and other worldly these mangrove forests, caverns, caves and clearings are.

Taking a Private Speedboat Day Trip   A private snorkeling day trip is a great way to be romantic. This trip features a private boat, lunch with wine, a lovely bouquet of flowers, and an itinerary of isolated beaches where you can enjoy the beauty while escaping the Phuket crowds. All trips are in stellar settings at either Kai Nok Island or Racha Yai Island. Reliable operators are **Coral Seekers** (© **66/76-221-442;** www.coralseekers.com), **Off Spray Leisure** (© **66/81-894-1274;** www.offsprayleisure.com), and **Charter Yachts Phuket** (© **66/76-360-876;** charteryachtsphuket.com).

HOTELS WITH HEART

Aleenta $$$ If you want a romantic beach place, and you like the clean modern lines of glass-box houses right on the water or ocean views from a split-level with ceiling-to-floor glass, this is paradise. Gorgeously positioned beside a clean endless beach, Aleenta is far from the crowd, slightly off Phuket Island, on the mainland. The landscaping has Asian sensibilities, and the small ocean-side spa is remarkable, surrounded by the sound of crashing waves. (The spa menu is inventive: Water buffalo milk bath treatment anyone?)

The range of guest rooms are almost Scandinavian in spareness, with outdoor showers, Jacuzzis, and private pools. Most are oriented to the beach and water, but a few sacrifice an ocean view for privacy and a nice-sized private or semi-private pool. There's a choice of three good restaurants on property.

On Natai (Pilai) Beach. ℂ **66/2-514-8112.** www.aleenta.com.

B-Lay Tong Phuket $ This reasonable hotel is on the quiet end of a popular beach; most rooms offer modern low-slung beds and Eames chairs— and direct access to the pool or a view of the Andaman Sea.

198 Taveewong Rd, Patong, Kathu. ℂ **66/86519-0556.** www.b-laytong.com.

Paresa $$$ In a major engineering feat, villas appear to be gently strewn down the hill, each with a view, a pool, and a Frank Lloyd Wright sensibility that feels international but warm. We love the outdoor showers with the oversized heads and granite walls, and the fact that you get your own infinity pool whose horizon is linked with the dynamite view of the sea. Down several levels is the hotel pool, which is very large, shaded by an old Banyan tree, and has an 8-pound crystal at its center for balance and harmony, always good for romance! Don't miss the fantastic rooftop restaurant (actually two restaurants in one: Thai and Italian). Note: Paresa is expensive, but prices drop sharply in the low season.

49 Moo 6, Layi-Nakalay Ro., Kamala. ℂ **66/76-302-000.** www.paresaresorts.com.

The Pavilions Resort $$$ From the moment you turn into Pavilions, romance is in view. The long driveway is a bower of feathery bamboo as you climb up the hilltop (though you remain just 5 minutes from a lovely beach). Everything here is geared toward romance. Each pavilion has its own pool and sala (outdoor room and lounging area); not only that, your expansive and ultra-modern villa has its own spa and steam room! The living room is huge, and the equally big bedroom has a gauzy surround, and a chic black-walled shower and tub area. A tapas and grill restaurant higher up on the hill is part of the **360 Bar**, which is *the* place to be at sunset. Warning: Pavilions is built on a steep hill. The golf cart service can take you to breakfast or other meals, but if you prefer to walk, you'd better be in good shape.

31/1 Moo 6, Cherngtalay, Thalang. ℂ **66/7631-7600.** www.thepavilionsresorts.com.

MOST ROMANTIC RESTAURANTS

This atmospheric China Inn Café (**$;** 20 Thalang Rd., in Old Phuket; ✆ **66/76-356-239**) serves excellent Chinese-inspired specialties at everyday prices. If you want a break from Thai food, try Diavolo (**$;** Paresa Resort, 49 Moo 6, Layi-Nakalay Rd., Kamala; ✆ **66/76-302-000**) for Italian delicacies.

Baan Rim Pa $ ROYAL THAI   Baan Rim Pa provides dining in a romantic indoor setting or overlooking the scenic bay from open-air outdoor terraces close enough to the sea to hear the waves below. This two-story restaurant is popular, so reserve a table early. Take a seat at the piano bar and enjoy fine cocktails and wines from a celebrated cellar. The owner operates a few good neighboring spots on the cliff side, including **Joe's Downstairs,** for cocktails and tapas (✆ **66/7634-4254**).

223 Prabaramee Rd., Patong Beach. ✆ **66/7634-0789.** www.baanrimpa.com.

Mom Tri's Kitchen $$ INTERNATIONAL/THAI   Fine dining in an open-air garden terraces or covered patio, plus a "Wine Spectator" award-winning wine cellar. Two menus offer inventive international dishes and Thai favorites, both with local seafood, in a setting overlooking the crystal waters, ringed by the white crescent of Kata Noi Beach.

12 Kata Noi Rd., Kata Noi. ✆ **66/76-333-568.** www.momtriphuket.com.

Siam Indigo $$ THAI FUSION   Fabulous Thai cuisine, and atmosphere are the lure here, though the American-style steaks are also standout.

8 Phang Nga Rd., in old Phuket. ✆ **66/76-256-697.** www.siamindigo.com.

360, Eastland, & Plantation Club $ MEDITERRANEAN/THAI   The food at Pavilion Resort's restaurants is essentially Thai with some international dishes—and we've enjoyed each dish we've tried here. Especially recommended are the pan-seared foie gras, the perfect sirloin, and the tasty tuna carpaccio. The 360 restaurant is particularly romantic.

At the Pavilions Resort, 31/1 Moo 6, Cherngtalay, Thalang. ✆ **66/7631-7600.** www.thepavilionsresorts.com.

33Mu5 & The Edge $; $$ ASIAN/THAI   The cuisine at Aleenta's mostly Asian restaurants tend toward the healthful but carefully tease out fabulous traditional Thai flavors using herbs and exotic spices in the hands of chefs who know what they are doing. Extra special variations are available for special moments. Private dining is the perfect choice: a romantic dinner for two at a restaurant or on the beach.

At the Aleenta Resort. www.aleenta.com.

PHUKET BY NIGHT

Sky-lanterns on the Beach   Make a wish as your sky-lantern (*khom loi*) lifts up into the air and watch it together as it drifts over the sea. Try to

POPPING THE question

Pepper was proposed to in Koh Samui while researching this book. Fred took her down to the beach at The Banyan Tree hotel and, with the water lapping at their feet, popped the question. To honor that moment and her fiancé, we place this advice in this destination.

A proposal is a signature moment in your life. How many times do people tell the story of how they engineered the perfect proposal, or how blown away they were by the place or way their partner presented the question

and ring? It doesn't matter if the answer is a forgone conclusion—women want the moment of the proposal to be a significant event, and many men strive to guarantee it a special place in both their memories. It doesn't have to be the man who proposes (unless, of course, it's a gay male couple) but it's one of those traditions that seems to hang on.

Make your proposal in any way you see fit, but see our Romantic Interest Index starting on p. 391 for some fairly awesome locations in which to do the deed.

guess what each other wished for! Setting off sky-lanterns is a Thai tradition for good luck. These days, you can buy sky lanterns cheaply from beach vendors year round. *Tip:* This activity is best at night.

Canoe Tour by Starlight   Explore the sea caves, or *hongs,* which can be entered only by canoe when the tide is right, and then enjoy a sunset Thai seafood dinner. The **Hong by Starlight tour** begins after dark with three natural light sources that can create a memory for life. Contact **John Gray's Sea Canoe** (✆ **66/76-254-5057;** www.johngray-seacanoe.com).

Siam Niramit Phuket Show   This tastefully done cultural extravaganza is located just off the By-Pass Road, in the outskirts of Phuket Town. The show features singing, dancing, and traditional martial arts with more than 100 performers in lavish costumes. It's over-the-top with wild special effects. See it on a gigantic stage listed in the Guinness World Records. 55/81 Moo 5, Rassada, Muang. ✆ **66/76-335-001-2.** www.siamniramit.com.

Koh Samui

Located in the gulf of Thailand, Koh Samui is Thailand's third largest island—a third the size of Phuket and less developed. The *New York Times* tagged it one of the "41 Places to Go" in 2011, and a lot of people listened. The hotels are heavily booked, even in the low (rainy) season, mid-June through August. That's a good time to go: It's substantially cheaper, and the weather can be very good. You might get three days of rain, but you also can get weeks with no rain at all!

In any season, the beaches and coves are glorious, and the water is barely cool. Palms and lush vegetation are everywhere, as are some of the most amazing luxury resorts ever imagined. You can also stay very cheaply here, but if you can afford the first two hotels we mention here—for an anniversary, wedding or proposal—we heartily recommend it.

KEY ATTRACTIONS

Water Fun   You can kayak, sail, swim, snorkel, and beach it: This is the perfect place just to relate to the water. Because healthy coral reefs are here and good swimming beaches (**Lamai Beach** is a good place to start), snorkeling is particularly rewarding. The water is so warm that the two of you may need a cold shower, if you prefer your water below bath temperature. For watersports rentals, contact **Koh Samui Sports Center** (© **66/77-419-909;** www.wateredgesports.com) or **Saard's Water Sports Center** (© **66/77-247-656;** www.saardswatersport.com).

Island-hopping   Beautiful islands are all over this area, and **Kol Tao** is an eye-full. A day trip can take you there quite easily for snorkeling and picnics. Ang Thong Marine Park is close enough for a day trip, but deserted enough to offer unspoiled Crusoe charm. *The Beach* may have been filmed elsewhere, but we can't help but think this 42-island archipelago was the inspiration. One of the park's islands, **Maekoh,** has its own inland lake—with challenging steps that give thighs a workout. Most Koh Samui hotels and travel agencies can arrange tours to Kol Tao and Ang Thong. Consider using **Samuii Boat Charter** (© **66/87276-7598;** www.samuiboatcharter.com); **Oceans Elite Charters** (© **66/77-427-244;** www.oceanselitecharters.com), or **Koh Samui Speedboat Charters and Tours** (© **66/7742-5262;** www.samuispeedboat. com).

The X-rated Rocks   At the southern end of Lamai Beach lie Koh Samui's two famous rocks, **Hin Ta** and **Hin Yai,** Grandfather and Grandmother Stone. The rocks are seen as strong fertility symbols due to their likeness to male and female genitalia.

Hitting the Spa   The spa scene has rocketed here. All the international five-star resorts, such as **Anantara** (© **66/77-428-300;** www.samui.anantara. com), **The Four Seasons** (© **66/77-243-000;** www.fourseasons.com/ kohsamui), and **The Banyan Tree** (© **66/77-915-333;** www.banyantree.com/ en/samui), offer pricey, top-range treatments by well-trained staff in beautiful spas.

A number of excellent day spas also may be perfect for couples who want to share a treat:

- **Ban Sabai**, 59 Moo 4, Bohut, Bang Rak, on Big Buddha Beach (© **66/ 7724-5175;** www.ban-sabai.com), has a wide range of therapies given in teak Thai houses or beachside.
- **Eranda Herbal Spa,** 9/37 Moo 2, North Chaweng Road (© **66/7730-0323;** www.erandaspa.com), is a delightful escape perched in tropical gardens

with plunge pools, steam rooms, and Jacuzzis with views of Chaweng Bay. Choose from an open communal sala or private pavilions with their own steam rooms and Jacuzzis.

o **Tamarind Springs,** 205/7 Thong Takian (© **66/77-424-221;** www.tamarindsprings.com), just above the beach at Lamai, is a gem takes you back to nature. After the herbal steam room, you slip into the outdoor plunge pool. Must book in advance.

HOTELS WITH HEART

Four Seasons enthusiasts will not be disappointed with the luxe Phuket location (**$$$;** 219 Moo 5, Angthong; © **66/77-243-000;** www.fourseasons.com/kohsamu). From the small open-air lobby, you see the view of a lifetime: a hill that spirals down to the roaring endless sea. Inside, the perfection continues with superb service (your own butler, of course), signature spa treatments, and villas staggered along steep hillsides, most with a view of a turquoise sea, with your own pool. It's expensive, but significantly less so in low season.

The Amari Palm Reef $ Ask for the newer seaside suites that meld contemporary with traditional Thai decor. If you are watching your budget, go for the newer mid-range units in the small "village" across the road from the beach with separate pool. The main pool area is appealing, as is the dining terrace overlooking it. Far enough from the Chaweng strip to be quiet and comfortable but close enough to party for those looking for nightlife. Though it's a short walk to a less rocky beach, this beach is beautiful. **Prego,** the excellent Italian restaurant, is located here.

Chaweng Beach. © **66/77-30-0306-09.** www.amari.com/palmreef.

The Banyan Tree $$$ The Banyan Tree has the same hilltop appeal as the Four Seasons. You look out at a huge view: the bay framed by boulders and the resort cascading down the steep hills, each villa tucked into the hillside beside its fairly large pool. The roomy villas are incredibly elegant with 15-foot ceilings and outdoor showers of tile and black slate that rival the bathroom's stylishness. Sitting rooms and floor-to-ceiling windows—most look out to the sea—are standard, and each villa has privacy from the others. With the steep location and the distance to the restaurants—the casual sand-floored Sands and the prestigious Saffron are both memorable—you will call for your "buggy" to get around.

The pool area, not far from the white sand beach, possesses what may be the biggest, longest, and loveliest pools we have seen anywhere. The spa offers a wildly innovative, hydrotherapeutic rainforest experience.

99/9 Moo 4, Maret. © **800/591-0439** or 66/77-915-333. www.banyantree.com.

The Library $$$ Designed by a Bangkok architect, this minimalist retreat offers a startlingly different contemporary slant, with namesake library.

If you love high-tech, these state-of-the-art rooms provide a range of luxuries, from huge plasma TVs to self-controlled colored lights and delightful rain showers.

14/1 Moo 2, Chaweng Beach. ℂ **66/7742-2767-8.** www.thelibrary.co.th.

Six Senses Hideaway $$$ Located on 20 tropical acres, the resort has a relaxing wellness orientation, and naturally, it's also dedicated to romance, even offering a "Rediscover the Romance" package. The program includes a three-hour couples spa package (with a consultation, herbal steam, sauna, "romance flower" bath, aroma massages and dehydration facial treatments), lodging in a luxury villa and a private dinner in a romantic spot at the resort's signature restaurant, Dining on the Rocks. The sophisticated hotel prides itself on responsible environmental stewardship of its grounds and provides extraordinary views and a variety of leisure activities. Villas include private pools, and couples can sign up for tours, diving trips, and cooking classes together. Of course, your personal butler will attend to you.

9/10 Moo 5, Baan Plai Laem, Bophu. ℂ **66/7724-5678.** www.sixsenses.com.

MOST ROMANTIC RESTAURANTS

The Pier $ FRENCH/INTERNATIONAL This fine French restaurant offers great food and atmosphere. Try the crab salad, followed by roasted salmon with lime butter sauce. Don't scrimp on dessert. Save room for the perennial French classics: rich chocolate mousse or crème brûlée.

Next to Bophut Pier in Fisherman's Village, Chaweng Beach. ℂ **66/77-430-681.**

Zico's $ BRAZILIAN This lively Brazilian-style restaurant combines music, drink, and authentic sexy Brazilian dance for a great night out. Food comes on massive skewers of meat and trays of delicacies (also graze along the enticing salad bar). The price is preset, so eat whatever and as much as you like. For more, simply slap a small coin green-side-up on the table. The red side signals "enough." This can be your wild night out!

38/2 Moo 3, Tambon Bo Phut. ℂ **66/7723-1560-3.** www.zicossamui.com.

KOH SAMUI BY NIGHT

Koh Samui is famous for its nightlife, which is concentrated in **Chaweng** and **Lamai.** A variety of bars and nightclubs can suit all tastes, and a trip to Koh Samui isn't complete without sampling some Mekong, the famous Thai whiskey. Certain monthly outdoor events can be fun, such as the **Full Moon Party**, where revelers dance the night away on the beach. The island of Koh Pha Ngan, a short boat ride away, also hosts a Full Moon party that has become world famous.

9 Gems Lounge and Restaurant $$$ Overlooking Chaweng Beach and Chaweng Lake, this dreamy lounge restaurant provides exclusive dining and wining with world fusion food. A great place to stop for some peppy cocktails and tapas. 141/190 Moo 6, Tambon Bophut. © **66/80-6920-520.** www.9gemssamui.com.

The Three Monkeys Pub and Restaurant $$ This bar seems to have it all for the casual traveler: free Internet, a pool table, great food, and fun atmosphere. Its menu exceeds typical pub grub; for example, the Sneezing Monkey is prepared with sliced beef filet, black pepper, and asparagus in a black soya sauce. Easy to find on Chaweng Road, the pub is open from 10:30am to 1am. 13/11, Moo 2, Tambon, Bophut. © **66/7742-2584.**

Adventure
Romance

13 Amorous Adventures: North America
14 Amorous Adventures: Exotic Lands

AMOROUS ADVENTURES: NORTH AMERICA

13

The thrill of white-water rafting, climbing rugged mountains, or being in the heart of nature, with no sign of humankind for miles—that adrenaline charges every part of our beings. Adventure makes us depend on each other and watch out for each other. In some ways it's the most intimate kind of vacation because it reminds us how much we love life and love each other, and, frankly, how much we need each other. We are never more aware, more focused, or more fully present than when we have adrenaline coursing through our veins. To share this with the one you love is magical and, if you're not too scared, romantic. The trick is finding something that is perhaps slightly dangerous, but not so dangerous that it is folly to do it. In this chapter we offer destinations and activities that provide a thrill but, if the rules are followed, do not create unreasonable vulnerability.

ALASKAN CRUISE
Into the Wild

We think that everyone, at some point in their lives, should witness the majesty of the Inside Passage, the network of waterways that weaves through the islands on the Pacific Coast of North America from Puget Sound into southeastern Alaska. The best, and really the only, way to see it is from a ship during the summer, the only time you are likely to get predictably good weather. A huge number of cruise ships are lined up to take you there. They vary in size, and smaller ships can explore areas the larger ships cannot. Still, especially for couples with children, we like the larger ones that offer many romantic services and give parents, and grandparents, some romantic time for themselves, not to mention great programs that keep the kids entertained from sunrise to sunset.

Routes vary, but the American cruise ships typically start and end in Seattle (see p. 61) or Juneau. Ferries are inexpensive but bare-bones; however, the good news is that they make many small stops where luxury cruises do not. You can catch the **British Columbia ferries** (℡ **250/381-1401;** www.bc ferries.com) from Vancouver Island to Prince Rupert, BC, and then board the **Alaska Marine Highway System** (℡ **800/642-0066** or 907/465-3941; www. dot.state.ak.us/amhs).

Following is a conglomeration of the stops that often are included in typical itineraries by cruise ships, and the special activities and excursions that you can arrange (often done long before your sail date). These destinations are also accessible by ferry should you choose to design your own tour.

Juneau

The capital of Alaska is a lovely city with the usual tourist shops at the pier, but here you have Mount Juneau and Mount Roberts as your backdrop, and you are surrounded by wilderness. A real thrill, though a pretty hefty bite at your wallet, is a helicopter ride to the **Juneau icefields** (a mere 1,500 square miles that offers more than 140 glaciers).

The **Tracy Arm Fjord**, a startlingly beautiful 22-mile-long fjord of continuous waterfalls spilling down glacial walls, is just south of Juneau and a worthwhile day trip or overnight excursion if your cruise line doesn't already visit the fjord. The magnificent scale of the fjord is visually hypnotic, but you will also observe wildlife (bear, mountain goats, eagles) on the shoreline and the cliffs above. Mile-high peaks line the narrow, twisting waterway, and waterfalls cascade thousands of feet down the mountains. It's very likely you'll see marine mammals, and in season, whales.

HOTELS WITH HEART

The Capital Inn $$ This restored 1906 mansion near the capital takes you back to the romantic 19th century. Period decorations and antiques in the lobby hint at the fineries in your room: high ceilings, a fireplace, and, of course, a claw-foot tub! The inn is a friendly place where people meet and greet over breakfast and in the afternoon, wine and cheese. The $339 suite gets you the entire top floor of the house.

113 W. 5th St. ℡ **888/588-6507** or 907/586-6507. www.alaskacapitalinn.com.

Pearson's Pond Luxury Inn and Adventure Spa $$$ There is a bit of artifice here: You feel like you are in the wilderness, but you really are in suburban Juneau. This "as if" approach might bother purists, but these are lovely accommodations, with kitchenettes, feather beds, luxurious bathrooms, and a good spa and health club. Enjoy the inn's genteel hospitality, plus afternoon events in the lounge and plenty of privacy when you want it. Its off-site condo is squarely in the $$ category.

4541 Sawa Circle. ℡ **888/658-6328** or 907/789-3772. www.pearsonspond.com.

MOST ROMANTIC RESTAURANTS

Twisted Fish Company $$ SEAFOOD   This casual but romantic spot, with a light oak interior, scenery-packed views, and an open kitchen, overlooks Gastineau Channel at the cruise ship dock. This is the place to get cedar-smoked salmon or fresh halibut or whatever is on the chef's fresh menu that evening.

550 S. Franklin St. ✆ **907/463-5033.** www.twistedfish.hangaronthewharf.com. Closed Oct–Apr.

Zephyr $$ MEDITERRANEAN   This restaurant's planked floors, high ceilings, and large storefront windows create the illusion of being in an historic room, even though it is a relatively new restaurant. Zephyr is a great place for a special date; each table has privacy, and the fine service tells you a lot about the restaurant's ambitions. The continental cuisine is inspired by Italy with classic dishes like grilled calamari and osso buco. Other more local offerings like scallops and salmon are prepared well. Desserts are excellent.

200 Seward St. ✆ **907/780-2221.** http://zephyrrestaurant.com.

Petersburg on Mitkof Island

Visiting another colorful town every day is partly why cruising Alaska is so much fun. Petersburg is a pretty town with fishing boats and pleasure cruisers dominating its winding waterways. The murals, totems, and sculpture of local artists and crafts people line the downtown streets, and you'll find its Norwegian heritage in the architecture. Wander the town, take a floatplane expedition to the **Le Conte Glacier** (weather permitting), or hike in the nearby forest. Petersburg's bay offers amazing sights: icebergs, whales, sea lions, and seals. Kayaking in these waters can be a private romantic experience of discovery and wonder. Small ships carry their own kayaks, while larger ships have vendors on shore.

Point Adolphus

Smaller ships stop here, particularly because Point Adolphus is a premier Alaskan feeding area for humpback whales. The cruising area follows the coastline of **Chichagof Island** and usually reveals marine mammals and eagles along the huge and wild **Tongass National Forest.**

Glacier Bay National Park

Glacier Bay is on almost every cruise itinerary with good reason. The ice fields are receding (and this can be depressing) but the sight of these massive walls of snow and ice are still magnificent. The calving of the glaciers (when a huge mass of ice breaks off and crashes into the sea) and the accompanying roar are nothing short of amazing. Some expeditions will let you get close in kayaks; others keep you safely away to avoid the danger of falling ice and the possibility of waves swamping the boat. Smaller boats will stop at the park preserve for walks in old-growth forests. This is also whale country, and you might see them surfacing any time!

Admiralty Island

About 25 miles from Juneau at the opening of Gastineau Channel is Admiralty Island, which includes the **Kootznoowoo Wilderness** and may have the highest number of brown bears on Earth. If you find this romantic rather than scary as hell, you will enjoy the island's **Pack Creek Bear Viewing Area.** Guides will show you how to spot bears; best viewing is in July and August. Amazingly, the bears pay no attention to tourists, which is good because there are no barriers of any kind. Bear sightings are common from boats as well, and tour operators can organize fly-overs, camping with guides, or circling the island by rented kayak to see wildlife, including bald eagles.

Sitka

Many, but not all, tour boats will stop at tiny Sitka to see this picturesque island with visible Russian traditions. Sitka's docks can't accommodate mammoth ships; only ship's tenders (small boats) can use the dock, which helps control the crowds. As a result, Sitka feels like a real town and not a Disneyland facsimile. The Russian fur traders have moved on, but their influence endures. The small **St. Michael's Russian Orthodox Cathedral** (240 Lincoln St.; ✆ **907/747-8120;** services Mon–Sat 6pm, Sun 9:30am) is the gem of any landing here, and there is also an old Russian Orthodox Cemetery. **The Russian Bishops House** of Innocent Veniaminov, a 19th-century priest who translated scripture into native languages and helped found the continuing Russian Orthodox community, has been preserved at 501 Lincoln St.; the tour is worth taking. Still, Alaska's Russian past is not the most romantic reason to get to Sitka. That honor goes to the coastal and mountain beauty, including the dormant volcano **Mt. Edgecombe**, and the astounding richness of the native **Tlingit art** collected and displayed here.

KEY ATTRACTIONS

Sheldon Jackson Museum   This fine collection of native art and cultural treasures was amassed in the 19th century by Sheldon Jackson, a missionary. The extensive collections are often mindboggling and can be viewed as true art and not just artifacts. The gift shop represents top-notch Native American artists, and this is an extremely good place to buy a mask, box, or ivory carving.

104 College Dr. ✆ **907/747-8981.** www.museums.state.ak.us. Mid-May to Sept 14 admission $5, $4 for seniors; Sept 15 to mid-May admission $3.

Sitka National Historical Park   Created in the late 19th century, this park is very touching and perhaps the best place in Alaska to learn about Tlingit culture. Antique totem poles are displayed in a lovely high-ceilinged hall, and many reproduction poles are outside. During the summer, artists at the **Southeast Alaska Indian Cultural Center** demonstrate traditional methods of craft, sculpture, beading, and basketry. You can share a few private moments strolling a trail bounded by tall spruce and hemlock that displays more totems and ultimately leads you to an important Tlinglit battle site. You can also sign up for tours and tribe activities here.

106 Metlakatla St. ℭ **907/747-6281.** www.nps.gov/sitk. Free admission.

Wildlife Watching In season, you have a very good chance of seeing whales and marine mammals in this area; in fact, the wildlife is so abundant that some tour operators *guarantee* sightings of sea lions, orcas, humpback whales, bears, otters, and so on—or they will refund your money! If animals touch your hearts, you will fall in love with the **Raptor Rehabilitation Center** (1000 Alaska Raptor Way; ℭ **800/643-9425** or 907/747-8662; www.alaskaraptor.org; May–Sept admission $12 adults, $6 children 12 and under; call for info Oct–Apr), where injured eagles, owls, and hawks are nursed back to health. You can view the animals up close or inside the exceptional aviary, where a flight-training center helps the raptors soar again. The center's wheelchair-accessible nature trail leads to a salmon stream where free eagles often feed.

Sea Kayaking Sitka's protected waters and bays are perfect for kayaking. Here's another near guarantee to see marine mammals, such as otters and seals, and raptors, such as eagles and hawks. You might glimpse whales, too! Kayaking around here is a romantic interlude, especially in a two-person kayak.

HOTELS WITH HEART
Fly-In Fish Inn $ This very romantic inn offers excellent views right on the water. Enter your room or suite from a covered walkway and cozy up in bed with down comforters and pillows. Later, walk down to the classy waterfront bar for a drink in front of the fireplace before bedtime. In nice weather, you can linger on the bar's deck over the harbor. You also get your custom breakfast here in the morning. As the name implies, there is an air taxi on the dock (**Air Sitka;** ℭ **907/747-7920**).

485 Katlian St. ℭ **907/747-7910.** www.flyinfishinn.com. Rate includes full breakfast.

Totem Square Hotel and Marina $ The use of Tlingit colors (red, black, and white) and Tlingit art define this hotel, which offers great service and ambience and provides lovely rooms and views (and a waterfront suite) at decent rates. And if you get the munchies in the middle of the night, snacks are available at the Dock Shack Cafe. A dock for tour and fishing charter boats is attached.

201 Katlian St. ℭ **866/300-1353** or 907/747-3693. www.totemsquarehotel.com.

MOST ROMANTIC RESTAURANTS
The Channel Club $$ STEAK & SEAFOOD Enjoy the ocean views from this simple but elegant dining room. There's fresh grilled fish and an ample salad bar, but the real star here is steak. The restaurant provides a shuttle if you don't have a car.

2906 Halibut Point Rd. ℭ **907/747-7440.** www.sitkachannelclub.com.

Larkspur Caffe $ CAFE   This little, happy cafe, with seating indoors and out, has an eclectic menu and winning waterfront views. Located in an historic cable house, the decor is funky, but in a good way. Check out the excellent local lox and smoked fish.

2 Lincoln St. ℂ **907/966-2326.** www.facebook.com/larkspurcafe.

Skagway

Skagway is probably the most historically preserved town in Alaska. The downtown buildings have been restored to the look and feel of the gold rush days. While many of them are filled with inappropriate merchandise for a frontier town, there is still enough romance to beguile visitors. If you are on a ferry rather than a ship that is moving on, you can take the ferry from Skagway to **Haines**, which is less touristed and a prime spot for eagles and other wildlife. Some of the luxury ships stop at Haines, too.

From May to September, the **White Pass and Yukon Route narrow-gauge railroad line** (231 2nd Ave.; ℂ **800/343-7373;** www.wpyr.com) is a romantic way to witness Skagway's scenery and wildlife. Some of the cars are as old as the railroad (completed in 1900), and the antique touches include the train's speed: The train kind of creeps up the mountain (lovely sights on a clear day!). Most enticing are Friday and Monday afternoons, when the steam trains go over the pass and 6 miles beyond to Fraser Meadows; it's a taste of history and can be a sweet time to talk and enjoy each other for about 3 hours.

A romantic place to stay is **Chilkoot Trail Outpost ($;** ℂ **907/983-3799;** www.chilkoottrailoutpost.com), located a half-mile from the head of the Chilkoot Trail; the outpost has romantic log cabins and some suites; all rooms come with breakfast. They are located 8½ miles outside of town and beyond the press of other cruise ship tourists. If weather permits, there are nightly campfires and s'mores. Dinner is served in a fine log building. Another good choice is the **Skagway Inn Bed & Breakfast ($;** 655 Broadway; ℂ **888/752-4929** or 907/983-2289; www.skagwayinn.com), a Victorian Inn with a past (it was a brothel at the turn of the 20th century), and 10 antiques-appointed guestrooms. The Inn's quiet and lovely fine-dining spot, **Olivia's ($;** 655 Broadway; ℂ **907/983-2289;** www.skagwayinn.com) at the Skagway Inn, is worth a visit even if you don't stay there—they specialize in Alaskan crab dishes and offer a choice of excellent wines.

Ketchikan

Ketchikan is often shrouded in mist or saturated by a downpour. Its small downtown is smothered when the big cruise ships drop off everyone on Front Street. But there is a good reason to see this place: **Totem Bight State Historical Park** (ℂ **907/247-8574;** dnr.alaska.gov). Here a clan house and totem poles are preserved in a beautifully plotted area, reached after a short walk in the woods. Downtown is the **Southeast Alaska Discovery Museum** (ℂ **907/228-6220;** www.fs.fed.us/r10/tongass/districts/discoverycenter), a lively educational resource on the local Tlingit and Haida cultures. **The Totem Heritage Center** (℡ **907/225-5900;** www.city.ketchikan.ak.us) has a uniquely precious stand of 19th-century totem poles, the largest collection in existence. Because of their age and the need to protect these antique treasures from the elements, they are, unlike most totem poles, displayed (beautifully) indoors. If you want to see an authentic native village and actual totem carvers in action, visit **Saxman Native Village** (℡ **907/225-4846;** www.capefoxtours.com), a few miles outside Ketchikan. Here, a cultural show and tour features the Cape Fox Dancers, who perform traditional storytelling through song and dance; the show is usually timed to cruise visits, so if you are on a big boat, it's likely they will direct you there. The totems are not as dramatically arranged as the ones in Ketchikan, but the carving and the performances make it a worthy excursion.

Also in Ketchikan, look for Creek Street, known as the **Boardwalk** because it really is an antique boardwalk looming over Ketchikan Creek; it's lined by restaurants, shops, a museum, and private homes, plus some excellent salmon viewing areas. For the romantic pay-off, follow the boardwalk through the old growth forest. These giants humble us and make us want to celebrate Earth's gifts on such generous display here. **Deer Mountain Tribal Hatchery and Eagle Center** (℡ **800/252-5158** or 907/228-5530; www.dmthec.org) also makes for a stirring visit where you can view the salmon cycle in Ketchikan Creek. Salmon are programmed by their DNA to return to the place where they were spawned, and you can see that here, as salmon work against the current to get back "home" to spawn (and die). Depending on the season, you'll see the salmon cruising in or feeding the little hatchlings before they depart for the ocean. You can also enter the eagle enclosure and get close to these magnificent birds.

If you have time, see **Misty Fjords National Monument** (℡ **907/225-2148;** www.gorp.com/parks), 22 miles from Ketchikan. A few cruises go here, but seeing Misty Fjords by seaplane (always ready at the docks) is a huge thrill and scores high for romance. Called the Yosemite of the North for its glacier-cut granite mountains, this 2-million-acre area also has lots of deep saltwater fiords. Mountain goats, bears, orcas, porpoises, and eagles are among the wildlife on view. Hope for clear weather; Ketchikan is rarely dry.

HOTELS WITH HEART

Black Bear Inn $ This unexpectedly luxurious inn reflects the best of Alaskan traditions and places your right on the water with access to a private beach. Fireplaces, decorative wood, and native art merge with leather couches and chairs to set a mood of luxury and leisure. The rooms have a feeling of privacy and relationship to the outdoors. You can sit on your porch and cuddle! You might prefer the especially romantic separate cabin that overlooks the water. The cabin has its own kitchen; otherwise, guests breakfast in a communal kitchen.

5528 North Tongass Highway. ℡ **907/225-4343.** stayinalaska.com.

Cape Fox Lodge $ This gorgeous, even fabled, place, is nestled in the trees above downtown, and you need to take a funicular to get here. Big windows give you treetop views, while you are surrounded by serious Tlinglit art and sculpture. The place has almost a spiritual quality. Ask for a room with a view of the sea and the islands. The rooms are cheerful and big and have very nice bathrooms.

800 Venetia Ave. ⓒ **800/325-4000** or 907/225-8001. www.capefoxlodge.com.

MOST ROMANTIC RESTAURANTS

Bar Harbour Restaurant $$ AMERICAN Try to reserve a table on this spot's romantic deck, complete with views of the harbor, narrows, and mountains. The ambitious menu features seafood, meats (steak, lamb, pork), and numerous vegetarian entrees.

2813 Tongass Highway. ⓒ **907/225-2813.** wwwbarharborrestaurantketchikan. com.

The Heen Kahidi $$ AMERICAN This eatery is the perfect translation of stylish rustic. A charming fireplace dominates the dining room, and lots of windows with gorgeous views make it romantic as well as welcoming. The food is simple but very good and is served from breakfast through dinner.

In the Cape Fox Lodge, 800 Venetia Ave. ⓒ **800/325-4000** or 907/225-8001. www. capefoxlodge.com.

Inland Excursion to Denali

Most cruises from Seattle to Alaska offer expeditions to **Denali National Park** (www.nps.gov/dena), lasting from 3 to 7 days. Some hardy people camp and hike through the 6-million-acre park, while others prefer to stay at a lodge. If the latter is your preference, we like the simple but cozy **North Face Lodge**, which has gorgeous views from every room, well-organized hiking and bicycle tours, and a truly hospitable atmosphere. They will pick you up at the train station and narrate the beautiful 5-hour drive to this well-situated lodge. Don't expect luxury or Wi-Fi, but the scenery and food will wow you (**$$;** ⓒ **907/683-2290;** rates include tours and meals, 3 night minimum). Denali is the perfect place to take guided day trips to see Dall sheep, caribou, wolves, moose, grizzly bears, eagles, and the other wild inhabitants of this majestic park. Touring Denali is aided by its great shuttle-bus system (www. reservedenali.com); you reserve a seat way in advance of your trip, especially for the morning buses that take you to see the most wildlife. You can take the bus out, hike, and then catch a bus back. **Mount McKinley,** one of the highest and most impressive peaks in the world, is here. Among the more thrilling Alaskan adventures: Drive about 3 hours from Denali to the historic town of **Talkeetna** and board a morning flight over Mount McKinley. Both **Talkeetna air taxi** (ⓒ **800/533-2218** or 907/733-2218) and **K2 Aviation** (ⓒ **800/764-2291**) have several options, ranging from a trip to McKinley's base camp (from $205 per person) to the glacier ($265) to landing on the summit ($365–$440).

Note: Weather often interferes, and you must be there early before the clouds mass.

TOP HOTELS

Earthsong $ This is the authentic Alaska lodge experience. It's located on open tundra with vast views of the Alaska Range, 17 miles north of Denali National Park, which is to say, out in the big lonesome. The 10 rustic log cabins are cozy and warm and have quilts on the beds and sometimes hanging on the walls. Cabin sizes range from tiny (with a full bed) to commodious (queen beds, or 2 bedrooms, plus living space). The lodge includes a library and coffeehouse, **Henry's,** which serves breakfast and dinner and packs lunches. Earthsong is the dog-sledding concessionaire for the national park—romantic *and* cool. You can ride during the winter and tour the kennel during summer. Mush!

✆ **907/683-2863.** www.earthsonglodge.com.

Kantishna Roadhouse $$ If you are not here to rough it, this would be a good choice. The Kantishna feels more like a hotel than a lodge, which might be most attractive to less active couples and those who want more amenities. Rooms vary, but the main lodge options are generally spacious and luxurious; cabins, not so much. Activities include ranger lectures, biking, gold panning (it's a former mining area), and sled-dog demonstrations. The rack rates are high (around $450 for a double), but they include all meals and activities, plus transportation from the Denali train station, knocking it into the moderate category.

✆ **800/942-7420** or 907/683-1475 (907/459-2120 in winter). www.kantishnaroad house.com.

COLONIAL MEXICO: GUANAJUATO, SANTIAGO DE QUERÉTARO & SAN MIGUEL DE ALLENDE
Small Exquisite Cities

The old silver mining cities in the ruggedly handsome mountains of the Sierra Madre Occidental in Western Mexico have a very specific romantic allure. The architecture shows its Spanish roots, and the charming leafy squares and cobblestone streets are unique in this country. These days, U.S. ex-pats have discovered their charms and created boutique lodgings that augment the romance of these historic towns, just a two-hour drive northwest of Mexico City.

We recommend three cities: **Guanajuato** (Gwah-nah-*whah*-toh), **Santiago de Querétaro,** and **San Miguel de Allende.** When combined, they make for a wonderful road trip, but if you are driving from Guadalajara to Mexico City, you could add **Morelia** as a stopover. You could also start in Mexico City, drive to Morelia, and work back toward Guadalajara for easy flights in and out. The climate is universally lovely, and each town has its own appeal. While drivers visiting Mexico should be observant and careful, you will feel and be quite safe here.

Guanajuato

This postcard pretty town sits in a highland valley at a 6,586-foot elevation. Its streets seem planned by a throw of the dice and can be a little frustrating but that's part of what makes them so interesting. It's a charming, unpredictable city—almost a metaphor for romance.

KEY ATTRACTIONS

The Plazas This is a town of fountains and squares, and a good place to slow down time together. A beautiful fountain (bestowed by Emperor Maximilian) is at the centerpiece of the **Plazuela del Baratillo** (close to the Jardín Unión). People gather here, and the languid yet cheery atmosphere is very likable. We love the shaded plazas of Mexico; they are the heartbeat of small towns. In this town it's also the best spot for people-watching and eating. You'll find even more plazas immediately to the west: Walk along Juárez and Calle Positos streets, and you'll find three linked plazas—**Plaza San Roque, Jardín de la Reforma,** and **Plaza San Fernando**—perfect for romantic strolling. Outdoor coffee shops abound here, so sit down together for a sip of *José* in this aged and charming setting.

The Ranch Museum Back in the day, almost 200 haciendas were scattered around Guanajuato. Many are gone, but some of these former homes of rich agricultural and mining entrepreneurs are a restored, and some are public. The **Museo Exhacienda San Gabriel de Barrera** (Carr Guanajuato-Marfil Km 2.5; ℭ **52/473-732-0619;** admission 284 MXN [US$22] for students, 194 MXN [US$15] for children 7–12) is one that is now a museum. Not far from Marfil, this romantic survivor features an intricate and interesting garden derived from many international styles of planting, The hacienda is also worth visiting because it provides a window into 18th-century life on a *hacendado.* The hacienda has a beautiful baroque-styled chapel with an ornate *retablo* (altarpiece). The state-operated shop (open Wed–Sun) offers handicrafts produced today in the state.

Touring You will need a car or taxi to see some of the best sights and towns in this area. Take the highway route around the city; it offers super views and will lead you to the colorful areas of La Valenciana, La Cata, La Raya, and El Pípila. In La Valenciana, don't miss the magnificent 16th-century baroque **Church of San Cayetano,** which is quite grand inside, with numerous gilded statues and carving. Sometimes the sun will hit them just right, and the effect is glorious.

HOTELS WITH HEART

Casa Estrella de la Valenciana $$ Ascend the mountain above La Valenciana church to reach this adorable guest house. Sweeping views of the city and rural valley make it storybook perfect, and the American owners have added to the delightful tone with comfy and roomy interiors accented by regional handicrafts and art, plus terraces for each room. Room upgrades can include soaking tubs or even a steam room; opt for the two-bedroom casita. Public spaces include a lovely terrace and pool area.

Callejon Jalisco #10, Col. Valenciana. ✆ **866/983-8844** or 52/473-732-1784. www.mexicaninns.com. Rates include breakfast.

La Casa de Espíritus Alegres B&B $ Go here for a sense of real Mexico, down to its soul. The eccentric, 16th-century hacienda is filled with folk art, and ethnic atmosphere abounds. The affordable rooms have unexpected touches, such as the fireplaces in each unit. The real charm, however, derives from the art and colorful decorations. Day of the Dead papier-mâché incarnations are everywhere: humorous and festive, but somber, too. The garden outside is as colorful and attractive as the interior. You may not want to leave this place—especially after you taste the breakfast, an array of delicious Californian and Mexican options.

La Ex-Hacienda La Trinidad no. 1. ✆ **52/473-733-1013.** www.casaspirit.com.

MOST ROMANTIC RESTAURANTS

La Casa del Conde de la Valenciana $ Housed in the former home of a count, and just opposite another of his major contributions, La Valenciana Church. You will want to linger in the romantic shade of the outdoor patio. The menu harmoniously blends tradition with new recipes. So don't miss their take on chicken mole, tortillas, or the way they blend squash flowers into various dishes.

Carretera a Dolores Hidalgo. ✆ **52/473-731-2550.**

México Lindo y Sabroso $ This is nothing less than a shrine to Mexican—particularly Yucatan—cooking. Located in a quiet Paseo de la Presa neighborhood, you can avoid crowds if you arrive shortly after 5pm (though reservations are accepted). Seating is in three locations including a lovely dining room and the front veranda overlooking the street; for romance, we like the attractive interior courtyard. On the menu are many Mexican favorites: tostadas, green *pozole*, and excellent *flautas*. But as long as you are here, consider the scrumptious Yucatan specialties: The *cochinita pibil* and *panuchos* are wonderful.

154 Paseo de la Presa. ✆ **52/473-731-0529.**

GUANAJUATO BY NIGHT

La Clave Azul   This small bar, just off Plaza San Fernando, makes for an enjoyable evening and affords a glimpse of the Bohemian side of Guanajuato.

Two smallish cockeyed rooms have been carved out of rock walls and outfitted with rough-hewn furniture. It's really quite charming and something to share, like discovering a treasure together. The bar snacks can be pretty interesting, starting with the tapas and roast suckling pig. Segunda de Cantaritos 31, Zona Central. ⓒ **52/473-732-1561.**

Santiago de Querétaro

This historic city (in the small state of Querétaro) is only about an hour from San Miguel. It has a lovely square, and it immediately invites wandering. The square, which leads to tempting streets that are lined with attractive colonial buildings, is a good place to start. The charm runs so deep that you might want to schedule more than just a drive-by visit.

KEY ATTRACTIONS

Jardin Zenea This city's character springs from its many plazas, churches, and convents. This central plaza is a great gathering place, and it is especially fun on Sundays, when music is performed in a turn-of-the-20th-century bandstand. Join in the dancing if the spirit moves you.

Walking History This city is so pedestrian-friendly. Walk from Anador Libertad to the Plaza de Independencia for your choice of shaded patio dining and architectural eye candy. The colonial mansions are beautiful. Nearby is the **Galería Libertad,** which has changing exhibits of high quality art. Also on the plaza is the **Casa de la Corregidora** (Andador 5 de Mayo), the home of a female patriot in Mexico's fight for Independence from Spain. As you approach the plaza, don't miss the **Casa de Ecala** (Pasteur SN, Centro; ⓒ **52/442-238-5108**), a dramatic 18th-century home that is immediately recognizable because of its extensive use of wrought iron. The plaza's fountain centerpiece celebrates the architect of the city's most famous landmark, the aqueduct. You can see it from a distance from a small plaza behind the Casa la Corregidora—or you can explore it on your won.

Colonial Art The **Museo de Arte** (Allende no. 14 Sur; ⓒ **52/442-212-3523;** http://museodeartequeretaro.com/nueva/en; admission 388 MXN [US$30], free for children 11 and under, free for all on Tues). The museum houses one of the world's great collections of Mexican colonial art, plus it's located in the former convent of San Agustín, an architectural beauty worth visiting in its own right.

While exploring the town and walking the lovely, bougainvillea-laden streets, visit the historically interesting convent of **Santa Rosa de Viterbo** and the church of **Santa Clara** to see architectural masterpieces. They represent the best of Querétaro sacred architecture and include and an imaginative tower. Both churches have magnificent gilt altars, pictures, and carvings.

Opals Who knew? The state of Querétaro is second only to Australia for mining iridescent opals commercially. Shop the *lapidarias* (gem shops) in Querétaro for these local gems. Shops such as **Lapidaria de Querétaro** (Corregidora Norte 149-A; ⓒ **52/442-212-0030**) and **El Artesano**, on Corregidora

Norte near the Jardín Zenea, are worth checking out. For more affordable mementos (not opals), visit the state-sponsored arts and crafts center, **Casa Queretana de Artesanía** (Andador Libertad no. 52; © **52/442-224-3456;** http://artesanias.queretaro.gob.mx). Don't miss the shops' three-room annex just a little farther up the walkway.

HOTELS WITH HEART

The Gran Hotel $ Grand spaces mark this lovely hotel. A monumental stairway and spacious galleries enliven the pathway to your room. The large and homey rooms with lofted ceilings have independently controlled air-conditioning and beautiful bathrooms. Most of the rooms have views of at least one of the two adjacent plazas, which remain surprisingly quiet. But for those who especially want peace and quiet, ask for one of their interior rooms, which offers extra amenities, for about the same price as the others.

Juaréz Sur no. 5. © **52/442-251-8050.** www.granhoteldequeretaro.com.mx.

La Casa de la Marquesa $ This gorgeous colonial mansion-hotel is reason enough to visit Querétaro. It has stunning Moorish/Spanish architecture that make it a stand out in all of Mexico. Built by an adoring Marqués for his bride, the groom went all out and threw in about every opulent touch you could want. Walk amid the Moorish arches and intricately tiled walls and spend time in the courtyard, even if you are just visiting it for a cup of coffee or drink. Still, you might want to spring for a room; the, large elegantly appointed rooms have are a step back in time with their rich colonial decor. Cross the street to find the less expensive rooms (merely deluxe) in a second colonial house, **La Casa Azul.**

Calle Francisco I. Madero no. 41. © **52/442-212-0092.** www.lacasadelamarquesa. com.

MOST ROMANTIC RESTAURANTS

San Miguelito $$ Once the Casa de los Cinco Patios, a famous colonial mansion, this grand dining spot is near the main square. The main dining area is an inviting patio, marked by high arches and wrought iron under warm romantic lighting. In this meat-eater's paradise, start with the *infladitas* (puffed up tostadas with various fillings) and move on to the fine beef steaks with tasty sauces. You also can dine and listen to live music (weekends only) at the bar **La Viejoteca.** While you are there, try out some superb tacos at the adjacent **La Antojería,** which offers a less-expensive menu than you find in the main dining room.

Andador 5 de Mayo 39. © **52/442-224-2760.** www.lacasona5patios.com/san miguelito.html.

SANTIAGO DE QUERÉTARO BY NIGHT

For twosomes, this lovely city is for strolling in the evening and giving in to impulse! After sunset, join the city-stroll, where everyone is out seeing friends, looking at the rest of the town, and being with family; for locals, this is the time to have dinner at the cafes or meet friends for drinks. You can do the same, except with just the two of you it becomes quite romantic. As for the many street vendors along the way: Local public health authorities are vigilant, so these tempting stands are generally safe to sample.

San Miguel de Allende

This city of colonial Mexico is the most famous in the United States because so many Americans spend their winters, or fully transplant, to this amazing little town. Some come to relax, others to study art or a language. Still others have landed here because of how many other interesting people have gathered to make this place a hub of writers, musicians, and artists.

San Miguel de Allende (elevation 1,862m/6,107 ft.) is a tasty mix of small-town life and big city pleasures and possibly the most relaxed of the colonial cities covered here. It has all the right ingredients for both intellectual and playful leisure time: A real depth of events, boutiques, and art and craft shops are all easily accessible by foot. The town center has historic gravitas: Many of the building are from colonial times, but contemporary building laws preserve the center's charm by mandating that new building have the same scale and feel as older ones. The ruling goes right down to the cobblestone streets. Best of all, this city holds festivals at the drop of a hat. One note: This is not a private, quiet getaway kind of place. It has been discovered many times over and is a quick jaunt by super-highway from Mexico City, so you can count on company on weekends. (September 29 is also a good time to avoid; it's a big celebration for the patron Saint of San Miguel and the streets and restaurants are packed.)

KEY ATTRACTIONS

Walking, Shopping & Admiring   There's so much to do in this little town, and it's all in an atmosphere that's dripping with romance! Shop and dine in style, and then check out the fine colonial architecture, which centers on residences and their traditional courtyards, decorative interiors, and rich architectural details. Outside, the narrow cobblestone streets beg you to wander them. The **House and Garden Tour**, offered through the local library (www.bibliotecasma.com; © **52/415-152-0293;** tickets 233 MXN [US$18]), is very popular, focusing on the city's large number of historic and charming mansions and houses. Most strolls in this town are at least somewhat romantic, but our favorites all lead to El Mirador, a high point that allows beautiful sunset views over the town and lake. **Parque Juárez,** an expansive, shady park, is also worth strolling.

Masks of Mexico   Mexican masks are justly admired all over the world and **La Otra Cara de México** (The Other Face of Mexico; Cuesta de San Jose no. 32; © **52/415-154-4324;** www.casadelacuesta.com/gallery.html; by appointment) is a private, well-curated museum that has a great selection of masks paired with thoughtful commentary that helps the visitor understand how they emerged from Mexican culture, dance, and religious rituals. Take time to see the films the museum shows to illustrate how these artifacts and art in performances.

Festivals   With some 40 festivals every year, it's hard to miss some kind of festival in San Miguel. Some of our favorites include the Blessing of the Animals (Jan 17), during which proud owners of dogs, sheep, horses, and cows trot out their beloved animals to be blessed by a priest. The first Friday in March kicks off Our Lord of Conquest, which begins with a mass and ends with fireworks, traditional dances, and teams of oxen. June brings Saint Anthony's Day, and the Fiesta de los Locos, which is just what it sounds like, everyone acting as if they were crazy, wearing colorful, kooky costumes and dancing and parading in character. During Dias de la Muertas (Day of the Dead; Nov 1), deceased relatives and friends are celebrated. The day has a festive mood, with skeletal costumes, crafts, and food that looks like body parts, but there is a very serious veneration aspect to the holiday as well.

Mineral Springs   One of the most rewarding aspects of San Miguel is often missed by tourists: the hot mineral springs, located right outside the city limits. To visit these relaxing soaking pools, head out the road that leads to Dolores Hidalgo; you encounter three worth visiting: La Taboada, La Gruta, and Escondido. La Gruta and La Taboada are perhaps the most atmospheric and La Taboada, with its attached spa hotel, exudes a certain amount of charm.

MOST ROMANTIC RESTAURANTS

Café Ibérico $ TAPAS   We love the tapas here, particularly the fried calamari, and the paella (seafood or rabbit with chorizo) transports you to Spain. If you plan ahead, you can try *lechón al horno* (roast suckling pig) with a 24-hour notice. Dine outdoors on the large patio, or in the dining room with a fireplace. A happy hour runs from 4 to 7pm; live music performances, Friday (variable) and Saturday (Spanish guitar) evenings.

Mesones 101 Centro San Miguel de Allende. ✆ **415/152-6154.** http://frank110. wix.com/123.

Jackie's San Antonio $ CONTEMPORARY   This restaurant is in a very pretty suburb near Colonia San Antonia church. You can't walk there from town but it's worth the drive (or taxi fare) because it's a serious gourmet experience. They do wonders with duck and prepare fruit sauces and compotes to bring out the sweetness of meat and fish.

Plaza San Antonio 4. ✆ **52/415-110-2223.**

The Restaurant $$ INTERNATIONAL   Romance alert! This courtyard is made for holding hands and looking into each other's eyes. The mix of colonial and Moorish details works well together, especially in the courtyard that is bounded by the classic Arabian/Spanish–inspired arches. A serious chef cooks seasonal menus here but not at high prices. Food is traditional but with unexpected and imaginative flourishes. You might find an Asian spice in a classic Mexican dish—and it all works brilliantly! If that's a bit more inventive than you like, settle in for some really good hamburgers.

Centro Sollano 16. © **52/415-154-7862** in Mexico, or 213/471-2833 in the U.S. www.therestaurantsanmiguel.com.

SAN MIGUEL DE ALLENDE BY NIGHT

This town offers a simple nightlife, typically live music along with your dinner or after dinner, If you are a jazz fan, head over to **Tío Lucas** (Mesones 105; © **52/415-512-4996**) or **Mama Mía** (Umarán 8; © **52/415-152-2063;** www. mamamia.com.mx) on the weekend. When the weather is good, Mama Mía has another draw: a pretty rooftop terrace. If that's crowded or closed, next-door neighbor **La Azotea Bar** (Umarán 6; © **52/415-152-4977;** www.azoteasan miguel.com) can get serve you that romantic drink on their roof top bar.

HOTELS WITH HEART

Casa de Sierra Nevada $$ This lovely hotel has been top of the line in this city for many years. On a picturesque street in a quiet neighborhood, it offers luxury, service, and one of the few pools in the city. Suites have their own plunge pools and patios, and most rooms are spacious and have a terrace and fireplace. All are beautifully decorated. Rooms have ceiling fans as well as air conditioning. Bathrooms are luxurious, some with both in- and outdoor showers. The **Andanza** restaurant is excellent and serves both Mexican and International specialties. People rave about the cooking school, and it's pretty romantic to learn to cook together here.

Hospicio 35. © **800/701-1561** or 52/415-152-7040. www.casadesierranevada.com.

Casa Luna Boutique Hotel $ One of the things we like best about Mexico is seeing bright, happy colors almost everywhere we go. That's especially true in this colonial hacienda house, which is enlivened with a playful decor, and filled with local art, traditional artifacts, and local crafts. There's greenery everywhere, plus inviting places to sit and read or just relax. The rooms are large, and some feature private patios. If there's a chill in the air, settle around the gas fireplace or soak in the comodious tub. Casa Luna also offers accommodations at its ranch on the outskirts of town; it's a more rural, but still chic, experience.

Quebrada 117. © **52/210-200-8758** or 415/152-1117 (U.S.) www.casaluna.com.

Casa Misha $$ This small hotel is all about service and customization. The owners, Edward George and Richard Samuel, assist in making your visit as romantic as you want it to be, so they happily arrange private dinners and make suggestions about how best to see the area's best sights. This is an expansive property and you can wander it looking for an intimate patio or rooftop terrace to relax in, share the view, or have a drink. The public rooms exude elegance and the guest rooms, too, are decorated tastefully and with quality antiques and oil paintings. Request a terrace; most rooms have them and they are generally private—just right for romance.

Chiquitos no. 15. ℂ **646/688-4862** in U.S. or 52/415-152-2021 in Mexico. www. casamisha.com. 2-night minimum stay.

Rosewood San Miguel Allende $$ This gorgeous three-story resort with romantic archways, roof gardens, and a lovely spa, opened in 2011. Just walking in feels good. The common areas are gracious and open up to views, gardens, or patios with fountains. Guest rooms, and bathrooms, are large, and the bath has both tub and a separate shower. The bedrooms have hardwood floors and a spare but elegant style, typical of restored hacienda hotels. Most romantic are the double doors that open to your own, very private terrace, looking out over manicured gardens. Suites are lavish, and if you are in that market, ask for one of the ones on the third floor that view the town's cathedral. To top it off, the service is phenomenal.

Nemesio Diez 11. ℂ **888/767-3966** in U.S. & Canada or 52/415-152-9700 in Mexico. www.rosewoodsanmiguel.com.

MONTANA: THE LUXURY RANCH EXPERIENCE
Glamping the American West

There are fifty shades of green in Montana from spring through fall: the lighter chartreuse leaves of spring, the darker evergreen shades, and the gray-greens that cover the velvety hills and link the lower landscape to the scrub pines and massive evergreens.

This is a land of rushing rivers, fine fishing, and endless cattle and horse ranches punctuating the valleys and hills. Not everyone wears a cowboy hat, far from it, but the cowboy ethos is in the air. It lives in that particular Montana twang and in the no-nonsense, friendly way you are likely to be greeted.

Much of this world is about cattle, some of it about timber, and a little about mining (it used to be a lot). But come summertime, tourists flock to Montana. They come to fish, to camp, and to hike. They want the whole Western experience, which often means a stay at a guest ranch.

We think guest ranches are romantic because they hearken back to a way of life that our collective imagination treasures. Most of us grew up watching cowboy movies where the clean-cut, clean living, heart-of-gold guy saves the girl, saves the ranch, and goes silently into the sunset (sometimes with, sometimes without, the girl). But the romance is also in the scenery: mountains still young enough to be jagged, rivers turbulent and free, and men and women teaming up to make the land work for them. When you visit a guest ranch you get a slice of this, and it feels authentic. The cowboys are still here, fences still need to be fixed, and hunting and packing are still a way of life.

The Ranches

Guest ranch stays can range from mom-and-pop affairs with a few simple cabins to all-out rustic-chic escapes with the most luxurious experiences you can imagine. Here are two of our faves. But whatever you do, *don't* call them dude ranches—that's so 1970s!

McGinnis Meadows Cattle & Guest Ranch $$
This gorgeous, smaller ranch—with accommodations for about 25 people—is all about the horses. Almost 10 miles off the highway and highlighted by beautiful meadows, the ranch has simple Amish-built pine cabins, but a complex equestrian program. Each horse is exquisitely trained for riding, cow penning, and any other skill they need on a working cattle ranch. The main lodge is more like a log home, with a limited number of guest rooms (several of which have outdoor toilets). Cabins are more upscale, some of them featuring whirlpool baths and peaked roofs with second-story lounging areas. The ambience throughout is laid back, and you dine on fine Montana comfort food, plus heavenly desserts. Dinners are a group affair, so if you wanted a ranch getaway where you wouldn't have to deal with other people, you might look elsewhere. (That said, you do get a packed lunch daily, so you can sneak away to a meadow together). You can start the day moving cattle or working on your horsemanship (sometimes in an indoor arena), fly-fishing, or just floating on a river. *Horse lovers, note:* For 2 weeks a year, the famous Buck Brannaman holds a 2-week clinic here. He is one of the original "horse whisperers," and subject of the documentary "Buck."

6220 McGinnis Meadows Rd, Libby, Montana. ℭ **866-764-5569** or 406-293-5000. www.mmgranch.net. Weekly rates vary by season but include meals and activities.

The Resort at Paws Up $$$
This 37,000-acre Greenough, Montana, spread is the real deal—a working ranch, but with maximum luxury. In a lovely valley cut by the Clark Fork River, the ranch is a half-hour drive from downtown Missoula and 45 miles from the airport. There are two kinds of accommodations, spread over four locations. You can choose from handsome two- or three-bedroom log cabins for families or a few couples and well-appointed one- or two-bedroom tents, some overlooking the Blackfoot River (Pinnacle Camp), some right beside it (River Camp) and others by a small creek (Creekside). Another luxury six-tent group, Moonlight Camp, offers an expansive meadow view near an excellent fly-fishing spot. The tent camps remind us of African luxury camps, but without the nearby predators. The tents have king beds and a chic American West decor; tents in the Creekside and Pinnacle camps have en suite bathrooms and Jacuzzi tubs. (There's a tent at Pinnacle that's custom-made for lovers, with an old-fashioned two-person copper tub at the foot of the bed, and enough privacy that you can leave your

door open to get a peek-a-boo river view from the tub.) At breakfast and dinner in the tent camps, your butler reserves your place in the camp pavilion, a remarkable free-standing canopied deck, which at Pinnacle and Creekside is equipped with a romantic stone fireplace and drapes to keep out the wind and rain if necessary.

In the evenings, as you return to your tent you feel the wilderness around you. Maybe you chat about having earlier sighted a cougar (the shy creatures are busy stalking the abundant deer and elk in the area and, so far, seem to be uninterested in ranch guests) or an elk herd. Sitting in front of a blazing fire at night or in the morning, you hear the burble of a creek or the steady rush of the Blackfoot river. Rise early for a morning excursion, and you'll have a breakfast cooked to order at your campsite but will still hear the call of the wild. (If you've ever considered an African safari, a stay here might not be a bad place to test your aptitude for the experience.) Couples can expect to feel more genuine, more integrated with the natural world and, we think, feel blessed you can share it together.

You can be as solitary or as busy as you like. The place has more daytime choices than you can think of: It is both a kids' camp for grown-ups and a camp for kids, within limits. You can try skeet-shooting, fly-fishing, riding lessons, sightseeing on horseback, cattle drives (where you learn how to separate and guide cattle), downhill dirt-bike tours, ATV rides, balloon trips, helicopter sightseeing (weather permitting) and more—all rated for kids, novices, or experts. Or go easy on the activities and grab a book and be still by the river, listening to the birds, or simply take a walk together in the woods. One must-do: Visit the resort's Spa Town, where treatments are done in a colony of white tents in the pines whose soundtrack is the natural sounds of the forest.

Note: The activities at Paws Up can be wonderful if you are looking for a getaway that provides romantic opportunities plus family fun—this place is super kid friendly. But if you are here without kids, and it's a totally adult world you seek, stay in **Moonlight Camp,** which only books adults.

40060 Paws Up Rd., Greenough. ℭ **877-588-7151.** www.pawsup.com. Rates include 3 meals daily and round-trip transportation from Missoula International Airport.

EXCURSIONS FROM PAWS UP

Just driving around Montana is inspiring. Twenty minutes away from Paws Up is **Garnet** (www.garnetghosttown.net), the oldest ghost town in Montana and a center for cross-country skiing in winter. With more than 50 miles of trails, it is an awe-inspiring backcountry spot to stir your senses together. **Seeley Lake** and **Lobo Pass** also have beautiful groomed or backcountry trails. In fair weather, this is the area for spotting white tail deer, elk, the occasional moose, plenty of marmots, bald eagles, and other birds and, not infrequently, black bear and cougar.

VANCOUVER ISLAND
From British Formality to Absolute Wilderness

This island has it all. From Victoria to its tip, it varies from a wannabe English town to unmitigated wilderness. There really is something stirring for both of you: extremely English formal gardens, a grand old hotel, and quaint streets in Victoria—and then a few hours away by car, increasingly wilder coasts and forests until, 350 miles in, you are in a wilderness with more bears than people. This huge, diverse, and easily accessible island should rank high on your summer and fall romance list. (Winters are hard, and spring is a bit uncertain.)

Victoria

You want the historic city next to the waterfront, but you also want the small-town suburbs for additional good dining and cozying up. There are gloriously scenic and quick Kenmore Air (© **866/435-9524**) flights from Seattle to Victoria and car ferries between Vancouver and Tsawwassen (www.bcferries.com) just across the Washington border about 90 minutes from Seattle. If, instead, you choose to zip by Hydrofoil from Seattle (about three hours), you will be on the *Victoria Clipper* (© **800/888-2535;** www.clippervacations.com) in very comfortable seats, with a bar with alcoholic or soft drinks and snacks and island views the whole way. Occasionally hanging out in the boat's wake are handsome black and white Orcas, usually called killer whales, although they aren't even whales, but gigantic and highly social dolphins. You will arrive at the waterfront with a splendid view of the aged hotels and homes on either side, and as you close in, the dowager Empress Hotel will be your focal point. In the summer, you will likely hear the bagpipes as costumed players welcome you to the town. If you are staying at the Empress, it's only a short walk from the dock. But you might consider other choices just because large tour groups use the hotel, and the overwhelming clamor can be a disagreeable soundtrack for a romantic getaway.

KEY ATTRACTIONS

Shopping for Treasures If you enjoy shopping together for unusual finds, you will like old Victoria. Walk the streets and ogle the historic 19th-century buildings, English shops (a great place to buy a tea service), and galleries (Inuit and other First Nation galleries often have museum-quality art work). Don't be shocked at the prices of Northwest Indian Art—a good mask or small sculpture will start at several thousand dollars.

Royal BC Museum We think museums can exhaust you pretty quickly, and what started out as a date can spiral into the blahs. But some museums are irresistible: awe-inspiring or just plain fun. This provincial museum is a bit of both, particularly the fun part, with lots of Northwest artifacts, culture, and history, beautifully displayed.

675 Belleville St. ✆ **250/356-7226.** www.royalbcmuseum.bc.ca.

Butchart Gardens   The wife of an industrialist restored this former quarry into a magnificent, world-class, 55-acre garden in Brentwood Bay. A rose garden, a Japanese garden, and gardens with Italian and English themes—there are plots for every taste. Plant exhibits change every season, so you and your honey could go several times a year and not be bored. But steal down to the water and a quiet cove and make it your own. It's a romantic place to take pictures against the profusion of flowers and water features in the background.

800 Benvenuto Ave. ✆ **250/652-4422.** www.butchartgardens.com.

HOTELS WITH HEART

Sooke Harbour House $$$ This boutique luxury hotel on the water offers individualized rooms, some with soaking tubs or outside tubs and fireplaces. Views vary, but many are extraordinary, looking broadly over the Strait of Juan de Fuca and to the mountain peaks in the distance. There is a lot of wildlife on the beach, and you can easily see seals or eagles up close. Ramble around the wonderful English flower garden and take in another ocean view. Then there is the matter of feeding each other very, very well (see later).

1528 Whiffin Spit Rd., Sooke. ✆ **800/889-9688.** www.sookeharbourhouse.com.

The Victoria Empress Hotel $$$ The grand old lady of the harbor has had some touch-ups and is looking good. As with many older hotels, be careful which room you get; you can't go wrong with the elegant, concierge-level Gold Rooms and Suites and a room with a harbor view adds romantic oomph. Other pluses: the Willow Spa, the famed lavish afternoon tea, and other traditional touches like the curry buffet at the Bengal Lounge. Most of all, you are perfectly situated for all the downtown attractions.

721 Government St. ✆ **866/540-4429.** www.fairmont.com/Empress.

MOST ROMANTIC RESTAURANTS

Aura Waterfront Restaurant $$ CANADIAN REGIONAL   This great fish restaurant at Laurel Point Inn has expert service, a romantic view of the harbor, and very nice outdoor seating. You will want to order the calamari and share it. Just pick up the daintily seasoned lightly battered morsels, dunk in the incredible dipping sauce, pop it in your true love's mouth, and, voila! Now it's your turn.

680 Montreal St. ✆ **250/414-6739.** http://aurarestaurant.ca.

Blue Crab Bar and Grill $$ SEAFOOD   We would recommend the Blue Crab for the excellent fresh seafood alone. Add the quiet ambience, fine service, and beautiful views of the sea-through floor-to-ceiling windows, and you've set the perfect stage for romance.

In the Coast Victoria Hotel, 146 Kingston St. ☎ **250/480-1999.** http://bluecrab.ca.

The Restaurant at Sooke Harbor House $$$ PACIFIC NORTH-WEST   This restaurant has been a destination for foodies for years. Reviews are sometimes raves, sometimes not—but most people agree this place oozes romance. The restaurant sits on the edge of the water, with beautiful views and gardens. It is not in Victoria proper, but 45 minutes away, so you will need a car.

1528 Whiffin Spit Rd., Sooke. ☎ **800/889-9688.** www.sookeharbourhouse.com.

VICTORIA BY NIGHT

Walking Victoria   Victoria is a sophisticated city with cool bars and plenty of live music and places to dance. You'll find them with no trouble. What may not be obvious is that you can take a fabulous evening walk or drive after dinner. Drive up Victoria's scenic causeway to the top of Beacon Hill and eyeball the breathtaking Strait of Juan de Fuca. Or grab your partner and have a stroll along the Inner Harbour Causeway, starting on Government Street in front of the Empress Hotel and follow the water in either direction. There's plenty going on along the way, from puppeteers and musicians to friendly pubs.

Touch Lounge   After you've absorbed history, younger lovers may want to seek out their own at this spot that attracts a 20s and 30s crowd; three DJs spin in separate rooms. 751 View St. ☎ **250/384-2582.** http://touchlounge.ca.

Vancouver Island Interior

Tofino   Aim for this tremendously romantic spot about a 4-hour drive from Victoria, but a quick hop from Vancouver. A delightful small town gathered around a harbor, it has become a getaway for Vancouverites, but still feels charming and undeveloped. It has a first-class art gallery and a few good places to eat at nearby resorts, but you'll come for its haunting and dramatic rocky coast. The wide beach and its picturesque outcroppings take a beating from the rough waves. You'll want to be inside when the big storms come in. Luckily, there are places here to do that in style.

Campbell River & Beyond   This is salmon and bear country. Campbell River and its namesake city are said to be the salmon capital of the world. They also mark where Vancouver Island turns more sylvan and less full of tourists. This northern part is said to have the highest number of Black bears in North America. It is quite likely you will see at least one bear, presenting a fine reason for couples to unite! (Hey, a little adrenaline can help your romance!) Bears wander through the small towns, and you often can spot them from the road. They are not aggressive, but are not big doggies either. Give them wide berth.

If you keep on keeping on, you'll end up at one of the most romantic and ethereal bays in the world. En route, your first marker will be Port Hardy—it has good B&Bs and a few galleries—and campers can stock up on supplies here. Drive 39 miles to Cape Scott Provincial Park—where you can't drive any further. Undaunted, you take a 3-mile hike on a gravel trail to idyllic San Josef Bay. You are very much on your own here, so watch for wildlife. But once you get there, all you will think about is the view, which is almost unreal. The white sand defines upright sea stack rocks as if they were carefully placed in a Zen garden. Many have windblown trees atop them as if a Bonsai master planted them there, and the sand is littered with driftwood. A light fog is not unusual, and the total picture is breathtaking. The sea beyond has more sea stacks and small islands and haze. This may be among the most mysteriously romantic places you have been, but check the tides and don't tarry too long; it could be tricky to find your way back in the dark.

> ## Perfect Place to Propose
>
> Butchart Gardens, 800 Benvenuto Ave., Brentwood Bay (℡ **250/652-4422;** www.butchartgardens.com). The exhibits change every season, so you can propose any time. If you steal down to the waters of Brentwood Bay, there's a quiet cove where you can be alone for the big moment.

HOTELS WITH HEART

Both the restaurant and pub at **Glen Lyon Inn** ($; 6435 Hardy Bay Rd.; ℡ 877/949-7115; www.glenlyoninn.com) have great bay views.

Bear Cove Cottages $ This Port Hardy spot is good for a fishing trip, but it's perfect for a couple that wants to get away from the world in a sweet, private cottage up on a hilltop. With a Jacuzzi tub, fireplace, and kitchen, you'll want to spend serious playtime in your adorable, affordable cottage with views of Hardy Bay.

6715 Bear Cove Hwy. ℡ **877/949-7939.** www.bearcovecottages.ca.

The Long Beach Lodge Resort $$ The rooms at this spectacular spot are simple Northwest elegant, with fireplaces and tubs-for-two that are in prime position for sunset views overlooking the ocean, and sometimes surging waves. Cottages for two are available with private hot tubs. The restaurant gets high marks and offers fresh Northwest fish and local produce. The cedar rooms decorated with First Nation art are so romantic, and so many people have wanted weddings here, that the lodge has a resident wedding planner, should that be your wish. The hotel's Great Room is cozy and comfortable, and the views of the ocean and surfers are so engaging that you might head over to the surf club and take a lesson. (*Caution:* This is frigid water; you will be wearing a wet or dry suit). If you want a more Zen relationship to the ocean, take a walk on the very long silver beach.

1441 Pacific Rim Hwy. ℡ **877/844-7873.** www.longbeachlodgeresort.com.

The Wickaninnish Inn $$$ This wonderful place in Tofino recently became more wonderful with new rooms on the point that have better views than before. The rooms are love nests with fireplaces, soaking tubs, cuddling nooks, and even a teapot to help cozy you in. The main restaurant, **The Pointe**, is excellent and offers a view from every table; the breakfast place is also scenic. This hotel really tries to be romantic, and succeeds. The nightly turn-down service includes turning your lights low and putting on romantic music. Staff will arrange a beach picnic with fresh oysters ready to eat or shuck. The Ancient Cedars Spa has the Cedar Sanctuary for a memorable hot stone massage for two. They often have yoga classes with the ocean as your backdrop. You won't want to leave.

Osprey Lane, at Chesterman Beach. ⓒ **250/725-3100.** www.wickinn.com.

AMOROUS ADVENTURES: EXOTIC LANDS

This chapter is for couples who like pushing the envelope—people who find their senses most aroused when they place themselves in situations that are utterly foreign to them and which just might have a hint of risk (if not actual danger). If you and your lover are true adventurers of this sort, read on. We have some great suggestions for you!

14

BOTSWANA
Get in the Game

This is a relatively new identity for a very old piece of earth. In 1966, diamonds were discovered in Bechuanaland in southern Africa, and a new economy, as well as a new name, flourished. The land itself is both desert and aquatic, the Kalahari Desert and the Okavango River Delta, and offers just about any dramatic landscape a couple could ask for. It is a land of great beauty and raw power that puts you in close contact with a lot of different wildlife species. As you whisk through the waters in small craft, you'll experience a gasp-worthy appreciation of the elements.

One of Africa's most stable governments, Botswana has a mind for conservation. A number of amazing places to visit have been well prepped for tourists, but our favorite for romance is the Delta region. Many camps lie within the huge span of land and water that comprise the Delta, and it is definitely worth spending time in several different locations. Camps vary from simple inland tents to luxury villas hovering over the water. All of them have something great to offer. Be warned, however, that tours of this area are *pricey;* the fees go toward protecting the country's natural resources so, if you can swing it, and get there, you get to feel good about supporting the environment. Wherever you go in this region, you can assume the land and its people are being protected by the best practices the country can afford.

The Okavango Delta

The Delta is a river world and a most romantic one at that. However hard to believe, it is part of the vast Kalahari Desert. Basically, the Okavango Delta of Botswana is formed by rainwater that drains from Angola via the Okavango River and forms lakes and marshes that attract wildlife. The flooding peaks between June and August. You will want to come in the non-rainy season, from the fall through November for the best game viewing, although most of the lions appear January through March.

GETTING THERE

Getting to your camp is part of the adventure: Arriving from Bostwana's capital, **Maun** (the only town of any size in the country), you'll head for an obscure landing strip, where your plane (usually big enough for 4, plus a pilot) may have to approach a few times; apparently the elephants don't abide the rule to keep off the runway! From there, you pile into Land Rovers or Land Cruisers and head to the delta where a boat awaits. Speeding through waterways that only a very practiced guide could understand, you are in a world of reeds, tall grasses, and lily pads by the thousands (creating beautiful orange, copper, and green patterns) along a route of sinuous twists and turns. And, yes, you have to be on the lookout for submerged hippopotamuses.

The passage is exciting: Your hair blows in the wind as your motorboat dodges in and out of reeds higher than your head, opening up to ponds and then closing in again. Above, white-headed eagles swoop down for hapless fish along the water's edge where river otters play and elephants congregate. When you finally reach your destination, chances are the staff will be waiting, singing you into your new home. Your camp will provide safe but adventurous outings, candlelight, exciting stories, and all the necessary trappings for romantic adventures, dining, and lodging. We describe two of our favorite camps below.

Note: As always in interior Africa, be on the lookout: Huge numbers of elephants inhabit Botswana, and some do not phone ahead to book their appearances in camp. You are on notice from the moment you walk where they walk: This is their world. But it's not just elephants you'll observe; lions, crocs, lots of hippos (generally hiding in the water during the day), and leopards all make a showing.

CAMPS

Nxabega $$$ Pronounced (roughly) *nah-beh-kah* (but it's got a click in there, too), this tented river camp of **& Beyond Nxabega Okavango Tented Camp** is a vibrant mix of luxury and African rustic. You are out in the wild, to be sure, but you are also seriously pampered. The canvas roofs of the tents are industrial strength, and you have a flush toilet and a shower inside. You are elevated, which is a good thing because elephants will be grazing on the trees overhead, and you don't really want them in your bedroom.

Game drives (excursions to see wildlife) go out twice daily with intermittent scenic (and safe) stops. You get up very early, while it's still dark, and have hot beverages and some snacks. Then you go out while many animals are still hunting or have not settled down into the noonday sun. You return to a lavish breakfast, which includes some local dishes. The land tours are usually in open-top Jeeps (very unnerving until you get used to it) and by motor boats or small, indigenous (and very tippy) canoes if you are in quiet waters. You will view game from morning to evening, stopping for lunch (often in picturesque places) and an afternoon rest (usually until 2–4pm). The latter drives become night drives, and you tool around until dinnertime using big infrared search lights to highlight the game (but not blind them or interfere in their hunts). If something special is sighted by your guides, or guides from nearby camps, you will venture out with your guides again after dinner. Our trip yielded an unusual sight: a group of male lions and their cubs at twilight climbing trees to get a better lookout for game.

After witnessing these stirring sights, you are fed extensive and delicious bush meals: All meals here are lavish, but dinners are especially so. Sometimes the camp will surprise you by setting a fancy table, white linen and silver in a special *Boma* (a center space surrounded by logs and other obstructions to keep you safe from predators); other times they will create special places to eat within the camp (poolside, perhaps, illuminated by candles and lanterns). Spreads are extensive with copious quantities of game meats, beef, and chicken, many kinds of vegetables, locally spiced dishes and wonderful choices for desserts.

✆ **27/11-809-4314.** www.andbeyond.com. Rates include all meals and safari.

horseback EXPLORATION

The **Okavango Horse Safaris** (**$$$**; ✆ **267/6861-671**; www.okavangohorse.com; rates include all meals and safari) explore a section of the delta that is part of the Moremi Game reserve, from March through November. You are in the saddle 4 to 6 hours a day, so this tour isn't for novices. While you are only required to know the basics, remember that this is a wildlife area, and it's useful to know how to control a horse should you need to make a hasty exit (and your horse is feeling a certain amount of well-earned panic). Guided trail riders move from the tented Kujwana Camp (shower and flush toilets en suite) to Moklowane (romantic but rustic tree houses with flush toilets and hot showers) to Fly Camp (spacious but really rustic tents with bush toilets and buckets for showers). At most, 8 riders can participate, and the safaris run 5 to 10 days. You will also get game drives and bush walks and venture into the river via *mokoros* (local, flat-bottomed dug-out canoes). This is serious adventure travel: romantic if you both are brave, but *not* if the idea of riding horses in a predator's country chills you.

Xudum $$$ On another piece of the river is the luxurious **&Beyond Xudum Okavango Delta Lodge.** Here at Xudum (pronounced *koo-dum*), guests stay in villas with mixed African and European sensibilities. The villas are European on their first level, with elegant, netted beds and fine furnishings in the sitting area with a gorgeous bathroom and a huge tub facing an outdoor plunge pool. The rooftop lookout has an area for observation and elegant dining, but it is thatched and rustic, an African touch. The main lodge itself, a short walk from the path that leads to the villas, has a rustic, but luxe, feel. Meal service is an elegant affair, and you are treated as an honored guest. The overall effect at here is both beguiling and adventurous. You can expect wonderful guides, fine meals, and a hippo serenade at night. The camps are open to animals, so even though you can walk to the main lobby for meals during the day, be alert (elephants are frequent visitors). Still, while there is a real need for caution, you get used to living with animals that, at least here, are definitely above you on the food chain. After coming back from a bush outing, few moments are more warmly shared than breaking for tea or a beer together after glimpsing a pride of female lions tending their 12-week-old cubs or sighting a leopard on the prowl. At night, the African world is torch lit, and your staff may perform, dancing informally to African music. At journey's end, after watching life, and the end of life, in the bush, the two of you have a new sense of how precious life can be.

℗ **27/11-809-4314.** www.andbeyond.com. Rates include all meals and safari.

GREAT BARRIER REEF & BEYOND (AUSTRALIA)
Exploring an Endless Ocean

Mention the Whitsunday Islands to people who have been there, and they get a bit glassy-eyed with nostalgia. This group of 74 islands, an hour's flight from Cairns, lies off the coast of Queensland, Australia, and is the gateway to **Great Barrier Reef Marine Park.** Almost all these islands have quiet bays, thriving coral reefs, and warm snorkel-friendly waters; the subtropical climate ensures moderate air and water temperatures all year, and the islands have plentiful wildlife and bird species. Impeccable weather, clear blue water with silica beaches, plus exquisite resorts combine to make this part of the world a top romantic destination. Lovers here will be pampered, well fed, relaxed, and rejuvenated.

Shute Harbour and nearby Airlie Beach are the mainland departure points for boats en route to the Whitsundays. Some islands have resorts, but most are day-trip destinations for beach picnics, hikes in the bush, or simply ogling the scenery. Nearly all are outfitted for all sorts of water sports. People in the know go here to snorkel and dive at the area's stunning reefs. The

Whitsundays are lesser known, and, therefore, lesser crowded than the areas surrounding the Great Barrier Reef, which means you could have an area all to yourself. Whitsunday beaches are famous for their white, pure silica sand. And although the entire island group is worth exploring, Hayman Island and Hamilton Island win for the most exquisite experiences.

Airlie Beach & The Whitsundays
KEY ATTRACTIONS

Charter a Powerboat The main reason to visit the Whitsundays is to explore the water and the islands themselves. Having your own captain and cook, with the sea as your playground, provides a romantic value second to none. If you are a serious boater, you can charter your own boat and handle all the details, but for pure pampering, hire a boat with a crew just for you or book a more affordable semi-private luxury cruise. Both **Descarada** (✆ 61/2-9699-2214; www.descarada.com.au; call for rates) and **Cruise Whitsundays** (✆ 61/7-4946-4662; www.cruisewhitsundays.com; A$130–A$225 per person) organize cruises with a maximum of 12 guests in four private cabins. It is a perfect way to experience majestic views, the freedom of the open sea, and the full variety of experiences the Whitsundays offer. **Cumberland Charter Yachts** (www.ccy.com.au) has a fleet of 23 boats based in Airlie Beach, including sailing yachts, catamarans, and powerboats for self-charter, ranging in size from 32 to 47 feet. You can set your own itinerary, and they will back you up with radio contact.

Sailing Around the Islands It's hard to beat the romance of sailing these isles. Most are uninhabited, and you can locate your own secluded beaches, quietly set anchor, and be alone together in this enchanted world. Sailboats are quiet and peaceful, and nothing quite matches the smooth transit of a sailing vessel and feeling the power of the wind while sipping drinks together, bathed in a spectacular sunset in a secluded cove. The Whitsundays have many sheltered bays where you can sail, snorkel, and swim safely. Popular anchorages are Blue Pearl, Butterfly, and Hook Island Bays. Following are three companies that can help you set sail:

- **Explore Whitsundays**, 4 Airlie Esplanade, Airlie Beach. ✆ 61/07-4946-5782; www.explorewhitsundays.com. Shared charters cost A$400–A$834 per person; private charters from A$2,500 and up.
- **Sailfree**. ✆ 800-911-244 or 61/07-3852-2449; www.sailfree.com.au. Call for rates.
- **Sailing Whitsundays**, 259 Shute Harbour Rd., Airlie Beach. ✆ 800-677-119 or 61/07-4946-5299; www.sailingwhitsundays.com. Shared charters cost A$295 to A$755 per person.

Visiting Whitehaven Beach The most famous of all area landmarks, this uninhabited paradise on Whitsunday Island stretches for miles of powdery white sand, offering spectacular views, sun, sea, and relaxation. Most of the year it is sheltered from the southeasterly trade winds, which means shallow waters are transparent and swimming is safe and enjoyable. It's an easy ferry ride from the mainland or Hamilton Island. Your hotel can help you set it up.

Scuba Diving   You can't do much better than this spectacular area for seeing exotic colored fish, coral structures, and marine mammals, including whales, dolphins, and turtles. **Wings Diving Adventures** (G/6 Airlie Esplanade, Airlie Beach; ☏ **300-859-853** or 6/17-4948-2034; www.whitsunday dive.com.au) is a dive operator that charges A$70 for single dives and A$490–A$840 for multi-day charters. If you're game to learn how to scuba dive together, contact the **Whitsunday Dive Center** at 16 Commerce Close, Cannonvale (☏ **61/07-4948-1117** or 61/07-4948-1239; www.whitsundaydive centre.com). Full PADI certification courses are available for A$399–A$599 and require a 4-day commitment.

Golfing on Hamilton Island   Hamilton Island Golf Club is an 18-hole championship course that's perched at the edge of the Great Barrier Reef. There simply is no other golf course on the planet with this kind of drop-dead panoramic views.

Hamilton Island. ☏ **61/2-9433-0444.** www.hamiltonislandgolfclub.com.au. Greens fee: A$100 9 holes, A$150 18 holes.

HOTELS WITH HEART
Countless excellent resorts are scattered among the islands; some occupy entire islands themselves. Below are two suggestions.

Airlie Beach Hotel $ In the heart of Airlie Beach, this large hotel complex offers fairly standard accommodations but puts you in the thick of things. The hotel straddles an entire block, giving it frontage on both the Esplanade and the main street. Rooms are spacious and well appointed, with views over the inlet. There are standard motel rooms, as well as newer hotel rooms and executive-style suites with kitchens. Our pick would be any of the rooms at the front, which have small balconies and overlook the Esplanade and the inlet. The hidden charm here is the dining—all the restaurants serve locally sourced food.

16 The Esplanade, Airlie Beach. ☏ **800/466-233** or 61/7-4964-1999. www.airlie beachhotel.com.au.

Hayman Island Resort $$$ If you're craving a private world-class uber-deluxe getaway—exquisite service, elegance, and fine dining—pick this resort. After you are met at Hamilton Island airport with a drink, you climb aboard a handsome powerboat and speed toward the resort. (Yes, you will feel like you are in a Bond movie). The property reeks of exclusivity and good taste. The beautifully landscaped grounds offer small waterfalls and ponds and a slick collection of swimming pools. The dress is casual, but the prices are not. Rooms are expensive, but beach villas are through the roof (A$1,990–A$10,600). The extensive range of activities includes sailing, snorkeling, fishing, and even cooking lessons.

Hayman Island, Queensland. ☏ **61/7-4940-1838.** www.hayman.com.au.

Whitsunday Moorings B&B $ This small place is a great bargain and a lovely place to stay. Mango and frangipani trees envelop the house itself, and there are two open-plan suites with kitchens, terra-cotta floors, ceiling fans, and fantastic views overlooking Abel Point Marina. A bountiful gourmet breakfast is included and served on a romantic terrace with a pretty view of Airlie's Beach.

37 Airlie Crescent, Airlie Beach. ℂ **61/77-4946-4692.** www.whitsundaymoorings bb.com.au.

MOST ROMANTIC RESTAURANTS

Armada Loungebar & Restaurant $$$ MODERN AUSTRA-LIAN   Sexy decor, romantic lighting, and Asian and Balinese touches create a sensual mood. You can eat outside upstairs under a canopy and enjoy excellent food and cocktails with a seaside vibe. This chic restaurant will feed you well with local fish, exotic game, or vegetarian specialties.

350 Shute Harbor Rd., Airlie Beach. ℂ **61/7-4948-1600.**

Déjà Vu $$ MODERN AUSTRALIAN CUISINE   A tropical breeze combines with the seaside view for fine dining over Airlie Beach, the turquoise water nearly at your table. Déjà vu is a lovely place for dinner and is justly famous for its Sunday Brunch, an eight-course, seemingly endless feast (A$45).

At the Waters Edge Resort, 4 Golden Orchid Drive, Airlie Beach. ℂ **6/17-4948-4309.** www.dejavurestaurant.com.au.

On Aqua Restaurant and Bar $$ AUSTRALIAN   This small place is set for romance: Diners collect around a lovely, candlelit pool adjacent to the Coral Sea. The sophisticated, chef-driven cuisine includes Australian traditional favorites with a modern touch.

Shute Harbour Rd., Airlie Beach. ℂ **07-4948-2782.**

Whitsunday Sailing Club $$ CONTEMPORARY   This casual club is a popular hangout for locals, with one of the best views in the Whitsundays, overlooking Pioneer Bay and the islands. The menu includes light meals such as tortillas or a steak sandwich; for something heartier go for roast duck, lamb rogan josh, or a veal filet. If you're feeling really hungry, go for the A$95 "Grand Catch," a platter of oysters, crispy soft-shell crab, prawns, salt 'n'pepper calamari, scallop-and-prawn stir-fry, French fries, salad, and a piece of both the daily fish of the day and the house battered fish.

Airlie Point (enter from The Esplanade), Airlie Beach. ℂ **61/07-4946-6138.** www. whitsundaysailingclub.com.au.

AIRLIE BEACH BY NIGHT

Airlie Beach is a party town at night, so the truly romantic moments may be made most memorable by enjoying the starlight or walking on the marina. For something livelier, the many pubs won't disappoint. Charter boat passengers often wind down together after their cruises at the pubs on the main street. The

Great Barrier Reef & Beyond (Australia)

AMOROUS ADVENTURES: EXOTIC LANDS

tribally themed club **Mama Africa,** at 263 Shute Harbour Rd. (☏ **61/07-4948-0438;** www.facebook.com/mamaafricaniteclub), is the late-night place to be. It's where restive vacationers congregate after most watering holes close down at midnight.

Hamilton Island

More than 70% of Hamilton remains as nature made it, although it is the most developed of the Whitsundays. The island offers vast expanses of unspoiled beach (we love the gently arcing Catseye Beach), walking paths, and fantastic views. Even so, Hamilton is more of a festive holiday site than a place to escape from society.

Activity centers on the village around the marina, with its many eateries and shops, tourist services, and a yacht club. But the real action is at the resorts, each with its own personality, prices, and style. The range of activities and services is enormous, and you'll likely find one that you like and that fits your budget. Choices range from a high-rise hotel and one-bedroom apartments to Polynesian-style bungalows to private super-deluxe pavilions. There are no cars allowed on this island so rent a golf buggy or hop the free bus to explore. **Hamilton Island Buggy Rental** (☏ **61/07-4946-8263;** www.hamiltonisland.com.au/golf-buggy), located on the grounds of the Hamilton Resort, charges A$45 for 1 hour or A$85 for 24 hours.

KEY ATTRACTIONS

Night Snorkeling   A particularly romantic option for snorkel enthusiasts is to spend a night in a cabin on a pontoon floating in the sea. **Cruise Whitsundays** (☏ **61/07-4946-4662;** www.cruisewhitsundays.com; A$898 per couple) offers a 2-day, 1-night ReefSleep. You snorkel at night, partly lit by coral reflecting the moonlight. Your trip includes breakfast, lunches, and best of all, a romantic dinner with wine under the stars. The reef is all yours, and you can also see it through an underwater viewing chamber! If you just want a great day snorkeling at one of the many gorgeous islands or beaches in the areas, you can find inexpensive sail or motor launches to take you there through **Whitsundays.com** (☏ **61/07-4946-5299** or at info@whitsundays.net.au); day trips cost A$65 to A$165 per person.

Go Sailing   Hamilton Island, the largest inhabited island in the Whitsundays, lies off the east coast of Australia, close to the Queensland mainland. Sailing enthusiasts rank it among the top sailing destination is the world—you navigate around 74 islands and islets in the protection of the Great Barrier Reef. Sunsail Australia, located at the Hamilton Island Marina (☏ **800/803-988** or 61/2-8912-7040; www.sunsail.com.au) is a charter boat outfit that offers optional extras including a professional skipper and cook, kayaks, and dinghies. A 5-day charter for two passengers starts at A$3500.

HOTELS WITH HEART

More a vacation village than a single resort, Hamilton has the widest range of accommodations styles of any Great Barrier Reef island resort.

The accommodations choices are extra-large rooms and suites in the high-rise hotel; high-rise one-bedroom apartments; Polynesian-style bungalows (**Palm Bungalow; $$**) in tropical gardens (ask for one away from the road for real privacy); and glamorous rooms in the two-story, adults-only **Beach Club ($$$),** with a personal "host" to cater to every whim, and private restaurant, lounge, and pool for exclusive use of Beach Club guests; as well as one-, two-, three-, and four-bedroom apartments and villas, including villas at the waterfront Yacht Club. The best sea views are from the second-floor Beach Club rooms, from floors 5 to 18 of the **Reef View Hotel,** and from most apartments and villas. If your budget is huge, the poshest part of the resort is the ultraluxe **qualia ($$$),** an exclusive, adults-only retreat on the northern part of the island. It has 60 one-bedroom pavilions, each with a private swimming pool and a guest pavilion. There's a spa and two restaurants, and none of these facilities are available to other Hamilton Island guests.

Hamilton Island, Whitsunday Islands. www.hamiltonisland.com.au or www.qualia resort.com.au. ✆ **13-73-33** in Australia, 61/02-9433-3333 (Sydney reservations office), or 07/4946 9999 (the island).

MOST ROMANTIC RESTAURANTS

Beach Club Restaurant $$$ MODERN AUSTRALIAN

This intimate restaurant creates a mood and ambience that are hard to resist. The lighting is low and romantic, the setting is beachfront, and the rule is: adults only. Cocktails are served poolside, on the beach, or at a cozy bar. Great care is taken to provide exquisite seasonal menus with local ingredients. There is also an excellent wine list.

Cats Eye Beach, Beach Club Resort on Hamilton Island. ✆ **61/07-4946-8000.** www.hamiltonisland.com.au/beach-club-restaurant.

Bommie Restaurant $$$ MODERN AUSTRALIAN

A smartly designed place at the Hamilton Yacht Club, Bommie has a country-club feel with carpeted floors, gleaming wood, and classic Eames chairs. But the sail-shaped tables and fine seafood remind you it's a yacht club. The menu has a wide selection of fresh-caught fish, plus steaks and other meat dishes. Dine on the deck for romance—the restaurant's policy of no kids under 12 helps.

Hamilton Island Yacht Club. ✆ **61/07-4948-9433.** www.hamiltonisland.com.au/bommie-restaurant.

Marina Tavern $$ GASTRO PUB

This pub is a twilight destination for a lot of people. Great for casual camaraderie, it will also serve you a meal, early or late, overlooking the Hamilton harbor.

Front Street, Marina Side on Hamilton Island. ✆ **61/07-4946-9999.** www.hamilton island.com.au/marina-tavern.

HAMILTON ISLAND BY NIGHT

Sunset & Dinner Cruises

Dinner cruises have received a tarnished reputation because so many have bad food. But when the package works, it is romantic and gratifying. You can satisfy all your senses with **Cruise Indigo** aboard the *Denison Star* (Hamilton Island; *©* **61/07-4946-9664;** www.explore group.net/en/unique-experiences/sunset-cruise-and-dine; $A294 per couple). Dinner is excellent, the sounds and smells of the water and air are heavenly, and you will see spectacular islands and water, lit beautifully at sunset.

THE GREAT RIFT VALLEY & ZANZIBAR (TANZANIA & KENYA)
The Experience of a Lifetime

The Great Rift Valley should be on everyone's bucket list. Aside from the absolute beauty of the place—long plains sprinkled with acacia trees, rivers, and lakes and the fearsome power of the great animal migrations—it is filled with meaning for couples. It is the cradle of human existence, and there is a sense of having been here in some dream, some other life, or, perhaps just in one's imagination. It's a moving, even life-changing, experience. To come here with someone you love is all this, plus an enhanced sense of the passage of time and the preciousness of each other.

Africa alone is a potent experience, but this giant valley, which stretches across Kenya and Tanzania, down to Congo, Rwanda, and Uganda and includes Lake Victoria, stands out even among the other amazing places we recommend. You stay in bush camps that are beyond luxurious and discover the hospitality and majesty of the Masai and their extraordinary way of life. You will be stunned, drawn together by the scale of it all.

Phenomenal animal sights occur every month of the year. But we urge you to visit during the **Great Migration** (June through October for most animals) at **Serengeti National Park,** during which animals make the long trip to new grazing areas ultimately to have their young (typically in January). Miles and miles of herds form and intensify in spring as they move through a western corridor that leads many to a predictable crossing in June at the Grumeti River, where crocs are waiting, and in September or October through the Mara River. The babies, of course, attract predators. Obviously, witnessing "a kill" does not fall within our romantic parameters, but it is an unforgettable experience.

The drama of the migration is played out in a minor way year round, but during the migrations, the scale is truly unimaginable until you see it. Thousands of walking, then thundering, animals create a Noah's Ark procession that renders most people speechless, snapping hundreds of pictures, still awestruck when they return to camp. You and your partner will witness the basics of life: Eat or be eaten, survive among the herd or be picked off if you are not fast or alert enough. It makes life and love that much more precious.

Note: Rates in this section are in US$.

KEY ATTRACTIONS

Campfires, Singing & Stars   Every camp offers dinners lit by campfires and starlight, but not all are accompanied by a singing staff. The &Beyond camps host singing competitions so their staffers tend to be particularly able. The beat of Africa is in everything you see, but it rings loudest in its people; the music is a stirring part of the trip and goes directly to the heart.

Picnics   After a long morning watching game, you pull into a shaded grove for breakfast or lunch—and there sits a table, set with a white cloth, surrounded by beaming staff ready to serve an elegant lunch in the most spectacular of areas and views. The camps know how to delight and surprise you with elaborate buffets of grilled game, vegetables, fruits, freshly baked breads, juice or wine, and sweets.

Staying in Camp   No one wants to miss a game drive, but if it's your second or third camp, you may feel the need to relax, stay by the pool, or linger in bed. The camps can run you a bit ragged, and if you want a romantic retreat you will need to resist at least one game drive and pay attention to each other and to the peace and beauty of your camp. You can also get some extras. Most camps are the masters of a romantic surprise. Tell them you are on your honeymoon, anniversary, or romantic getaway (whatever it is) and watch them surprise you with a **special dinner** in your bungalow or alone together at the pool, on a bridge, or some other place that will be romantic—and safe.

Sundowners   Almost all tours will have a stop in the late afternoon—and usually in a protected and romantic spot—where the setting sun and you combine satisfyingly with a cup of coffee, some jerky, and perhaps some spirits. We have had sundowners in front of a small natural pool with hippos calling and yawning in the distance; on top of a rock ledge surrounded by elephant tracks; and in our car, watching hyenas circle cautiously, perhaps hopefully.

Your Itinerary

The big travel companies usually follow a few set itineraries—but you can also create a custom journey with individual travel planners. And even if you go with a big company with lots of camps, you are usually free to visit a different camp.

TANZANIA

Tanzania is the most expensive African country to visit, and it's especially expensive during migration season. We think it's worth it to save up for this exciting destination, but you might also consider joining a smaller tour group through **Overseas Adventure Travel** (© **800/955-1925;** www.oattravel.com). In 2014 they offered a Safari Serengeti, staying at the Tanzania Lodge on a tented Safari (with a side trip to Zanzibar) for $2,495 for 12 days (not including airfare)—see their website for other tours, including Botswana (p. 356).

Serengeti National Park   Contiguous with Kenya's Masa Mara, the Serengeti National Park is the main attraction here, and it will be the focus of any trip to Tanzania, especially during the Great Migration. But in any season its long plains and high and low grasses will charm.

© **255/028-262-1515**. www.tanzaniaparks.com/serengeti.html. $60 park fee per person.

Lake Manyara National Park   This is the land of Flamingos, and if you have never seen dozens and dozens of them spread out like a Chinese fan, you have missed one of the most romantic sights of the world. Their pink loveliness and strange yet graceful stance against the blue lake and the green foliage move the heart. This is a primary bird-watching place—and it is also famous for the lions that, unlike most, have learned to climb trees to scope out their prey. Big herds of elephants also call this small but beautiful park home, but the flamingos are the emblematic sight.

The only lodge here in this park is the intimate **Lake Manyara Tree Lodge** located on the southern edge of Lake Manyara ($$$; © **888-882-3742** or 27/11-809-4300; www.andbeyond.com; closed April); it offers lakeside picnics and a few fantastic treehouses amid the mahogany branches. Public areas are all elevated, the better to watch the game. Few people overnight here, but do, if you want the silence of Africa! In the early morning, the land is yours. Like all the camps, dinner under the stars, protected by the boma (wood enclosure) and lit by dozens of lanterns, is extremely romantic, no matter how many times you experience it. The food is also fantastic and sophisticated, a combination of continental desserts (like crème anglaise) and local game and vegetables.

© **255/272-253-9112**. www.tanzaniaparks.com/manyara.html. $45 park fee per person.

Ngorongoro Crater   Located in the **Ngorongoro Conservation Area** (www.ngorongorotanzania.com), a world heritage site, this is considered by many to be among of the seven wonders of the modern world. The crater encircles the wildlife, and its floor is rich in lions, elephants, zebra, rhino—everything you want to see on a game drive. The downside is that every other safari group is here too, and unless you come in the low season, or very early or late, you are likely to be cheek and jowl with other Land Rovers. Still, it is an awesome place.

For your stay, the **Ngorongoro Crater Lodge,** along the southern edge of the Ngorogoro Crater ($$$; © **888/882-3742** [U.S. toll-free] or 27/11-809-4300; www.andbeyond.com), is a love or hate place. It is a fantasy built on the idea of a Masai village, and the fantasy is far more glamorous than any village could possibly be. Still, if you are romantics who want a flight of fancy, this could be the most romantic place on earth. You will have your own *Ascari* (Masai warrior) to guide you to your house and be your "butler." You will need him because the animals are all around you, and it would be dangerous to leave your lodging without a brave and savvy escort.

Open your door and you enter an English drawing room, with leather chairs, a fireplace, and a big mosquito-netted bed awash in fresh flowers and elegant lighting. But wait, there's more: Likely, you will see a trail of rose petals leading to a closed door. When you open it, you'll see an astounding paneled room with a bathtub in the center, possibly with a bubble bath already drawn and cold champagne beside it—in addition to two showers and floor-to-ceiling windows. Even more splendid suites exist, but this average "hut" is more than enough, and the views over the crater are sublime.

The public rooms maintain the theme: The mirrored dining room has chandeliers and fine furniture, but still there are also campfires with enchanting Masai dancing and singing—distinctive, tall Masai silhouettes, proud and strong, women in beautiful beaded necklaces, headdresses, and decorated clothes, athletic rhythmic leaping—you can expect to be captivated and thrilled. As you might imagine, this lodge is a popular choice for honeymoons, weddings, and wedding parties. The decorous dining room is more than up to the task of staging an elegant dinner with rose petals flooding the floor, and roses covering the room and on the tables. A silver service and fine cuisine make this the experience of a lifetime.

Olduvai Gorge and Shifting Sands Near most camps in northern Tanzania on the Serengeti Plain is the steep-sided Olduvai Gorge, the original and still active archeological site where Louis and Mary Leakey and their family discovered our earliest ancestors. Sometimes a Leakey family member is there to show you around while other times, graduate students and colleagues will lead you. Not far from the gorge is a strange and slightly magical place, **Shifting Sands,** the English name for the sacred Masai area where magnetized sands gather and form high mounds. Over the course of years, when the wind blows some sand away, the rest of the sand follows so the mounds "walk" through the desert. Markers show where the mounds were in any given year. It is just amazing.

Most Romantic Camps

Grumeti River Camp $$$ This camp is right in the migration path, at the edge of the river; you warily watch the giant crocodiles. This is such a wonderful place to experience the migration that you must book way ahead. Hippos grace this landscape any time of year, and you'd better not be a light sleeper; their roars wake almost anyone. The camp is decorated in a light-hearted fashion: Colorful rooms are playful rather than the traditional colonial English style of most camps. Amazing dinners served in surprise locations in the Masira Hills are a romantic highlight.

✆ **888/882-3742** (U.S. toll-free) or 27/11-809-4300. www.andbeyond.com.

Singita Sabora Plains, Faru Faru & Sasakwa $$$ Singita signifies three things: the most luxurious camps, the most expensive camps, and usually, the best locations you can find. The rooms are gorgeous, dressed with fine linens, textiles, and artifacts. The suites are worth spending an extra day for, just to fully take advantage of the large and ultra-luxurious bathrooms, sitting rooms, decks and often, pools. Game viewing is particularly good here because they have a private concession from the Masai, meaning private sightings, unhindered by other safari groups.

☏ **27/021-683-3424** or 27/013-735-5500. www.singita.co.za.

KENYA

Kenya is also in the path of the Great Migration and part of the Great Rift Valley. In addition, it is home to the **Masai Mara National Reserve** (www.masaimaranationalpark.org), a 5- to 6-hour drive from Nairobi. Masai Mara's ecosystem has one of the highest concentrations of lions in the world, and it sustains more than 95 mammal species and 570 species of birds.

Most Romantic Camps

Kichawa Tembo Tented Camp $$ & Bateleur Camp at Kichwa Tembo $$$ These storied camps in the path of the migration are on the banks of the Mara River, with all the charm of traditional camps. Whether in migration season or not, you are here to watch the herds of giant elephants, the crocs silently lurking (even if they look like they are snoozing), and, in the plains beyond, devilishly fast cheetahs, black-maned lions, elegant and powerful giraffes, and uncountable masses of monkeys and baboons. Onsite naturalists lead you on walks and morning and afternoon game drives. You are on Masai ground, so many of your hosts will be tribal members. A special romantic treat: This camp is located at the foot of the Oloololo Escarpment, which is very near where "Out of Africa" was filmed. You can almost hear the haunting music from the movie in your head.

☏ **888/882-3742** (U.S. toll-free) or 27/11-809-4300. www.andbeyond.com. Classic Kichwa Tembo tents closed from Oct 15–July 1.

Klein's Camp $$$ Bordered by the Masai Mara on the north and the Serengeti on the west, this isolated camp is what Africa is all about. You are high on an escarpment looking down at the valley from the lodge's timbered living room, and almost constant animal traffic is on your horizon descending from the Kuka Hills. As you have a cocktail or lunch in your deep leather chairs, you witness huge African elephants, a small troupe of zebra, or a lone giraffe cross your sight lines in a particularly moving panorama. The lodge is small and unbothered by other visitors because it is in a private Masai concession. The rooms are either luxury tents with hardwood floors or round stone huts modeled after Masai habitats. They are not uber-luxurious, but are very nice indeed with elegant showers, but sadly no tubs (we romantics like tubs everywhere—even on safari), warm wood furniture, and king-sized beds. Rooms look out into the green forest, but it's not quite the perfect view you will see from the main gathering place, a short walk away. The camp is not fenced, so after you are escorted to your place at night, you stay there. (Keep your tents zipped or baboons will almost certainly ransack it). This place feels like the real Africa.

☏ **888-882-3742** (U.S. toll-free) or 27/11-809-4300. www.andbeyond.com.

Lemala Camps $$ If you are looking for a more affordable option and a first-class wildlife experience, these camps could be your best choice, especially if you avoid high season. Commodious tents, with all the necessary bath and bedroom creature comforts (no more than 10 tents per camp) are near a main game river crossing on the Mara, so the migration here can be spectacular. Lemala's private location is special; you will not feel crowded by other tourists.

℃ **255/027-254-8966** or 255/027-254-8952. www.lemalacamp.com. Closed Apr–May.

A ROMANTIC EXCURSION TO ZANZIBAR

The island of Zanzibar (really two islands) has an intriguing world heritage town (**Stone Town**), stunning beaches, hospitable and diverse people, and ready access to getaway islands. The sea is a shockingly true turquoise, and the traditional, colorful costumes worn by men and women complete the feast for the eyes. Speaking of feasts, the cuisine here is excellent, with local exotic species, and contributions from Arabic and Indian traditions as well as from Africa in this semi-autonomous part of Tanzania.

Labyrinthine streets, seafood restaurants, and white-sand beaches make Stone Town a romantic place with a soundtrack of the melodic call to prayer to its mostly Muslim population. A certain amount of "deferred maintenance" can take some getting used to. A satisfying pursuit is to find a *taarab* orchestra in performance. Taarab is a delightful blend of African and Middle Eastern music, and you can take a cruise with a taarab band, and taarab artists usually perform at Zanzibar's cultural festivals. In Stone Town, a taarab group performs some evenings on the seaside terrace of the **Serena Inn** (see below), and also at the seafood restaurant, **Mercury's** (Mizingani Road, Stone Town; *℃* **255/777-413-081**), named for Zanzibar native son, rock star Freddie Mercury of Queen.

Key Attractions

Getting in the Water   This is a great place to dive, and there are many outfits to help you. It is also a great place to snorkel. Even more romantic, there is **snorkeling with dolphins**. Go very early in the morning to **Kizmkazi**, a small historically important village on the southern part of the island where Islam first took root in East Africa. Almost immediately offshore you will find a large number of bottlenose dolphins that often let people swim close to them. Patience and calm will be rewarded with at least sightings of the animals—don't press them, and their natural curiosity will drive them to investigate *you*. They are allowed to come to you, not vice versa! Think about staying at nearby **Unguja Lodge** ($$; Near Kizmkazi Village; *℃* **255/774-857-234;** www.ungujalodge.com) to get an early start and help from guides who know what they are doing and won't hassle the dolphins.

Hotels with Heart

Mnemba Island Lodge $$$ After an introductory visit to the stone buildings and streets, the romantic excursion we prefer is the private Mnemba Island: isolation, white sand, vivid sunsets, turquoise water, and impeccable service at this &Beyond property. It is the quintessential honeymoon place, where tropical fruits, coconuts, and fresh fish are the mainstay of your diet. Fewer than a dozen cottages claim the island as their own, and your days will be spent in the warm, clear waters of the ocean diving or snorkeling, investigating healthy coral reefs with an amazing number and variety of wildly colored fish. It is a quiet place, where you can kayak, fish, swim, or go deep-sea cruising or fishing, or do nothing at all. The rooms are up to the caliber of other five-star lodges, and the food is delicious, leaning heavily on the exotic spices of the area.

Mnemba Island. ☎ **888-882-3742** (U.S. toll-free) or 27/11-809-4300. www.mnemba-island.com. Closed Apr–June.

Serena Inn $$ With a classic water view, a pool, fine service, and a perfect location on the ocean, this is the place to stay in Stone Town. All the rooms, in two lovely historical buildings, have sea views. Even if you don't stay here, get a dinner reservation for a Friday night and have an authentic and delicious Swahili dinner. End your day at the bar overlooking the water.

☎ **255/24-223-3587**. www.serenahotels.com.

Seyyida Hotel & Spa $ This hotel has an elegant lobby, a spa, and large rooms with marble accents. Near the Zanzibar Palace Museum and overlooking the ocean, it is a lovely place to stay or to have dinner and drinks. A romantic choice would be one of the sea view rooms, and be sure to visit the rooftop terrace.

Off Mizingani Rd., Old Stone Town next to Palace Museum. ☎ **866/538-0187** or 255/24-223-8352. www.theseyyida-zanzibar.com.

KERALA & COCHIN (KOCHI), INDIA
Cruising Through Cultures

If you are familiar with only northern India, the South will be a revelation. You wait for the crowds, the dust, the—let's face it—chaos of the big Northern cities like Mumbai, and it's just not there. It's a different landscape and a different mood. The people here are poorer than many parts of the country, but they have the highest literacy rate (96%) and the lowest birth rate in India. Many practice Ayurveda, India's ancient science of wellness. But time your visit well: The best time to go is November through March, when it is not so torrid; avoid the monsoons in June and October.

Kerala

Visit the state of Kerala for a more romantic India than you ever imagined. Grossly mislabeled "the Venice of India," Kerala is nothing of the sort; it has its own kind of watery magic. On the Arabian Sea, Kerala is a network of villages, lagoons, and natural canals, but it's also plantations and small farms. Kerala's famous "backwaters" are lush tropical canals best navigated aboard stunning houseboats called *kettuvallam* that you can rent for a day or longer. Covered by woven bamboo and wicker roofs that are works of art, they can be simple, just a covered top; or elaborate with several bedrooms, a kitchen, bathrooms, and four men to operate them, including a guide and a chef. Reserve your *kettuvallam* ahead of time (through a travel agent or your hotel) and pick it up in Alleppey (Alappuzha) or Kottayam. You'll slowly cruise the waterways, sitting or lounging together in the front of the boat along small channels (so crowded with weeds that your boatman will have to clear them along the way) to canals so large that they look like lakes. The scenery slowly changes, but depending on the route, you will see locals fishing or farming; temples, mosques, and huts; and water buffalo, an occasional elephant, and other animals amid the lush foliage. It's very slow, sensual, and absorbing—*very* romantic.

Cochin (Kochi)

Cochin is an old colonial city in Kerala with an intermittent history of tolerance that is now primarily a fishing village. Explore the waterfront: You'll be fascinated by the fishing nets and boats that use traditional 14th-century technologies we haven't seen elsewhere. The triangular sails and nets are quite beautiful and are hoisted with a pulley and lever system that seems to be quite effective. Along the shore, small local restaurants grill the catch as it comes in. In the village you'll witness more reminders that the city wasn't born yesterday. Consider the little park near the charming St. Francis Church; it was once a repository for the buried remains of the famous Portuguese explorer Vasco da Gama (before being shipped back to Portugal about 500 years ago).

KEY ATTRACTIONS

Paradesi Synagogue   This beautiful little synagogue, dating from 1568, is in the heart of what is still startlingly labeled Jew Town. The area itself is adorable and full of energy and commerce. It has quite a few interesting antique and souvenir shops. The synagogue is bedecked with gorgeous blue and white Chinese tiles (on the floor, on the walls) and ornate hanging oil lamps. A series of paintings unveils a fiery history of how a Maharajah saved the Jews as they ran from the rabid hatred of Portugal's colonial government. The Jewish community lived in harmony with the Indian state until quite late in the 20th century, when most Jews emigrated to Israel. When we were there, the feeling of tolerance still seemed active: Numerous school groups were visiting to hear the story. It's pretty heartwarming, which we think is always good for a relationship!

Mattancherry Synagogue Lane, Jew Town Rd., Kappalandimukku, Kochi. ℂ **91/ 471-232-1132.**

Kathakali   Kerala in general has high quality arts, but these performances are unique to the area and very special. It is more than dancing; each facial expression portrays a world of cultural meaning. Get there an hour or so early to see the actors apply their make up (an effort that takes up to 5 hours) and to get a short and worthwhile education on what various expressions and costumes mean. There are no words in these dances and plays; instead, everything is conveyed by the body and the face. Traditionally, the actors are men (they were in our show, but we were told that women now perform in other troupes), and they play roles in which great transformations take place. Some actors play demons and spirits; others play women. The make-up is fantastic and might even change the shape of the face. The plays often portray humor, violence, and transformation (from a comely temptress, for example, to a demon) and are exciting, even gripping, to watch—and fun to talk about later.

K.B. Jacob Rd., Fort Kochi. ℂ **91/484-221-7552.** www.kathakalicentre.com. INR250–INR350).

Shopping   We think India is one big shopping orgy, with its gorgeous stuff at extremely tempting prices. There are small treasures you can cram into your bag (silver and gold bangles, scarves and throws, small relics of Hindu worship, etc.) and big magnificent things (antique doors, furniture, large blankets, and weavings) that shops can ship (in our experience the treasures actually turn up once you get home). Some beguiling choices, both on Jew Town Road in Jew Town, are at **Leen's Exports** (at no. 6/92; ℂ **91/98-47-011901**) and **Heritage Arts** (ℂ **91/484-221-1145**). The latter has a huge warehouse with a mind-boggling spread of merchandise. Shop together and create memories with the things you desire—it's not the same as shopping in the real Venice, where you lust after things you could never afford!

Spice Market   We love Asian spice markets, with their sacks of spices in the most vivid colors. This one is near town on Bazaar Road. Why not be experimental and buy a bunch of little bags of new spices and try them at home? (They will make your clothes smell exotic!)

Festivals   It's hard not to come upon a festival in Kerala. You can check with the India tourist center to find out which ones are going on while you are there. They usually have fascinating ceremonies, dancing, music, decorated elephants, and diverse pageantry. Sometimes you'll see men carrying planks hung with large but intricate papier-mâché figures of animals or gods. For the festival of Onam, celebrated in August and September, women create great big colorful floral carpet presentations. The Kochi-Muziris Biennale, inaugurated in 2012, is a celebration of painting, film, sculpture, and performances, held on even years.

HOTELS WITH HEART

The Malabar House $ This inexpensive but stylish boutique hotel in Fort Cochin, is housed in an old colonial building that at the Parade Ground. The modern guestrooms are punctuated by antiques along with some examples of local crafts. The restaurant offers big buffets of tasty regional food, and more than you could ever eat. It has a small pool in a tropical courtyard that adds a dash of romance. The hotel also offers delightful rooms and suites in its neighboring **Malabar House Escapes**, but the suites will bump you up to the $$$ category.

1/268 Parade Rd., Fort Cochin. ☏**91/484-221-6666.** www.malabarhouse.com.

The Marari Beach Resort $ This resort and Ayurvedic center (with a complete Ayurvedic spa) is located in Alleppey (Alappuzha), south of Cochin. Perched on the side of a canal, the resort's buildings—handsome cottages with huge thatched roofs over white stucco—are arranged as though they were a fishing village.

North S.L Puram, Mararikulam. ☏ **91/478-286-3801.** www.cghearth.com/marari-beach.

The Taj Malabar $$ This luxury property on Willingdon Island is a 20-minute car or ferry trip from Cochin. It's renowned kitchen will prepare a private romantic dinner for you; all you need to do is ask (in advance, of course). Sometimes they will set the table at the end of a pier—very romantic if you don't look back at the people watching you from the hotel.

Willingdon Island, Cochin. ☏**91/484-664-3000.** www.vivantabytaj.com/Malabar-Cochin.

MOST ROMANTIC RESTAURANTS

The Kashi Art Café $ CAFE   A delightful mixture of open-air restaurant, art gallery, and tropical garden, this casual place thoroughly expresses the vacation vibe of Kerala. Breakfast is served throughout the day, and lunch comes from a selection of sandwiches, salads, and a hearty soup of the day. Freshly made cakes and pies top off the light meals nicely, especially with a nice cup of coffee or spot of tea.

Burgher Street, Fort Kochi. ☏**91/484-221-5769.** www.kashartgallery.com. Closed June.

Oceanos $ SEAFOOD   Oceanos may specialize in seafood, but it does all of the traditional Kerala dishes well, and at reasonable prices. The menu is extensive with special veggie dishes with eggplant and tamarind. The staff is especially helpful and prompt, which fits in with the pleasant, romantic setting.

Elphinstone Road, Near Bishop House, Fort Kochi. ☏**91/97-46-034739.**

THE SOSSUSVLEI (NAMIBIA)
Splendor in the Dunes

This Namibian desert reserve presents one of the most awesome sights anywhere: a collection of the highest sand dunes on the planet. These sinuous, majestic orange/red dunes change shape and color with the time of day. The Sossusvlei itself covers a huge expanse of the Namib Desert (19,305 square miles and federally protected as the **Namib-Naukluft Park**), thought to be the Earth's oldest desert. **Sossusvlei** translates to *the gathering place of water,* and one must-see destination here is the "clay pan," an ancient riverbed that every 10 years or so holds rainwater as a lake.

The dunes are magical. They "walk" to the western coast, and the wind deposits the grains of sand into the Atlantic; eventually eastward winds take them back inland—over millions of years. Their shapes slowly undulate and grow, and in pictures of the largest ones, people look like tiny apostrophes.

The dunes' changing tones result from iron oxides and other pigments reflecting light differently as the day passes—a major part of their romantic appeal. Guides will rouse you early to see them as the sun comes up, and thus your early pictures are quite different from later ones. The color also changes according to the age of the dune—older ones are more brilliant. As you photograph the dunes—and you must bring a camera here—you will find yourself uncontrollably snapping hundreds of pictures because the dunes seem to change while you are watching them! Come sunset or the next sunrise, you are seeing a new landscape. It's like a living painting.

In and out of the park, the harsh desert landscapes have a profound beauty you won't want to miss. Most lodges are outside the actual park and make the arrangements for you to see the dunes and the other stunning attractions of the area.

GETTING THERE

Major airlines—such as United, South African Airways, and Swiss Air—can fly you to Windhoek, Namibia's fairly pleasant capital. From there it's a long drive to the Sossusvlei, so your travel agent can set up a charter flight to your lodge. Namibia is among the least populated countries in the world, and the flight over this sparsely settled desert is truly awesome. The desert has a few rivers with occasional human habitats near them, but the canyons, mesas, brutal cliffs, and mountain ranges tell you this is wild, untamable turf. In its raw forbidding way, Namibia's extreme beauty will give you a stunning memory together, watching from the plane with just three or four passengers (the maximum). Finally, seeing your lodge all alone in a desert canyon, requiring your pilot to circle around a few times to put down, is a breathtaking experience. You land in what seems like the middle of "nowhere." You might not even be able to see your lodge from this vantage point, but there, next to the runway, is your guide with his Land Rover. Romantic? Oh, my.

KEY ATTRACTIONS

Your lodge can set up guides and make the arrangements for all of the excursions below.

The Clay Pan   For this trip—an experience that may make you feel as though you are walking on the moon—your lodge will set you up with a driver and an all-terrain vehicle. The trek in isn't difficult, although it can be very hot. Black ghostly trees, as if ancient markers of long-forgotten events, greet you at the prehistoric lake for a great photo-op: the terracotta colored dunes, the black trees, and the bluest of skies. *Click!* The empty clay pan is an eerie sight, filling with rainwater or river water only once in 10 years. After plodding around, you'll be ready for a picnic, and if you stay at the places we recommend, your guide will find a tree and, in its shade, cook you a delicious hot breakfast right out of the back of his van! *Warning:* Beyond the boulevard of mega-dunes, you will come to a sign that says only four-wheel drive vehicles are allowed. Believe it; we saw several cars totally stuck in the sand.

www.sossusvlei.org/attractions/deadvlei.

Dune 45   Each dune has a number, and this one is famous because you are allowed to climb it. Easier said than done. The dune is more solid than you would think, but there is still slippage, and it's steeper than you'd like it to be. (It's also pretty windy out there.) Climbing Dune 45 is a very popular endeavor, and even if you get to the park exactly when it opens, you'll see a long line of cars with people who got up earlier than you did. As you climb and look up, you see the dune is larger and more contoured than you imagined. People on it look like tiny dots. Before you reach the top, you might choose a moment when you consider it "climbed." (We did.) It is an amazing experience.

www.sossusvlei.org/attractions/dune-45.

The Dunes from Above   Flights aboard these colorful hot-air balloons take off at sunrise, and most float along only about 10 miles, but it's the perspective that thrills. Then you land and celebrate with a champagne breakfast! You can also hire a plane to see the dunes (a particularly awesome sight), canyons, and the more distant seashore. You can arrange to land in a few places—or stop to have a picnic lunch. It's the experience of a lifetime, but it doesn't come cheap. All the main lodges in the area can set up balloon and airplane rides.

www.sossusvlei.org/activities/namib-sky-balloon-safaris.

Ancient Pictographs & Other Mysteries   This land of mystery has both human and ecological secrets; some become known, while others still puzzle even the most committed researchers. Ancient pictures survive in hidden caves; some require a scramble up a mountain to see. Closer, but more confusing, are the "fairy circles," recurring circles of grass that dot the plains so consistently that you can see them when you fly in. They look like agricultural shapes made by haying machines, but no one knows why they are here and why nothing else grows on the land they cover.

Beyond the Park   The vast open spaces here, with piles of boulders like so much ancient rubble, hide exotic animals. The leopards are secretive and hard to find, but rides out into the great beyond will reveal handsome black and white oryx, springbok, ostriches, bat-eared foxes and birds of prey. Some rustic places are not off-road simply because there is no road. The emptiness of it all imparts a kind of Zen feeling. Your guide will stop for a sundowner (an enjoyable ritual snack!), and there will be no other life as far as the eye can see. It's a good time to exhale and draw closer.

MOST ROMANTIC HOTELS & RESTAURANTS

The summer months here are extremely hot. Most upscale places, and certainly the ones we recommend here, have air conditioning but, naturally, you won't have that luxury on your excursions. Therefore, the winter months are the most popular time for travel here, requiring that you reserve far in advance. There are no freestanding restaurants to speak of in this part of the world—meals are taken at your resort and are often included in your rate.

Little Kulala $$$ This property offers 11 spacious, modern thatched cottages and—important in the summer—climate-controlled rooms. Each bungalow has a rooftop skylight for romantic stargazing. It also offers innovative places for romantic dinners.

✆ **27/11-807-1800** or 27/21-702-7500. www.wilderness-safaris.com/camps/little-kulala.

Sossusvlei Desert Lodge $$$ As you arrive by plane your resort looks small against the rugged Nubib Mountains, boulders, and the expanse of uninhabited land, the **NamibRand Nature Reserve** (✆ **264-61-224882**; www.namibrand.com). The reserve looks inhospitable to life, and yet walking close to the landing strip is a family of ostrich. The huge birds calmly ignore your Land Rover as you embark on the 10-minute drive to your lodging. The long road in reveals hardly a hint of the luxury inside and the privacy of your villas. Inside, it's all rock and modernity and an open view to the vast plain and mountains. You can't see them with the naked eye, but there are trails through the grasslands between you and the mountains, and petroglyphs in the mountains that are hundreds, perhaps thousands, of years old. Later, you will hike to them.

Check-in is in the public rooms where there is a gift shop (with wonderful shell jewelry), an intimate bar, and a dining room that faces an illuminated watering hole where wild animals come to drink at all hours. The food is excellent and often features exotic game such as springbok or kudu. The serious wine cellar can double as a private room for romantic dining tête-à-tête. You can also dine at an outdoor pool and a patio where an occasional animal, such as a heron, may appear. No other human settlement is nearby, and the tranquility is almost overwhelming.

The 10 lodgings are in large stone-and-glass villas spaced far apart with private outdoor stone showers and large marble bathrooms that are open, but shielded from other guests. The air-conditioned bi-level suites are adorned in neutral tones with a dash of rose; downstairs is a living room, which leads to an outside sitting room, and inside is a skylit bedroom (it can be covered for light sleepers) that lets you lie in bed and gaze at the stars. You have a fireplace for dips in temperature, cool mornings, and winter's chill. The front of the villa is almost all glass, and very little blocks your connection with the amazing scenery.

Stargazing is a big deal here. The lodge has its own planetarium and a visiting astronomer on duty. Every night you can go up to the observatory and get a talk and lesson on the skies—it makes a nice date night! The odds and conditions make it likely that you will experience many stars you have never seen before. Other activities include observing petroglyphs, wildlife, and other nature; for more physical challenge, consider hiking and quad biking in the dunes area. Or just lounge in front of your villa, taking in the dramatic scenery and letting serenity wash over your minds and bodies. For a romantic thrill, the staff will spirit you away to a private canopied dining extravaganza by candle- or lantern-light, the only illumination except for the ever-present stars.

✆ **888-882-3742** or 27/11-809-4300. www.andbeyond.com. Rates include meals.

Wolwedans Boulder Camp $$ The company Wolwedans offers several different camps with a number of options, and this one seems right for honeymooners or couples who want something intimate and exclusive. Wolwedans recommends that you split your stay with a few nights in one of their resorts near the reserve and 2 nights at this luxurious camp.

The setting is quite romantic: The camp overlooks the stunning reserve with its huge boulders. The main area includes a breakfast deck and inviting open fireplace. The tent "houses" are surrounded by glass and have stylish and comfortable lounge areas plus commodious outdoor decks, beds with mosquito netting, and elegant bathrooms. The chef prepares gourmet meals and serves dinner (with fine wines) in different places each night for maximum romance and mystery. Expanding on the luxury theme, there is a resident massage professional who offers a variety of therapies. Sundowners are held on excursions or at the top of a rock plateau with glorious views.

✆ **264/61-230-616.** www.wolwedans.com. Park fees are extra.

RAJASTHAN: JAIPUR & UDAIPUR (INDIA)
The Royal Treatment

West of Agra en route to Jaipur is the red sandstone city of **Fatehpur Sikri** (www.fatehpursikri.org; admission INR250 per person), your first taste of Rajasthan's Mogul magnificence with its breathtaking arches, courtyards, and harem quarters that a good guide can enliven for you. Seek out **Jama Masjid,** a spectacular mosque here, to see its beautiful inlaid stones and watercolor paintings. A grand gateway leads to the white marble tomb of the Sufi Saint Salim Chishti and some of the most beautiful carved screens in India. This is a mere sampling of what is on extravagant display throughout Rajasthan, the region of shahs, kings, queens, and dreamers. The historical shrines and buildings on display form an open-air museum with antiquities so well preserved your imaginations can run wild. Very near the historical works are parks and vast wildlife preserves with scenery of heart-stopping beauty. The great cities for romance are Jaipur and Udaipur, each with hidden and apparent charms for lovers.

Jaipur

This is one of the most decorative cities in India, which is saying something. Called the pink city for the color of its historic buildings, it is seductive and has that wonderful bustle of crowds, a random elephant or two, and the dense retail that defines most cities in this desert region. The busy tourist season runs September to March; April is also a great time to visit, but expect Jaipur to become uncomfortably hot beginning in May.

KEY ATTRACTIONS

The Amber Fort   About 11 kilometers (6.8 miles) from Jaipur, this complex on Maota Lake is rich in beautiful sandstone and marble appointments in a Hindu style. It is best reached by a short elephant ride (romantic because it is fun and short!). The views are somewhat stark but the interior erupts with celebrations of deities and battles in the extravagant form of mirrored ceilings, frescoes, and stone carvings. An evening sound & light show covers the history from 1070 'til today.

Amer. ✆ **91/141-253-0293.** www.rajasthantourism.gov.in. Admission: INR200 per person.

The City Palace   The palace is also the residence of the Jaipur Royal Family; an enthralling part of it is the **Maharaja Sawai Man Singh II Museum.** Let your imagination go wild as you look behind the curtain of royal life in the 1600s and beyond.

Behind Tripolia Gate. ✆ **91/141-408-8888.** www.msmsmuseum.com. Admission: INR300 per person.

The Gem Palace   This is no palace, but some of its treasures may cost as much. It is one of the best places to buy gems new (cut and polished here) or antique (sloughed off by royal families on hard times) and could be just the place to make a very special and meaningful romantic purchase. Don't be intimidated by the huge emeralds on display; there are affordable jewels here as well as something Brad might pick up for Angelina. If you are going whole-hog in India, buy jewels. But don't expect subtlety: This is the world of extravagant creations!

M.I. Road. ✆ **91/141-237-4175.** www.gempalacejaipur.com.

Ranthambore National Park   Give your senses a romp in nature. Picturesque ruins dot this 116-square-mile wildlife park that is famous for tigers. Sightings aren't guaranteed, but taking a tiger tour improves your chances. The park is a 4-hour drive from Jaipur in a mountainous region and heavily treed, so you'll spot plenty of other species, especially birds.

✆ **91/847-401-2050.** www.ranthamborenationalpark.com. Closed July–Sept.

HOTELS WITH HEART

Amanbagh $$$ Any Aman is a splurge, but this location 2 hours from Jaipur is an especially beautiful offering; it is an idealized local village with marble villas walled off from each other to provide complete privacy (especially wonderful if you go for broke and get a villa with a private pool). Staff can take you (by camel, part way) to the ruins of a lost city, and give you yoga lessons and a picnic on an ancient terrace.

Ajabgarh, Jaipur. ✆ **91/1465-223-333.** www.amanresorts.com.

Oberoi Rajvilas $$$ This fabled, expensive, and much awarded resort is about 20 minutes outside of the city. You will see gorgeous grounds, lavish rooms, and supreme hospitality. Dine here, even if you don't stay here (see Surya Mahal, below).

Goner Road. ✆ **800-562-3764** or 91/11-2389-0606. www.oberoihotels.com.

Samode Haveli $ This affordable heritage hotel has been updated and offers charming, romantic rooms, several of which surround the pool's courtyard. The most inspired rooms are elaborately decorated and located in the part of the house where women were once sequestered. If you choose the Sheesh Mahal Suite, you will be dazzled by a mosaic of tiny mirrors that totally surround you.

Gangapole. ✆ **91/141-263-2407.** www.samode.com.

MOST ROMANTIC RESTAURANTS

Niros $ TRADITIONAL INDIAN   This is real India—a memory to share. It is quite famous, and celebrities from around the world flock here for truly fine interpretations of Rajasthan cuisine (and at good prices!). Opt for curries, kebabs, lamb, and mutton but, really, you can't go wrong here—and there are nearly 300 selections!

M. I. Road, Ashok Nagar. ✆ **91/141-237-4493.** www.nirosindia.com.

Surya Mahal Courtyard at Oberoi Rajvilas $ INTERNATIONAL   This elegant eatery is among the most romantic in Jaipur. Ask to dine under the stars in the courtyard against the backdrop of the Rajvilas Fort. Huge braziers illuminate the courtyard, which features Rajasthani women performing traditional dances (Sept 15 through March only). The food is traditional, too, with many beautiful preparations of lamb with regional spices. However, if you want to stick with western cuisines, they do that well, too. We thought their rack of lamb was perfect.

Goner Rd, near Agra Rd, Jaipur. ✆ **91/141-268-0101.** www.suryamahal.com.

JAIPUR BY NIGHT

Sunset from Nahargarh Fort or "Tiger Fort"   See the pink city at its rosiest when the sun sinks behind the Aravalli Hills and Jaipur turns into twinkling jewels. The view is always a winner, but during the festival of Diwali in November, when firecrackers explode above the city, it becomes one you will never forget. ✆ **91/141-513-4038.** Admission: INR50.

Udaipur

Some say Udaipur is India's most romantic city, with its enchanting gardens, sparkling lakes, and abundant supply of beautiful palaces overlooking them. We won't argue. The lakes and the aged buildings in and around them give the place an otherworldy aura. A 5-hour drive from Jaipur (by an experienced Indian driver, not you), the city sometimes seems more heaven than earth. You may already know a part of it: The white City Palace in the lake has been photographed almost as much as the Taj Mahal.

KEY ATTRACTIONS

The City Palace & Museum   This is the largest of Rajasthan's 11 fairytale city palace complexes. Located on Lake Pichola it boasts lavish interiors. The gardens are charming with romantic courtyards to discover. The original family still occupies a substantial part of the palace. Delve into the palace's fascinating history at the museum.

City Palace Rd. ✆ **91/294-241-9021.** www.rajasthantourism.gov.in. Admission: INR50 + INR200 camera fee.

The Ranakpur Jain Temples   A 2½-hour drive from Udaipur, these temples, with their detailed, carved pillar, are a sight to behold. Chaumukha Temple, dating from 1446, includes 66 subsidiary shrines. Built by the Jains, the temple rules must be followed according to the religion's strict dictates. Jains are vegetarian and mean it: No leather items (including belts and handbags) are allowed. As in many other temples, you are requested to dress conservatively (legs and shoulders must be covered). No cuddling or funny stuff here.

Ranakpur, near Sadri Town. ✆ **91/2934-28-5019.**

HOTELS WITH HEART

The Oberoi Udaivilas $$$ This hotel draws consistent raves. A new construction modeled on an imagined royal palace, it succeeds. On the banks of Lake Pichola, a bit outside of Udaipur, it is an imposing sight and an experience of absolute luxury. Reserve a lake view room and porch (with semi-private infinity pool) that separates you from the rest of the hotel. The views of the lake and verdant grounds are stunning.

Mulla Talai, Haridasji Ki Magri, near Lake Pichola. ✆ **91/294-243-3300.** www. oberoihotels.com.

Shiv Niwas Palace $ The Palace Rooms in this Grand Heritage hotel are reasonably priced and some even have balconies overlooking Lake Pichola.

City Palace Complex, Udaipur. ✆ **91/294-2528016-19.** www.hrhhotels.com.

Taj Lake Palace Hotel $$$ Even if you don't stay at this 18th-century charmer, take a boat out for tea or a meal. But don't settle for lunch if you can swing a stay here, which is divine. You are ferried by boat, serenaded at the close of the day, and bedded down in opulently decorated wood-paneled rooms with murals, commodious marble bathrooms, and fine linens. The views are sensational from most rooms (make sure you request one with a lake view. For the royal treatment, request one of the opulent suites (116 and 117) that actually once housed the queen and king. Don't miss a chance to dine here, either. The food is as good as the superlative views from the hotel's rooftop terrace, as the sunset background turns the City Palace pink and gold.

Lake Pichola. ✆ **91/294-252-8800.** www.tajhotels.com.

MOST ROMANTIC RESTAURANTS

Sheesh Mahal $$ INDIAN Located on the roof of the Leela Palace hotel beside a lake, the restaurant is exquisitely decorated with fine Indian artifacts, and the food here shows the creative and talented imprint of a celebrated Parisian chef, Karim Hassene.

Leela Palace, Like Pichola, Udaipur. ✆ **91/294-670-1234.** www.theleela.com.

UDAIPUR BY NIGHT

14

Cocktails on the Rooftop Choose a rooftop restaurant (they are some-what plentiful here) and toast each other. We recommend the **Sunset Terrace** at the Fateh Prakash Palace (**$$;** Lake Pichola; ✆ **91/1594-252-8016;** www.heritagehotelsofindia.com). At sunset here the sun ducks behind the Aravalli Hills and the atmosphere teems with romance, as candles are lit and the Lake Palace, floating in the foreground, shines like a ghost ship on Lake Pichola. The food is only adequate so let appetizers suffice. The terrace at the nearby **Jagat Niwas Palace Lakeside Restaurant** (**$;** Behind Jagdish Temple, Udaipur; ✆ **91/294-242-2860;** www.jagatniwaspalace.com) is open to the breeze but has a roof. One level up is an open-air deck with sublime lake views.

THE RED CENTRE (AUSTRALIA)
Unforgettable Night Skies

The Red Centre, a mostly empty red desert in the center of Australia, is among the world's great landscapes. This area is mystical, and if this is your kind of landscape, it's incredibly romantic, too.

At the heart of the Red Centre is The Rock, a huge monolith plunked in the middle of nowhere—actually **Uluru Kata Tjuta National Park** (✆ **61/2-6274-2220;** www.environment.gov.au/parks/uluru; A$25 for a 3-day pass). It is a religious place, *Uluru* to the Aboriginal people who have lived here for tens of thousands of years and have an intense spiritual connection to their land. Visit Uluru, and it is hard not to feel emanations from this sandstone formation. Travelers do not expect to be as touched as they are. (We certainly didn't expect it during our visit; but in fact we, like most the other pilgrims, found ourselves quite worshipful.)

The Red Centre is also home to big cattle ranches, sheep stations, rugged mountain ranges, and the scenic Kings Canyon. Kangaroos roam the canyon the way buffalo once roamed the American West. This magical land, however, is much older, though it is younger in terms of its untamed natural challenges. Exploring the Red Centre takes care and planning. The weather can be brutal, and you need to know where the next water hole or community will be.

If you visit the only big town in this part of Australia, Alice Springs, the mood is completely different—it's more of a rough-and-ready yet sociable experience. But whatever you do, travel in the temperate season: The desert's summer heat, from November through March, will melt you.

Uluru

You've likely seen pictures of this place before, but they leave you unprepared for how the rock will affect you. Give in to your instincts and emotions. Stop thinking in a linear way and plan to spend enough time to see Uluru at both dawn and dusk. It's not just the size of the ochre-colored mountain, although it is massive, more than six miles long. It's the aura, the shape, the way the light hits it, and its improbable one-off placement. It's not quite like anything you have experienced before.

Uluru is most intense at sunset, when different shades of orange and ochre pinks, red, and purple appear, never quite the same one day to the next. You will want to experience each of its moods.

Some people climb it, and you can see them daisy-chained together by ropes over the top. But Aboriginal people feel that is a sacrilege and, honestly, it seemed disrespectful to us, so we opted not to climb. Rather, take a walk with an Aboriginal guide and hear creation stories and more local lore. If you climb, know that it can be quite vertical, has a lot of ruts and unstable surfaces, and can get very hot, windy, or cold. There are tales of heat stroke, and traumatic, even fatal, falls here. We think that the easy, 2-hour base walk is the better shared moment.

KEY ATTRACTIONS

Silent Dinner in the Desert   Ayers is the non-Aboriginal name for The Rock. Ayers Rock Resort (below) offers a "Sounds of Silence" dinner in the desert and is not at all hokey. At a desert clearing you enjoy champagne and hors d'oeuvres. Didgeridoo music is performed, and its deep tones and laments put you in a meditative state. The Australian barbecue buffet includes local exotic foods (kangaroo, emu, crocodile, etc.) and after dinner, the lights dim, and you listen to the silence of the desert and appreciate the brilliance of the stars. A resident astronomer helps you interpret what you are seeing, now that you are in the Southern Hemisphere.

Yulara Dr. ℭ **61/2-8296-8010** or 1300-134-044. www.ayersrockresort.com.au. A$195 per person.

Flying Over the Monolith   If a bird's-eye view is the vantage point you want, you can rent a plane or helicopter and get that perspective without endangering yourself on a climb. Several companies arrange scenic flights by light aircraft or helicopter over the whole area; for example, **Professional Helicopter Services** (ℭ **61/8-8956-2003** or 08/8956-2003; www.phs.com.au)

offers a 15-minute flight over Uluru for A$145 per person (or a 30-minute ride for A$275).

A Camel's-eye View Some really nice camels live here, and they are available daily for touring the desert through **Uluru Camel Tours** (Ayers Rock Resort, Yulara; ℂ **61/8-8956-3333;** ulurucameltours.com.au; A$80–$125 per person). The gait takes a little getting used to, and the guide may simply lead rather than teach you how to steer, but, still, you can ride to Uluru by sunrise or sunset, and have tea in the morning or champagne in the evening. Tours leave from the Camel Depot at Ayers Rock Resort.

HOTELS WITH HEART

Ayers Rock Resort community is the only place to stay here. We recommend you stick with hotels for both lodging and dining, which can be quite good. If money is truly no object, **Longitude 131°** ($$$; Outback Pioneer Wilderness Camp, Yulara; ℂ **61/2-9918-4355;** or 08-8957-7888; www.longitude131.com.au) provides luxurious tents as your window to Uluru's enchantment. If price, in fact, does matter, read on—but do consider a special dinner in the sand dunes under the stars at **Table 131°**.

Ayres Rock Resort/Sails in the Desert Hotel $$$ This modern oasis offers stylish rooms that overlook the pool's dramatic white shade canopies, which resemble sails. Views are few, but the living is easy (if pricey), and good restaurant choices are plentiful: **Mayu a la Carte** for fine dining, the **Ilkari Restaurant** buffet, and the poolside **Pira Pool Bar.** After a day in the sun, it's nice to hit the **Red-Ochre Spa** (ℂ **61/8-8957-7036** for appointments); treatments run from A$60 to A$285.

ℂ **61/2-8296-8010**. www.ayersrockresort.com.au/sails.

Desert Gardens $$ The only hotel with room views of Uluru, this place is slightly more affordable than the others. It isn't quite as lavish, but it is set in a lovely desert landscape and provides what is arguably Australian's best sunset. The resort's **Arnquli Grill** specializes in flame-grilled meats.

Yulara Dr., Yulara. ℂ **08/8957-7714**. www.ayersrockresort.com/au/desert.

Kings Canyon

While you are in the neighborhood (in Australia, a 200-mile range is neighborly), you'll want to visit Kings Canyon, also known as **Watarrka National Park** (ℂ **61/8-8956-7460;** www.parksandwildlife.nt.gov.au/parks/find/watarrka). You may have seen it before: The camp movie "Priscilla, Queen of the Desert" was partly shot here. The area's sandstone canyon and ochre-hued sand dunes are impressive. Hikers should go with a professional guide, and those who are not exactly canyon-ready can book guided and self-drive tours on stable quad bikes (or even a helicopter canyon tour) at Kings Canyon Resort (below). Expect to see cattle, but also camels and kangaroos and, if you are lucky, the canny Australian dingo.

HOTELS WITH HEART

Kings Canyon Resort $$ If you want a romantic roof over your head, this is it. The deluxe rooms are very, very romantic, so we recommend the added splurge if you can swing it. The best rooms are quite private, with big desert views. Spa rooms also have balconies with truly dramatic views of rock ledges that have been romantically lit, plus you can soak together in your oversized Jacuzzi. The resort's family-oriented Holiday Park offers quad-bike tours and camel rides—time for you and your sweetie to have a sunrise camel ride if you haven't done one yet!

☏ **61/3-9426-7550** or 300-863-248. www.kingscanyonresort.com.au.

SIEM REAP, CAMBODIA
Mysterious Ancient Temples

Some places are romantic because they feel like a forbidden world, where you've entered another civilization; you are visitors from another century, perhaps another planet. **Angkor Wat,** a vast Hindu and Buddhist temple complex about 4 miles north of Siem Reap, is such a place.

Driving from the airport, you see the temple ruins rising, grand and mysterious, behind a lake. You head toward Siem Reap, but you'll want to come back at sunset and sunrise to see the temples bathed in celestial or morning light.

We first saw the temples at sunrise driving through the jungle, so we had the thrill of emerging from the thick tangle of flora to behold the ancient walls and stone carvings as though we were rediscovering a lost civilization. At sunrise other tourists aren't distracting; the beauty of the reflected sun hushes all. You are glad you are with your partner: This is one of life's semi-sacred moments that should be shared. There is no better introduction to Siem Reap, where you come for the temples situated among scenic jungles, rice paddies, estuaries, and bird sanctuaries. Dating from the 9th century, the ornate shrines were elaborated on in the 11th and 12th centuries. Some are in good condition, others a crumbling mess. Surrounded by a mix of scrub and heavy jungle, many are tortured by trees that have grown up and around the buildings, wrapping them in sinuous branches and roots, seeming to squeeze them into submission, but yet they survive.

TOP ATTRACTIONS

Bayon Temple   If you want to be stunned, see the huge mysterious stone faces that embellish the Bayon temple, said to be the intersection of heaven and earth. The jungle has reclaimed some of these awesome figures, believed to represent the bodhisattva Avalokiteshvara. Also appealing to the senses are the wonderful carvings of dancing women and the Terrace of the Elephants, with massive reliefs of elephants and the Garuda, the mythical national (part-human) bird of Thailand that guards temples, houses, and people from evil spirits. One could get melancholy here amidst the decay of extraordinary art and craftsmanship of a great Khmer culture. But instead they make us cling even closer together, acknowledging the passage of precious time, and perhaps vowing to use it well.

Angkor Thom, Siem Reap.

The Psah Chaa Market   This market is great fun for couples to mutually discover fresh new aromas, tastes, and feasts for the eyes. We recommend this not-too-large market, located a little east of Siem Reap near the river, for its exoticism, variety, and ease. You'll find sumptuous local produce plus textiles and carvings for memorable souvenirs. The merchants are friendly, the prices fair, and you can safely get lost together in a foreign country. It's also good for sampling Cambodian (Khmer) dishes.

Old Market, Psar Chaa Rd, Siem Reap.

HOTELS WITH HEART

Amansara $$$ This stunning Aman property was first built as a retreat for King Sihanouk. Unlike other hotels in the chain that decorate in native craft style, the Amansara's style is mid-century modern. It comes with the Aman price tag, but the extras fit our romantic expectations. The resort picks you up at the airport in a classic Mercedes limo that, so the story goes, belonged to the king. At the resort, staffers line up to help, tailoring your stay according to your desires and your stamina. Beautiful, modern, freestanding cottages cluster with others around a central green. You can have an in-room spa treatment, then slip out a glass door to your private pool, which is surrounded by 10-foot walls that give confidence to would-be skinny dippers.

Road to Angkor, Siem Reap. ✆ **855/63-760-333.** www.amanresorts.com. Additional board charge of US$150 per person per day.

Heritage Suites Hotel $ This well-priced haven offers a 2-day Romantic Escape that includes airport pickup in a vintage Mercedes, a candlelit dinner, a monk's blessing ceremony, and a temple day trip by *tuk tuk* (bicycle rickshaw) with a personal guide. Its 26 rooms and suites epitomize Eastern elegance and offer the chance to bathe with a view of your tropical garden, or shower outside in privacy. The dining room draws raves for both Asian and international cuisine and you can eat by the pool (romantic). This place feels much more expensive than it is.

Near Wat Po Lanka, Slokram Village, Khum Slok Kram. ✆ **855-6396-9100.** heritage suiteshotel.com.

La Residence D'Anghor $$$ Sure, the rooms are air conditioned, but you have mosquito netting in case you want to rely on the evening breezes to cool down together. The lushness here centers on a swimming pool amid gardens that reach to the Siem Reap River. The hotel is built in traditional Khmer style, inside and out; the 54 rooms, all with lavish terrazzo bathrooms, are decorated with dark hardwood and bamboo. It's close to the ruins (a 10-minute drive), but not the crowds, and its lovely restaurant has a poolside terrace.

River Road, Siem Reap. ℂ **855/63-963-390.** www.residencedangkor.com.

Raffles Grand Hotel D'Angkor $$ This is a majestic place from an earlier era, with old elegance, eight restaurants, and nightly cultural shows that conveniently keep you close to your room—if impulse should strike. The best destination for romancers are the choice Landmark rooms overlooking the pool.

Vithei Charles de Gaulle, Khum Svay Dang Kum. ℂ **855/63-963-888.** www.raffles. com/siem-reap.

Shinta Mani $ For passionate couples, quiet can be a visa to romance. This affordable hotel on a peaceful side street near the river is decorated with hardwoods and pale, calm colors that suggest a Zen quietude. You will feel at peace with the world, and each other, at this gentle place. The best of the rooms open onto the patio and pool, so request one. Good inexpensive massages are available at the spa.

Oum Khun and 14th St., Siem Reap. ℂ **855/63-761-998.** shintamani.com.

MOST ROMANTIC RESTAURANTS

The Khmer Kitchen $ THAI/CAMBODIAN   We love this informal, extremely inexpensive open-air restaurant in downtown Siem Reap for its good Khmer food and a chance to enjoy each other's company without effort. It's also great for people-watching.

Modul I, Sangkat Svay Dangkum. ℂ **855/63-964-154.** www.khmerkitchens.com.

The Red Piano $ CAMBODIAN   Here you can dine on the roof terrace, absorb a captivating view of Siem Reap, and linger over a menu with a wide variety of international dishes, specializing in Thai and Khmer. Table for two, please.

341 Street 8, Pub Street, Siem Reap. ℂ **855/63-964-750.** www.redpianocambodia. com.

The Soup Dragon $ VIETNAMESE   It can be sexy to find each other among strangers. Travel to this three-story open-air Vietnamese cafe for rice noodles and breakfast on the ground floor or Asian and international specialties on the next floor up (try the Soup Ch'nang Dae). After dinner you can party down at the top-floor bar, where locals and tourists mix at night.

369 Street 8, Near Pub Street, Siem Reap. ℂ **855/63-964-933.**

SIEM REAP BY NIGHT

We recommend leisurely open-air dinners (see above), but if dancing gets you connected, check out the discos on **Pub Street, Sivatha Road,** and in the **Old Market** and **Wat Bo** areas. They start late, but stay open until 3am.

UTTAR PRADESH: AGRA & THE TAJ MAHAL (INDIA)

An Iconic Monument to Everlasting Love

India has more history and glamour than the eye can handle, but also more poverty. For some, the country's overcrowding and it's noises, congestion, and intensity are simply too much. We understand—yet India remains one of our favorite places in the world. To feel its romance, focus instead on the culture, the pungent colors of the saris (even on the poorest women), the richness of diverse religions and traditions, and the beauty the ruling classes have given to the ages.

The most romantic pearl of the Indian oyster is, of course, Agra's **Taj Mahal,** the universally known monument to love. You can fly, or be driven from, Delhi, a city we like but do not find especially romantic. It's possible to make a day-trip from Delhi only to see the Taj Mahal (closed Fridays), but don't short yourself. The area is rich in monumental tombs of Mogul Shahs that will make an exotic backdrop for your personal love story.

If experiencing the Taj Mahal is on your bucket list, don't immediately dismiss it as too expensive. At the time of writing, we've seen group travel outfits like Friendly Planet offering trips to India, including Delhi, Jaipur, and Agra, starting at $1,499 (based on double occupancy), inclusive of airfare. Keep your eyes open on social media, or ask a travel agent, for group tours that make the most exotic places affordable.

Heads up: A modern divided highway connects Delhi and Agra, and the drive takes about 5 hours, much of it spent navigating the clogged roads around Delhi to get to the highway. Do not think about driving yourself, unless you have a knack for dodging oncoming elephants and goats in your lane. Please, hire a car with a driver. It may be better for your relationship as well!

KEY ATTRACTIONS

The Taj Mahal   Some storied places are a disappointment when you see them. This one is not. The famed marble and jeweled building may be a bit smaller than you imagined, but it is perfect (and note that that term is used with restraint in this book). Treat yourself by spending 24 hours with the Taj to see it in varied light, especially at dawn and sunset. The story is well known: The Taj was an act of love by Shah Jahan in remembrance of his beloved dead wife. It took 20 years to build and severely strained the finances of the Mogul Empire, but the result is very moving. An Indian poet called it "a teardrop on the cheek of eternity." The Taj's linear gardens introduce the fairytale building, originally set completely with precious stones, overlooking the Yamuna River and the fort, from which Jahan later would view the memorial after he was deposed and imprisoned. The story is bittersweet, but this serene masterpiece makes us feel the passion and completeness of perfect love—and want to be in that same, rarified air.

Agra, Uttar Pradesh. ℆ **91/562-222-6431.** www.tajmahal.gov.in. Admission INR750. Closed Fri.

Agra Fort   After the white marble Taj, it can be refreshing to see these 70-foot-high red sandstone walls, polished to a sheen. Surrounded by a moat (1½ miles around), this secure retreat for royalty contains beautiful, richly decorated inner courtyards. You can also see the small chamber where Shah Jahan was imprisoned beside the Yamuna River.

Rakabganj, Agra. ℆ **91/562-222-6431.** agrafort.gov.in. Admission INR300.

HOTELS WITH HEART

ITC Mughal Agra $ This beautiful luxury hotel near the Taj costs far less than other luxury hotels in the area. The hotel's use of marble in a modern version of traditional architecture stirs the senses. Spa services are very good, especially the Mughal mix—a sensuous blend of Persian and Indian treatments.

Taj Ganj, Agra. ℆ **91/562-402-1700.** www.starwoodhotels.com.

The Oberoi Amarvilas $$ Inspired by the local Mogul architecture, this luxurious hotel on Agra's fringes is pricey but not over the top, and *every* room offers a view of the Taj Mahal. Excellent Indian food is served at its Esphahan restaurant (below). You will feel a sense of magic as you walk through the inlaid walkways and gaze upon the reflecting pools and terraced gardens.

Taj East Gate Rd. ℆ **91/562-223-1515.** www.oberoihotels.com.

Wyndham Grand Agra $ This quite reasonable hotel is palatial in feel, with marble walls and floors with traditional heritage rooms. It is a huge resort with meeting rooms, lovely grounds, excellent food, and a large pool. Fair warning: Service here has been called into question by quite a few visitors, but for the price, you are way ahead. It is approximately 2½ miles to the Taj Mahal, so no view. If you can, spring for the better rooms or suites.

Fatehabad Rd., Agra. ℆ **855/201-7819.** www.wyndhamgrandagra.com

MOST ROMANTIC RESTAURANTS

Esphahan $$ TRADITIONAL INDIAN   You can expect extraordinary cuisine, service, and live Indian music here, but what will stick in your memories will be the view upon arrival: The glorious illuminated palace is set amid the resort's Mogul-inspired architecture and lush terraced lawns, fountains, and reflection pools, and also affords a view of the Taj Mahal. Consider pre-dinner cocktails on the veranda and experience sunset over the Taj. You can't go wrong with cauliflower appetizers followed by tandoori prawns or the succulent chicken *tikka* in saffron and garlic. Also try the *rogan josh* (lamb braised in Kashmiri chilies) or the delicious Persian-style quail. Or order a *thali* (platter), and feed each other samples of local specialties. This is a stirring place to celebrate seeing the Taj.

In the Oberoi Hotel, Amarvilas. ℂ **91/562-223-1515.** www.oberoihotels.com.

Saniya Palace $$ INDIAN At the inn of the same name, this lovely rooftop restaurant is a 3-minute walk from the Taj Mahal, with incredible unobstructed close-up views of the Taj. Offering a delicious variety of Indian cuisines, it is also good place to sip a cocktail or a ginger-lemon-honey-tea at sunset.

Chowk Kagziyan, South Gate, Agra. ℂ **91/562-327-0199.**

AGRA BY NIGHT

Evening entertainment is restrained in Agra, but there are plenty of movies, cafes, restaurants, and pubs to explore. And you'll find shopping for gorgeous Indian fabrics and precious jewelry in the **Chhipitola and Sadar Bazar** areas. For pure romance, try a walk down the Taj Mahal complex by moonlight. The Light and Sound Show at the **Agra Fort** (www.agrafort.gov.in), on Yamuna Kinara Road, is a dramatic showcase for the glorious past of Agra and perhaps some inadvertent hand holding.

ROMANTIC INTEREST INDEX

Not sure where to go on your romantic adventure? Here are a few (hundred) ideas to help you focus in on the paradise of both your dreams.

MOST PRIVATE PARADISES

Amansara
Siem Reap, Cambodia (p. 385)

&Beyond Desert Lodge
Soussevhei, Namibia (p. 377)

Amandari
Ubud, Indonesia (p. 306)

Four Seasons at Sayan
Ubud, Bali (p. 307)

Klein's Camp
Kenya (p. 369)

Outermost Inn (winter)
Martha's Vineyard, MA (p. 733)

Over-water Bungalows
Four Seasons, Bora Bora (p. 310)

Whitsundays Private Charter Boat Tour
The Whitsundays, Australia (p. 360)

HIKER'S PARADISE

Bamboo Forest
Along the way to Hana, Maui (p. 235)

Beach & Cliffwalk Lanai
Four Seasons Lana'i at Manele Bay, Lanai, Hawaii (p. 236)

Bell Rock Pathway
Sedona, Arizona (p. 149)

Bermuda Railway Trail
Hamilton, Bermuda (p. 263)

County Mayo, Ireland
(p. 190)

Griffith Park
Los Angeles, California (p.36)

Hoh Rainforest
Jefferson County, Washingon (p. 63)

Johnston Canyon
Banff, British Columbia (p. 170)

Na Pali Coast
Kauai, Hawaii (p. 238)

Valle dei Mulini (Valley of the Mills)
Amalfi Coast, Italy (p. 284)

Zion & Bryce National Parks
Springdale & Bryce Canyon, Utah (p. 164, 166)

BEST PLACES TO STROLL

The Avenidas
Buenos Aires, Argentina (p. 100)

Charleston's Battery Park
Charleston, South Carolina (p. 26)

Gay Head Cliffs
Martha's Vineyard, Massachusetts (p. 233)

High Line
New York, New York (p. 51)

La Ramblas
Barcelona, Spain (p. 69)

Marina District
San Francisco, California (p. 54)

Walk Atop the Old City Wall
Dubrovnik, Croatia (p. 291)

Shore Walk (Oak Street to Lincoln Park)
Chicago, Illinois (p. 30)

Walkway along the Seine
Paris, France (p. 83)

Vieux Montréal
Montréal, Canada (p. 43)

Village Walks
The Cotswolds, England (p. 182)

BEST FOR BIKE RIDING

Ancient Balinese Villages
Bali, Indonesia (p. 304)

Icefields Parkway
(Banff to Jasper)
Alberta, Canada (p. 170)

Loire Valley
France (p. 193)

Willamette Valley
Willamette, Oregon (p. 159)

MOST SPLURGE-WORTHY GETAWAYS

Banyan Tree
Koh Samui, Thailand (p. 328)

Hayman Island Resort
Airlie Beach, Australia (p. 361)

Hotel Danieli
Venice, Italy (p. 88)

Jade Mountain
St. Lucia (p. 281)

La Residence
Franschhoek, South Africa (p. 104)

Le Bristol
Paris, France (p. 84)

Mandarin Oriental Dara-Devi
Chiang Mai, Thailand (p. 95)

Ngorogoro Crater Lodge
Resort
Tanzania (p. 367)

One&Only Pamilla
San Jose del Cabo, Mexico (p. 268)

Phinda Private Game Reserve
South Africa (p. 106)

Pinnacle Camp at The Resort at
Paws Up
Greenough, Montana (p. 349)

Post Ranch Inn
Big Sur, California (p. 219)

BEST SHOPPING DESTINATIONS

Ubud & Nearby Towns
Bali, Indonesia (p. 304)

Cape Town Waterfront
Cape Town, South Africa (p. 104)

Istanbul Grand Bazaar
Istanbul, Turkey (p. 73)

Marrakech Souks
Marrakech, Morocco (p. 107)

Magnificent Mile
Chicago, Illinois (p. 30)

Paris Flea Markets
Paris, France (p. 307)

San Miguel Allende
San Miguel Allende, Mexico (p. 345)

Santa Fe
Santa Fe, New Mexico (p. 58)

New York City
New York, New York (p. 49)

BEST ANTIQUES OGLING

Bucks County
Bucks County, Pennsylvania (p. 125)

The Cotswolds
Cotswolds, England (p. 181)

Paris (Left Bank & flea markets)
Cligancourt (18th arrondise-
ment) and Porte de Vanves
(14th arrondisement)
Paris, France (p. 307)

Provence
Provence, France (p. 198)

San Francisco (especially
Valencia, Polk, Sutter area, and
Telegraph Avenue in Oakland)
(p. 54)

MOST JAW-DROPPING VISTAS

Amalfi Coastal Drive
Amalfi Coast, Italy (p. 284)

Belvedere Outlook
Moorea, Society Islands (p. 315)

Cliffs of Moher
Liscannor, County Clare Ireland
  (p. 186)

Dalmation Coast
Split to Dubrovnik (p. 292)

Dunes at Namib-Naukluft Park
Soussevhei Namibia (p. 37)

Going to the Sun Highway
Glacier National Park, Montana
  (p. 144)

Helicopter views over Kilauea
Hilo, Big Island, Hawaii (p. 225)

The Icefields Parkway
Alberta, Canada (p. 171)

**Lake Louise from the Fairmont
Chateau**
Lake Louise, Alberta, Canada
  (p. 174)

Na-Pali Coast
Kauai, Hawaii (p. 238)

Santorini by Sea
Santorini, Greece (p. 301)

Uluru, The Red Center
Uluru, Australia (p. 382)

Zion National Park
Springdale, Utah (p 164)

BEST NIGHTLIFE

Buenos Aires
(p. 103)

Chicago
(p. 33)

Lisbon
(p. 81)

Los Angeles
(p. 39)

New Orleans
(p. 49)

New York City
(p. 54)

Rio de Janeiro
(p. 114)

Venice
(p. 90)

BEST FOODIE DESTINATIONS

Bali
(p. 303)

Barcelona
(p. 69)

Buenos Aires
(p. 100)

Chicago
(p. 29)

Los Angeles
(p. 33)

Napa Valley
(p. 131)

New Orleans
(p. 47)

New York City
(p. 49)

Paris
(p. 82)

San Francisco
(p. 54)

Seattle
(p. 61)

Tuscany
(p. 202)

BEST SPOTS FOR A DESTINATION WEDDING

Ashford Castle
County Mayo, Ireland (p. 191)

Fiesta Americana
Cancún, Mexico (p. 272)

The Grand Wailea Resort
Maui, Hawaii (p. 236)

Halekulani Hotel
Oahu, Hawaii (p. 242)

The Inn at Orcas
Orcas Island, Washington (p. 253)

Kenwood Inn and Spa
Sonoma, California (p. 130)

Live Aqua
Cancún, Mexico (p. 272)

The Little Nell
Aspen, Colorado (p. 123)

The Lodge at Koele
Lanai City, Hawaii (p. 236)

Salish Lodge
Snoqualmie, Washington (p. 64)

Wauwinet
Nantucket Island, Massachusetts
 (p. 230)

BEST ALL-INCLUSIVE GETAWAYS

Azamara Cruise
Athens to Istanbul (p. 296)

Azul Sensatori Jamaica
Negril, Jamaica (p. 277)

**Four Seasons Kuda Huraa &
Four Seasons Llardaa Giraavatu**
Maldives (p. 313)

Live Aqua
Cancún, Mexico (p. 272)

Rancho La Puerta
Tecate, Mexico (p. 178)

BEST FOR CULTURE VULTURES

Chicago
(p. 29)

Festival di Ravello
Amalfi Coast, Ravello, Italy (p. 286)

Los Angeles
(p. 33)

New York City
(p. 49)

Paris
(p. 82)

**Santa Fe, New Mexico
(summertime)**
(p. 54)

Venice
(p. 86)

Vienna
(p. 90)

BEST ALL-OUT AMAZING ADVENTURES

Angkor Wat & Bayon Temple
Near Siem Reap, Cambodia
 (p. 385)

Camel Riding
The Red Centre, Australia (p. 384)

**Charter Sailing in the
Whitsundays**
Australia (p. 360)

**Diving & Snorkeling at Great
Barrier Reef**
Australia (p. 361)

Elephant Experiences
Four Seasons Chiang Mai (p. 97)

Manta Ray Adventure
Bora Bora (p. 309)

Mayan Temples
The Mayan Coast to Tulum
 (p. 273); Cancún to Chichén Itzá
 ruins (p. 271); and Maya Riviera
 (p. 273)

Safari Camps
Botswana (p. 357) South Africa
 (p. 106), and Namibia (p. 377)

Witnessing The Migration
Great Rift Valley (the Masa Mara &
 Serengeti), Kenya, and Tanzania
 (p. 365)

BEST OFF-SEASON GETAWAYS

Bali (January & February)
(p. 303)

Bermuda (late fall & winter)
(p. 261)

California Winelands (late fall)
(p. 257)

**Catalina Island (late fall &
winter)**
Near Los Angeles, California (p. 35)

**Martha's Vineyard & Nantucket
(winter)**
Massachusetts (p. 228)

Maui (summer)
Maui, Hawaii (p. 235)

Negril & St. Lucia (after Thanksgiving but before Christmas)
Jamaica (p. 275)

Paris (at Christmastime)
(p. 82)

San Francisco (late fall)
(p. 54)

San Juan Islands (late fall &winter)
(p. 252)

Vail & Aspen (just before & after ski season)
(p. 120)

Wickanannish Inn (fall & winter)
Tofino, British Columbia (p. 355)

PERFECT PLACES TO PROPOSE

Over Stunning Panoramic Views Aboard a Hot-Air Balloon
Sedona, Arizona (p. 148)
Napa Valley, California (p. 128)
Shenandoah Valley near Washington, DC (p. 67)
Loire Valley, France (p. 193)

In a Private Cove
Amankila, Bali (p. 306)
Cambridge Beaches, Bermuda (p. 263)
Swan Lake at the Hotel Bel-Air, Los Angeles (p. 38)

In Front of a Waterfall or Water View
Aleenta Resort, Phuket, Thailand (p. 324)
Salish Lodge (nearby waterfall) Snoqualmie, Washington (p. 64)
Paressa, Phuket, Thailand (p. 324)
Mauna Lani, Hawaii, Big Island (p. 226)
Banyan Tree Beach, Koh Samui, Thailand (p. 327)
Floating Dinner at Kayumanis at Jimbaran Bay (p. 307)
The Four Seasons Koh Samui, Thailand (p. 328)
Shanti, Bali (with your own private waterfall) (p. 307)

Seine bridge with Eiffel Tower backdrop, Paris (p. 83)
Harbor & Bridge, Sydney, Australia (p. 116)
Waimoku Fall, Haleakola National Park, Maui (p. 235)

With A World-Class Urban View
The Eiffel Tower, Paris (p. 83)
Top of the Rock, New York City (p. 50)
The Space Needle, Seattle (p. 61)
Le Bristol Hotel, Paris (at the hotel pool) (p. 84)
San Marco Square (late at night), Venice, Italy (p. 87)
Willis Tower (Sky Deck), Chicago (p. 5)

With the Best Meal Ever
Auberge du Soleil, Napa Valley California (p. 133)
Dasheene at Ladera, St. Lucia (p. 282)
The French Laundry, Yountville, Napa Valley (p. 133)
The Inn at Little Washington, near Washington, DC (p. 68)
Le Pre Catelan, Paris (p. 85)
Post Hotel, Lake Louise, Alberta, Canada (p. 175)

BEST PLACES TO COMMUNE WITH WILDLIFE

Four Seasons Tented Camp Golden Triangle
Chiang Mai, Thailand (p. 98)

Glacier National Park
Glacier, Montana (p. 143)

The Great Migration
Tanzania (p. 365)

Jackson Hole & Grand Teton National Park
Jackson Hole, Wyoming (p. 136)

Ranthambore National Park
Jaipur, India (p. 379)

Safari Camps
Botswana (p. 357), Kenya (p. 369), South Africa (p. 106)

BEST OFFBEAT ROMANTIC ADVENTURES

Bull "Dancing" in Arles
Provence, France (p. 199)

Caving at Aktun Chen
Mayan Coast (p. 273)

Cosmic Ray Station & Observatory
Banff, Canada (p. 171)

Crystal Cave & Fantasy Cave
Bermuda (p. 263)

St. George Open Air Cinema
Sydney, Australia (p. 118)

MOST GLORIOUS GARDENS

Butchart Gardens
Vancouver, Canada (p. 352)

Chicago Botanical Gardens
Glencoe, Illinois (p. 30)

City Palace & Museum
Udaipur, India (p. 379)

Gardens of Augustus
Capri, Italy (p. 289)

Giverny & Roserie de la Hay
Outside Paris, France (p. 82)

BEST GETAWAYS FOR WINE LOVERS

Abeja
Walla Walla, Washington (p. 157)

Allison Inn
Willamette Valley, Oregon (p. 162)

Bardessono
Napa Valley, California (p. 134)

Black Walnut Inn
Willamette Valley, Oregon (p. 162)

Le Quartier Francais
Franschhoek, South Africa (p. 105)

Porto, Portugal
(p. 20)

Santa Ynez Valley
Near Santa Barbara, California
(p. 257)

Tuscany & Umbria
(p. 202)

ROMANCE ON A FAMILY HOLIDAY

Aboard an Alaska Cruise
(p. 332)

Azul Sensatori Jamaica
Negril, Jamaica (p. 277)

Club Med
Cancún, Yucatan (p. 315)

The Conrad
Bali, Indonesia (p. 306)

Fairmont Chateau
Whistler, BC (p. 174)

Grand Hyatt
Kauai, Hawaii (p. 239)

Kayumanis
Jimbaran, Bali (p. 307)

Lux Resort
Maldives (p. 315)

Paws Up
Greenough, Montana (p. 350)

Ritz Carlton
Kapalua, Maui (p. 237)

Westin Lagunamar
Mayan Riviera, Mexico (p. 267)

Index

See also Accommodations and
Restaurant indexes, below.

General Index

A

Accommodations. *See also*
    specific destinations;
    Accommodations Index
    gestures that facilitate
        romance, 7
    getting the best room, 21–22
    money-saving tips, 16
    price categories, 20
Admiralty Island (Alaska), 335
Agra, 388–390
Agra Fort, 389, 390
Airlie Beach, 360–363
Aix-en-Provence (France), 199–202
Aktun Chen (Mexico), 273
Alaska cruises, 332–340
Alfama (Lisbon), 76
Al Jamal (Istanbul), 75
All-inclusive resorts, 14
Amalfi (Italy), 284–286
Amalfi Coast (Italy), 283–290
The Amber Fort (Jaipur), 379
Anderson Family Vineyard
    (Newberg), 159
Angkor Wat (Siem Reap), 385
Anniversaries, celebrating, 266
Archery Summit (Dayton), 160
Architecture River Cruise
    (Chicago), 30
Argosy Evening Cruises
    (Seattle), 64
Argyle Winery (Dundee), 160
Arles (France), 199–202
Artesa Vineyards & Winery
    (Napa), 132
Art Institute of Chicago, 30
Arts and Crafts movement, 182
Aspen, Colorado, 120–125
Aspen Music Festival, 122
Assisi (Italy), 207, 209–210
Astoria (Oregon), 243–246
Astronomy, stargazing, 168
Athens, 297–299
Austrian National Library
    (Vienna), 90
Avalon (Catalina Island), 35
Ayasofya (Istanbul), 73

B

Bairro Alto (Lisbon), 77
Bairro Alto Hotel Rooftop Terrace
    (Lisbon), 81
Bali, 16, 303–308
Ballooning
    Jackson Hole, 136
    Loire Valley (France), 193
    Tuscany (Italy), 203
    Willamette Valley (Oregon),
        160–161

Bandon (Oregon), 250–252
Banff, 170–173
Bangkok, 93–96
Barcelona, 19, 69–72
Barnsdall Park (Los Angeles), 36
A Bar with a View (Istanbul), 76
Basilica di San Francesco
    Assisi, 207
Basilique Notre-Dame
    (Montréal), 47
Bateau Parisiens (Paris), 82
Bateaux-Mouche (Paris), 82
Bath products, 18
Bathrooms, 22
Bayon Temple (Siem Reap),
    385–386
Beach Blanket Babylon (San
    Francisco), 58
Beaches, 11–12
    Bali, 304
    Bermuda, 262
    Bora Bora, 309
    Cabo San Lucas, 267
    Moorea, 316
    nude (Martha's Vineyard), 232
    Santa Barbara, 257
Beaver Creek, 122
Bebek Balikci (Istanbul), 76
Bermuda, 16, 261–266
Bigfork, 144–145
Big Sur, 219
Biking
    Aspen, 121
    Bali, 304
    Banff, 170
    Loire Valley (France), 193
    Martha's Vineyard, 232
    Monterey, 218
    Montréal, 43
    Nantucket, 229
    Santa Barbara, 258
    Sedona, 150
    Walla Walla, 157
    Willamette Valley (Oregon), 161
Bill Marriott's Hideaway
    (Virginia), 67
Bird-watching, 232, 251
Birthdays, 63
Blue Mosque (Istanbul), 73
Bluesalt Bar (Sydney), 117
Boqueria Market (Barcelona), 69
Bora Bora, 308–311
Botswana, 356–359
Bowman's Hill Wildflower Preserve
    (New Hope), 126
Bradbury Building (Los Angeles),
    34, 36
Bromont Mountain, 45
Bryce Canyon National Park,
    166–168
Bucks County, Pennsylvania,
    125–128
Bucks County Playhouse (New
    Hope), 128
Buenos Aires, 100–103
Bullards Beach State Park, 251
Burano, 88
The Burren (Ireland), 186
Butchart Gardens (Victoria),
    352, 354

C

Cable cars (San Francisco), 55
Cabo San Lucas, 266–270
Cafe Carlyle (New York City), 54
Café Luso (Lisbon), 77
Café Majestic (Oporto), 81
Cafe Tortoni (Buenos Aires), 101
Cağaloğlu Hamami (Istanbul), 74
Calhoun Mansion (Charleston), 27
Campbell Apartment (New York
    City), 51
Campbell River, 353–354
Canal St. Martin (Paris), 82
Cancún, 270–273
Cannon Beach (Oregon), 246–248
Canoeing, Banff, 171
Cantons-de-l'Est region, 45
Cape Town, 103–107
Capital Crescent Trail
    (Washington, D.C.), 65
Capri (Italy), 288
Carmel-by-the-Sea, 212–214
Carmel Valley, 215–216
Carnaval, Rio de Janeiro, 112
Carpentras (France), 200
Casa Batlló (Barcelona), 70
Casa de Casal de Loivos
    (Oporto), 81
Cas-en Bas Beach (St. Lucia), 279
Castelo da Sao Jorge (Lisbon), 78
Castillo de Feliciana (Milton-
    Freewater, Oregon), 156
Castillo Gallery (Cordova), 60
Catalina Island, 16, 35
Catalina Tours (Avalon), 35
Cathedral Sagrada Familia
    (Barcelona), 70
Céide Fields, 191
Çemberlitaş, Hamam (Istanbul), 74
Central Park (New York City), 50
Chaco Culture National Historic
    Park, 59
Chappellet (St. Helena), 132
Charleston (South Carolina), 26–29
Charlottesville (Virginia), 67
Château d'Amboise, 194
Château de Blois, 194
Château de Chambord, 194
Château de Chaumont, 194–195
Château de Chenonceau, 195
Château de Cheverny, 195
Château de Valençay, 195
Château de Villandry, 195
Chiang Mai, 97–100
Chicago, 29–33
Chicago Architecture
    Foundation, 30
Chicago Blues & Jazz, 33
Chicago Botanic Gardens, 30
Chicago Summer Dance, 29
Chichén Itzá (Mexico), 271
Chihuly Glass Garden (Seattle),
    61–62
Christ the Redeemer (Rio de
    Janeiro), 111
Churchill Downs, 141
Cirque du Soleil (Montréal), 47

City Lights Bookstore (San Francisco), 56
The City Palace & Museum (Udaipur), 381
The Clay Pan (The Sossusvlei), 375–376
Cliff Castle Casino Hotel (Camp Verde), 149
Cliff House (San Francisco), 56
Cliffs of Moher (Ireland), 186–187
The Cloisters (New York City), 51
Cochin (Kochi), 372–374
Concierge, 23
Cotswolds, England, 181–185
County Clare (Ireland), 186–188
County Kerry (Ireland), 188–190
County Mayo (Ireland), 190–193
Cruises, 14–15, 22
    Alaska, 332–340
    Cabo San Lucas, 268
    Greek isles, 295–297
    Hamilton Island, 364–365
    Moorea, 318
    Negril, 276–277
    St. Lucia, 281
    the Whitsundays, 360
Culinary Institute of America at Greystone (St. Helena), 132

D

Dalmatian Coast (Croatia), 20, 290–295
DaMa Wines (Walla Walla), 156
Deer Mountain Tribal Hatchery and Eagle Center, 338
Denali National Park, 339–340
Deruta (Italy), 208
De Young Museum (San Francisco), 55–56
Diamond Falls Botanical Gardens & Mineral Baths (St. Lucia), 279
Die Rote Bar (Vienna), 92
Dingle Peninsula (Ireland), 189
Dingle Town (Ireland), 189
Dock Street Theatre (Charleston), 29
Dog sledding, Jackson Hole, 137
Dolphins, swimming with, 241, 269, 370
Domaine Serene (Dayton), 160
Dorothy Chandler Pavilion (Los Angeles), 39
Drayton Hall (near Charleston), 27
Dubrovnik, 290–292
Dune 45 (The Sossusvlei), 376
D'vino Wine Bar (Dubrovnik), 292

E

Edison (Los Angeles), 36
Edisto Beach (Charleston), 27
Edmund Rainforest (St. Lucia), 279
El Credito Cigar Factory (Miami), 41
El Farol (Santa Fe), 61
Empire State Building (New York City), 50
Estremoz, 80
The Everglades, 40–41

Evergreen Aviation and Space Museum (McMinnville), 161
Evora, 80

F

Family holidays, 314–315
Festival di Ravello, 286
Fishing
    Banff, 172
    County Mayo (Ireland), 191
    Key Largo, 221
Flathead Lake, 144
Flathead River, 144, 145
Florence (Italy), 203
Florence (Oregon), 249–250
Florida Keys, 220–224
Fond Doux Estate (St. Lucia), 280
Four Seasons' Tented Camp Golden Triangle (Chiang Mai), 97
Franschhoek, 104

G

Galeria dell'Accademia (Venice), 88
Garden District (New Orleans), 48
Gardens, the Cotswolds, 183–184
Garland Ranch Regional Park, 215
Garnet (Montana), 350
Garrison Creek (near Walla Walla), 156
Gearhart (Oregon), 246
The Gem Palace (Jaipur), 379
Georgia O'Keeffe Museum (Santa Fe), 59
Getty Center (Los Angeles), 37
Getty Villa (Los Angeles), 37
Glacier Bay National Park (Alaska), 334
Glacier National Park, 143–144, 148
Glaciers, Lake Louise, 174
Gleneden Beach (Oregon), 248
Golden Age Passport, 17
Golden Gate Bridge (San Francisco), 54
Golden Gate Park (San Francisco), 55
Golf
    Bandon, 251
    Bermuda, 262
    County Mayo, 191
    Hamilton Island, 361
    Jackson Hole, 136
    Jamaica, 276
Gondolas, Venice, 87–88
Grand Bazaar (Istanbul), 73
Grand Canyon, 149
Grand Central Terminal (New York City), 51
Grand Circle Travel, 17
Great Barrier Reef (Australia), 359–365
Great Point Lighthouse (Nantucket), 229
Great Rift Valley (Tanzania and Kenya), 365–366
Greek isles, 295–302
Greenlake (Seattle), 62

Greenwich Village (New York City), 51
Griffith Observatory (Los Angeles), 34
Griffith Park (Los Angeles), 36
Guanajuato (Mexico), 341–343
Guggenheim Museum (New York City), 52
Gullah Tours (Charleston), 27

H

Hamilton Island, 363–365
Hanalei Beach (Kauai), 238
Harbor Bridge (Sydney), 116
Harry's Bar (Venice), 90
Hawaii (Big Island), 224–228
Hawaii Volcanoes National Park, 225
Healdsburg, 129
Hedonism II (Jamaica), 279
The High Line (New York City), 51
High Road Marketplace (Truchas), 60
Hiking and walking
    Amalfi, 284
    Banff, 170–171
    Bermuda, 263
    Cannon Beach (Oregon), 246–247
    the Cotswolds, 182
    County Mayo, 191
    Dubrovnik, 290–291
    Jackson Hole, 136
    Jasper, 176
    Martha's Vineyard, 232
    Montana, 144
    Moorea, 316
    Nantucket, 229
    Oregon Dunes, 250
    Palouse Falls State Park, 157
    Paradise Valley/Larch Valley, 174
    Rancho La Puerta, 179
    Ravello (Italy), 286
    Santa Barbara, 258
    Sedona, 149–150
    St. Lucia, 280
    Victoria, 353
    Zion National Park, 165
Hoh Rainforest, 63
Hollywood Bowl (Los Angeles), 39
Horseback riding
    Aspen, 122
    Banff, 171
    Botswana, 358
    Bryce Canyon, 167
    Cabo San Lucas, 267–268
    Jasper, 176
    Lake Louise, 174
    Moorea, 317
    Negril, 276
    Santa Barbara, 258
    Sedona, 150
Hotels, See Accommodations Index
Hot springs
    Banff, 173
    Jasper, 176–177
Hunter Valley, 116
Hvar, 293

I

Icefields
Banff, 171
Juneau, 333
Il Palio (Siena), 203
Indian Market (Santa Fe), 58–59
Ink48 (New York City), 54
Internet discounts, 18
Ipogeo dei Volumni (near Perugia), 208
Ireland, 186–193
Isla Mujeres (Mexico), 271
Istanbul, 72–76
Istiklal Caddesi (Istanbul), 75

J

Jackson Hole (Wyoming), 135–140
Jaipur, 378–381
Japanese Tea Garden (San Francisco), 55
Jardin Botanique (Montréal), 44
Jardin Botanique (Tahiti), 320
Jasper (Canadian Rockies), 175–178
Jazz (Charleston), 29
Jessup Cellars (Yountville), 132
Jewell Meadows Wildlife Area (Oregon), 246–247
Juneau, 333–334

K

Kailua Beach (Oahu), 241
Kalalau Trail (Kauai), 238–239
Kathakali (Kerala), 372–373
Kauai, 238–240
Kayaking
Bermuda, 262–263
Key Largo, 221
Montana, 144
Phuket, 323
Santa Barbara, 258
Sitka, 336
Keeneland, 141
Kentucky horse country, 140–143
Kentucky Horse Park, 141
Kenya, 369–371
Kerala, 371–374
Ketchikan, 337–339
Key Largo, 220–223
Key West, 223–224
Killarney (Ireland), 189
Kings Canyon (Australia), 384–385
Koh Samui, 326–330
Koranic Ben Youssef Medersa (Marrakech), 108–109
Korcula Island, 294–295
Koutoubia Mosque (Marrakech), 108
Kruger National Park, 106

L

La Chocolaterie de Jacques Genin (Paris), 83
La Conner, 62
Lahaina (Maui), 235
Lake Louise, 173

Lake Manyara National Park (Tanzania), 367
Lake Massawippi, 45
Lake Washington, 62
Lanai, 235–236
La Pedrera (Barcelona), 70
La Rambla (Barcelona), 69
La Soufriere Volcano (St. Lucia), 280
La Tartine (Paris), 83
L'Atelier Saint-Germain de Joel Robuchon (Paris), 86
The Laurentians, 45
Leavenworth, 62
Le Bar Churchill (Marrakech), 110
Le Comptoir Darna (Marrakech), 110
Le Conte Glacier (Alaska), 334
Le Procope (Paris), 86
Lewis and Clark National Historical Park, 244
Lido Restaurant and Bayside Grill (Miami), 43
Lisboa Regency Chiado (Lisbon), 81
Lisbon, 20, 76–81
Little Havana (Miami), 41
Loire Valley (France), 193–198
Lopez Island, 252–253
Los Angeles, 33–39

M

Majorelle Garden (Marrakech), 108
MALBA (Buenos Aires), 100
Maldives, 312–313
Mama Africa's (Cape Town), 106–107
Maple Leaf Bar (New Orleans), 49
The Marais (Paris), 82–83
Marrakech, 107–110
Martha's Vineyard, 16, 231–234
Masai Mara National Reserve (Kenya), 369
Massages
Bali, 305
Cannon Beach, 246
Marrakech, 108
Maui, 235–238
Maun (Botswana), 357
Mayan Coast (Mexico), 270, 273
Medina Spa (Marrakech), 108
Mercer Museum (Doylestown), 126
Metropolitan Museum (New York City), 51
Miami, 39–43
Michigan Avenue (Chicago), 30
Middleton Place (near Charleston), 27
Mikla Bar (Istanbul), 76
Milion (Buenos Aires), 103
Miraval (Catalina), 153
Misty Fjords National Monument, 338
Money-saving tips, 15–20
Montagne Ste.-Victoire, 199
Montana, 348–350

Monterey, 218–219
Monterey Bay Aquarium, 218
Monteriggioni (Italy), 205
Montréal, 43–47
Mont Royal (Montréal), 44
Mont-Tremblant, 45
Moorea, 314–319
Mt. Si, 64
Mountain Road (High Road; New Mexico), 59
Mount McKinley, 339
Mulholland Drive (Los Angeles), 36–37
Murano, 88
Musée Carnavalet (Paris), 83
Musée des Beaux-Arts (Montréal), 45
Museo de Arte (Santiago de Querétaro), 343
Museo Exhacienda San Gabriel de Barrera (Guanajuato), 341
Museu Calouste Gulbenkian (Lisbon), 77
Museu Europeu d'Art Modern (Barcelona), 70
Museum of Art and Design (New York City), 52
Museum of Modern Art (New York City), 52
Museum of Natural History (New York City), 51
Museum of Sex (New York City), 52
Museu Picasso (Barcelona), 70
Music, 18–19
Mykonos, 300

N

Namibia, 374–378
Nantucket, 16, 229–231
Napa Valley, 131–135
National Elk Refuge, 137
National Tile Museum (Lisbon), 77
Natural Science Museum (San Francisco), 55
Nauplion, 300
Navy Pier (Chicago), 29
Negril, Jamaica, 275–279
Nerano, 288
Neue Galerie ((New York City), 52
New Hope, 126–128
New Orleans, 47–49
New York City, 49–54
Ngorongoro Crater (Tanzania), 367
Night Bazaar (Chiang Mai), 100
Nikai (Jackson), 140
Nikki Beach (Cabo San Lucas), 270
Nokia Theater (Los Angeles), 39
North Beach (San Francisco), 56

O

Oahu, 241–243
Oceanario de Lisboa (Lisbon), 77–78
Off-season, 15
Okavango Delta, 357–359
Old Town Plaza (Santa Fe), 58

Olduvai Gorge and Shifting Sands
(Tanzania), 368
Opals, Querétaro (Mexico),
343–344
Oporto, 80–81
Orcas Island, 253–254
Oregon coast, 243–252
Oregon Dunes National
Recreation Area, 249–250
Ortaköy Mosque (Istanbul), 75
Orvieto (Italy), 206–207, 210
Ouarzazate, 109
Ourika Valley, 109
Overseas Adventure Travel, 17,
107, 366

P

Pacific Coast Highway
(California), 37
Package deals, 17, 18
Palace of the Governors (Santa
Fe), 58
Palais Soleiman (Marrakech), 110
Palau de la Música Catalana
(Barcelona), 72
Palau Güell (Barcelona), 70
Palazzo Ducale (Venice), 88
Pantages Theater (Los
Angeles), 39
Paradesi Synagogue (Kerala), 372
Paragon Bar and Grill (Seattle),
64–65
Parc d'Attraccions del Tibidabo
(Barcelona), 70
Paris (France), 82–86
Paris (Kentucky), 142
Parker Ranch (Hawaii), 225
Patera Elephant Conservation
Farm (Chiang Mai), 97
Peggy Guggenheim Collection
(Venice), 88
Perugia (Italy), 207–210
Petersburg (Alaska), 334
Phuket, 322–326
Pienza (Italy), 209
The Pietons (St. Lucia), 280
Pike Place Market (Seattle), 62
Pioneer Square (Seattle), 62
Plaka (Athens), 298
Planning your vacation, 9–24
on a budget, 15–20
choosing your destination,
10–15
getting off to a romantic start,
23–24
price categories, 20–21
Playa del Carmen (Mexico),
274–275
Point Adolphus (Alaska), 334
Pokolbin, 116
Polly Hill Arboretum (Martha's
Vineyard), 233
Pololu Valley Lookout
(Hawaii), 226
Pont des Arts (Paris), 83
Port Wine Institute (Lisbon), 78
Preservation Hall (New
Orleans), 48

Provence (France), 198–202
Psah Chaa Market (Siem
Reap), 386

R

Rajasthan (India), 378–382
The Ranakpur Jain Temples
(Udaipur), 381
Rancho La Puerta (Tecate,
Mexico), 178–180
Ranthambore National Park, 379
Rattlesnake Ridge, 64
Ravello, 286–288
Ravinia, 33
The Red Centre (Australia),
382–385
Refrigerator, 22
Restaurants. *See also specific
destinations;* Restaurants Index
price categories, 20
Revolving Carousel (New
Orleans), 49
Rhodes, 301
Rice's Market (New Hope), 126
Ring of Kerry (Ireland), 188–189
Rio de Janeiro, 111–115
River float, Xel-Há National Park
(Mexico), 274
Riverfront Park (Charleston), 26
River rafting and floating
Banff, 171
Jasper, 177
RLS Gallery (Charleston), 26
Robben Island (Cape Town), 104
The Rocky Mountaineer, 169
Rodin Museum (Paris), 86

S

Safari camps (South Africa),
106–107
Sailing
Bermuda, 262–263
Hamilton Island, 363
Nantucket, 230
the Whitsundays, 360
St. George Open Air Cinema
(Sydney), 118
St. George's Castle (Lisbon), 78
St. Helena, 131–134
St. Lucia, 279–282
Saint Lawrence River (Montréal),
43–44
Salad dressings, Bermuda, 263
San Francisco, 54–58
San Gimignano (Italy), 205, 209
San Juan Island (Washington
State), 255
San Juan Islands (Washington
State), 16, 252–256
San Miguel de Allende, 345
Santa Barbara (California),
257–260
Santa Fe, 58–61
Santa Fe Opera, 60
Santa Monica Pier (Los
Angeles), 36
Santiago de Querétaro, 343–345
Santorini, 301

Sausalito, 55
Saxman Native Village, 338
Sazerac Bar (New Orleans), 49
Schramsberg Vineyards
(Calistoga), 132
Scirocco's Sky Bar (Bangkok), 96
Scuba diving
Airlie Beach and the
Whitsundays, 361
Bora Bora, 309
Cancún, 271
Hawaii, 226
Key Largo, 220
Miami, 41
Moorea, 316
Tahiti, 320
Zanzibar, 370
Seattle, 61–65
Second City (Chicago), 33
Sedona, Arizona, 148–154
Seniors Home Exchange, 17
Serengeti National Park, 365–367
Setai Hotel (Miami), 43
17-Mile Drive (California), 213
Shaker Village of Pleasant
Hill, 142
Sheldon Jackson Museum
(Sitka), 335
Shenandoah National Park, 67
Shenandoah Valley, 67–68
Shipwreck diving, Miami, 41
Shoshone National Forest, 136
Shoulder season, 15–16
Siem Reap (Cambodia), 385–387
Siena (Italy), 204–205
The Signature Room (Chicago), 33
The Silver Dollar Bar and Grille
(Jackson), 140
Sitka, 335
Skagway, 337
Skiing and other winter sports
Aspen, 121
Banff, 171
Jackson Hole, 137
Jasper, 177
Lake Louise, 174
Montréal area, 44, 45
Seattle area, 62
near Sydney, 121
Whitefish Mountain Resort, 145
Skyline Drive (Virginia), 67
Snorkeling
Bermuda, 263
Bora Bora, 309
Hamilton Island, 363
Hawaii, 226
Key Largo, 221
Moorea, 316
Negril, 276
Phuket, 323
St. Lucia, 280–281
Tahiti, 320
Zanzibar, 370
SoHo (New York City), 51
Sonoma, 129
Sonoma County, 129–131
The Sossusvlei (Namibia), 374–378
Soundproofing, 21
Space Needle (Seattle), 61

Spanish Riding School (Vienna), 91
Speedy's Airboat Tours
(Everglades City), 40–41
Spice Market (Istanbul), 73
Split (Croatia), 292–293
Sr. Vinho (Lisbon), 81
Staatsoper (Vienna), 92
Stargazing. See also Astronomy
   Bora Bora, 311
   Bryce Canyon, 168
   Sedona, 154
   The Sossusvlei, 378
Staten Island Ferry (New York
City), 50
Sugar Loaf Mountain (Rio de
Janeiro), 111
Sulphur Mountain gondola
(Banff), 171
Sultan Ahmet Camii (Istanbul), 73
Surfing, 258, 320
Swimming, Tahiti, 320
Swing 46 (New York City), 54
Sydney, 115–118

T

Table Mountain (Cape Town), 104
Tahiti, 319–322
Taj Mahal (Agra), 388–389
Tanah Lot Temple (Bali), 306
Tango, Buenos Aires, 103
Tanzania, 366–369
Teatro Colón (Buenos Aires), 101
Ten Thousand Waves (near Santa
Fe), 59
Théâtre Antique (Arles), 199
Third Street Promenade (Los
Angeles), 36
Three Chimneys Farm, 142
360 Istanbul, 76
Tiburon, 55
Todi (Italy), 206, 210
Tofino, 353
Topkapi Palace (Istanbul), 74
Top of the Rock (New York
City), 50
Totem Bight State Historical Park,
337–338
Tours, 14–15
Townhouse Hotel's Bar (Miami), 42
Tracy Arm Fjord (Alaska), 333
Trubadur Hard Jazz Cafe
(Dubrovnik), 292
Truchas Peak, 60
Tulum, 275
Tuscany (Italy), 204–205

U

Udaipur, 379, 381–382
Uluru (Australia), 383–384
Uluru Kata Tjuta National Park
(Australia), 382–383
Umbria (Italy), 206–210
University of California Botanical
Garden (Berkeley), 55
University of Virginia, 67
Upper King Street
(Charleston), 29

V

Vail, 122
Valentine's Day, 34–35
Vancouver Island, 351–355
Vendue Inn (Charleston), 29
Venice, 86–90
Venice Boardwalk (Los
Angeles), 36
Victoria (British Columbia),
351–353
Vienna, 90–92
Viking Cruises, 17
Villa Rufolo (Ravello), 286–287
The Violet Hour (Chicago), 33
Vizcaya (Miami), 41

W

Waimea Canyon (Kauai), 239
Waimea Valley (Oahu), 241–242
Walla Walla winelands
(Washington State), 155–158
Walt Disney Concert Hall (Los
Angeles), 36, 39
Warwick Wine Estate, 105
Washington, D.C., 65–68
Washington Park Arboretum
(Seattle), 63
Watarrka National Park
(Australia), 384
Watersports
   Koh Samui, 327
   Tahiti, 320
Waterton Lakes National Park,
143–144
Wat Phra Kaew (Bangkok), 94
Wat Phra Singh (Chiang Mai), 97
Weddings, 216–217, 225, 242
Wendella (Chicago), 30
Whale-watching, 238, 255,
259, 268
Wheeler Opera House (Aspen),
124–125
Whitehaven Beach (Whitsunday
Island), 360–361
White Pass and Yukon Route
railroad, 337
White-water rafting
   near Aspen, 122
   Jackson Hole, 136
The Whitsundays, 360–361
Willamette Valley (Oregon),
159–164
Winderlea Vineyard & Winery
(Dundee), 160
Wines and wineries
   Carmel Valley, 215
   Carpentras (France), 200
   Napa Valley, 132
   Santa Barbara, 257–258
   Sonoma County, 129–130
   Tuscany (Italy), 204
   Walla Walla, 155–157
   Willamette Valley (Oregon),
   159–160
Woodinville, 63

Y

Yachats (Oregon), 248–249
Yellowstone National Park,
136–137
Yountville, 131–135

Z

Zanzibar, 370–371
Zion National Park, 164–166

Accommodations

Adriana (Hvar), 293
An African Villa (Cape Town), 105
Airlie Beach Hotel, 361
Aleenta (Phuket), 324
Alexander's Guesthouse (Key
West), 223
Algodon Mansion (Buenos
Aires), 101
The Allison Inn and Spa
(Newberg), 162
Alstadt Vienna, 91
Altis Avenida Hotel (Lisbon), 78
Amanbagh (Jaipur), 380
Amandari Ubud (Bali), 306
Amangani (Jackson), 138
Amankila at Nusa Dua (Bali), 306
Amansara (Siem Reap), 386
The Amari Palm Reef (Koh
Samui), 328
Anantara Chiang Mai Resort and
Spa (Chiang Mai), 97–98
Antica Torre (Siena), 209
Arch Cape Inn (Cannon
Beach), 247
The Argonaut (San Francisco), 56
Arun Residence (Bangkok), 94
Ashford Castle (Cong), 191–192
As Janelas Verdes (Lisbon), 78–79
Auberge Bonaparte (Montréal), 45
Auberge du Bon Laboureur
(Chenonceaux), 196
Auberge du Vieux-Port
(Montréal), 45
Ayres Rock Resort/Sails in the
Desert Hotel, 384
Azul del Mar (Key Largo), 221
Azul Sensatori Jamaica
(Negril), 277
Baan Orapin (Chiang Mai), 98
Bandon Dunes Golf Resort, 251
Bandon Inn, 251
The Banyan Tree (Koh Samui), 328
Banyan Tree Maldives
Vabbinfaru, 312
Bardessono (Yountville), 134
Barnsely House (Cirencester), 184
The Bar W Guest Ranch
(Whitefish), 145
Bateleur Camp at Kichwa Tembo
(Kenya), 369
Beach Club (Hamilton Island), 364
Beach Plum Inn (Martha's
Vineyard), 233
Bear Cove Cottages (Vancouver
Island), 354

Becker's Chalets (Jasper), 177
Belmond Charleston Place Hotel, 27
The Benson (Portland), 161–162
Bernardus Lodge (Carmel Valley), 215
The Bervie (Achill), 192
Best Western Plus Elm House Inn (Napa), 135
The Biltmore in Coral Gables (Miami), 41
The Bishop's Lodge (Santa Fe), 60
Black Bear Inn (Ketchikan), 338
Black Walnut Inn (Dundee), 162
B-Lay Tong Phuket, 324
Bridgeton House on the Delaware (Upper Black Eddy), 126–127
Britania Hotel (Lisbon), 79
Buenos Aires Park Hyatt, 102
The Cabo Surf Hotel (Cabo San Lucas), 268
Caesar Augustus, 289
Cambridge Beaches Resort & Spa (Bermuda), 263–264
The Canary Hotel (Santa Barbara), 259
Cannery Pier Hotel (Astoria), 244
Canyon Villa Bed and Breakfast Inn of Sedona, 151
Cape Fox Lodge (Ketchikan), 339
The Capital Inn (Juneau), 333
Capri Palace (Italy), 289
The Carriage House Inn (Carmel), 213
Carrig Country House (Caragh Lake), 189
Casa Calma (Buenos Aires), 102
Casa de Sierra Nevada (San Miguel), 347
Casa Estrella de la Valenciana (Guanajuato), 342
Casa Luna Boutique Hotel (San Miguel), 347
Casa Malibu Inn (Los Angeles), 37
Casa Marina, A Waldorf Astoria Resort (Key West), 223
Casa Misha (San Miguel), 347–348
Casa Morada (Key Largo), 221
Castello Delle Quattro Torra (Siena), 209
Castello di Monterone (Perugia), 210
Castle Kiahuna Plantation (Kauai), 239
Channel Road Inn (Los Angeles), 37
Charingworth Manor (near Chipping Campden), 184
The Charming House (Venice), 88
Château de Pray (Amboise), 196
The Cheeca Lodge (Key Largo), 221
Chilkoot Trail Outpost, 337
China Beach Retreat (Iwaco, Washington), 244
The Ciragan Palace Kempinski in Istanbul, 74
Cliffside Beach Club (Nantucket), 230

Coco La Palm (Negril), 277
Colony Hotel (Miami), 41–42
The Conrad at Nusa Dua (Bali), 306
Copacabana Palace (Rio de Janeiro), 112–113
Coqui Coqui (Tulum), 275
The Culver Hotel (Los Angeles), 38
The Cypress Inn (Carmel), 213
Dar Ayniwen (Marrakech), 109
Dar Kantzaro (Marrakech), 109
Desa Seni-A Village Resort (Bali), 306–307
Desert Gardens (Yulara), 384
Divani Apollon Palace & Spa (Athens), 298
Domaine des Hauts-de-Loire (Chaumont sur Loire), 196
Dr. Wilkinson's Hot Springs Resort (Calistoga), 134
The Drake Hotel (Chicago), 31
Dromoland Castle Hotel and Country Estate (Newmarket-on-Fergus), 187
Earthsong (Denali), 340
El Portal Sedona, 151
Embassy Circle Guest House (Washington, D.C.), 65–66
Embudu Village (Maldives), 313
Empress Zoe (Istanbul), 74
Enchantment (Sedona), 151
Enniscoe House (Castlehill Ballina), 192
Esencia Estate (Playa del Carmen), 274
Establishment Hotel (Sydney), 116
The Fairmont Banff Springs Hotel, 172
The Fairmont Chateau Lake Louise, 174–175
The Fairmont Jasper Park Lodge (Jasper), 177
Fiesta Americana Grand Coral Beach Cancún Resort & Spa, 272
Flanigan's Inn (Springdale), 165
Fly-In Fish Inn (Sitka), 336
Fonte Cesia (Todi), 210
Four Seasons (Koh Samui), 328
The Four Seasons (Bangkok), 94
Four Seasons at Hualalai (Hawaii), 226
The Four Seasons at Kuda Huraa (Maldives), 313
Four Seasons at Sayan (Bali), 307
The Four Seasons Biltmore (Santa Barbara), 259
Four Seasons Chiang Mai, 98
Four Seasons Hotel Ritz (Lisbon), 78
Four Seasons Jackson Hole, 138
Four Seasons Resort Bora Bora, 310
Friday Harbor House (San Juan Island), 255
Fulton Lane Inn (Charleston), 27
Gearhart Ocean Inn, 246
Glacier Park Lodge (East Glacier), 145–146

Gramercy Park Hotel (New York City), 52
Grande Bretagne (Athens), 298
Grand Hotel Continental (Siena), 209
Grand Hotel Nord-Pinus (Arles), 200
The Grand Hyatt Kauai, 239
The Grand Wailea Resort and Spa (Maui), 236
The Gran Hotel (Santiago de Querétaro), 344
Gran Hotel La Florida (Barcelona), 70
The Green House Yeşil Ev (Istanbul), 75
Gregans Castle Hotel (Ballyvaughan), 188
Grumeti River Camp (Tanzania), 368
Hacienda Temozón (Uxmal), 275
Halekulani (Oahu), 242
Harbor View Hotel (Martha's Vineyard), 233
Harvest House Bed & Breakfast (Springdale), 165–166
Hayman Island Resort, 361
The Heathman (Portland), 162
Heritage Suites Hotel (Siem Reap), 386
Hilton Imperial Dubrovnik, 291
Hilton Moorea Lagoon & Spa (Moorea), 317
Holualoa Inn (Hawaii), 226
Hostel D'Uxelles (Barcelona), 70–71
Hostellerie Pierre du Calvet (Montréal), 46
Hotel Arts (Barcelona), 71
Hotel Bel-Air (Los Angeles), 38
Hotel Brufani Palace (Perugia), 210
Hotel Caron de Beaumarchais (Paris), 84
Hotel Casa Fuster (Barcelona), 71
Hotel Danieli (Venice), 88
Hôtel Diderot (Chinon), 196
Hotel Elliott (Astoria), 244–245
Hotel España (Barcelona), 71
The Hotel Excelsior (Dubrovnik), 291
Hotel Fasano (Rio de Janeiro), 113
Hotel Gavea Tropica (Rio de Janeiro), 113
Hotel Graal (Ravello), 287
Hotel Il Chiostro di Pienza (Pienza), 209
Hotel Imperial (Vienna), 91
Hôtel Jeanne d'Arc le Marais (Paris), 84
The Hotel Jerome (Aspen), 123
Hotel Korcula (Korcula), 295
Hotel La Badia (Orvieto), 210
Hotel Lenado (Aspen), 123
Hôtel Le St-James (Montréal), 46
Hotel Lido Mare (Amalfi), 285
Hotel Lucia (Portland), 162
Hotel Luna Convento (Amalfi), 285

Hotel Lunata (Playa del Carmen), 274
Hotel Marina Riviera (Amalfi), 285
Hotel Monaco (San Francisco), 56
Hotel Monteriggioni, 205
Hotel Oceana (Santa Barbara), 259
Hotel Santa Caterina (Amalfi), 285
Hotel Subasio (Assisi), 210
Hotel Umbra (Assisi), 209–210
Hotel Vestibul Palace (Split), 293
The Hyatt Carmel Highlands, 214
Indigo Inn (Charleston), 28
The Inn at Abeja (Walla Walla), 157
Inn at Barley Sheaf Farm (New Hope), 127
Inn at Bowman's Hill (New Hope), 127
The Inn at Fairfield Farm (Hume, VA), 68
The Inn at Irving Place (New York City), 52
The Inn at Little Washington (Washington, VA), 68
The Inn at Loretto Downtown (Santa Fe), 60
The Inn at the Market (Seattle), 64
The Inn on Orcas Island, 253–254
InterContinental Resort and Thalasso Spa Bora Bora, 310
InterContinental Resort & Spa (Moorea), 317
InterContinental Resort Tahiti, 320–321
Iskeroon (Caherdaniel), 190
ITC Mughal Agra, 389
The Jalousie Plantation (St. Lucia), 281
The Jefferson, Dupont Circle (Washington, D.C.), 66
The Jenny Lake Lodge (Grand Teton), 138
Kahala Hotel (Oahu), 242
Kandahar Lodge (Whitefish), 146
Kantishna Roadhouse (Denali), 340
The Kenwood Inn and Spa, 130
Kichawa Tembo Tented Camp (Kenya), 369
King George IV Inn (Charleston), 28
Kings Canyon Resort (Australia), 385
Klein's Camp (Kenya), 369
Kona Kai Resort and Gallery (Key Largo), 222
La Casa de Espíritus Alegres B&B (Guanajuato), 342
La Casa de la Marquesa (Santiago de Querétaro), 344
Ladera (St. Lucia), 281
La Guardia Bed & Breakfast (Italy), 289
Lake Crescent Lodge (Olympic National Park), 63–64
Lakedale Resort at Three Lakes (San Juan Island), 255–256
Lake McDonald Lodges & Cabins, 146

L'Antico Pozzo (San Gimignano), 209
La Residence D'Anghor (Siem Reap), 386
La Tortuga Hotel & Spa (Playa del Carmen), 274
L'Auberge de Sedona, 151–153
Lebau Hotel (Bangkok), 94
Le Citizen Hotel du Canal Paris, 84
Le Fleuray (near Amboise), 196–197
Lemala Camps (Kenya), 370
Le Manoir (Aix), 200
Le Meridien Tahiti, 321
Le Puy Inn (Newberg), 163
Lesic Dimitri Palace (Korcula), 295
The Library (Koh Samui), 328–329
Limelight Hotel (Aspen), 123
Little Kulala (The Sossusvlei), 377
The Little Nell (Aspen), 123
Live Aqua (Cancún), 272
The Lodge at Bryce Canyon, 167
The Lodge at Whitefish Lake, 146
The Long Beach Lodge Resort (Vancouver Island), 354
Lord of the Manor Hotel (Upper Slaughter), 184–185
Lost Creek Ranch & Spa (Moose), 138
Lumeria Maui, 236–237
Luna Hotel (Italy), 289
Lux Resort (Maldives), 315
The Lygon Arms (Broadway), 185
Magnolia Mansion (New Orleans), 48
Maison Fleurie (Yountville), 135
Majestic View Lodge (Springdale), 167–168
The Malabar House (Fort Cochin), 373–374
Mandarin Oriental (Bangkok), 95
The Mandarin Oriental (Chiang Mai), 98–99
The Mandarin Oriental (San Francisco), 56
Many Glacier Hotel (Babb), 147
The Marari Beach Resort (Mararikulam), 374
The Marcus Whitman (Walla Walla), 157–158
Marina Inn (San Francisco), 56
Marjorie's Kauai Inn, 240
Matahari Beach Resort & Spa (Bali), 307
Mauna Lani Bay Hotel (Hawaii), 226
McGinnis Meadows Cattle & Guest Ranch, 147
Meadowood (St. Helena), 134
The Michelangelo (New York City), 52
Millennium Knickerbocker Hotel (Chicago), 31
Mnemba Island Lodge (Zanzibar), 370–371
The Moana Surfrider (Oahu), 242–243
The Moorings Village (Key Largo), 222

Moy House (Lahinch), 188
Ngorongoro Crater Lodge (Tanzania), 367–368
The Normandy Hotel (Washington, D.C.), 66
North Face Lodge (Denali), 339
Novecento (Venice), 89
Nxabega (Botswana), 357
The Oberoi Amarvilas (Agra), 389
Oberoi Rajvilas (Jaipur), 380
The Oberoi Udaivilas (Udaipur), 381
The Ocean Lodge (Cannon Beach), 247
Old Monterey Inn, 218
Oltre Il Giardino (Venice), 89
One&Only Palmilla (Cabo San Lucas), 268
Oriental Residence Bangkok, 95
The Outermost Inn (Martha's Vineyard), 233
Overleaf Lodge & Spa (Yachats), 249
Oxford House (Bermuda), 264
Palácio Belmonte (Lisbon), 79
Palazzo Abadessa (Venice), 89
Palazzo Avino (Ravello), 287
Palazzo di Valli (Siena), 209
Palazzo Piccolomini (Orvieto), 210
Palm Bungalow (Hamilton Island), 364
Palms Cliff House Inn (Hawaii), 227
Paradise Inn (Key West), 223
Paresa (Phuket), 324
Park Hotel Kenmare, 190
The Pavilions Resort (Phuket), 324
Pearson's Pond Luxury Inn and Adventure Spa (Juneau), 333
Peninsula Bangkok, 95
Pestana Porto Hotel (Oporto), 81
The Pierre (New York City), 52
Planters Inn (Charleston), 28
The Post Hotel & Spa (Banff), 175
The Post Ranch Inn (Big Sur), 219
Prince of Wales Lodge (Waterton Lakes), 147
Pullman Quay (Sydney), 117
qualia (Hamilton Island), 364
Raffles Grand Hotel D'Angkor (Siem Reap), 387
The Raleigh (Miami), 42
The Reefs (Bermuda), 264
Reef View Hotel (Hamilton Island), 364
Regents Court (Sydney), 117
The Resort at Paws Up (San Miguel), 349–350
Riad Kniza (Marrakech), 109–110
Rimrock Resort Hotel (Banff), 172
Ritz Carlton at Bachelor Gulch (Avon), 16, 122
Ritz-Carlton Chicago, 31
Riva (Hvar), 294
Roche Harbor (San Juan Island), 256
The Rockhouse Hotel (Negril), 278
Rohutu Fare Lodge (Bali), 310–311

Rosewood Inn of the Anasazi (Santa Fe), 60
Rosewood San Miguel Allende, 348
Royal Hideaway Playacar (Playa del Carmen), 274–275
The Rusty Parrot Lodge (Jackson), 138–139
Salishan Spa & Golf Resort (Gleneden Beach), 248
Salish Lodge & Spa (Snoqualmie), 63, 64
Samode Haveli (Jaipur), 380
Sea Quest Inn Bed and Breakfast (Yachats), 249
Serena Inn (Zanzibar), 371
Seyyida Hotel & Spa (Zanzibar), 371
Shangri-La Hotel (Sydney), 117
Shanti Natural Panorama View Hotel (Bali), 307
Shinta Mani (Siem Reap), 387
Shiv Niwas Palace (Udaipur), 381
Shutters on the Beach (Los Angeles), 38
Silver Oaks Guest Ranch (Hawaii), 227
The Simpson House Inn (Santa Barbara), 259
Singita Sabora Plains, Faru Faru & Sasakwa (Tanzania), 368–369
Six Senses Hideaway (Koh Samui), 329
Skagway Inn Bed & Breakfast, 337
Snug Hollow Farm Bed & Breakfast (Irvine), 142
Sofitel Moorea la Ora Beach Resort, 318
The Sonoma Mission Inn, 130
Sonoma's Best Guest Cottages, 131
Sooke Harbour House (Victoria), 352
Sossusvlei Desert Lodge, 377–378
The Spindrift Inn (Monterey), 218
Spring Creek Ranch (Jackson), 138
Stephanie Inn (Cannon Beach), 247
Stone Canyon Inn (Tropic), 168
Stonefield Resort and Estates (St. Lucia), 281
Stonepine Ranch (Carmel Valley), 215
The Storm Mountain Lodge (Banff), 172–173
A Storybook Inn (Versailles), 143
Sukantara Cascade Resort and Spa (Chiang Mai), 99
Sunset Beach Resort & Spa (Cabo San Lucas), 268–269
Sunset Tower (Los Angeles), 38
The Swan Hotel (Bibury), 185
Swann's Nest Inn (Lexington), 143
Taj Lake Palace Hotel (Udaipur), 381–382
The Taj Malabar (Cochin), 374
Talbott Hotel (Chicago), 32
Tandjung Sari (Bali), 307

Terre di Nano Monticchiello Pienza, 209
A Teton Tree House (Wilson), 139
Totem Square Hotel and Marina (Sitka), 336
Tucker's Point Hotel and Spa (Bermuda), 264
Turtleback Farm Inn (Orcas Island), 254
Turtle Bay Resort (Oahu), 243
Twelve Apostles (Cape Town), 105
Unguja Lodge (Zanzibar), 370
Victoria and Alfred Hotel (Cape Town), 105
The Victoria Empress Hotel, 352
Villa del Parmar Cancún, 272
Villa Dubrovnik, 291
Villa Gallici (Aix), 201
Villa Maria Hotel (Ravello), 287
Villa Monte Solare (Perugia), 210
Waimea Plantation Cottages (Kauai), 240
Walla Faces, 158
Wauwinet Inn (Nantucket), 230
The Westin (Cabo San Lucas), 269
White Swan Inn (San Francisco), 56–57
Whitsunday Moorings B&B (Airlie Beach), 362
The Wickaninnish Inn (Vancouver Island), 355
The Willard Intercontinental Washington, D.C., 66
Windsor Court Hotel (New Orleans), 48
W Istanbul, 75
Wolwedans Boulder Camp (Namibia), 378
Wyndham Grand Agra, 389
Wyoming Inn (Jackson), 139
Xudum (Botswana), 359
Zion Lodge, 166

Restaurants Index

Achill Cliff House, 192
Ad Hoc (Yountville), 133
Ai Fiori, 53
Alloro Wine Bar (Bandon), 251–252
American Seasons (Nantucket), 230
Andina in Portland, 163
An Port Mor (Westport), 192
Antico Osteria da Divo (Siena), 204–205
Apsara at Trou Au Diable Soufriere (St. Lucia), 281–282
Area 31 (Miami), 42
Aria (Sydney), 117
Armada Loungebar & Restaurant (Airlie Beach), 362
Atlantic's Edge (Key Largo), 222
Auberge du Bon Laboureur (Chenonceaux), 197
Auberge du Soleil (Rutherford), 133
Aubergine (Carmel), 214

Au Pied de Cochon (Paris), 86
Aura Waterfront Restaurant (Victoria), 352
Azul (Miami), 42
Baan Rim Pa (Phuket), 325
Backdoor Kitchen (San Juan Island), 256
Baked Alaska (Astoria), 245
Bar Harbour Restaurant (Ketchikan), 339
Bar Uriarte (Buenos Aires), 102
Beach Club Restaurant (Hamilton Island), 364
The Beach House Restaurant (Kauai), 240
Beach Plum Inn Restaurant (Martha's Vineyard), 234
Becker's Gourmet Restaurant (Jasper), 177–178
Belcanto (Lisbon), 79
The Bison Restaurant and Terrace (Banff), 173
Bistro (Cannon Beach), 248
Bloody Mary's Restaurant & Bar (Bora Bora), 311
Blue Crab Bar and Grill (Victoria), 352–353
Blue Duck Tavern (Washington, D.C.), 67
Bommie Restaurant (Hamilton Island), 364
Book Restaurant and Bar (Oporto), 81
Boucan in the Hotel Chocolat (St. Lucia), 282
Bouchon (Santa Barbara), 259–260
Bow Valley Grill (Banff), 173
Brasserie T (Montréal), 46–47
Bridgewater Bistro (Astoria), 245
Brophy Bros. Clam Bar and Restaurant (Santa Barbara), 260
Brown's Beach House (Hawaii), 227
Cabbages and Condoms (Bangkok), 95
Café de L'Acadèmia (Barcelona), 71
Café du Monde (New Orleans), 47–48
Café Ibérico (San Miguel), 346
Café Pasqual's (Santa Fe), 60–61
Café Spiaggia (Chicago), 32
Can Majo (Barcelona), 71
Canoehouse at the Mauna Lani Bay Resort (Hawaii), 227
Casa da Comida (Lisbon), 79
Casa da Feijoada (Rio de Janeiro), 113
Casa Tua (Miami), 42
Cavell's Restaurant & Terrace (Jasper), 178
Celadon (Bangkok), 95–96
Centre Street Bistro (Nantucket), 231
The Channel Club (Sitka), 336
Charleston Grill, 27, 28
The Chart House, 190
Chez Nenesse (Paris), 85
Chez Panisse (Berkeley), 55

Chicago Alinea, 32
Chiribiri (San Gimignano), 205
Churrascaria Carretao (Rio de Janeiro), 113
Club Jalapeño (Carmel), 214
Cochon (New Orleans), 48
Cocotte (Portland), 163
Commander's Palace (New Orleans), 48–49
Company of the Cauldron (Nantucket), 231
Confeitaria Columbo (Rio de Janeiro), 114
Côté Jardin Restaurant (Gien), 197
Cucina Rústica, 154
Cullinan's Restaurant & Guesthouse (Doolin), 188
Cyrano's Cafe & Wine Bar (Chicago), 32
Dahl & DiLuca (Sedona), 154
Dar Yacout (Marrakech), 110
Da Salvatore (Ravello), 287
Dasheene at Ladera (St. Lucia), 282
The Deck (Bangkok), 96
Déjà Vu (Airlie Beach), 362
De Pisis (Venice), 89
The Depot Restaurant (Seaview, Washington), 245
Diafani Garden (Rhodes), 301–302
Dordota Vartal (Hvar), 294
The Dove Parlour (New York City), 53
Dr. Ali's (Maldives), 313
Duck Soup Inn (San Juan Island), 256
Ebenezer's Barn & Grill (Bryce Canyon), 168
Echo Lake Café (near Bigfork), 147
Edith's Restaurant (Cabo San Lucas), 269
Edwin K Bed & Breakfast (Florence, Oregon), 250
El Farallón (Cabo San Lucas), 269
Els Quatre Gats (Barcelona), 71
Emily's Restaurant and Cooking School (Cape Town), 106
Esphahan (Agra), 389–390
Etoile at Domaine Chandon, 133
Ferrara Bakery & Café (New York City), 51
Floating Dinner (Bali), 307
Flora Farms (Cabo San Lucas), 269
Flying Fish Grill (Carmel), 214
Foz Velha (Oporto), 81
The Freight House (Doylestown), 128
Fremont Diner (Sonoma), 131
The French Laundry (Yountville), 133
Gadsby's Tavern (Washington, D.C.), 67
Galatoire's (New Orleans), 49
Geoffrey's (Los Angeles), 37
Gero (Rio de Janeiro), 114
Geronimo (Santa Fe), 61
The Girl & the Fig (Sonoma), 131
Grand Café (San Francisco), 57

Grand Central Oyster Bar (New York City), 51
Green Turtle Inn (Key Largo), 222
Hali'Malie General Store (Maui), 237
Hamdi Restaurant (Istanbul), 75
Hamilton's Grill Room (Lambertville), 128
The Harbourfront Restaurant & Komodaru Sushi Lounge (Bermuda), 265
The Heartline Café (Sedona), 154
Heaven's Peak Dining and Spirits (West Glacier), 147
The Heen Kahidi (Ketchikan), 339
HG (Buenos Aires), 102
Hominy Grill (Charleston), 28
Honey 1 BBQ (Chicago), 32
Honey Restaurant (Doylestown), 128
The Hotel Tugu Bali's Javanese Cooking Experience (Bali), 308
Huen Huay Keaw Restaurant (Chiang Mai), 99
Icebergs (Sydney), 117
Ideale Ristorante (San Francisco), 57
Il Falchetto (Perugia), 208–209
Il Postale (Perugia), 208
Il Terrasso (Seattle), 62
Inlaa'Kech Lobster & Grill (Cancún), 272–273
The Inn at Little Washington (Washington, VA), 68
Inn at Ship Bay (Orcas Island), 254
Ivan's Bar (Negril), 278
Jackie's San Antonio (San Miguel), 346
Jenny Lake Lodge Dining Room, 139
Justice Snow's (Aspen), 124
Kamuela Provision Company at the Hilton Waikoloa (Hawaii), 227–228
The Kashi Art Café (Fort Kochi), 374
The Khmer Kitchen (Siem Reap), 387
Koi (Cape Town), 106
Konoba Adio Mare (Korcula), 295
Konoba Lokanda Peskarija (Dubrovnik), 291–292
Konoba Menego (Hvar), 294
Krabloonik (Aspen), 124
Ksar Char-Bagh (Marrakech), 110
La Caravella (Amalfi), 285
La Casa del Conde de la Valenciana (Guanajuato), 342
La Charcuterie (Aix), 201–202
La Coupole (Paris), 85
La Cuisine de Bar (Paris), 85
La Folie (San Francisco), 57
La Fortezza (Assisi), 207
La Gueule du Loup (Aix), 202
L'Anice Stellato (Venice), 89
La Plage de Maui Restaurant (Tahiti), 321
La Plantation (Moorea), 318
Larkspur Caffe (Sitka), 337

La Stalla (Assisi), 207
L'Atelier de Jean Luc Rabanel (Aix), 202
La Villa Mahana (Bora Bora), 311
Le Basilic (Cancún), 273
Le Belvédère (Tahiti), 321
Le Bistro Latin (Aix), 201
Le Carré (Tahiti), 321
Le Club Chasse et Pêche (Montréal), 46
Le Grenier (Martha's Vineyard), 234
Le Lotus (Tahiti), 321–322
Le Meurice (Paris), 84–85
Le Petit Canard (Paris), 85
Le Pigeon (Portland), 163
Le Pre Catelan (Paris), 85
Les Délices du Château (Saumur), 197
Les Gueules Noires (Vouvray), 197
L'etoile (Martha's Vineyard), 234
L'Express (Montréal), 46
Lido Azzurro (Amalfi), 286
Lido del Faro (Capri), 289
Lilly's (Louisville), 143
The Little Door (Los Angeles), 38
L'O à la Bouche (Tahiti), 322
The Lodge at Bryce Canyon Restaurant, 168
L'Olivo (Capri), 289–290
L'Orangerie du Chateau (Blois), 197–198
Lord Baker's (Dingle), 190
Louie's Backyard (Key West), 223–224
Madrona Manor (Healdsburg), 131
Mama's Fish House (Maui), 237
Manolis Dinoris Fish Taverna (Rhodes), 302
The Marc Restaurant (Walla Walla), 158
Marina Tavern (Hamilton Island), 364
Matsuhisa Athens, 298–299
Mavrikos (Rhodes), 302
Medio Evo (Assisi), 207
Merriman's (Maui), 237
México Lindo y Sabroso (Guanajuato), 342
Milos (Athens), 299
Mom Tri's Kitchen (Phuket), 325
Montrio Bistro (Monterey), 218–219
Morada Bay Beach Café (Key Largo), 222
More (Dubrovnik), 292
Mustards Grill, 134
Nepenthe (Big Sur), 219
Newman's at 988 (Cannon Beach), 248
Newport House Hotel Restaurant, 192–193
9 Gems Lounge and Restaurant (Koh Samui), 329–330
nine one five (Key West), 224
Niros (Jaipur), 380
North Pond (Chicago), 32
The Oakroom (Louisville), 143
Oceanos (Fort Kochi), 374

On Aqua Restaurant and Bar (Airlie Beach), 362
One if by Land, Two if by Sea (New York City), 53
Osteria a Priori (Perugia), 208
Osteria le Logge (Siena), 204
Pacific Way Café and Bakery (Gearhart), 246
Painapo (Pineapple) Beach (Moorea), 318
The Painted Lady (Newberg), 163–164
Palaca Paladini (Hvar), 294
Palacio de los Jugos (Miami), 42
Pasticceria Sandri (Perugia), 208
Pavilions Resort (Phuket), 325
Peninsula Grill (Charleston), 28
Per Se (New York City), 53
Pfarrwirt (Vienna), 91
The Pier (Koh Samui), 329
Pierre Reboul (Aix), 201
Pink Door (Seattle), 62
Piñons (Aspen), 124
The Place (San Juan Island), 256
Place Pigalle (Seattle), 62
The Post Hotel Dining Room (Lake Louise), 175
Proto (Dubrovnik), 292
Rancho de Chimayó, 59
The Red Hills Provincial Dining (Dundee), 164
The Red Piano (Siem Reap), 387
Red Rock Grill in Zion Lodge, 166
The Restaurant (Chiang Mai), 99
The Restaurant (San Miguel), 346–347
The Restaurant at Sooke Harbor House (Victoria), 353
Restaurant at the Getty Center (Los Angeles), 37
The Restaurant at Villa Maria Hotel (Ravello), 288
Restaurant du Terass Hotel (Paris), 86
Restaurante Gabbiano Al Mare (Rio de Janeiro), 114
Restaurant Fare Manuia (Bora Bora), 311
Restaurant Korso (Vienna), 91–92
Restaurant Lucca (Istanbul), 75
Restoran Boban (Split), 293
Restoran Sumica (Split), 293

Ristorante Dorando (San Gimignano), 205
Ristorante Latini (San Gimignano), 205
Ristorante Santa Caterina (Amalfi), 286
Ristorante Umbria (Todi), 206
River Café (New York City), 53
The Rockhouse Restaurant and Bar (Negril), 278
Rossellinis (Ravello), 287
Russell's of Broadway, 185
Saddle Peak Lodge (Los Angeles), 39
Saffron Mediterranean Kitchen (Walla Walla), 158
Salathip (Bangkok), 96
Salt (Maldives), 313
Sam's Anchor Cafe (Tiburon), 55
Saniya Palace (Agra), 390
San Miguelito (Santiago de Querétaro), 344
Santa Café (Santa Fe), 61
Scoma's (Sausalito), 55
By the Sea Restaurant (Maldives), 313
Serrano's (East Glacier), 148
Sheesh Mahal (Udaipur), 382
The Shelburne Inn (Seaview, Washington), 245
Siam Indigo (Phuket), 325
Sidewalk Café (Los Angeles), 36
Skal (New York City), 53
The Smoke Daddy (Chicago), 32
Snake River Grill (Jackson), 139
The Soup Dragon (Siem Reap), 387
Spago (Los Angeles), 39
The Spotted Dog Cafe (Springdale), 166
Stella Mare (Santa Barbara), 260
Strogili (Santorini), 301
Sunrise Buffet (Bali), 308
Surya Mahal Courtyard at Oberoi Rajvilas (Jaipur), 380
Takumi (Sydney), 117
The Tankard (Tralee), 190
Tapa at The Bale Resort (Bali), 308
Te Honu Iti (Moorea), 318
Tekarra Lodge Restaurant (Jasper), 178

The Terrace (Maui), 237
Terrasses des Epices (Marrakech), 110
Thai (Cancún), 273
Thao Nam Restaurant (Chiang Mai), 99
1300 Taberna (Lisbon), 79
33Mu5 & The Edge (Phuket), 325
The Three Monkeys Pub and Restaurant (Koh Samui), 330
Tidepools (Kauai), 240
Tipica Trattoria Etrusca (Orvieto), 206–207
Tom Moore's Tavern (Bermuda), 265
Tomo1 (Buenos Aires), 102–103
Toqué (Montréal), 46–47
Trattoria del'Orso (Orvieto), 206
Tribe Road Kitchen (Bermuda), 265
Trio, 139–140
Tupelo Grille (Whitefish), 148
Twin Anchors Tavern (Chicago), 32
Twisted Fish Company (Juneau), 334
'Ulu Ocean Grill and Sushi Lounge (Hawaii), 228
Upperline (New Orleans), 49
Valle Flor (Lisbon), 79
Varoulko (Athens), 299
Versailles Cuban Restaurant (Miami), 41
Vertigo and Moon Bar (Bangkok), 96
Via Veneto (Barcelona), 72
Waterbar (San Francisco), 57
Waterfront Depot Restaurant & Bar (Florence, Oregon), 250
The Waterlot Inn (Bermuda), 265
Wesley House (Winchcombe), 185
Whitehouse-Crawford Restaurant (Walla Walla), 158
Whitsunday Sailing Club (Airlie Beach), 362
Wild Rose (Bandon), 252
Wine Cask (Santa Barbara), 260
Yank Sing (San Francisco), 57
Yaxché (Playa del Carmen), 275
Zephyr (Juneau), 334
Zico's (Koh Samui), 329